JOHN F. TANNER, JR.

Dr. Tanner is the research director of Baylor University's Center for Professional Selling and professor of marketing. He earned his PhD from the University of Georgia. Prior to entering academia, Dr. Tanner spent eight years in industry with Rockwell International and Xerox Corporation, as both sales-person and marketing manager.

Dr. Tanner has received several awards for teaching effectiveness and research. His sales teaching efforts have been recognized by *Sales & Marketing Management* and the *Dallas Morning News.* Dr. Tanner has authored or co-authored 10 books, including *Business Marketing: Connecting Strategy, Relationships, and Learning* with Bob Dwyer.

Research grants from the Center for Exhibition Industry Research, the Institute for the Study of Business Markets, the University Research Council, the Texas Department of Health, and others have supported his research efforts. Dr. Tanner has published over 45 articles in the *Journal of Marketing, Journal of Business Research, Journal of Personal Selling and Sales Management,* international journals, and others. He serves on the review boards of several journals, including *Marketing Education Review, Journal of Personal Selling and Sales Management,* and *Journal of Marketing Theory and Practice.*

Dr. Tanner writes a bimonthly column on sales and sales management topics for *Sales and Marketing Strategies & News.* His other trade publications include *Advertising Age's Business Marketing, Decisions, Sales Managers' Bulletin, American Salesman,* and *Potentials in Marketing.* A nationally recognized speaker and author on issues regarding customer relationships, Dr. Tanner has presented seminars at international conventions of several trade organizations, including the International Exhibitor's Association and the Canadian Association of Exposition Managers. More recently, he has taught executive and graduate programs in India, France, and Mexico.

Jeff_Tanner@BAYLOR.EDU
http://hsb.baylor.edu/html/tanner

CENTRAL MISSOURI STATE UNIVERSITY

Property of University Store
Elliott Union 128
Warrensburg, MO 64093
660-543-4370 or 800-330-7698
ustore@cmsu1.cmsu.edu

Renter Responsibility

By accepting this rental text from the University Store,
students agree to the following:

- **Return rental books by close of business on the last day of finals.**
  A late fee will be charged equal to the current rental fee beginning
  on the first regular business day following finals. No returns will be
  accepted beginning on the second regular business day following
  finals, and a charge will be placed on the student's university bill
  equal to the replacement cost of a new textbook.

- **Exercise reasonable care while the book is in your possession.**
  Students are expected to protect rental books from theft, moisture,
  chemical, fire or other sources of damage. Failure to do so will result
  in assessment of a damage fee, which may include the replacement
  cost of a new textbook.

- **Make no marks except yellow highlighting.** The textbook rental
  program depends on multiple circulations; it is important that
  markings in university-owned books be minimized.

CMSU 973-05

Selling

Building Partnerships

FIFTH EDITION

Selling
Building Partnerships

Barton A. Weitz
University of Florida

Stephen B. Castleberry
University of Minnesota, Duluth

John F. Tanner, Jr.
Baylor University

Boston   Burr Ridge, IL   Dubuque, IA   Madison, WI   New York   San Francisco   St. Louis
Bangkok   Bogotá   Caracas   Kuala Lumpur   Lisbon   London   Madrid   Mexico City
Milan   Montreal   New Delhi   Santiago   Seoul   Singapore   Sydney   Taipei   Toronto

SELLING: BUILDING PARTNERSHIPS

Published by McGraw-Hill/Irwin, an imprint of The McGraw-Hill Companies, Inc.
1221 Avenue of the Americas, New York, NY, 10020. Copyright © 2004, 2001, 1998, 1995, 1992, by The McGraw-Hill Companies, Inc. All rights reserved. No part of this publication may be reproduced or distributed in any form or by any means, or stored in a database or retrieval system, without the prior written consent of The McGraw-Hill Companies, Inc., including, but not limited to, in any network or other electronic storage or transmission, or broadcast for distance learning.
Some ancillaries, including electronic and print components, may not be available to customers outside the United States.

This book is printed on acid-free paper.

domestic   3 4 5 6 7 8 9 0 DOW/DOW 0 9 8 7 6 5 4
international 1 2 3 4 5 6 7 8 9 0 DOW/DOW 0 9 8 7 6 5 4 3

ISBN 0-07-254928-9

Publisher: *John E. Biernat*
Executive editor: *Linda Schreiber*
Developmental editor: *Sarah Crago*
Marketing manager: *Kim Kanakes*
Media producer: *Craig Atkins*
Senior project manager: *Kari Geltemeyer*
Lead production supervisor: *Heather D. Burbridge*
Designer: *Adam Rooke*
Photo research coordinator: *Jeremy Cheshareck*
Photo researcher: *Billie Porter*
Lead supplement producer: *Cathy L. Tepper*
Senior digital content specialist: *Brian Nacik*
Interior design: *Kay Fulton*
Cover photograph: *© Copyright 2002 Getty Images, Inc.*
Typeface: *10/12 Sabon*
Compositor: *Precision Graphics Services, Inc.*
Printer: *R. R. Donnelley*

Library of Congress Cataloging-in-Publication Data
Weitz, Barton A.
    Selling : building partnerships / Barton A. Weitz, Stephen B. Castleberry, John F. Tanner, Jr.—5th ed.
        p. cm.—(McGraw-Hill/Irwin series in marketing)
    Includes bibliographical references and index.
    ISBN 0-07-254928-9 (alk. paper)
    1. Selling. I. Castleberry, Stephen Bryon. II. Tanner, John F. III. Title. IV. Series.
  HF5438.25.W2933 2004
  658.85—dc 21   2002030945

INTERNATIONAL EDITION ISBN 0-07-121519-0
Copyright © 2004. Exclusive rights by The McGraw-Hill Companies, Inc. for manufacture and export. This book cannot be re-exported from the country to which it is sold by McGraw-Hill. The international edition is not available in North America.

www.mhhe.com

To Edward Weitz, a great father and salesperson.

—Bart Weitz

To Andrew Patrick Castleberry, the latest little "partner" in our home, and to Christ, who makes all things new.

—Steve Castleberry

To those most precious: My God, my wife Karen, my children, my parents.

—Jeff Tanner

The Irwin/McGraw-Hill Series in Marketing

Arens
Contemporary Advertising
Ninth Edition

Arnould, Price & Zinkhan
Consumers
Second Edition

Bearden, Ingram & LaForge
**Marketing: Principles &
Perspectives**
Fourth Edition

Belch & Belch
**Advertising & Promotion: An
Integrated Marketing
Communications Approach**
Sixth Edition

Bingham & Gomes
**Business Marketing
Management**
Second Edition

Boyd, Walker, Mullins &
Larreche
**Marketing Management: A
Strategic Decision-Making
Approach**
Fourth Edition

Cateora & Graham
International Marketing
Eleventh Edition

Cole & Mishler
**Consumer and Business Credit
Management**
Eleventh Edition

Cravens & Piercy
Strategic Marketing
Seventh Edition

Cravens, Lamb & Crittenden
**Strategic Marketing
Management Cases**
Seventh Edition

Crawford & Di Benedetto
New Products Management
Seventh Edition

Dolan
**Marketing Management: Text
and Cases**
First Edition

Duncan
**IMC: Using Advertising and
Promotion to Build Brands**
First Edition

Dwyer & Tanner
Business Marketing
Second Edition

Eisenmann
**Internet Business Models: Text
and Cases**
First Edition

Etzel, Walker & Stanton
Marketing
Twelfth Edition

Forrest
Internet Marketing Intelligence
First Edition

Futrell
ABC's of Relationship Selling
Eighth Edition

Futrell
Fundamentals of Selling
Seventh Edition

Hair, Bush & Ortinau
Marketing Research
Second Edition

Hawkins, Best & Coney
Consumer Behavior
Ninth Edition

Johansson
Global Marketing
Third Edition

Johnston & Marshall
**Churchill/Ford/Walker's Sales
Force Management**
Seventh Edition

Kerin, Hartley & Rudelius
Marketing: The Core
First Edition

Kerin, Berkowitz, Hartley &
Rudelius
Marketing
Seventh Edition

Lehmann & Winer
Analysis for Marketing Planning
Fifth Edition

Lehmann & Winer
Product Management
Third Edition

Levy & Weitz
Retailing Management
Fifth Edition

Mason & Perreault
The Marketing Game!
Third Edition

McDonald
Direct Marketing: An Integrated Approach
First Edition

Mohammed, Fisher, Jaworski & Cahill
Internet Marketing: Building Advantage in a Networked Economy
Second Edition

Monroe
Pricing
Third Edition

Pelton, Strutton & Lumpkin
Marketing Channels: A Relationship Management Approach
Second Edition

Peppers & Rogers
Managing Customer Relationships to Build Competitive Advantage
First Edition

Perreault & McCarthy
Basic Marketing: A Global Managerial Approach
Fourteenth Edition

Perreault & McCarthy
Essentials of Marketing: A Global Managerial Approach
Ninth Edition

Peter & Donnelly
A Preface to Marketing Management
Ninth Edition

Peter & Donnelly
Marketing Management: Knowledge and Skills
Seventh Edition

Peter & Olson
Consumer Behavior
Sixth Edition

Purvis & Burton
Which Ad Pulled Best?
Ninth Edition

Rayport & Jaworski
Introduction to e-Commerce
Second Edition

Rayport & Jaworski
e-Commerce
First Edition

Rayport & Jaworski
Cases in e-Commerce
First Edition

Richardson
Internet Marketing
First Edition

Roberts
Internet Marketing: Integrating Online and Offline Strategies
First Edition

Spiro, Stanton & Rich
Management of a Sales Force
Eleventh Edition

Stock & Lambert
Strategic Logistics Management
Fourth Edition

Ulrich & Eppinger
Product Design and Development
Second Edition

Walker, Boyd, Mullins & Larreche
Marketing Strategy: A Decision-Focused Approach
Fourth Edition

Weitz, Castleberry & Tanner
Selling: Building Partnerships
Fifth Edition

Zeithaml & Bitner
Services Marketing
Third Edition

Preface

In spite of the growth of the Internet, face-to-face meetings and personal relationships between sellers and buyers seem more important than ever before. Over the past 10 years, *Sales & Marketing Management* has determined that the average cost of a sales call has come down, while average compensation for salespeople has gone up. Salespeople are more productive, seeing more customers and making more sales. The profession has changed, and is changing, at a rapid pace. Salespeople have growing responsibilities to manage the entire value chain within their company, with suppliers, and with customers. All of these factors make the skills of partnering more important now than ever before.

OUR PHILOSOPHY

The skills of partnering go well beyond the arena of selling a product. Strategic alliances are important to virtually all businesses and all aspects of business. That is why we are excited to see professional selling continue to grow in numbers of schools teaching the course, to grow as a required course for marketing majors at many schools, and to become part of the core curriculum for all business majors at a few institutions (see Greg Marshall and Ron Michaels' article in *Marketing Education Review,* Summer 2002, for more on the state of sales education).

Our assumption, though, is not that all students of sales will become salespeople. Students in this course should learn principles of selling so well that they would have enough confidence in themselves to begin making calls if provided no additional training by their employer, even if those calls occurred in a nonselling field (for example, an accountant soliciting new business). At the same time, more students than ever before are being exposed to selling who have no plans to enter the sales profession. One of our objectives in this book is to provide sound partnering and communication skills that will be useful no matter what their occupation may become.

Another objective is to integrate material from other "theory-driven" courses. While nothing may be more practical than a good theory, students sometimes say that this is the only class in which they learned something they could use. That is unfortunate. We continue to work on integrating material from other courses and disciplines to illustrate the application of theories in the practice of selling. Several of you have told us that you have had the same experience and found this book to be useful in integrating material. We're glad that we have been successful and hope you find this edition to do an even better job.

SPECIAL OFFER

The Center for Professional Selling at Baylor University and McGraw-Hill have teamed up to prepare a magazine called *Careers in Professional Selling.* The magazine profiles successful salespeople and companies that hire college graduates for sales positions. If you would like *free* copies to pass out to your students, let your rep know and you can get it shipped directly to you in multiples of 50 copies. You may want to order copies for the Principles of Marketing class to encourage enrollment in your selling class, or use it to counsel sales students about jobs.

PARTNERING AND SALES EDUCATION

The importance of partnering and partnering skills to students and business has changed the way sales is taught. Several unique features place this book at the cutting edge of sales technology and partnering research:

1. A revision of the traditional selling process—approach, opening, making a presentation, demonstrating benefits, overcoming objections, and closing—into the new partnering process. The new process includes strategically planning each sales call within a larger account strategy, making the sales call, strengthening communications, responding helpfully to objections, obtaining commitment, and building partnerships.

2. A thorough description of the partnering and buying processes used by business firms and the changes occurring in these processes, along with methods of internal and external partnering to deliver total quality.

3. An emphasis throughout the text on the need for salespeople to be flexible—to adapt their strategies to customer needs and buyer social styles.

4. A complete discussion of how effective selling and career growth are achieved through planning and continual learning.

5. The growing role of salespeople in learning organizations to carry the voice of the customer to all parts of the organization, and beyond to suppliers and facilitators.

6. A thorough examination of the ways in which salespeople use technology to learn about, connect with, and build relationships with customers.

These unique content features are presented in a highly readable format, supported with examples from current sales programs and salespeople, and illustrated with four-color exhibits and photographs. If you've used this book before, you'll find that many Selling Scenario and Building Partnerships field examples are new to this edition, and nearly all Profiles of salespeople (that open each chapter) are brand new. With so many changes in selling over the past few years, a new edition must, necessarily, be *new*. Yet you will find the same practicality and theory of the previous editions.

PARTNERING: FROM THE FIELD TO THE CLASSROOM

Textbooks are generally developed, reviewed, and edited by academicians. In that respect, this book is no different. We have improved the text based on feedback from users and reviewers. What is different is that sales executives and field salespeople who are locked in the daily struggle of adapting to the new realities of selling also reviewed *Selling: Building Partnerships*. They have told us what the field is like now, where it is going, and what students must do to be prepared for the challenges that will face them.

Students have also reviewed chapters. They are, after all, the ones who must learn from the book. We asked for their input before and during the revision process. And judging by their comments and suggestions, this book is effectively delivering the content.

As you can see in About the Authors, we have spent considerable time in the field in a variety of sales positions. We continue to spend time in the field engaging in personal selling ourselves, as well as observing and serving professional salespeople. We believe the book has benefited greatly because of such a never-ending development process.

Users of the earlier editions will find several improvements in this edition:

A renewed emphasis on ethics. Professional sales ethics have always been a hallmark of *Selling: Building Partnerships*, but you'll now find ethics issues discussed in every chapter,

as well as discussion questions devoted to ethical issues at the end of each chapter. Many of these ethics discussions are identified by a special icon in the margin.

Continued emphasis on Canadian and Mexican examples, and more global and cultural diversity sales examples. We want to reflect both the reality of NAFTA and the global nature of selling. This means including not only Canadian and Mexican examples throughout the text but also examples of global account management, particularly in Chapters 16 and 17.

An expanded emphasis on technology. Technology continues to change how buyers and sellers interact, and we've continued to emphasize the role technology plays in supporting sales activities. As you will see, we've added discussions on technology in virtually every chapter, as well as incorporated technology issues into Selling Scenario and Thinking It Through features. By including technology throughout the book, students can understand the impact it has on every facet of selling.

An updated CD-ROM supplement. Don McBane, technical wizard and great sales teacher, has again prepared a CD-ROM package that significantly improves what you can do in the classroom. Transparencies are available in PowerPoint; but more important, video clips are now available. This means you can illustrate individual techniques of selling quickly and easily.

TEXT FEATURES AND SUPPLEMENT

Everything in this edition of *Selling: Building Partnerships* is designed to help teachers be more effective and to help students develop skills they can use every day and in the field. Several features help both students and teachers achieve their objectives.

Profiles of field salespeople set the stage for each chapter in the text. In each profile, the salesperson discusses his or her experiences and how they relate to the material that follows. Almost all profiles are new for this edition. Each chapter begins with a series of questions that will guide the student's reading experience.

In each chapter, Selling Scenarios present the real-life experiences of professional salespeople and issues such as the impact of technology. Most Selling Scenarios are new to this edition; many were written specifically for the text. The Selling Scenarios are tied to the material within each chapter, reinforcing the concepts and presenting applications of selling principles.

Building Partnership field examples focus on the partnership aspects of selling. These scenarios examine case studies of how salespeople were able to build relationships through the application of concepts presented in the chapter.

A feature called Thinking It Through helps students internalize key concepts. Each Thinking It Through feature is an involving exercise that could be the start of wonderful classroom dialogue or a short essay exam question. But most important for students, reading and using Thinking It Through is a method of experiencing the concepts as they read, which increases their comprehension and retention. Based on user feedback, we have expanded the number of Thinking It Through features, and we've tried to tie at least one in each chapter to technology.

Most chapters have at least two global references that apply the material to other cultures or settings or consider diversity issues. A prime example is the negotiations chapter. All chapters have expanded international coverage, as well as coverage of the multicultural diversity within the United States. These expanded global diversity references are marked with global symbols.

Key terms at the end of each chapter are followed by page references so the student can look up the definitions. The list of key terms will help students prepare for exams; the page references will improve their retention because they will be more likely to read supporting material, not just definitions. You'll find many new terms, such as digital asset management, privacy laws, virtual sales calls, data mining, and more discussed in detail in this new edition.

The questions and problems at the end of each chapter are also designed to involve the student, but in a slightly different manner. The first question (and sometimes more) deals with ethics issues. The questions are designed to (a) integrate concepts and definitions, (b) require the student to apply a concept to a selling situation, or (c) start discussion during class. Therefore, students will want to review the questions to study for exams, while the teacher will use the questions to stimulate classroom discussion. These questions are more than just look up a list in the chapter—they will require thought and help develop critical thinking skills. And since many are new to this edition, students cannot rely on libraries of answers.

Cases are also available at the end of each chapter. We have found these cases to work well as daily assignments and as frameworks for lectures, discussion, or small group practices. Some cases are tied to the videotapes for complete integration. Many of them have been tested in our classes and have been refined based on student feedback. A few user favorites have been revised and updated, but many are new cases.

New role-play scenarios are also provided in the text, with various buyer roles in the Instructor's Manual. One set of role-plays makes use of ACT! software, increasing students' knowledge of what contact management software is and how it helps salespeople manage their time and territory. These role-plays serve two functions. First, students practice their skills in a friendly environment. They can try out their partnering skills in an environment that will encourage personal growth. Second, and this is unique, the role-plays are written to serve as minicases. Student observers will see situations that call for application of many of the concepts and principles from the book. Both vicarious and experiential learning are enhanced for the observers. These role-play scenarios are all completely new for this fifth edition, and we've included in the text an essay for students on how to prepare for role-plays.

We've updated this book's website, and we hope you'll take a look at www.mhhe.com/business/marketing/weitz. The password-protected area for instructors (ask your rep for the password) includes an Instructor to Instructor bulletin board, along with lots of great links and downloadable supplements, like the Instructor's Manual, Test Bank, and PowerPoint slides. You'll also find role-playing information, including information to help create your own buying scenarios, if you wish. In the student area, you can find all of the URLs that appear in the text, business cards for role-plays from the text, examples of entry-level sales jobs, and more. Sample test questions are also there for students to check their understanding of the material in each chapter.

Instructor's manuals are available with any text, but the quality often varies. Because we teach the course every semester, as well as presenting and participating in basic sales seminars in industry, we feel that we have created an Instructor's Manual that can significantly assist the teacher. We've also asked instructors what they would like to see in a manual. In addition to suggested course outlines, chapter outlines, lecture suggestions, answers to questions and cases, and transparencies (many that are not from exhibits in the book), we include helpful suggestions on how to use the video and the CD-ROM. You can also find information on how to use the book with The Sales Connection telecourse, for which Steve Castleberry was the content advisor and appears in eight segments. We also include many of the in-class exercises we have developed over the years. These have been subjected to student critique, and we are confident you will find them useful. You will also find a number of additional role-play scenarios.

Students do need to practice their selling skills in a selling environment. And they need to do this in a way that is helpful. Small group practice exercises, complete with instructions for student evaluations, are provided in the Instructor's Manual. These sessions can be held as part of class but are also designed for out-of-class time for teachers who want to save class time for full-length role-plays.

The Test Bank has been carefully and completely rewritten. Questions are directly tied to the learning goals presented at the beginning of each chapter and the material covered in the questions and problems. In addition, key terms will be covered in the test questions. Application questions are available so students can demonstrate their understanding of the key concepts by applying those selling principles.

Teachers and students alike have been thrilled with the videotapes that have been created especially for this package. Corporate training videos, Achieve Global's Professional Selling Skills seminar, and customized videos developed expressly for this new edition (e.g. new ethics videos, new video sales calls, and a new day-in-the-life video) have been carefully integrated with material from the text. Each segment is short, generally under 10 minutes, with opportunities for stopping and discussing what has been viewed. Or students can watch the videos outside class and still learn. Video information, including in-class and homework exercises, is incorporated for the teacher in the Instructor's Manual so that all can make the most of the video.

ACKNOWLEDGMENTS

Staying current with the rapidly changing field of professional selling is a challenge. Our work has been blessed with the excellent support of reviewers, users, editors, salespeople, and students. Reviewers who also added important insights are:

Casey Donoho—Northern Arizona University

Margery Fetters—North Central College

Shawn Green—Aurora University

Larry Fuhrer—College of DuPage, et al.

Susan Thompson—Palm Beach Community College

Gary Ernst—North Central College

Robert Mullenbach—Loyola University

Annette Jajko—Triton College

Readers will become familiar with many of the salespeople who contributed to the development of the fifth edition through various Selling Scenario or Profile features. But other salespeople and sales executives contributed in less obvious, but no less important, ways. For providing video material, reviewing chapters, updating cases, providing material for Selling Scenarios, or other support, we'd like to thank:

Ted Barnett, McGraw-Hill

Tracey Brill, Abbott Labs

Brian Cobb, Glaxo Smith-Kline Pharmaceutical

Matt Haberle, Maximum Impact

Shirley Hunter, NCR–Teradata

Kris Jacobson, Procter & Gamble

Barb Kellgren, Lutron Electronics

Rhonda Killen, Quaker Tropicana Gatorade

Danielle Lord, US Foodservice

Angie Main, Magic 95.7 FM

Alex Marquette, PartStock Computer Solutions

Tom McCarty, Motorola

Vince Nall, Ideal Industries

Tim Pavlovich, Carleton-Bates

Jeff Pope, Edward Jones Co.

Glenn Price, Northwest Financial Network

Mark Prude, Wallace

Jeremy Villareal, Spenco Medical

Virginia Wichern, 3M

In addition to the support of these individuals, many companies also provided us with material. We'd like to express our sincere gratitude for their support.

There are some folks who are very easy to work with, yet get the job done well. Linda Schrieber and Sarah Crago both fit that bill. For some reason, becoming absent-minded is an occupational hazard for us, but with Sarah and Linda on the ball, the details, crises, and creative needs get handled with equal flair. Kari Geltemeyer was superb as project manager. We mentioned Don McBane's outstanding work earlier, and we'd like to thank Craig Atkins, media tech manager, and Cathy Tepper, who coordinated the supplements—we've heard so many good things about Cathy, and now we know they're all true! Billie L. Porter is the photo researcher, new for this edition, and we appreciate the fresh approach that was taken. Thanks also to Cole-Martens Media, who prepared the video.

Several people assisted in manuscript preparation, and we gratefully appreciate their help: Jeannie Castleberry, Jon Hoel, and Ted and John R. Tanner, who worked on research.

Many students and teachers have made comments that have helped us strengthen the overall package. They deserve our thanks, as do others who prefer to remain anonymous.

Bart Weitz
Steve Castleberry
Jeff Tanner

Guided Tour

Selling: Building Partnerships was the first text to bring a partnership/relationship approach into the selling course, offering a solid framework on which to hang plenty of practice and real-world application. The Fifth Edition of this popular text builds on that foundation with updated content, improved hands-on exercises, and powerful technology that's sure to make the material more engaging for professors and students alike.

CHAPTER OPENING PROFILES

The **Chapter Opening** profiles in this edition are the product of strong selling partnerships. The authors approached the McGraw-Hill sales representatives with an innovative proposal and the opportunity to involve their selling faculty in this revision. Steve Castleberry and Jeff Tanner asked the reps to request that their customers contact former students, who had gone on to careers in sales. Many faculty and past students agreed to participate, and the results are exciting new profiles to which we hope current students can relate.

"You have to pay attention to body language to see if you've lost someone. If so, you stop, go back and break things down even further so they understand."

Barbara S. Kellgren, Lutron

PROFILE

Barbara S. Kellgren graduated from Middle Tennessee State University with a BBA in marketing and a minor in Spanish. She works for Lutron Electronics, a high-tech firm that manufactures and designs lighting controls for residential, commercial, and institutional applications. As a marketing representative in the ... calls on interior ... XPO Design ... educate them ...

... y audiences I ... needs, so the ... ent. The sales ... in to a cus- ... ners in their ... more time to ... . The project ... to install at a ... b site. Then ... who need to ... electricians, ... all of these ... arily to keep ... ducts so they ... st full year in ... 38 percent ... r because of ... s.

... selling. For ... to understand ... em, I explain ... lights from a ... e. But you've ... dark outside ... of groceries ... ling with, or ... rying to get ... little Johnny ... magine never

having to come into a dark house again. With our lighting system, you can turn lights on from your car and create a pathway of light to get you from your garage, down a hall, and into your kitchen, or on into your bedroom—however you normally come into your home, all without doing any special wiring in your home." I can often win over customers by painting these pictures because these are images they are familiar with. Almost everyone has had these experiences and can easily relate to them. Most people just don't realize they can do something about it.

"Watching customers' body language is very important. I know our products back and forth, but many things that I take for granted with lighting controls, I must realize many other people don't understand. You have to pay attention to body language to see if you've lost someone. If so, you stop, go back, and break things down even further so they understand. I've learned to explain the same concepts in different ways because people are so different.

"My position takes me to southeast Florida twice a month, and the communication that takes place there is different from anywhere else. The store in Miami does a lot of export business with lots of customers from Mexico, Puerto Rico, and South America. People with Spanish/Hispanic backgrounds have a different idea of proxemics than most Americans. For instance, men and women stand much closer to a stranger than what most Americans find comfortable. Plus, there is a different sense of camaraderie there than at other stores I call on. Like when I arrive at the Miami store, the sales associates will give me a peck on each cheek—which is a standard greeting in the Spanish world when you see friends. Other locations would probably take this as sexual harassment, but it's not. It's just varying the communication style depending on what your customer is comfortable with."

Visit Our Website @ www.lutron.com.

"My success in publishing is built on the principle of partnerships."

Ted Barnett, McGraw-Hill

PROFILE

Not everyone goes directly from college to sales; for some, sales positions are taken after a start in another career. Such was the case for Ted Barnett, who began teaching right after college. As he learned, however, teaching and sales require very similar skills. "Teaching in the public schools for nine years taught me many selling skills: listening, analyzing needs, gathering information, making effective presentations, relationship building, and managing time." When Barnett decided to leave the classroom, he didn't want to leave education all together. As he says, "Strong commitments to education lead me into the educational publishing industry," where he now combines his educational background with his sales expertise for McGraw-Hill, the publisher of this textbook.

"My teaching experience gave me a unique perspective on the problems and concerns faced by professors and instructors in the classroom." Because of that experience, he's been able to generate consistent revenue growth for 17 of his 19 years in sales. "My success in publishing is built on the principle of partnerships. Understanding that customers rely on me for information, academic trends, market activity, and most importantly, service," Barnett works hard to build partnerships with his customers.

Barnett believes that effective customer service is the distinguishing characteristic that turns his customers into partners. The service supplied may range from reliable delivery of product and support resources to seminars on academic trends or technology training programs, or from problem solving to future program strategy planning.

A feature of customer service is the advocacy that a salesperson takes back to the company on behalf of the customer. "Many times I found myself negotiating with the company (in departments such

as) editorial, production, or sales management on the value of recognizing the customer priorities and changing our operations to meet those needs. In some cases it might take long-term operational or scheduling changes to meet the professor's planning needs, or it might mean pushing for consistent technology support and training or bringing new technology into the classroom. Each case is a matter of demonstrating the value of delivering the service to the customer. The revenue follows."

Barnett also believes that establishing a reputation as an advocate for customer service among clients is a two-way street. "When customers become partners, they are willing to help you out," notes Barnett. In 2001 Barnett had surgery and was on medical leave for over a month. When he returned, a paralyzed vocal cord made speech nearly impossible. "In my case, I built enough credit with clients to sustain a growing revenue base in spite of a period of absence due to spinal surgery and a paralyzed vocal cord that took months of therapy to overcome. Using technology, I was able to maintain contact with customers and growth opportunities. The decision makers granted me the leeway that kept me in the running until I could again deliver the service they relied on. It didn't guarantee that I would win, but gave me the opportunity to compete." Some of his customers had no idea he was out; the level of service they received didn't change due to his hard work and use of e-mail and other technology. "That was a tough year, but revenue goals were achieved," notes Barnett.

Barnett's relationships with his clients are perhaps his most satisfying reward. "Sales growth over a long period of time can only occur when all the pieces are in place: great customer service, great products, and great relationships."

Visit Our Website @ www.mhhe.com.

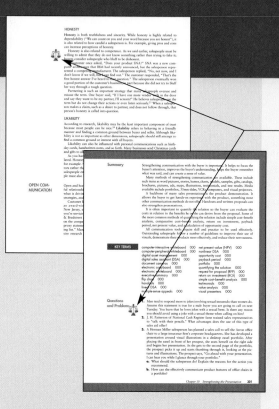

ETHICS

Professional sales **ethics** have always been the hallmark of this text. The new edition integrates ethics throughout each chapter, as well as in discussion questions devoted to this topic. Many of the discussion questions are identified by a special icon in the margin, underscoring the importance of ethics in professional sales.

GLOBAL AND CULTURAL DIVERSITY EMPHASIS

Current and continued emphasis on selling examples from Canada, Mexico, and all around the globe, as well as the impact of cultural diversity, serve to reflect the reality of the true nature of selling.

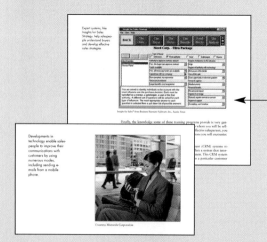

TECHNOLOGY EMPHASIS

The text analyzes the way technology impacts the salesperson's life. The authors discuss PDAs, cell phones, virtual sales calls, the Internet and email as a source of leads; presentation software; and voice mail; as well as ways to manage these technologies to achieve the highest level of success.

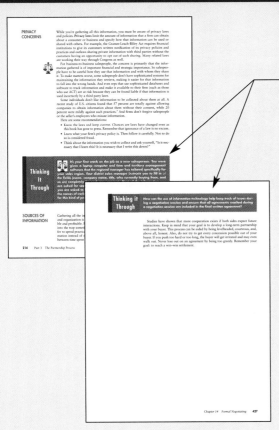

THINKING IT THROUGH

Thinking It Through boxes (two per chapter, one featuring a technology discussion) are engaging exercises that can inspire classroom dialogue or serve as a short-essay exam question to help students experience concepts as they read.

SELLING SCENARIOS &
BUILDING PARTNERSHIPS

Featured in each chapter, **Selling Scenarios** reinforce the concepts and present applications of selling principles through realistic examples. **Building Partnerships** boxes examine how successful salespeople build relationships.

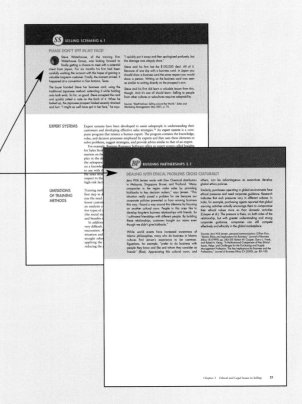

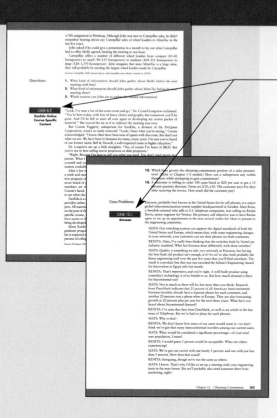

MINI-CASES

Class-tested **mini-cases** at the end of each chapter work well as daily assignments and as frameworks for lectures, discussion, or small-group practices. Some cases are tied to the videotapes for complete integration. The cases encourage the student to apply theories and skills learned in the text to solve sales situations.

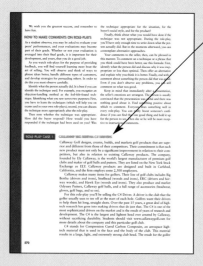

ROLE-PLAY EXERCISES

Students can practice their partnering skills in **role-play exercises** that encourage personal growth and experiential learning. Additional role-plays are included in the Instructor's Manual

Supplements

ACT! EXPRESS CD-ROM

Included with the textbook is **ACT! Express,** a real-world business tool. Based on the best-selling ACT! contact management system, ACT! Express shows students how to become more productive—resulting in better business relationships and greater business opportunities.

INSTRUCTOR'S RESOURCE CD-ROM

The **Instructor's Resource CD** contains the Instructor's Manual, the Test Bank (and computerized test bank) and the PowerPoint Lecture slides. The IM includes a course outline, chapter outlines, lecture suggestions, answers to discussion and case questions, video case suggestions, Wilson CD tips, lecture transparencies, in-class exercises, and additional role-plays. The PowerPoint slides feature video clips, exhibits from the text, and additional lecture support.

VIDEO LIBRARY

The **Video Library** features nine brand new video segments customized for the text, including four from Achieve Global's Professional Selling Skills Seminar (PSS), three new ethics segments, a new "Day in the Life," and a new "Anatomy of a Sales Call."

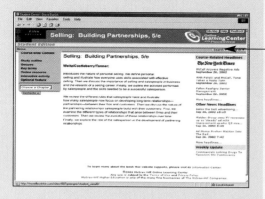

ONLINE LEARNING CENTER

The **Online Learning Center** houses the Instructor's Manual, PowerPoint slides and a link to McGraw Hill's course management system, PageOut for the Instructor and study outlines, quizzes, key terms, career information, and online resources for the student.

Contents in Brief

Preface   ix

PART 1

The Field of Selling   1

Chapter 1
Selling and Salespeople 2

Chapter 2
Building Partnering Relationships 30

PART 2

Knowledge and Skill Requirements   55

Chapter 3
Ethical and Legal Issues in Selling   56

Chapter 4
Buying Behavior and the Buying Process   82

Chapter 5
Using Communication Principles to Build
Relationships 120

Chapter 6
Adaptive Selling for Relationship Building   152

PART 3

The Partnership Process   177

Chapter 7
Prospecting   178

Chapter 8
Planning the Sales Call   208

Chapter 9
Making the Sales Call   238

Chapter 10
Strengthening the Presentation   274

Chapter 11
Responding to Objections   308

Chapter 12
Obtaining Commitment   340

Chapter 13
After the Sale: Building Long-Term
Partnerships   370

PART 4

Special Applications   405

Chapter 14
Formal Negotiating   406

Chapter 15
Selling to Resellers   434

PART 5

The Salesperson as Manager   467

Chapter 16
Managing Your Time and Territory   468

Chapter 17
Managing within Your Company   502

Chapter 18
Managing Your Career   536

Role-Play Cases   569

Endnotes   N

Glossary   G-1

Indexes   I

Contents

Preface   ix

PART 1

The Field of Selling   1

Chapter 1
Selling and Salespeople   2

Why Learn about Personal Selling?   3

Role of Salespeople in Business   5
   Salespeople Communicate to Customers and
      Prospects   6
   Salespeople Acquire and Share Information with the
      Seller's Firm   8
   Salespeople Serve as Relationship Managers   9

What Do Salespeople Do?   9
   Selling   9
   Servicing Customers   10
   Coordinating Activities   11
   Providing Information to the Company and
      Preparing Information for Customers   11

Types of Salespeople   12
   Selling and Distribution Channels   12
   Describing Sales Jobs   14
   The Sales Jobs Continuum   16
   Examples of Sales Jobs   16

Characteristics of Successful Salespeople   18
   Motivation   18
   Dependability and Trustworthiness   18
   Ethical Sales Behavior   18
   Customer and Product Knowledge   18
   Communication Skills   19
   Flexibility   19
   Creativity   19
   Emotional Intelligence   20
   Are Salespeople Born or Made?   21

Rewards In Selling   21
   Independence and Responsibility   22

Financial Rewards   22
Management Opportunities   23
The Building Partnerships Model   24
   Summary   25
   Key Terms   25
   Questions and Problems   25
   Case Problems   26
   Additional References   28

Chapter 2
Building Partnering Relationships   30

The Evolution of Personal Selling   32

Types of Relationships   33
   Market Exchanges   33
   Partnerships   35
   Summary   38

Characteristics of Successful Relationships   38
   Mutual Trust   40
   Open Communication   43
   Common Goals   44
   Commitment to Mutual Gain   44
   Organizational Support   45

Phases of Relationship Development   46
   Awareness   46
   Exploration   47
   Expansion   47
   Commitment   47
   Dissolution   47

Managing Relationships and Partnering   47
   Choosing the Right Relationship   47
   Using Technology to Increase Efficiency   49
   Summary   50
   Key Terms   50
   Questions and Problems   50
   Case Problems   51
   Additional References   52

PART 2

Knowledge and Skill Requirements 55

Chapter 3
Ethical and Legal Issues in Selling 56

Ethics and Personal Selling 58
   Ethics and Partnering Relationships 59

Factors Influencing the Ethical Behavior of
   Salespeople 59
   Personal, Company, and Customer Needs 60
   Company Policies 60

A Personal Code of Ethics 62

Selling Ethics and Relationships 62
   Relationships with Customers 63
   Relationships with the Salesperson's Company 67
   Relationships with Colleagues 68
   Relationships with Competitors 69

Legal Issues 69
   Uniform Commercial Code 70
   Misrepresentation or Sales Puffery 72
   Illegal Business Practices 73
   Legal Guidelines 75

Ethical and Legal Issues in International Selling 75
   Resolving Cultural Differences 76
   Legal Issues 76

      Summary 78
      Key Terms 78
      Questions and Problems 78
      Case Problems 80
      Additional References 81

Chapter 4
Buying Behavior and the Buying Process 82

Types of Customers 84
   Producers 84
   Resellers 86
   Government Agencies 86
   Institutions 87
   Consumers 88

Organizational Buying and Selling 88
   Complexity of the Organizational Buying Process 88
   Derived versus Direct Demand 89

How Do Organizations Make Buying Decisions? 89
   Steps in the Buying Process 89
   Creeping Commitment 92

Types of Organizational Buying Decisions 93
   New Tasks 93
   Straight Rebuys 93

Modified Rebuys 95

Who Makes the Buying Decision? 95
   Users 96
   Initiators 96
   Influencers 96
   Gatekeepers 96
   Deciders 97

Supplier Evaluation and Choice 98
   Organizational Needs and Criteria 98
   Individual Needs of Buying Center Members 100
   Vendor Analysis 102

Trends in Organizational Buying 102
   Increasing Importance of Purchasing Agents 104
   Centralized Purchasing 104
   Global Sourcing 104
   Outsourcing 105
   Supply Chain Management 105
   The Internet and Business-to-Business Selling 106
   Long-Term Customer–Supplier Relationships 108

      Summary 109
      Key Terms 109
      Questions and Problems 110
      Case Problems 111
      Appendix: Multiattribute Model of Product
         Evaluation and Choice 114
      Additional References 118

Chapter 5
Using Communication Principles to Build
Relationships 120

Building Relationships through Two-Way Communication
   122
   The Communication Process 122
   Communication Breakdowns 122
   Communication Methods 124

Sending Verbal Messages 125
   Effective Use of Words 125
   Voice Characteristics 127
   Asking Questions 129

Listening to Verbal Communications from Customers 131
   Active Listening 131

Reading Nonverbal Messages from Customers 135
   Body Language 135
   Detecting Customers' Hidden Emotions and
      Feelings 137

Sending Messages with Nonverbal Communication 138
   Using Body Language 138
   The Role of Space and Physical Contact in
      Communication 140
   Appearance 141

Communicating in a High-Technology Environment   143

Adjusting for Cultural Differences   145
Use of Language   145
Time and Scheduling   146
Body Language   146

Summary   147

Key Terms   148

Questions and Problems   148

Case Problems   149

Additional References   150

Chapter 6
Adaptive Selling for Relationship Building   152

Types of Presentations   154
Standard Memorized Presentation   154
Outlined Presentation   154
Customized Presentation   154

Adaptive Selling and Sales Success   154

Knowledge and Adaptive Selling   157
Product and Company Knowledge   157
Organizing Knowledge of Sales Situations and
Customers into Categories   158
Approaches for Developing Knowledge   158

The Social Style Matrix: A Training Program for Building
Adaptive Selling Skills   161
Dimensions of Social Styles   161
Categories of Social Styles   162
Identifying Customers' Social Styles   165
Social Styles and Sales Presentations   165
Versatility   167
The Role of Knowledge   168

Alternative Training Systems for Developing Adaptive
Selling Skills   168
Expert Systems   169
Limitations of Training Methods   169

Customer Relationship Management (CRM) Systems   170

Summary   171

Key Terms   171

Questions and Problems   171

Case Problems   172

Additional References   174

PART **3**

The Partnership Process   177

Chapter 7
Prospecting   178

The Importance of Prospecting   180

Characteristics of a Good Prospect   180
Does a Want or Need Exist?   181
Does the Lead Have the Ability to Pay?   182
Does the Lead Have the Authority to Buy?   182
Can the Lead Be Approached Favorably?   182
Is the Lead Eligible to Buy?   182
Other Criteria   184

How and Where to Obtain Prospects   184
Satisfied Customers   184
Endless-Chain Method   185
Center-of-Influence Method   186
Networking   187
The Internet   188
Ads, Direct Mail, Catalogs, and Publicity   189
Shows   190
Seminars   191
Lists and Directories   191
Data Mining and CRM Systems   193
Cold Calling   193
Spotters   194
Telemarketing   194
Sales Letters   196
Other Sources of Leads   198

Lead Qualification and Management Systems   198

Overcoming a Reluctance to Prospect   201

Summary   203

Key Terms   203

Questions and Problems   203

Case Problems   204

Additional References   206

Chapter 8
Planning the Sales Call   208

Why Plan the Sales Call?   210

Obtaining Precall Information   210
The Prospect/Customer as an Individual   212
The Prospect's/Customer's Organization   212
Privacy Concerns   214
Sources of Information   214

Setting Call Objectives   218
Criteria for Effective Objectives   219
Setting More than One Call Objective   220
Setting Objectives for Several Calls   221
Buyers May Be Setting Goals Also   223

Making an Appointment   223
How to Make Appointments   223
The Right Person   224
The Right Time   226
The Right Place   226

Cultivating Relationships with Subordinates   227

Telephoning for Appointments   229

Additional Planning   231

    Summary   233

    Key Terms   233

    Questions and Problems   233

    Case Problems   234

    Additional References   236

Chapter 9
Making the Sales Call   238

Making a Good Impression   240
    Waiting for the Prospect   240
    The Entrance   241
    Very First Impressions   241
    Handshaking   242
    Selecting a Seat   242
    Getting the Customer's Attention   243
    Developing Rapport   246
    When Things Go Wrong   247

Identifying the Prospect's Needs: The Power of Asking
    Questions   248
    Remember to Communicate Effectively   250
    Asking Open and Closed Questions   250
    SPIN® Technique   252
    Reiterating Needs You Identified before the
        Meeting   254
    Additional Considerations   255
    Developing a Strategy for the Presentation   256

Offering the Solution to the Buyer's Needs   256
    Relating Features to Benefits   256
    Assessing Reactions   259

Building Credibility during the Call   261

Selling to Groups   264

    Summary   266

    Key Terms   266

    Questions and Problems   267

    Case Problems   268

    Additional References   270

Chapter 10
Strengthening the Presentation   274

Characteristics of a Strong Presentation   276
    Keeps the Buyer's Attention   276
    Improves the Buyer's Understanding   276
    Helps the Buyer Remember What Was Said   276
    Offers Proof of the Salesperson's Assertions   277
    Creates a Sense of Value   277

How to Strengthen the Presentation   278

Verbal Tools   278
Visual Tools   280
Product Demonstrations   289
Handouts   292
Written Proposals   293
Value Analysis: Quantifying the Solution   296

Dealing with the Jitters   299

    Summary   301

    Key Terms   301

    Questions and Problems   301

    Case Problems   303

    Additional References   305

Chapter 11
Responding to Objections   308

When Do Buyers Raise Objections?   310
    Setting Up an Initial Appointment   310
    The Presentation   310
    Attempting to Obtain Commitment   310
    After the Sale   311

Common Objections   311
    Objections Related to Needs   311
    Objections Related to the Product   312
    Objections Related to the Source   313
    Objections Related to the Price   315
    Objections Related to Time   316
    Other Objections   317

Preparing to Respond   318
    Develop a Positive Attitude   318
    Commit to Always Tell the Truth   319
    Anticipate Objections   319
    Relax and Listen—Do Not Interrupt   320
    Forestall Known Concerns   321
    Evaluate Objections   321

Effective Response Methods   322
    Direct Denial   324
    Indirect Denial   324
    Compensation Method   325
    Feel–Felt–Found Method   326
    Boomerang Method   327
    Pass-Up Method   327
    Postpone Method   328
    Using the Methods   329
    Objections When Selling to a Group of Buyers   330

The Price Objection   330
    Use Up-to-Date Information   331
    Establish the Value   331
    Use Communication Tools Effectively   332

Dealing with Tough Customers   334

Summary 335

Key Terms 335

Questions and Problems 335

Case Problems 337

Additional References 339

Chapter 12
Obtaining Commitment 340

Obtaining Commitment Today 342
Part of the Process 342
The Importance of Securing Commitment 343

Financial Terms and Conditions 344
Discounts 344
Credit Terms 345
Shipping Costs 345
Presenting Price 346

When to Attempt to Obtain Commitment 346
Buyer Comments 346
Nonverbal Cues 348

How to Successfully Obtain Commitment 349
Maintain a Positive Attitude 349
Let the Customer Set the Pace 349
Be Assertive, Not Aggressive 349
Sell the Right Item in the Right Amounts 350

Effective Methods 351
Direct Request 352
Benefit Summary 352
Balance Sheet Method 353
Probing Method 354
Alternative Choice 355
Other Methods 355

If Commitment Is Obtained 355
No Surprises 356
Confirm the Customer's Choice 356
Get the Signature 357
Show Appreciation 357
Cultivate for Future Calls 358
Review the Actions to be Taken 358

If Commitment Is Not Obtained 358
Some Reasons for Lost Opportunities 359
Discovering the Cause 360
Suggestions for Dealing with Rejection 360

Bringing the Interview to a Close 361
Summary 363
Key Terms 363
Questions and Problems 364
Case Problems 365
Additional References 368

Chapter 13
After the Sale: Building Long-Term
Partnerships 370

The Value of Customers 372

Exploration 374
Set the Right Expectations 375
Monitor Order Processing 375
Ensure Proper Initial Use of the Product or
Service 376
Follow Up 377
Make Personal Visits 378
Handle Customer Complaints 378
Achieve Customer Satisfaction 384

Expansion 385
Generating Repeat Orders 385
Upgrading 387
Full-Line Selling 387
Cross-Selling 388
Total Quality Management and Account
Relationships 388

Commitment 389
Securing Commitment to a Partnership 390
The Salesperson as Change Agent 392

Causes of Dissolution 395
Limited Personal Relationships 395
Failing to Monitor Competitor Actions 396
Failing to Monitor the Industry 396
Falling into Complacency 396
Conflict 397
Summary 399
Key Terms 399
Questions and Problems 399
Case Problems 400
Additional References 403

PART 4

Special Applications 405

Chapter 14
Formal Negotiating 406

The Nature of Negotiation 408
Negotiation versus Nonnegotiation Selling 408
What Can Be Negotiated? 409
Are You a Good Negotiator? 409

Planning for the Negotiation Session 411
Location 411
Time Allotment 412
Negotiation Objectives 412

Team Selection and Management   414
Individual Behavior Patterns   416
Information Control   418

The Negotiation Meeting   418
Preliminaries   419
General Guidelines   420
Dealing with Win–Lose Negotiators   421
Making Concessions   424
Recap of a Successful Negotiation Meeting   426

Summary   428
Key Terms   428
Questions and Problems   428
Case Problems   430
Additional References   431

Chapter 15
Selling to Resellers   434

Resellers and the Distribution Channel   436
Who Are Resellers?   436
The Role of Resellers in a Distribution Channel   437

Getting Resellers to Sell Your Products   438
Share of Space   439
Share of Mind   440

Reseller Buying Considerations   440
Return on Inventory—Strategic Profit Model   440
Return on Space   444
Image   444
Other Factors to Consider   445

Selling to Resellers   445
Using the Strategic Profit Model   446
Improving Turnover   446
Proving Sales   447
Selling Profit Margin   451
Selling Image   453

Merchandise Markets, Trade Shows, and Trade Fairs   455
Merchandise Markets   455
Trade Shows   455

Supporting the Sales Efforts of Resellers   456
Promotions to Build Demand   457
Motivating Reseller Salespeople   459
Training Resellers   459

Partnering with Resellers   460
Category Management   460

Summary   462
Key Terms   462
Questions and Problems   463
Case Problems   463
Additional References   465

PART **5**

The Salesperson as Manager   467

Chapter 16
Managing Your Time and Territory   468

The Value of Time   470

The Self-Management Process   470

Setting Goals   471
The Need for Goals   471
The Nature of Goals   471
Types of Sales Goals   473
Setting Sales Goals   475

Allocating Resources   475
Resources to Be Allocated   475
Where to Allocate Resources   475
Account Classification and Resource Allocation   476
Investing in Accounts   481

Implementing the Time Management Strategy   482
Daily Activity Planning   482
Planning Process   483
Making More Calls   485
Handling Paperwork and Reports   489

Evaluating Performance   490
Postcall Analysis   491
Activity Analysis   491
Performance Analysis   492
Productivity Analysis   492

Summary   494
Key Terms   494
Questions and Problems   494
Case Problems   495
Additional References   500

Chapter 17
Managing within Your Company   502

Building Internal Partnerships   504
The Importance of Internal Partnerships   504
Selling Internally   505

Company Areas Important To Salespeople   507
Manufacturing   507
Administration   508
Shipping   509
Customer Service   509
Marketing   509
Sales   510

Partners in the Sales Organization   510
Sales Management   510

Field Sales Managers   515
Managing Ethics in Sales   517
Salespeople as Partners   520
Sales Teams   523
Technology and Teamwork   525

    Summary   527

    Key Terms   527

    Questions and Problems   528

    Case Problems   529

    Additional References   534

Chapter 18
Managing Your Career   536
Opportunities in Selling   538
Making a Good Match   539
    Understanding Yourself   539
    Understanding the Company   541
The Recruiting Process   543
    Selecting Salespeople   543
    Selling Your Capabilities   545
Managing Your Career Goals   556
    Making the Transition from College to Career   556
    Managing Your Career   557
    Developing Your Skills   560
    Managing Stress   561

    Summary   564

    Key Terms   564

    Questions and Problems   565

    Case Problems   565

    Additional References   568

Role-Play Cases   569

Endnotes   N

Glossary   G-1

Indexes   I

The Field of Selling

Part 1 introduces the nature of personal selling. In Chapter 1, we define personal selling and illustrate how everyone uses skills associated with effective selling. Then we discuss the importance of selling and salespeople in business and the rewards of a selling career. Finally, we outline the activities performed by salespeople and the skills needed to be a successful salesperson.

In Chapter 2, we review the different roles that salespeople have and illustrate how many salespeople now focus on developing long-term relationships—partnerships—between their firm and customers. Then we discuss the nature of the partnering relationships salespeople build with their customers. First, we examine the different types of relationships that arise between firms and their customers. Then we review the evolution of these relationships over time. Finally, we explore the role of the salesperson in the development of partnering relationships.

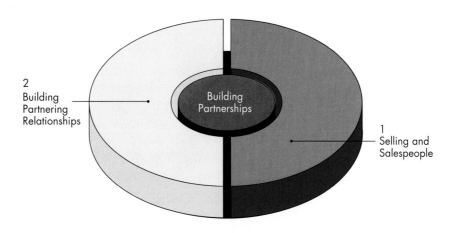

2
Building
Partnering
Relationships

Building
Partnerships

1
Selling and
Salespeople

Chapter

1

Selling and Salespeople

SOME QUESTIONS ANSWERED IN THIS CHAPTER ARE:

- What is selling?
- Why should you learn about selling even if you do not plan to be a salesperson?
- What is the role of personal selling in a firm?
- What are the different types of salespeople?
- What are the rewards of a selling career?

Business has changed dramatically over the last 20 years. Now firms compete in global markets, using sophisticated communication, transportation, and management information systems. More customers are demanding **24/7 service** (which means they expect a selling firm to be available for them 24 hours a day, seven days a week). These changes in the business environment have expanded the responsibilities of salespeople and increased their importance to the success of their firms.

This chapter discusses the importance of personal selling to business firms and how the nature of selling is changing from persuading prospects to buy products to managing the firm's relationships with its customers. The chapter concludes by describing the activities salespeople perform, the skills needed to be a successful salesperson, and the rewards of a sales career.

"I have observed that top salespeople are great at simplifying matters, not complicating them."

Glenn R. Price Jr., Northwestern Mutual Financial Network

PROFILE

Glenn R. Price Jr. graduated from MTSU in the spring of 1994 with a BBA degree and a major in marketing. He started with Northwestern Mutual Life as a college intern in February 1994 selling life and disability insurance, and then joined the firm full-time upon graduation. In his first year he had the highest sales in the country among his college intern peers. Why? He absolutely loved what he did and had fun working hard.

"I learned early in my sales career that to maintain long-term success you must first believe in what you are selling, and then it's just a matter of disciplining yourself to master the fundamentals. What are the fundamentals? For me it starts with planning my day. I've learned to focus only on the things that I can control. I focus each day on the inputs (i.e., number of calls, number of referrals, number of cases, number of fact finders), realizing that the outputs (i.e., sales) will take care of themselves. This helped me to stop taking it personally when someone said no. Keeping a positive mental attitude is key in personal selling, and once I realized that selling was a science, a number's game, then my emotional roller coaster leveled out and I became more productive.

"Today, the financial services industry is very complex, as are the needs of my clients. With hundreds of insurance and equity products I must have an excellent understanding of my clients' needs so I can make the right recommendation with the right product. I realize that in this complex world I live in I can't be all things to all people. I can, however, become a guru or a specialist in a couple of things and surround myself with specialists in all the other areas to create a team of specialists. For areas outside of my expertise all I have to do is identify which specialists are needed and bring them in. This approach allows me to operate at maximum efficiency while providing the highest level of expertise and service to my clients. It's also good from a business perspective because each specialist is like a profit center with no overhead. Whatever the specialist does for my clients I share in 50 percent of the revenue. Successful salespeople are good at time management, and being a specialist has helped me improve this skill by leveraging my time so I can focus my energy on what I do best. It also allows me to spend more time doing the things that are very important to me, like spending time with my family, being involved with my church, and community, as well as fishing a stream or in the woods hunting.

"Another area I focus on involves my communication skills. I have observed that top salespeople are great at simplifying matters, not complicating them. Many salespeople today purposefully add complexity to their presentation, thinking it raises their stature and indispensability in the eyes of their clients. This complicated approach, however, works against, not for, the salesperson. My observation is that top salespeople do just the opposite. They use simple illustrations, anecdotes, and metaphors; they bring themselves and their ideas into the mental grasp of every client. Consequently, when I practice these skills, clients enjoy talking with me and are willing to refer me to their friends. This technique is called storyselling. We all enjoy a good story. I believe that a big part of my success as a salesperson hinges on my ability to communicate and make the complex simple and understandable. I also believe that my success does not hinge on being a better analyst, but rather on being a better teacher, a better storyteller, and a master of the metaphor.

"Success truly is in learning the fundamentals and in doing the things that unsuccessful people are not willing to do. I do wish you success!"

Visit Our Website @ www.nmfn.com/glennprice.

WHY LEARN ABOUT PERSONAL SELLING?

What's the first thing that pops into your mind when you hear this phrase: "personal selling"? Do you conjure up images of fast-talking, nonlistening, pushy guys who won't take "no" for an answer? Does the cartoon in Exhibit 1.1 resonate with your idea of a seller? Maybe your definition would be something like this: "Personal selling is the craft of persuading people to buy what they do not want and do not need for more than it is worth."[1]

If that's what you think selling is, then please read and study this book carefully. You're going to learn things about selling that you never knew before. Let's start with a more accurate definition of a professional salesperson, which is quite different from the one just mentioned. **Personal selling** is a person-to-person business activity in which a salesperson uncovers and satisfies the needs of a buyer to the mutual, long-term benefit of both parties. This definition stresses that selling is more than making a sale and getting an order. The objective is to build a relationship—a partnership—that provides long-term benefits to both the seller and the customer. Thus selling involves helping customers identify problems, offering information about potential solutions, and providing after-the-sale service to ensure long-term satisfaction. Quite a bit different from the image of the seller in the cartoon, isn't it?

The days of salespeople carrying briefcases overstuffed with brochures and knocking on every door they can find to drum up interest in their companies'

Ralph Harrison, king of salespersons

products are waning. Today's professional salespeople coordinate the resources of their companies to help customers solve problems. They use e-mail, faxes, and videoconferencing to communicate with customers and support staff around the world; download information from their firms' data warehouses into laptop computers so they can know more about their prospects and customers; and develop client-specific multimedia presentations to illustrate the benefits of their firms' products and services.

This text discusses personal selling as a business activity undertaken by salespeople. But keep in mind that the principles of selling are useful to everyone, not just people with the title of salesperson. Developing mutually beneficial, long-term relationships is vital to all of us. Thus the principles discussed in this book will be useful even if you never plan to work as a salesperson.

As a college student, you might use selling techniques when asking another student to go out on a date or to ask a professor to let you enroll in a course that is closed out. When you near graduation, you will certainly confront a very important sales job: selling yourself to an employer.

To get a job after graduation, you will go through the same steps used in the sales process (discussed in Part 3, Chapters 7 through 13). First you will identify some potential employers (customers). On the basis of an analysis of each employer's needs, you will develop a presentation to demonstrate your ability to satisfy their needs. During the interview you will listen to what the recruiter says, ask and answer questions, and perhaps alter your presentation based on the new information you receive during the interview. At some point you might negotiate with the employer over starting salary. Eventually you will try to secure a commitment from the employer to hire you. This process is selling at a very personal level. Chapter 18 reviews the steps you need to undertake to get a sales job.

People in business use selling principles all the time. Engineers convince managers to support their R&D projects; industrial relations executives use selling approaches when negotiating with unions; and aspiring management trainees sell themselves to associates, superiors, and subordinates to get raises and promotions.

Traditionally, lawyers, accountants, doctors, and architects believed it was unprofessional to sell their services. They waited for customers to come to them. But times are changing. Faced with increased competition and more cost-conscious customers, even these professionals are becoming salespeople. A growing number of professional service firms are hiring salespeople to help them develop new business and teach their service providers how to sell. Salespeople in these situations are typically called *business development managers* or *business consultants*.

But it's not just businesspeople who practice the art of selling. Presidents encourage politicians in Congress to support certain programs; charities solicit contributions and volunteers to run organizations; scientists try to convince foundations and government agencies to fund research; and doctors try to get their patients to adopt healthier lifestyles. People skilled at influencing others and developing long-term relationships are usually leaders in our society.

ROLE OF SALESPEOPLE IN BUSINESS

Firms exist only when their products and services are sold, and salespeople are usually one of the most important elements in making that happen. They play a critical role in linking the firm and its customers by speaking on behalf of the selling firm, by acquiring and sharing valuable information about buyers with various groups within the selling firm, and by serving as relationship managers.

SALESPEOPLE COMMUNICATE TO CUSTOMERS AND PROSPECTS

Marketing textbooks usually treat salespeople as an element in the firm's marketing communications program—the firm's effort to tell customers about its products and services and where and how they can be bought, and to influence customers to buy them. Exhibit 1.2 classifies communication methods based on whether they're impersonal or personal and paid or unpaid.

METHODS FOR COMMUNICATING WITH CUSTOMERS

Advertising and promotions are examples of paid impersonal communications. Advertising uses impersonal mass media such as newspapers, TV, radio, direct mail, and the Internet to give information to customers. Sales promotions offer extra value and incentives to customers to purchase products during a specific period of time. For example, McDonald's offered special prices and gifts when the Disney movie *Return to Never Land* was first shown in theaters. Chapter 15 will provide more information on promotions to retailers.

Salespeople are the primary vehicles for providing paid personal communications to customers. Many people think—incorrectly—that advertising is the most important part of the firm's promotion program. However, industrial companies place far more emphasis on personal selling than on advertising.[2] Even in consumer products firms such as Lever Brothers, which spends more than $1 billion annually on advertising, personal selling plays a critical role. Although advertising informs customers about Lever Brothers' products, salespeople make sure the products are available and properly displayed in retail stores. All marketing people at Lever Brothers spend considerable time in the field with salespeople, learning about the needs of the retail stores as well as those of the ultimate consumers.

The primary method for generating unpaid impersonal communication is publicity. Publicity is communication through significant unpaid presentations about the firm (usually a news story). An example of publicity is Pennzoil's sponsorship of NASCAR racing teams.

Finally, firms communicate with their customers at no cost through word of mouth (communication among buyers about the selling firm). For example, salespeople often ask a customer to recommend their firms' products to other customers (see Chapter 7).

EXHIBIT 1.2

Communication Methods

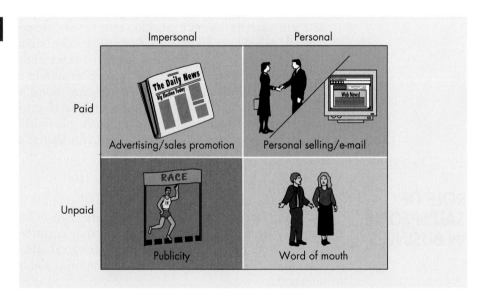

STRENGTHS AND WEAKNESSES OF COMMUNICATION METHODS

Exhibit 1.3 compares communication methods in terms of control, flexibility, credibility, and cost. Firms have more control when using paid versus unpaid methods. When using advertising, Internet websites, and sales promotions, companies can determine the message's exact content and the time of its delivery. They have less control over the communications delivered by salespeople and have very little control over the content or timing of publicity and word-of-mouth communications.

Personal selling is the most flexible communication method because salespeople can talk with each customer, discover the customer's specific needs, and develop unique presentations for that customer. Internet websites are less flexible than advertising but, due to their interactivity, more flexible than other communication methods. Mass media ads deliver the same message to all customers, but websites can be tailored to the needs of specific customers.

Because publicity and word of mouth are communicated by independent sources, their information is usually more credible than the information in paid communication sources. For example, because they know that retailers are trying to promote their merchandise, customers tend to doubt claims made by a store's salespeople and in its ads; however, the same customers may trust information provided by a person from another firm they meet at a trade show.

Personal selling is the most costly method of communication. A presentation by a salesperson costs more than $100—almost 10,000 times more than exposing a customer to a newspaper, radio, or TV ad.[3] However, the effectiveness of personal selling, due to its advantages in flexibility and control, justifies its high cost.

INTEGRATED MARKETING COMMUNICATIONS

Because each communication vehicle has strengths and weaknesses, many firms are developing communication programs that coordinate the use of various vehicles to maximize the impact of the program on customers. These coordinated efforts are called **integrated marketing communications.**[4]

For example, NationsBank used an integrated marketing communication program when it launched its Money Manager Account product. Money Manager is a combination brokerage, checking, savings, and money market account that allows a customer to quickly transfer money from one area to another to improve his or her rate of return. To launch the product, a direct mail piece urged selected customers to call the bank. When calls came in, NationsBank sent the callers a kit describing the program and assigned them to a broker. The broker telephoned and met with the callers to make the sale. The direct-marketing and personal-selling effort was reinforced with an advertising campaign on radio and television.[5]

Some have the mistaken notion that the growing world of e-commerce is causing the demise of salespeople. Studies have shown, however, that customers still

EXHIBIT 1.3	Communication Method	Control	Flexibility	Credibility	Cost
Comparison of Communication Methods	Personal selling	Moderate to high	High	Low	High
	Internet website	High	Moderate to high	Low	Moderate to high
	Mass media advertising	High	Low	Low	Moderate
	Publicity	Low	Low	High	Low to moderate
	Word of mouth	Low	Low	High	Low

Salespeople share important market information with their boss and others in their firm.

SuperStock

want to interact with a salesperson and value their interactions with salespeople.[6] As you will learn as you read through this book, salespeople add value that the buyer can't get by simply relying on e-commerce.

SALESPEOPLE ACQUIRE AND SHARE INFORMATION WITH THE SELLER'S FIRM

But salespeople are more than one of the methods companies use to communicate with their customers. Salespeople are the eyes and ears of the company in the marketplace. They are a critical element in the development of a learning organization.

A **learning organization** acquires information about its environment and remembers this information so that it can guide organizational decisions and actions even if the employees in the organization change.[7] Two types of organizational learning are adaptive learning and generative learning. *Adaptive learning* refers to developing knowledge to do the present activities better. For example, when Bob Meyer, a salesperson at Ballard Medical Products, was demonstrating a medical device, a surgeon commented that he could not tell whether the device was working properly because the tube was opaque. Meyer relayed this information to the vice president of engineering, and the product was redesigned, substituting a clear tube for the opaque tube. Meyer also learns a lot about customer needs when he conducts training sessions for the nurses in hospitals that use Ballard devices. This information provides valuable input to distribution, pricing, and advertising decisions for Ballard's present product lines.

Generative learning occurs when firms go beyond their present products, markets, policies, and procedures to develop new insights. Salespeople also provide critical input to this type of learning that affects strategic decision making by their firms. They are often the first to know when their customers' needs are changing. For example, at Flexatard, a manufacturer of fitness bodywear, salespeople relay customer reactions to changing fashions, new styles introduced by competitors, and approaches the company is considering to satisfy activewear users' needs. Salespeople know what the trends are and what new ideas will capture the imaginations of their customers.

Two critical processes of organizational learning are information acquisition and information dissemination. Because salespeople are in constant contact with the marketplace, they play an important role in information acquisition. They are typically the firm's best source of information about what customers want and what competitors are doing. They provide a critical input to the firm's strategic intelligence system.[8]

But to be effective members of a learning organization, salespeople need to be skillful at disseminating the knowledge they have acquired to other people in their companies. By communicating this information, salespeople play an important role in new product development, pricing decisions, and channel management. Chapter 17 discusses the relationship between salespeople and their companies in great detail.

Although salespeople are intimately involved in organizational learning, they still need to continually learn how to do their jobs better.[9] Issues related to self-improvement are discussed in Chapters 5 and 18.

SALESPEOPLE SERVE AS RELATIONSHIP MANAGERS

Rather than buying from the lowest-cost suppliers, many firms now are building competitive advantages by developing and maintaining close, cooperative relationships with a select set of suppliers. Through these relationships the firms provide superior value to their customers. Because of this increased attention to long-term partnering relationships, marketing scholars believe that **relationship marketing**—the focus of marketing activities on establishing, developing, and maintaining cooperative, long-term relationships—is the new marketing philosophy.[10]

Salespeople play a key role in the development, growth, and maintenance of these long-term buyer–seller relationships. They are the primary link between the buying and selling firms. Salespeople's performance has considerable effect on the value customers get from the relationship and the customers' interest in continuing the relationship. Customers often have greater loyalty to salespeople than to the firms employing the salespeople.[11]

When firms focus on developing partnering relationships, salespeople become relationship managers. They are responsible for identifying opportunities for creating value and organizing the resources of their companies to make sure these opportunities are exploited. For example, Ray Arckey is responsible for managing Procter & Gamble's relationship with Publix, the fourth-largest supermarket chain in the United States. His team of 25 people, located in an office close to Publix corporate headquarters, includes experts in advertising and promotion, data analysis, and supply chain management. They work with their counterparts at Publix to develop better approaches for promoting Procter & Gamble products and lowering inventory levels. Exploiting this opportunity to find innovative approaches for running the business improves sales and profits for both Procter & Gamble and Publix.

Many buyer–seller relationships are not partnerships. However, because of the importance of this emerging strategy, we focus on building partnerships in this textbook. The next chapter examines the different types of buyer–seller relationships and the role of salespeople in managing partnering relationships.

WHAT DO SALESPEOPLE DO?

The activities of salespeople depend on the type of selling job they choose. The responsibilities of salespeople selling financial services for General Electric differ greatly from those of salespeople selling pharmaceuticals for Merck or paper products for James River. But certain basic activities are common to all types of selling. In addition to face-to-face and telephone contact with customers, all salespeople have to undertake servicing, internal selling, and reporting activities.

SELLING

Sales jobs involve prospecting for new customers, increasing sales to existing customers, making sales presentations, demonstrating products, negotiating price and delivery terms, and writing orders. Selling Scenario 1.1 provides an example of some of these activities. But these sales-generating activities (discussed in Chapters 7 through 13) are only part of the job. Exhibit 1.4 shows how salespeople spend their time. Less than 35 percent of their time is spent on-site in a face-to-face meeting with customers and prospects. It is interesting to note that for world-class firms, that percentage rises to 40 percent, while for poorly performing firms, the percentage drops to just 20 percent.[12] The rest of salespeople's time is spent in meetings,

SELLING IS MUCH MORE THAN PUSHING A PRODUCT OR SERVICE

Matt Haberle is owner of and salesperson for Maximum Impact, a promotional services company that focuses on client appreciation, employee recognition, and brand awareness. Matt is in the business for the long run, desiring to develop long-term relationships with customers. As Matt puts it, "There are several ways in which I differentiate myself from the myriad of so-called promotional agencies. The primary way is the process of needs discovery and presentation of options. My industry, sometimes referred to as 'the trash-n-trinkets industry,' is very heavily laden with catalogs and literature. Most companies simply send out thousands of catalogs, wait for the phone to ring, be the cheapest they can be, and try to handle the order as cost-effectively as possible." That's not Matt's method, though.

"When a client has a project coming up, I do not arm myself with catalogs for that first meeting. I arm myself with questions: Who is the target audience? What is the message? How do you want them to feel? What do you want them to do? How important are they to your overall success? What is the scope, time frame, and estimated budget?"

For example, Target, a major national retailer, wanted to appropriately show thanks to employees (from part-timers to executives from all over the country) for the time they volunteered on various Habitat for Humanity projects. By discovering their needs, Matt determined that Target's original idea would not convey the message thoroughly. He returned with several options and presented them to Target from the viewpoint of the intended recipients. The ensuing promotion was declared a success on all levels. In fact, the promotion was received so well that it is still evident today.

Selling is an important blend of finding out what the customer really needs and then providing a solution to that need. In the long run, it's the only way to do business.

Source: Matt Haberle, personal correspondence, used with permission.

---

working with support people in their companies (internal selling), traveling, waiting for a sales interview, doing paperwork, and servicing customers.

SERVICING CUSTOMERS

The salesperson's job does not end when the customer places an order. Sales representatives must make sure customers get the benefits they expect from the product. Thus salespeople work with other company employees to ensure that

---

EXHIBIT 1.4

How Salespeople Spend Their Time Each Week

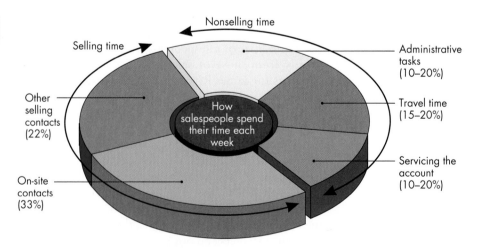

Source: Adapted from The Alexander Group, Inc. SalesTime Maker, Software Services, February 8, 2002 <http://tools.saleslobby.com/perfMgmt/2001_STM_Presentation.pdf>

An important role of many salespeople is to aid customers in installation of products.

Mary Kate Denny/PhotoEdit

deliveries are made on time, equipment is properly installed, operators are trained to use the equipment, and questions or complaints are resolved quickly. Providing these services is critical to developing partnerships, the long-term objective of selling. Chapter 13 will provide more insights on developing partnerships through customer services.

Making sales and servicing customers can be very challenging in less developed countries where many customers are difficult to reach. For example, Sabritas, Mexico's largest snack food company, has an extensive distribution system to reach customers in isolated mountain and jungle villages. Salespeople drive specially equipped vans to make weekly calls on these remote villages and often sleep in their vans or in customers' stores. Salespeople reach villages in the lake region by canoe and ride donkeys into some mountain villages.[13]

COORDINATING ACTIVITIES

Salespeople also spend time in meetings, coordinating the activities of their firms to solve customer problems. Dick Holder, president of Reynolds Metal Company, spent five years "selling" Campbell Soup Company on using aluminum cans for its tomato juice products. He coordinated a team of graphic designers, marketing people, and engineers to educate Campbell about a packaging material it had not used before.

To provide solutions and build relationships, salespeople need to thoroughly understand the operations of all areas in their firm. Tom Wolven, regional president for Ailing & Cory, a paper supplier, says that his salespeople are effective because "They really get involved from one end of the business to the other. They understand credit, they understand finances, they understand shipping systems, and they understand product knowledge . . . at times problems crop up in various areas, and our salespeople know where to go and who to go to and how things work in the different areas."[14] Approaches for improving efficiency in performing these nonselling activities are discussed in Chapter 16.

PROVIDING INFORMATION TO THE COMPANY AND PREPARING INFORMATION FOR CUSTOMERS

In their reporting activities salespeople provide information to their firms about expenses, calls made, future calls scheduled, sales forecasts, competitor activities, business conditions, and unsatisfied customer needs. Much of this information is now transmitted electronically to the company, its salespeople, and its customers. For example, each night salespeople at Curtin Matheson Scientific, a distributor of clinical and laboratory supplies in Baton Rouge, Louisiana, enter call report information and download all the ordering and shipping information for their customers from the company mainframe to their laptop computers. This information helps salespeople make sure that their customers' needs are being fulfilled. It also comes in handy in correcting misperceptions. Scott Salling called on one of his accounts and met the buyer. The buyer immediately began criticizing Curtin Matheson for its poor service and delivery. So Salling took out his laptop and showed her the records for her company's recent purchases. Only one order had not been delivered on time. Because Salling had the information at his fingertips, he was able to correct the buyer's unfavorable image.[15]

TYPES OF SALESPEOPLE

Almost everyone is familiar with people who sell products and services to consumers in retail outlets. Behind these retail salespeople is an army of salespeople working for commercial firms. Consider a DVD player you might purchase in a store. To make the DVD player, the manufacturer bought processed material, such as plastic and electronic components, from various salespeople. In addition, it purchased capital equipment from other salespeople to mold the plastic, assemble the components, and test the player. Finally, the DVD player manufacturer bought services such as an employment agency to hire people and an accounting firm to audit the company's financial statements. The manufacturer's salespeople then sold the players to a wholesaler. The wholesaler purchased transportation services and warehouse space from other salespeople. Then the wholesaler's salespeople sold the players to a retailer.

SELLING AND DISTRIBUTION CHANNELS

As the DVD player example shows, salespeople work for different types of firms and call on different types of customers. These differences in sales positions come from the many roles salespeople play in a firm's distribution channel. A **distribution channel** is a set of people and organizations responsible for the flow of products and services from the producer to the ultimate user. Exhibit 1.5 shows the principal types of distribution channels used for business-to-business and consumer products and the varied roles salespeople play.

BUSINESS-TO-BUSINESS CHANNELS

The two main channels for producers and providers of business-to-business, or industrial, products and services are (1) direct sales to a business customer and (2) sales through distributors. In the direct channel salespeople working for the manufacturer call directly on other manufacturers. For example, Nucor salespeople sell steel directly to automobile manufacturers, Dow Chemical salespeople sell plastics directly to toy manufacturers, and Nielsen salespeople sell marketing research services directly to business customers.

In the distributor channel the manufacturer employs salespeople to sell to distributors. These salespeople are referred to as **trade salespeople** because they sell to firms that resell the products rather than using them within the firm. Distributor salespeople sell products made by a number of manufacturers to businesses. For example, some Intel salespeople sell microprocessors to distributors such as Arrow Electronics, and Arrow salespeople then resell the microprocessors and other electronic components to customers such as Compaq. Chapter 15 focuses on the special issues confronting trade salespeople.

Many firms use more than one channel of distribution and thus employ several types of salespeople. For example, Motorola and Dow Chemical have trade salespeople who call on distributors and direct salespeople who call on large companies.

In the second business-to-business channel (see Exhibit 1.5), a missionary salesperson is employed. **Missionary salespeople** work for a manufacturer and promote the manufacturer's products to other firms. However, those firms buy the products from distributors or other manufacturers, not directly from the

EXHIBIT 1.5

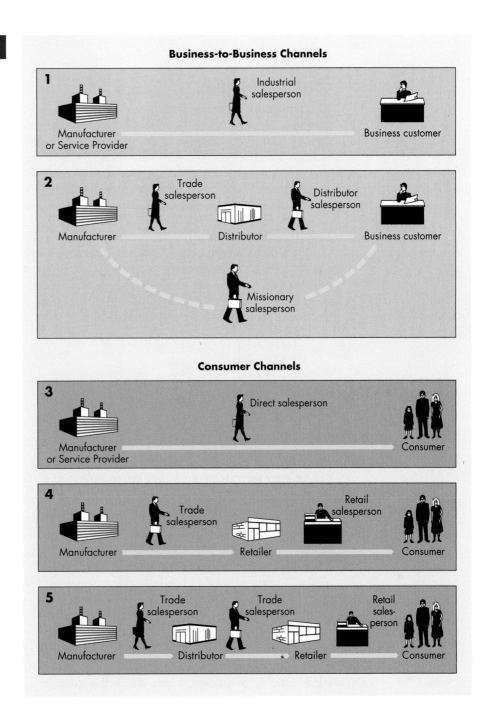

Business-to-Business Channels

1   Manufacturer or Service Provider   Industrial salesperson   Business customer

2   Manufacturer   Trade salesperson   Distributor   Distributor salesperson   Business customer   Missionary salesperson

Consumer Channels

3   Manufacturer or Service Provider   Direct salesperson   Consumer

4   Manufacturer   Trade salesperson   Retailer   Retail salesperson   Consumer

5   Manufacturer   Trade salesperson   Distributor   Trade salesperson   Retailer   Retail salesperson   Consumer

salesperson's firm. For example, sales representatives at Driltech, a manufacturer of mining equipment, call on mine owners to promote their products. The mines, however, place orders for drills with the local Driltech distributor rather than with Driltech directly. Normally, missionary and local distributor salespeople work together to build relationships with customers.

Frequently, missionary salespeople call on people who influence a buying decision but do not actually place the order. For example, Du Pont sales representatives call on clothing designers to encourage them to design garments made with nylon, and Merck sales representatives call on physicians to encourage them to prescribe Merck pharmaceutical products.

CONSUMER CHANNELS

The remaining channels shown in Exhibit 1.5 are used by producers and providers of consumer products and services. The third channel shows a firm, such as State Farm Insurance, whose salespeople sell insurance directly to consumers. The fourth and fifth channels show manufacturers that employ trade salespeople to sell to either retailers or distributors. For example, Revlon uses the fourth channel when its salespeople sell directly to Wal-Mart. However, Revlon uses the fifth channel to sell to small, owner-operated stores through distributors.

Some of the salespeople shown in Exhibit 1.5 may be manufacturers' agents. **Manufacturers' agents** are independent businesspeople who are paid a commission by a manufacturer for all products or services sold. Unlike distributors and retailers, agents never own the products. They simply perform the selling activities and then transmit the orders to the manufacturers.

DESCRIBING SALES JOBS

Descriptions of sales jobs focus on six factors:

1. The stage of the customer–firm relationship.
2. The salesperson's role.
3. Importance of the customer's purchase decision.
4. Location of salesperson–customer contact.
5. The nature of the offering sold by the salesperson.
6. The salesperson's role in securing customer commitment.

STAGE OF CUSTOMER–FIRM RELATIONSHIP: NEW OR CONTINUING

Some sales jobs emphasize finding and selling to new customers. Selling to prospects requires different skills than selling to existing customers. To convince prospects to purchase a product they have never used before, salespeople need to be especially self-confident and aggressive. They must be able to deal with the inevitable rejections that occur when making initial contacts with potential customers. On the other hand, salespeople responsible for existing customers place more emphasis on building relationships and servicing customers than on selling to them.

SALESPERSON'S ROLE—TAKING ORDERS OR CREATING NEW SOLUTIONS

Some sales jobs focus primarily on taking orders. For example, most Frito-Lay salespeople go to grocery stores, check the stock, and prepare an order for the store manager to sign.

However, some Frito-Lay salespeople sell only to buyers in the headquarters of supermarket chains. Headquarters selling requires a much higher level of skill and creativity to do the job effectively. These salespeople work with buyers to develop new systems and methods to increase the retailer's sales and profits.

IMPORTANCE OF CUSTOMER'S PURCHASE DECISION

Consumers and businesses make many purchase decisions each year. Some decisions are important to them, such as purchasing a home or a business telephone system. Others are less crucial, such as buying candy or cleaning supplies.

SuperStock

Selling intangibles, like Internet service solutions, can be harder than selling tangible products.

Sales jobs involving important decisions for customers differ greatly from sales jobs involving minor decisions. Consider the company that needs a computer-controlled drill press. Buying the drill press is a big decision. The drill press sales representative needs to be knowledgeable about the customer's needs and the features of drill presses. The salesperson will have to interact with a number of people involved in the purchase decision.

LOCATION OF SALESPERSON–CUSTOMER CONTACT: FIELD OR INSIDE SALES

Field salespeople spend considerable time in the customer's place of business, communicating with the customer face to face. **Inside salespeople** work at their employer's location and typically communicate with customers by telephone or letter.

Field selling typically is more demanding than inside selling because the former entails more intense interactions with customers. Field salespeople are more involved in problem solving with customers, whereas inside salespeople often respond to customer-initiated requests.

THE NATURE OF THE OFFERING SOLD BY THE SALESPERSON: PRODUCTS OR SERVICES

The nature of the benefits provided by products and services affects the nature of the sales job. Products such as chemicals and trucks typically have tangible benefits: Customers can objectively measure a chemical's purity and a truck's payload. The benefits of services, such as business insurance or investment opportunities, are more intangible: Customers cannot easily see how the insurance company handles claims or objectively measure the riskiness of an investment.[16]

Intangible benefits are harder to sell than tangible benefits because it is difficult to demonstrate intangible benefits to customers. It is much easier to show a customer the payload of a truck than the benefits of carrying insurance.

SALESPERSON'S ROLE IN SECURING CUSTOMER COMMITMENT

Sales jobs differ by the types of commitments sought and the manner in which they are obtained. For example, the Du Pont missionary salesperson might encourage a clothing designer to use Du Pont synthetic fibers. The salesperson might ask the designer to consider using the fiber but does not undertake the more difficult task of asking the designer to place an order. If the designer decides to use nylon fabric in a dress, the order for nylon will be secured by the salesperson calling on a company that makes the fabric.

Thinking It Through

How do you think the greater use of technology—use of laptop computers and communicating over the Internet—will affect the different types of sales jobs? Will some types of sales jobs decline in importance? Why?

THE SALES JOBS CONTINUUM

Exhibit 1.6 uses the factors just discussed to illustrate the continuum of sales jobs in terms of creativity. Sales jobs described by the responses in the end column require salespeople to go into the field and call on new customers who make important buying decisions. These selling assignments emphasize selling to new customers rather than building relations with old customers, promoting products or services with intangible benefits, and/or gaining commitments from customers. These types of sales jobs require the most creativity and skill and, consequently, offer the highest pay.

For example, Gene Choi, director of business operations, Asia, for Cisco Systems, spent three years selling switches worth $10 million to the Chinese government for China's Internet backbone. The sales process started in 1994 when Cisco opened an office in Beijing and began to build a reputation for reliability and trustworthiness in the government's eyes. In 1996 the government finally asked Cisco to install a pilot demonstration but gave Cisco only 30 days to complete the installation. Choi says, "Understanding cultural differences is integral to selling in China. A lot of repetition, hand holding, dedication, and commitment is what it takes."[17]

The next section examines the responsibilities of specific types of salespeople in more detail.

EXAMPLES OF SALES JOBS

JCPENNEY RETAIL SALESPERSON

JCPenney salespeople sell to customers who come into their stores. In many cases the customers know what they want; the salesperson just rings up the sale. However, JCPenney, like most department stores, is upgrading its salespeople from order takers to relationship builders. The company is encouraging salespeople to keep customer books, notify customers of new merchandise, and make special appointments with key customers to present merchandise selected to meet their needs.

KRAFT/GENERAL FOODS PACKAGED GOODS SALESPERSON

Kraft salespeople increase the sales of their firm's products by influencing retailers and distributors to stock Kraft/General Foods brands and then servicing them. Most Kraft salespeople typically make regularly scheduled calls on existing

---

EXHIBIT 1.6

Creativity Level of Sales Jobs

Factors in Sales Jobs	Lower Creativity	Higher Creativity
1. Stage of the customer–firm relationship	Existing customer	New customer
2. The salesperson's role	Order taking	Creating new solutions
3. Importance of the customer's purchase decision	Low	High
4. Location of salesperson–customer contact	Inside company	Field customer
5. Nature of the offering sold by the salesperson	Products	Services
6. Salesperson's role in securing customer commitment	Limited role	Significant role

customers in an assigned territory and generally are not expected to find new customers. Some of the responsibilities of a Kraft trade salesperson are

1. Convincing retailers to buy and display all Kraft products in their stores.
2. Making sure that retailers have enough stock displayed on shelves and stored in the back room so that an out-of-stock condition will not arise.
3. Counting stock and preparing orders for store managers if inventories are low.
4. Checking to see that Kraft products are priced competitively.
5. Trying to get Kraft products displayed on shelves where consumers can see them easily.
6. Encouraging managers to develop special displays for Kraft products and helping to build the displays.
7. Convincing store managers to feature Kraft products in advertising and place in-store ads and signs to promote the sale of Kraft products.

In Chapter 15 we discuss the issues in selling to resellers in more detail.

MERCK PHARMACEUTICAL SALESPERSON

Traditionally, salespeople working for pharmaceutical companies such as Merck have been classic examples of missionary salespeople. They provide information on their products to physicians, surgeons, and other people licensed to provide medical services in their territories. Typically they make about eight calls on doctors each day, usually without an appointment.[18]

The salespeople spend 2 to 15 minutes with doctors on each call. The presentations include accurate information about the symptoms for which a pharmaceutical is effective, how effective it is, and the side effects that might occur. Doctors consider these presentations an important source of information about new products.

However, the world of pharmaceutical selling is changing. With the growing importance of cost reduction, many Merck salespeople are calling on hospitals and health maintenance organizations (HMOs). These Merck salespeople are working with customers to develop creative solutions for halting the rising cost of health care.

DELL COMPUTER SALESPERSON

Some of the most challenging sales jobs involve selling capital goods. Dell salespeople sell computers and support systems to large companies. The salespeople outline the benefits of developing a customized computer configuration for each department in the company. Each configuration is stored on a Web page that employees access when they need a new computer. When the orders are placed electronically with Dell, Dell builds the customized computers with appropriate network cards and software so the customer can simply plug in the computer and turn it on.

Because these capital equipment sales are made infrequently, Dell salespeople often approach new customers. The selling task requires working with customers who are making a major investment and are involved in an important buying decision. Many people are involved in this sort of purchase decision. Dell salespeople need to demonstrate both immediate, tangible benefits and future, intangible benefits to executives ranging from the chief information officer (CIO) to the chief financial officer (CFO).

The next section reviews the skills required to be effective in the sales positions just discussed.

CHARACTERISTICS OF SUCCESSFUL SALESPEOPLE

For the last 100 years, many people have written books and articles discussing why some people are successful in selling and others are not. After all of this research, no one has identified the profile of the "perfect" salesperson because sales jobs are so different. As the job descriptions in the preceding section show, the characteristics and skills needed for success when selling for Kraft differ from those needed for success when selling for Dell.

In addition, each customer is unique. Some like to interact with aggressive salespeople, whereas others are turned off by aggressive behavior. Some are all business and want formal relationships with salespeople, whereas others look forward to chatting with salespeople in an informal way. Thus the stereotype of the hard-driving, back-slapping sales personality will not succeed with all customers. No magic selling formula works in all sales jobs or with all customers.

Although no one personality profile exists for the ideal salesperson, successful salespeople are hard workers and smart workers. They are highly motivated, dependable, ethical, knowledgeable, good communicators, flexible, creative, and emotionally intelligent.

MOTIVATION

Most salespeople work in the field without direct supervision. Under these conditions they may be tempted to get up late, take long lunch breaks, and stop work early. But successful salespeople do not succumb to these temptations. They are self-starters who do not need the fear inspired by a glaring supervisor to get them going in the morning or to keep them working hard all day.[19]

Spending long hours on the job is not enough. Salespeople must use their time efficiently. They need to maximize the time spent in contacting customers and minimize the time spent in traveling and waiting for customers. To do their job effectively, salespeople must organize and plan their work (a subject discussed in more detail in Chapter 16).

Finally, successful salespeople are motivated to learn as well as work hard. They must continually work at improving their skills by analyzing their past performance and using their mistakes as learning opportunities.

DEPENDABILITY AND TRUSTWORTHINESS

In some types of selling, such as used-car sales, the salesperson rarely deals with the same customer twice. However, this book focuses on business-to-business selling situations in which the customer and salesperson have a continuing relationship—a partnership. Such salespeople are interested not just in what the customers will buy this time but also in getting orders in the years to come.

Customers develop long-term relationships only with salespeople who are dependable and trustworthy.[20] When salespeople say the equipment will perform in a certain way, they had better make sure the equipment performs that way! If it doesn't, the customer will not rely on them again. Chapter 2 focuses on the development of long-term relationships with customers.

ETHICAL SALES BEHAVIOR

Honesty and integrity are important components of dependability. Over the long run, customers will find out who can be trusted and who cannot. Good ethics is good business. Ethical sales behavior is such an important topic that Chapter 3 is devoted to it.

CUSTOMER AND PRODUCT KNOWLEDGE

Effective salespeople need to know how businesses make purchase decisions and how individuals evaluate product alternatives. In addition, effective salespeople need product knowledge—how their products work and how the products' features are related to the benefits customers are seeking. Chapter 4 reviews the buying process, and Chapter 6 discusses product knowledge.

COMMUNICATION SKILLS

The key to building strong long-term relationships is to be responsive to a customer's needs. To do that, the salesperson needs to be a good communicator. But talking is not enough; the salesperson must also listen to what the customer says, ask questions that uncover problems and needs, and pay attention to the responses.

To compete in world markets, salespeople need to learn how to communicate in international markets. For example, business is conducted differently in Europe than in the United States. In the United States business transactions generally proceed at a rapid pace, whereas Europeans take more time reaching decisions. European customers place more emphasis on the rapport developed with a salesperson, whereas U.S. firms look more at the size and reputation of the salesperson's company. Because Europeans want to do business with salespeople they like and trust, the latter devote a lot of time to building close personal relationships with customers. Chapter 5 is devoted to developing communication skills, with considerable emphasis on communicating in other cultures.

FLEXIBILITY

The successful salesperson also realizes that the same sales approach does not work with all customers; it must be adapted to each selling situation. The salesperson must be sensitive to what is happening and flexible enough to make those adaptations during the sales presentation.

As mentioned earlier in this chapter, personal selling is the most costly marketing communication vehicle. Why do companies spend money on personal selling when it is so expensive? The higher cost is justified by its greater effectiveness. Personal selling works better than any other communication vehicle because salespeople are able to develop a unique message for each customer. Salespeople can do "market research" on each customer by asking questions and listening carefully. They then use this information to develop and deliver a sales presentation tailored to the needs and beliefs of each customer. In addition, salespeople can observe verbal and nonverbal behaviors (body language) in their customers and, in response, adjust their presentation. If the customer is uninterested in the contents of the presentation or turned off by the salesperson's style, the salesperson can make changes quickly.

In contrast, advertising messages are tailored to the typical customer in a segment and thus are not ideally suited to many of the customers who may see the ad. Advertisers are also limited in how fast they can make adjustments. Salespeople can adjust on the spot, but it may take months to determine that an advertisement is not working and then to develop a new one.

Only personal selling provides the opportunity to be truly adaptive in making presentations. Consequently, selling effectiveness hinges on the salesperson's ability to practice adaptive selling and exploit this unique opportunity. Adaptive selling is treated in detail in Chapter 6.

CREATIVITY

Successful salespeople use their creative juices to build bridges to their customers, gain long-term commitments, and effectively manage relationships.[21] **Creativity** is the trait of having imagination and inventiveness and using it to come up with new solutions and ideas. Sometimes it takes creativity in order to get an appointment with a prospect. Or it takes creativity to develop a long-remembered presentation in the buyer's mind. Or it takes creativity to solve a sticky installation problem after the product is sold.

Some people don't see themselves as creative because they've been told by family, friends, or teachers that they're not creative. Others refuse to allow their natural creativity to flow, due to fears of being laughed at or fears of having the

GET CREATIVE!

Here are some ideas to improve your creativity:

- Look at the problem from a totally different viewpoint. Thus you could pretend to be the buyer and think of all sorts of solutions that would not only be useful but also downright exciting for you.

- Have a brainstorming session with your fellow salespeople or friends with regard to the problem or opportunity. The rules: No suggestion is to be considered a dumb one, don't embrace any idea until all ideas are on the table, no one is allowed to try to influence others' opinions, and no ideas can be criticized until the idea-creating process is done.

- Keep a journal of your thoughts and ideas. It is surprising to most people how much creativity they actually possess. They've just been too busy to remember and reflect on the solutions they've toyed with.

- Keep a small box on your desk that is full of odd objects (such as a golf ball, an empty spool of thread, a nail, fingernail clippers, or a sock). When faced with an issue you don't know how to handle, randomly pick up an item from the box and try to see how it might offer insight into your problem.

- Pretend in your mind that the problem has been totally resolved. Now try working backward to see what things could have brought about that solution.

- Ask a child what he or she would do in a situation or how he or she would solve a problem. It is amazing how a totally distant third party can sometimes spark a creative thought in your own mind.

Sources: Personal experience; Julie Hill, "Genius at Work: How to Be More Creative in the World of Business," *Presentations*, November 2001, pp. 34–42.

---

idea fail. Still other salespeople come up with creative ideas, but fail to act on them. We can probably all improve our creative genius. Building Partnerships 1.1 provides some hints on how to break out of your mold and improve your creativity. Top salespeople use these and other techniques to increase their creativity and hence their success.

EMOTIONAL INTELLIGENCE

Salespeople span the boundary between their companies and the companies' customers. At times the objectives of the company can differ from those of the customers. The company wants the salesperson to make profits, and the customer wants to buy a product that meets his or her needs at the lowest price. Dealing with these conflicting objectives can be very stressful for salespeople.

To cope with conflicting company and customer objectives, rude customers, and indifferent support staff members, effective selling requires a high degree of emotional intelligence. **Emotional intelligence** is the ability to effectively understand and use one's own emotions and the emotions of people with whom one interacts. Emotional intelligence has four aspects: (1) knowing one's own feelings and emotions as they are experienced, (2) controlling one's emotions to avoid acting impulsively, (3) recognizing customers' emotions (called empathy), and (4) using one's emotions to interact effectively with customers.[22] We discuss aspects of emotional intelligence as they relate to adaptive selling and effective verbal and nonverbal intelligence in Chapters 5 and 6.

Thinking It Through

Which of the characteristics listed in this section are needed to be an effective teacher, engineer, banker, or actor?

Salespeople need emotional intelligence to be able to recognize customers' emotions.

Francesco Cruz/SuperStock

ARE SALESPEOPLE BORN OR MADE?

On the basis of the preceding discussion, you can see that the skills required to be a successful salesperson can be learned. People can learn to work hard, plan their time, and adapt their sales approach to their customers' needs. Research has shown that innate characteristics such as personality traits, gender, and height are largely unrelated to sales performance. In fact, companies show their faith in their ability to teach sales skills by spending more than $10 billion each year on training programs.[23] The next section discusses the rewards you can realize if you develop the skills required for sales success.

REWARDS IN SELLING

Personal selling offers interesting and rewarding career opportunities. More than 7 million people in the United States currently work in sales positions, and the number of sales positions is growing.[24] Exhibit 1.7 provides a breakdown of

EXHIBIT 1.7

Employment in Sales Positions

Type of Sales Job	Number Employed
Retail salespeople	4,100,000
Manufacturers' and wholesale sales representatives	1,800,000
Insurance sales agents	378,000
Securities, commodities, and financial sales agents	367,000
Real estate agents	339,000
Real estate brokers	93,000
Sales engineers	85,000
Total number of salespeople	7,162,000

Source: *Occupational Outlook Handbook*, 2002–2003 edition, U.S. Department of Labor, Bureau of Labor Statistics.

employments by the type of sales job. Sales positions are challenging, exciting, and financially rewarding. They can provide the base for promotion to management positions in a firm or for launching a new business.

INDEPENDENCE AND RESPONSIBILITY

Many people do not want to spend long hours behind a desk, doing the same thing every day. They prefer to be outside, moving around, meeting people, and working on various problems. Selling ideally suits people with these interests. The typical salesperson interacts with dozens of people daily. Most of these contacts involve challenging new experiences.

Selling also offers unusual freedom and flexibility. It is not a nine-to-five job. Most salespeople decide how to spend their time; they do not have to report in. They have the freedom to determine what they do during a day, to decide which customers to call on and when to do paperwork. Long hours may be required on some days, and other days may bring fewer demands.[25]

Because of this freedom, salespeople are like independent entrepreneurs. They have a territory to manage and few restrictions on how to do it. They are responsible for the sales and profits the territory generates. Thus their success or failure rests largely on their own skills and efforts.

FINANCIAL REWARDS

Exhibit 1.8 shows the annual compensation for average and top sales performers. As you can see, successful salespeople often earn more than $100,000 a year; some earn more than $1 million. Occasionally the top salespeople in a firm will even earn more than the sales executives, as the exhibit indicates.

EXHIBIT 1.8

Average Annual Compensation for Salespeople and Managers

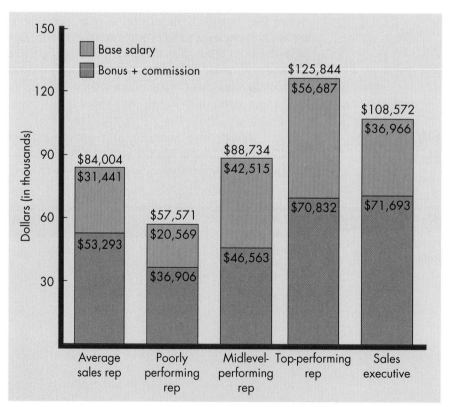

Source: 2001 Salary Survey, *Sales & Marketing Management*, May 2001, pp. 47–50.

The financial rewards of selling depend on the level of skill and sophistication needed to do the job. For example, salespeople who sell to businesses typically are paid more than retail salespeople because the buying process in businesses is more complex and difficult to manage. Exhibit 1.9 shows the average compensation for salespeople in various jobs.

MANAGEMENT OPPORTUNITIES

Selling jobs provide a firm base for launching a business career. For example, Mark Alvarez started his sales career in the Medical Systems Division at General Electric (GE) selling diagnostic imaging equipment to hospitals in central Illinois. Over the years he held positions in the firm that included district and regional sales manager and product manager; at one point he had responsibility for all Medical Systems Division business in Latin America. Sixteen years later, he was in corporate marketing and was responsible for managing the relationships between GE's 39 divisions and key customers in the southeastern United States. These include such accounts as Federal Express, Disney, and Home Depot. Some of his businesses do more than $500 million worth of business with GE annually. His entry-level job in selling provided great experience for his current assignment.

Even though selling offers opportunities for advancement, many salespeople promoted to management positions eventually return to selling. Ed Nunn sold for Enerpac Group, a Wisconsin tool manufacturer, for six years and was offered the position of national sales manager—at a $10,000 pay cut. Everyone told him, "Oh, Ed, you gotta take it; it's good for your career." At first he liked training salespeople and working in the field with them. But as time passed, the administrative work, the meetings, and being tied to a schedule made him long to return to selling. One morning he realized the managerial life was not for him: "I was standing in an office getting chewed out because I came in at 8:20 instead of 8:00. I looked at my

EXHIBIT 1.9	Sales Occupation	Average Annual Compensation
Average Compensation for Salespeople in Various Positions	Retail salespeople (department stores)	$7.63 per hour
	Retail salespeople (new and used car dealers)	$17.81 per hour
	Real estate agents and managers	$27,770
	Life insurance sales agents	$35,920
	Mortgage bankers and brokers	$36,590
	Grocery and related products salespeople	$37,220
	Medical service and health insurance salespeople	$38,900
	Industrial distribution salespeople	$47,000
	Electrical goods salespeople (technical products)	$51,650
	Machinery, equipment, and supplies salespeople (technical products)	$52,820
	Drug salespeople	$56,660
	Professional and commercial equipment salespeople (technical products)	$56,840
	Computer and data processing service salespeople	$62,310
	Sales engineers—electrical goods	$67,810
	Security brokers and dealers	$69,550

Note: These are just the averages. Some salespeople in these positions make much more than these averages indicate.

Sources: *Occupational Outlook Handbook*, 2002–2003 edition, U.S. Department of Labor, Bureau of Labor Statistics; Bridget McCrea, "Industrial Distributors Should Have in Place an Incentive Sales Program to Motivate Sales Agents to Boost Sales," *Industrial Distribution* 90 (June 2001), p. 73.

This young manager learned the ropes as a salesperson before moving into product management at his firm.

boss and said, 'What difference does it make? Sometimes I'm here till seven or eight at night.' And he said, 'But Ed, no one sees you then.' I've never been big on details or hanging around the factory [office] for show. I want to be out doing something." So Nunn quit and went to work for another company as a salesperson.[26]

THE BUILDING PARTNERSHIPS MODEL

This book is divided into five parts, as illustrated in Exhibit 1.10. Part 1 discusses the partnering landscape—the field of selling. Topics include the nature, role, and rewards of selling and what partnering really means.

The knowledge and skills needed for successful partnerships are covered in Part 2. You will learn about the legal and ethical responsibilities of salespeople, the buying process, the principles for communicating effectively, and methods for adapting to the unique styles and needs of each customer.

In Part 3 you will explore the partnership development process and the activities needed for this to occur. After completing this section, you should have enhanced skills and understanding about prospecting, planning, discovering needs, using visual aids and conducting demonstrations effectively, responding to objections, obtaining commitment, and providing excellent after-sale service.

Partnering in special applications is covered in Part 4. You will learn about formal negotiating as well as the somewhat unique role of selling to resellers.

Finally, Part 5 discusses the role of the salesperson as a manager. You'll learn how you can improve your effectiveness as a salesperson by managing your time and territory and by managing the relationships within your own company. This section also discusses ways to manage your career.

| EXHIBIT 1.10 | The Building Partnerships Model |

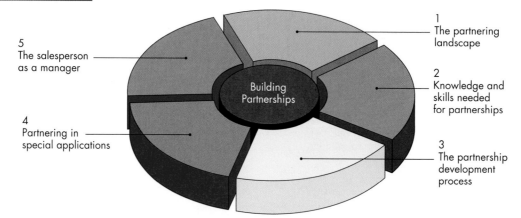

5 The salesperson as a manager

4 Partnering in special applications

Building Partnerships

1 The partnering landscape

2 Knowledge and skills needed for partnerships

3 The partnership development process

Summary

You should study personal selling because we all use selling techniques. If you want to work in business, you need to know about selling because salespeople play a vital role in business activities. Finally, you might become a salesperson. Selling jobs are inherently interesting because of the variety of people encountered and activities undertaken. In addition, selling offers opportunities for financial rewards and promotions.

Salespeople engage in a wide range of activities, including providing information on products and services to customers and employees within their firms. Most of us are not aware of many of these activities because the salespeople we meet most frequently work in retail stores. However, the most exciting, rewarding, and challenging sales positions involve building partnerships—long-term win–win relationships with customers.

The specific duties and responsibilities of salespeople depend on the type of selling position. However, most salespeople engage in various tasks in addition to influencing customers. These tasks include managing customer relations, working with other people in their firms, reporting on activities in their territories, and traveling.

Sales jobs can be classified by the roles salespeople and their firms play in the channel of distribution. The nature of the selling job is affected by whom salespeople work for and whether they sell to manufacturers, distributors, or retailers. Other factors affecting the nature of selling jobs are the customer's relationship to the salesperson's firm, the salesperson's duties, the importance of the buying decision to the customer, where the selling occurs, the tangibility of the benefits considered by the customer, and the degree to which the salesperson seeks a commitment from customers.

Research on the characteristics of effective salespeople indicates that many different personality types can be successful in sales. However, successful salespeople do share some common characteristics: All successful salespeople are highly motivated, dependable, ethical, knowledgeable, good communicators, flexible, creative, and emotionally intelligent.

KEY TERMS

creativity   19
distribution channel   12
emotional intelligence   20
field salespeople   15
inside salespeople   15
integrated marketing communications   7
learning organization   8

manufacturers' agents   14
missionary salespeople   12
personal selling   4
relationship marketing   9
trade salespeople   12
24/7 service   2

Questions and Problems

1. Some buyers are now demanding 24/7 response (24 hours a day, seven days a week) from their suppliers. What impact do you think that would have on a salesperson's job? On his or her personal life?
2. Is attending college necessary in order to be successful in selling today? Why or why not?
3. Discuss the following myths about selling:
   a. Salespeople do not serve a useful role in society.
   b. Salespeople are born, not made.
   c. Selling is just a bag of tricks.
   d. A salesperson should never take no for an answer.
   e. A good salesperson can sell anything to anybody.
4. Christine Walker has been teaching English in high school for two years since graduating from college. She is considering taking a job with a pharmaceutical

company. The job involves calling on doctors and explaining the benefits of the firm's products. What are the similarities and differences between her teaching job and the selling job she is considering?

5. Cindy Alvarez worked her way through college by selling in a local department store. She has done well on the job and is one of the top salespeople in the jewelry department. Last week Black & Decker offered her a job selling consumer appliances to retailers. Explain the differences between selling in a department store and the Black & Decker sales job.

6. Poll at least five students who are not taking your selling course (and who, better yet, are outside the business school or program). What are their opinions about salespeople? How accurate are their opinions based on what you've read in this chapter?

7. Think about what you want in your first job out of college. Based on what you know so far from this chapter, how well does selling match your desires in a job?

8. According to the text, some sales jobs require less creativity. Why would anyone want a job that requires less creativity?

9. Would society benefit if large insurance companies eliminated salespeople and sold insurance through the mail at a lower price to the customer?

10. Assume you are a sales manager and you need to recruit someone for the following sales positions. For each position, list the qualities you would want in the recruit:
   a. Salesperson selling computers to businesses.
   b. College textbook salesperson.
   c. Used-car salesperson.
   d. Salesperson selling laundry detergent to supermarkets.

11. Some predictions about the future of personal selling and the role of salespeople are as follows:
   a. Salespeople will spend more time selling new applications of their products and services to existing customers rather than cultivating new customers.
   b. Salespeople will become more financially oriented, selling the financial benefits and costs of their products and services.
   c. Salespeople will be part of a team of company employees selling to customers.
   Do you agree with these predictions? Why?

Case Problems

CASE 1.1

JDE Electrical Corporation

Jim Morrison, vice president of sales for JDE Electrical Corporation in Wichita Falls, Texas, has experienced the problem of enticing university graduates to the sales profession. This year he needed to hire 12 new salespeople for his growing electrical wiring firm. Looking for recent university graduates that JDE could train and mold into successful salespeople, Morrison placed want ads in university newspapers and local magazines and newspapers. The response was minimal. The ad said, "Looking for entry-level salespeople," but Morrison said people were "turned off" by it. He placed another ad in the same papers and magazines looking for "entry-level marketing people," and suddenly the responses came pouring in. When students came for interviews, Morrison made it clear that the position was for sales, but he presented the job in a way they could relate to. "I knew college kids would need money, so I stressed the opportunity to earn a lot of money," he said. "I also showed them the responsibility they would have in a sales position, and they were impressed with that.

Growing up, they had heard bad things about sales. You need to make it more glamorous than they think it is."

Questions

1. What are some of the "bad things" about selling that students might have heard?
2. What are some possible causes of the negative stereotype of the salesperson that some people have?
3. What other rewards in selling could Morrison stress in the interview beyond financial rewards and responsibility?

This case was written by Dr. Jack Eure, Professor of Marketing, Southwest Texas State University, San Marcos, Texas.

CASE 1.2

Salespeople, Direct Mail, or the Internet?

Greg Briddick Jr. has just completed his undergraduate degree at Millikin University. In the last semester of the program, Greg took a course on entrepreneurship. During the class Greg worked with a team of other students to develop a plan for a business he wants to start when he graduates. His idea was to develop a website targeting Millikin University college students. The site would provide information to students, such as good classes to take and apartments available for rent. It also would offer discount coupons to local stores and restaurants. The business would generate revenues by charging local companies for advertising on the site.

Greg is very interested in technology. He has an undergraduate degree in computer sciences and has been fascinated by the rapid increase in Internet surfing to search for information. Greg is a creative multimedia computer programmer. He has developed some unique techniques for incorporating three-dimensional diagrams and full-motion videos into websites. His classmates frequently comment that his personal home page, which he designed, is very exciting and attractive.

On the basis of some market research performed by the class group, Greg is confident that he can generate considerable student traffic for his site. The research also indicates interest among local merchants in using the site to attract students. Greg's parents are willing to lend him $25,000 to start his business.

Greg's concern is how to build student traffic for the site and how to get merchants to buy advertising space and offer coupons on the site. He is not very confident in his own ability to sell the site to businesses through face-to-face meetings. He is very good at analyzing business situations and had excellent grades in his undergraduate program, but is not very aggressive.

He considered hiring a salesperson, but anyone Greg thought was qualified for the job wanted to make at least $35,000 a year. Several candidates were willing to work on a 20 percent commission, but Greg thought that was too much money to pay just to sell his service. Rather than paying for a salesperson, he is considering creating a Web page that describes the benefits of advertising on his site. But he's concerned that some of the older merchants in town might not be very Web-savvy. So he's also considering making up a brochure describing his site and mailing the brochure to potential customers. The cost for setting up his advertising Web page plus direct mail costs is less than $3,000—about 1/10 of the cost of hiring a salesperson.

Questions

1. What should Greg do to explain his website and business to prospective advertisers?
2. Should he emphasize personal selling, direct mail, or electronic advertising? Why?

Additional References

"America's 500 Largest Sales Forces." *Selling Power*, October 1999, pp. 68–104.

Baldauf, Artur, and David W. Cravens. "Improving the Effectiveness of Field Sales Organizations: A European Perspective." *Industrial Marketing Management* 28 (January 1999), pp. 63–66.

Beverland, Michael. "Contextual Influences and the Adoption and Practice of Relationship Selling in a Business-to-Business Setting: An Exploratory Study." *Journal of Personal Selling and Sales Management* 21, Summer 2001, pp. 207–15.

Clopton, Stephen W.; James E. Stoddard; and Jennifer W. Clay. "Salesperson Characteristics Affecting Consumer Complaint Responses." *Journal of Consumer Behaviour* 1, November 2001, pp. 124–40.

Comer, Lucette; J. A. F. Nicholls; and Leslie J. Vermillion. "Diversity in the Sales Force: Problems and Challenges." *Journal of Personal Selling and Sales Management* 18 (Fall 1998), pp. 1–20.

Cross, James; Steven W. Hartley; William Rudelius; and Michael J. Vassey. "Sales Force Activities and Marketing Strategies in Industrial Firms: Relationships and Implications." *Journal of Personal Selling and Sales Management* 21, Summer 2001, pp. 199–206.

DelVecchio, Susan, and Earl D. Honeycutt, Jr. "Explaining the Appeal of Sales Careers." *Journal of Marketing Education* 24, April 2002, pp. 56–63.

Duncan, Tom, and Sandra Moriarty. "A Communication-Based Marketing Model for Managing Relationships." *Journal of Marketing* 62 (April 1998), pp. 1–12.

Johnson, Julie T.; Hiram C. Barksdale, Jr.; and James S. Boles. "The Strategic Role of the Salesperson in Reducing Customer Defection in Business Relationships." *Journal of Personal Selling and Sales Management* 21, Spring 2001, pp. 123–34.

Ridnour, Rick E.; Felicia G. Lassk; and C. David Shepherd. "An Exploratory Assessment of Sales Culture Variables: Strategic Implications within the Banking Industry." *Journal of Personal Selling and Sales Management* 21, Summer 2001, pp. 247–54.

Satterfield, Mark. "Selling to the Top: Traits and Characteristics of Senior Level Business Developers." *The American Salesman* 46, December 2001, pp. 3–17.

Schultz, Don E. "Summit Explores Where IMC, CRM Meet." *Marketing News*, March 4, 2002, pp. 11–12.

"The Seven Secrets of Great Salespeople." *Training*, January 2000, p. 14.

Sirgy, M. Joseph. *Integrated Marketing Communications: A Systems Approach*. Upper Saddle River, NJ: Prentice Hall, 1998.

Smith, J. Brock, and Donald W. Barclay. "Selling Partner Relationships: The Role of Interdependence and Relative Influence." *Journal of Personal Selling and Sales Management* 19, Fall 1999, pp. 21–40.

Sojka, Jane Z., and Dawn R. Deeter-Schmeiz. "Enhancing the Emotional Intelligence of Salespeople." *Mid-American Journal of Business* 17, Spring 2002, pp. 43–53.

Tanner, John Jr., and Melissa Schmitt. "Quality Salespeople: Sell, Service and . . ." *American Salesman,* January 1999, pp. 18–23.

"The Top 25 Sales Forces." *Sales & Marketing Management*, November 1999, p. 38.

Weitz, Barton, and Kevin Bradford. "Personal Selling and Sales Management: A Relationship Marketing Perspective." *Journal of the Academy of Marketing Science* 27 (Spring 1999), pp. 251–63.

2 Building Partnering Relationships

SOME QUESTIONS ANSWERED IN THIS CHAPTER ARE:

- What different types of relationships exist between buyers and sellers?
- When is each type of relationship appropriate?
- What are the characteristics of successful partnerships?
- What are the benefits and risks in partnering relationships?
- How do relationships develop over time?
- What are the responsibilities of salespeople in partnerships?

Buyers are demanding higher levels of service and product quality from fewer suppliers than ever before. To compete in this complex and dynamic environment, companies are looking for partners to help gain an advantage over their competitors. For example, companies involved with the Internet, from Netscape to Microsoft, are partnering with Sun Microsystems to utilize Java in their applications.

In the first chapter we briefly discussed the activities of salespeople in general. In this chapter we explore in more depth the role of salespeople in building relationships in the partnering era. We begin by examining the different types of exchange relationships in which salespeople are involved. Then we cover the characteristics of successful buyer–seller relationships. We conclude with a discussion of how relationships develop over time and the activities salespeople perform in relationship development. The specific activities salespeople engage in to develop and maintain good relationships with customers are discussed in more detail in Chapter 13.

"I don't have any sales secrets. I just do the basics."

Tim Pavlovich, Carlton-Bates

PROFILE

In the high-technology world, companies like Microsoft, Intel, Dell, and Gateway grab all the glamour. But deep in that world are electronics distributors, companies that supply the electronic parts that go into all types of products. Most college students are probably not aware of that field—certainly that was the case for Tim Pavlovich when he began interviewing for sales positions before graduating in the spring of 1997. At the end of his first four years selling for Carlton-Bates, though, Pavlovich is glad he stumbled into it.

His first position was as a sales representative covering a territory in Atlanta. Before the year was out, however, he had created a reputation as one of the new breed of successful salespeople who adapt and embrace the changing demands of the industry. He was promoted to run the Fort Smith branch office, and now the Austin branch.

"Like many industries, electronics distribution is changing," says Pavlovich. "Supply chain management, where vendors like Carlton-Bates have greater responsibilities for managing customers' inventories, sourcing parts, and reducing transaction costs, is demanded by an ever-growing number of our customers. Smaller distributors who don't have the resources to do that are being driven out."

Pavlovich also notes that these changes mean greater reliance on vendors like Carlton-Bates, which means that relationships with those vendors are more important than ever before. "I'm lucky in that I haven't had to learn a new way to sell. Partnering with customers is the only way I know how to sell."

"On a normal day-to-day basis, I don't sell an individual fuse or switch; I sell me. I sell my company and its service second, and I sell the part third." Pavlovich believes, "It's my job to add value and make it easy for that customer to buy from me."

He focuses on the largest accounts and requires that his salespeople do the same. "The 80/20 rule works—80 percent of my business comes from 20 percent of my customers, and I go after those 20 percent. I focus only on those that have the return—but it means that I have to build relationships. For each account, my goal is to have four levels of contact—to get to know someone from at least four of these areas: manufacturing, upper-level executive, production, maintenance, engineering, or purchasing."

But relationship selling is more than just knowing people. "Every customer is unique, with a unique culture, and I have to blend in. You have to take their mission statement; put it at the front of your folder; and say, 'I have to start thinking the way my customer thinks.'" He believes that this approach helps his salespeople meet the buyers' needs more effectively, which includes selling the way they want to buy as well as what they want to buy.

"I also do things others don't do. I send thank-you notes, flowers to a customer on a bad day, follow-up e-mails, and so on. No one takes the time for common courtesy any more, but I do. It's reaching out to my customers. It shows respect for them." As Pavlovich says, no one has time for these activities any more, so these actions separate him from his competitors.

In a very short time, Pavlovich has been very successful. "I don't have any sales secrets," he claims. "I just do the basics." But he is committed to adding value for his customers, and he is able to understand how to do that because of the relationships he's built with them. "If you get into a situation where price is the deciding factor and a buyer says 'Can you beat $450 for these controllers?' then you aren't doing your job. Your entire effort and relationship has now come down to the price of that item. What happened to the value of you and your company? The challenge is selling the product for more."

Visit Our Website @ www.carlton-bates.com

THE EVOLUTION OF PERSONAL SELLING

The selling function has been a part of humankind since the beginning. There were two ways to get something from another human being: by force or by trade. **Bartering,** or trading goods, meant that each person had to sell the other that what was offered for trade was worthwhile.

In the 1800s came the Industrial Revolution and the development of the canned sales pitch. For the first time, barter was replaced primarily by monetary transactions, although barter continues in developed economies. Salespeople for National Cash Register (NCR) and Singer Sewing Machines (among other companies) learned effective sales presentations and hit the road, looking for customers.

The nature of business and the role of salespeople have changed a lot since those early days. Bill Gardner, a retired computer salesperson, confesses, "I sold systems that people didn't want, didn't need, and couldn't afford." At one time Gardner would have been admired for his skill in convincing customers to buy things they did not need. Now Gardner's statement is embarrassing to many professional salespeople.[1] As award-winning salesperson Eileen Shay says, "People don't want to be sold anything. They want you to help them make good buying decisions."[2] Exhibit 2.1 illustrates how the role of the salesperson has evolved from taking orders through persuading customers to building partnerships.[3]

As Exhibit 2.1 shows, the orientations of salespeople emerged in different time periods. However, all these selling orientations still exist in business today. For example, inbound telephone salespeople working for direct mail catalog retailers like Lands' End and Spiegel are providers with a production orientation. They answer an 800 number and simply take orders. Many outbound telephone, real estate, and insurance salespeople are persuaders with a sales orientation. They use high-pressure selling techniques to get prospects to place orders. However, partnering-oriented selling is becoming more common as companies make strategic choices about the type of selling best suited to their situation. Selling Scenario 2.1 illustrates how one company uses several forms of relationships to meet the varying relationship needs of its customers.

Even though many sales jobs do not involve building long-term partnerships, we stress the concept of developing partnering relationships throughout this textbook because the roles of salespeople in many companies are evolving toward a partnering orientation. Further, salespeople are called upon to build partnerships with some accounts and other types of relationships with other accounts. Understanding partnerships is critical to understanding the professional selling process, as will become apparent as the book unfolds.

Traditionally, telephone salespeople have engaged in market relationships with their customers, while account managers in industries such as office equipment build partnerships with their customers. However, even telephone salespeople are now placing more emphasis on long-term customer relationships.

Spencer Grant/PhotoEdit

David P. Hall/Masterfile

EXHIBIT 2.1

The Evolution of
Personal Selling

	Production	Sales	Marketing	Partnering
Time Period	Before 1930	1930 to 1960	1960 to 1990	After 1990
Objective	Making sales	Making sales	Satisfying customer needs	Building relationships
Orientation	Short-term seller needs	Short-term seller needs	Short-term customer needs	Long-term customer and seller needs
Role of Salesperson	Provider	Persuader	Problem solver	Value creator
Activities of Salespeople	Taking orders, delivering goods	Aggressively convincing buyers to buy products	Matching available offerings to buyer needs	Creating new alternatives, matching buyer needs with seller capabilities

Many students may have heard of relationships marketing and wonder what the difference is between relationships marketing and building partnerships. *Relationships marketing* is a term with several meanings, but all reflect companies' attempts to develop stronger relationships with their customers. For example, relationships marketing to Coca-Cola may mean using a database to target different consumers for different direct mail campaigns. American Airlines may think of its AAdvantage frequent flyer program as the heart of relationships marketing. But in professional selling, relationships marketing refers to creating the type of relationship that best suits the customer's need, which may or may not require a partnership.

TYPES OF RELATIONSHIPS

Each time a transaction occurs between a buyer and a seller, the buyer and the seller have a relationship. Some relationships may involve many transactions and last for years; others may exist only for the few minutes during which the exchange of goods for money is made.

This section describes two basic relationship types: market exchanges and partnerships.[4] There are two types of each, summarized in Exhibit 2.2.

MARKET EXCHANGES

A **market exchange** is a transaction between a buyer and a seller in which each party is concerned only about that party's benefit. The seller is concerned only with making the sale; the buyer with getting the product at the lowest possible price. Most business transactions are market exchanges, and there are two types: solo market exchanges and functional relationships.

SOLO MARKET EXCHANGES

For example, suppose you are driving on a highway to Florida for a spring vacation. The generator light in your car comes on. You stop at the next gas station, and the service attendant says your car needs a new generator. The generator will cost $250, including installation. At this point you might pay the quoted price, bargain with the service attendant for a lower price, or drive to another service station a block away and get a second opinion. After you select a service station,

OFFICE DEPOT'S BUSINESS SERVICE DIVISION: SELLING THE WAY PEOPLE WANT TO BUY

Office Depot is familiar to many students because of the company's retail stores. You may even have purchased your school supplies at one of Office Depot's 800 stores. But the world's largest seller of office supplies also has a large commercial sales division (using direct mail, online sales, and seven national telemarketing facilities) and an even larger business services division (BSD) that serves corporate customers through a field sales force. Why?

"The simple reason is that's the way our customers want to buy," says Tom Willis, BSD manager. BSD, for example, represents 20 percent of Office Depot's sales and has 1,100 salespeople calling on medium and large accounts. These salespeople seek relationships with their buyers and develop personalized services that enable customers to receive the office supplies they want, delivered when and where they want them, packaged the way they need.

Customers who don't need personalized service, though, can visit a store or visit the company's website. Contract pricing and other terms are still available. Thus the BSD representative has to recognize what type of relationship is desired and then bring all of Office Depot's resources to bear on making that relationship work.

Source: Tom Willis, "Opportunities: Career for a Lifetime," *Careers in Professional Selling,* Fall 1999, pp. 14–15; Tom Willis, personal correspondence, used with permission.

agree on a price, have the generator replaced, and pay for the service, you have completed a one-shot market exchange. Neither you nor the service station attendant expects to engage in future transactions.

Because the parties in the transaction do not plan on doing business together again, both the buyer and the seller in a **solo market exchange** pursue their own self-interests. In this example, you try to pay the lowest price for the generator, and the service station tries to charge the highest price for it. The service station is not concerned about your welfare, just as you are not concerned about the service station's welfare.

FUNCTIONAL RELATIONSHIPS

Functional relationships are long-term market exchanges in which the buyer purchases out of habit or routine. Buyers in this type of relationship tend to have the

---

| EXHIBIT 2.2 | Types of Relationships between Buyers and Sellers |

Factors Involved in the Relationship	Type of Relationship			
	Solo Market Transaction	**Functional Relationship**	**Relational Partnership**	**Strategic Partnership**
Time horizon	Short term	Long term	Long term	Long term
Concern for other party	Low	Low	Medium	High
Trust	Low	Low	High	High
Investments in the relationship	Low	Low	Low	High
Nature of the relationship	Conflict, bargaining	Cooperation	Accommodation	Coordination
Risk in relationship	Low	Medium	High	High
Potential benefits	Low	Medium	High	High

same orientation as they do in solo market exchanges, but the previous purchase does influence the next purchase. As long as the product is available at a reasonable price and does what it is supposed to do, the buyer will continue to buy.

Sometimes firms buy from the same supplier for a long time because the buyers find it easier to buy repeatedly from the same supplier rather than search for a new supplier every time they need an item. For example, a Nortel buyer purchases janitorial supplies—paper towels, soap, cleanser, and mops—for the company. However, the buyer and the janitorial supply distributor have little interest in working closely together. The relationship between the buyer and the distributor's salesperson is not critical to Nortel's success as a corporation. The purchase and sale of janitorial supplies is routine. The buyer can decide to deal with another distributor. Research indicates that as long as the buyer is satisfied with the supplier's performance, switching is unlikely.[5] It is the salesperson's responsibility to make sure that the buyer stays satisfied.

Even in these long-term market exchanges, both parties are interested primarily in their own profits and are unconcerned about the welfare of the other party. In market exchanges price is the critical decision factor. It serves as a rapid means of communicating the bases for the exchange. Basically, the buyer and the salesperson in a market exchange are always negotiating over how to "split up the pie"—who is going to make more in the transaction. Thus a market exchange is a **win–lose relationship:** When one party gets a larger portion of the pie, the other party gets a smaller portion.

On the positive side market exchanges offer buyers and sellers a lot of flexibility. Buyers and sellers are not locked into a continuing relationship, and thus buyers can switch from one supplier to another to make the best possible deal. However, these minimal relationships do not work well when buyers and sellers have an opportunity to increase the size of the pie by developing products and services tailored to their needs. These more complex transactions cannot be conducted solely on the basis of price. A high level of trust and commitment is needed to manage these types of relationships, since buyers and sellers need to share sensitive information.

PARTNERSHIPS

There are two types of partnerships: relational and strategic. In partnerships both parties are concerned about each other's welfare and in developing **win–win relationships.** By working together, both parties benefit because the size of the pie increases.

RELATIONAL PARTNERSHIPS

Many times the buyer and the salesperson have a close personal relationship that allows them to communicate effectively. These personal relationships create a cooperative climate between the salesperson and the customer. When both partners feel safe and stable in the relationship, open and honest communication takes place. Salesperson and buyer work together to solve important problems. The partners are not concerned about little details because they trust each other enough to know these will be worked out. These types of partnerships are not necessarily strategic to either organization, although they may be to the individuals involved, and are called **relational partnerships.**

The benefits of a relational partnership go beyond simple increased short-term profits. Although both partners are striving to make money in the relationship, they are also trying to build a working relationship that will last a long time. For example, Traci Jensen had one prospect who mentioned that he played underwater hockey every Friday night. "Being a good sales rep, if you find somebody is interested in something, you ask about it." She asked him what it was, and he asked if she wanted to learn how to play. "So I went one Friday night. I didn't want to. But there came a time when I couldn't turn him down anymore." What she found is a game played at the bottom of a pool that she really enjoyed. "I've been doing it (playing the game) for about a year. We started getting his account immediately. And we've hung onto it, even after they signed a contract with our largest competitor." Traci says that they keep buying because her friend was willing to fight for her and show how her products were better quality.[6]

Relational partnerships can occur between a buyer and seller not only because of personal ties but also because each is important to the other professionally. For example, a trade show program may not be important enough to the organization to demand a strategic partner but is very important to the trade show manager. That manager may seek a relational partnership with a supplier, complete with personal investment of time and departmental resources, rather than a strategic organizational investment and commitment.

In Asian countries, the personal relationship is an important precursor to strategic partnerships. Several studies have found that social bonding and interpersonal commitment are necessary ingredients to any long-term partnership between Asian organizations.[7] In one study examining relationships between Australians and Chinese, interpersonal commitment was a precursor to organizational relationships, so without friendship, there was no partnership.[8]

In this chapter we talk about relationships between buyers and sellers, but these concepts also apply to personal relationships. A relational partnership is like a close friendship. In a close friendship you are not concerned with how the pie is split up each day because you are confident that, over the long run, each of you will get a fair share. You trust your friend to care about you, and she or he trusts you in return. The founder of the country's largest department store chain, James Cash Penney, once said, "All great businesses are built on friendship."

STRATEGIC PARTNERSHIPS

Strategic partnerships are long-term business relationships in which the partner organizations make significant investments to improve the profitability of both parties. In these relationships the partners have gone beyond trusting each other to "putting their money where their mouths are." They take risks to expand the pie, to give the partnership a strategic advantage over other companies.[9]

For example, Michael DiMartino, national account executive at Starbucks, developed a strategic relationship with United Airlines. United agreed to serve Starbucks coffee exclusively on all flights, and Starbucks developed a special blend available only on United flights. Starbucks went the extra mile to make the partnership work. "A lot of companies will roast coffee and ship it to you, but we were interested in training flight attendants and inspecting and modifying the on-board brewing equipment," DiMartino says. Through the partnership, United is able to increase the satisfaction of its customers by giving them an excellent cup of coffee, and Starbucks is able to sell more coffee.[10]

Strategic partnerships are created for the purpose of uncovering and exploiting joint opportunities.[11] Members of strategic partnerships have a high level of dependence on and trust in each other; share goals and agree on how to accomplish those goals; and show a willingness to take risks, share confidential information, and make significant investments for the sake of the relationship. An example is the partnership between American Airlines and Wallace, as discussed in Building Partnerships 2.1.

Wollin, a small plastic parts manufacturer, developed a strategic relationship with Whirlpool, a much larger corporation. Whirlpool shared confidential infor-

"TAG—YOU'RE IT"

When asked how long it took to get the business, Harry Murphy sat back and laughed. "From start to finish, the sale took 18 months. But frankly, it took us over a decade to get the business." The business he's talking about is American Airlines' luggage tag business. Wallace, Murphy's company, is now American's sole vendor for baggage tags, or bagtags as they're called.

Wallace is an integrated supply and total print management company. The company produces and distributes business forms, labels, direct response or direct mail pieces, commercial printing products, and office supplies.

"Back in the eighties, we targeted several vertical markets, including transportation and distribution," notes Murphy. American Airlines was targeted because they were beginning to consider automation through the use of barcoding. Wallace's considerable experience in retail barcoding positioned the company to capture a large portion of the transportation barcode business.

When Amercian became serious about automating the baggage handling process, Murphy and the account manager built a team that included product development people, sales management, and production. In addition, they had to work with other suppliers. As Murphy says,

"We had to involve other companies from a technology standpoint—conveyers, printers, scanners—and we did the consumables."

From American Airlines' perspective, the decision was as much about choosing a business partner as it was a bagtag supplier. "It was 18 months from the time American began seriously looking at automating their luggage handling to when we won the business. But we earned the right to compete for that business by proving we could serve their needs with earlier, smaller sales." Three years after the bagtag sale, American chose Wallace as a single vendor for many more printing applications. A team of Wallace specialists even has offices at American's headquaters.

As Murphy notes, "It has taken us from a product-based business within the relationship to a business-to-business service, even though there is a product. It [the product] is just a commodity, but the service is not. We are selling distribution, functionality, and administration—the complete partnership. This is what has really positioned us, and the model has been adapted to over 350 companies across the country."

Source: Gilbert Churchill, Neil Ford, Orville Walker, Mark Johnston, and John Tanner, *Sales Force Management,* 6th ed. (San Francisco: McGraw-Hill, 2000), pp. 48–49.

---

mation about its design plans for a new, energy-efficient washing machine with Wollin. Wollin then used its expertise to develop some plastic parts tailored to the design plans. These unique parts were superior to the standard parts that could be purchased from other parts suppliers. Whirlpool took a risk in sharing the information about its new product and eventually buying parts that were available from only one supplier. Wollin took a risk in designing parts without a firm order and producing parts that could be sold to only one customer. However, by taking these risks the performance and eventual sales of the new washing machine were enhanced, and both parties benefited.[12]

Similarly, Levi Strauss teams worked with JCPenney to create a specially designed area in its stores to display Dockers merchandise. Then teams from each company developed sophisticated inventory control systems to make sure that the stores were always stocked with the styles and sizes that were selling well. As a result, JCPenney is now Levi Strauss's largest customer worldwide. JCPenney also increased its own profits because it was able to offer merchandise to its customers that was not available from its competitors.[13]

Many students wonder about the exclusivity of strategic partnerships. Does a strategic partnership mean, for example, that JCPenney cannot carry Wranglers or that United can't serve Folgers? In the United situation the agreement was for an exclusive arrangement that tied the two companies together. But Penney also sells Wrangler jeans as well as a private-label brand. Strategic partnerships do not necessarily mean exclusivity for either buyer or seller—Levi can still sell to customers that compete with Penney.

In cultures outside the United States, long-term relationships are very important. In Japan, for example, several organizations may join together to form a *keiretsu,* or family of companies. These families of companies may include a bank, a transportation company, a manufacturing company, and distribution companies that share risks and rewards and jointly develop plans to exploit market opportunities. *Keiretsus* are thus strategic partnerships among several companies rather than between only two.

SUMMARY

Most salespeople are involved in either market exchanges or functional relationships. Strategic partnerships are rare. Exhibit 2.3 illustrates the differences in the nature of selling in market exchanges and long-term relationships.

Each type of relationship has its pluses and minuses.[14] Companies cannot develop a strategic advantage from a market exchange, but they do get the flexibility to buy products from the supplier with the lowest cost when the order is placed. On the other hand, strategic partnerships create a win–win situation, but the companies are committed to each other and flexibility can be reduced. In the next section we talk about the characteristics of successful relationships, relationships that have the potential to develop into strategic partnerships.

Thinking It Through

Think about a close relationship you have. How did it develop? How is it like a strategic partnership? How do you and the other person act differently in this relationship than you both do in other relationships with passing acquaintances? Think also about your close relationships in general. How often and by what means do you stay in contact? Does e-mail play a role in maintaining the relationship?

CHARACTER-ISTICS OF SUCCESSFUL RELATIONSHIPS

Some companies use the term *partnering* but do not really understand what it means. For example, Allan Weydahl, a regional sales director at Nalco, likes to work with a customer that says, " 'Please quit talking about money; that's not the issue we're talking about. We're talking about product and how you're going to get it here and how we're going to use it.' That kind of partner is a joy to do business with. On the other hand, you get a company that calls us in and says, 'We want a partnership,' and what the buyers really want is to use their purchasing power to get the lowest possible price."[15] Some salespeople question the ethics of browbeating suppliers to lower price.

One reality of partnerships is that one party is usually bigger than the other, or has the potential to wield more power. Weydahl's comment is a statement about the use of power by the buyer, but the statement can be fairly applied to either side. The issue in a partnership is not who has power, but that power is used equally. As we'll see in the rest of this section, the characteristics of successful relationships do have ethical implications, but perhaps the most important is that the partnership not be used unfairly.

Successful relationships involve cultivating the mutual benefits as the partners learn to trust and depend on each other more and more. As trust develops,

EXHIBIT 2.3

Selling in Market Exchanges and Long-Term Relationships

Market Exchange Selling Goal: Making a Sale	Long-Term Relationship Selling Goal: Building Trust
Making Contact	**Initiating the Relationship**
• Find someone to listen.	• Engage in strategic prospecting and qualifying.
• Make small talk.	• Gather and study precall information.
• Ingratiate and build rapport.	• Identify buying influences.
Closing the Sale	• Plan the initial sales call.
• Deliver a sales pitch to:	• Demonstrate an understanding of the customer's needs.
• Get the prospect's attention.	• Identify opportunities to build a relationship.
• Create interest.	• Illustrate the value of a relationship with the customer.
• Build desire.	**Developing the Relationship**
• Get the prospect to take action.	• Select an appropriate offering.
• Stay alert for closing signals.	• Customize the relationship.
• Use trial closes.	• Link the solution to the customer's needs.
• Overcome objections.	• Discuss customer concerns.
• Close early and often.	• Summarize the solution to confirm benefits.
Following Through	• Secure commitment.
• Reestablish contact.	**Enhancing the Relationship**
• Resell self, company, and products.	• Assess customer satisfaction.
	• Take actions to ensure satisfaction.
	• Maintain open, two-way communications.
	• Expand collaborative involvement.
	• Work to add value and enhance mutual opportunities.

Source: Adapted from Thomas Ingram, "Relationship Selling: Moving from Rhetoric to Reality," *Mid-American Journal of Business* 11 (1996), p. 6.

buyer and salesperson are able to resolve conflicts as they arise, settle differences, and compromise when necessary. The foundations of successful, long-term relationships are (1) mutual trust, (2) open communication, (3) common goals, (4) a commitment to mutual gain, and (5) organizational support (see Exhibit 2.4).

EXHIBIT 2.4

Foundations of Successful Relationships

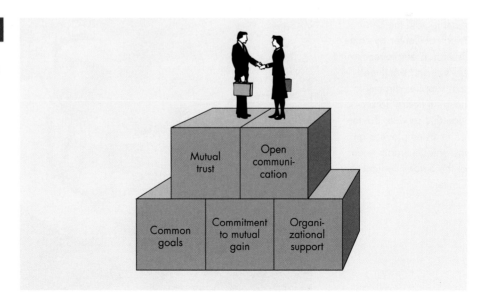

MUTUAL TRUST

The key to the development of successful, long-term customer relationships is trust. Lou Pritchett, former senior vice president of sales at Procter & Gamble, once said, "Cost reduction throughout the total system can be accomplished when trust replaces skepticism. Trusting suppliers, customers, and employees is one of the most effective, yet most underutilized, techniques available to management."[16] Daniel Fries, account executive for Relizon, agrees. "A little trust and confidence go a long way in motivating the supplier to go beyond the single requirements of a contract."[17]

Trust is a belief by one party that the other party will fulfill its obligations in a relationship.[18] When salespeople and buyers trust each other, they are more willing to share relevant ideas, clarify goals and problems, and communicate more efficiently. Information shared between the parties becomes increasingly comprehensive, accurate, and timely. There is less need for salesperson and buyer to constantly monitor and check up on each other's actions because both believe the other party would not take advantage of them if given the opportunity.[19]

Trust is an important building block for long-term relationships. A study of partnerships in Switzerland found trust to be the most important variable that contributes to the success of the relationship.[20] Trust is a combination of five factors: dependability, competence, customer orientation, honesty, and likability. In this section we discuss these factors and how salespeople demonstrate their own trustworthiness.

DEPENDABILITY

Dependability, the buyer's perception that the salesperson, and the product and company he or she represents, will live up to promises made, is not something a salesperson can demonstrate immediately. Promises must be made and then kept. Early in the selling process, a salesperson can demonstrate dependability by calling at times agreed to, showing up a few minutes early for appointments, and providing information as promised.

Third-party references can be useful in proving dependability, especially if the salesperson has not yet had an opportunity to prove it personally. If the seller can

Baxter cements its partnership with the Seton Medical Center by committing its employees to deliver and stock medical supplies directly to hospital floors. To provide this service, Baxter trains its employees on the unique supply needs of the Seton Medical Center.

John Storey

point to a similar situation and illustrate, through the words of another customer, how the situation was resolved, the buyer can verify the seller's dependability. Some companies also prepare case studies of how they solved a particular customer's problem to aid salespeople in proving the company's dependability.

Product demonstrations, plant tours, and other special types of presentations can also illustrate dependability. A product demonstration can show how the product will work, even under difficult conditions. A buyer for component parts for appliances was concerned about one company's ability to produce the large volumes required. The salesperson offered a plant tour to prove that the company could live up to its promises of on-time delivery. When the buyer saw the size of the plant and the employees' dedication to making quality products, she was convinced.

The salesperson's prior experience and training can also be used to prove dependability. For a company (and a salesperson) to remain in business, there must be some level of dependability. Length of experience, however, is a weak substitute for proving dependability with action.

As time goes on and the relationship grows, the buyer assumes dependability. For example, a buyer may say, "Well, let's call Sue at Mega. We know we can depend on her." At this point the salesperson has developed a reputation within the account as dependable. But reputations can spread beyond that account through the buyer's community. A reputation for dependability, however, can be quickly lost if the salesperson fails to continue to deliver as promised.

COMPETENCE

Salespeople demonstrate **competence** when they can show that they know what they are talking about. Knowledge of the customer, the product, the industry, and the competition are all necessary to the success of the salesperson. It is through the use of this knowledge that a salesperson demonstrates competency. For example, when a pharmaceutical representative can discuss the treatment of a disease in medical terms, the physician is more likely to believe that the rep is medically competent.

Salespeople recognize the need to appear competent. Unfortunately, their recognition of the importance of competence may lead them to try to fake knowledge. Because buyers test the trustworthiness of a seller early in the relationship, they may ask questions just to see the salesperson's response.

Competence is demonstrated through the use of accurate information. Salespeople should never make up a response to a tough question; at the same time, salespeople should try to present information objectively. Buyers can tell when salespeople are exaggerating the performance of their products.

Arrow Electronics, a global distributor of electronics parts, creates competence through intensive training. Each salesperson undergoes 90 days of training before going into the field. Once in the field, salespeople undergo an additional six months of training, including two weeks at the company's headquarters in Melville, New York (see Exhibit 2.5). The result is a highly competent sales force that works in partnership with retailers, helping them to run their businesses more successfully.[21]

CUSTOMER ORIENTATION

Customer orientation is the degree to which the salesperson puts the customer's needs first. Salespeople who think only of making sales are sales oriented rather than customer oriented. Buyers perceive salespeople as customer oriented when sellers stress benefits and solutions to problems over features.

Phase 1		Phase 2		Phase 3
Classroom Training Corporate HQ Melville, NY (Three Weeks)	**Field Training Branches throughout United States** (Two Months)	**Classroom Training Corporate HQ Melville, NY** (Two Weeks)	**Field Training Branches throughout United States** (Three months)	**Field Training Assigned to Business Group** (Three Months)
• Introduction to the electronics distribution industry. • Customer and supplier dynamics. • Technical product training. • Introduction to Arrow Electronics, Inc. • Exceeding customer and supplier expectations. • Field visit: touring a customer's facility. • Professional development. • Business savvy—having impact on day 1. • Customer service, teambuilding, communication skills.	• Work with active accounts under supervision of field sales managers. • Participate in sales calls with customers and suppliers. • Work in Arrow facilities at customer's manufacturing facility.	• Arrow sales system. • Roles and responsibilities. • Intergroup selling strategies. • Inventory management. • Professional selling skills. • Collaborative selling. • Account management. • Financial management—creating profitable businesses. • Professional development. • Career development and personal learning. • Presentation skills.	• Work with active accounts under supervision of field sales managers. • Research account potential and formulate account strategies. • Collaborate with suppliers on strategies for assigned accounts.	• Based on demonstrated expertise and company staffing needs, associates are assigned a sales territory. • Associates continue with training specific to their assigned business group. • Associates are eligible for rewards and incentives for meeting or exceeding sales goals.

Source: Jeffrey Uschok, "Pathways: Putting Your Career on the Fast Track," *Careers in Professional Selling,* Fall 1999, pp. 16–17.

Buyers who perceive that the product is tailored to their unique requirements are likely to infer a customer orientation. Stating pros and cons can be perceived as being customer oriented because understanding the cons also indicates that the salesperson understands the buyer's needs.

Emphasizing the salesperson's availability and desire to provide service also indicates a customer orientation. For example, the statement "Call me anytime for anything that you need" indicates availability. Offering the numbers for toll-free hot lines, voice mail, and similar concrete information indicates a desire to respond promptly to the buyer and can serve as proof of a customer orientation.

Listening skills are essential for developing a customer orientation. Linda Zitka, a buyer for General Motors Acceptance Corporation, says this about Carrie Thomas, who sells for Duplex Products: "She picks up on things I never even realized I told her." Zitka appreciates the way Thomas keeps track of every detail and follows through. "When we had a little blip [problem] in the project, I felt that she understood my frustration. I get the feeling that it's her project as well as mine, that she's with me all the way."[22] This level of listening, listening to feelings as well as facts, is difficult but essential to building long-term relationships.

HONESTY

Honesty is both truthfulness and sincerity. While honesty is highly related to dependability ("We can count on you and your word because you are honest"), it is also related to how candid a salesperson is. For example, giving pros and cons can increase perceptions of honesty.

Honesty is also related to competence. As we said earlier, salespeople must be willing to admit that they do not know something rather than trying to fake it; buyers consider salespeople who bluff to be dishonest.

A customer once asked, "Does your product SNA?" SNA was a new computer architecture that IBM had recently announced, but the salesperson represented a competing manufacturer. The salesperson replied, "No, not now, and I don't know if we will, but I can find out." The customer responded, "That's the first honest answer I've heard to that question." The salesperson eventually won a good portion of the customer's business, in part because she did not try to bluff her way through a tough question.

Partnering is such an important strategy that many salespeople overuse and misuse the term. One buyer said, "If I have one more vendor walk in the door and say they want to be my partner, I'll scream!" He believes salespeople use the term but do not change their actions or even listen seriously.[23] When a salesperson makes a claim, such as a desire to partner, and does not follow through, that person's honesty is called into question.

LIKABILITY

According to research, likability may be the least important component of trust because most people can be nice.[24] **Likability** refers to behaving in a friendly manner and finding a common ground between buyer and seller. Although likability is not as important as other dimensions, salespeople should still attempt to find a common ground or interest with all buyers.

Likability can also be influenced with personal communications such as birthday cards, handwritten notes, and so forth. Many businesses send Christmas cards and gifts to all customers, but personal touches make these gestures meaningful.

As you have probably noticed, the five dimensions of trust are tightly interrelated. Honesty affects customer orientation, which also influences dependability, for example. Salespeople should recognize the interdependence among these factors rather than simply focusing on one or two. For example, at one time many salespeople emphasized only likability. In today's market, professional salespeople must also be competent, dependable, honest, and customer oriented.

OPEN COMMUNICATION

Open and honest communication is a key building block for developing successful relationships. Buyers and salespeople in a relationship need to understand what is driving each other's business, their roles in the relationship, each firm's strategies, and any problems that arise over the course of the relationship.

Customer knowledge facilitates communication and builds trust. Ellen Manzo, an award-winning area manager at AT&T Computer Systems in Parsippany, New Jersey, explains, "It's critical to do a lot of account research, especially if you're servicing a small number of accounts. I go to the library, I go through Dun & Bradstreet and news clipping services, and I get the last 18 months of articles on the company. I buy a share of stock in the company so that I receive all the proxy statements and quarterly information. I try to get on the customer's mailing list." Manzo also requires all of her new salespeople to go through an extensive research exercise before they ever call on a customer, and she develops strategies for visits with her reps on major accounts.[25] (Chapter 5 focuses on approaches for improving communication.)

An important aspect of open and honest communication is the use of such communication when conflict arises. Conflict can occur even in the strongest of partnerships, and how it is handled says more about the relationship than if or when it happens. Joint problem solving and cooperation when there is conflict are much more likely to strengthen a partnership; whereas blaming, demanding, and the like are likely to lead to a breakup.[26] We'll talk more about breakups later, but it is important to recognize the importance of open communication, especially when there is conflict.

Cultural differences in communication style can be easily misunderstood and thus hinder open and honest communication. For example, all cultures have ways to avoid saying no when they really mean no. In Japan maintaining long-lasting, stable relationships is very important. To avoid damaging a relationship, customers rarely say no directly. Some phrases used in Japan to say no indirectly are *It's very difficult, We'll think about it,* and *I'm not sure;* alternatively, customers may leave the room with an apology. In general, when Japanese customers do not say yes or no directly, it means they want to say no.[27]

COMMON GOALS

Salespeople and customers must have common goals for a successful relationship to develop. Shared goals give both members of the relationship a strong incentive to pool their strengths and abilities. When goals are shared, the partners can focus on exploiting opportunities rather than arguing about who will benefit the most from the relationship.

Donna Crowell is an account executive for Hewlett-Packard (HP) and has only one account, Texas Instruments (TI). Her primary job is to see that HP computers are the primary platform for TI software, so every sale of TI software is a potential sale for HP computers. Crowell spends most of her time coordinating the efforts of HP and TI salespeople selling to end users, but it is important that she understands TI's goals and that she makes sure that everyone in HP understands and shares those goals.

Shared goals also help to sustain the partnership when the expected benefit flows are not realized. If one HP shipment fails to reach a TI customer on time because of an uncontrollable event, such as misrouting by a trucking firm, TI will not suddenly call off the whole arrangement. Instead, TI is likely to view the incident as a simple mistake and will remain in the relationship. TI knows that it and HP are committed to the same goal in the long run.

Clearly defined, measurable goals are also very important. Crowell has a sales budget that she has to meet; but more important, the two organizations set joint goals such as sales revenue, on-time delivery, service response time, and others. Performance is assessed monthly to determine if these goals are being met, so that the two organizations can work together to rectify any problems quickly.

Effective measuring of performance is particularly critical in the early stages of the partnership. The achievement of explicitly stated goals lays the groundwork for a history of shared success, which serves as a powerful motivation for continuing the relationship and working closely together into the future.

COMMITMENT TO MUTUAL GAIN

Members of successful partnerships actively work to create win–win relationships by looking for overlapping areas of opportunity in which both can prosper. For example, Clark Equipment Company manufactures forklift trucks, pallet trucks, and other mobile material-handling equipment. It recently began to integrate its partnering suppliers into its design process by sharing detailed information on costs, cost targets, profitability targets, and business strategies. By working closely with its suppliers, Clark improved its product quality and sales, which increased its orders for the vendors' products, outcomes that were mutually satisfying to both parties.[28]

The most successful relationships involve mutual dependence. One party is not more powerful than the other party. Mutual dependence creates a cooperative spirit. Both parties search for ways to expand the pie and minimize time spent on resolving conflicts over how to split it.

CREDIBLE COMMITMENTS

As a successful relationship develops, both parties make credible commitments to the relationship. **Credible commitments** are tangible investments in the relationship. They go beyond merely making the hollow statement "I want to be a partner." Credible commitments involve spending money to improve the products and services sold to the other party.[29] For example, a firm may hire or train employees, invest in equipment, and develop computer and communication systems to meet the needs of a specific customer. These investments signal the partner's commitment to the relationship in the long run.

ORGANIZA-TIONAL SUPPORT

Another critical element in fostering good relationships is giving boundary-spanning employees—the purchasing agents and salespeople—the necessary support.[30]

STRUCTURE AND CULTURE

The organizational structure and management provide the necessary support for the salespeople and buyers in a partnering relationship. All employees in the firm need to "buy in"—in other words, accept the salesperson's and buyer's roles in developing the partnership. Partnerships created at headquarters should be recognized and treated as such by local offices, and vice versa. Without the support of the respective companies, the partnership is destined to fail.

Firms interested in developing long-term customer relationships build a partnering culture throughout the organization. Creating and maintaining this culture can be difficult, however. Joe Durrett, senior vice president of sales at Kraft

To effectively build partnerships, salespeople must make sure that their products offer important benefits to the customers of retailers and distributors. Here, a salesperson for a shoe manufacturer is training a customer's sales staff so that they can deliver greater value to the store's customers.

Richard Pasley/Stock, Boston

General Foods (KGF), notes that "the biggest difficulty is changing attitudes. You must reengineer what you have because there are no experienced salespeople you can bring into the company who relate to this team approach."[31]

TRAINING

Special training is required to sell effectively in a relationship-building environment. Salespeople need to be taught how to identify customer needs and work with the customer to achieve better performance.

KGF uses a program called Navigator to train its salespeople in partnering. In this program salespeople pretend to work for a KGF clone, Pathfinder Foods. Pathfinder sells to three hypothetical customers. Salespeople are asked early on which retailer has a competitive advantage in today's market. Inevitably, every person falls into the trap of trying to pick only one, when the right answer is that each has the opportunity to be successful. The lesson is that every salesperson should develop a unique sales strategy that will help the customer outsell its competition.[32]

Training is critical in helping salespeople identify ways to make it easier for the customer to do business with them. At Alcoa Aluminum sales representatives are trained to look at what their customers do to a product that Alcoa could make for them. For example, one salesperson noticed that customers stack materials in skids in various-size stacks, sometimes 10 feet tall. When an order is pulled from inventory, a forklift driver must go into the stacks and pull a particular skid. Sometimes the skids are not stacked with a packing ticket on the outside, so the driver has a hard time identifying the right skid. Alcoa began to put a packing ticket on both ends of the skid so that the driver can always see the package number, no matter how the skid is stacked.

REWARDS

Reward systems on both sides of the relationship should be coordinated to encourage supportive behaviors. In market exchanges buyers are rewarded for wringing out concessions from the salespeople, and salespeople are rewarded on the basis of sales volume. In a partnering relationship rewarding short-term behaviors can be detrimental. Thus companies are beginning to reward salespeople and buyers based on the quality of the relationships they develop.[33]

For example, IBM changed its sales compensation to base bonuses and commissions on the profitability of the sales to IBM and the satisfaction of the customers buying IBM products and services. Salespeople are given information about product costs and some authority to adjust prices. Any price reductions salespeople make affect their compensation. In addition, customer satisfaction information is collected periodically, and 40 percent of the salesperson's compensation is based on the results of these surveys.[34]

PHASES OF RELATIONSHIP DEVELOPMENT

Although not all relationships should become partnerships, strategic partnerships tend to go through several phases. These phases are (1) awareness, (2) exploration, (3) expansion, (4) commitment, and sometimes (5) dissolution. Although there are cultural differences in the way buyers and sellers move through these phases, strategic partnerships go through these stages in most situations.

AWARENESS

In the **awareness** stage no transaction has taken place. During the awareness phase salespeople locate and qualify prospects, while buyers identify various sources of supply. Buyers may see a booth at a trade show, an ad in a magazine, or some other form of marketing communication and seek additional information. Reputation and image in the marketplace can be very important for sellers at this point.

EXPLORATION

The **exploration** stage is a search and trial phase for both buyer and seller. Both parties may explore the potential benefits and costs. At this point the buyer may make purchases, but these are in the form of market exchanges as neither side has committed to the relationship. Each purchase, though, can be thought of as a test of the supplier's capability.

EXPANSION

At this point the supplier has passed enough tests to be considered for additional business. The **expansion** stage involves efforts by both parties to investigate the benefits of a long-term relationship. The relationship can still devolve into a functional relationship rather than a strategic partnership, but the intention of both parties is to develop the appropriate type of relationship. The buyer's dependence on the seller as a primary source of supply grows and may lead to the purchase of additional products.

COMMITMENT

In the **commitment** stage the customer and seller have implicitly or explicitly pledged to continue the relationship for a period of time. Commitment represents the most advanced stage of the relationship. Investments are made in the relationship, especially in the form of sharing proprietary information, plans, goals, and the like.

In later chapters we discuss obtaining commitment as a stage in the sales process. In that sense we are talking about asking the buyer to make a decision, either a decision to buy the product or to take the next step in the decision process. The commitment stage in a relationship involves a promise by both buyer and seller to work together over many transactions, not just the one decision.

DISSOLUTION

Dissolution can occur at any time in the relationship process, though it doesn't necessarily have to occur at all. Dissolution is the process of terminating the relationship and can occur because of poor performance, clash in culture, change in needs, and other factors. When dissolution occurs in latter stages of the relationship, the loss of investments made in the relationship can be significant and have an impact throughout both organizations.

In the next section we explore the factors used in selecting partners. Not every customer should become a strategic partner, but the general principles of creating value by satisfying needs do apply to all customer types. Thus understanding some of the issues involved in evaluating potential partners is important to salespeople.

MANAGING RELATIONSHIPS AND PARTNERING

Today's salespeople are **relationship managers.** They are responsible for making sure that their companies develop the appropriate types of relationships with each customer. In other words, some customers want, and need, a market exchange; others need a functional relationship; and still others need a strategic partnership. Relationship managers must assess a number of characteristics of their customers to develop the most appropriate relationship.

CHOOSING THE RIGHT RELATIONSHIP

As you can see from the discussion about what makes for a strategic relationship, at least one factor that influences a salesperson's choice of relationship is the type of relationship the customer desires. Becoming a strategic partner requires investment by both parties, and if the customer isn't willing to make that investment, then another type of relationship is called for. But even then, as Weydahl's comment about what makes a partner a joy to do business with illustrates, not every customer who wants a strategic partnership should become your strategic partner. Some of the factors to consider are size of the account, access and image in the market, and access to technology.

SIZE

JCPenney has a strategic partnership with Levi Strauss. Would Levi Strauss have a similar partnership with Kestner's Department Store, a three-store chain in central Texas? Probably not. The return could not be great enough to justify the investment. The thought is that by partnering with large accounts, the accounts invest in the supplier and become locked in. Economies of scale can often justify lower prices and higher investments. Size of the account, then, is one aspect to consider. But that doesn't mean that one should partner only with the largest accounts. In some cases larger accounts are not necessarily the most profitable, particularly when the seller's investments are factored in.[35] In other cases smaller accounts provide important benefits that larger accounts cannot, as we will discuss.

ACCESS AND IMAGE

A strategic partnership may be called for if an account can provide access to a specific, desired market or can enhance the image of the seller. For example, Heineken was shocked to discover that Albert Heijn, the largest supermarket chain in the Netherlands, placed Heineken beer on the store's "mega-losers" list. Heineken could not afford the damage to its image that such a list would cause with all retailers in Europe, so it quickly made major commitments to meet Albert Heijn's needs and to rebuild the relationship it had taken for granted.[36] Thus Heineken believed it was important to partner with Albert Heijn because working with the leader in the market was critical to Heineken's image.

Similarly, Oasis Technology Ltd., a small Canadian software company, partnered with the National Commercial Bank of Jamaica. As a result of this partnership, hardware vendors such as NCR and Hewlett-Packard developed partnerships with Oasis. Ashraf Dimitri, Oasis CEO, says, "We were (then) able to go into the smaller countries and say, 'These people have chosen us, you can have confidence in us.'"[37]

ACCESS TO TECHNOLOGY

Some companies are called **lead users** because they face and resolve needs months or years ahead of the rest of the marketplace. These companies often develop innovations, either in the way they use a product or by altering a product, that the supplier can copy. Diamond Shamrock, for example, has a vice president of future systems who works closely with technology suppliers. Diamond Shamrock actively codevelops software with its suppliers to meet its own needs, while the suppliers can then market the products to other potential users. Other companies seek to jointly develop products with their customers.[38]

Other lead users may develop technologies in other areas of the business, such as logistics, that suppliers can copy. For example, Florida Furniture Industries (FFI) works closely with customer Rooms To Go, with the benefit of learning logistics methods that reduce FFI's shipping costs for all customers. Astute salespeople can identify such companies and develop strategic partnerships that lead to joint development of new products or technologies, important outcomes regardless of the size of the account.

8. Assume you have a functional relationship with a buyer. You have been informed that the next order placed by the buyer is going to be shipped late. The buyer has already told you that the order must be delivered on time. You contact the factory and cannot do anything to speed up delivery. What should you do next?

9. We all know a store we used to do business with regularly but don't visit much any more. Think of one or two establishments from your own experience. What did the salesperson do to contribute to your current lack of interest? What could the salesperson do to keep your business? (Don't include a store that you stopped visiting because you moved or because the store went out of business.)

10. What can salespeople do to increase the level of trust a buyer has in them?

Case Problems

CASE 2.1

Old Account or Lost Account?

Morgan Pope, an account executive for Freeman Companies, believes in long-term relationships with customers. Her 10 years of selling trade show services have resulted in a list of clients she can count on to use her company's services over and over. "Some of the customers I work with were actually first called on by Buck Freeman, our company's founder, before I was born!" This "customer for life" philosophy has guided Freeman Companies, and Morgan, to a level of success few other competitors can enjoy.

But recently, Morgan developed problems with one of her major accounts. "First, the exhibit manager I worked most directly with left the company. Then the director of marketing communications left. What I didn't realize is that these were people leaving a company in distress; while the company isn't likely to go bankrupt any time soon, this is a tough time for their industry and they have to have results."

Morgan believes that Freeman's trade show consulting services can help the company increase sales from prospects met at trade shows, and for less money than the company was spending. But she's getting nowhere with the new management team. "Suddenly, I'm dealing with two new people, plus a VP of marketing who thinks all trade shows are just one big party and don't really produce results. So now they've thrown all exhibit services out for bid."

A committee was formed to make the decision, including the new exhibit manager, the new director of marketing communications, and the account executive from the company's advertising agency. Also participating was the director of sales, with whom Morgan had worked many trade shows, and who confided that he thought she didn't have much of a chance.

The committee will hear presentations from Morgan, from the company that did trade show services for the marketing communications director's previous company, and from a company that is Freeman's largest competitor. Morgan is wondering what to stress in the presentation: how trade shows can deliver sales when done the Freeman way; how Freeman can help save money on trade shows; or Freeman's creativity and ability to integrate trade shows with advertising campaigns.

Questions

1. Which approach should Morgan take to save this account? Why? (Note: Do not choose a combination of all three—pick the most important and justify your choice.)

2. Could Morgan prevent this problem from occurring?

3. Check out the website CEIR.org. What information can they provide that Morgan can use? Why is that information better than information from Freeman's own experience or research?

Monica Gutierrez has always believed she could never make too many sales. Then came the day she made one sale too many. Monica is the owner and president of AdTech, a company that manages product sampling and promotional programs targeted toward children, teens, and teachers in elementary and secondary schools. Companies use these programs to get potential customers to try their products and to increase sales.

Most of the programs AdTech manages are cooperative. Groups of products and coupons from various manufacturers are assembled and distributed to children in specific age groups. AdTech offers an exclusive guarantee for each cooperative program. Once a firm has decided to participate in a program, competitive products will not be included in the package.

Monica's oldest and largest client, VibraCare, often used AdTech to introduce new products. But Monica was called by the product manager for a competitor of VibraCare, Thompson's, who wanted to take part in a teen promotion program with a shampoo sample for a new product. Monica told the Thompson's product manager that she would first have to check with VibraCare, but if it was not going to participate, then Thompson's could.

After a week of deliberation, VibraCare said it was not prepared to make a decision about participating in the teen promotion package. The client told Monica, "Do what you have to do." And she did. Monica told Thompson's, a new client for her company, that it had the shampoo slot in the promotion. And that was that until VibraCare phoned a week later, after the contract with Thompson's was signed. VibraCare had changed its plans and wanted to be in the promotion package. Yes, it was late. Yes, there was one shampoo too many. Yes, it was Monica's largest client.

Questions

1. Monica believes she has two options. First, she could ask Thompson's to withdraw. After all, VibraCare was Monica's largest and oldest client. Second, she could tell VibraCare the truth and honor the contract with Thompson's. She could say she had given VibraCare the chance, and she was now obligated to stand by her new client. What should Monica do?

2. What other options, if any, might be better than those mentioned in question 1?

Additional References

Anderson, Helen; Virpi Havila; and Asta Salmi. "Can You Buy a Business Relationship? On the Importance of Customer and Supplier Relationships in Acquisitions." *Industrial Marketing Management* 30 (2001), pp. 575–86.

Bello, Daniel C.; Ritu Lohtia; and Shrish P. Dant. "Collaborative Relationships for Component Development: The Role of Strategic Issues, Production Costs, and Transaction Costs." *Journal of Business Research* 45 (1999), pp. 15–31.

Blois, Keith J. "Trust in Business Relationships: An Evaluation of Its Status." *Journal of Management Studies,* March 1999, pp. 197–212.

de Ruyter, Ko; Luci Moorman; and Jos Lemmik. "Antecedents of Commitment and Trust in Customer–Supplier Relationships in High Technology Markets." *Industrial Marketing Management* 30 (2001), pp. 271–86.

Donnan, Michael P., and James Comer. "Insights into Relationship Structures: The Australian Aluminum Industry." *Industrial Marketing Management* 30 (2001), pp. 255–69.

Dorsch, Michael J.; Les Carlson; Mary Anne Raymond; and Robert Ranson. "Customer Equity Management and Strategic Choice for Sales Managers." *Journal of Personal Selling & Sales Management* 21 (2), Spring 2001, pp. 157–66.

Ellram, Lisa. "Partnering Pitfalls and Success Factors." *International Journal of Purchasing and Materials Management,* April 1995, pp. 36–44.

Fournier, Susan; Susan Dobscha; and David Glen Mick. "Preventing the Premature Death of Relationship Marketing." *Harvard Business Review,* January/February 1998, pp. 42–51.

Laneros, Robert; Robert Beck; and Richard Plank. "Maintaining Buyer–Supplier Partnerships." *International Journal of Purchasing and Materials Management,* July 1995, pp. 3–11.

Lemon, Katherine N.; Tiffany Barnett White; and Russell S. Winer. "Dynamic Customer Relationship Management: Incorporating Future Consideration into the Service Retention Decision." *Journal of Marketing* 66 (1), January 2002, pp. 1–14.

Morgan, Robert, and Shelby Hunt. "The Commitment–Trust Theory of Relationship Marketing." *Journal of Marketing,* July 1994, pp. 20–38.

Sirdeshmuckh, Deepak; Jagdip Singh; and Barry Sabol. "Consumer Trust, Value, and Loyalty in Relational Exchanges." *Journal of Marketing* 66 (1), January 2002, pp. 15–37.

Smith, J. Brock, and Donald W. Barclay. "Selling Partner Relationships: The Role of Interdependence and Relative Influence." *Journal of Personal Selling & Sales Management* 19 (4), Fall 1999, pp. 21–40.

Swan, John E.; Cathy Goodwin; Michael Mayo; and Lynne Richardson. "Customer Identities: Customers as Commercial Friends, Customer Coworkers, or Business Acquaintances." *Journal of Personal Selling & Sales Management* 21 (1), Winter 2001, pp. 29–37.

Turner, Gregory B.; Stephen LeMay; Mark Hartley; and Charles M. Wood. "Interdependence and Cooperation in Industrial Buyer–Supplier Relationships." *Journal of Marketing Theory and Practice* 8 (1), Winter 2000, pp. 16–24.

Tuten, Tracy L., and David J. Urban. "An Expanded Model of Business-to-Business Partnership Formation and Success." *Industrial Marketing Management* 30 (2001), pp. 149–64.

Walter, Achim; Thomas Ritter; and Hans Georg Gemünden. "Value Creation in Buyer–Seller Relationships: Theoretical Considerations and Empirical Results from a Supplier's Perspective." *Industrial Marketing Management* 30 (2001), pp. 365–77.

Weitz, Barton A., and Kevin Bradford. "Personal Selling and Sales Management: A Relationship Marketing Perspective." *Journal of the Academy of Marketing Science* 27, no. 2 (Spring 1999), pp. 241–54.

2 Knowledge and Skill Requirements

The basis of effective personal selling is understanding the customer's needs and communicating how your products and services satisfy those needs. Part 2 provides information about the knowledge and skills needed to be an effective salesperson.

In Chapter 3, we focus on ethical and legal responsibilities confronting salespeople. Partnership relationships are based on mutual trust and respect; both are more likely to exist when salespeople have a strong code of ethics and behave in accordance with their ethical principles. In this chapter, we discuss the ethical choices confronting salespeople and the principles that salespeople can use when faced with these situations, as well as the laws that govern selling activities. These laws define the appropriate behavior in relationships; however, they indicate only a minimum acceptable level of conduct.

Chapter 4 focuses on customers—the process they go through in making purchase decisions and the factors they consider in evaluating alternatives. The chapter also outlines changes occurring in the way businesses buy products and services, and shows how these changes will affect what salespeople do.

Chapter 5 reviews communication principles. It explains how salespeople collect information about their customers by listening, asking questions, and observing nonverbal behaviors. Methods for using verbal and nonverbal communication to influence customers are also discussed.

Effective selling requires salespeople to adapt both the style and the content of their sales presentations to satisfy the needs of a customer. Chapter 6 discusses why flexibility is important and how salespeople can develop the knowledge to effectively practice adaptive selling.

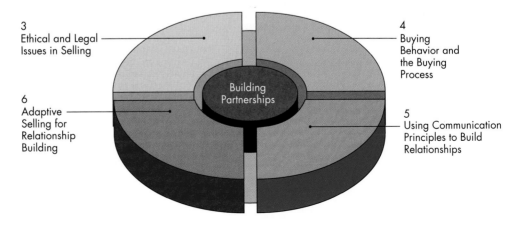

3
Ethical and Legal
Issues in Selling

4
Buying
Behavior and
the Buying
Process

6
Adaptive
Selling for
Relationship
Building

Building
Partnerships

5
Using Communication
Principles to Build
Relationships

3 Ethical and Legal Issues in Selling

SOME QUESTIONS ANSWERED IN THIS CHAPTER ARE:

■ Why do salespeople need to develop their own codes of ethics?

■ Which ethical responsibilities do salespeople have toward themselves, their firms, and their customers?

■ Do ethics get in the way of being a successful salesperson?

■ Which guidelines should salespeople consider when confronting situations involving an ethical issue?

■ Which laws apply to personal selling?

Consider the following situation. A salesperson for a consumer electronics manufacturer is negotiating a $100,000 sale with the buyer for a discount store chain. The buyer says, "I like your new, large-screen TVs. I would really appreciate getting one as a gift." If the salesperson makes the sale, he will get a commission of $7,000. It would cost him $2,000 to buy the TV and give it to the buyer. What should he do? Would it be illegal to give the gift to the buyer? Would it be ethical?

Everyone confronts situations that involve making ethical choices. However, ethics are particularly important in personal selling. Salespeople often have to balance their personal needs with the needs of their companies and their customers. This chapter examines the salesperson's personal code of ethics and the laws that should govern the salesperson's personal behavior when conflicts arise.

"We preach always keeping our promises, promising little and delivering a lot, and only recommending solutions we would choose for ourselves."

Jeff Reeter, Northwestern Mutual Financial Network

PROFILE

Wholly develop a team of champions dedicated to excellence in serving others. That mission describes the focus of the Reeter Financial Group. Jeff Reeter, the Managing Partner of the Reeter Financial Group, has been in a leadership role with Northwestern Mutual Financial Network in every major city in Texas. Currently Reeter owns an organization responsible for "The Quiet Company" operations in Houston, Austin, San Antonio, and all of South Texas

But before this successful career, Jeff Reeter spent his college summers working in a Christian athletic camp and preparing for what seemed to be a career in youth ministry. When he announced his intention to enter the field of insurance and financial services sales, this decision was quite controversial. It was thought that Jeff might be very successful in sales, but one of his mentors challenged this decision based on his experience. The truth is, many aspiring students graduate embracing a definition of success equated only to financial gain.

Each year, hundreds of students like Reeter graduate from college with a desire to pursue a career in professional selling. Undoubtedly the opportunity for income and an outstanding vocational life is available in exchange for hard work and perseverance. Many of the highest-income businesspeople in America are salespersons who have paid the price and climbed the ladder of success. But is income the principal issue for determining success? Are success and income to be achieved at any cost? How should success be defined?

Various factors affect success in sales, and several of those factors involve ethics. Statutory and administrative laws provide legal guidelines. These, along with company policies, protect clients and establish business standards. Equally important are the personal principles "that direct us to uphold a high ethical standard. Our personal code of ethics affects our actions not only in dealing with clients but also in relationships with colleagues. Honesty and integrity in all levels of our lives provide trust that results in significant strides toward success. Competency and lifelong learning are other factors that impact the standard by which you serve your clients."

Jeff Reeter has taught his "team of champions" to forget about income and short-term success. In their company's culture, ethical behavior is a critical precursor to making a difference and having a long-term impact. "We build trust relationships focused on serving our clientele over a 20+-year period of time. These relationships start with listening to a client or prospect's feelings and facts and then responding accordingly. The profit is in the relationship, not in the sale or the commission," says Reeter, "so ethics are critical to our success. We preach always keeping our promises, promising little and delivering a lot, and only recommending solutions we would choose for ourselves."

Interestingly, with a focus on ethics and impact (not income), the financial representatives in the Reeter Financial Group are among the highest paid in all of the selling industry. Along with solid income, the firm retains clients at a 96 percent rate, which is at the top of the financial service industry. Another by-product of truly serving the clientele is repeat business. When a person makes an initial purchase with the firm, on an average, he or she will make seven additional purchases. The bottom line is that ethical behavior is just good business. Many organizations across various selling disciplines take the path of high-pressure closing and quick commission-based sales. Others take the longer-term approach of listening, building lifelong relationships, and truly seeking to serve the clientele. Prospects and clients in today's marketplace are smarter than you may think regarding whom they choose to deal with. Today's clients don't care how much you know until they know how much you care.

Visit Our Website @ www.nmfn.com.

ETHICS AND PERSONAL SELLING

Ethics are the principles governing the behavior of an individual or a group. These principles establish appropriate behavior indicating what is right and wrong. Defining the term is easy, but determining what the principles are is difficult. What one person thinks is right another may consider wrong. For example, 58 percent of sales managers in one poll report believing that sales contests between salespeople do not generate unethical behavior—such as asking customers to take unwanted orders and then return the merchandise after the contest is over—but 42 percent do believe that unethical behaviors are a consequence of sales contests.[1] So the feelings and experiences of sales managers are mixed when it comes to a commonly accepted practice.

What is ethical can vary from country to country and from industry to industry. For example, offering bribes to overcome bureaucratic roadblocks is an accepted practice in Middle Eastern countries but is considered unethical, and even illegal, in the United States. An ethical principle can change over time. For example, some years ago doctors and lawyers who advertised their services were considered unethical. Today such advertising is accepted as common practice.

Here are some examples of difficult situations that salespeople face:

- Should you give an expensive gift to a buyer?
- If a buyer tells you it is common practice to pay off purchasing agents to get orders in his or her country, should you do it?
- Is it acceptable to use a high-pressure sales approach when you know your product is the best for the customer's needs?
- Should you attempt to sell a product to a customer if you know a better product exists for that application?
- If you know about the poor performance features of a competing product, should you tell the customer about them?
- Should you put the cost of a hotel room on your expense account even though you stayed at a friend's house during a business trip?

Enron's questionable business tactics destroyed many careers and the savings of thousands of workers when these tactics were brought to the public. The cost of poor ethics can be quite high.

Reuters NewMedia, Inc./CORBIS

Thinking It Through

How would you respond to the statements in the preceding list? Why? How do you think your friends and your family would respond?

ETHICS AND PARTNERING RELATIONSHIPS

Ethical principles are particularly important in personal selling. As discussed in Chapter 2, most businesses try to develop long-term, mutually beneficial relationships with their customers. Salespeople are the official representatives of their companies, responsible for developing and maintaining these relationships, which are built on trust. Partnerships between buyers and sellers cannot develop when salespeople behave unethically or illegally.[2]

Legal principles guide market exchange relationships. The issues governing buying and selling in these relationships are typically straightforward. The terms and conditions are well defined and can easily be written into a traditional contract.

Ethical principles become increasingly important as firms move to strategic partnerships. Because of the high levels of investment and uncertainty, the parties in these relationships cannot accurately assess the potential benefits—the size of the pie—accruing from strategic investments in the relationships or the contributions of each party in producing those benefits. Many issues cannot be reduced to contractual terms. For example, a salesperson might make a concession for a buyer with a special problem, anticipating that the buyer will reciprocate on future orders. Thus the parties in a strategic partnership have to trust one another to divide the pie fairly.

FACTORS INFLUENCING THE ETHICAL BEHAVIOR OF SALESPEOPLE

Exhibit 3.1 illustrates the factors that affect the ethical behavior of salespeople. The personal needs of salespeople, the needs of their companies and customers, company policies, the values of significant others, and the salesperson's personal code of ethics affect their ethical behaviors.[3]

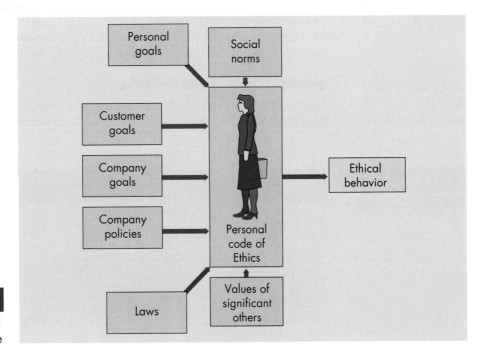

EXHIBIT 3.1

Factors Affecting Ethical Behavior of Salespeople

PERSONAL, COMPANY, AND CUSTOMER NEEDS

Exhibit 3.2 shows how the personal needs of salespeople can conflict with needs of their firms and their customers. Both the salesperson's company and its customers want to make profits. But sometimes these objectives are conflicting. For example, should a salesperson tell a customer about problems his or her firm is having with a new product? Concealing this information might help to make a sale, increase the company's profits, and enhance the salesperson's chances of getting a promotion and a bonus, but doing so could also decrease the customer's profits when the product does not perform adequately. In the situation described at the beginning of the chapter, the salesperson's moral values concerning bribes may be in conflict with his desire to succeed in his new job and the buyer's personal needs for a large-screen TV.[4]

Deb Farrell, now with Lanyon Ltd., a software company in London, England, understands well the pressure of being caught in the middle. In her previous job, managers browbeat reps, shaming them publicly for not reaching quota. To meet revenue projections shortly before the company went public, salespeople pursued an overly aggressive approach. Farrell admits that the atmosphere put her and her colleagues in a compromising position. As she says, "The pressure was ungodly." The reps' actions were not always right for the customer. "You're the one that's always squarely in the middle." To her credit, she left that employer and is much happier with the ethical climate at Lanyon.[5]

Farrell's not alone, either. Research shows that a positive ethical climate is related to job satisfaction, commitment to the organization, and intention to stay among salespeople.[6] Organizations that have a positive ethical climate also have salespeople more committed to meeting the organization's goals—somewhat ironic in light of Farrell's experience.

Ethical conflicts often are not covered by company policies and procedures, and managers may not be available to provide advice. Thus salespeople must make decisions on their own, relying on their ethical standards and understanding of the laws governing these situations.

COMPANY POLICIES

To maintain good relationships with their companies and customers, salespeople need to have a clear sense of right and wrong so that their companies and customers can depend on them when questionable situations arise. Many companies have codes of ethics for their salespeople to provide guidelines in making ethical decisions. An outline of Motorola's policy appears in Exhibit 3.3.

VALUES OF SIGNIFICANT OTHERS

People acquire their values and attitudes about what is right and wrong from the people they interact with and observe. Some important people influencing the

EXHIBIT 3.2 Conflicting Objectives	Company Objectives	Salesperson Objectives	Customer Objectives
	Increase profits	Increase compensation	Increase profits
	Increase sales	Receive recognition promotion	Solve problems, satisfy needs
	Reduce sales costs	Satisfy customers	Reduce costs
	Build long-term customer relationships	Build long-term customer relationships	Build relationships with suppliers
	Avoid legal trouble	Maintain personal code of ethics	Avoid legal trouble

EXHIBIT 3.3

Ethics Policy for
Motorola Salespeople

Improper Use of Company Funds and Assets

The funds and assets of Motorola may not be used for influential gifts, illegal payments of any kind, or political contributions, whether legal or illegal.

The funds and assets of Motorola must be properly and accurately recorded on the books and records of Motorola.

Motorola shall not enter into, with dealers, distributors, agents, or consultants, any agreements that are not in compliance with U.S. laws and the laws of any other country that may be involved, or that provide for the payment of a commission or fee that is not commensurate with the services to be rendered.

Customer/Supplier/Government Relationships

Motorola will respect the confidence of its customers. Motorola will respect the laws, customs, and traditions of each country in which it operates but, in so doing, will not engage in any act or course of conduct that may violate U.S. laws or its business ethics. Employees of Motorola shall not accept payments, gifts, gratuities, or favors from customers or suppliers.

Conflict of Interest

A Motorola employee shall not be a supplier or a competitor of Motorola or be employed by a competitor, supplier, or customer of Motorola. A Motorola employee shall not engage in any activity where the skill and knowledge developed while in the employment of Motorola is transferred or applied to such activity in a way that results in a negative impact on the present or prospective business interest of Motorola.

A Motorola employee shall not have any relationship with any other business enterprise that might affect the employee's independence of judgment in transactions between Motorola and the other business enterprise.

A Motorola employee may not have any interest in any supplier or customer of Motorola that could compromise the employee's loyalty to Motorola.

Compliance with the Code of Conduct is a condition of employment. We urge you to read the complete code.

Should any questions remain, you are encouraged to consult your Motorola law department. In the world of business, your understanding and cooperation are essential. As in all things, Motorola cannot operate to the highest standards without you.

Source: Company document.

ethical behavior of salespeople are their relatives and friends, other salespeople, and their sales managers. Sales managers are particularly important because they establish the ethical climate in their organization through the salespeople they hire, the ethical training they provide for their salespeople, and the degree to which they enforce ethical standards.[7]

Some people hesitate to pursue a sales career because they think selling will force them to compromise their principles. For example, students often think salespeople and sales managers are unethical. However, some studies suggest that sales managers have a greater concern for ethical standards than college students do.[8] Good ethics are good business! Sales managers and salespeople know that.

LAWS

In this chapter we examine ethical and legal issues in personal selling. *Laws* dictate which activities society has deemed to be clearly wrong, the activities for which salespeople and their companies will be punished. These laws are reviewed later in the chapter. However, most sales situations are not covered by laws. Salespeople have to rely on their own codes of ethics and/or their firms' and industries' codes of ethics to determine the right thing to do.

A PERSONAL CODE OF ETHICS

Long before salespeople go to work they develop a sense of what is right and wrong—a standard of conduct—from family and friends. Although salespeople should abide by their own codes of ethics, they may be tempted to avoid difficult ethical choices by developing "logical" reasons for unethical conduct. For example, a salesperson may use the following rationalizations:[9]

- All salespeople behave unethically in this situation.
- No one will be hurt by this behavior.
- This behavior is the lesser of two evils.
- This conduct is the price one has to pay for being in business.

Salespeople use such reasoning to avoid feeling responsible for their behavior and being bound by ethical considerations. Even though the pressure to make sales may tempt salespeople to be unethical and act against their internal standards, maintaining an ethical self-image is important. Compromising ethical standards to achieve short-term gains can have adverse long-term effects. When salespeople violate their own principles, they lose self-respect and confidence in their abilities. They may begin to think that the only way they can make sales is to be dishonest or unethical.

Short-term compromises also make long-term customer relationships more difficult to form. As discussed earlier, customers will be reluctant to deal with the salespeople again. Also, they may relate these experiences to business associates in other companies.

Exhibit 3.4 lists some questions you can ask yourself to determine whether a sales behavior or activity is unethical. The questions emphasize that ethical behavior is determined by widely accepted views of what is right and wrong. Thus you should engage only in activities about which you would be proud to tell your family, friends, employer, and customers.

Your firm can strongly affect the ethical choices you will have to make. When you view your firm's policies or requests as improper, you have three choices:

1. *Ignore your personal values and do what your company asks you to do.* Self-respect suffers when you have to compromise principles to please an employer. If you take this path, you will probably feel guilty and be dissatisfied with your job in the long run.
2. *Take a stand and tell your employer what you think.* Try to influence the decisions and policies of your company and supervisors.
3. *Refuse to compromise your principles.* Taking this path may mean you will get fired or be forced to quit.

You should not take a job with a company whose products, policies, and conduct conflict with your standards. Before taking a sales job, investigate the company's procedures and selling approach to see whether they conflict with your personal ethical standards. The issues concerning the relationship between salespeople and their companies are discussed in more detail in Chapter 17, while methods for evaluating companies are presented in Chapter 18.

SELLING ETHICS AND RELATIONSHIPS

In the following sections we discuss the ethical situations salespeople may confront in their relationships with their customers, competitors, and colleagues (other salespeople).[10]

EXHIBIT 3.4

Checklist for Making
Ethical Decisions

1. Would I be embarrassed if a customer found out about this behavior?
2. Would my supervisor disapprove of this behavior?
3. Would most salespeople feel that this behavior is unusual?
4. Am I about to do this because I think I can get away with it?
5. Would I be upset if a salesperson did this to me?
6. Would my family or friends think less of me if I told them about engaging in this sales activity?
7. Am I concerned about the possible consequences of this behavior?
8. Would I be upset if this behavior or activity were publicized in a newspaper article?
9. Would society be worse off if everyone engaged in this behavior or activity?

If the answer to any of these questions is yes, the behavior or activity is probably unethical and you should not do it.

RELATIONSHIPS WITH CUSTOMERS

Areas of ethical concern involving customers include using **deception**; offering gifts, bribes, and entertainment; divulging confidential information; and back-door selling.

DECEPTION

Deliberately presenting inaccurate information, or lying, to a customer is illegal. However, misleading customers by telling half-truths or withholding important information is a matter of ethics. Frequently salespeople believe it is the customer's responsibility to uncover potential product problems. These salespeople answer questions but don't offer information that might make a sale more difficult. For example, a salesperson selling satellite communication systems might tell a customer that the system will work in all weather but fail to inform the customer about problems in locations surrounded by tall buildings.

Customers expect salespeople to be enthusiastic about their firm and its products and recognize that this enthusiasm can result in a certain amount of exaggeration. Customers also expect salespeople to emphasize the positive aspects of their products and spend little time talking about the negative aspects. But practicing deception by withholding information or telling white lies is clearly unethical. Such salespeople take advantage of the trust customers place in them. When buyers uncover these deceptions, they will be reluctant to trust such salespeople in the future.

Salespeople who fail to provide customers with complete information about products lose an opportunity to develop trust. By revealing both positive and negative information, salespeople can build credibility. Selling Scenario 3.1 illustrates how being honest and straightforward pays off in the long run.

BRIBES, GIFTS, AND ENTERTAINMENT

Bribes and kickbacks may be illegal. **Bribes** are payments made to buyers to influence their purchase decisions, whereas **kickbacks** are payments made to buyers based on the amount of orders placed. A purchasing agent personally benefits from bribes, but bribes typically have negative consequences for the purchasing agent's firm because the product's performance is not considered in buying decisions.

Taking customers to lunch is a commonly accepted business practice. More than 85 percent of salespeople take customers to lunch occasionally or frequently. However, fewer than half occasionally take customers to dinner or for a drink, and only 25 percent entertain customers with leisure activities such as golf or fishing.[11]

Determining which gifts and entertainment activities are acceptable and which are not brings up ethical issues. To avoid these issues, more than half of the U.S.

GOOD ETHICS ARE GOOD BUSINESS

The most difficult ethical dilemmas arise when competitive pressure is intense and the stakes are high. In these situations salespeople are tempted to say and do things that achieve short-term results but sacrifice long-term relationships.

Rick Shih-Hsieh is an IBM marketing specialist in Chicago. One of his biggest customers was ready to place a $500,000 order for PCs but wanted delivery of 500 units in two months. Rick knew IBM and his competitors would not be able to meet this delivery schedule because of an industry shortage of a critical microprocessor. Rick told the customer he could not meet the delivery requirements, but one of his competitors made the commitment and got the order.

"One good thing about working for IBM is that the company has a strong ethical code of conduct. I kept management informed about the situation, and they supported me all the way even though we lost the order. The competitors didn't deliver as promised. Now the purchasing agent really respects me, and this situation will strengthen our relationship. He knows that I'm going to be straight with him."

Source: Personal communication.

companies in a recent survey have set policies that forbid employees to accept gifts (more than pencils or coffee cups) or entertainment from suppliers. These firms require that all gifts sent to the employee's home or office be returned. Wal-Mart, the largest retailer in the world, goes one step further, allowing contact between buyers and vendors only at business meetings at Wal-Mart's or the vendor's headquarters. On the other hand, many companies have no policy on receiving gifts or entertainment. Some unethical employees will accept and even solicit gifts, even though their company has a policy against such practices.

One reason that salespeople find lavish gift giving so tempting is that it often works. One study compared customer satisfaction and sales with the level of gift given. A $40 gift (gold desk set) resulted in significantly greater repurchases than did a similar $20 gift (silver desk set). But even the silver gift resulted in greater resales than a simple thank-you letter after the initial purchase.[12] While none of these gifts were too lavish for the situation, the research indicates how effective thank-you gifts can be at influencing future sales.

To develop a productive, long-term relationship, salespeople need to avoid embarrassing customers by asking them to engage in activities they might see as unethical. If a salesperson wants to give a gift out of friendship or invite a customer to lunch to develop a better business relationship, she or he should phrase the offer so that the customer can easily refuse it. For example, a salesperson with a large industrial firm might have this conversation with a customer:

SALESPERSON: John, we have worked well together over the last five years, and I would like to give you something to show my appreciation. Would that be OK?

BUYER: That's very nice of you, but what are you thinking of giving me?

SALESPERSON: Well, I want to give you a Mont Blanc pen. I really enjoy using my pen, and I thought you might like one also. Is that OK?

BUYER: I would appreciate that gift. Thank you.

Buyers typically are sensitive about receiving expensive gifts, according to Debra Sieckman, director of sales at Allied Van Lines. "It's a bit like getting roses

Most salespeople take customers to lunch. However, paying for a lavish meal can make a customer feel uncomfortable and is considered unethical.

Michael Gracco/Stock, Boston

after a first date. You appreciate the gesture, but you wonder, What is the motive?"[13] Some guidelines for gift giving are as follows:

- Check your motives for giving the gift. The gift should be given to foster a mutually beneficial, long-term relationship, not to obligate or pay off the customer for placing an order.
- Make sure the customer views the gift as a symbol of your appreciation and respect with no strings attached. Never give customers the impression that you are attempting to buy their business with a gift.
- Make sure the gift does not violate the customer's or your firm's policies.
- The safest gifts are inexpensive business items imprinted with the salesperson's company's name or logo.

Even when customers encourage and accept gifts, lavish gifts and entertainment are both unethical and bad business. Treating a customer to a three-day fishing trip is no substitute for effective selling. Sales won this way are usually short-lived. Salespeople who offer expensive gifts to get orders may be blackmailed into continually providing these gifts to obtain orders in the future. Customers who can be bribed are likely to switch their business when presented with better offers.

Giving gifts in other countries requires special attention. Exhibit 3.5 lists some suggestions.

SPECIAL TREATMENT

Some customers try to take advantage of their status to get special treatment from salespeople. For example, a buyer asks a salesperson to make a weekly check on the performance of equipment even after the customer's employees have been thoroughly trained in the operation and maintenance of the equipment. Providing this extra service may upset other customers who do not get the special attention. In addition, the special service can reduce the salesperson's productivity. Salespeople should be diplomatic but careful about undertaking requests to provide unusual services.

EXHIBIT 3.5

It's Not the Gift That Counts, but How You Present It

Japan

Do not open a gift in front of a Japanese customer unless asked, and do not expect the Japanese customer to open a gift in front of you.

Avoid ribbons and bows as part of the gift wrapping. Bows are viewed as unattractive, and different ribbon colors can have different meanings.

Do not offer a gift depicting a fox or a badger. The fox is a symbol of fertility, and the badger a symbol of cunning.

Europe

Avoid red roses and white flowers, even numbers, and the number 13. Do not wrap flowers in paper.

Do not risk the impression of bribery by spending too much on the gift.

Arab World

Do not give a gift when you first meet a customer. It may be misinterpreted as a bribe.

Give a gift in front of others when you do not have a personal relationship with the customer.

Latin America

Gifts should be given on social occasions, not in the course of business.

Avoid the colors black and purple. Both are associated with the Catholic Lenten season.

China

Never make an issue of a gift presentation, either publicly or privately.

Source: Phillip Catoera, *International Marketing*, 10th ed. (New York: Irwin/McGraw-Hill, 1999), p. 100.

CONFIDENTIAL INFORMATION

During sales calls salespeople often encounter confidential company information such as new products under development, costs, and production schedules. Offering information about a customer's competitor in exchange for an order is unethical.

Long-term relationships can develop only when customers trust salespeople to maintain confidentiality. By disclosing confidential information, a salesperson will get a reputation for being untrustworthy. Even the customer who solicited the confidential information will not trust the salesperson, who will then be denied access to information needed to make an effective sales presentation.

BACKDOOR SELLING

Sometimes purchasing agents require that all contacts with the prospect's employees be made through them because they want to be fully informed about and control the buying process. The purchasing agent insists that salespeople get his or her approval before meeting with other people involved in the purchase decision. This policy can make it difficult for a new supplier to get business from a customer using a competitor's products.

Salespeople engage in **backdoor selling** when they ignore the purchasing agent's policy, go around his or her back, and contact other people directly involved in the purchasing decision. Backdoor selling can be very risky and unethical. If the purchasing agent finds out, the salesperson may never be able to get an order. To avoid these potential problems, the salesperson needs to convince the purchasing agent of the benefits to be gained by direct contact with other people in the customer's firm.

Exhibit 3.6 summarizes some research revealing specific sales behaviors that buyers think are unethical and/or inappropriate. The research suggests that buyers will go out of their way to avoid salespeople who engage in these practices.[14]

EXHIBIT 3.6

Buyers' View of
Unethical Sales
Behaviors

- Exaggerates benefits of product.
- Passes the blame for something he or she did to someone else.
- Lies about product availability.
- Misrepresents guarantees.
- Lies about competition.
- Sells products that people do not need.
- Makes oral promises that are not legally binding.
- Is not interested in customer needs.
- Answers questions even when he or she does not know the correct answer.
- Sells hazardous products.

Source: Adapted from William Bearden, Thomas Ingram, and Raymond LaForge, *Marketing: Principles and Perspectives* (New York: Irwin/McGraw-Hill, 1998), p. 512.

RELATIONSHIPS WITH THE SALESPERSON'S COMPANY

Because salespeople's activities in the field cannot be closely monitored, their employers trust them to act in the company's best interests. Professional salespeople do not abuse this trust. They put the interests of their companies above self-interest. Taking this perspective may require them to make short-term sacrifices to achieve long-term benefits for their companies and themselves. Some problem areas in the salesperson–company relationship involve expense accounts, reporting work-time information and activities, and switching jobs.

EXPENSE ACCOUNTS

Many companies provide their salespeople with cars and reimburse them for travel and entertainment expenses. Developing a reimbursement policy that prevents salespeople from cheating and still allows them the flexibility they need to cover their territories and entertain customers is almost impossible. Moreover, a lack of tight control can tempt salespeople to use their expense accounts to increase their income.

To do their jobs well, salespeople need to incur expenses. However, using their expense accounts to offset what they consider to be inadequate compensation is unethical. A salesperson who cannot live within the company compensation plan and expense policies has two ethical alternatives: (1) persuade the company to change its compensation plan or expense policy or (2) find another job.

In using the company's expense account, you should act as though you are spending your own money. Eat good food, but don't go to the most expensive restaurant in town. Stay in clean, comfortable, safe lodgings, but not in the best hotel or the best room in a hotel. When traveling, you should maintain the same standards of living and appearance that you do at home.

REPORTING WORK-TIME INFORMATION AND ACTIVITIES

Employers expect their salespeople to work full-time. Salespeople on salary are stealing from their employers when they waste time on coffee breaks, long lunches, or unauthorized days off. Even salespeople paid by commission cheat their companies by not working full-time. Their incomes and company profits both decrease when salespeople take time off.

To monitor work activities, many companies ask their salespeople to provide daily call reports. Most salespeople dislike this clerical task. Some provide false information, including calls they never made. Giving inaccurate information or bending the truth is clearly unethical. A failure to get an appointment with a customer is not a sales call. Providing a brief glimpse of a product is not a demonstration.

SWITCHING JOBS

When salespeople decide to change jobs, they have an ethical responsibility to their employers. The company often makes a considerable investment in training salespeople and then gives them confidential information about new products and programs. Over time, salespeople use this training and information to build strong relationships with their customers.

A salesperson may have good reasons to switch jobs. However, if a salesperson goes to work for a competitor, she or he should not say negative things about the past employer. Also, disclosing confidential information about the former employer's business is improper. The ethical approach to leaving a job includes the following:[15]

- Give ample notice. If you leave a job during a busy time and with inadequate notice, your employer may suffer significant lost sales opportunities.
- Offer assistance during the transition phase. Help your replacement learn about your customers and territory.
- Don't burn your bridges. Don't say things in anger that may come back to haunt you. Remember that you may want to return to the company or ask the company for a reference in the future.

RELATIONSHIPS WITH COLLEAGUES

To be effective, salespeople need to work together with other salespeople. Unethical behavior by salespeople toward their coworkers, such as engaging in sexual harassment and taking advantage of colleagues, can weaken company morale and have a negative effect on the company's reputation.

SEXUAL HARASSMENT

Sexual harassment includes unwelcome sexual advances, requests for sexual favors, jokes or graffiti, and physical conduct. Harassment is not confined to requests for sexual favors in exchange for job considerations such as a raise or promotion; creating a hostile work environment can be considered sexual harassment. Some actions that are considered sexual harassment are engaging in suggestive behavior, treating people differently because they are male or female, making lewd sexual comments and gestures, joking that has a sexual content, showing obscene photographs, staring at a coworker in a suggestive manner, alleging that an employee got rewards by engaging in sexual acts, and spreading rumors about a person's sexual conduct.

Customers as well as coworkers can sexually harass salespeople. Salespeople are particularly vulnerable to harassment from important customers who may seek sexual favors in exchange for their business. Following are some suggestions for dealing with sexual harassment from customers:

- Don't become so dependent on one customer that you would con-

Persistent, unwelcome advances are one form of sexual harassment. It is illegal and unethical.

Bob Daemmrich/The Image Works

sider compromising your principles to retain the customer's business. Develop a large base of customers and prospects to minimize the importance of one customer.

- Tell the harasser in person or write a letter stating that the behavior is offensive, is unacceptable, and must be stopped. Clearly indicate that you are in control and will not be passive.
- Utilize the sexual harassment policies of your firm and your customer's firm to resolve problems. These policies typically state the procedure for filing a complaint, the person responsible for investigating the complaint, the time frame for completing the investigation, and the means by which the parties will be informed about the resolution.[16]

TAKING ADVANTAGE OF OTHER SALESPEOPLE

Salespeople can behave unethically when they are too aggressive in pursuing their own goals at the expense of their colleagues. For example, it is unethical to fail to relay a customer's phone message to another salesperson or to make critical comments about a colleague to one's boss. Colleagues usually discover such unethical behavior and return the lack of support.

RELATIONSHIPS WITH COMPETITORS

Making false claims about competitors' products or sabotaging their efforts is clearly unethical and often illegal. For example, a salesperson who rearranges the display of a competitor's products to make it less appealing is being unethical. This type of behavior can backfire. When customers detect these practices, the reputation of the salespeople and their companies may be permanently damaged.

Another questionable tactic is criticizing a competitor's products or policies. Although you may be tempted to say negative things about a competitor, this approach usually does not work. Customers will assume you are biased toward your own company and its products and discount negative comments you make about the competition. Some customers may even be offended. If they have bought the competitor's products in the past, they may regard these comments as a criticism of their judgment.

LEGAL ISSUES

Society has determined that some activities are clearly unethical and has decided to use the legal system to prevent people from engaging in these activities. Salespeople who violate these laws can cause serious problems for themselves and their companies—problems more serious than just being considered unethical by a buyer. By engaging in illegal activities, salespeople expose themselves and their firms to costly legal fees and millions of dollars in fines.[17]

The activities of salespeople in the United States are affected by three forms of law: statutory, administrative, and common. **Statutory law** is based on legislation passed either by state legislatures or by Congress. The main statutory laws governing salespeople are the Uniform Commercial Code and antitrust laws. **Administrative laws** are established by local, state, or federal regulatory agencies. The Federal Trade Commission is the most active agency in developing administrative laws affecting salespeople. However, the Securities and Exchange Commission regulates stockbrokers, and the Food and Drug Administration regulates pharmaceutical salespeople. Finally, **common law** grows out of court decisions. Precedents set by these decisions fill in the gaps where no laws exist.

This section discusses current laws affecting salespeople, but every year important new laws are developed and court decisions rendered. Thus you should contact your firm for advice when a potential legal issue arises.

UNIFORM COMMERCIAL CODE

The **Uniform Commercial Code (UCC)** is the legal guide to commercial practice in the United States. The UCC defines a number of terms related to salespeople.

AGENCY

A person who acts in place of his or her company is an **agent.** Authorized agents of a company have the authority to legally obligate their firm in a business transaction. This authorization to represent the company does not have to be in writing. Thus, as a salesperson, your statements and actions can legally bind your company and have significant financial impact.

SALE

The UCC defines a **sale** as "the transfer of title to goods by the seller to the buyer for a consideration known as price." A sale differs from a **contract to sell.** Any time a salesperson makes an offer and receives an unqualified acceptance, a contract exists. A sale is made when the contract is completed and title passes from the seller to the buyer.

The UCC also distinguishes between an offer and an invitation to negotiate. A sales presentation is usually considered to be an **invitation to negotiate.** An **offer** takes place when the salesperson quotes specific terms. The offer specifically states what the seller promises to deliver and what it expects from the buyer. If the buyer accepts these terms, the parties will have established a binding contract.

Salespeople are agents when they have the authority to make offers. However, most salespeople are not agents because they only have the power to solicit written offers from buyers. These written offers, called **orders,** become contracts when they are signed by an authorized representative in the salesperson's company. Sometimes these orders contain clauses stating that the firm is not obligated by its salesperson's statements. However, the buyer usually can have the contract nullified and may even sue for damages if salespeople make misleading statements, even though they are not official agents.

TITLE AND RISK OF LOSS

If the terms of the contract specify **free on board (FOB) destination,** the seller has title until the goods are received at the destination. In this case any loss or damage incurred during transportation is the responsibility of the seller. The buyer assumes this responsibility and risk if contract terms call for **FOB factory.** The UCC also defines when titles transfer for goods shipped cash on delivery (COD) and for goods sold on consignment. Understanding the terms of the sale and who has title can be useful in resolving complaints about damaged merchandise.

The buyer is inspecting a shipment of bananas. Because the produce was shipped FOB destination, the buyer is not responsible for the merchandise until it is delivered to the buyer's warehouse and can turn down the sale even now if the product is not up to standard.

Syracuse Newspapers/The Image Works

ORAL VERSUS WRITTEN AGREEMENTS

In most cases oral agreements between a salesperson and a customer are just as binding as written agreements. Normally, written agreements are required for sales over $500. Salespeople may be the legal representatives of their firms and thus must be careful when signing written agreements.

OBLIGATIONS AND PERFORMANCE

When the salesperson and the customer agree on the terms of a contract, both firms must perform according to those terms in "good faith." In addition, both parties must perform according to commonly accepted industry practices. Even if salespeople overstate the performance of their products, their firms have to provide the stated performance and meet the terms of the contract.

WARRANTIES

A **warranty** is an assurance by the seller that the products will perform as represented. Sometimes a warranty is called a *guarantee*. The UCC distinguishes between two types of warranties, expressed and implied. An **expressed warranty** is an oral or a written statement by the seller. An **implied warranty** is not actually stated but is still an obligation defined by law. For example, products sold using an oral or a written description (the buyer never sees the products) carry an implied warranty that the products are of average quality. However, if the buyer inspects the product before placing an order, the implied warranty applies only to any performance aspects that the inspection would not have uncovered. Typically, an implied warranty also guarantees that the product can be used in the manner stated by the seller.

Salespeople can create a warranty for their products through inadvertent comments and actions. For example, a chemical company was liable for a product that did not meet the performance standards the salesperson promised, even though the sales brochure contradicted the salesperson's claims for the product. Salespeople can also create an implied warranty when they are knowledgeable about the customer's specific application and recognize that the customer is relying on their judgment.

Salespeople can also offset the effects of warnings provided by a firm. For example, when securities salespeople indicated that legally required warnings in the documents describing the investment were unimportant and could be ignored, the company offering the securities was liable for millions of dollars when customers were disappointed with the financial returns from the securities.

Problems with warranties often arise when the sale is to a reseller (a distributor or retailer). The ultimate user—the reseller's customer—may complain about

Factual statements made by this sales representative to a pharmacist about the product are an explicit warranty. They legally bind the salesperson's company, particularly when the customer has limited knowledge about the product.

Custom Medical Stock

a product to the reseller. The reseller, in turn, tries to shift the responsibility to the manufacturer. Salespeople often have to investigate and resolve these issues.

MISREPRESENTATION OR SALES PUFFERY

In their enthusiasm salespeople may exaggerate the performance of products and even make false statements to get an order. Over time, common and administrative laws have defined the difference between illegal misrepresentation and sales puffery. Not all statements salespeople make have legal consequences.[18] However, misrepresentation, even if legal, can destroy a business relationship and may involve salespeople and their firms in lawsuits.

Glowing descriptions such as "Our service can't be beat" are considered to be opinions or **sales puffery.** Customers cannot reasonably rely on these statements. Some examples of puffery are

- This is a top-notch product.
- This product will last a lifetime.
- Our school bus chassis has been designed to provide the utmost safety and reliability for carrying the nation's most precious cargo—schoolchildren.
- The most complete line of reliable, economical gas heating appliances.

However, statements about the inherent capabilities of products or services, such as "Our system will reduce your inventory by 40 percent," may be treated as statements of fact and warranties. Here are examples of such statements found to be legally binding:

- Mechanically, this oil rig is a 9 on a scale of 10.
- Feel free to prescribe this drug to your patients, doctor. It's nonaddicting.
- This equipment will keep up with any other machine you are using and will work well with your other machines.

Factual statements become particularly strong indicators of an expressed warranty when salespeople sell complex products to unsophisticated buyers. In these situations buyers rely on the technical expertise and integrity of the salespeople. However, when salespeople deal with knowledgeable buyers, the buyers are obligated to go beyond assertions made by the salespeople and make their own investigation of the product's performance.

 U.S. salespeople need to be aware of both U.S. laws and laws in the host country when selling internationally. All countries have laws regulating marketing and selling activities. In Canada all claims and statements made in advertisements and sales presentations about comparisons with competitive products must pass the **credulous person standard.** This standard means the company and the salesperson have to pay damages if a reasonable person could misunderstand the statement. Thus a statement like "This is the strongest axle in Canada" might be considered puffery in the United States but be viewed as misleading in Canada unless the firm had absolute evidence that the axle was stronger than any other axle sold in Canada.

To avoid legal and ethical problems with misrepresentation, you should try to educate customers thoroughly before concluding a sale. You should tell the customer as much about the specific performance of the product as possible. Unless your firm has test results concerning the product's performance, you should avoid offering an opinion about the product's specific benefits for the customer's application. If you don't have the answer to a customer's question, don't make a guess. Say that you don't know the answer and will get back to the customer with the information.

ILLEGAL BUSINESS PRACTICES

The Sherman Antitrust Act of 1890, the Clayton Act of 1914, the Federal Trade Commission Act of 1914, and the Robinson-Patman Act of 1934 prohibit unfair business practices that may lessen competition. The courts used these laws to create common law that defines the illegal business practices discussed in this section.

BUSINESS DEFAMATION

Business defamation occurs when a salesperson makes unfair or untrue statements to customers about a competitor, its products, or its salespeople. These statements are illegal when they damage the competitor's reputation or the reputation of its salespeople.

Following are some examples of false statements made about competitors that have been found to be illegal:

- Company X broke the law when it offered you a free case of toilet paper with every 12 cases you buy.
- Company X is going bankrupt.
- You shouldn't do business with Company X. Mr. Jones, the CEO, is really incompetent and dishonest.

You should avoid making negative comments about a competitor, its salespeople, or its products unless you have proof to support the statements.

RECIPROCITY

Reciprocity is a special relationship in which two companies agree to buy products from each other. For example, a manufacturer of computers agrees to use microprocessors from a component manufacturer if the component manufacturer agrees to buy its computers. Such interrelationships can lead to greater trust and cooperation between the firms. However, reciprocity agreements are illegal if one company forces another company to join in the agreement. Reciprocity is legal only when both parties consent to the agreement willingly.

TYING AGREEMENTS

In a **tying agreement** a buyer is required to purchase one product in order to get another product. For example, a customer who wants to buy a copy machine is required to buy paper from the same company, or a distributor that wants to stock one product must stock the manufacturer's entire product line. Because they reduce competition, tying agreements typically are illegal. They are legal only when the seller can show that the products must be used together—that is, that one product will not function properly unless the other product is used with it.

Tying agreements are also legal when a company's reputation depends on the proper functioning of equipment. Thus a firm can be required to buy a service contract for equipment it purchases, although the customer need not buy the contract from the manufacturer.

CONSPIRACY AND COLLUSION

An agreement between competitors before customers are contacted is a **conspiracy**, whereas **collusion** refers to competitors working together while the customer is making a purchase decision. For example, competitors are conspiring when they get together and divide up a territory so that only one competitor will call on each prospect. Collusion occurs when competitors agree to charge the same price for equipment that a prospect is considering. These examples of collusion and conspiracy are illegal because they reduce competition.

INTERFERENCE WITH COMPETITORS

Salespeople may illegally interfere with competitors by

- Trying to get a customer to break a contract with a competitor.
- Tampering with a competitor's product.
- Confusing a competitor's market research by buying merchandise from stores.

RESTRICTIONS ON RESELLERS

Numerous laws govern the relationship between manufacturers and resellers—wholesalers and retailers. At one time it was illegal for companies to establish a minimum price below which their distributors or retailers could not resell their products. Today this practice, called **resale price maintenance**, is legal in some situations.

Manufacturers do not have to sell their products to any reseller that wants to buy them. Sellers can use their judgment to select resellers as long as they announce their selection criteria in advance. One sales practice considered unfair is providing special incentives to get a reseller's salespeople to push products. For example, salespeople for a cosmetics company may give a department store's cosmetics salespeople prizes based on the sales of the company's product. These special incentives, called **spiffs** (or **push money**), are legal only if the reseller knows and approves of the incentive and it is offered to all of the reseller's salespeople.

PRICE DISCRIMINATION

The Robinson-Patman Act became law because independent wholesalers and retailers wanted additional protection from the aggressive marketing tactics of large chain stores. Principally, the act forbids price discrimination in interstate commerce. Robinson-Patman applies only to interstate commerce, but most states have passed similar laws to govern sales transactions between buyers and sellers within the same state.

Court decisions related to the Robinson-Patman Act define **price discrimination** as a seller giving unjustified special prices, discounts, or services to some customers and not to others. To justify a special price or discount, the seller must prove that it results from (1) differences in the cost of manufacture, sale, or delivery; (2) differences in the quality or nature of the product delivered; or (3) an attempt to meet prices offered by competitors in a market. Thus a seller must treat all customers equally. If a seller offers a price discount or special service to one customer, the seller must offer the same price or service to all customers. Different prices can be charged, however, if the cost of doing business is different. For example, a customer who buys in large volume can be charged a lower price if the manufacturing and shipping charges for higher-volume orders are lower than they are for smaller orders.

Firms also may not offer special allowances to one reseller unless those allowances are made available to competing resellers. Because most resellers compete in limited geographic areas, firms frequently offer allowances in specific regions of the country.

LEGAL GUIDELINES

To reduce the chances of violating laws governing sales practices, you should adopt the following guidelines:[19]

- Be sure that all specific statements about your product's performance, such as technical characteristics and useful life, are accurate.

- Be sure that all specific positive statements about performance can be supported by evidence. If you make strong positive statements that cannot be supported, use very general wording, such as *high quality* and *great value.*

- If your customers do not pay attention to warnings and operating instructions, remind them to read this information. Never suggest that this information can be ignored.

- If customers contemplate using your product incorrectly or in an inappropriate application, caution them specifically about how the product should be used.

- Assess your customer's experience and knowledge. Your legal obligations are greatest with unsophisticated customers.

- Don't make negative statements about a competitor's product, financial condition, or business practices. Never pass along rumors about competitors.

ETHICAL AND LEGAL ISSUES IN INTERNATIONAL SELLING

Ethical and legal issues are very complex when selling in international markets. Value judgments and laws vary widely across cultures and countries. Behavior that is commonly accepted as proper in one country can be completely unacceptable in another country. For example, a small payment to expedite the loading of a truck is considered a cost of doing business in some Middle Eastern countries but may be viewed as a bribe in the United States.

Many countries make a clear distinction between payments for lubrication and payments for subordination. **Lubrication** involves small sums of money or gifts, typically made to low-ranking managers or government officials, in countries where these payments are not illegal. The lubrication payments are made to get the official or manager to do the job more rapidly—to process an order more quickly or to provide a copy of a request for a proposal. **Subordination** involves paying larger sums of money to higher-ranking officials to get them to do something that is illegal or to ignore an illegal act. Even in countries where bribery is common, subordination is considered unethical.[20]

RESOLVING CULTURAL DIFFERENCES

What do you do when the ethical standards in a country differ from the standards in your country? This is an age-old question. Cultural relativism and ethical imperialism are two extreme answers to this question. **Cultural relativism** is the view that no culture's ethics are superior. If the people in Indonesia tolerate bribery, their attitude toward bribery is no better or worse than that of people in Singapore who refuse to give or accept bribes. When in Rome, do as the Romans do. But is it right for a European pharmaceutical company to pay a Nigerian company to dispose of the pharmaceutical company's highly toxic waste near Nigerian residential neighborhoods, even though Nigeria has no rules against toxic waste disposal?

On the other hand, **ethical imperialism** is the view that ethical standards in one's home country should be applied to one's behavior across the world. This view suggests that Saudi Arabian salespeople working for a U.S. firm should go through the same sexual harassment training U.S. salespeople do, even though the strict conventions governing relationships between men and women in Saudi Arabia make the training meaningless and potentially embarrassing.

Adopting one of these extreme positions is probably not the best approach. To guide your behavior in dealing with cultural differences, you need to distinguish between what is merely a cultural difference and what is clearly wrong. You must respect core human values that should apply in all business situations but also respect local traditions and use the cultural background to help you decide what is right and what is wrong. For example, exchanging expensive gifts is common in Japanese business relationships, although it may be considered unethical in Western cultures. Most Western firms now accept this practice as an appropriate local tradition. On the other hand, exposing people in less developed countries to hazardous waste is clearly wrong no matter where it takes place. However, selling some fungicides banned in the United States may be acceptable in equatorial countries, since the chemicals may be harmless in high-temperature, humid environments.[21]

Research indicates that salespeople, particularly those who operate in foreign cultures, are in significant need of corporate support and guidance in handling cultural ethical differences. Even a high level of personal morality may not prevent an individual from violating a law in a sales context, so it is imperative that companies establish specific standards of conduct, provide ethical training, and monitor behavior to enforce standards as uniformly as possible around the globe.[22] Building Partnerships 3.1 illustrates some of the cultural differences in ethics and offers other suggestions for resolving those differences.

LEGAL ISSUES

Regardless of the country in which U.S. salespeople sell, they are subject to U.S. laws that prohibit participating in unauthorized boycotts, trading with enemies of the United States, or engaging in activities that adversely affect the U.S. economy. Under the antiboycott law, it is illegal for U.S. firms and their salespeople to be involved in an unauthorized boycott of a foreign country. Any approach to cooperate in such a boycott must be reported. For example, a large hospital supply company was found guilty of violating this law when it closed its manufacturing plant in Israel to remove its name from an Arab blacklist.

The **Foreign Corrupt Practices Act** makes it illegal for U.S. companies to pay bribes to foreign officials. Violations of the law can result in sizable fines for company managers, employees, and agents who knowingly participate in or authorize the payment of such bribes. However, an amendment to the act permits small lubrication payments when they are customary in a culture.[23]

The U.S. laws concerning bribery are much more restrictive than laws in other countries. For example, in Italy and Germany bribes made outside the countries are clearly defined as legal and tax deductible.

DEALING WITH ETHICAL PROBLEMS CROSS-CULTURALLY

Jens Wiik Jensen works with Dow Chemical distributors in Malaysia, Singapore, Brunei, and Thailand. "Many companies in the region make sales by providing kickbacks to key decision makers," says Jensen. "This situation really posed a problem for me because our corporate policies prevented us from winning business this way. I found a way around this dilemma by focusing on another cultural norm. People in this area like to develop long-term business relationships with friends. So I cultivated friendships with different people. By building these relationships, customers bought our resins even though we didn't give kickbacks."

While world events have increased awareness of Islamic philosophies, many who do business in Islamic cultures find Jensen's experience to be common. Egyptians, for example, "prefer to do business with people they know and like and whom they consider as friends" (Rice). Appreciating this cultural norm, and others, can be advantageous as executives develop global ethics policies.

Similarly, purchasers operating in global environments face ethical pressures and need corporate guidance. Research indicates that such pressures vary in different cultures. In India, for example, purchasing agents reported that global sourcing activities actually encourage them to compromise their ethical values more so than domestic activities (Cooper et al.). The pressure is there, on both sides of the relationship, but with greater understanding and strong corporate guidance, companies can still compete effectively and ethically in the global marketplace.

Sources: Jens Wiik Jensen, personal communication; Gillian Rice, "Islamic Ethics and Implications for Business," *Journal of Business Ethics* 18 (1999), pp. 345–58; Robert W. Cooper, Garry L. Frank, and Robert A. Kemp, "A Multinational Comparison of Key Ethical Issues, Helps, and Challenges for the Purchasing and Supply Management Profession: The Key Implications for Business and the Professions," *Journal of Business Ethics* 23 (2000), pp. 83–100.

Summary

This chapter discussed the legal and ethical responsibilities of salespeople. These responsibilities are particularly important in personal selling because salespeople may face conflicts between their personal standards and the standards of their firms and customers.

Salespeople's ethical standards determine how they will conduct relationships with their customers, employers, and competitors. Relations with customers involve the use of entertainment and gifts and the disclosure of confidential information. Relations with employers involve expenses and job changes. Finally, salespeople must be careful in how they talk about competitors and treat competitive products.

Many companies have ethical standards that describe the behavior expected of their salespeople. In evaluating potential employers, salespeople should consider these standards.

Salespeople also encounter many situations not covered by company statements and therefore must develop personal standards of right and wrong. Without personal standards, salespeople will lose their self-respect and the respect of their company and customers. Good ethics are good business. Over the long run, salespeople with a strong sense of ethics will be more successful than salespeople who compromise their own and society's ethics for short-term gain.

Statutory laws (such as the Uniform Commercial Code) and administrative laws (such as Federal Trade Commission rulings) guide the activities of salespeople in the United States. Selling in international markets is quite complex, however, because of cultural differences in ethical judgments and laws that relate to sales activities in various countries.

KEY TERMS

administrative law   69
agent   70
backdoor selling   64
bribes   63
business defamation   73
collusion   74
common law   69
conspiracy   74
contract to sell   70
credulous person standard   73
cultural relativism   76
deception   63
ethical imperialism   76
ethics   58
expressed warranty   71
free on board (FOB) destination   70
FOB factory   70
Foreign Corrupt Practices Act   76

implied warranty   71
invitation to negotiate   70
kickbacks   63
lubrication   75
offer   70
orders   70
price discrimination   75
reciprocity   73
resale price maintenance   74
sale   70
sales puffery   72
sexual harassment   68
spiffs (push money)   74
statutory law   69
subordination   75
tying agreement   74
Uniform Commercial Code (UCC)   70
warranty   71

Questions and Problems

1. There are certainly many ethical and legal issues in selling, as this chapter demonstrates. Do you think there are more in selling than other jobs, such as accounting, finance, retail store management, or the like? Why or why not?

2. For centuries the guideline for business transactions was the Latin term *caveat emptor* (let the buyer beware). This principle suggests that the seller is not responsible for the buyer's welfare. Is this principle still appropriate in modern business transactions? Why or why not?

3. What should a salesperson do if he or she believes a competitor is making unethical statements about his or her product?

4. Which factors influence the ethical conduct of salespeople?

5. What is the relationship between the UCC and ethics?

6. Consider the following situations and indicate whether the salesperson behaved illegally, unethically, or inappropriately or whether the behavior was appropriate.

   a. The buyer's secretary asks you out as you are leaving the plant after making a sales call, and you accept.

   b. You have a customer who is about to place an order. You know the product's price will be reduced in two weeks, and if the buyer knew about the price reduction, she would wait two weeks to place the order. Therefore, you don't inform the buyer about the impending price reduction.

   c. You accept an invitation from a buyer to take you out to dinner in appreciation for all the support you have provided over the last three months.

   d. You ask a buyer about the experiences he has had with a competitor's products.

   e. You go directly to see the head of the engineering department because the buyer will not see you.

   f. You take the afternoon off after making a big sale.

7. Consider this statement: Sales managers, not salespeople, have to be concerned with the legal implications of selling activities. Do you agree with this statement? Why or why not?

8. For each of the following situations, evaluate the salesperson's action and indicate what you think the appropriate action would be.

   a. A power tool manufacturer begins a program of providing extra incentives to retail clerks in home improvement centers. The salespeople for the power tool company are instructed to contact retail clerks and offer them $1 for each item they sell from the manufacturer's product line. The company instructs the salespeople not to mention this program to the management of the retail stores.

   b. In some Latin American countries, a cash payoff to customers who do a favor for a salesperson is considered normal. A young, inexperienced salesperson is given the responsibility for sales in one such country. When a buyer confronts the salesperson with a demand for a cash payoff in return for a larger order, the salesperson complies.

   c. A customer asks a salesperson selling small business computers in Canada whether the computer has software for an inventory control system. The salesperson replies that an inventory control software package is available as part of the standard software system that comes with each unit. The salesperson has answered the question truthfully but has failed to mention that the inventory control software is useful only in a few special situations and probably will not meet the customer's needs.

   d. A salesperson picks up an order at a customer's plant but forgets to turn it in to the order-processing department. After a few weeks, the customer calls to complain about the slow delivery. The salesperson realizes the order has not been turned in and immediately submits it. Then the salesperson tells the customer that the slow delivery is the result of a mistake by the order-processing department because the truth may jeopardize her future relations with the customer.

   e. The custom of the trade is that competitive firms submit bids based on specifications provided by the buyer; then the buyer places an order with the firm offering the lowest bid. After a salesperson submits a bid, the purchasing agent calls him and indicates that the bid is $100,000 too high. The buyer asks the salesperson to submit another bid at a price $100,000 lower.

f. A customer gives a salesperson a suggestion. The salesperson does not turn in the idea to her company, even though the company's policy manual states that all customer ideas should be submitted with the monthly expense report. Instead, the salesperson quits her job and starts her own business using the customer's suggestion.

g. Jim Hanson is a sales representative for a plastics manufacturer. His company has always had a policy of uniform pricing for all customers. One of his largest customers, Hoffman Container, always tries to bargain for special prices. The buyer is now threatening to use another supplier unless Jim agrees to a special price concession. Jim's sales manager has agreed to the concession. Jim has just gotten a similar-size order from one of Hoffman's competitors at a price 10 percent higher than Hoffman is demanding. What should Jim do? Does Jim have any responsibility to Hoffman's competitor?

h. A few months after joining a company, you learn about a Diner's Club card that gives you a 20 percent cash refund on meals at certain restaurants. You get the card and start taking clients to restaurants offering the rebate, pocketing the rebate.

Case Problems

CASE 3.1
Headhunting

"You start off by cold-calling, calling people who when they first hear your voice, think they don't want to talk to you. Then you prove them wrong."

So says Sylvia Colter, successful employment counselor, or headhunter. Her job is to convince people they want a new job or to convince other people to hire the ones who want the job. "You call a company, and instead of saying that you are a personnel consultant and asking if they have any staffing needs, you say, 'Hi, I'm Sylvia and I've got a great candidate for your company, came straight from your competitor.' Even though you just made that up, it sounds pretty good, right? And that's the point, you want them to think it sounds good and they want to hear more."

As she says, if the company you just called wants to hear more about this candidate, you pick up the phone and call until you find one. Call all the company's competitors if you have to.

But if the company says they're not interested in this "competitor's employee," then ask what are they interested in. "You're always looking for jobs that need filling," states Sylvia. "Or people who want a job." She uses the same approach when calling potential employees. "Say, 'I know a company that's looking for someone with your skills and experience.' You say this even though you don't have any such client. You just say it. At the very least, he'll send a resume so you can add him to your database and you can begin to look for a position."

Questions

1. Apply the checklist in Exhibit 3.4 to this situation. Are there any ethical issues with Sylvia's practices?

2. How widespread do you think such behavior is in this business?

CASE 3.2
Rosewood Boat

Mary Demail is a purchasing agent for Rosewood Boat, a family-owned business that specializes in manufacturing wooden fishing and pleasure boats. The company sells about 500 boats a year, usually for $100,000 and up. She works with a number of vendors, including companies who provide finishing products (resins, varnishes, and the like). One in particular, American Chemical, supplies almost 60 percent of Rosewood's needs.

On the Thursday before the Final Four collegiate basketball tournament, Bill Nether called. Bill is Rosewood's VP of sales, and he had an interesting proposition for Mary.

After the usual hellos, Bill got right to it. "Mary, you know that we've been trying to land the Kingshead Bay account for several years. With their chain of 20 stores, they could sell 100 boats a year for us, which would grow us by more than 20 percent. But to get this business, I need your help. Max Fischer, their buyer, has asked if I can get him tickets to the Final Four, and I've tried everything I can. Is there any way you could call Frank Walker over at American and see if they have any?" He went on to hint how important this account is and that perhaps a purchasing agent was too much overhead for the company at its current size.

Mary wondered immediately if Bill had heard about the offer of tickets that Frank had made earlier that week. Mary had turned Frank down, thinking it was too generous an offer; and besides, she didn't really like basketball all that much.

Questions

1. Should she tell Bill about the tickets and should she offer to get them for Bill?
2. The company could benefit greatly from her decision. Could she personally benefit? Should either of these issues of who benefits matter?
3. If she gets the tickets, what is the impact on her relationship with American, assuming they don't find out that Bill and Max went? If they do find out?
4. What should she do if she decides not to get the tickets? Be specific.

Additional References

Bass, Ken; Tim Barnett; and Gene Brown. "The Moral Philosophy of Sales Managers and Its Influence on Ethical Decision Making." *Journal of Personal Selling and Sales Management* 18 (Spring 1998), pp. 1–18.

Chonko, Lawrence; John Tanner; and William Weeks. "Ethics in Salesperson Decision Making: A Synthesis of Research Approaches and an Extension of the Scenario Method." *Journal of Personal Selling and Sales Management*, Winter 1996, pp. 35–52.

Cooper, Robert W.; Garry L. Frank; and Robert A. Kemp. "A Multinational Comparison of Key Ethical Issues, Helps, and Challenges for the Purchasing and Supply Management Profession: The Key Implications for Business and the Professions." *Journal of Business Ethics* 23 (2000), pp. 83–100.

Dunfee, Thomas; N. Craig Smith; and William Ross. "Contracts and Marketing Ethics." *Journal of Marketing* 63 (Summer 1999), pp. 14–32.

Ferrell, O. C.; Thomas N. Ingram; and Raymond W. LaForge. "Initiating Structure for Legal and Ethical Decisions in a Global Sales Organization." *Industrial Marketing Management* 29 (2000), pp. 555–64.

Fine, Leslie; C. David Shephard; and Sally Josephs. "Insights into Sexual Harrassment of Salespeople by Customers: The Role of Gender and Customer Power." *Journal of Personal Selling and Sales Management* 19 (Spring 1999), pp. 19–34.

Hotchkiss, Carolyn. "The Sleeping Dog Stirs: New Signs of Life in Efforts to End Corruption in International Business." *Journal of Public Policy & Marketing* 17 (Spring 1998), pp. 108–21.

Rallapalli, Kumar C.; Scott J. Vitell; and James H. Barnes. "The Influence of Norms on Ethical Judgments and Intentions: A Study of Marketing Professionals." *Journal of Business Research* 43 (1998), pp. 157–68.

Rice, Gillian. "Islamic Ethics and Implications for Business." *Journal of Business Ethics* 18 (1999), 345–58.

Schwepker, Charles W., Jr. "Ethical Climate's Relationship to Job Satisfaction, Organizational Commitment and Turnover Intention in the Salesforce." *Journal of Business Research* 54 (2001), pp. 39–52.

Buying Behavior and the Buying Process

SOME QUESTIONS ANSWERED IN THIS CHAPTER ARE:

■ What are the different types of customers?

■ How do organizations make purchase decisions?

■ Which factors do organizations consider when evaluating products and services?

■ Who is involved in the buying decision?

■ What should salespeople do in the different types of buying situations?

■ Which changes are occurring in organizational buying, and how will these changes affect salespeople?

To be effective, salespeople must know what their customers need, who will be involved in the purchase decision, and how the purchase decision will be made. The more salespeople know about their customers, the more effective those salespeople will be in satisfying their customers' needs. This chapter describes how businesses decide to buy products and services and how salespeople can influence this decision-making process.

PROFILE

For some people, selling is a career. For others, selling is a launching pad from which their career takes off into other areas. Howard Stroud, though, has neither made a career from sales nor completely left sales.

Stroud is now the director of merchandising and purchasing for Grocery Supply Company, Sulphur Springs, Texas. Grocery Supply Company is a grocery distributor to convenience stores. Stroud got his start in the industry with Southland Corporation while completing his BS in business at LeTourneau University. Stroud explains, "Southland Corporation was the parent corporation for 7-11 convenience stores. I was working in distribution, and when I graduated, they asked me to stay."

But after a few years, a company lured Stroud into sales. "I joined Sav-A-Stop, a company selling health and beauty aids, for a year and found that I really enjoyed sales." When Southland called him to come back and join their sales force, he did. "We sold Southland's distribution services to convenience stores other than 7-11."

Then came the switch. "After 17 years, total, with Southland, I got an intriguing offer." That offer was to join Grocery Supply Company as their chief buyer. It isn't often that someone makes the switch from salesperson to buyer, but in Stroud's case, the sales experience is a tremendous value. With that sales experience, Stroud understands the needs of GSC's customers. After all, he sold to them for nearly 17 years. So when Stroud is working with a manufacturer to develop a merchandising program for GSC to sell to its customers, he can call on his field experience to know what will work, how it will work, and why.

"Our partnerships are really three-way partnerships—GSC is in the middle between our manufacturers and our customers," says Stroud. "Some manufacturers want us to handle everything for our customers—they won't work with us on marketing and promotional programs. Others may go directly to the retailers and try to exclude us. Neither of those situations is a partnership, and neither works well for the manufacturer." Stroud believes that when the manufacturer chooses not to get heavily involved but lets GSC handle everything, GSC can do a good job for the customer. But when a manufacturer tries to go around GSC directly to the convenience store, "That is frustrating. Someone [a manufacturer] who develops a program and sells it to the retailers without involving us means that we don't know what's going on. Then someone has to coordinate distribution, stocking, allowances, deals, promotional rates, etc., and we can't because we don't know anything about it. The manufacturer still needs us to get the product there, to get it on the shelf, and to get the POS [point-of-sale] materials right. Someone still needs to do our job, but there isn't anyone there to do it because the manufacturer went direct."

Stroud does say, "There are manufacturers who get it right—Hershey Chocolate does it right. Their field reps, their upper management, and their marketing people work together to coordinate their marketing programs with us and our customers. We involve our salespeople in these partnerships, too." Stroud believes that this type of coordinated effort is why companies like Hershey do so well in the market. In a true partnership, GSC is a valuable player that helps both manufacturer and retailer succeed.

Does Stroud miss sales? Yes and no—Stroud says that, in a way, he's still doing sales. "You have to do a lot of sales in purchasing, because all of our marketing programs have to be sold to our vendors, and I have to interact with customers a lot to make sure we have the right marketing programs and products for them." And that's where that sales experience pays off.

Visit Our Website @ www.grocerysupply.com.

TYPES OF CUSTOMERS

Salespeople interact with a wide of variety of customers, including producers, resellers, government agencies, institutions, and consumers. Each of these customer types has different needs and uses a different process to buy products and services. Thus salespeople need to use different approaches when selling to different types of customers.

PRODUCERS

Producers buy products and services to manufacture and sell their products and services to customers. Buyers working for producers are involved in two types of buying situations: buying products that will be included in the products the company is manufacturing or buying products and services to support the manufacturing operation.

OEM PURCHASES

Buyers for **original equipment manufacturers (OEMs)** purchase goods (components, subassemblies, raw and processed materials) to use in making their products. For example, General Motors (GM) buys glass windshields from PPG and uses them in the automobiles GM sells to consumers. The windshields directly affect the performance and cost of GM's cars. GM spends more than $60 billion annually—more than $170 million each day—for products such as steel, upholstery, and tires.

Salespeople selling OEM products need to demonstrate that their products help their customers produce products that will offer superior value. For example, Intel microprocessors have such a strong reputation for quality and performance that personal computer manufacturers advertise that Intel microprocessors are inside their computers.

Most OEM products are bought in large quantities on an annual contract. The purchasing department negotiates the contract with the supplier; however, engineering and production departments play a major role in the purchase decision. Engineers evaluate the products and may prepare specifications for a custom

Salespeople sell products to OEMs such as the shipbuilder on the left. The salespeople working for the shipbuilder then sell the ships (which are capital equipment) to ocean transport firms, who then sell their services to other businesses.

Paul Chesley/Stone

Lester Lefkowitz/The Stock Market

design. The production department works with the supplier to make sure that the OEM products are delivered "just in time."

OEM customers are building long-term relationships with a limited number of OEM suppliers. Thus relationship building with more than one department in a customer firm is particularly important when selling OEM products.

END-USER PURCHASES

When producers buy goods and services to support their own production and operations, they are acting as **end users.** End-user buying situations include the purchase of capital equipment; maintenance, repair, and operating (MRO) supplies; and services. **Capital equipment** items are major purchases, such as mainframe computers and machine tools, that the producer uses for a number of years. **MRO supplies** include paper towels and replacement parts for machinery. **Services** include Internet and telephone connections, employment agencies, consultants, and transportation.

Because capital equipment purchases typically require major financial commitments, capital equipment salespeople need to work with a number of people involved in the purchase decision, including high-level corporate executives. These salespeople need to demonstrate the reliability of their products and their support services because an equipment failure can shut down the producer's operation. Capital equipment buying often focuses on lifetime operating cost rather than the initial purchase price because the equipment is used over a long period of time. Thus capital equipment salespeople need to present the financial implications as well as the operating features and benefits of their products.

MRO supplies and services are typically a minor expense and therefore are usually less important to businesses than are many other items. Purchasing agents typically oversee MRO buying decisions. Because they often do not want to spend the time to evaluate all suppliers, they tend to purchase from vendors who have performed well in the past.

Grainger uses field salespeople, telemarketing salespeople, catalogs, and the Internet to sell MRO products.

© 2000 W.W. Grainger, Inc.

Although the cost of MRO supplies is typically low, availability can be critical. For example, the failure of a $10 motor in an industrial robot can shut down an entire assembly line. Some professional services, such as accounting, advertising, and consulting, also are important to the company and may be purchased in a manner similar to capital equipment purchases.

RESELLERS

Resellers buy finished products or services with the intention to resell them to businesses and consumers. For example, Barnes & Noble buys large quantities of books from publishers and resells the books to consumers at its retail locations. McKesson Corporation is a wholesaler that buys heath care products from manufacturers and resells those products to drugstores.

Because resellers do not use the products, they are interested primarily in the attractiveness of the products to their customers. For example, Du Pont promotes the benefits of Stainmaster™ carpets to stimulate consumer demand and thus encourage carpet distributors and retailers to stock and sell the carpets. Resellers are also interested in services provided by suppliers that make the resale of the product profitable.[1]

For example, Dan Fleshman is responsible for selling Nike footwear worth $70 million to the 700 exchange stores operated around the world by the U.S. military. He worked with the buyers to tailor assortments to individual bases. Training bases would get more men's and women's running shoes, and regular bases would get merchandise for families. Then he developed a system to bypass the government warehouses so that bases receive shoes directly from Nike within 10 days after an order is placed. "We have to be partners and help customers plan their business," Fleshman says. "Instead of just identifying problems, we have to propose solutions and make sure the solutions get implemented."[2] Selling to resellers is discussed in more detail in Chapter 15.

Note that the same customer can act as an OEM manufacturer, an end user, and a reseller. For example, Dell Computer makes OEM buying decisions when it purchases microprocessors for its computers, acts as an end user when it buys materials handling equipment for its warehouse, and functions as a reseller when it buys software to resell to its computer customers when they place orders.

GOVERNMENT AGENCIES

The largest customers for goods and services in the United States are federal, state, and local governments, which collectively purchase goods and services valued at more than $1 trillion annually. More than half of these purchases are made by the federal government, making it the largest customer in the world.[3] Government buyers typically develop detailed specifications for a product and then invite qualified suppliers to submit bids. A contract is awarded to the lowest bidder. However, government agencies are beginning to use less bureaucratic procedures when they purchase commercial products.[4]

Effective selling to government agencies requires a thorough knowledge of their unique procurement procedures and rules. Salespeople also need to know about projected needs so they can influence the development of the buying specifications. For example, Harris Corporation worked for six years with the Federal Aviation Administration and finally won a $1.7-billion contract to modernize air traffic communication systems.

Some resources available to salespeople working with the federal and state governments are

- Guidelines for selling to the government published by the U.S. Government Printing Office.
- The *Commerce Business Daily*, which contains all invitations for bids issued by the federal government.

Selling weapons to a government requires thorough knowledge of the government's procedures and regulations.

Richard Baker-IPG/Matrix

- The National Association of State Purchasing Officials in Washington, D.C., which publishes information on all 50 states, including the availability of vendor guides, registration fees, and how to get on bidder lists.
- The Procurement Automated Source System (PASS), the Small Business Administration database with information on more than 900 federal purchasing agents and prime contractors working on federal contracts.[5]

 Many international salespeople are selling to government agencies, even though private companies may be the biggest buyers of these products and services in the United States. For example, Nortel, a Canadian company that manufactures telephone equipment, sells to private companies such as Verizon and IBM in the United States but to the post, telephone, and telegraph (PTT) government agency in many countries in Europe, Asia, and Africa.

Selling to foreign governments is very challenging. The percentage of domestic product (countries may require that a certain percentage of the product be manufactured or assembled locally) and exchange rates (the value of local currency in U.S. dollars) are as important as the characteristics of the product. Different economic and political systems, cultures, and languages also can make international selling difficult.

INSTITUTIONS

Another important customer group consists of public and private institutions such as churches, hospitals, and colleges. Often these institutions have purchasing rules and procedures that are as complex and rigid as those used by government agencies.

Packaged goods manufacturers, such as Heinz, sell to both resellers (supermarkets) and institutional customers (restaurants and hospitals). These customers have different needs and buying processes. Thus Heinz has one sales force calling on supermarkets and another sales force selling different products to restaurants.

CONSUMERS

Consumers purchase products and services for use by themselves or by their families. A lot of salespeople sell insurance, automobiles, clothing, and real estate to consumers. However, college graduates often take sales jobs that involve selling to business enterprises, government agencies, or institutions. Thus the examples in this text focus on these selling situations, and this chapter discusses organizational rather than consumer buying behavior.

In the next section we contrast the buying processes of consumers and organizations. Then we describe the buying process that organizations use in more detail, including the steps in the process, who influences the decisions, and how salespeople can influence the decisions.

ORGANIZA-TIONAL BUYING AND SELLING

Salespeople who sell to consumers and salespeople who call on organizations have very different jobs. Because the organizational buying process typically is more complex than the consumer buying process, selling to organizations often requires more skills and is more challenging than selling to consumers.[6]

COMPLEXITY OF THE ORGANIZA-TIONAL BUYING PROCESS

The typical organizational purchase is much larger and more complex than the typical consumer purchase. Organizations use highly trained, knowledgeable purchasing agents to make these decisions. Many other people in organizations are involved in purchase decisions, including engineers, production managers, business analysts, and senior executives.

Organizational buying decisions often involve extensive evaluations and negotiations over a period of time. The average time required to complete a purchase is five months, and during that time salespeople need to make many calls to gather and provide information.

For example, Chuck Smith, a salesperson at Walker Interactive Systems, took three years to sell a $1 million general ledger system to an aircraft-manufacturing division of a large corporation. The process began when the customer issued a request for information (RFI). On the basis of Smith's response to the RFI, the customer selected Walker as a potential supplier. A year after the initial RFI, Smith's team had developed strong relationships with the division's contact people, but Smith discovered they did not have authority to sign off on the order. Then he "trained" the division personnel to sell the concept to their corporate counterparts and finally closed the sale, three years after the RFI. Smith's tips for long cycle selling are

- Stay in touch. Call the customer, check on the status, and mail information so the customer will remember you.

- Stay energized. Keep things moving on your side. Bring the team up to date. Ask for suggestions on how to move things along.

- Stay busy. Always have several sales going.[7]

The complexity of organizational purchase decisions means that salespeople must be able to work effectively with a wide range of people working for their customer and their company. For example, when selling a new additive to a food processor such as Nabisco, an International Flavors and Fragrances salesperson may interact with advertising, product development, legal, production, quality control, and customer service people at Nabisco. The salesperson needs to know the technical and economic benefits of the additive to Nabisco and the benefits to consumers.

In addition, the salesperson coordinates all areas of his or her own firm to assist in making the sale. The salesperson works with research and development to provide data on consumer taste tests, with production to meet the customer's delivery requirements, and with finance to set the purchasing terms. (Working effectively within the salesperson's organization is discussed in more detail in Chapter 17.)

The complexity of organizational selling is increasing as more customers become global businesses. For example, Deere and Company has a special unit to coordinate worldwide purchases. The unit evaluates potential suppliers across the globe for each of its product lines and manufacturing facilities. Thus a salesperson selling fan belts to Deere must work with the special corporate buying unit as well as with the employees at each manufacturing location around the world.[8] There's no doubt that global competitiveness is a key factor increasing the complexity of organizational buying, but global sourcing is also a key factor for achieving a sustainable competitive advantage. [9]

DERIVED VERSUS DIRECT DEMAND

Salespeople selling to consumers typically can focus on the individual consumer or family needs. Organizational selling often requires salespeople to know about the customer's customers. Sales to OEMs and resellers are based on derived demand rather than direct demand. **Derived demand** means that purchases made by these customers ultimately depend on the demand for their products—either other organizations or consumers. For example, J.R. Simplot sells 1.5 billion pounds of potatoes to McDonald's restaurants. Simplot's sales depend on how many french fries McDonald's sells.[10] When demand is derived, salespeople must understand the needs of the ultimate user as well as those of the immediate customer.

HOW DO ORGANIZA-TIONS MAKE BUYING DECISIONS?

To effectively sell to organizations, salespeople need to understand how organizations make buying decisions. This section discusses the steps in the organizational buying process, the different types of buying decisions, and the people involved in making the decisions.[11]

STEPS IN THE BUYING PROCESS

Exhibit 4.1 shows the eight steps in an organizational buying process.

RECOGNIZING A NEED OR A PROBLEM (STEP 1)

The buying process starts when someone realizes that a problem exists. Employees in the customer's firm or outside salespeople can trigger this recognition. For example, a supermarket cashier might discover that the optical scanner is making mistakes in reading the bar code labels. Salespeople often trigger the buying process by demonstrating how their products can improve the efficiency of the customer's operation.

DEFINING THE TYPE OF PRODUCT NEEDED (STEP 2)

After identifying a problem, organization members develop a general approach to solving it. For example, a production manager who concludes that the factory is not running efficiently recognizes a problem, but this insight may not lead to a purchase decision. The manager may think the inefficiency is caused by poor supervision or unskilled workers.

Spenco encourages consumer demand through advertising like this. Spenco then encourages retailers to carry the product in order to handle the derived demand.

Courtesy Spenco Medical Corporation

EXHIBIT 4.1

Steps in the
Organizational Buying
Process

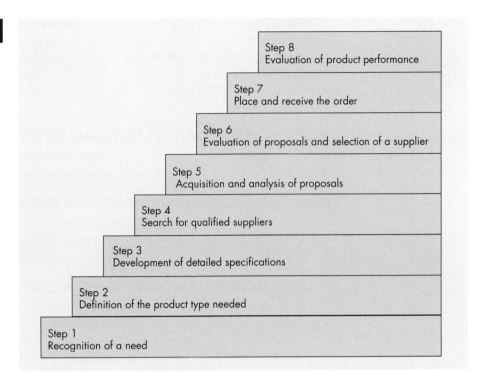

However, a production equipment salesperson might work with the manager to analyze the situation and show how efficiency could be improved by purchasing some automated assembly equipment. Thus the problem solution is defined in terms of purchasing a product or service—the automated assembly equipment needed—and the buying process moves to step 3.

DEVELOPING PRODUCT SPECIFICATIONS (STEP 3)

In step 3 the specifications for the product needed to solve the problem are prepared. Potential suppliers will use these specifications to develop proposals. The buyers will use them to objectively evaluate the proposals.

Steps 2 and 3 offer great opportunities for salespeople to influence the outcome of the buying process. Using their knowledge of their firm's products and the customer's needs, salespeople can help develop specifications that favor their particular product. For example, a Hyster forklift might have superior performance in terms of a small turning radius. Knowing this advantage and the customer's small, tightly packed warehouse, the Hyster salesperson might influence the customer to specify a very small turning radius for forklifts, a turning radius that only Hyster forklifts can provide. Competing salespeople, who first become aware of this procurement after the specifications are written, will be at a severe disadvantage.

SEARCHING FOR QUALIFIED SUPPLIERS (STEP 4)

After the specifications have been written, the customer looks for potential suppliers. The customer may simply contact previous suppliers or go through an extensive search procedure: calling salespeople, asking for a list of customers, and checking with the customers on each supplier's financial stability and performance. Many purchasing agents now use the Internet to find suppliers. Worldwide Internet Solutions Network's website (www.wiznet.com) provides access to a library of product catalogs from 80,000 manufacturers around the world.[12]

A survey reported in July 2001 by the Institute for Supply Management indicates that many organizations use the Internet to locate suppliers, and the percentage is rising. Nearly half use the Internet to ask suppliers for proposals, but that figure will be over 80 percent by the end of 2003. In Canada, the rate of new companies using the Internet to find suppliers is growing much faster than in the U.S.[13]

ACQUIRING AND ANALYZING PROPOSALS (STEP 5)

In step 5 qualified suppliers are asked to submit proposals. Salespeople work with people in their company to develop their proposal.

EVALUATING PROPOSALS AND SELECTING A SUPPLIER (STEP 6)

Next the customer evaluates the proposals. After a preferred supplier is selected, further negotiations may occur concerning price, delivery, or specific performance features. The appendix to this chapter shows a model used in evaluating proposals.

PLACING AN ORDER AND RECEIVING THE PRODUCT (STEP 7)

In step 7 an order is placed with the selected supplier. The order goes to the supplier, who acknowledges receipt and commits to a delivery date. Eventually the product is shipped to the buying firm, which inspects the received goods and then pays the supplier for the product. During this step salespeople need to make sure the paperwork is correct and their firm knows what has to be done to satisfy the customer's requirements.

EVALUATING PRODUCT PERFORMANCE (STEP 8)

In the final step of the purchasing process, the product's performance is evaluated. The evaluation may be a formal or an informal assessment made by people involved in the buying process.[14]

Salespeople play an important role in this step. They need to work with the users to make sure the product performs well. In addition, salespeople need to work with purchasing agents to ensure that they are satisfied with the communications and delivery.

This after-sale support ensures that the salesperson's product will get a positive evaluation and that he or she will be considered a qualified supplier in future procurement.[15] This step is critical to establishing the successful long-term relationships discussed in Chapter 2. (Building relationships through after-sale support is discussed in more detail in Chapter 13.)

CREEPING COMMITMENT

Creeping commitment means that a customer becomes increasingly committed to a particular course of action while going through the steps in the buying process. As decisions are made at each step, the range of alternatives narrows; the customer becomes more and more committed to a specific course of action and even to a specific vendor. Thus it is critical that salespeople be very involved in the initial steps so they will have an opportunity to participate in the final steps.

An example of creeping commitment occurred when Coca-Cola introduced its Diet Coke with lemon flavor. As the company examined the market and considered the new product, it brought in potential suppliers for various flavorings. These companies were part of the strategic planning process at Coke. Coke then narrowed the choices among flavorings, which also narrowed the vendor list. So as Coke was developing the new product, it was also making decisions that ultimately led to the selection of the actual supplier.

TYPES OF ORGANIZATIONAL BUYING DECISIONS

Many purchase decisions are made without going through all the steps just described. For example, a Frito-Lay salesperson may check the supply of his or her products in a supermarket, write out a purchase order to restock the shelves, and present it to the store manager. After recognizing the problem of low stock, the manager simply signs the order (step 6) without going through any of the other steps. However, if the Frito-Lay salesperson wanted the manager to devote more shelf space to Frito-Lay snacks, the manager might go through all eight steps in making and evaluating this decision.

Exhibit 4.2 describes three types of buying decisions—new tasks, modified rebuys, and straight rebuys—along with the strategies salespeople need to use in each situation. In this exhibit the "in" company is the seller that has provided the product or service to the company in the past, and the "out" company is the seller that is not or has not been a supplier to the customer.[16]

NEW TASKS

When a customer purchases a product or service for the first time, a **new-task** situation occurs. Most purchase decisions involving capital equipment or the initial purchase of OEM products are new tasks.

Because the customer has not made the purchase decision recently, the company's knowledge is limited and it goes through all eight steps of the buying process. In these situations customers face considerable risk. Thus they typically seek information from salespeople and welcome their knowledge. For example, when NBC decided to upgrade the technology of its studio equipment, it assembled a nationwide team of engineers, production supervisors, and buyers. It asked seven major electronics manufacturers from around the world to submit proposals.[17]

From the salesperson's perspective, the initial buying process steps are critical in new-task situations. During these steps the alert salesperson can help the customer define the characteristics of the needed product and develop the purchase specifications. By working with the customer in these initial steps, the salesperson can take advantage of creeping commitment and gain a significant advantage over the competition. The final step, postpurchase evaluation, is also critical. Buyers making a new purchase decision are especially interested in evaluating results and will use this information in making similar purchase decisions in the future.

STRAIGHT REBUYS

In a **straight rebuy** situation, the customer buys the same product from the same source it used when the need arose previously. Because customers have purchased the product or service a number of times, they have considerable knowledge about their requirements and the potential vendors. MRO supplies and services and reorders of OEM components often are straight rebuy situations.

Typically, a straight rebuy is triggered by an internal event, such as a low inventory level. Because needs are easily recognized, specifications have been developed, and potential suppliers have been identified, the latter steps of the buying process assume greater importance.

EXHIBIT 4.2

Types of Organizational
Buying Decisions

	New Task	Modified Rebuy	Straight Rebuy
Customer Needs			
Information and risk reduction	Information about causes and solutions for a new problem; reduce high risk in making a decision with limited knowledge	Information and solutions to increase efficiency and/or reduce costs	Needs are generally satisfied
Nature of Buying Process			
Number of people involved in process	Many	Few	One
Time to make a decision	Months or years	Month	Day
Key steps in the buying process (Exhibit 4.1)	1, 2, 3, 8	3, 4, 5, 6, 8	5, 6, 7, 8
Key decision makers	Executives and engineers	Production and purchasing managers	Purchasing agent
Selling Strategy			
For in-supplier	Monitor changes in customer needs; respond quickly when problems and new needs arise; provide technical information	Act immediately when problems arise	Reinforce relationship with customers; make sure all of customer's needs are satisfied
For out-supplier	Suggest new approach for solving problems; provide technical advice	Respond more quickly than present supplier when problem arises; encourage customer to consider an alternative; present information on how new alternative will increase efficiency	Convince customer of potential benefits from reexamining choice of supplier; secure recognition and approval as an alternative supplier

Some straight rebuys are computerized. For example, many hospitals use an automatic reorder system developed by Baxter, a manufacturer and distributor of medical supplies. When the inventory control system recognizes that levels of supplies such as tape, surgical sponges, or IV kits have dropped to prespecified levels, a purchase order is automatically generated and transmitted electronically to the nearest Baxter distribution center.

When a company is satisfied and has developed a long-term supplier relationship, it continues to order from the same company it has used in the past. Salespeople at in-companies want to maintain the strong relationship; they do not want the customer to consider new suppliers. Thus these salespeople must make sure that orders are delivered on time and that the products continue to get favorable evaluations.

Salespeople trying to break into a straight rebuy situation—those representing an out-supplier—face a tough sales problem. Often they need to persuade a customer to change suppliers, even though the present supplier is performing satisfactorily. In such situations the salesperson hopes the present supplier will make a critical mistake, causing the customer to reevaluate suppliers. To break into a

A salesperson takes inventory in a supermarket to prepare a refill order for the manager to sign. In this situation, the manager will make a straight rebuy decision without going through all eight steps in the buying process.

Mitch Kezar/Stone

straight rebuy situation, salespeople need to provide very compelling information to motivate the customer to treat the purchase as a modified rebuy.

MODIFIED REBUYS

In a **modified rebuy** situation, the customer has purchased the product or a similar product in the past but is interested in obtaining new information. This situation typically occurs when the in-supplier performs unsatisfactorily, a new product becomes available, or the buying needs change. In such situations sales representatives of the in-suppliers need to convince customers to maintain the relationship and continue their present buying pattern. In-suppliers with strong customer relationships are the first to find out when requirements change. In this case customers provide the supplier's salespeople with information to assist them in responding to the new requirements.

Salespeople with out-suppliers want customers to reevaluate the situation and to actively consider switching vendors. The successful sales rep from an out-supplier will need to influence all the people taking part in the buying decision.

WHO MAKES THE BUYING DECISION?

As we discussed previously, a number of people are involved in new-task and modified rebuy decisions. This group of people is called the **buying center,** an informal, cross-department group of people involved in a purchase decision. People in the customer's organization become involved in a buying center because they have formal responsibilities for purchasing or they are important sources of information. In some cases the buying center includes experts who are not full-time employees. For example, consultants usually specify the air-conditioning equipment that will be used in a factory undergoing remodeling. Thus the buying center defines the set of people who make or influence the purchase decision.[18]

Salespeople need to know the names and responsibilities of all people in the buying center for a purchase decision. For example, Gus Maikish heads a 21-person sales team responsible for IBM's business with a major New York City bank. He says, "There are many people involved in a major sale, and each one has a specific

The buying center for an MRI scanner in a hospital includes the technicians operating the equipment (the users), the radiologists (gatekeepers and influencers), and the hospital administrator (the decision maker).

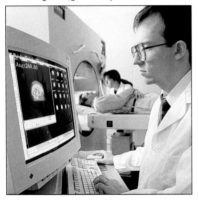

Roger Tully/Stone

Charles Gupton/The Stock Market

Bruce Ayres/Stone

stake in the outcome. One will be concerned with reliability, another with processing speed, someone else with obsolescence."

To coordinate a major sale, Maikish uses a matrix. Each vertical column is labeled with the name of key influencers in a specific area of the bank, such as investment banking, securities trading, or data processing. Along the side of the matrix, he lists all of the factors that might be considered in evaluating the proposal (e.g., software availability, ease of user interface). Then, in the matrix squares, he checks off the factors important to each influencer.[19]

USERS

Users, such as the manufacturing-area personnel for OEM products and capital equipment, typically do not make the ultimate purchase decision. However, they often have considerable influence in the early and late steps of the buying process—need recognition, product definition, and postpurchase evaluation. Thus users are particularly important in new-task and modified rebuy situations. Salespeople often attempt to convert a straight rebuy to a modified rebuy by demonstrating superior product performance or a new benefit to users.

INITIATORS

Another role in the buying process is that of **initiator,** or the person who starts the buying process. A user can play the role of the initiator, as in "This machine is broken, we need a new one." Or the initiator could be an executive making a decision, such as to introduce a new product (like lemon-flavored Diet Coke), which starts the buying process.[20]

INFLUENCERS

People inside or outside the organization who directly or indirectly provide information during the buying process are **influencers.** These members of the buying center may provide details on product specifications, criteria for evaluating proposals, or information about potential suppliers. For example, the marketing department can influence a purchase decision by indicating that the company's products would sell better if they included a particular supplier's components. Architects can play the critical role in the purchase of construction material by specifying suppliers, even though the ultimate purchase orders will be placed by the contractor responsible for constructing the building.

GATEKEEPERS

Gatekeepers control the flow of information and may limit the alternatives considered. For example, the quality control and service departments may determine which potential suppliers are qualified sources.

SELLING TO THE NBA

Gene Fay has one of the most interesting sales jobs. As an account manager for Avid Sports, he is responsible for selling digital video systems and software to teams in the National Basketball Association (NBA). Rather than looking through videotapes of games, teams now use computers to scan digitized video footage.

Avid Sports' systems help teams prepare better for games, but the systems cost between $50,000 and $400,000, so it's not an easy sell. Teams spend millions of dollars in player salaries, so the team accountants try to cut costs in other areas. Therefore, Fay must "show value, how the systems can help solve the problems of coaches and general managers." Coaches use the systems to improve their teams' play, and general managers use the systems to check out players they might want to recruit or get in a trade.

The buying center for these systems consists of the video coordinator, coach, general manager, and accountant.

The video coordinator is the technical expert, but Fay tries to set up a meeting with the general manager first. Then he brings in a technical support person to demonstrate the system to the video coordinator in a follow-up meeting.

Fay finds that selling to NBA teams can be difficult because "the teams have more money and more people between me and the person I want to reach. In hockey and baseball it's easier to get the right person. It's a 'good ole boy' network. On the other hand, the NBA teams are more technically sophisticated. Baseball and hockey teams are used to spending $3,000 for some VCRs and cameras," not systems in the $50,000+ range. That's why Fay focuses on the NBA.

Source: Ken Liebeskind, "Sporting Chance," *Selling Power,* June 1998, pp. 14–16.

Purchasing agents often play a gatekeeping role by determining which potential suppliers are to be notified about the purchase situation and are to have access to relevant information. In some companies all contacts must be made through purchasing agents. They arrange meetings with other gatekeepers, influencers, and users. When dealing with such companies, salespeople often are not allowed to contact these members of the buying center directly. When purchasing agents restrict access to important information, salespeople are tempted to bypass the purchasing agents and make direct contact. This backdoor selling approach can upset purchasing agents so much that they may disqualify the salesperson's company from the purchase situation. In Chapter 8 we discuss strategies that salespeople can use to deal with this issue.[21]

DECIDERS

In any buying center one or more members of the group, **deciders,** make the final choice. Determining who actually makes the purchase decision for an organization is often difficult. For straight rebuys the purchasing agent usually selects the vendor and places the order. However, for new tasks many people influence the decision, and several people must approve the decision and sign the purchase order. Selling Scenario 4.1 illustrates the challenges of selling digital video systems to professional sports teams.

In general, senior executives get more involved in important purchase decisions, those that have a greater effect on the performance of the organization. For example, the chief executive officer (CEO) and chief financial officer (CFO) play an important role in purchasing a telephone system because this network has a significant impact on the firm's day-to-day operations.

To sell effectively to organizations, salespeople need to know the people in the buying center and their involvement at different steps of the buying process.

Consider the following situation. Salespeople selling expensive intensive care monitoring equipment know that a hospital buying center for the type of equipment they sell typically consists of physicians, nurses, hospital administrators, engineers, and purchasing agents. Through experience, these salespeople also know the relative importance of the buying center members in various stages of the purchasing process (see Exhibit 4.3). With this information the intensive care equipment salespeople know to concentrate on physicians throughout the process, nurses and engineers in the middle of the process, and hospital administrators and purchasing agents at the end of the process.

In some countries identifying the members of the buying center is a difficult task. For example, in China, Craig McLaughlin of Texaco reports that salespeople frequently negotiate with representatives of the customer who do not have the authority to make a decision. In some cases the delegation of authority is not clearly defined within the company. To identify the decision makers in the buying center, McLaughlin emphasizes that there is no point in discussing the situation unless the customer is willing to reveal its chain of command. "Customers may not necessarily give you a straight answer, and sometimes they may not even know themselves, but it's a step in the right direction."[22]

SUPPLIER EVALUATION AND CHOICE

At various steps in the buying process, members of the buying center evaluate alternative methods for solving a problem (step 2), the qualifications of potential suppliers (step 4), proposals submitted by potential suppliers (step 5), and the performance of products purchased (step 8). Using these evaluations, buyers select potential suppliers and eventually choose a specific vendor.

The needs of both the organization and the individuals making the decisions affect the evaluation and selection of products and suppliers (see Exhibit 4.4). Often these organizational and personal needs are classified into two categories: rational needs and emotional needs. **Rational needs** are directly related to the performance of the product. Thus the organizational needs discussed in the next section are examples of rational needs. **Emotional needs** are associated with the personal rewards and gratification of the person buying the product. Thus the personal needs of buying center members often are considered emotional needs.

ORGANIZATIONAL NEEDS AND CRITERIA

Organizations consider a number of factors when they make buying decisions, including economic factors such as price, product quality, and supplier service.

| EXHIBIT 4.3 | Importance of Hospital Buying Center Members in the Buying Process for Intensive Care Monitoring Equipment |

Step in Buying Process	Physicians	Nurses	Hospital Administrators	Engineers	Purchasing Agents
Need recognition (step 1)	High	Moderate	Low	Low	Low
Definition of product type (step 2)	High	High	Moderate	Moderate	Low
Analysis of proposal (step 5)	High	Moderate	Moderate	High	Low
Proposal evaluation and supplier selection (step 6)	High	Low	High	Low	Moderate

EXHIBIT 4.4

Factors Influencing
Organizational Buying
Decisions

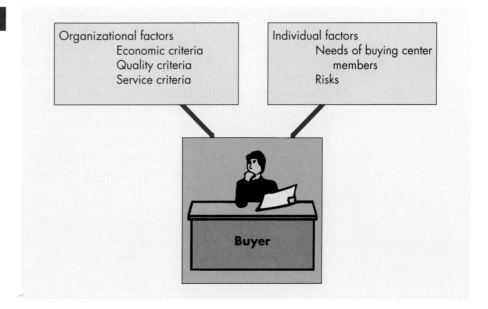

Organizational factors	Individual factors
Economic criteria	Needs of buying center
Quality criteria	members
Service criteria	Risks

Buyer

ECONOMIC CRITERIA

The objective of businesses is to make a profit. Thus businesses are very concerned about buying products and services at the lowest cost. Organizational buyers are now taking a more sophisticated approach to evaluating the cost of equipment. Rather than simply focusing on the purchase price, they consider installation costs, the costs of needed accessories, freight charges, estimated maintenance costs, and operating costs, including forecasts of energy costs.

Life-cycle costing, also referred to as the total cost of ownership, is a method for determining the cost of equipment or supplies over their useful lives. Using this approach, salespeople can demonstrate that a product with a higher initial cost will have a lower overall cost. An example of life-cycle costing appears in Exhibit 4.5. (Approaches salespeople can use to demonstrate the value of their products to customers are discussed in more detail in Chapter 10.)

QUALITY CRITERIA

Many firms now recognize that the quality and reliability of their products are as important to their customers as price.[23] Firms expect their suppliers to support

---

EXHIBIT 4.5

Life-Cycle Costing

	Product A	Product B
Initial cost	$35,000	$30,000
Life of machine	10 years	10 years
Power consumption per year	150 MWh*	180 MWh*
Power cost at $30/MWh	$45,000	$54,000
Estimated operating and maintenance cost over 10 years	$25,000	$30,000
Life-cycle cost	$105,000	$114,000

Note: A more thorough analysis would calculate the net present value of the cash flow associated with each product's purchase and use.

*MWh = megawatt hour

their efforts to provide quality products. Salespeople often need to describe how their firms will support the customer's quality objectives.

To satisfy customer quality needs, salespeople need to know what organizational buyers are looking for. For example, Giddings & Lewis Measurement Systems made a technological breakthrough that enabled it to provide superior precision measuring devices at lower prices. However, the firm could not sell its systems to European automobile manufacturers. When visiting the Mercedes-Benz plant in Stuttgart, Germany, salespeople found out why. They were told that the unattractive casing for the equipment demonstrated a lack of concern for product quality and customer needs. Giddings & Lewis hired an industrial design firm to develop a new package, and sales increased dramatically.[24]

SERVICE CRITERIA

Organizational buyers want more than products that are low cost, perform reliably, and are aesthetically pleasing. They also want suppliers that will work with them to solve their problems. One primary reason firms are interested in developing long-term relationships with suppliers is so they can learn about each other's needs and capabilities and use this information to enhance their products' performance. Value analysis is an example of a program in which suppliers and customers work together to reduce costs and still provide the required level of performance.[25]

Representatives from the supplier and the purchasing department and technical experts from engineering, production, or quality control usually form a team to undertake the analysis. The team begins by examining the product's function. Then members brainstorm to see whether changes can be made in the design, materials, construction, or production process to reduce the product's costs but keep its performance high. Some questions addressed in this phase are the following:

- Can a part in the product be eliminated?
- If the part is not standard, can a standard (and presumably less expensive) part be used?
- Does the part have greater performance than this application needs?
- Are unnecessary machining or fine finishes specified?

Salespeople can use **value analysis** to get customers to consider a new product. This approach is particularly useful for the out-supplier in a straight rebuy situation. Scott Paper Company's salespeople use value analysis to sell hand towels and toilet paper. Because Scott products are of high quality and sell at a premium price, Scott sales representatives have to prove that the products are worth the extra money. The salespeople use value analysis to help purchasing agents determine how much it costs to use the product, rather than how much the product costs. They focus on the price per use, such as the number of dries per case of paper towels, rather than the price per case. Scott even designed a paper towel dispenser to reduce the number of refills needed and thus reduce maintenance labor cost.

Each year, *Purchasing Magazine* asks its 100,000 readers to nominate an outstanding salesperson with whom they work. The top salespeople all help buyers increase the profits of their companies (see Exhibit 4.6).

INDIVIDUAL NEEDS OF BUYING CENTER MEMBERS

In the preceding section we discussed criteria used to determine whether a product satisfies the needs of the organization. However, buying center members are people. Their evaluations and choices are affected by their personal needs as well as the organization's needs.

EXHIBIT 4.6

Top Salespeople Add
Value

Frank Mastrodonato, Kenneth Crosby Co, Rochester, New York

"He knows our business as well as we do and always goes the extra mile to get the job done . . . holds 'lunch and learn' sessions for our technical groups to learn about what's going on in our areas, and brings new products and ideas to us. His substitution for existing products has saved thousands of dollars."

Mary Fahland, Ryerson Coil Processing, New Hope, Minnesota

"[She] has been a leader in developing an inventory program to deliver materials the same day they are used in production. She is creative in her approach to our company's partnership, and she's always upbeat and knowledgeable."

Timothy Shanahan, Weldstar Company, University Park, Illinois

"We had a problem with a separation of a particular gas mix we use. Shanahan got his company to install special mixer tubes in the cylinders and then had them put on a rolling mixer machine prior to delivery of the product. It's hard to put a dollar value on it, but . . . the less than perfect welds were largely eliminated by this measure."

Lawrence Hobbs, J&L, Anaheim, California

"We were experiencing a high level of shipping damage and freight claims with customers. We worked together for five months developing cost-effective yet strong packaging. Shortly after our final changes, corporate adopted our specifications."

Bill Besser, Chicago Rawhide, New Castle, Indiana

"[He is] very proactive: He really stays on top of our orders and keeps me informed . . . has been successful in changing the contents of some bearing kits. This eliminated our having to buy extra bearings and return excess bearings. [He has] driven from his home to the national distribution center [more than 100 miles from his home] to pick up parts and deliver them to us to be sure we had them the next morning."

Frank Subach, Gaylord Container Corporation, Deerfield, Illinois

"Whenever we have a Quality Assurance (QA) problem with Gaylord's products, we notify Frank. He picks up the samples in person, reviews the problem, and makes sure the problem is fixed in his factory. This improves the quality of our products and saves us the time and energy of dealing with inside QA."

Source: Lisa Van Der Pool, "Follow-up Is Number One with Buyers," *Purchasing*, November 18, 1999, pp. 97–100.

TYPES OF NEEDS

Buying center members, like all people, have personal goals and aspirations. They want to get a raise, be promoted to a high-level position, have their managers recognize their accomplishments, and feel they have done something for their company or demonstrated their skills as a buyer or engineer.

Salespeople can influence members of the buying center by developing strategies to satisfy individual needs. For example, demonstrating how a new product will reduce costs and increase the purchasing agents' bonus would satisfy the purchasing agents' financial security needs. Encouraging an engineer to recommend a product employing the latest technology might satisfy the engineer's need for self-esteem and recognition by his or her engineering peers.

RISK REDUCTION

Members of the buying center tend to be more concerned about losing benefits they have now than about increasing their benefits. They place a lot of emphasis on avoiding risks that may result in poor decisions, decisions that can adversely affect their personal reputations and rewards as well as their organization's performance. To reduce risk, buying center members may collect additional information, develop a loyalty to present suppliers, and/or spread the risk by placing orders with several vendors.[26]

Because they know that suppliers try to promote their own products, customers tend to question information received from vendors. Customers usually view information from independent sources such as trade publications, colleagues, and outside consultants as more credible than information provided by salespeople and company advertising and sales literature.

Advertising and sales literature tends to be used more in the early steps of the buying process. Word-of-mouth information from friends and colleagues is very important in the proposal evaluation and supplier selection steps. Word-of-mouth information is especially important for risky decisions, decisions that will have a significant impact on the organization and/or the buying center member.[27]

Another way to reduce uncertainty and risk is to display **vendor loyalty** to suppliers—that is, to continue buying from suppliers that have proven satisfactory in the past. By converting buying decisions into straight rebuys, the decisions become routine, minimizing the chances of a poor decision. Organizations tend to develop vendor loyalty for unimportant purchase decisions. In these situations the potential benefits from new suppliers do not compensate for the costs of evaluating these suppliers.[28]

The consequences of choosing a poor supplier can be reduced by using more than one vendor. Rather than placing all orders for an OEM component with one supplier, for example, a firm might elect to purchase 75 percent of its needs from one supplier and 25 percent from another. Thus if a problem occurs with one supplier, another will be available to fill the firm's needs. If the product is proprietary—available from only one supplier—the buyer might insist that the supplier develop a second source for the component.

These risk reduction approaches present a major problem for salespeople working for out-suppliers. To break this loyalty barrier, these salespeople need to develop trusting relationships with customers. They can build trust by offering performance guarantees or consistently meeting personal commitments. Another approach is to encourage buyers to place a small trial order so that the salesperson's company can demonstrate the product's capabilities. On the other hand, the salesperson for the in-supplier wants to discourage buyers from considering new sources, even on a trial basis.

VENDOR ANALYSIS

Organizational buyers frequently use a formal method, called **vendor analysis,** to summarize the benefits and needs satisfied by a supplier. When using this procedure, the buyer rates the supplier and its products on a number of criteria such as price, quality, performance, and on-time delivery.[29] Note that the ratings of suppliers can be affected by the perceptions and personal needs of the buyers. Then the ratings are weighted by the importance of the characteristics, and an overall score or evaluation of the vendor is developed. Exhibit 4.7 shows a vendor evaluation form used by Chrysler Corporation. The appendix to this chapter describes the multiattribute model, which is useful in analyzing how members of the buying center evaluate and select products. The model also suggests strategies salespeople can use to influence these evaluations.

TRENDS IN ORGANIZATIONAL BUYING

The business environment is changing dramatically as firms enter the new millennium. Major changes include the increasing cost of raw materials, the development of new technologies, and increased competition from international firms and in deregulated industries. These changes put organizations under pressure to improve product quality, control the cost of purchased material, and minimize

EXHIBIT 4.7

Sample Vendor
Analysis Form

Supplier Name: _____   Type of Product: _____

Shipping Location: _____   Annual Sales Dollars: _____

	5 Excellent	4 Good	3 Satisfactory	2 Fair	1 Poor	0 N/A
Quality (45%)						
Defect rates	—	—	—	—	—	—
Quality of sample	—	—	—	—	—	—
Conformance with quality program	—	—	—	—	—	—
Responsiveness to quality problems	—	—	—	—	—	—
Overall quality	—	—	—	—	—	—
Delivery (25%)						
Avoidance of late shipments	—	—	—	—	—	—
Ability to expand production capacity	—	—	—	—	—	—
Performance in sample delivery	—	—	—	—	—	—
Response to changes in order size	—	—	—	—	—	—
Overall delivery	—	—	—	—	—	—
Price (20%)						
Price competitiveness	—	—	—	—	—	—
Payment terms	—	—	—	—	—	—
Absorption of costs	—	—	—	—	—	—
Submission of cost savings plans	—	—	—	—	—	—
Overall price	—	—	—	—	—	—
Technology (10%)						
State-of-the-art components	—	—	—	—	—	—
Sharing research & development capability	—	—	—	—	—	—
Ability and willingness to help with design	—	—	—	—	—	—
Responsiveness to engineering problems	—	—	—	—	—	—
Overall technology	—	—	—	—	—	—

Buyer: _____   Date: _____

Comments: _____

Source: Chrysler Corporation

inventories. Some changes in organizational buying stimulated by these changes are discussed next.

INCREASING IMPORTANCE OF PURCHASING AGENTS

Most large firms have elevated their directors of purchasing to the level of senior vice president to reflect the increasing importance of this function. A survey of decision makers reports that purchasing agents made 35 percent of the buying decisions five years ago and now make 58 percent of the buying decisions.[30] In addition, to improve efficiency and coordination of logistical activities, firms are combining purchasing, transportation, inventory control, and warehouse activities into an all-encompassing materials management department.[31]

In response to these new responsibilities, purchasing managers are upgrading their skills and developing partnering relationships with their suppliers. For example, Al Mulvey, vice president of purchasing and administration at J. I. Case (located in Racine, Wisconsin), is one of a new breed of purchasing managers. He has a degree in engineering and an MBA and has taught courses in negotiating skills, international business, and value analysis. Mulvey emphasizes that in the past, purchasing agents and salespeople focused on "beating each other up over the amount of profit." Now he is more interested in discovering ways to reduce Case's manufacturing costs: "The ability to negotiate manufacturing costs requires an even stronger relationship with suppliers than it has in the past."

Mulvey wants salespeople to make a "technical infusion" into J. I. Case. A salesperson who spoke with him about Case's involvement in financial leases illustrates the concept. The salesperson had done his homework. He could talk knowledgeably about Case's customers and current suppliers, how prices were set, how leases were structured, and the tax advantages. The salesperson presented an opportunity for Case to carve a niche in the truck-leasing business. According to Mulvey, "His work amounts to a technical infusion on the management side. His company is making a contribution to our business mission instead of coming to me and simply saying, 'Give me your business.'"

CENTRALIZED PURCHASING

Purchasing is becoming more centralized. Rather than having each manufacturing facility contract for supplies to meet its own production needs, more purchasing is done at a central location, such as corporate headquarters. Through centralization, purchasing agents can become specialists, concentrating on particular items and developing extensive knowledge about the uses, specifications, and suppliers for those items.

To effectively sell to a centralized purchasing department, many firms use a national account management organization concept. In this type of sales organization, a **national account manager (NAM)** is responsible for coordinating the firm's efforts to satisfy the needs of a major customer. The NAM works directly with the centralized purchasing department and coordinates the activities of salespeople calling on decentralized locations and finance, logistics, and technical support people from the corporate headquarters. When strong relationships exist, customers may actually determine who will call on their accounts. For example, Sherwin-Williams, a large paint supplier, lets Sears select the sales team that will service the Sears account.[32]

GLOBAL SOURCING

Corporations no longer focus on buying from suppliers in their own countries. Purchasing agents consider potential suppliers from around the globe. For example, the costs for one General Motors car consisted of

- Labor and assembly in South Korea: $3,000.
- Engines, transaxles, and electronics made in Japan: $1,850.

- Styling and design engineering in Germany: $700.
- Small components from Japan, Singapore, and Taiwan: $400.
- Advertising done in Britain: $250.
- Data processing in Barbados and Ireland: $50.

Not all suppliers are independent companies. Some are General Motors subsidiaries and joint ventures. But the global sourcing used by General Motors illustrates the growing need for salespeople to recognize the global nature of competition and the importance of understanding a customer's network of relationships.[33]

OUTSOURCING

Another major trend in business is outsourcing. **Outsourcing** is the purchasing of goods and services that were previously made by the firm. In an effort to reduce costs, firms are buying more and more goods and services from more efficient suppliers. Some common activities that are being outsourced are computer systems operation and maintenance, trucking and transportation services, and jobs that can be completed in a specific time frame.[34]

SUPPLY CHAIN MANAGEMENT

A major concern of producers and resellers is to reduce the amount of inventory they have in stock. For example, a study of the supermarket inventory found that if packaged goods manufacturers and supermarket chains coordinated their production, shipping, transportation, and receiving activities, the amount of inventory in the stores and warehouses could be reduced by $40 billion.[35] **Supply chain management** is a set of programs undertaken to increase the efficiency of the distribution channel that moves products from the producer's facilities to the end user.[36] The **just-in-time (JIT) inventory control** system is an example of a supply chain management system used by a producer to minimize its inventory by having frequent deliveries, sometimes daily, just in time for assembly into the

In situations where the buyer is engaged in just-in-time inventory management, supply chain management coordination is critical to the success of the relationship, requiring salespeople to develop partnering relationships.

Courtesy Benelux Press/e-Stock Photos

final product. In theory each product delivered by a supplier must conform to the manufacturer's specifications every time. It must be delivered when needed, not earlier or later, and it must arrive in the exact quantity needed, not more or less. The ultimate goal is to eventually eliminate all inventory except products in production and transit.[37]

To develop the close coordination needed for JIT systems, manufacturers tend to rely on one supplier. The selection criterion is not the lowest cost, but the ability of the supplier to be flexible. As these relationships develop, employees of the supplier have offices at the customer's site and participate in value analysis meetings with the supplier. The salesperson becomes a facilitator, coordinator, and even marriage counselor in developing a selling team that works effectively with the customer's buying center. (The manufacturer and supplier develop a strategic partnership, which we discussed in Chapter 2.)

Resellers are also interested in managing their inventories more efficiently. Retailers and distributors work closely with their suppliers to minimize inventory investments and still satisfy the needs of customers. These JIT inventory systems are referred to as **quick-response** or **efficient consumer response (ECR) systems** in a consumer product distribution channel.[38] (Partnering relationships involving these systems are discussed in more detail in Chapter 15.)

Material requirements planning (MRP) systems are an important element in JIT programs. These systems are used to forecast sales, develop a production schedule, and then order parts and raw materials with delivery dates that minimize the amount of inventory needed, thereby reducing costs. Effective JIT requires that customers inform suppliers well in advance about production schedules and needs.

Automatic replenishment (AR) is a form of JIT where the supplier manages inventory levels for the customer. The materials are provided on consignment, meaning the buyer doesn't pay for them until they are actually used. These types of arrangements are used most often in industrial settings, where the product being consumed is a supply item used in a manufacturing process.[39]

Many firms use elaborate computer systems to keep track of inventories, orders, and deliveries. These systems help firms uncover and eliminate suppliers whose late deliveries and defective products cause scheduling problems. Many customers and suppliers link computer systems, sharing information about sales, production, and shipment and receipt of products. These computer-to-computer linkages between suppliers and buyers are referred to as **electronic data interchange (EDI)**.[40] Exhibit 4.8 illustrates the communications associated with placing orders and receiving products that are transmitted electronically through EDI.

THE INTERNET AND BUSINESS-TO-BUSINESS SELLING

Companies like Amazon.com and eBay that sell products to consumers over the Internet are well known, but the number of business-to-business transactions over the Internet is 10 times greater than the number of business-to-consumer transactions.[41] Electronic ordering through EDI has been a common practice in business for more than 10 years. However, until recently this EDI activity was transacted over private networks that required buyers and sellers to use specialized software to communicate with each other. Now companies are using the Internet to interact with each other. Although private networks are more secure than the Internet, the Internet lets companies communicate with each other by using readily available browsers such as Netscape's Communicator® and Microsoft's Internet Explorer®. Secure Internet-based networks connecting buyers and suppliers are called **extranets.**

How is the Internet going to affect salespeople? Most businesses view their websites on the Internet as a tool for supporting salespeople rather than replacing them.[42] Buyers will go to supplier websites to get information about product

USING THE INTERNET AT NATIONAL SEMICONDUCTOR

National Semiconductor segments its customers into two groups. The company's largest customers, representing more than 60 percent of its annual revenue, buy through its direct sales force. The majority of customers, however, buy through a network of distributors.

For customers buying through the sales force, the company's website is a customer service tool. Salespeople have worked with these customers to set up customized websites on National's extranet. Design engineers and purchasing agents use the extranet to review specifications and prices for products they buy, analyze their order history, and check on order status.

National Semiconductor uses its public site to supports its distributors. Customers can research products, sort lists of

potential purchases, and link directly to distributors' sites to place orders. Customers use this site to get information about all of National's products, not just the products carried by a specific distributor. Many of these smaller customers probably never dealt directly with the company before using the site.

National is not using the public site to bypass its distributors. Its intent is to use the site to build its brand image and pass along leads to its distributors. Each month the company passes more than 50,000 leads generated by visits to its website to its distributors.

Source: Chad Kaydo, "You've Got Sales," *Sales & Marketing Management,* October 1999, pp. 34–35.

specifications and availability, place orders, and check on the status of orders. Thus salespeople will be able to spend less time on transactions and more time building relationships. Building Partnerships 4.1 illustrates how National Semiconductor uses the Internet to support its salespeople.

EXHIBIT 4.8

EDI Transactions

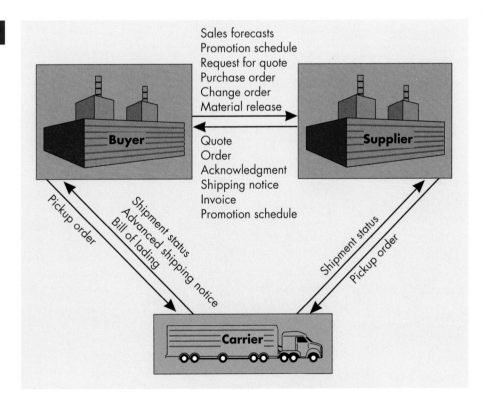

LONG-TERM CUSTOMER–SUPPLIER RELATIONSHIPS

As we discussed in Chapters 1 and 2, organizational customers and suppliers are developing mutually dependent partnering relationships. The supplier needs the customer's orders to meet financial objectives; the customer needs the supplier and its salespeople to make sure that products are delivered when needed, that products perform to specifications and are reliable, and that spare parts and service are provided. This interdependence makes obtaining a specific purchase order only one point in a long-term relationship between the organizational buyer and the seller.

All the trends we have discussed in this chapter can be implemented only when buyers and sellers have strong relationships. For example, effective supply chain management can be realized only when companies share sensitive information about their long-term plans and short-term production and sales. The general trend in organizational buying is to reduce the number of suppliers and to develop strategic partnerships with the remaining suppliers.[43]

Summary

Salespeople sell to many different types of customers, including consumers, business enterprises, government agencies, and institutions. This text focuses on selling to organizations rather than to consumers. Selling to organizations differs from selling to consumers because organizations are more concentrated, demand is derived, and the buying process is more complex.

The organizational buying process consists of eight steps, beginning with the recognition of a need and ending with the evaluation of the product's performance. Each step involves several decisions. As organizations progress through these steps, decisions made at previous steps affect subsequent steps, leading to a creeping commitment. Thus salespeople need to be involved in the buying process as early as possible.

The length of the buying process and the role of various participants depend on the customer's past experiences. When customers have had considerable experience in buying a product, the decision becomes routine—a straight rebuy. Few people are involved, and the process is short. However, when customers have little experience in buying a product—a new task—many people are involved and the process can be quite lengthy.

The people involved in the buying process are referred to as the buying center. The buying center is composed of people who are initiators, users, influencers, gatekeepers, and deciders. Salespeople need to understand the roles buying center members play to effectively influence their decisions.

Individuals in the buying center are concerned about satisfying the economic, quality, and service needs of their organization. In addition, these people have personal needs they want to satisfy.

Organizations are facing an increasingly dynamic and competitive environment. Organizational buying practices are changing to help firms cope with growing uncertainties. Some of these changes are the increasing importance of purchasing agents, the longer-term orientation in evaluating costs and vendors, the use of computer systems for planning and inventory control, and the development of long-term relationships with selected vendors.

The Internet is playing a much more important role in business-to-business transactions than it plays in the widely publicized business-to-consumer e-businesses. Business-to-business applications of the Internet are designed to support salespeople's ability to build relationships with major customers.

KEY TERMS

automatic replenishment (AR)   106
buying center   95
capital equipment   85
creeping commitment   92
deciders   97
derived demand   89
efficient consumer response (ECR)
   system   106
electronic data interchange (EDI)   106
emotional needs   98
end users   85
extranet   106
gatekeepers   96
influencers   96
initiators   96
just-in-time (JIT) inventory control   105

life-cycle costing   99
material requirements planning
   (MRP)   106
modified rebuy   95
MRO supplies   85
national account manager
   (NAM)   104
new task   93
original equipment manufacturer
   (OEM)   84
outsourcing   105
producers   84
quick-response system   106
rational needs   98
resellers   86
services   85

straight rebuy   93
supply chain management   105
users   96

value analysis   100
vendor analysis   102
vendor loyalty   102

Questions and Problems

1. The production superintendent at Gulf States Paper called you to ask about a new dust-handling system your company just introduced. You suggested a meeting, and she agreed to see you. During the meeting, you discovered that the plant needs two such systems, and the production superintendent agreed to recommend your system to her boss. After your initial sales call at her plant, you got a call from the director of purchasing accusing you of back-door selling. He yells at you for ignoring their policy of registering all sales calls through the purchasing department. Specifically, what would you say to the director of purchasing? Why is this person so upset?

2. You are talking about this class to someone who isn't very familiar with business. When you mention you are studying how people make buying decisions and that this information will help you be a better salesperson, your friend says that you are just trying to learn how to manipulate people more effectively. How do you respond?

3. How would the purchasing decision process differ in the following situations? Which situation is a new task? A modified rebuy? A straight rebuy? How likely is the buyer to get other people in the organization involved? Which types of people are likely to get involved in each decision? Which situation is likely to produce the slowest decision?

   a. The organization is purchasing a custom-designed machine to be used in the manufacturing of automobile engines.

   b. An organization buys CD drives from a regular supplier, a supplier that it has bought from in the past.

   c. The organization is buying an improved and updated microprocessor for its PCs. It is considering its past suppliers as well as some suppliers that it has not bought from before.

4. A chain of home improvement centers wants to buy new electronic cash registers. Which criteria for evaluating supplier proposals might be used by (a) the purchasing agent, (b) the engineering department, (c) the sales manager, and (d) the head of the legal department?

5. Sally Brown, a purchasing agent, views her decision to buy chemicals used to clean the plant floors as a routine purchase decision. Assume you are a salesperson working for a chemical distributor from which Brown does not currently order. How would you try to make a sale to Brown?

6. Assume you are calling on a customer for the first time. You have just learned that the customer needs a product such as the one you are selling. Which questions would you ask to learn how to sell your product to this customer?

7. Why might management place pressure on purchasing agents to buy from the lowest bidder? Why might a purchasing agent ignore this pressure and buy from a higher-priced bidder?

8. Under what conditions might loyalty to a supplier be economically efficient? When might it be inefficient or wasteful?

9. Assume you work for a manufacturer that sells plumbing supplies and equipment to dealers (resellers). In the opinion of your company, would you be more successful if you sold as much supplies or equipment to a dealer as possible or if you helped the dealer sell supplies and equipment to its customers? Would there be any difference between the long- and short-term effects of

these two approaches? Why or why not? How could you, as a salesperson, help the dealer sell its inventory of your products? Would your answers vary for supplies versus equipment? Why or why not?

10. You are selling a health care plan to a company. You attend a meeting of people in the company who will participate in the buying decision. Based on the following conversation, which type of buying center person do you think each individual is?

Buying center — "We need a health plan for our employees. The plan must have doctors who are close to where our employees work, not close to the plant," says Fred, the plant manager.

organize — "I'll work with you to develop the specifications for the plan," offers Mark, the human resource director.

risk reduction — "I want to make sure that my doctor is covered under the plan," notes Rachael, a production supervisor.

org — "I will review the plan and let you know what my final decision is," says Shirley, the CEO.

Based on your classification of these people, at which stages in the buying process will each have the most influence?

Case Problems

CASE 4.1

General Electric Streamlines Its Purchasing Practices

General Electric (GE), along with Whirlpool, Frigidaire, Maytag, and Raytheon, dominates the white-goods market. GE spends in excess of $20 billion annually on products and services bought from over 45,000 suppliers worldwide. It spends over $7 billion on OEM components alone. Like many companies, GE is developing stronger relationships with key suppliers and reducing the number of suppliers.

GE's purchasing is both centralized and decentralized. Each of the company's 12 divisions does its own buying, except when products are used by several divisions. The company has a single computer supplier and a single travel agency. Purchase decisions for these types of products and services are made by a "council of users," a group consisting of a representative from each division.

The manager of purchasing activities emphasizes to potential suppliers that if they cannot provide GE with the best, GE cannot provide the best products to its customers.

Questions

1. What criteria are most important to GE representatives when they make decisions to buy OEM parts for GE appliances?
2. Who are likely to be the members of the buying center when GE buys aluminum for one of its appliances?

Source: William Bearden, Thomas Ingram, and Raymond LaForge, *Marketing: Principles and Perspectives* (Burr Ridge, IL: Richard D. Irwin, 1995), p. 150.

CASE 4.2

Fleet Management

Fleet Management, Inc., is a supplier of custom-built panel vans (trucks like those FedEx uses for deliveries) for companies to deliver products, move trade show or other special equipment, or carry service equipment and parts. Pat Nelson, senior account executive, is working with Data Telecom, a company whose North American operations are based in Toronto but with significant operations located across the United States and Mexico. Data Telecom's primary business is selling and servicing telephone switching systems to companies for internal phone systems. The switches range in cost from $500,000 to $5 million.

DATA TELECOM

Data Telecom is a well-established company, having been in business for over 70 years. Conservative, the company entered the U.S. and Mexican markets only 20 years ago, and it is often referred to as the "IBM of telecommunications" for its blue-suits-and-white-shirts image. This carefully cultivated image is believed to lower the perceived risk among buyers when they choose Data Telecom. On the other hand, the company has experienced severe competition over the last 10 years and actually lost money in domestic (Canadian) operations last year. The U.S. business barely breaks even, and the Mexican operations carry the profit ball for DT.

At the end of last year, the company announced a 10 percent reduction in workforce, along with a significant restructuring. One area that has been restructured is corporate marketing; and the company, which was known as a leader in manufacturing quality, is now applying TQM principles to marketing.

Jack Truitt is the service vehicle director for DT. His job is to manage all of the service vehicles in North America. He told Pat that he is the strategist; his primary job is to work with service (the actual technicians, plus the call center and Internet support staff) and upper management to determine service strategy, then oversee the groups that carry out the strategy. Pat has labeled Jack as a driver, and he has been the subject of a lot of press in the industry magazines as a maverick who likes to be innovative for its own sake. Jack came to DT's North American operations from Europe, where he headed marketing and was very successful. Company pundits predict he will be the next VP of customer satisfaction.

Jack wants to own no trucks, which is the opposite of past DT policy. DT has always purchased custom-built trucks, usually buying about 50 per year at a price of about $80,000 to $125,000. Each truck has a life of about five years. Jack wants his fleet vendor to buy the existing trucks back at book value (except for the ones that need replacing, which will be trashed), then lease them to him. He believes that this will lower his costs substantially. Jack expects the rent to be about 20 percent of current fleet costs because Fleet Management would be responsible for service and maintenance costs of the trucks.

Betty Franklin is the technical service manager. She has worked her way up to the North American corporate office over a 20-year career, which she began as a secretary in her mid-thirties. She earned her college degree while with DT, and Pat classifies her as an expressive. Pat has sensed some tension between Betty and Jack, which she has put down to the fact that Betty may feel passed over by Jack's promotion. Betty has very strong relations with the field technical force, which has always made customer service very effective. She can express the company's service strategy in the same terms as the customer and the technician, which is useful when creating new service policies. Jack, being new to NA Ops, doesn't have the same type of relationship with the technicians.

Jack reports to the VP of customer satisfaction, a man who is nearing retirement. The VP came out of sales, so he focuses more time on sales than on service. He is entirely responsible for the allocation of budget to the various marketing areas, including new product development, customer service, and marketing communications. All marketing research is outsourced. Pat has met this man several times, and feels that he is very conservative, particularly in terms of financial decisions. Pat also feels that he patronizes women, and a quick glance at the management structure indicates that women have a tough time getting promoted at DT.

There are four fleet managers (FM) who each manage one of the regional areas. They make sure there are enough trucks to support the technicians. They also coordinate all aspects of service part inventory (a large part of which is carried on the trucks), tools, and so forth. They work closely with the service force to plan ahead for critical periods such as new product introductions.

Bill Bradley is the most senior of the FMs. He is also an expressive, and has been with DT for about 12 years. His background is software, and he is very strong with debugging problems. He is the least detail-oriented person, which always causes Betty problems because he'll forget stuff and depend on Betty to take care of him.

Toniqua Davis has been with DT for eight years, beginning right out of college. She has a bachelor's degree in management and wants to move into sales. Pat figures Toniqua is a driver, but she hasn't worked much with her.

Shawn Gale is the youngest of the fleet managers, at 27, and has been with DT five years. Shawn is an analytical, has the firmest grasp on how to evaluate a region's performance, and has probably the dullest personality. Senior management always likes Shawn's reports because it is so obvious if a region is doing well, but the technicians don't think much of her.

Gerry MacDonald is the newest member of the DT service staff, having joined the company from Giltspur, a competitor of Fleet Management. She has been with DT for about six months and has been in the fleet industry for over 10 years. Pat hasn't classified Gerry's personality yet. Gerry doesn't have a college degree, but seems to make up for it with her experience.

One issue that hasn't been considered is what happens to DT's maintenance crew. The company has its own truck maintenance operations (employing 120 truck mechanics) in several Canadian and U.S. cities, though it also outsources maintenance in areas where the company doesn't have a large service staff.

FLEET MANAGEMENT, INC.

Pat managed to win the DT business two out of the last three years, but two years ago, it was won by a Volvo distributorship out of Quebec. Before that, the business was held exclusively by a Mercedes distributor in Toronto, a company that is no longer in business.

Fleet Management is a family-owned business founded in 1920 by a young WWI veteran, Ted Ruch. Ted's daughter, Sally R. Massy, took over the company in 1960 and is about to retire, passing the reins to her two children, Gil, who runs the manufacturing side, and Nancy, who runs the sales and service part of the business.

COMPETITION

Parker Peterbilt is the only competitor that offers comparable services. Parker, based in Chicago, offers one advantage that Fleet does not—it also provides in-house leasing. Fleet has always sold vehicles, using a third-party company (GE Capital) for leasing.

Most custom truck builders are small, serving a limited geographic area, meaning that while they may ship trucks anywhere in the world, their customers come from a limited area. Parker is the only one that does its own leasing.

Questions

1. What will the buying center look like? Who will participate, and what role do you expect each person to take?
2. What will the buying criteria likely be? Why is the company making such a change?
3. What strategy should Pat follow to strengthen her position with DT?

APPENDIX: MULTI-ATTRIBUTE MODEL OF PRODUCT EVALUATION AND CHOICE

The multiattribute model is a useful approach for understanding the factors individual members of a buying center consider to evaluate products and make choices. The multiattribute model is just one approach that companies can take to making purchases, and is most often used in complex decisions involving several vendors.[44] Many business decisions are straight rebuys, but the original vendor selection decision may have involved a multiattribute approach. The vendor analysis form used by Chrysler (see Exhibit 4.7) illustrates the use of this model in selecting vendors. The model also provides a framework for developing sales strategies.

The multiattribute model is based on the idea that people view a product as a collection of characteristics or attributes. Buyers evaluate a product by considering how each characteristic satisfies the firm's needs and perhaps their individual needs. The following example examines a firm's decision to buy laptop computers for its sales force. The computers will be used by salespeople to keep track of information about customers and provide call reports to sales managers. At the end of each day, salespeople will call headquarters and transmit their call reports through a modem.

PERFORMANCE EVALUATION OF CHARACTERISTICS

Assume the company narrows its choice to three hypothetical brands: Apex, Bell, and Deltos. Exhibit A.1 gives information the company collected about each brand. Note that the information goes beyond the physical characteristics of the product to include services provided by the potential suppliers.

Each buying center member, or the group as a whole in a meeting, might process this objective information and evaluate the laptop computers on each characteristic. These evaluations appear in Exhibit A.2 as ratings on a 10-point scale, with 10 being the highest rating and 1 the lowest.

How do members of the buying center use these evaluations to select a laptop computer? The final decision depends on the relationship between the performance evaluations and the company's needs. The buying center members must consider the degree to which they are willing to sacrifice poor performance on one attribute for superior performance on another. The members of the buying center must make some trade-offs.

No one product will perform best on all characteristics. For example, Apex excels on size, weight, and availability of convenient service; Bell has superior speed; and Deltos provides the best reliability and internal memory.

EXHIBIT A.1

Information about Laptop Computers

Characteristic/Brand	Apex	Bell	Deltos
Reliability rating	Very good	Very good	Excellent
Weight (pounds)	3.0	4.5	7.5
Size (cubic inches)	168	305	551
Speed (clock rate in megahertz)	332	500	400
RAM memory (in megabytes)	64	64	128
Display visibility	Good	Very good	Excellent
Number of U.S. service centers	140	60	20

EXHIBIT A.2

Performance Evaluation of Laptop Computers

Characteristic/Brand Rating	Apex	Bell	Deltos
Reliability	5	5	8
Weight	8	5	2
Size	8	6	4
Speed	3	8	6
RAM memory	3	5	8
Display visibility	2	4	6
Service availability	7	5	3

IMPORTANCE WEIGHTS

In making an overall evaluation, buying center members need to consider the importance of each characteristic. These importance weights may differ from member to member. Consider two members of the buying center: the national sales manager and the director of management information systems (MIS). The national sales manager is particularly concerned about motivating his salespeople to use the laptop computers. He believes the laptops must be small and lightweight and have good screen visibility. On the other hand, the MIS director foresees using the laptop computers to transmit orders and customer inventory information to corporation headquarters. She believes expanded memory and processing speed will be critical for these future applications.

Exhibit A.3 shows the importance these two buying center members place on each characteristic using a 10-point scale, with 10 representing very important and 1 representing very unimportant. In this illustration the national sales manager and the MIS director differ in the importance they place on characteristics; however, both have the same evaluations of the brands' performance on the characteristics. In some cases people may differ on both importance weights and performance ratings.

EXHIBIT A.3

Information Used to Form an Overall Evaluation

	Importance Weights		Brand Ratings		
Characteristic	Sales Manager	MIS Director	Apex	Bell	Deltos
Reliability	4	4	5	5	8
Weight	6	2	8	5	2
Size	7	3	8	6	4
Speed	1	7	3	8	6
RAM memory	1	6	3	5	8
Display visibility	8	5	2	4	6
Service availability	3	3	7	5	3
Overall evaluation					
Sales manager's			167	152	143
MIS director's			130	169	177

OVERALL EVALUATION

A person's overall evaluation of a product can be quantified by multiplying the sum of the performance ratings by the importance weights. Thus the sales manager's overall evaluation of Apex would be as follows:

$$
\begin{array}{rcl}
4 \times 5 & = & 20 \\
6 \times 8 & = & 48 \\
7 \times 8 & = & 56 \\
1 \times 3 & = & 3 \\
1 \times 3 & = & 3 \\
8 \times 2 & = & 16 \\
\underline{3 \times 7} & = & \underline{21} \\
& & 167
\end{array}
$$

Using the national sales manager's and MIS director's importance weights, the overall evaluations, or scores, for the three laptop computer brands appear at the bottom of Exhibit A.3. These scores indicate the benefit levels the brands provide as seen by these two buying center members.

VALUE OFFERED

The cost of the computers also needs to be considered in making the purchase decision. One approach for incorporating cost calculates the value—the benefits divided by the cost—for each laptop. The prices for the computers and their values are shown in Exhibit A.4. The sales manager believes Apex provides more value. He would probably buy this brand if he were the only person involved in the buying decision. On the other hand, the MIS director believes that Bell and Deltos offer the best value.

SUPPLIER SELECTION

In this situation the sales manager might be the key decision maker, and the MIS director might be a gatekeeper. Rather than using the MIS director's overall evaluation, the buying center might simply ask her to serve as a gatekeeper and determine whether these computers meet her minimum acceptable performance standards on speed and memory. All three laptops pass the minimum levels she established of a 332-megahertz clock rate and a 64-megabyte internal memory. Thus the company would rely on the sales manager's evaluation and purchase Apex laptops for the sales force.

EXHIBIT A.4 Value Offered by Each Brand	Overall Evaluation (Benefits Points)	Computer Cost	Assigned Value (Benefit/Cost)
Sales manager			
Apex	167	$1,600	$0.10
Bell	152	1,800	0.08
Deltos	143	1,800	0.08
MIS director			
Apex	130	$1,600	0.08
Bell	169	1,800	0.09
Deltos	177	1,800	0.10

Even if a buying center or individual members do not go through the calculations described here, the multiattribute model is a good representation of their product evaluations and can be used to predict product choices. Purchase decisions are made as though a formal multiattribute model were used.

Thinking It Through

If you were selling the Bell computer to the national sales manager and MIS director depicted in the text and in Exhibits A.3 and A.4, how would you try to get them to believe that your computer provides more value than Apex or Deltos does? What numbers would you try to change?

IMPLICATIONS FOR SALESPEOPLE

How can salespeople use the multiattribute model to influence their customers' purchase decisions? First, the model indicates what information customers use in making their evaluations and purchase decisions. Thus salespeople need to know the following information to develop a sales strategy:

1. The suppliers or brands the customer is considering.
2. The product characteristics being used in the evaluation.
3. The customer's rating of each product's performance on each dimension.
4. The weights the customer attaches to each dimension.

With this knowledge salespeople can use several strategies to influence purchase decisions. First, salespeople must be sure their product is among the brands being considered. Then they can try to change the customer's perception of their product's value. Some approaches for changing perceived value are

1. Increase the performance rating for your product.
2. Decrease the rating for a competitive product.
3. Increase or decrease an importance weight.
4. Add a new dimension.
5. Decrease the price of your product.

Assume that you are selling the Bell computer and you want to influence the sales manager so that he believes your computer provides more value than the Apex computer. Approach 1 involves altering the sales manager's belief about your product's performance. To raise his evaluation, you would try to have the sales manager perceive your computer as small and lightweight. You might show him how easy it is to carry—how well it satisfies his need for portability. The objective of this demonstration is to increase your rating on weight from 5 to 7 and your rating on size from 6 to 8.

You should focus on these two characteristics because they are the most important to the sales manager. A small change in a performance evaluation on these characteristics will have a large impact on the overall evaluation. You would not want to spend much time influencing his performance evaluations on speed or internal memory because these characteristics are not important to him. Of course, your objectives when selling to the MIS director would be different because she places more importance on speed and internal memory.

This example illustrates a key principle in selling. In general, salespeople should focus primarily on product characteristics that are important to the customer—characteristics that satisfy the customer's needs. Salespeople should not focus on the areas of superior performance (such as speed in this example) that are not important to the customer.

Approach 2 involves decreasing the performance rating of Apex. This strategy can be dangerous. Customers prefer dealing with salespeople who say good things about their products, not bad things about competitive products.

In approach 3 you change the sales manager's importance weights. You want to increase the importance he places on a characteristic on which your product excels, such as speed, or decrease the importance of a characteristic on which your product performs poorly, such as display visibility. For example, you might try to convince the sales manager that a fast computer will decrease the time salespeople need to spend developing and transmitting reports.

Approach 4 encourages the sales manager to consider a new characteristic, one on which your product has superior performance. For example, suppose the sales manager and MIS director have not considered the availability of software. To add a new dimension, you might demonstrate a program specially developed for sales call reports and usable only with your computer.

Approach 5 is the simplest to implement: Simply drop your price. Typically, firms use this strategy as a last resort because cutting prices decreases profits.

These strategies illustrate how salespeople can adapt their selling approach to the needs of their customers. Using the multiattribute model, salespeople decide how to alter the content of their presentation—the benefits to be discussed—based on customer beliefs and needs. (Chapter 6 describes adaptive selling in more detail and illustrates it in terms of the form of the presentation—the communication style the salesperson uses.)

Additional References

Deeter-Schmelz, Dawn R., and Rosemary Ramsey. "A Conceptualization of the Functions and Roles of Formalized Selling and Buying Teams." *Journal of Personal Selling and Sales Management,* Spring 1995, pp. 47–60.

Faes, Wouter; Paul Matthyssens; and Koen Vendenbempt. "The Pursuit of Global Purchasing Synergy." *Industrial Marketing Management* 29, November 2000, pp. 539–54.

Fitzgerald, Kevin. "Profile of a Purchasing Professional." *Purchasing Magazine,* July 15, 1999, pp. 74–84.

Fitzgerald, Kevin. "What Buyers Want from Suppliers." *Purchasing Magazine,* November 18, 1999, pp. 17–19.

Ford, John; Michael LaTour; and Tony Henthorne. "Cognitive Moral Development and Japanese Procurement Executives: Implications for Industrial Marketers." *Industrial Marketing Management* 29, November 2000, pp. 589–600.

Ghinggold, Morry. "Buying Center Research and Business Marketing Practice Meeting the Challenge of Dynamic Marketing." *Journal of Business & Industrial Marketing* 13, Spring 1998, pp. 96–107.

Guinipero, Larry; David Dawley; and William P. Anthony. "The Impact of Tacit Knowledge on Purchasing Decisions." *Journal of Supply Chain Management* 35, Winter 1999, pp. 42–49.

Handfield, Robert, and Ernest Nichols. *Introduction to Supply Chain Management.* Upper Saddle River, NJ: Prentice Hall, 1998.

Hult, G. Tomas M. "Cultural Competitiveness in Global Sourcing." *Industrial Marketing Management* 31, January 2002, pp. 25–34.

Lorge, Sarah. "Purchasing Power." *Sales & Marketing Management*, June 1998, pp. 43–46.

Ray, Dana. "Value-Based Selling." *Selling Power*, September 1999, pp. 33–36.

Schorr, John E. *Purchasing in the 21st Century: A Guide to State-of-the-Art Techniques and Strategies*. 2nd ed. New York: John Wiley & Sons, 1998.

Stremersch, Stefan; Stefan Wuyts; and Ruud T. Frambach. "The Purchasing of Full-Service Contracts: An Exploratory Study within the Industrial Maintenance Market." *Industrial Marketing Management* 30, January 2001, pp. 1–12.

Tanner, John F. Jr. "Organizational Buying Theories: A Bridge to Relationships Theory." *Industrial Marketing Management* 28, May 1999, pp. 245–46.

5 Using Communication Principles to Build Relationships

SOME QUESTIONS ANSWERED IN THIS CHAPTER ARE:

■ What are the basic elements in the communication process?

■ Why are listening and questioning skills important?

■ How can salespeople develop listening skills to collect information about customers?

■ How do people communicate without using words?

■ What are the barriers to effective communication?

A stockbroker is telling a client about the benefits of buying Wal-Mart stock. The broker says, "Wal-Mart is an excellent buy. Its price–earnings ratio is depressed because of uncertainties in GDP growth. But NAFTA offers great opportunities for expansion into Mexico." The stockbroker wants to communicate the benefits of buying stock in Wal-Mart, but the client may not interpret this message correctly because he is not familiar with the terms NAFTA, GDP, and depressed price–earnings ratio. The stockbroker may recognize the lack of understanding by observing the client's facial expression and then say, "Let me explain my reasoning in more detail." Or the client might try to understand the stockbroker's message by asking, "What does depressed price–earnings ratio mean?" But the client may be embarrassed by his lack of understanding and respond, "I don't think I am interested in buying stocks now."

Effective communication is a key element in building close personal and business relationships. To adapt your sales presentation to customers and to communicate product benefits to them, you need to learn about customers' needs. The communication principles discussed in this chapter can help everyone, including salespeople, avoid misunderstandings and improve relationships.

"You have to pay attention to body language to see if you've lost someone. If so, you stop, go back and break things down even further so they understand."

Barbara S. Kellgren, Lutron

PROFILE

Barbara S. Kellgren graduated from Middle Tennessee State University with a BBA in marketing and a minor in Spanish. She works for Lutron Electronics, a high-tech firm that manufactures and designs lighting controls for residential, commercial, and institutional applications. As a marketing representative in the Design Center Channel at Lutron, she calls on interior designers, architects, and the EXPO Design Centers (a Home Depot company) to educate them and get them to specify Lutron products.

"Within the EXPOs, there are many audiences I have to address, each with different needs, so the way I teach and educate must be different. The sales floor associates need to quickly explain to a customer why they should have dimmers in their homes, while the in-house designer has more time to talk to a client about lighting controls. The project managers must know what product to install at a moment's notice because they're at a job site. Then there are the trade services people, who need to know how to present our products to electricians, contractors, and builders. I work with all of these people, one-on-one or in groups, primarily to keep them updated and educated on our products so they feel more confident selling them. My first full year in the field, my territory experienced a 38 percent increase in sales over the previous year because of the personal attention I give my accounts.

"I like to use word pictures when selling. For example, when trying to get someone to understand the value of a whole-house lighting system, I explain the convenience of having control of lights from a car by telling them, 'You leave the house. But you've been gone longer than you thought, it's dark outside and in your home. Maybe you have bags of groceries or other shopping bags you're fumbling with, or even kids. Do you fumble around trying to get into the house and not step on the truck little Johnny left in front of the door? Well, now imagine never having to come into a dark house again. With our lighting system, you can turn lights on from your car and create a pathway of light to get you from your garage, down a hall, and into your kitchen, or on into your bedroom—however you normally come into your home, all without doing any special wiring in your home.' I can often win over customers by painting these pictures because these are images they are familiar with. Almost everyone has had these experiences and can easily relate to them. Most people just don't realize they can do something about it.

"Watching customers' body language is very important. I know our products back and forth, but many things that I take for granted with lighting controls, I must realize many other people don't understand. You have to pay attention to body language to see if you've lost someone. If so, you stop, go back, and break things down even further so they understand. I've learned to explain the same concepts in different ways because people are so different.

"My position takes me to southeast Florida twice a month, and the communication that takes place there is different from anywhere else. The store in Miami does a lot of export business with lots of customers from Mexico, Puerto Rico, and South America. People with Spanish/Hispanic backgrounds have a different idea of proxemics than most Americans. For instance, men and women stand much closer to a stranger than what most Americans find comfortable. Plus, there is a different sense of camaraderie there than at other stores I call on. Like when I arrive at the Miami store, the sales associates will give me a peck on each cheek—which is a standard greeting in the Spanish world when you see friends. Other locations would probably take this as sexual harassment, but it's not. It's just varying the communication style depending on what your customer is comfortable with."

Visit Our Website @ www.lutron.com.

BUILDING RELATIONSHIPS THROUGH TWO-WAY COMMUNICATION

As we discussed in Chapter 2, open and honest communications are a key to building trust and developing successful relationships. To develop a good understanding of each other's needs, buyers and sellers must effectively communicate with each other by actively talking and listening. If the communication is successful, the seller's firm not only will benefit by knowing the customer's current needs but also will see what changes it needs to enact to meet unfilled and future needs.

THE COMMUNICATION PROCESS

Exhibit 5.1 illustrates the communication process. Note that this is an example of **two-way communication,** since both parties act as senders and receivers of information. The process begins when the sender, either the salesperson or the customer, wants to communicate some thoughts or ideas. Because the receiver cannot read the sender's mind, the sender must translate these ideas into words. The translation of thoughts into words is called **encoding.** Then the receiver must decode the message and try to understand what the sender intended to communicate. **Decoding** involves interpreting the meaning of the received message.

Consider a salesperson who is demonstrating a complex product to a customer. At some point in the presentation, a perplexed look flits across the customer's face. The salesperson receives this nonverbal message and then asks the customer what part of the presentation needs further explanation. The feedback the customer's expression provides tells the salesperson that the message is not being received. The customer then sends verbal messages to the salesperson in the form of questions concerning the operation and benefits of the product.

COMMUNICATION BREAKDOWNS

Communication breakdowns can be caused by encoding and decoding problems and the environment in which the communications occur.[1] The following sales interaction between a copier salesperson and a prospect illustrates problems that can arise in encoding and decoding messages:

What the salesperson wants to say: We have an entire line of copiers. But I think the model 900 is ideally suited for your needs because it provides the basic copying functions at a low price.

What the salesperson says (encodes): The model 900 is our *best-selling* copier. It is designed to economically meet the copying needs of small businesses like yours.

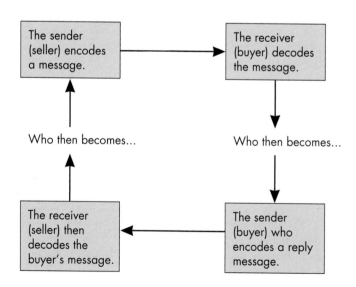

EXHIBIT 5.1

Two-Way Flow of Information

Background noise from traffic can hinder effective communication. The salesperson should attempt to move the discussion to a quieter location so the traffic noise will not distract the customer.

Tom and DeeAnn McCarthy/The Stock Market

What the customer hears: The model 900 is a *low-price* copier for small businesses.

What the customer thinks (decodes): This company makes low-price copiers with limited features. They are designed for businesses that don't have much money to spend for a copier. We need a copier with more features. We should invest in a better copier that will meet our future needs.

What the customer says: I don't think I'm interested in buying a copier now.

In this situation the salesperson assumed that price was very important to the prospect, and the prospect thought (incorrectly) that the salesperson's company made only low-price, low-performance copiers.

Communication can also be inhibited by the environment in which the communication process occurs. For example, noises can distract the salesperson and the customer. **Noises** are sounds unrelated to messages being exchanged by the salesperson and the customer, such as ringing telephones or other conversations nearby. To improve communication, the salesperson should attempt to minimize the noises in the environment by closing a door to the room or suggesting that the meeting move to another, quieter place.

Other environmental issues must be dealt with before effective communication can occur. For example, people communicate most effectively when they are physically comfortable. If the room is too hot or too cold, the salesperson should suggest changing the temperature controls, opening or closing a window, or moving to another room. Other environmental issues might include items such as the following: The buyer is preoccupied with something that she was thinking about before the seller entered the room, the seller can't easily see the buyer due to some obstruction like a lamp or a chair that is too low, the buyer isn't feeling well, the buyer is angry about something that has happened since the last sales call, or the buyer is tired and starts to nod off as the seller talks. Many of these environmental issues and possible solutions will be discussed in Chapters 9 and 10. For now, realize that effective communication can't occur without the proper environment.

Thinking It Through

Think of a recent face-to-face interaction you had with another person when a communication problem occurred. What caused the miscommunication? Was it a two-way communication with feedback? Did noises affect the interaction?

COMMUNICA-TION METHODS

Salespeople communicate with customers in face-to-face interactions and by using the telephone, e-mail, and letters. As shown in Exhibit 5.2, these methods vary in terms of the interactivity of the communications, the ability to use verbal and nonverbal communication channels, and the quantity of information that can be conveyed. **Response time** is the time between sending a message and getting a response to it. **Verbal communication** involves the transmission of words in face-to-face communication, over a telephone, or through written messages. **Nonverbal communications** are forms of expression—body language, space, and appearance—that communicate thoughts and emotions without using words.

Because of the fast response time and the ability to use both verbal and nonverbal channels, face-to face interactions are the most effective method for communication with customers. Salespeople in face-to-face interactions can get immediate feedback from customers and quickly make adjustments to correct any miscommunications.

Telephone interactions are not as effective as face-to-face communication for communicating with customers because the only nonverbal communications that salespeople can send or receive over the telephone are voice characteristics. When two people communicate with each other, spoken words play a surprisingly small part in the communication process. Words are responsible for only 40 percent of the information people acquire in face-to-face communication. Voice characteristics account for 10 percent of the message received, and the remaining 50 percent comes from nonverbal communications.[2]

Nonverbal communications provide a lot of information to the receiver because the sender has difficulty controlling them. Because senders have less control over nonverbal communication than over verbal communication, receivers tend to trust nonverbal communications more than verbal statements. For example, a customer claims to be happy about a salesperson's proposal and indicates her happiness by smiling. However, people can detect fake smiles very accurately. The salesperson who feels the smile is not genuine will discount the customer's words and think the customer really is not pleased by the proposal.

In addition, some nonverbal communications have more universal meaning than do verbal communications. The same facial muscles are used to communicate emotions such as happiness, anger, surprise, and fear in many cultures. The cultural differences in nonverbal communications arise not from the meanings of the expressions but from when to appropriately display the expressions.

Both e-mail messages and letters have limited effectiveness because of the slow level of response time. These communication methods involve **one-way communication.** However, when people send an e-mail message, they generally expect to receive a return e-mail the next time they turn on their computer. Thus e-mail communication tends to have faster response time than communication through letters. However, even proponents of e-mail admit that it is not effective at sending and receiving information about emotions.[3]

In face-to-face interactions, salespeople can use visual aids, such as brochures and computer displays, to support the messages they deliver verbally. Some of

EXHIBIT 5.2 Effectiveness of Various Methods of Communications	Face to Face	Telephone	E-mail	Letter
Response time	Fast	Fast	Slow	Slowest
Verbal channel	Yes	Yes	Yes	Yes
Nonverbal channel	Yes	Limited	No	No
Quantity of information	Highest	Low	Lowest	Moderate

these visual aids can also accompany letters and e-mails sent to customers. But the visual aids cannot be used in telephone interactions.

In the next sections we discuss techniques that salespeople can use to effectively send verbal messages to customers, receive (listen to) verbal messages from customers, receive (read) customers' nonverbal messages, and send nonverbal messages to customers.

SENDING VERBAL MESSAGES

Messages communicated verbally are encoded into symbols called *words*. Words, however, are just symbols; they have different meanings to different people. Consider a presentation by a salesperson working for a fabric manufacturer. During the presentation the salesperson indicates that the fabrics the company makes are of high quality and durable and their colors are fast. But will the prospect know what *fast* means? The dictionary lists more than 30 definitions of *fast*. Some of them have to do with very different things, including eating habits, running, or behavior on a date. In this case, of course, the salesperson is pointing out that the colors will not fade despite frequent washing or dry cleaning.

EFFECTIVE USE OF WORDS

Each industry has its own trade jargon. A college textbook sales representative, for example, must know the meaning of technical expressions such as *test bank, transparency, semester,* and *instructor's manual.* But salespeople cannot assume that all customers will be familiar with this trade jargon. Salespeople need to check with their customers continually to determine whether they are interpreting sales messages properly.

Words have different meanings in different cultures and even in different subcultures of the United States. In England the hood of a car is called the *bonnet*, and the trunk is called the *boot*. In Boston a *milkshake* is simply syrup mixed with milk, whereas a *frappe* is ice cream, syrup, and milk mixed together. Similarly, the words *ship* and *boat* have very different meaning to sailors. Studies show that about half of blacks over the age of 40 prefer the designation "black," while those 18–39 years old prefer "African American."[4]

CHARACTERISTICS OF WORDS

Words can be either abstract or concrete as well as emotional or neutral. Concrete, fact-oriented words and expressions usually convey more information and are less likely to be misinterpreted than are abstract, conceptual words. The purity of water is communicated more effectively by using the concrete expression "The mineral content of this water is under one part per million" than by abstractly saying "This water is pure."

Many words related to politics, gender, and race elicit strong emotional responses that inhibit effective communication. Politicians are particularly adept at using words that typically involve a positive emotional response. Who could be against programs such as Truth in Lending, the Fair Deal, or the Right to Work?

USING EFFECTIVE WORDS

Words are tools. Word artists have the power to be soft and appealing or strong and powerful. They can use short words and phrases to demonstrate strength and force or to provide charm and grace (like, *clean, crisp copies* and *library quiet*). With practice, words may be used, like the notes of a musical scale, to create the proper mood.

Words in sales presentations should have strength and descriptive quality. Avoid words such as *nice, pretty, good,* and *swell* and phrases that make you

"TROY TRIES HARD, BUT HE'S NOT THE SHARPEST CRAYON IN THE BOX"

"Not the sharpest knife in the drawer." "Lights are on, but nobody's home." "A few bricks short of a load." "Elevator doesn't go to the top." "In the pinball game of life, his flippers were a little farther apart." "A few fries short of a happy meal." What do all of these statements have in common? They're metaphors, denoting one kind of object in place of another—in this case, to describe someone who is not all that smart.

Most salespeople use metaphors (such as "We're making it possible for you to raise the bar in terms of what you can expect from your suppliers" or "Our computerized help desk will be a sturdy bridge to your important customers"). Want some tips for improving their use?

- Use the fewest words possible. For example, say "swimming with sharks," not "swimming in a great big ocean that has a number of sharks swimming around you at the same time."

- Use metaphors that listeners can easily picture. Most people can visualize swimming with sharks around them, but would have more trouble picturing themselves swimming in a pool of asphalt.

- Make sure they're appropriate for the topic. "Swimming with dolphins" wouldn't make quite the same impression as using the word "sharks" if you're trying to convey a predatory situation.

- Make sure they're appropriate for the audience and do not offend. Don't use the shark metaphor if talking to someone whose son was attacked in Florida by a shark. The opening examples could easily be offensive to someone sensitive or someone who has a child with a mental disability.

- Don't overdo their use. It can get distracting if someone talks *only* in metaphors.

Now you can return to reading the chapter, and learn communication principles that may someday "save your skin"!

Sources: Peter J. Leone, Jr., Scott Luostari, and Tad Simons, "Mastering the Art of Metaphor," *Presentations,* June 2001, pp. 43–52.

sound like an overeager salesperson such as *a great deal, I guarantee you will . . .,* and *No problem!* Also, avoid using complicated words and phrases. Don't say, "Typically, the often complicated value chain relationships don't have a concrete paradigm for learning and cross-pollination of ideas," when you could just as easily say, "Often, suppliers and customers don't talk to each other." The first phrase was actually used recently by a business![5]

Avoid using off-color language, slang, and foul language. Jim O'Conner, author of *Cuss Control,* encourages salespeople to stop using foul language, even when talking to established clients. "I don't care who I'm talking to . . . You never know when a certain word is going to make someone feel uncomfortable. Why risk it?"[6] And sales managers understand this. In a recent study, over 75 percent of managers would avoid hiring a rep who used salty language.[7]

Every salesperson should be able to draw on a set of words to help present the features of a product or service. The words might form a simile, such as This battery backup is like a spare tire; a metaphor, such as This machine is a real workhorse; or a phrase drawing on sensory appeal, such as *smooth as silk* and *strong as steel.* Building Partnerships 5.1 gives some valuable tips for using metaphors. Exhibit 5.3 illustrates how positive, pacifying words can be used in place of negative words.

PAINTING WORD PICTURES

Salespeople can use word pictures to help customers understand the benefits of a product or a feature of the product. A **word picture** is a story designed to help the buyer visualize a point. For example, Exhibit 5.4 provides a word picture

In order for this older salesperson to communicate with these younger buyers, he must use words and metaphors that are meaningful and interesting to the buyers.

Juanne Gual Carborell/AGE Fotostock

that a Jeep Cherokee salesperson might use when calling on the owner of a commercial real estate firm.

To use a word picture effectively, the salesperson needs to paint as accurate and reliable a picture as possible. No attempt at puffery should be made. Word pictures should be honest attempts to help the buyer accurately visualize the situation.

TAILORING WORDS TO THE CUSTOMER

Customers can have different styles of communicating. Some people may be very visual; others may prefer an auditory communication mode; and still others communicate in a feeling mode. Salespeople need to adapt their word choices to the customer's preferred communication style.[8] For example, customers with a visual orientation prefer words like *see, observe, demonstrate,* and *clarity;* customers with an auditory orientation prefer words like *announce, hear,* and *mention;* and customers who communicate in a feeling mode like words such as *touch, sensitive,* and *grasp.* A key goal is to use words that allow buyers to catch and retain details, which they will often need to share with others in a buying group (see Chapters 4 and 7 for more details on the activities of buying groups).[9]

VOICE CHARACTERISTICS

A salesperson's delivery of words affects how the customer will understand and evaluate his or her presentations. Poor voice and speech habits make it difficult for customers to understand the salesperson's message. **Voice characteristics** include rate of speech, loudness, inflection, and articulation.

SPEECH RATE

Customers have a tendency to question the expertise of salespeople who talk slower or faster than the normal rate of 140 words per minute. Salespeople who talk faster

EXHIBIT 5.3		
Using Positive Rather than Negative Words	**Don't Say**	**Do Say**
	Cost or price	Investment
	Down payment	Initial investment
	Contract	Agreement or paperwork
	Buy	Own
	Sell	Get involved
	Sign	Okay, approve, or authorize
	Deal	Opportunity
	Problem	Challenge
	Objection	Area of concern
	Customer	People, companies we serve
	Cheaper	More economical
	Appointment	Visit
	Prospect	Future client
	Commission	Fee for service

Source: Francy Blackwood, "Back to Basics," *Selling,* April 1996, p. 39. Reprinted with permission from Institutional Investors, Inc.

EXHIBIT 5.4

Example of a Word
Picture

Situation

A Jeep Cherokee salesperson is calling on Jill, the owner of a commercial real estate firm. The goal of the word picture is to demonstrate the value of the four-wheel-drive option.

Word Picture

Jill, picture for a moment the following situation. You have this really hot prospect—let's call him Steve—for a remote resort development. You're in your current car, a Cadillac DeVille. You've been trying to get Steve up to the property for months, and today is his only free day for several weeks. The property, up in the northern Georgia mountains, is accessible only by an old logging road. The day is bright and sunny, and Steve is in a good mood. When you reach the foot of the mountains, the weather turns cloudy and windy. As you wind up the old, bumpy road, a light rain begins. You've just crossed a small bridge when a downpour starts; the rain is pelting your windshield. Steve looks a little worried. Suddenly your car's tires start spinning. You're stuck in the mud.

Now let's replay the story, assuming that you buy the Jeep Cherokee we've been talking about. [Salesperson quickly repeats the first paragraph of this story, substituting Jeep Cherokee for Cadillac DeVille.] Suddenly your car tires start spinning. You're stuck in the mud. Calmly you reach down and shift into four-wheel drive. The Jeep pulls out easily, and you reach the destination in about five minutes. Although it's raining, the prospect looks at the land and sees great potential. On the way back down the mountain, you discuss how Steve should go about making an offer on the property. Jill, I hope I've made a point. Can you see why the four-wheel-drive option is important for you, even though it does add to the base price of the car?

or slower than the normal rate should consciously try to slow down or speed up when first meeting a customer and then gradually return to their normal rate.

Salespeople should also vary their rate of speech, depending on the nature of the message and the environment in which the communication occurs. Simple messages can be delivered at faster rates, and more difficult concepts should be presented at slower rates. Salespeople should speak more slowly in a noisy area and when calling on customers in a region of the country where speech is normally slower than average.

Telephone calls should be conducted at a lower speech rate because the listener lacks visual information to help interpret the words. In general, varying the rate of speech helps to maintain attention.[10]

LOUDNESS

Loudness should also be tailored to the communication situation. To avoid monotony, salespeople should learn to vary the loudness of their speech. Loudness can also be used to emphasize certain parts of the sales presentation, indicating to the customer that these parts are more important.

Salespeople should use customer reactions to determine the appropriate loudness. For example, if a customer backs away, the salesperson may be talking too loudly; if a customer leans closer, the salesperson may be talking too softly.

INFLECTION

Inflection is the tone of speech. At the end of a sentence, the tone should decrease, indicating the completion of a thought. When the tone goes up at the end of a sentence, listeners often sense uncertainty in the speaker. Use inflection to reduce monotony.

ARTICULATION

Articulation refers to the production of recognizable sounds. Articulation is best when the speaker opens his or her mouth properly; then the movements of the lips and tongue are unimpeded. When the lips are too close together, the enunciation of certain vowels and consonants suffers.

ASKING QUESTIONS

Asking questions is a critical element in effective verbal communications. Questioning gets customers to participate in the sales interview. They have a chance to actively engage in conversation rather than just listen to a presentation. This technique holds the attention of the customer, who ends up learning and remembering more about the product. Questioning also builds relationships by showing the salesperson's interest in the customer's problems. Asking questions also enables salespeople to demonstrate their expertise. Suppose a customer says, Our computers are crashing too often. One salesperson says, I'll have our tech rep call you. The other starts asking questions: When do they typically crash? Are you running several programs and an Internet browser when they crash? Which salesperson will appear to have greater expertise?

Finally, by asking questions, salespeople are able to collect information about customers and test their assumptions during all phases of the sales interaction, from prospecting to closing. In this text we focus on using the SPIN® method for uncovering customer needs. **SPIN** stands for questions about **s**ituation, **p**roblems, **i**mplications, and **n**eed payoffs. The SPIN® method is discussed in Chapter 9. Some guidelines for asking good questions follow.

ENCOURAGE FULL RESPONSES

Closed questions can be answered with a word or short phrase. Such questions draw little information from the customer. **Open questions,** questions for which there are no simple answers, encourage greater communication.

For example, the closed question Have you heard of our company? will probably result in a simple yes or no answer. Then the salesperson will need to ask a follow-up, open question, such as Why haven't you heard of our company? or What have you heard about our company? Here are some examples of closed and open questions:

Closed Questions	Open Questions
Are you interested in buying laptop computers for your sales force?	Why haven't you bought laptop computers for your sales force?
Are you satisfied with your present supplier of aluminum cans?	What problems are you having with your present supplier of aluminum cans?

More information on the use of open and closed questions is presented in Chapter 9.

Thinking It Through

If open questions are so much better at drawing out more information from buyers, why would anyone ever ask closed questions? Why not encourage salespeople to just ask open questions and never use closed ones?

SPACE OUT YOUR QUESTIONS

When salespeople ask several questions, one right after another, customers may feel threatened. They may think they are being interrogated rather than participating in a conversation. Some customers react by disclosing less rather than more information. For this reason, questions should be spaced out so the customer has time to answer each question in a relaxed atmosphere. One method for spacing out questions is to encourage prospects to elaborate on their responses. In this way customers realize they are volunteering information rather than being forced to divulge it.

If several questions are really necessary, the salesperson might ask a permission question first, such as Do you mind if I ask you some questions about your operations so we can see whether my company's products might be of use to you?

ASK SHORT, SIMPLE QUESTIONS

Questions that have two or more parts should be avoided. The customer may not know which part to answer, and the salesperson may not know which part has been answered. For example:

> SALESPERSON: How much time do you spend making your annual budget and your sales forecasts?
>
> CUSTOMER: Oh, about three weeks.

Does this answer mean that the customer spends three weeks on both tasks or only on one?

Long questions are hard to remember and to answer. For example: With so many complicated reports to prepare and review, is it difficult for you to determine your direct material and labor costs and to determine how much shelf space to allocate to laundry detergent in the 20,000- and 40,000-square-foot stores? Long questions can confuse the customer. Some customers may be annoyed by questions that force them to ask the salesperson for clarification.

AVOID LEADING QUESTIONS

Questions should not suggest an appropriate answer. Such questions may put words into the customer's mouth rather than drawing out what the customer actually thinks. For example:

> SALESPERSON: Why do you think this is a good product?
>
> CUSTOMER: Well, you said it has a low price and is very reliable.

The salesperson's question encouraged a positive response and discouraged a negative one. Even though such questions may get the responses the salesperson wants to hear, they may mask the customer's true feelings.

USE QUESTIONS TO MAINTAIN THE FLOW OF INFORMATION

A good way to maintain the flow of information is to offer verbal and nonverbal encouragement, such as saying Really? Uh-huh, That's interesting, and Is that so? and nodding your head. Let's look at the effect of a sequence of these encouragement signals:

> CUSTOMER: Then this salesperson asked whether I was interested in getting lower costs than I was getting from Delta.
>
> SALESPERSON: That's interesting. Tell me more.
>
> CUSTOMER: Well, he said that at my current usage level he could save me about $25 a month.
>
> SALESPERSON: Is that right?
>
> CUSTOMER: Then came the kicker.

SALESPERSON: Uh-huh.

CUSTOMER: When I asked about service, the whole picture changed.

SALESPERSON: I see.

CUSTOMER: In short, he was going to give me a lower cost, all right. But he wasn't going to give me much in the way of service.

Another approach for maintaining the flow of information is to make positive requests for additional information, such as

Can you give me an example of what you mean?

Please, tell me more about that.

The third type of approach for maintaining the flow of information is to make neutral statements that reaffirm or repeat a customer's comment or emotion. They allow the salesperson to dig deeper, and they stimulate customers to continue their thoughts in a logical manner. By reaffirming a customer's statement, the salesperson can respond to the customer without agreeing or disagreeing with him or her. Some examples of these questions are

You said you were dissatisfied with your present service?

So you need the self-correcting feature?

Reaffirming a customer's statement is particularly effective with customers who are angry, upset, or in some other highly emotional state. Often these emotions persist until the customer recognizes that the emotions are being acknowledged. For example:

CUSTOMER: Look, I've just about had it with you, your company, and your pumps!

SALESPERSON: It's pretty obvious you're upset, Ms. Roberts.

CUSTOMER: Of course I am. That's the third time this week the pump has gone on the fritz!

By acknowledging customers' emotional states, salespeople let customers know they are being heard, which usually reduces the level of negative feelings. This approach allows salespeople to focus on the problem causing the emotion.

LISTENING TO VERBAL COMMUNICATIONS FROM CUSTOMERS

Many people believe effective communication is achieved by talking a lot. Inexperienced salespeople often go into a selling situation thinking they have to outtalk the prospect. They are enthusiastic about their product and company, and they want to tell the prospect all they know. However, salespeople who monopolize conversations cannot find out what customers need.

People can speak at a rate of only 120 to 160 words per minute, but they can listen to more than 800 words per minute. This difference is referred to as the **speaking–listening differential**. Because of this differential, people often become lazy listeners. They do not pay attention and often remember only 50 percent of what is said immediately after they hear it.

ACTIVE LISTENING

Effective listening is not a passive activity. Good listeners project themselves into the mind of the speaker and attempt to feel the way the speaker feels. If a customer says she needs a small microphone, the salesperson needs to listen carefully to find out what the term *small* means to this particular customer, how small the microphone has to be, why she needs a small microphone, and what she will be willing

To be an effective listener, the salesperson on the right demonstrates an interest in what the customer is saying and actively thinks about questions for drawing out more information.

IT Internationa/e-Stock Photo

to sacrifice to get a small microphone. Effective listening enables the salesperson to recommend a type of microphone that will meet the customer's specific needs.

Effective listeners actively think while they listen. They think about the conclusions toward which the speaker is building, evaluate the evidence being presented, and sort out important facts from irrelevant ones. **Active listening** also means the listener attempts to draw out as much information as possible. Gestures can motivate a person to continue talking. Head nodding, eye contact, and an occasional I see, Tell me more, and That's interesting all demonstrate an interest in and understanding of what is being said. Take a moment and complete the questionnaire in Exhibit 5.5 to rate your active listening skills.

Suggestions for active listening include (1) repeating information, (2) restating or rephrasing information, (3) clarifying information, (4) summarizing the conversation, (5) tolerating silences, and (6) concentrating on the ideas being communicated.[11]

REPEATING INFORMATION

During a sales interaction the salesperson should verify the information she or he is collecting from the customer. A useful way to verify information is to repeat, word for word, what has been said. This technique minimizes the chance of misunderstandings. For example:

> CUSTOMER: I'll take 15 cases of personal-size Ivory soap and 12 cases of the family size.
>
> SALESPERSON: Sure, Mr. Johnson, 15 cases of personal size and 12 cases of family size.
>
> CUSTOMER: Wait a minute. I got that backward. I want 12 cases of personal size and 15 cases of family size.
>
> SALESPERSON: Fine. Twelve personal, 15 family. Is that right?
>
> CUSTOMER: Yes. That's what I want.

Salespeople need to be careful when using this technique, however. Customers can get irritated with salespeople who echo everything.

RESTATING OR REPHRASING INFORMATION

To verify a customer's intent, salespeople should restate the customer's comment in their own words. This step ensures that the salesperson and customer understand each other. For example:

> CUSTOMER: The service isn't quite what I had expected.
>
> SALESPERSON: I see, you're a little bit dissatisfied with the service we've been giving you.

EXHIBIT 5.5

Test Your Active
Listening Skills

	My performance could be improved substantially			My performance needs no improvement	
During a typical conversation:					
1. I project an impression that I sincerely care about what the person is saying.	1	2	3	4	5
2. I don't interrupt the person.	1	2	3	4	5
3. I don't jump to conclusions.	1	2	3	4	5
4. I ask probing questions.	1	2	3	4	5
5. I ask continuing questions like "Could you tell me more?"	1	2	3	4	5
6. I maintain eye contact with the person.	1	2	3	4	5
7. I nod to show the person that I agree or understand.	1	2	3	4	5
8. I read the person's nonverbal communications.	1	2	3	4	5
9. I wait for the person to finish speaking before evaluating what has been said.	1	2	3	4	5
10. I ask clarifying questions like "I'm not sure I know what you mean."	1	2	3	4	5
11. I restate what the person has stated or asked.	1	2	3	4	5
12. I summarize what the person has said.	1	2	3	4	5
13. I make an effort to understand the person's point of view.	1	2	3	4	5
14. I try to find things I have in common with the person.	1	2	3	4	5

Scoring: 60–70=Outstanding; 50–59=Good; 40–49=Could use some improvement; 30–39=Could definitely use some improvement; Under 30=Are you listening?

Source: An adaptation of the ILPS scale. Stephen B. Castleberry, C. David Shepherd, and Rick E. Ridnour, "Effective Interpersonal Listening in the Personal Selling Environment: Conceptualization, Measurement, and Nomological Validity," *Journal of Marketing Theory and Practice*, Winter 1999, pp. 30–38.

CUSTOMER: Oh, no. As a matter of fact, I've been getting better service than I thought I would.

CLARIFYING INFORMATION

Another way to verify a customer's meaning is to ask questions designed to obtain additional information. These can give a more complete understanding of the customer's concerns. For example:

CUSTOMER: Listen, I've tried everything. I just can't get this drill press to work properly.

SALESPERSON: Just what is it that the drill press doesn't do?

CUSTOMER: Well, the rivets keep jamming inside the machine. Sometimes one rivet is inserted on top of the other.

SALESPERSON: Would you describe for me the way you load the rivets onto the tray?

CUSTOMER: Well, first I push down the release lever and take out the tray. Then I push that little button and put in the rivets. Next, I push the lever again, put the tray in the machine, and push the lever.

SALESPERSON: When you put the tray in, which side is up?

CUSTOMER: Does that make a difference?

This exchange shows how a sequence of questions can clarify the problem and help the salesperson determine its cause.

SUMMARIZING THE CONVERSATION

An important element of active listening is to mentally summarize points that have been made. At critical spots in the sales presentation, the salesperson should present his or her mentally prepared summary. Summarizing provides both salesperson and customer with a quick overview of what has taken place and lets them focus on the issues that have been discussed. Summarizing also lets the salesperson change the direction of the conversation. For example:

CUSTOMER: So I told him I wasn't interested.

SALESPERSON: Let me see whether I have this straight. A salesperson called on you today and asked whether you were interested in reducing your costs. He also said he could save you about $25 a month. But when you pursued the matter, you found out the dollar savings in costs were offset by reduced service.

CUSTOMER: That's right.

SALESPERSON: Well, I have your account records right here. Assuming you're interested in getting more for your dollar with regard to data transmission costs, I think there's a way we can help you—without having to worry about any decrease in the quality of service.

CUSTOMER: Tell me more.

TOLERATING SILENCES

This technique could more appropriately be titled "Bite your tongue." At times during a sales presentation, a customer needs time to think. This need can be triggered by a tough question or an issue the customer wants to avoid.

While the customer is thinking, periods of silence occur. Salespeople may be uncomfortable during these silences and feel they need to say something. However, the customer cannot think when the salesperson is talking. By tolerating silences, salespeople give customers a chance to sell themselves. The following conversation about setting an appointment demonstrates the benefits of tolerating silence:

SALESPERSON: What day would you like me to call on you?

CUSTOMER: Just a minute. Let me think about that.

SALESPERSON: [silence]

CUSTOMER: Okay, let's make it on Monday, the 22nd.

SALESPERSON: Fine, Ms. Quinn. What time would be most convenient?

CUSTOMER: Hmmm . . .

SALESPERSON: [silence]

CUSTOMER: Ten o'clock would be best for me.

CONCENTRATING ON THE IDEAS BEING COMMUNICATED

Frequently what customers say and how they say it can distract salespeople from the ideas the customers are actually trying to communicate. For example, salespeople may react strongly when customers use emotion-laden phrases such as *bad service* or *lousy product*. Rather than getting angry, the salesperson should try to find out what upset the customer so much. Salespeople should listen to the words from the customer's viewpoint instead of reacting from their own viewpoint.

READING NONVERBAL MESSAGES FROM CUSTOMERS

In addition to asking questions and listening, salespeople can learn a lot from their customers' nonverbal behaviors. John Napier, author of the book *Hands,* put it this way: "If language was given to men to conceal their thoughts, then gesture's purpose was to disclose them. Experts on nonverbal behavior say we literally leak our true or masked feelings through our body language and movements."[12] In this section we discuss how salespeople can collect information by observing their customers' body language. Later in the chapter we examine how salespeople can use the three forms of nonverbal expression—body language, space, and appearance—to convey messages to their customers.

BODY LANGUAGE

Customers provide a lot of information through their **body language.** The elements of body language are body angle, facial expressions, arms, hands, and legs. Each element is important in face-to-face communication; however, combinations of elements are needed to accurately interpret body language.

BODY ANGLE

Back-and-forth motions indicate a positive outlook, whereas side-to-side movements suggest insecurity and doubt. Body movements directed toward a person indicate a positive regard; in contrast, leaning back or away suggests boredom, apprehension, or possibly anger. Changes in position may indicate that a customer wants to end the interview, strongly agrees or disagrees with what has been said, or wants to place an order.

FACE

The face has many small muscles capable of communicating innumerable messages. Customers can use these muscles to indicate interest, expectation, concern, disapproval, or approval. The eyes are the most important area of the face. The pupils of interested or excited people tend to enlarge. Thus by looking at a customer's eyes, salespeople can often determine when their presentations have made an impression. For this reason many Chinese jade buyers wear dark glasses so they can conceal their interest in specific items and bargain more effectively.

Even the rate at which someone blinks can tell a lot about a person. The average blink rate for a relaxed person is 10 to 20 blinks per minute (bmp). During normal conversation, it increases to about 25 bmp. Bmp over 50, and particularly over 70 bmp, indicates high stress levels.[13]

Eye position can indicate a customer's thought process. Eyes focused straight ahead mean a customer is passively receiving information but devoting little effort to analyzing the meaning and not really concentrating on the presentation. Intense eye contact for more than three seconds generally indicates customer displeasure. Staring indicates coldness, anger, or dislike.

Customers look away from the salesperson while they actively consider information in the sales presentation. When the customer's eyes are positioned to the left or right, the salesperson has succeeded in getting the customer involved in the presentation. A gaze to the right suggests the customer is considering the logic and facts in the presentation, and gazing to the left suggests more intense concentration based on an emotional consideration. Eyes cast down offer the strongest signal of concentration. However, when customers cast their eyes down, they may be thinking, How can I get my boss to buy this product? or How can I get out of this conversation? When customers look away for an extended period, they probably want to end the meeting.

Significant cultural differences dictate the appropriate level of eye contact between individuals. In the United States salespeople look directly into their customers' eyes when speaking or listening to them. Direct eye contact is a sign of interest in what the customer is saying. In other cultures looking someone in the eye may be a sign of disrespect. For example:

- In Japan looking directly at a subordinate indicates that the subordinate has done something wrong. When a subordinate looks directly into the eyes of his or her supervisor, the subordinate is displaying hostility.

- Arabs dislike eye contact, and Americans often believe that Arabs' eyes dart around. This behavior, unfortunately, gives some Americans the impression that Arabs are shifty.

- Brazilians look at people directly even more than Americans do. Americans tend to find this direct eye contact, when held over a long period of time, to be disconcerting.[14]

Skin color and skin tautness are other facial cues. A customer whose face reddens is signaling that something is wrong. That blush can indicate either anger or embarrassment. Tension and anger show in a tightness around the cheeks, jawline, or neck.

ARMS

A key factor in interpreting arm movements is intensity. Customers will use more arm movement when they are conveying an opinion. Broader and more vigorous movement indicates the customer is more emphatic about the point being communicated verbally.

HANDS

Hand gestures are very expressive. For example, open and relaxed hands are a positive signal, especially with palms facing up. Self-touching gestures typically

Customers communicate through body language. The customer (left panel) on the right is giving a negative signal by raising her hand with her palm turned away from the salesperson on the left. The doctor (right panel) is giving positive signals indicating interest in what the salesperson is saying.

Double Exposure/The Image Bank

Jon Feingersh/The Stock Market

indicate tension. Involuntary gestures, such as tightening of a fist, are good indicators of true feelings. The meanings of hand gestures differ from one culture to another. For example, in the United States the thumbs-up expression means everything is all right, but in the Middle East it is an obscene gesture. In Japan the OK sign made by holding the thumb and forefinger in a circle symbolizes money, but in France it indicates that something is worthless.

LEGS

When customers have uncrossed legs in an open position, they send a message of cooperation, confidence, and friendly interest. Legs crossed away from a salesperson suggest that the sales call is not going well.

BODY LANGUAGE PATTERNS

No single gesture or position defines a specific emotion or attitude. To interpret a customer's feelings, salespeople need to consider the pattern of the signals via a number of channels. As one nonverbal expert put it, "Research shows that many men are most comfortable in conversations with their arms crossed in front of their bodies. It doesn't necessarily mean they're disbelieving or resisting a message. And many women, when they're feeling slightly chilled, will cross their arms in front of them during a conversation."[15] Exhibit 5.6 illustrates the patterns of signals that indicate the customer is reacting positively and negatively to a salesperson's presentation.[16]

DETECTING CUSTOMERS' HIDDEN EMOTIONS AND FEELINGS

In business and social situations, people treat one another politely and are considerate of one another's feelings. Thus salespeople often have difficulty knowing what a customer is really thinking. For example, smiling is the most common way to conceal a strong emotion.

During a product demonstration, salespeople should know which benefits and features are attractive to the customer. Thus salespeople need to know whether a customer's smile is real or just a polite mask. The muscles around the eyes reveal whether a smile is real or polite. When a customer is truly impressed, the muscles around the eyes contract, the skin above the eyes comes down a little, and the eyelids are slightly closed.

Some signals that customers may be hiding their true feelings are as follows:

- Contradictions and verbal mistakes. People often forget what they said previously. They may leak their true feelings through a slip of the tongue or a lapse in memory.
- Differences in two parts of a conversation. In the first part of a conversation, a customer may display some nervousness when asked about the performance of a competitor's product and give a flawless response outlining

EXHIBIT 5.6	Positive Signals	Negative Signals
Patterns of Nonverbal Reactions to Presentation	Uncrossed arms and legs	Crossed arms or legs
	Leaning forward	Leaning backward or turned away from you
	Smiling or otherwise pleasant expression	Furrowed brow, pursed lips, frowning
	Nodding	Shaking head
	Contemplative posture	Fidgeting, distracted
	Eye contact	No eye contact
	Animated, excited reaction	Little change in expression, lifeless

the product's benefits. Later in the conversation, the evaluation of the competitor's product may be much more convoluted.

- Contradictions between verbal and nonverbal messages. For example, facial expression may not match the enthusiasm indicated by verbal comments. Also, a decrease in nonverbal signals may indicate that the customer is making a cautious response.
- Nonverbal signals such as voice tone going up at the end of a sentence, hesitation in the voice, small shrugs, increased self-touching, and stiffer body posture suggest that the customer has concerns.

When customers disguise their true feelings, they are often trying to be polite, not deceptive. To uncover the customer's true feelings and build a relationship, the salesperson needs to encourage the customer to be frank by emphasizing that she or he will benefit from an open exchange of information.

Here are some comments a salesperson can make to encourage forthright discussion:

- Perhaps there is some reason you cannot share the information with me.
- Are you worried about how I might react to what you are telling me?
- I have a sense that there is really more to the story than what you are telling me. Let's put the cards on the table so we can put this issue to rest.

SENDING MESSAGES WITH NONVERBAL COMMUNICATION

USING BODY LANGUAGE

The preceding section described how salespeople can develop a better understanding of their customers by observing their body language. Salespeople can also use body language, voice characteristics, spacing, and appearance to send messages to their customers. This section will explore this aspect of body language. More discussion (such as of handshaking) will occur in future chapters.

During a 30-minute sales call around 800 nonverbal signals are exchanged.[17] Astute salespeople use these signals to communicate more effectively with customers. For example, salespeople should strive to use the positive signals shown in Exhibit 5.6. Cooperative cues indicate to customers that the salesperson sincerely wants to help them satisfy their needs. On the other hand, salespeople should avoid using negative cues. These cues will intimidate customers and make them uncomfortable.

One authority on nonverbal communication issues this important warning: "Be your own counsel and do what comes naturally, becuase the most effective gestures are spontaneous ones. Trying to apply the numerous and often-contradictory 'rules' and guidelines of body language that the experts hand down can turn you into a quivering mass of self-consciousness, steering you way off of your message."[18]

FACE

Nonverbal communications are very difficult to manage. Facial reactions are often involuntary, especially during stressful situations. Lips tense, foreheads wrinkle, and eyes glare without salespeople realizing they are disclosing their feelings to a customer. Salespeople will be able to control their facial reactions only with practice.

As with muscles anywhere else in the body, the coordination of facial muscles requires exercise. Actors realize this need and attend facial-exercise classes to learn to control their reactions. Salespeople are also performers to some extent and need to learn how to use their faces to communicate emotions.

Nothing creates rapport like a smile. The smile should appear natural and comfortable, not a smirk or an exaggerated, clownlike grin. To achieve the right smile, stand before a mirror or a video camera and place your lips in various smiling positions until you find a position that feels natural and comfortable. Then practice the smile until it becomes almost second nature.

EYE CONTACT

Appropriate eye contact varies from situation to situation. People should use direct eye contact when talking in front of a group to indicate sincerity, credibility, and trustworthiness. Glancing from face to face or staring at a wall has the opposite effect. However, staring can overpower customers and make them uncomfortable.

HAND MOVEMENTS

Hand movements can have a dramatic impact. For example, by exposing the palm of the hand, a salesperson indicates openness and receptivity. Slicing hand movements and pointing a finger are very strong signals and should be used to reinforce only the most important points. In most cases pointing a finger should be avoided. This gesture will remind customers of a parent scolding a child. When salespeople make presentations to a group, they often use too few hand gestures. Gestures should be used to drive home a point. But if a salesperson uses too many gestures, acting like an orchestra conductor, people will begin to watch the hands and miss the words.

POSTURE AND BODY MOVEMENTS

Shuffling one's feet and slumping give an impression of a lack of both self-confidence and self-discipline. On the other hand, an overly erect posture, such as that of a military cadet, suggests rigidity. Salespeople should let comfort be their guide when searching for the right posture.

To get an idea of what looks good and feels good, stand in front of a mirror and shift your weight until tension in your back and neck is at a minimum. Then gently pull your shoulders up and back and elevate your head. Practice walking by taking a few steps. Keep the pace deliberate, not halting; deliberate, controlled movements indicate confidence and empathy.[19]

MATCHING THE CUSTOMER'S COMMUNICATION STYLE

Salespeople develop better rapport when they match the verbal and nonverbal behavior of their customers. Consider a salesperson from New York selling to a

The open hands on the left are a positive signal by a salesperson. The intertwined fingers in the middle indicate that the salesperson is expressing his power and authority. On the right the salesperson is playing with his hands, indicating underlying tension.

Michael J. Hruby

customer in Texas. Communication in this sales interaction will be effective only if the salesperson slows his or her rate of speech and avoids using expressions only another New Yorker would understand.

This matching process also extends to body language. Michael McCasky, writing in the *Harvard Business Review,* notes, "In moments of great rapport, a remarkable pattern of nonverbal communication can develop. Two people will mirror each other's movements—dropping a hand, shifting their body at exactly the same time." The more customers and salespeople share language, speech patterns, and nonverbal behavior, the greater the sense of rapport and mutual understanding they will have. However, a little mirroring goes a long way. Customers may become irritated if they realize you are using this technique.

THE ROLE OF SPACE AND PHYSICAL CONTACT IN COMMUNICATION

The physical space between a customer and a salesperson can affect the customer's reaction to a sales presentation.

DISTANCE DURING INTERACTIONS

Exhibit 5.7 shows the four distance zones people use when interacting in business and social situations. The intimate zone is reserved primarily for a person's closest relationships; the personal zone for close friends and those who share special interests; the social zone for business transactions and other impersonal relationships; and the public zone for speeches, teachers in classrooms, and passersby. The exact sizes of the intimate and personal zones depend on age, gender, culture, and race. For example, the social zone for Latinos is much closer than that for North Americans. Latinos tend to conduct business transactions so close together that North Americans feel uncomfortable.

Customers may react negatively when they believe that salespeople are invading their intimate or personal space. To show the negative reaction, customers may assume a defensive posture by moving back or folding their arms. Although approaching too close can generate a negative reaction, standing too far away can create an image of aloofness, conceit, or unsociability.

In general, salespeople should begin customer interactions at the far end of the social zone and not move closer until an initial rapport has been established. If

| EXHIBIT 5.7 | Distance Zones for Interactions |

Intimate zone: 0–2 feet

Social zone: 4–12 feet

Personal zone: 2–4 feet

Public zone: beyond 12 feet

the buyer indicates that a friendlier relationship has developed, the salesperson should move closer.

TOUCHING

People fall into two touching groups: contact and noncontact. Contact people usually see noncontact people as cold and unfriendly. On the other hand, noncontact people view contact people as overly friendly and obtrusive.

Although some customers may accept a hand on their backs or a touch on their shoulders, salespeople should limit touching to a handshake. Touching clearly enters a customer's intimate space and may be considered rude and threatening—an invasion.

APPEARANCE

Physical appearance, specifically dress style, is an aspect of nonverbal communication that affects the customer's evaluation of the salesperson. Two priorities in dressing for business are (1) getting customers to notice you in a positive way and (2) getting customers to trust you. If salespeople overdress, their clothing may distract from their sales presentation. Proper attire and grooming, however, can give salespeople additional poise and confidence.

At one time dressing for work was simple: You just reached in the closet and picked from your wardrobe of blue, gray, and pinstripe suits. Today things are not that simple. With casual days and dress-down Fridays, styles and dress codes vary considerably from office to office. During a given day a salesperson may have to visit his or her company's and customers' offices, each of which may have a different dress code. Some suggestions for proper dress follow.

Business clothes project an image of the salesperson, the salesperson's company, and the product. Salespeople will feel most comfortable using their own natural style plus some common sense. Standards of acceptable business dress vary in different areas of the country, and salespeople should adapt their clothing styles accordingly. Consider corporate culture, too. How do the executives of the company dress? What image do they project? Finally, remember the customer: The salesperson's business dress should make both of them comfortable.

MATCH THE CUSTOMER'S DRESS

The appropriate style of dress depends on the person's occupation, social status, age, physical size, and geographic location. Salespeople can get some useful clues about appropriate styles by observing their customers. Salespeople should attempt to match the styles of their customers and avoid dressing more stylishly or expensively. Dressing better than their customers dress may create an impression of greater authority but also may make customers feel uncomfortable and defensive. Before visiting a new prospect, a salesperson should find out what the dress code is, particularly if visiting a branch office or a manufacturing site, where the formal standards that typically prevail at corporate headquarters may not apply.

Salespeople should wear classic dresses, suits, and accessories. High-fashion clothing should be avoided; it costs too much, goes out of style too soon, and may look unprofessional or unbusinesslike unless the salesperson works in the fashion industry.

CASUAL DRESS CODES

Many companies are adopting more casual dress codes or instituting dress-down days. Norm Pifer, national sales manager at Alco Chemical, believes dressing down is good for sales, particularly for salespeople working in heavy industry. "Dressing down gives the appearance of a willingness to get one's hands dirty.

And successful salespeople often get their hands dirty." On the other hand, Sean Ciemiewicz argues, "When a rep wears a suit, he blends in with all of the other people a buyer is going to meet in the day." Read Selling Scenario 5.1 to find out what happened to one rep who took "casual" too casually.

If you elect to dress casually, you need to pay greater attention to your clothes because the clothes will be more revealing than a business suit. You must remember that you are going to work, not shuffling around the house. Wearing shorts and sport shirts suggests that you are confusing the boundaries between work and play, your career and your social life. Knit shirts and khaki pants are the basics, but you might want to show more imagination and personal flair. Men can show more flair by wearing a dressier pair of pants and a long- or short-sleeve shirt made from a fabric with more color and texture. Women can show a sense of fun and self-confidence by adding more color and wearing skirts, blouses, and accessories.

HINTS FOR MEN

The suit is the focal garment in business dress, particularly when you are interacting with upper-level decision makers. In general, darker suits give a more authoritative image; lighter colors create a friendlier one. Pinstripes convey the most authority, followed in descending order by solids, chalk stripes, and plaids (which must be very subtle). Natural fibers such as wool (or wool-polyester blends that look and feel like wool) are preferable. They look better and wear better than most synthetics. Cottons and linens, while comfortable, wrinkle too easily.

Solid white shirts are the most effective, adding credibility; blues and other pale pastels are also popular. Shirts, as a rule, should be lighter than the suit, and the tie should be darker than the shirt. Shirt stripes should always be close together, clearly defined, and of one coordinating color on a white background.

Ties are important indicators of the salesperson's status, credibility, and personality. A good rule is to wear suits and shirts in basic colors and let the tie provide the accent color. The tie tip should come just to the belt buckle, and its width should harmonize with the width of the suit lapels. Bow ties give off negative signals, and tie pins and clasps are currently out of style. Silk is the best choice for tie material; it looks elegant and wears well.

As for accessories, the less, the better. Stay away from bracelets, earrings, and pins and wear simple, small cuff links. Shoes should be black, brown, or cordovan in lace-up, wingtip, Gucci-type buckle, or all-leather, slip-on styles. Never wear shoes with multiple colors, platforms, or high heels with business dress. Most belts are acceptable. Buckles should be small, clean, and traditional. Attaché cases are positive symbols of success.

HINTS FOR WOMEN

In 1977, when John Molloy wrote *Dress for Success*, businesswomen were advised to wear only very conservative navy or gray suits, tailored blouses, and string ties. They were entering professions dominated by men (such as selling), and they needed to give clear signals that they were serious about their jobs and were members of the company team. In those days the more women in these "uniforms" looked like men, the more easily they were accepted in the business world.

Today, thanks to those pioneers, women just beginning their careers have the luxury of dressing with more flair and style while still maintaining a dignified, professional look. Women in business can now signal that they are good at, and relaxed about, their jobs and that they know the difference between business and private life. A good business wardrobe still starts with navy, black, and gray suits

WHAT'S WRONG WITH THE WAY I'M DRESSED?

It didn't take Lawrence Mandel long to realize he had made a huge mistake. "Just get back from the links?" the prospect asked, eyeing Mandel's yellow golf shirt and khaki pants suspiciously.

"Uh—we're business casual in our office," Mandel weakly replied. During the remainder of his sales call, Mandel knew he wasn't going to get the business. What made it worse was the prospect's continual heel-tapping and watch-glancing. Mandel was right. He didn't get the business. "I lost all credibility by not coming in there in a suit."

In today's mixed-up world of fashion, it's often hard for a salesperson to know how to dress. Casual? Conservative?

According to Sam Parker, cofounder of Justsell.com, it's best to dress one level above your prospect. "If he's wearing a sportcoat, you put on a suit. Nobody is going to look at you poorly because you are slightly overdressed."

And that means one level greater, not two. Don't go overboard in dressing up. Bob Mander, while waiting for a prospect to see him, heard someone in the prospect's office yell to the prospect, "There's a suit here to see you!" "I went home and bought a sportcoat," Mander said.

Sources: Personal experience; Melinda Liogs, "Does Image Matter?" *Sales and Marketing Management*, March 2001, pp. 52–56.

worn with light-colored blouses. But you can also add suits in more cheerful shades, wool or silk dresses with jackets, and blazers with coordinated skirts. As with menswear, women's suits look and wear best in natural fibers or blends that look and feel like natural fibers. Women should choose a suit whose jacket and skirt lengths complement their figure shape and height. The suit should be stylish without being so trendy that it will look dated in a short time.

Women's blouses have a little more variety than men's shirts in color, style, and fabric. Cotton and silk are the best fabric choices; they are much more professional looking than sheer polyester or slithery silk imitations. Keep blouses businesslike, feminine but tailored, soft but not see-through, plain or with small prints.

Choose shoes and hose to complement the outfit. Black, brown, navy, or cordovan are always acceptable shoe colors. Tailored, classic pumps should have heels no higher than 1 or $1\frac{1}{2}$ inches (especially if the job requires walking) and should be combined with neutral or color-coordinated hose to look both professional and feminine. Fishnet or patterned hose, ankle straps, chunky loafers, and trendy boots are best left for after-hours wear.

Accessories such as ties, scarves, simple pins, gold chains, and plain watches can make even a plain, dark suit look dressy and businesslike. Chunky jewelry and clanking bracelets are out. Silk scarves can add flair and a touch of color if tied or draped attractively. Scarves are becoming more popular and acceptable today than the so-called ties that were formerly a required part of the uniform.

The businesswoman's hairstyle should share many of the same characteristics her clothes do: subtle, formal, comfortable, and easy to care for. Hair length is not an issue, but it must be managed effectively.

COMMUNICATING IN A HIGH-TECHNOLOGY ENVIRONMENT

Salespeople use technology like e-mail, fax, and voice mail to communicate with their customers. You call the customer and get his or her voice mail. You call again, and the secretary tells you to fax the information. You call again. The secretary says the prospect is out of town and suggests you e-mail him or her. Technology makes the transfer of information fast and easy. But it also holds the salesperson at arm's length and makes it difficult to develop rapport. High tech

Developments in technology enable salespeople to improve their communications with customers by using numerous modes, including sending e-mails from a mobile phone.

Courtesy Motorola Corporation

doesn't replace face-to-face interactions; it merely supplements and enhances personal exchanges. Following are some suggestions for putting a high touch into high tech:[20]

- Accept the need to communicate through electronic media, but don't be lulled into thinking that immediacy means the same thing as intimacy in communications.

- Learn the customer's preferences and find out which tools the customer uses and how she or he likes to communicate. Adapt the content to the customer's preferred communication style.

- Avoid "techno overkill"—use electronic communications when speed is critical, but written communication may be better when the customer wants to study the information at his or her leisure.

- Make the communication meaningful. Customers are drowning in information. Use visual graphs to reduce data. Don't send junk faxes and don't talk to your customer's voice mail until the time runs out. Busy customers like some chit-chat, but don't get carried away.

- Customize your messages. Replace a general reference with a meaningful specific, such as customer name, company name, and other details important to the customer. Develop a personal hallmark, such as a unique cover for a fax. Use a fresh message on voice mail each day. Tell callers in the message if a time limit exists for your voice mail. Offer the option to talk to someone immediately.

- Use speed to impress customers. Speed is invaluable for damage control. Use technology to exceed a customer's expectations, such as responding immediately to urgent calls via fax or e-mail.

- Don't deliver bad news via e-mail; rather, use e-mail to arrange a meeting to discuss the issue.

- Use short, clear sentences when communicating internationally. In some parts of the world, the written language is very formal and quite different from the spoken language. Err on the side of caution and write in a formal tone. It's easy and natural to progress from formal to friendly, but it weakens your position if you are forced to step backward from friendly to formal.

Because of its prevalence in selling, we will also discuss the appropriate use of technology in future chapters (prospecting in Chapter 7, interacting with voice mail in Chapter 8, strengthening the presentation in Chapter 10, and so on).

ADJUSTING FOR CULTURAL DIFFERENCES

Salespeople need to recognize that business practices differ around the world. For example, Americans tend to think that agreements require formal, written contracts. However, many other cultures have strong moral principles in which verbal agreements are just as binding as written agreements. People in these cultures may find an insistence on written contracts insulting because they believe their honor is being questioned.

Americans assume that all the terms in a contract, such as price and delivery, remain constant throughout the contract. However, Greek businesspeople view a contractual agreement as the initial step in the negotiation. After the agreement is signed, Greek customers keep negotiating until the products or services are delivered. In Korea the common practice is to adjust the terms of a contract if changes occur in the economy or in the price of raw materials.

Customers in different cultures also process verbal and nonverbal information differently. In **low-context cultures** such as the United States and Germany, words carry most of the information in communications. In **high-context cultures** such as Japan and Arab countries, more information is contained in factors surrounding the communications—for example, the background, associations, and basic values of the salesperson and customer. In a high-context culture, who the salesperson is has as much importance as or more importance than a formal analysis of the product benefits. Some other differences between high- and low-context cultures are shown in Exhibit 5.8.[21]

USE OF LANGUAGE

Communication in international selling often takes place in English because English is likely to be the only language salespeople and customers have in common. To communicate effectively with customers whose native language is not English, salespeople need to be careful about the words and expressions they use. People who use English in international selling should observe the following rules:

- Use common English words that a customer would learn during the first two years of studying the language. For example, use *expense* rather than *expenditure*, or *stop* instead of *cease*.

EXHIBIT 5.8

Differences between High- and Low-Context Cultures

Issue	High Context	Low Context
Person's word	Is his or her bond	Not to be relied on; "get it in writing"
Lawyers	Not very important	Very important
Space	People share common space and stand close to each other	People have a private space around themselves and resent intrusions into their space
Time	Everything is dealt with eventually	Wasting time is to be avoided
Negotiations	Lengthy so that the parties can get a chance to know one another	Accomplished quickly
Competitive bidding	Not very common	Very common

This American salesperson needs to recognize the differences between communicating in a high-context Arab culture versus a low-context American culture.

Derek Berwin/The Image Bank

- Use words that do not have multiple meanings. For example, *right* has many meanings, whereas *accurate* is more specific. When you use words that have several meanings, recognize that nonnative speakers will usually use the most common meaning to interpret what you are saying.
- Avoid slang expressions peculiar to American culture, such as "slice of life," "struck out," "wade through the figures," and "run that by me again."
- Use rules of grammar more strictly than you would in everyday speech. Make sure you express your thoughts in complete sentences, with a noun and a verb.
- Use action-specific verbs, as in *start the motor,* rather than action-general verbs, as in *get the motor going.*
- Never use vulgar expressions, tell off-color jokes, or make religious references.

Even if you are careful about the words you use, misunderstandings can still arise because terms have different meanings, even among people from different English-speaking countries. For example, in the United States *tabling a proposal* means "delaying a decision," but in England it means "taking immediate action." In England promising to do something by the end of the day means doing it when you have finished what you are working on now, not within 24 hours. In England, *bombed* means the negotiations were successful, whereas in the United States this term has the opposite meaning.

TIME AND SCHEDULING

International salespeople need to understand the varying perceptions of time in general and the time it takes for business activities to occur in different countries. For example, in Latin American and Arab countries people are not strict about keeping appointments at the designated times. If you show up for an appointment on time in these cultures, you may have to wait several hours for the meeting to start. Lunch is at 3:00 P.M. in Spain, 12:00 noon in Germany, 1:00 P.M. in England, and 11:00 A.M. in Norway. In Greece no one makes telephone calls between 2:00 P.M. and 5:00 P.M. The British arrive at their desks at 9:30 A.M., but like to do paperwork and have a cup of tea before getting any calls. The French, like the Germans, like to start early in the day, frequently having working breakfasts. Restaurants close at 9:00 P.M. in Norway, just when dinner is starting in Spain. The best time to reach high-level Western European executives is after 7:00 P.M., when daily activities have slowed down and they are continuing to work for a few more hours. However, Germans start going home at 4:00 P.M.[22]

BODY LANGUAGE

Gestures and body language can have different meanings across the globe. For example, the thumbs-up gesture is considered offensive in the Middle East, rude in Australia, and a sign of OK in France. It's rude to cross your arms in Turkey. Crossing your feet and showing the bottoms of your shoe soles is insulting in Japan. Also, the Japanese value the ability to sit quietly, and can view a fidgety American as uncontrolled. In Korea eye contact is considered rude, while in Muslim countries, eye contact is not supposed to occur between men and women.[23]

Summary

This chapter discussed the principles of communication and how they can be used to build trust in relationships, improve selling effectiveness, and reduce misunderstandings. The communication process consists of a sender, who encodes information and transmits messages, and a receiver, who decodes the messages. A communication breakdown can occur when the sender does a poor encoding job, when the receiver has difficulty decoding, and when noise and the environment interfere with the transmission of the message.

Effective communication requires a two-way flow of information. At different times in the interaction, both parties will act as sender and receiver. This two-way process enables salespeople to adapt their sales approach to the customer's needs and communication style.

Suggestions were provided for interpreting verbal and nonverbal communications from customers and for sending verbal and nonverbal communications to customers. Listening is a valuable communication skill that enables salespeople to adapt to various situations. To listen effectively, salespeople need to be actively thinking about what the customer is saying and how to draw out more information. Some suggestions for actively collecting information from customers are to repeat, restate, clarify, summarize the customer's comments, and demonstrate an interest in what the customer is saying.

More than 50 percent of communication is nonverbal. Nonverbal messages sent by customers are conveyed by body language. The five channels of body language communication are body angle, face, arms, hands, and legs. No single channel can be used to determine the feelings or attitudes of customers. Salespeople need to analyze the body language pattern composed of all five channels to determine when a customer is nervous, bored, or suspicious.

When communicating verbally with customers, salespeople must be careful to use words and expressions their customers will understand. Effective communication is facilitated through the use of concrete, neutral words, rather than abstract, emotional words.

Asking questions gets the customer involved in the interaction and provides additional information that can be used to develop and adapt the sales presentation. Open questions encourage complete and thoughtful responses. In addition, questions should be asked at intervals throughout the conversation, should be short and simple, and should not suggest an appropriate answer.

Salespeople can use nonverbal communication to convey information to customers. In addition to knowing how to use the five channels of body language, salespeople need to know the appropriate distances between themselves and their customers for different types of communications and relationships.

Salespeople should learn to use their physical appearance and dress to create a favorable impression on customers. In general, salespeople should try to match the dress of the customers they are calling on.

Finally, two-way communication increases when salespeople adjust their communication styles to the styles of their customers. In making such adjustments, salespeople need to be sensitive to cultural differences when selling internationally and in diverse subcultures.

KEY TERMS

active listening   132
articulation   128
body language   135
closed questions   129
decoding   122
encoding   122
high-context culture   145
inflection   128
loudness   128
low-context culture   145
noises   123

nonverbal communication   124
one-way communication   124
open questions   129
response time   124
speaking–listening differential   131
SPIN   129
two-way communication   122
verbal communication   124
voice characteristics   127
word picture   126

Questions and Problems

1. Suppose you're a male calling on a male prospect who uses language that is degrading to women. Should you mirror his language in order to make him like you and feel comfortable dealing with you?

2. Why is two-way communication preferable to one-way communication?

3. Make a chart with three columns: item of clothing, what I want my clothing to communicate to others, and what others will think my clothing is communicating. In the first column, list the clothing you are wearing now. In the second column, describe the message you want to communicate. Have someone else fill in the third column, describing what the clothing communicates to him or her.

4. Develop a metaphor that helps explain to a college student the merits of enrolling in your selling course.

5. What do the following body language cues indicate?
   a. Tapping a finger or pencil on a desk.
   b. Stroking the chin and leaning forward.
   c. Leaning back in a chair with arms folded across the chest.
   d. Sitting in the middle of a bench or sofa.
   e. Assuming the same posture as the person with whom you are communicating.

6. Understanding nonverbal communication is more important to salespeople than understanding verbal communication. Do you agree? Why or why not?

7. Many people do not like to hear the words *sell* or *sold*. Why would you be unlikely to say the following to a friend: Look at the new personal computer I was sold yesterday?

8. Why do you think lawyers wouldn't be as important in a high-context culture, as opposed to a low-context one?

9. Ross Thomas is a 25-year-old computer salesperson who calls on insurance companies, banks, and department stores. He views himself as a "free thinker," wears the latest apparel and hairstyles, and has both ears and his tongue pierced. At present his hair is quite long, giving him an "in" look. He buys casual clothing because he can wear it at work and for leisure activities. What advice would you give Ross about his appearance? Why? Should he dress differently when calling on banks versus department stores?

10. As a product category, carbonated drinks are referred to with many different labels, depending on where you live: pop, soda, coke, soda pop, and so on. Choose the word least like that you normally hear used. Now ask a friend if he or she would like to have a (use the selected word here) and record the reaction to your choice of words.

Karen Clements, a sales representative for Arco, calls on Thomas Coleman, the beverage buyer for Giant Markets, a chain of 12 supermarkets headquartered in Vancouver, British Columbia. Clements is trying to persuade Coleman to carry a new line of decaffeinated flavored coffees.

CLEMENTS: How's business?

COLEMAN: Well, now that you ask, sales have slowed down. I was just looking over our sales analysis and I am concerned about the number of different coffee brands we are carrying.

CLEMENTS: Thomas, maybe our new line of decaffeinated flavors will add some excitement to the beverage section. They are really attracting a lot of attention. Did you see our ad in *Progressive Grocer*?

COLEMAN: I saw the ad last week. I don't see how I can . . .

CLEMENTS: Good! Then you know all about the test market results for the six new decaffeinated flavors. Our research shows that a lot of elderly consumers like having flavored coffee after dinner but are afraid that the caffeine will keep them up. The new line has done particularly well with the elderly segment.

COLEMAN: Well, I can understand the concern about caffeine, but . . .

CLEMENTS: Everyone is more health conscious now. Customers really want more health foods—low fat, low cholesterol, no additives. We really think these decaffeinated coffees fit right into this trend. We have developed an exciting marketing program to get you to carry the new line. If you agree to stock four of the six decaffeinated flavors and feature the line in your weekly ad, we'll give you a 20 percent discount on your first order and pay for the space in your weekly ad.

COLEMAN: I have to stock four flavors?

CLEMENTS: I knew you'd be excited! We also can arrange a special in-store tasting for your customers.

COLEMAN: That sounds interesting. You know our target market is younger, blue-collar workers. Do you have any data on which flavor sells best to that segment?

CLEMENTS: Younger people like all the flavors. Pick the ones you like, and I'm sure they will sell well. The mocha and vanilla are excellent. Can I take your order?

COLEMAN: I've got an appointment coming in soon. Could you leave some material that I can look through? I'll get back to you.

CLEMENTS: Sure. I've got some brochures in my briefcase. Can we set up an appointment?

COLEMAN: Well, business has been really hectic. Let me give you a call. Thanks for stopping by.

Questions

1. Is Karen Clements a good listener? Why or why not?
2. What indicates that Clements has something to learn about communication skills?
3. Rewrite this dialogue to show how Clements should have handled this sales call.

Ann Robinson is a sales representative for OfficeMax, an office supply retailer and wholesaler. She has just walked into the office of Michelle Leder, the office manager at City of Walden. Robinson is 25 years old and has been working for OfficeMax for six months. She is dressed in a blue pinstripe suit. Leder is about 50 years old and is wearing a pair of slacks and a casual blouse. She is sitting behind her desk, leaning back with her arms crossed.

ROBINSON [walking around the desk to shake hands with Leder]: Good morning, Ms. Leder. It's a pleasure to meet you. How are you today?

LEDER [eye contact is mostly with some papers on her desk]: I'm fine, I suppose. Of course, I *was* expecting you 15 minutes ago. [looking at her watch and sighing] I have an appointment in 10 minutes, so I don't have much time.

ROBINSON: I'm only five minutes late. I got held up in the traffic around the mall. You know how it is this time of day. It's always backed up!

LEDER [moving around in her chair and crossing her arms again]: OK. Maybe it wasn't 15 minutes. What can I do for you?

ROBINSON: I would like to talk to you about our new program for providing office supplies more economically to our partners in the government sector. The program . . .

LEDER [interrupting, frowning]: Before you waste a lot of time, we just placed a large office supply order with Chestnut's. We really don't need supplies at this point.

ROBINSON [blinking rapidly, crossing her arms, speech rate increasing]: That's too bad. Our program could have reduced your office supply costs by 30 percent.

LEDER [uncrossing arms, leaning forward]: Really?

ROBINSON [starting to rise and putting on her coat]: Yes, but I guess I'm too late. Well, maybe next time. Goodbye.

Questions

1. How could Robinson have communicated better with Leder by using nonverbal methods?
2. How did Robinson make a mistake in reading the nonverbal messages sent by Leder?

Additional References

"Body Speak: What Are You Saying?" *Successful Meetings* 49, October 2001, p. 51.

Burgoon, Judee K.; David B. Buller; and W. Gill Woodall. *Nonverbal Communication: The Unspoken Dialogue.* New York: McGraw-Hill, 1996.

Castleberry, Stephen B.; C. David Shepherd; and Rick E. Ridnour. "Effective Interpersonal Listening in the Personal Selling Environment: Conceptualization, Measurement, and Nomological Validity." *Journal of Marketing Theory and Practice*, Winter 1999, pp. 30–38.

Comer, Lucette B., and Tanya Drollinger. "Active Empathetic Listening and Selling Success: A Conceptual Framework." *Journal of Personal Selling and Sales Management* 19, Winter 1999, pp. 15–29.

"Forget the Dog & Pony Shows." http://www.chally.com/enews/tip_forgetshows.html as viewed on March 30, 2002.

Fulfer, Mac. "Nonverbal Communication: How to Read What's Plain as the Nose . . . or Eyelid . . . or Chin . . . on Their Faces." *Journal of Organizational Excellence* 20, Spring 2001, pp. 19–27.

Johnson, Rob. "Body Talk." *Supply Management,* November 30, 2000, pp. 38–39.

Locker, Kitty O., and Stephen Kyo Kaczmarek. *Business Communication: Building Critical Skills.* New York: McGraw-Hill/Irwin, 2001.

Lustig, Myron, and Jolene Koester. *Intercultural Competence: Interpersonal Communication across Cultures.* 3rd ed. New York: Longman, 1999.

McKenzie, Samuel. "Break Nervous Habits Before They Become Distractions." *Presentations,* February 2002, p. 62.

Mornell, Pierre. "The Sounds of Silence." *Inc.,* February 2001, pp. 117–18.

Reid, David A.; Ellen Bolman Pullins; and Richard E. Plank. "The Impact of Purchase Situation on Salesperson Communication Behaviors in Business Markets." *Industrial Marketing Management* 31:3 (2002), pp. 205–13.

Sheppard, C. David; Stephen Castleberry; and Rick Ridnour. "Linking Effective Listening with Salesperson Performance: An Exploratory Study." *Journal of Business & Industrial Marketing* 12 (1997), pp. 315–32.

Simons, Tad. "Mastering the Art of Metaphor." *Presentations,* June 2001, pp. 43–52.

Woodward, Nancy. "Do You Speak Internet?" *HRMagazine,* April 1999, pp. S12–S17.

Young, Robert. *Understanding Misunderstandings: A Practical Guide to More Successful Human Interaction.* Austin, TX: University of Texas Press, 1999.

Zielinski, Dave. "Body Language Myths." *Presentations,* April 2001, pp. 36–42.

Chapter

6 Adaptive Selling for Relationship Building

SOME QUESTIONS ANSWERED IN THIS CHAPTER ARE:

- What is adaptive selling?

- Why is it important for salespeople to practice adaptive selling?

- What kind of knowledge do salespeople need to practice adaptive selling?

- How can salespeople acquire this knowledge?

- How can salespeople adapt their sales strategies, presentations, and social styles to various situations?

Personal selling is the most effective marketing communication medium because it allows salespeople to tailor their presentations to each customer. Salespeople can ask questions to determine the customer's needs and make a presentation to show how their products will satisfy those specific needs. By listening and observing nonverbal behaviors, they can tell when the presentation is not working and change their approach on the spot.

By comparison, advertising managers are restricted to delivering the same advertising campaign to all customers. The message in the campaign may work for the "typical" customer, but a lot of customers will have different needs and will not be influenced by the message. It may take months for an advertising manager to recognize and change a campaign that is not effective.

Effective salespeople take advantage of this unique opportunity. They use their knowledge of the customer's buying process (Chapter 4) and finely tuned communication skills (Chapter 5) to learn about their customers and select effective sales strategies. Effective salespeople adapt their selling strategies and approaches to the selling situation. This chapter examines how salespeople can communicate effectively with their customers by practicing adaptive selling.

"You really have a feeling of personal accomplishment when you make a big sale."

Maki Sartor, Delta

PROFILE

Maki Sartor came to the United States from Japan in 1981. After earning an undergraduate degree in psychology and an MBA from Louisiana Tech, she went to work for American Airlines. She started at the bottom, working her way up from telephone reservation agent and airport ticket counter agent to developing teaching manuals for the Sabre reservation system when it was introduced in Japan. Then she went to work for Delta in Atlanta, Delta's corporate headquarters, as the assistant to the regional manager in charge of the Asian Pacific market.

Maki now is an account manager for Delta in Dallas. She calls on travel agents and their corporate customers, encouraging them to use Delta's automation systems, such as WORLDSPAN and Delta, and its global airline alliance partners, such as Air France and AeroMexico, for travel services. In addition, she works with philanthropic organizations to build Delta's reputation and image in the local community.

"It's really challenging selling for Delta in Dallas. This is American's home base, and they have more than four times the number of daily flights than we have. What I do is look for companies that have heavy traffic to our hubs in Atlanta, Cincinnati, and Salt Lake City. When we are on equal footing in terms of flights, I can beat American by servicing the customer better. For example, we can offer substantial savings to customers if they make reservations over the Internet and use electronic ticketing. Electronic ticketing saves us money by reducing paperwork, and we pass this savings along to our customers.

"To be successful in selling you really need to be sensitive to the customers' needs, understand what is important to them, and then show them how you can satisfy their needs better than a competitor. A recent experience we had with a large corporate account illustrates this point.

"One of my colleagues asked me to help him with a large corporate account. The customer was a subsidiary of a Japanese company. All the managers were American except the two top officers, who were Japanese. These Japanese executives were making their airline reservations through a small local ethnic agency, even though the firm could get significantly lower prices by buying tickets on Delta through their corporate agency. My colleague asked me to make a call with him, since he had tried and failed repeatedly to get the Japanese executives to use the corporate agency.

"We met in the conference room. I apologized to the Americans in the room and started to talk with the executives in Japanese. They knew that the corporate agency offered lower fares through rebates on tickets purchased, but they didn't think that the savings would be credited to their expense budgets. They thought the purchasing travel department would get all the credit for the cost savings, and thus they had no personal incentive to use the corporate agency. They did not want to express this concern to Americans but were comfortable talking to me about it in Japanese. When I explained that each budget was credited with the rebates it generated, they started to use the corporate account and fly Delta.

"The thing I like about my job is the independence and flexibility. I have goals to meet, but it is up to me to develop a plan to meet my goals. I don't have to show up at an office every day and work from eight to five. I work longer than 40 hours a week, but I can set my own schedule. I liked working in the corporate office for the Asian Pacific regional manager, but it is more fun going out into the field and meeting with customers face to face. You really have a feeling of personal accomplishment when you make a big sale."

Visit Our Website @ www.delta-air.com

TYPES OF PRESENTATIONS

Salespeople can choose from a number of presentation types. This text will examine the three most common: (1) the standard memorized presentation, (2) the outlined presentation, and (3) the customized presentation.

STANDARD MEMORIZED PRESENTATION

The **standard memorized presentation,** also called a *canned presentation,* is a completely memorized sales talk. The salesperson presents the same selling points in the same order to all customers. Some companies insist that their salespeople memorize the entire presentation and deliver it word for word. Others believe that salespeople should be free to make some minor adjustments.

The standard memorized presentation ensures that the salesperson will provide complete and accurate information about the firm's products and policies. Because it includes the best techniques and methods, the standard memorized presentation brings new salespeople up to speed quickly and gives them confidence. Some pharmaceutical salespeople use a standard memorized presentation because they need to accurately communicate technical information to doctors in a short period of time. This type of presentation is also used in telemarketing and direct selling. However, the effectiveness of the standard memorized presentation is limited because it offers no opportunity for the salesperson to tailor the presentation to the needs of the specific customer.

OUTLINED PRESENTATION

The **outlined presentation** is a prearranged presentation that usually includes a standard introduction, standard answers to common objections raised by customers, and a standard method for getting the customer to place an order. An example of an outlined presentation appears in Exhibit 6.1.

An outlined presentation can be very effective because it is well organized. It is more informal and natural than the standard memorized presentation and provides more opportunity for the customer to participate in the sales interaction. It also permits some flexibility in the approach used to present the key points.

CUSTOMIZED PRESENTATION

The **customized presentation** is a written and/or oral presentation based on a detailed analysis of the customer's needs. This type of presentation offers an opportunity to use the communication principles discussed in the last chapter to discover the customer's needs and problems and propose the most effective solution for satisfying those needs. The customer recognizes the sales representative as a professional who is helping to solve problems, not just sell products. Cultivating this view is an important step in developing a partnering relationship.

Each of the presentation types just discussed involves a different level of skill, cost, and flexibility. Standard memorized presentations can be delivered at a low cost by unskilled salespeople with little training. On the other hand, the customized presentation can be very costly, requiring highly skilled people to analyze the customer's needs. Salespeople have the greatest opportunity to adapt their presentations to customer needs when using the customized presentation and the least opportunity when using the standard memorized presentation. The next section discusses the importance of adapting sales presentations.

ADAPTIVE SELLING AND SALES SUCCESS

Salespeople practice **adaptive selling** when they use different sales presentations for different customers and alter their sales presentation during a sales call based on the nature of the sales situation.[1] An extreme example of nonadaptive selling is using the standard memorized presentation, since the same presentation is used for all customers. The customized presentation illustrates adaptive selling because the presentation is tailored to the specific needs of the customer.

EXHIBIT 6.1

Example of an
Outlined Presentation

Scenario: A Procter & Gamble Salesperson Calling on a Grocery Store Manager

Step in Outlined Sales Presentation	Say Something Like This
1. Reinforce past success.	Good morning, Mr. Babcock. I was talking with one of your stockers, and he said our Crest end-of-aisle display was very popular with customers last weekend. He said he had to restock it three times. Looks like you made a wise decision to go with that program.
2. Reiterate customer's needs.	I know that profits and fast turns are what you are always looking for.
3. Introduce new Sure antiperspirant campaign.	We have a new campaign coming up for our Sure line.
4. Explain ad campaign and coupon drops.	We will be running a new set of commercials on all three network news programs . . . Also, we'll be adding an insert in the Sunday coupon section with a 35-cents-off coupon.
5. Explain case allowances.	We are going to give you a $1.20 case allowance for every case of Sure you buy today.
6. Ask for end-of-aisle display and order of cases.	I would propose that you erect an end-of-aisle display on aisle 7 . . . and that you order 20 cases.
7. Thank manager for the order.	Thank you, and I know the results will be just as good as they were for our Crest promotion.

Adaptive selling is featured in this textbook because this approach forces the salesperson to practice the marketing concept. It emphasizes the importance of satisfying customer needs and building long-term partnerships. And being adaptable increases buyer trust and commitment[2] and results in higher sales performance.[3] Building Partnerships 6.1 illustrates how international salespeople build better customer relationships by adapting their sales approaches.

The communication principles described in Chapter 5 are required to practice adaptive selling successfully. For example, a Briggs & Stratton sales representative

Remember that the world is made up of a wide variety of people, not all of whom think or reason the way you do.

K.C. Tanner/SupterStock

ADAPTABILITY CAN BE QUITE TIRING SOMETIMES

"Great, it looks good to me," the prospect summarized, gathering some papers from the table. "Oh, are we still on for dinner?"

The seller agreed, excited by the sale, and looking forward to building a stronger relationship and partnership with the company. "That would be great. But remember, it's my treat."

"Sure. Be ready at 2," the prospect said as he walked toward the door. "I'll pick you up at the hotel."

"Two?" the seller said, confused. "I thought we were going out this evening, not this afternoon."

"That's 2 A.M., not 2 P.M.," he said, laughing as he left the room.

Before you start rolling your eyes and thinking the prospect is probably overstepping propriety, you need to know the location of this little incident: Buenos Aires.

Nighttime is when Buenos Aires, Argentina, and much of South America comes alive. It's not uncommon for

business dinners to become "all-nighters." The challenge for salespeople not accustomed to this is to adapt to the situation.

There are other adaptations needed when selling in this country and in South America. Business dinners are much more common than business lunches, because many people like to go home for a few hours in the middle of the day. When in Argentina, don't plan on using the phone to conduct business. Not only are the phones less than reliable, but most Argentineans find phones to be too impersonal a form of communication. Meetings will probably occur after the time for which they were scheduled. And make sure your shoes are shined and your clothes pressed—how you look makes a much bigger impact than in America. Adapting is the way of life for salespeople selling in other cultures.

Sources: Jane Lasky, "How to Be Culturally Correct in South America," *The Secured Lender* 57, May/June 2001, pp. 38–42; *Argentina Business: The Portable Encyclopedia for Doing Business with Argentina* (San Rafael, CA: World Trade Press, 1986).

may believe that a customer is interested in buying an economical, low-horsepower motor. While presenting the benefits of a low-cost motor, the sales rep discovers, by observing nonverbal behaviors, that the customer is interested in discussing overall operating costs. At this point the rep asks some questions to find out whether the customer would pay a higher price for a more efficient motor with lower operating costs. Based on the customer's response, the rep may adopt a new sales strategy: presenting a more efficient motor and demonstrating its low operating costs.

It is sometimes hard for people to realize that the world is not made up of people just like them. Many people are much older than you, while some are younger than you. They practice different religions, like different foods, and shop at stores at which you would never think of shopping. They have different moral beliefs and different ideas about "the perfect product" and were raised in a totally different way. Their hopes and aspirations don't match yours. Many of them would be shocked to hear what your life's dreams and goals are. And we are not just talking about people in other countries that meet these criteria. We are talking about people who live next door to you, who may even be sitting next to you in your classroom. The sooner you realize that your world is made up of diverse people, the sooner you will realize the importance of becoming adaptive. Selecting the appropriate sales strategy for a sales situation and making adjustments during the interaction are crucial to successful selling.

Practicing adaptive selling does not mean that salespeople should be dishonest about their products or their personal feelings. It does mean that salespeople should alter the content and form of their sales presentation so that customers will be able to absorb the information easily and find it relevant to their situation.

Thinking It Through

Do you act differently when living on campus compared to living at home? How do you change your behavior when you go home for school breaks? How do you behave when you go to a restaurant with a date? With some friends? With your parents? Why do you behave this way in each situation?

The advantages and disadvantages of the three types of sales presentations illustrate the benefits and drawbacks of adaptive selling. Adaptive selling gives salespeople the opportunity to use the most effective sales presentation for each customer. However, uncovering needs, designing and delivering different presentations, and making adjustments require a high level of skills. The objective of this textbook is to help you develop the skills and knowledge required to practice adaptive selling.

KNOWLEDGE AND ADAPTIVE SELLING

A key ingredient in effective selling is knowledge.[4] Salespeople need to know about the products they are selling, the company they work for, and the customers they will be selling to. Knowledge enables the salesperson to build self-confidence, gain the buyer's trust, satisfy customer needs, and practice adaptive selling.

PRODUCT AND COMPANY KNOWLEDGE

Salespeople need to have a lot of information about their company and its products. For example, a buyer might say, "I'm satisfied with our present supplier. I see no reason to change." The informed salesperson might respond, "Company X is a fine company. But last year our firm sold three times as many units. IBM, General Electric, and Cisco gave us an outstanding vendor award. A *Purchasing* magazine survey of buyers reported that we were number one in on-time deliveries. Let me explain what this can mean for you."

Purchasing agents rate product knowledge as one of the most important attributes of good salespeople. Effective salespeople need to know how products are made, what services are provided with the products, how the products relate to other products, and how the products can satisfy customers' needs. For example, a

This Parker Hannifin valve salesperson has extensive knowledge about the operation of the customer's pneumatic control system and the features and benefits of various valves used in the system.

Courtesy Parker Hannifin

department store buyer for men's suits might want specific information to judge the quality of a suit. The salesperson may need to tell the buyer about the fabric used in making the suit and the method used to sew the garment to support claims about the quality of the suit.

In many situations the service provided is more important than the performance of the product. Efficient servicing of capital equipment assures the manufacturer that costly shutdowns will be minimized. Delays in providing service when equipment fails can result in substantial financial losses.

Customers often want salespeople to explain how their products will work with other products. For example, a salesperson selling a laser printer needs to know with which computers it can interface. The Kodak salesperson introducing a new film should know with which Kodak and Canon cameras it can and cannot be used.

But the most important knowledge is how the product will satisfy the customer's needs, not the technical details about the product. Customers are not interested in just the facts about a product; they are interested in what the product will do for them. The salesperson's job is to provide information about the features of a product and tell the customer how those features translate into benefits. For example, a wider hitting area (feature) in a golf club results in straighter and longer shots even when the ball is not hit perfectly (benefit).

Salespeople also need to know about their competitors' products as well as their own, since they are frequently asked to compare their products to competitors' offerings. A buyer for a meat-packing plant might say, "The model 41Z made by company X is one of the most energy-efficient refrigeration units in its size class"; in this case the salesperson might respond "The model 41Z certainly was a leader in energy efficiency when it was introduced in 1999. But our 800 series uses a new heat transfer technique that was not available in 1999. Tests show that our units have 10 to 15 percent greater energy efficiency than units that use the older technology."

ORGANIZING KNOWLEDGE OF SALES SITUATIONS AND CUSTOMERS INTO CATEGORIES

Even more important than product and company knowledge is detailed information about the different types of sales situations and customers salespeople may encounter and which sales presentation works best in each situation. Theoretically, salespeople can treat each sales situation differently. In practice, however, they typically do not have time to develop unique strategies for each sales situation. Hence effective salespeople tend to categorize sales situations. Each category contains a description of the customer and the most effective presentation for that customer type.

By developing categories, salespeople reduce the complexity of selling and free up their mental capacity to think more creatively; they also use knowledge gained through past experiences. When they encounter a customer whose needs differ from those the salespeople have dealt with previously—a customer who does not fit into an existing category—they add a new category to their repertoire. Salespeople with more categories, or customer types, have more selling approaches to use and thus have a greater opportunity to practice adaptive selling—to adjust their sales presentation to specific customer needs.[5]

The categories salespeople use can focus on the benefits the customer seeks, the person's role in the buying center, the stage in the buying process, or the type of buying situation. For example, Shelia Glazov divides people into four categories based on their thinking style. When selling to unstructured, resourceful buyers, salespeople need to be enthusiastic, engage in visual storytelling, and stress the immediate payoff of their products.[6]

Categories can help salespeople organize knowledge, but international salespeople need to avoid stereotyping buyers on the basis of their national origin. For example, North Americans are often viewed as cold and unfriendly by people from other countries. Yet, as you will see later in the section on social styles, some North Americans are amiables, some are drivers, some are expressives, and some are analyticals. The same holds true for buyers from other countries; when we see them as all being the same, we lose precious information that enables us to adapt. Categories are useful for organizing knowledge, but not when the categories become stereotypes.

APPROACHES FOR DEVELOPING KNOWLEDGE

Salespeople acquire most knowledge about company products and policies, customer needs, and selling situations through company training programs, analyses of company reports and trade publications, discussions with supervisors and other salespeople, and on-the-job learning. For example, Hewlett-Packard increases the knowledge of its 15,000 salespeople by providing them with an electronic sales partner (ESP). ESP has more than 30,000 documents that salespeople can access electronically from any computer, even during a sales call. These documents include product brochures, competitive information, graphical sales presentations, and answers to frequently asked questions. And, as you can imagine, the ESP system is used extensively: Every 1.2 seconds an HP salesperson accesses the system.[7]

TAP THE KNOWLEDGE OF SALES EXPERTS

Companies frequently tap the knowledge of their best salespeople and use this knowledge to train new salespeople. For example, a telecommunications company conducted in-depth interviews with its top performers. Through these interviews, it learned about the types of situations these salespeople encountered and what strategies they used in each situation. The company developed role-plays for each sales situation and used them when training new salespeople. Such role-playing enabled the new salespeople to experience the variety of situations they would actually encounter on the job. The strategies recommended by the top salespeople served as a starting point for the trainees to develop their own sales methods for handling these situations.

If your company does not tap the knowledge of its sales experts, you can do it. When you meet senior salespeople at a meeting, you should ask them how they handle difficult situations. For example, have they had any success selling product X? What types of customers are they selling it to? What do they emphasize in their presentations?

READ MANUALS AND TRADE PUBLICATIONS

Information about the salesperson's company, its products, and its competitors is available from many sources, including the Web, company sales manuals and newsletters, sales meetings, plant visits, and business and trade publications. Many large corporations provide this information to salespeople during periodic training classes and sales meetings. But salespeople cannot rely on these formal programs as their only source of information; learning new information is a process that never ends.

Knowledgeable salespeople read sales bulletins and announcements from their companies and articles in the trade publications about their customers and their industries. They ask company employees questions about new programs and products. They collect information about competitors from customers, by visiting customer displays at trade shows, and from viewing Web pages.

ASK FOR FEEDBACK ON WHAT YOU ARE DOING

Frequently the feedback salespeople get from their supervisors focuses on performance, called **performance feedback** (for example, Did you achieve your performance goals?). However, **diagnostic feedback** is much more useful than performance feedback for improving performance over the long run. Diagnostic feedback provides information about what someone is doing right and wrong.[8]

The following example illustrates the difference between performance and diagnostic feedback:

SALES MANAGER: You didn't do a good job of selling to that customer. You will need to improve if you want to sell to him in the future.

SALESPERSON: Why do you think I didn't make the sale?

SALES MANAGER: You stressed the low maintenance cost, but he wasn't interested in maintenance cost. Did you see how he kept looking around while you were talking about how cheap it is to maintain the product?

SALESPERSON: What do you think I should do next time?

SALES MANAGER: You might try spending more time finding his hot button. Maintenance cost isn't it.

The sales manager initially provided performance feedback, but the salesperson asked for diagnostic feedback. Such feedback provides reasons for sales successes and failures, helps salespeople build their knowledge of sales situations, and improves sales performance. Salespeople should ask their supervisors to analyze their performance, not simply evaluate it.

ANALYZE SUCCESSES AND FAILURES

Salespeople encounter many different types of selling situations; thus they have an opportunity to use different sales presentations. Sometimes they will use the wrong presentation and lose an order. Effective salespeople learn from their mistakes, using them to build a greater knowledge base. If salespeople disregard failures or blame the failures on someone else, they lose a valuable opportunity for learning. Salespeople should also try to learn from their successes. After making a sale, they should analyze what they did to achieve the outcome. Chapter 18 provides more information on how salespeople improve their skills throughout their careers.

When analyzing their performance, salespeople need to assign the right reasons for the outcomes. Salespeople have a natural tendency to take personal credit for successes and blame their company or competitors for failures. A salesperson might say, I made that sale because I am great, a super salesperson, or I lost that sale because my company's delivery was poor. Such reasoning does not

Successful sales managers provide their salespeople with diagnostic feedback.

IT International Ltd./e-Stock Photo

help salespeople learn. It doesn't show them what to do in the future to make sales or avoid failures. The performance analysis should focus on the sales strategies used, identifying the specific strategies causing the performance and determining whether and how they should be changed in the future.[9]

The key question when analyzing a sales situation is, Why? If you first offer some reason over which you have no control, such as the competition was too tough or your products don't work well, think deeper and come up with reasons to which you can respond. Formulate strategies you can use to overcome competition or limitations in product performance.

DEVELOP AN INTRINSIC ORIENTATION TOWARD YOUR WORK

People can have two types of orientation toward their jobs: intrinsic or extrinsic. People with an **intrinsic orientation** get rewards from doing the job itself. They enjoy their work; they find it challenging and fun. People with an **extrinsic orientation** view their jobs as something that has to be done, either to get extrinsic rewards (like more pay) or to avoid punishments (like getting fired). For these people, their jobs provide extrinsic rewards, but doing the job itself is not rewarding. Most people get both types of rewards from their jobs, but they tend to emphasize one type over the other.

Selling frequently emphasizes extrinsic rewards: If you do well, you will make more money, get promoted, or win awards. This emphasis encourages you to work hard, but it can distract you from learning how to do your job better. You may begin to think that you are just working for the money and your job is not fun.

When salespeople find their jobs challenging and fun, they want to learn how to do them better. They view their jobs as a challenge, like a video game. They want to try new sales methods and learn from their successes and failures, so they can improve their scores. Effective salespeople enjoy the challenge of selling. They like to try new selling methods, find new customers, sell new products, and figure out how to make a tough sale. If they find they do not enjoy their selling jobs, they probably will neither learn from their experiences nor improve their performance.

THE SOCIAL STYLE MATRIX: A TRAINING PROGRAM FOR BUILDING ADAPTIVE SELLING SKILLS

To be effective, salespeople need to use their knowledge about products and customers to adapt both the content of their sales presentations—the benefits they emphasize to customers and the needs they attempt to satisfy—and the style they use to communicate with customers. The **social style matrix** is a popular training program that companies use to assist salespeople in adapting their communication styles.

David Merrill and Roger Reid discovered patterns of communication behaviors, or social styles, that people use when interacting with one another.[10] Merrill and Reid found that people who recognize and adjust to these behavior patterns have better relationships with other people.

Here is a quick preview of what you will learn about the social style training program. As you know, the world is made up of diverse people. For example, some are fast decision makers, while others are very slow to make just about any kind of decision; some like to talk, while others are rather quiet. To make it easier, this system divides all people in the world into four different types or categories (based on just two dimensions). Your goal as a salesperson is to first identify which of those four types you are. Next, you figure out which of the four types your customer is. Finally, you adjust your behavior to mirror or match that of your customer. Now that you have a general idea of how the system works, let's look at it in more detail.

DIMENSIONS OF SOCIAL STYLES

This training program uses two critical dimensions to understand social behavior: assertiveness and responsiveness.

ASSERTIVENESS

The degree to which people have opinions about issues and publicly make their positions clear to others is called **assertiveness**. Simply having strong convictions does not make a person assertive; assertive people express their convictions publicly and attempt to influence others to accept these beliefs.

Assertive people speak out, make strong statements, and have a take-charge attitude. When under tension, they tend to confront the situation. Unassertive people rarely dominate a social situation, and they often keep their opinions to themselves. Exhibit 6.2 shows some verbal and nonverbal behavioral indicators of assertiveness.

RESPONSIVENESS

The second dimension, **responsiveness**, is based on how emotional people tend to get in social situations. Responsive people readily express joy, anger, and sorrow. They appear to be more concerned with others and are informal and casual in social situations. Less responsive people devote more effort toward controlling their emotions. They are described as cautious, intellectual, serious, formal, and businesslike. Exhibit 6.3 lists some indicators of responsiveness.

CATEGORIES OF SOCIAL STYLES

The two dimensions of social style, assertiveness and responsiveness, form the social style matrix shown in Exhibit 6.4. Each quadrant of the matrix defines a social style type.

DRIVERS

Drivers are high on assertiveness and low on responsiveness. The slogan of drivers, who are task-oriented people, might be "Let's get it done now, and get it done my way." Drivers have learned to work with others only because they must do so to get the job done, not because they enjoy people. They have a great desire to get ahead in their companies and careers.

Drivers are swift, efficient decision makers. They focus on the present and appear to have little concern with the past or future. They generally base their decisions on facts, take risks, and want to look at several alternatives before making a decision. As compared to analyticals, who also like facts and data, drivers want to know how the facts affect results—the bottom line. They are not interested in simply technical information.

EXHIBIT 6.2	Less Assertive	More Assertive
Indicators of Assertiveness	"Ask" oriented	"Tell" oriented
	Go-along attitude	Take-charge attitude
	Cooperative	Competitive
	Supportive	Directive
	Risk avoider	Risk taker
	Makes decisions slowly	Makes decisions quickly
	Lets others take initiative	Takes initiative
	Leans backward	Leans forward
	Indirect eye contact	Direct eye contact
	Speaks slowly, softly	Speaks quickly, intensely
	Moves deliberately	Moves rapidly
	Makes few statements	Makes many statements
	Expresses moderate opinions	Expresses strong opinions

EXHIBIT 6.3	Less Responsive	More Responsive
Indicators of Responsiveness	Controls emotions	Shows emotions
	Cool, aloof	Warm, approachable
	Talk oriented	People oriented
	Uses facts	Uses opinions
	Serious	Playful
	Impersonal, businesslike	Personable, friendly
	Moves stiffly	Moves freely
	Seldom gestures	Gestures frequently
	Formal dress	Informal dress
	Disciplined about time	Undisciplined about time
	Controlled facial expressions	Animated facial expressions
	Monotone voice	Many vocal inflections

EXHIBIT 6.4 Social Style Matrix

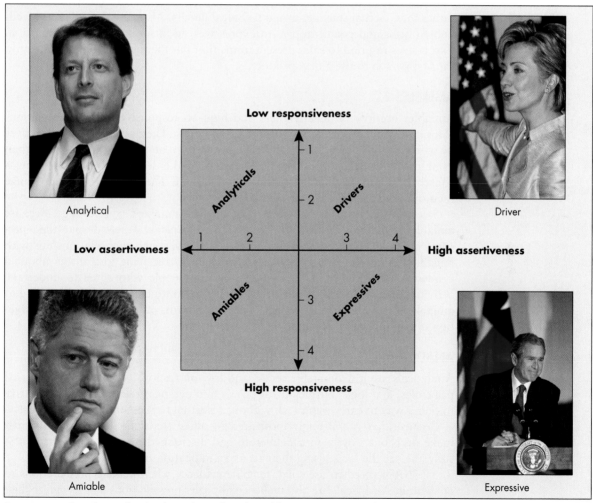

Some examples of social styles from the political world. Do you agree with where they are placed? Note that all of these people may switch to a different style under certain conditions.

Top left: Robert Maass/CORBIS. Top right: Rommel Pecson/The Image Works. Bottom left: Lynn Fernandez/The Image Works. Bottom right: Bob Daemmrick/The Image Works

To influence a driver, salespeople need to use a direct, businesslike, organized presentation with quick action and follow-up. Proposals should emphasize the effects of a purchase decision on profits.

EXPRESSIVES

Expressives are high on assertiveness and high on responsiveness. Warm, approachable, intuitive, and competitive, expressives view power and politics as important factors in their quest for personal rewards and recognition. Although expressives are interested in personal relationships, their relationships are primarily with supporters and followers recruited to assist expressives in achieving their personal goals.

People with an expressive style focus on the future, directing their time and effort toward achieving their vision. They have little concern for practical details in present situations. Expressives base their decisions on their personal opinions and the opinions of others. They act quickly, take risks, but tend to be impatient and change their minds easily.

When selling to expressives, salespeople need to demonstrate how their products will help the customer achieve personal status and recognition. Expressives prefer sales presentations with product demonstrations and creative graphics, rather than factual statements and technical details. Also, testimonials from well-known firms and people appeal to expressives' need for status and recognition. Expressives respond to sales presentations that put them in the role of innovator, the first person to use a new product.

AMIABLES

Amiables are low on assertiveness and high on responsiveness. Close relationships and cooperation are important to amiables. They achieve their objectives by working with people, developing an atmosphere of mutual respect rather than using power and authority. Amiables tend to make decisions slowly, building a consensus among people involved in the decision. They avoid risks and change their opinions reluctantly.

Salespeople may have difficulty detecting an amiable's true feelings. Because amiables avoid conflict, they often say things to please others despite their personal opinions. Therefore, salespeople need to build personal relationships with amiables. Amiables are particularly interested in receiving guarantees about a product's performance. They do not like salespeople who agree to undertake activities and then do not follow through on commitments. Salespeople selling to amiables should stress the product's benefits in terms of its effects on the satisfaction of employees.

ANALYTICALS

Analyticals are low on assertiveness and low on responsiveness. They like facts, principles, and logic. Suspicious of power and personal relationships, they strive to find a way to carry out a task without resorting to these influence methods.

Because they are strongly motivated to make the right decision, analyticals make decisions slowly, in a deliberate and disciplined manner. They systematically analyze the facts, using the past as an indication of future events.

Salespeople need to use solid, tangible evidence when making presentations to analyticals. Analyticals are also influenced by sales presentations that recognize their technical expertise and emphasize long-term benefits. They tend to disregard personal opinions. Both analyticals and amiables tend to develop loyalty toward suppliers. For amiables, the loyalty is based on personal relationships; analyticals' loyalty is based on their feeling that well-reasoned decisions do not need to be reexamined.

IDENTIFYING CUSTOMERS' SOCIAL STYLES

Exhibit 6.5 lists some cues for identifying the social styles of customers or prospects. Salespeople can use their communication skills to observe the customer's behavior, listen to the customer, and ask questions to classify the customer.

Merrill and Reid caution that identifying social style is difficult and requires close and careful observation. Salespeople should not jump to quick conclusions based on limited information. Some suggestions for making more accurate assessments are as follows:

- Concentrate on the customer's behavior and disregard how you feel about the behavior. Don't let your feelings about the customer or thoughts about the customer's motives cloud your judgment.
- Avoid assuming that specific jobs or functions are associated with a social style, such as he must be an analytical because he is an engineer.
- Test your assessments. Look for clues and information that may suggest you have incorrectly assessed a customer's social style. If you look for only confirming cues, you will filter out a lot of important information.

SOCIAL STYLES AND SALES PRESENTATIONS

In addition to teaching trainees how to assess social style, the Merrill and Reid program also assesses the trainees' social styles. Each person is asked to have a group of his or her customers complete a questionnaire and mail it to the director of the training program. These responses are used to determine the trainee's style. Trainees frequently are surprised by the difference between their self-perceptions and the perceptions of their customers. To get a rough idea of your own social style, you can complete the assessment in Exhibit 6.6.

EXHIBIT 6.5	**Analytical**	**Driver**
Cues for Recognizing Social Styles	Technical background Achievement awards on wall Office is work oriented, showing much activity Conservative dress Likes solitary activities (e.g., reading, individual sports)	Technical background Achievement awards on wall No posters or slogans on office walls Calendar prominently displayed Furniture is placed so that contact with people is across desk Conservative dress Likes group activities (e.g., politics, team sports)
	Amiable	**Expressive**
	Liberal arts background Office has friendly, open atmosphere Pictures of family displayed Personal momentos on wall Desk placed for open contact with people Casual or flamboyant dress Likes solitary activities (e.g., reading, individual sports)	Liberal arts background Motivational slogans on wall Office has friendly, open atmosphere Cluttered, unorganized desk Desk placed for open contact with people Casual or flamboyant dress Likes group activities (e.g., politics, team sports)

EXHIBIT 6.6

Self-Assessment of
Social Styles

Assertiveness Ratings I perceive myself as:				Responsiveness Ratings I perceive myself as:			
Quiet . . . . Talkative				Open . . . . Closed			
1	2	3	4	4	3	2	1
Slow to decide . . . . Fast to decide				Impulsive . . . . Deliberate			
1	2	3	4	4	3	2	1
Going along . . . . Taking charge				Using opinions . . . . Using facts			
1	2	3	4	4	3	2	1
Supportive . . . . Challenging				Informal . . . . Formal			
1	2	3	4	4	3	2	1
Compliant . . . . Dominant				Emotional . . . . Unemotional			
1	2	3	4	4	3	2	1
Deliberate . . . . Fast to decide				Easy to know . . . . Hard to know			
1	2	3	4	4	3	2	1
Asking questions . . . . Making statements				Warm . . . . Cool			
1	2	3	4	4	3	2	1
Cooperative . . . . Competitive				Excitable . . . . Calm			
1	2	3	4	4	3	2	1
Avoiding risks . . . . Taking risks				Animated . . . . Poker-faced			
1	2	3	4	4	3	2	1
Slow, studied . . . . Fast-paced				People-oriented . . . . Task-oriented			
1	2	3	4	4	3	2	1
Cautious . . . . Carefree				Spontaneous . . . . Cautious			
1	2	3	4	4	3	2	1
Indulgent . . . . Firm				Responsive . . . . Nonresponsive			
1	2	3	4	4	3	2	1
Nonassertive . . . . Assertive				Humorous . . . . Serious			
1	2	3	4	4	3	2	1
Mellow . . . . Matter-of-fact				Impulsive . . . . Methodical			
1	2	3	4	4	3	2	1
Reserved . . . . Outgoing				Lighthearted . . . . Intense			
1	2	3	4	4	3	2	1

Mark your answers above. Total the score for each side and divide each by 15. Then plot your scores on Exhibit 6.4 to see what social style you are. For fun, you may want to have several friends also score you.

Source: Based on work by David Merrill and Roger Reid, *Personal Styles and Effective Performance* (Radnor, PA: Chilton, 1981).

Interpreting self-ratings requires great caution. Self-assessments can be very misleading because we usually do not see ourselves the same way others see us. When you rate yourself, you know your own feelings, but others can only observe your behaviors. They don't know your thoughts or your intentions. We also vary our behavior from situation to situation. The indicators listed in Exhibits 6.2 and 6.3 merely show a tendency to be assertive or responsive.

Is there one best social style for a salesperson? No. None is "best" for all situations; each style has its strong points and weak points. Driver salespeople are efficient, determined, and decisive, but customers may also find them pushy and dominating. Expressives have enthusiasm, dramatic flair, and creativity but can also seem opinionated, undisciplined, and unstable. Analyticals are orderly, serious, and thorough, but customers may view them as cold, calculating, and stuffy. Finally, amiables are dependable, supportive, and personable but may also be perceived as undisciplined and inflexible.

The sales training program based on the social style matrix emphasizes that effective selling involves more than communicating a product's benefits. Salespeople must also recognize the customer's needs and expectations. In the sales interaction, salespeople should conduct themselves in a manner consistent with customer expectations. Exhibit 6.7 indicates the expectations of customers with various social styles.

Although each customer type requires a different sales presentation, the salesperson's personal social style tends to determine the sales technique he or she typically uses. For example, drivers tend to use a driver technique with all customer types. When interacting with an amiable customer, driver salespeople will be efficient and businesslike, even though the amiable customer would prefer to deal with a more relationship-oriented and friendlier salesperson.

This sales training program emphasizes that to be effective with a variety of customer types, salespeople must adapt their selling presentation to the *customer's* social style. Versatility is the key to effective adaptive selling.

VERSATILITY

The effort people make to increase the productivity of a relationship by adjusting to the needs of the other party is known as **versatility**. Versatile salespeople—those able to adapt their social styles—are much more effective than salespeople who do not adjust their sales presentations. Here is a comparison of behaviors of more versatile and less versatile people:

Less Versatile	More Versatile
Limited ability to adapt to others' needs	Able to adapt to others' needs
Specialist	Generalist
Well-defined interests	Broad interests
Sticks to principles	Negotiates issues
Predictable	Unpredictable
Looks at one side of an issue	Looks at many sides of an issue

---

EXHIBIT 6.7 Customer Expectations Based on Social Styles

Area of Expectation	Customer's Social Style			
	Driver	Expressive	Amiable	Analytical
Atmosphere in sales interview	Businesslike	Open, friendly	Open, honest	Businesslike
Salesperson's use of time	Effective, efficient	To develop relationship	Leisurely, to develop relationship	Thorough, accurate
Pace of interview	Quick	Quick	Deliberate	Deliberate
Information provided by salesperson	Salesperson's qualifications; value of products	What salesperson thinks; whom he/she knows	Evidence that salesperson is trustworthy, friendly	Evidence of salesperson's expertise in solving problem
Salesperson's actions to win customer acceptance	Documented evidence, stress results	Recognition and approval	Personal attention and interest	Evidence that salesperson has analyzed the situation
Presentation of benefits	*What* product can do	*Who* has used the product	*Why* product is best to solve problem	*How* product can solve the problem
Assistance to aid decision making	Explanation of options and probabilities	Testimonials	Guarantees and assurances	Evidence and offers of service

As just stated, sales training programs based on the social style matrix suggest that effective salespeople adjust their social styles to match their customers' styles. For example, salespeople with a driver orientation need to become more emotional and less assertive when selling to amiable customers. Analytical salespeople must increase their assertiveness and responsiveness when selling to expressive customers. Exhibit 6.8 shows some techniques for adjusting sales behaviors in terms of assertiveness and responsiveness.

THE ROLE OF KNOWLEDGE

The social style matrix illustrates the importance of knowledge, organized into categories, in determining selling effectiveness through adaptive selling. Sales training based on the social style matrix teaches salespeople the four customer categories, or types (driver, expressive, amiable, and analytical). Salespeople learn the cues for identifying them. Salespeople also learn which adjustments they need to make in their communication styles to be effective with each customer type.

ALTERNATIVE TRAINING SYSTEMS FOR DEVELOPING ADAPTIVE SELLING SKILLS

The social style matrix developed by Merrill and Reid is one of several sales training methods based on customer classification schemes. Rather than using assertiveness and responsiveness, V. R. Buzzotta and R. E. Lefton use the dimensions of warm–hostile and dominant–submissive,[11] and Gerald Manning and Barry Reece use dominance and sociability dimensions to classify customers.[12] Tony Alessandra, a sales guru, suggests that salespeople classify customers into four categories: relater, socializer, thinker, and director.[13] Marlane Miller proposes a scheme based on the following categories—logical (yellow), emotional (blue), conceptual (orange), and analytical (green) based on the customer's brain style.[14]

Regardless of the training system used, it is imperative that salespeople adjust to their audience. Selling Scenario 6.1 provides an excellent example of what can happen when you don't adapt when selling internationally. To repeat, it is also important to adjust your style when selling to diverse cultures even within your own country. For example, recent research shows that Hispanic salespeople need to alter their communication style when selling to Anglo-America customers.[15]

EXHIBIT 6.8	Adjusting Social Styles	

	Adjustment	
Dimension	**Reduce**	**Increase**
Assertiveness	Ask for customer's opinion.	Get to the point.
	Acknowledge merits of customer's viewpoint.	Don't be vague or ambiguous.
	Listen without interruption.	Volunteer information.
	Be more deliberate; don't rush.	Be willing to disagree.
	Let customer direct flow of conversation.	Take a stand.
		Initiate conversation.
Responsiveness	Become businesslike.	Verbalize feelings.
	Talk less.	Express enthusiasm.
	Restrain enthusiasm.	Pay personal compliments.
	Make decision based on facts.	Spend time on relationships rather than business.
	Stop and think.	Socialize; engage in small talk.
		Use nonverbal communication.

Steve Waterhouse, of the training firm Waterhouse Group, was looking forward to finally getting a chance to meet with a potential client from Japan. For six months his firm had been carefully working the account with the hopes of gaining a valuable long-term customer. Finally, the moment arrived. It happened at a convention in San Antonio, Texas.

The buyer handed Steve her business card, using the traditional Japanese method: extending it while holding onto both ends. So far, so good. Steve accepted the card and quickly jotted a note on the back of it. When he looked up, the Japanese prospect looked severely shocked and hurt. "I might as well have spit in her face," he says.

"I quickly put it away and then apologized profusely, but the damage was already done."

Steve and his firm lost the $100,000 deal. All of it. Because of one slip with a business card. In Japan you should show a business card the same respect you would show a person. Writing on the business card was seen as similar to writing directly on the prospect's arm.

Steve and his firm did learn a valuable lesson from this, though. And it's one all should learn: Selling to people from other cultures or subcultures requires adaptability.

Source: "BestPractices: Selling around the World," *Sales and Marketing Management,* May 2001, p. 70.

EXPERT SYSTEMS

Expert systems have been developed to assist salespeople in understanding their customers and developing effective sales strategies.[16] An **expert system** is a computer program that mimics a human expert. The program contains the knowledge, rules, and decision processes employed by experts and then uses these elements to solve problems, suggest strategies, and provide advice similar to that of an expert.

For example, Business Resource Software offers an expert system called Insights for Sales Strategy™. When using this computer program, salespeople input information on their objectives for an account, the decision makers and the roles they play in the decision, the competitors, the price and benefits of the products, and the salesperson's strategy. Then the program analyzes this information, drawing on a knowledge base of sales concepts to provide suggestions for a sales strategy to use with the customer. The output of the program includes an evaluation of the sales strategy, an analysis of the salesperson's strengths and weaknesses with respect to the account, a scoring of the probability of a close, an identification of high-risk factors, and suggested steps for improving strategy.

LIMITATIONS OF TRAINING METHODS

Training methods such as the social style matrix and expert systems are simply a first step in developing knowledge for practicing adaptive selling. They emphasize the need to practice adaptive selling—to use different presentations with different customers—and stimulate salespeople to base their sales presentations on an analysis of the customer. But these methods are limited; they present only a few types of customers, and classification is based on the form of communication (the social style), not on the content of the communication (the specific features and benefits stressed in the presentation).

In addition, accurately fitting customers into the suggested categories is often very difficult. Customers act differently and have different needs in different sales encounters: A buyer may be very amiable when engaging in a new-task buying situation and be analytical when dealing with an out-supplier's salesperson in a straight rebuy. Amiable buyers in a bad mood may act like drivers. By rigidly applying the classification rules, salespeople may actually limit their flexibility, reducing the adaptive selling behavior these training methods emphasize.

Expert systems, like Insights for Sales Strategy, help salespeople understand buyers and develop effective sales strategies.

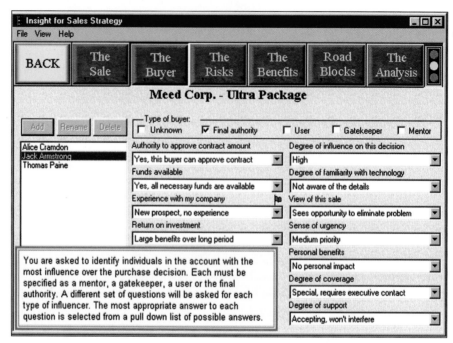

Insight for Sales® from Business Resource Software, Inc., Austin Texas

Finally, the knowledge some of these training programs provide is very general. It is not related to the specific types of customers to whom you will be selling or the specific products you will be selling. To be an effective salesperson, you need to develop knowledge about the specific sales situations you will encounter.

CUSTOMER RELATIONSHIP MANAGEMENT (CRM) SYSTEMS

Many companies have customer relationship management (CRM) systems to support their salespeople. For example, Wisdomware offers a system that interfaces with a firm's enterprise resource planning (ERP) system. This CRM system provides information and suggestions that are specific to a particular customer and product offered by the salesperson's company.

At the heart of the CRM system is the knowledge base: an online collection of information such as policy manuals, sales literature, analyses, price lists, and product descriptions. The knowledge base in the Wisdomware CRM system organizes this information into four categories: (1) key business issues facing the customer, (2) how the salesperson's company can meet these needs, (3) competitive offerings, and (4) the most effective sales presentation for a particular customer. For example, the information in the first category includes magazine articles and news releases about the salesperson's accounts.

The Sales Coaching™ module uses the first-hand experiences and observations of high-performance salespeople working for the company. The module provides a general presentation for each product the company offers (referred to as the "elevator speech"), the strengths and differentiators of the product, approaches for overcoming weaknesses and objections, answers to frequently asked questions about the product, and cross-selling and selling-up opportunities. Salespeople can also access sales presentations that emphasize specific benefits or address specific weakness about the product.[17]

Summary

Adaptive selling enables salespeople to exploit the unique properties of personal selling as a marketing communication tool: the ability to tailor messages to individual customers and make on-the-spot adjustments. Extensive knowledge of customer and sales situation types is a key ingredient in effective adaptive selling.

To be effective, salespeople need to have considerable knowledge about the products they sell, the companies for which they work, and the customers to whom they sell. In addition to knowing the facts, they need to understand how those facts relate to benefits their customers are seeking. Experienced salespeople organize customer knowledge into categories. Each category has cues for classifying customers or sales situations and an effective sales presentation for customers in the category.

To develop more extensive knowledge of customers, salespeople need to use information from their firms' market research studies, ask for feedback, analyze their successes and failures, and develop an intrinsic orientation toward their work.

The social style matrix, developed by Merrill and Reid, illustrates the concept of developing categorical knowledge to facilitate adaptive selling. The matrix defines four customer categories based on a customer's responsiveness and assertiveness in sales interactions. To effectively interact with a customer, a salesperson needs to identify the customer's social style and adapt a style to match. The sales training program based on the social style matrix provides cues for identifying social style as well as presentations salespeople can use to make adjustments.

The social style matrix is one example of a categorical scheme salespeople can use to improve their knowledge and adaptability. However, other schemes are used, and some have been incorporated into expert system computer programs. Although these schemes emphasize the need for flexibility, they are often very general and not directly related to the specific situation encountered by a salesperson. However, many companies now have customer relationship management (CRM) systems that provide knowledge and sales suggestions based on company information and the experiences of high-performance salespeople working for the company.

KEY TERMS

adaptive selling   154
amiable   164
analytical   164
assertiveness   162
customized presentation   154
diagnostic feedback   159
driver   162
expert system   169
expressive   164

extrinsic orientation   161
intrinsic orientation   161
outlined presentation   154
performance feedback   159
responsiveness   162
social style matrix   161
standard memorized presentation   154
versatility   167

Questions and Problems

1. As a salesperson, aren't you just using tricks when you adjust your presentation based on social styles? Is it ethical to do so? Are there any times when it would be unethical to do so?

2. How can the statement "Your greatest strength can become your greatest weakness" be applied to the social styles discussed in this chapter?

3. A salesperson who is a driver is preparing a presentation. What suggestions can you make to improve the salesperson's performance?

4. "A good salesperson can sell any customer." Do you agree? Why or why not?

5. Would a person with an analytical social style be better at selling than a person with a driver or an expressive style? Why or why not?

6. What do you think about the following statement? "Good salespeople need to be aggressive. They need to have powerful voices and a winning smile."

7. What social styles would you assign to the following people?
   a. President George W. Bush.
   b. Your selling instructor.
   c. Jay Leno on *The Tonight Show*.
   d. Your best friend.
8. What are the strengths and weaknesses of each of the four social styles in terms of effective selling?
9. Suppose that, during a sales call, a customer says, "Your computer software could never do everything you say it will." How would you respond if this were an analytical customer? An amiable?
10. The market research undertaken by a hospital supply company identified three types of hospitals. Traditional hospitals believe that patient satisfaction is based on the quality of medical staff and that hospital supplies are unimportant. Private hospitals believe that supplies are important because they affect the staff's efficiency. Marketing-oriented hospitals view supplies as an important element in creating a comfortable, customer service–oriented image. Which type of sales presentation would you use if you were selling bedsheets and pillowcases to each of these hospital types? Which product features and benefits would you emphasize in each case?

Case Problems

CASE 6.1

Using the Social Style Matrix to Develop Sales Presentations

TIM MORRIS

His office is pleasant and really looks "worked in." You notice a couple of file folders on the floor behind the desk. Two attractive nonbusiness posters (not framed) hang on the walls, along with four small, framed group photos. You notice a number of souvenirs on the desk. Chairs are comfortable and casually arranged. An assortment of snapshots is tucked in the frame of a family portrait on the desk.

HENRY WILLIAMS

His office is relatively neat. Some nicely framed diplomas and achievement certificates decorate the walls. Two reference posters with helpful business data are pinned to the wall nearest the desk. The desk holds several in–out baskets, all clearly labeled. Two chairs are set up so that Williams faces visitors directly across the desk.

BELINDA DALE

Her office walls contain one oil painting and some nicely framed prints. A large stack of business periodicals rests on the credenza behind the desk. The pen and pencil set on the desk has an achievement plaque with Dale's name on it. Although current work clutters the desk, the rest of the office is well organized. You notice a to-do list with today's date on it next to the telephone. The desk divides the room in two and separates you from the occupant.

BETH ATKINS

Lots of things cover her walls: framed, autographed photos of sports notables; a chamber of commerce citizenship citation; children's colorful crayon drawings; and a large newspaper ad with a clever headline. Propped against a cabinet full of trophies stands a tennis bag with a racquet. You count at least eight stacks of papers and magazines. The visitors' chairs are pulled close to the desk.

Questions

1. Identify each customer's social style.
2. How would you sell to each customer?

Angela DeFore is a salesperson at Comcast, the company with the cable TV rights for the city of Beloit and its surrounding suburbs. After DeFore graduated from Wayne State University with a BA in history, she went to work for the city in the community services department. When the economy slowed down, she was laid off and went to work for Comcast, where she has been working in sales for two years. DeFore is married, has two children, and is an active volunteer in programs for homeless persons.

DeFore is making her first call on Steve Sinor, the new director of advertising at Beloit National Bank. As DeFore enters Sinor's office, she notices several graphs on the wall indicating the number of new accounts opened, total deposits, and market share over time. A plaque signifying Sinor's selection as Southwestern Advertising Executive of the Year is prominently displayed.

DEFORE [extends her hand warmly and then takes a seat]: Good morning, Mr. Sinor. This is really a beautiful day. How are you?

SINOR [hesitates at first and then extends his hand]: I have just a few minutes to talk with you. My schedule is really tight today. Now tell me what you have to offer [sits down without demonstrating an emotional response].

DEFORE: Let me take a second to tell you why I made an appointment to see you. I was talking with Joan Waters at Fidelity Mutual Life Insurance. She said she met you at a recent Southwestern Advertising Executives luncheon. She has been using Comcast in her media plan and mentioned that you might be interested in advertising on cable TV.

SINOR: I really can't remember Ms. Waters. You meet so many people at these luncheons.

DEFORE: She really is an interesting person. We worked together as volunteers in the Homeless in America program last fall. Are you involved in many community activities?

SINOR: Not really [looks at his watch].

DEFORE: Well, Ms. Waters told me that you were developing a new advertising campaign for the bank. I hear the campaign will stress customer service. I really think that is a great idea. Banks should be more concerned about providing good service.

SINOR: We did a lot of market research to develop this new campaign. Our research shows that customer service is particularly important to people in the eastern suburbs. We hope to increase our share of new deposits by 3 percent over the next six months. Tell me something about what you can do for us.

DEFORE: I think we are the ideal media for your new campaign. Fidelity Mutual has been very pleased with the response to its commercials for homeowner insurance policies.

SINOR: That's interesting. What is its target market?

DEFORE: Fidelity has been targeting its campaign toward lower-income families in the western suburbs. Homeowner policy sales doubled six months after Fidelity placed the first ads on cable TV.

SINOR: Doubled?

DEFORE: At least doubled, I think.

SINOR: Could you be more specific about your reach in the eastern suburbs? How many families subscribe to your cable TV service? How often do they watch the cable channels?

DEFORE: I don't have the specific information with me, but I know that our coverage is very good. More and more people are watching cable channels. You know . . .

SINOR: Excuse me, but I have to go to another meeting. When you get some more specific information, you can leave it with my assistant.

Questions

1. What are DeFore's and Sinor's communication styles? On what do you base your assessments?
2. How effective do you think DeFore was on this sales call?
3. What adjustments should DeFore have made in her sales presentation to increase her effectiveness?

Additional References

Ainscough, Thomas; Thomas DeKeno; and Thomas Leigh. "Building Expert Systems from the Selling Scripts of Multiple Experts." *Journal of Services Marketing* 10, July/August 1996, pp. 23–41.

Alessandra, Anthony; Michael O'Connor; Tony Alessandra; and Michael O'Connor. *The Platinum Rule: Discover the Four Basic Business Personalities—And How They Can Lead You to Success.* New York: Warner, 1998.

Barker, A. Tansu. "Benchmarks of Successful Salesforce Performance." *Revue Canadienne des Sciences de l'Administration* 16, June 1999, pp. 95–104.

Boorom, Michael. "Relational Communication Traits and Their Effect on Adaptiveness and Sales Performance." *Journal of the Academy of Marketing Science* 26, Winter 1998, pp. 16–22.

Brennan, Ross, and Peter W. Trunbull. "Adaptive Behavior in Buyer–Seller Relationships." *Industrial Marketing Management* 28, September 1999, pp. 481–95.

Bush, Victoria D.; Gregory M. Rose; Faye Gilbert; and Thomas N. Ingram. "Managing Culturally Diverse Buyer–Seller Relationships: The Role of Intercultural Disposition and Adaptive Selling in Developing Intercultural Communication Competence." *Journal of the Academy of Marketing Science* 29:4 (2001), pp. 391–404.

Comer, Lucette B., and J. A. F. Nicholls. "Communication between Hispanic Salespeople and Their Customers: A First Look." *Journal of Personal Selling and Sales Management* 20, Summer 2000, pp. 121–27.

Comer, Lucette B.; J. A. F. Nicholls; and Leslie J. Vermillion. "Diversity in the Sales Force: Problems and Challenges." *Journal of Personal Selling and Sales Management* 18, Fall 1998, pp. 1–20.

Dwyer, Sean; Orlando Richard; and C. David Shepherd. "An Exploratory Study of Gender and Age Matching in the Salesperson–Prospective Customer Dyad: Testing Similarity–Performance Predictions." *Journal of Personal Selling and Sales Management* 18, Fall 1998, pp. 55–69.

Fang, Tony. "Culture as a Driving Force for Interfirm Adaptation: A Chinese Case." *Industrial Marketing Management* 30 (2001), pp. 51–63.

Laris, Alexis. "Software Lets Users Evaluate Sales Strategy." *InformationWeek,* December 13, 1999, pp. 100–102.

Lichtenthal, J. David, and Thomas Tellefsen. "Toward a Theory of Business Buyer–Seller Similarity." *Journal of Personal Selling and Sales Management* 21, Winter 2001, pp. 1–14.

Porter, Stephen S., and Lawrence W. Inks. "Cognitive Complexity and Salesperson Adaptability: An Exploratory Investigation." *Journal of Personal Selling and Sales Management* 20, Winter 2000, pp. 15–21.

Ray, Dana. "Work Your Brain." *Selling Power,* October 1999, pp. 119–23.

Rivers, L. Mark, and Jack Dart. "The Acquisition and Use of Sales Force Automation by Mid-sized Manufacturers." *Journal of Personal Selling and Sales Management* 19, Spring 1999, pp. 59–73.

Schultz, Roberta J.; Kenneth R. Evans; and David J. Good. "Intercultural Interaction Strategies and Relationship Selling in Industrial Markets." *Industrial Marketing Management* 28, November 1999, pp. 589–99.

"Selling to Small-Business Executives: Suppliers Must Recognize the Five Types of People They're Calling On." *Sales and Marketing Management,* January 2000, p. 14.

Sharma, Arun, and Rajnandini Pillai. "Customers' Decision-Making Styles and Their Preference for Sales Strategies: Conceptual Examination and Empirical Study." *Journal of Personal Selling and Sales Management,* Winter 1996, pp. 21–31.

Stafford, Thomas. "Conscious and Unconscious Processing of Priming Cues in Selling Encounters." *Journal of Personal Selling and Sales Management,* Spring 1996, pp. 37–44.

Sviokla, John. "Knowledge Workers and Radically New Technology." *Sloan Management Review* 37, Summer 1996, pp. 25–41.

Weitz, Barton; Harish Sujan; and Mita Sujan. "Knowledge, Motivation, and Adaptive Behavior: A Framework for Improving Selling Effectiveness." *Journal of Marketing,* October 1986, pp. 174–91.

3 The Partnership Process

Part 1 of this book provided a general introduction to the nature of selling jobs. In Part 2 we reviewed concepts of legal and ethical issues confronting salespeople, buyer behavior, communication principles, and the adaptive selling framework. In Part 3 we explore the activities required to build long-term relationships and partnerships. As the circular figure illustrates, these activities do not necessarily follow a step-by-step sequence; instead they occur throughout the partnership-building process.

Chapter 7 covers material on identifying prospects. Chapter 8 outlines how to gain precall information, plan each call, and make appointments effectively.

In Chapter 9 you will learn how to make a good impression. You will also discover techniques to effectively uncover the prospect's needs and then relate your solution to those needs.

Chapter 10 covers the use of communication tools such as visual aids, samples, and demonstrations. Chapter 11 will help you learn how to respond helpfully to concerns raised by the buyer, and Chapter 12 provides guidance in obtaining commitment. Finally, Chapter 13 summarizes methods and activities used to develop and enrich meaningful partnerships.

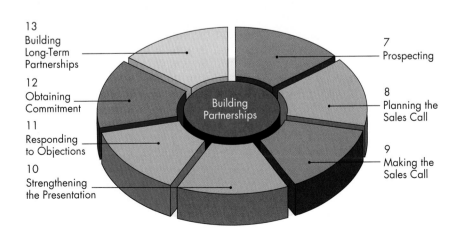

13
Building
Long-Term
Partnerships

12
Obtaining
Commitment

11
Responding
to Objections

10
Strengthening
the Presentation

Building
Partnerships

7
Prospecting

8
Planning the
Sales Call

9
Making the
Sales Call

Chapter

7 *Prospecting*

SOME QUESTIONS ANSWERED IN THIS CHAPTER ARE:

■ Why is prospecting important for effective selling?

■ Are all sales leads good prospects? What are the characteristics of a qualified prospect?

■ How can prospects be identified?

■ How can the organization's promotional program be used in prospecting?

■ How can an effective lead qualification and management system aid a salesperson?

■ How can a salesperson overcome a reluctance to prospect?

An important activity for nearly all salespeople is locating qualified prospects. In fact, the selling process generally begins with prospecting. You can be the best salesperson in the world in terms of listening, asking questions, discovering needs, giving presentations, helpfully responding to objections, and obtaining commitment, but if you are calling on the wrong person or organization, none of these skills do you any good! This chapter provides resources to help you prospect effectively and efficiently.

"What they don't tell you in school is that when you start out in radio advertising sales, you pretty much have to make your own account list."

Angie Main, Duluth Radio

PROFILE

Angie Main graduated from UMD in 2001 with a BBA in marketing. She began working at Midwest Communications as an account executive for Magic 95.7 FM; but she was quickly promoted to the promotions director position, where she sells radio advertising and handles promotions, events, PR, publicity, and advertising for the company's six Duluth radio stations.

"What they don't tell you in school is that when you start out in radio advertising sales, you pretty much have to make your own account list. All the people who have been there for five or more years have all the big accounts like car dealers, furniture stores, and grocery stores. For that reason, when you begin your career in sales, the most common word in your vocabulary is prospecting.

"So where do I find prospects? Here are a couple of sources I use: (1) With advertising sales I know who is advertising with my competitors. I see their ads in the paper, hear them on competitor radio stations or on TV. The best part about these prospects is that I know they already advertise, so I don't have to convince them to get their names out there; I just have to convince them to first use radio and second use my station. (2) I have created a network of friends (office suppliers, printers, convention center managers, movers, mall managers, and so on) and current clients who know a lot about what is going on in the community. I tap these folks for prospecting info. (3) Trade shows are an advertising sales heaven. Instead of spending an entire day and a tank of gas driving around town looking for my next client, I can find 200–300 potential clients sitting around just waiting for people to talk to them. (4) Looking at last year's newspapers gives me an idea of which companies have special sales/events and when would be best to call upon them. I buy a copy from our local newspaper. (5) The business section of the paper has a column of business happenings, and I can find out about new businesses, expanding businesses, and the like. (6) I like to set up a referral program with my clients. Every client that gives me the name of a prospect that buys radio from me within two months gets an incentive (approved by my general manager, of course). This way my own clients become my eyes and ears on the street. (7) Our stations run promotions to target a certain group of advertisers or to dovetail with community functions like women's expos, boat shows, and home shows. These promos help me to locate leads."

Qualifying and prioritizing prospects are also important for Angie. "I've found that the best advertising prospects are those who already advertise. Other factors help prioritize my leads as well: (1) Is their product a daily-needs item or something more unique? (2) How many locations does the business have? The more the better, because they can amortize the cost of advertising over, say, three locations instead of just one. (3) What is the demographics profile of the prospect's customers? I need to make sure that it roughly matches our station's listeners' demographics. (4) Does their service area match our station's signal? (5) Are their competitors advertising? If so, they are a stronger prospect. (6) Do they have some sale or special coming up? (7) Do they have potential co-op dollars from their distributors? (8) Does their personality match mine?"

How does she overcome the reluctance to prospect? "In my company we get to draw for cash for any new business we get. I can win between $5 and $100 for each new business. That creates a great incentive to prospect. Also, you can't get down if you lose a sale. Your job is to just keep on prospecting!"

Visit Our Website @ www.duluthradio.net

THE IMPORTANCE OF PROSPECTING

Prospecting, the important process of locating potential customers for a product or service, is critical whether you are a new or seasoned sales professional. In fact, many experts note that prospecting is the most important activity a salesperson does.

Why is it so important? Quite simply, the world is constantly changing. Consider the drastic changes in population movements, the creation of new businesses and products, the shifting of businesses to new lines and expansion of old-line companies, and changes in methods of distribution. These changes are resulting in an estimated 15 to 20 percent annual turnover of customers. In addition, salespeople must find new customers to replace those that switch to competitors, go bankrupt, move out of the territory, merge with noncustomers, or decide to do without the product or service. A salesperson often needs to prospect even in existing accounts because of mergers, downsizing by firms, and job changes or retirements of buyers. Sales trainer Joe Girard uses a ferris wheel metaphor to describe the important process of adding new customers (loading new accounts onto the ferris wheel) to replace customers you lose (people getting off the ferris wheel). Without replacing lost accounts, your ferris wheel will soon be running with no one on board.

Of course, prospecting is more important in some selling fields than in others. For example, the office products salesperson, stockbroker, or real estate sales representative with no effective prospecting plan usually doesn't last long in the business. Sales positions such as these may require 100 contacts to get 10 prospects who will listen to presentations, out of which one person will buy. Each sale, then, represents a great deal of prospecting. It is also important in these fields to prospect continually. Some sales trainers relate this process to your car's gas tank: You don't wait until you are on empty before you fill up!

Some sales positions require less emphasis on locating new contacts. For example, a Procter & Gamble sales representative in a certain geographic area would know all the potential prospects for Crest toothpaste (all the grocery stores, drugstores, convenience stores, and so on) because they are easy to identify. For the same reason, a Du Pont sales rep selling a new line of automobile finishes to auto manufacturers and body shops in Ontario can easily identify all of the main prospects. A Lockheed Martin salesperson assigned exclusively to sell the F16 tactical fighter jet to Taiwan, South Korea, Greece, and Singapore would not spend any time trying to locate new governments to call on. For these types of sales positions, prospecting as we normally think of it (that is, looking for new leads) is not an important part of the sales process. Nevertheless, salespeople cannot ignore these obvious leads, as the next section discusses. Salespeople still have to assess whether leads are good prospects.

CHARACTERISTICS OF A GOOD PROSPECT

Prospecting actually begins with locating a **lead,** a person or an organization that may or may not have what it takes to be a true prospect. Some salespeople mistakenly consider every lead a prospect without first taking the time to see whether these people really provide an opportunity to make a sale.

To avoid that mistake the salesperson must **qualify the lead.** Qualifying is the process of determining whether a lead is in fact a prospect.

If the salesperson determines that the lead is a good candidate for making a sale, that person or organization is no longer considered a lead and instead is called a **prospect.** Many leads do not become prospects. Exhibit 7.1 displays the relationship between the steps in the selling process and the terminology we use to refer to the "buyer." Note that qualifying can occur during several

EXHIBIT 7.1

Relationship between
the Steps in the Selling
Process and the
Designation of
the "Buyer"

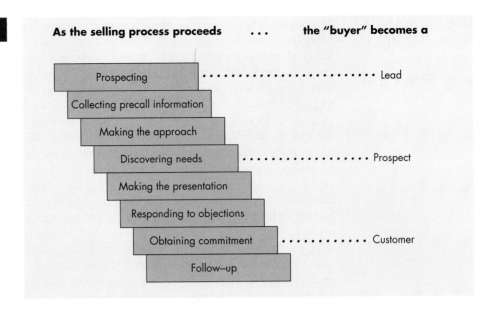

stages: prospecting, collecting precall information, making the approach, and discovering needs.

Naturally, the amount of time spent trying to determine which leads are prospects varies in different types of selling. It depends on such factors as the type of product or service, the value of the salesperson's time, and the profit per sale. The following five questions help to qualify leads and pinpoint the good prospects:

- Does the lead have a want or a need that the purchase of my products or services can satisfy?
- Does the lead have the ability to pay?
- Does the lead have the authority to buy?
- Can the lead be approached favorably?
- Is the lead eligible to buy?

These questions can be asked about the person who is a lead, the lead's firm, or both. Chapter 8 discusses how to begin gathering the information needed to answer these questions, and Chapter 9 provides further instruction on how to gather the remaining needed information during actual sales calls. For now, let's look at each question a little more closely.

DOES A WANT OR NEED EXIST?

Research has supplied no infallible answers to why customers buy, but it has found many reasons. As we pointed out in Chapter 4, customers buy to satisfy practical needs as well as intangible needs, such as prestige or aesthetics.

Determining whether leads need a salesperson's products or services is not always simple. Many firms use the telephone or e-mail to assess needs. Sometimes an exploratory interview is conducted to determine whether a lead has needs the seller's products can satisfy. Also, almost everyone has a need for some product lines; for example, practically every organization needs fax machines, copiers, paper, and a telephone system.

By using high-pressure tactics, sales may be made to those who do not need or really want a product. Such sales benefit no one. The buyer will resent making the purchase, and a potential long-term customer will be lost. The lead must want to solve his or her problem to be considered a qualified prospect.

DOES THE LEAD HAVE THE ABILITY TO PAY?

The ability to pay for the products or services helps to separate leads from prospects. For example, the commercial real estate agent usually checks the financial status of each client to determine the price range of office buildings to show. A client with annual profits of $100,000 and cash resources of $75,000 may be a genuine prospect for an office building selling in the $200,000 to $250,000 bracket. An agent would be wasting time, however, by showing this client an office building listed at $10 million. The client may have a real desire and need for the more expensive setting, but the client is still not a real prospect for the higher-priced office building if he or she doesn't have the resources to pay for it.

Ability to pay includes both cash and credit. Many companies subscribe to a credit-rating service offered by firms such as Dun & Bradstreet, Moody's, Value Line, and Standard & Poor's. This information is available on CD-ROM and can be accessed via the Web for a fee. Salespeople use information from these sources, often accessed directly from the salesperson's laptop or handheld PC, to determine the financial status and credit rating of a lead. They can also qualify leads with information obtained from local credit agencies, consumer credit agencies such as Experian, noncompetitive salespeople, and the Better Business Bureau. Salespeople are sometimes surprised at their leads' credit ratings. Some big-name firms have poor ratings.

DOES THE LEAD HAVE THE AUTHORITY TO BUY?

A lead may have a real need for a product and the ability to pay for it but lack the authority to make the purchase. Knowing who has this authority saves the salesperson time and effort and results in a higher percentage of closed sales. As discussed in Chapter 4, many people are typically involved in a purchase decision, and frequently it is unclear who has the most influence.

Because of downsizing, more firms are delegating their purchasing tasks to outside vendors. These vendors, often called **systems integrators**, have the authority to buy products and services from others. Systems integrators usually assume complete responsibility for a project, from its beginning to follow-up servicing. An example would be Lockheed Martin acting as a systems integrator for the complete mail-processing system of a new postal sorting facility in Germany. In that scenario every potential vendor would actually be selling to Lockheed Martin, not to the German government. When systems integrators are involved, salespeople need to delineate clearly who has the authority to purchase. Sometimes the overall buyer (the German government in this example) will retain veto power over potential vendors.

CAN THE LEAD BE APPROACHED FAVORABLY?

Some leads with a need, the ability to pay, and the authority to buy may still not qualify as prospects because they are not accessible to the salesperson. For example, the president of a large bank, a major executive of a large manufacturing company, or the senior partner in a well-established law firm normally would not be accessible to a young college graduate starting out as a sales representative for an investment trust organization. Getting an interview with these people may be so difficult and the chances of making a sale so small that the sales representative eliminates them as possible prospects.

IS THE LEAD ELIGIBLE TO BUY?

Eligibility is an equally important factor in finding a genuine prospect. For example, a salesperson who works for a firm that requires a large minimum order should not call on leads that could never order in such volume. Likewise, a representative who sells exclusively to wholesalers should be certain the individuals he or she calls on are actually wholesalers, not retailers.

Another factor that may determine eligibility for a particular salesperson is the geographic location of the prospect. Most companies operate on the basis of

exclusive sales territories, meaning that a particular salesperson can sell only to certain prospects (such as doctors in only a three-county area) and not to other prospects. A salesperson working for such a company must consider whether the prospect is eligible, based on location or customer type, to buy from him or her.

Salespeople should also avoid targeting leads already covered by their corporate headquarters. Large customers or potential customers that are handled exclusively by corporate executives are often called **house accounts.** For example, if Hilton Hotels considers PepsiCo a house account, a Hilton Hotel salesperson (who sets up events and conventions at the hotel) located in New York City should not try to solicit business from one of PepsiCo's divisions located in New York City. Instead, all PepsiCo business would be handled by a Hilton executive at Hilton corporate headquarters.

OTHER CRITERIA

Leads that meet the five criteria are generally considered excellent prospects. Some sellers, however, add other criteria. For example, DEI Management Group instructs its salespeople to classify leads by their likelihood of buying. Salespeople may have a long list of companies that need their product, can pay for it, have authority to buy it, and are approachable and eligible. If, however, these companies have absolutely no interest in buying, the salesperson should look elsewhere.

Criteria can include many things. Some firms look at the timing of purchase to determine whether a lead is really a good prospect.[1] Relevant questions to consider include When does the prospect's contract with our competitor expire? and Is a purchase decision really pending? How do we know? Still other firms look at the long-term potential of developing a partnering relationship with a lead. Some questions to ponder include What is the climate at the organization—is it looking to develop partnering relationships with suppliers? Do any of our competitors already have a partnering relationship there? Answers to these and other questions help a firm determine whether a lead is worth pursuing at this time.

HOW AND WHERE TO OBTAIN PROSPECTS

Prospecting sources and methods vary for different types of selling. A sales representative selling corrugated containers for Tenneco, for example, may use a system different than banking or office products salespeople would use. Exhibit 7.2 presents an overview of some of the most common lead-generating methods. Note that there is some overlap among the methods.

SATISFIED CUSTOMERS

Satisfied customers, particularly those who are truly partners with the seller, are the most effective sources for leads. In fact, one authority claims that successful salespeople should be getting about 75 percent of their new business through referrals from customers.[2] Referrals of leads in the same industry are particularly useful because the salesperson already understands the unique needs of this type of organization (If I have sold to a bank already, I have a better understanding of banks' needs). Referrals in some cultures (like Japan) are even more important than they are in North America.[3]

To maximize the usefulness of satisfied customers, salespeople should follow several logical steps. First, they should make a list of potential references (customers who might provide leads) from among their most satisfied customers. This task will be much easier if the salespeople have maintained an accurate and detailed database of customers. Next, they should decide what they would like each customer to do (such as have the customer write a personal letter of introduction, see whether the customer would be willing to take phone inquiries, have the customer directly contact prospects, or have the customer provide a generic letter of reference). Finally, salespeople should ask the customer for the names of leads and for the specific type of help she or he can provide. And because people have trouble coming up with a list of good leads, salespeople should give their customers time to think of names.

Salespeople shouldn't neglect the importance of getting leads from customers.[4] One study found that 80 percent of clients would be willing to give referrals, but only 20 percent are ever even asked to do so.[5] The study also found that one referral is as valuable as 12 unsolicited cold calls to leads.

Sometimes customers aren't willing to offer referrals. Why? At times it is because they know that if the salesperson somehow doesn't do a good job, they will be blamed. For this method of prospecting to work, the salesperson must continually keep the referring customer and the prospect fully satisfied. Also, asking for referrals when a new customer signs the order may be too soon. It would

EXHIBIT 7.2

Overview of Common
Sources of Leads

Source	How Used
Satisfied customers	Current and previous customers are contacted for additional business and leads.
Endless chain	Salesperson attempts to secure at least one additional lead from each person he or she interviews.
Center of influence	Salesperson cultivates well-known, influential people in the territory who are willing to supply lead information.
Networking	Salesperson uses personal relationships with those who are connected and cooperative to secure leads.
The Internet	Salesperson uses websites, e-mail, Listservs, bulletin boards, forums, roundtables, and newsgroups to secure leads.
Ads, direct mail, catalogs, and publicity	Salespeople use these forms of promotional activities to generate leads.
Shows	Salespeople use trade shows, conventions, and fairs for lead generation.
Seminars	Salespeople use seminars for prospects to generate leads.
Lists and directories	Salesperson uses secondary data sources, which can be free or fee-based.
Data mining and CRM systems	Salespeople use sophisticated data analysis software and the company's CRM system to generate leads.
Cold calling	Salesperson tries to generate leads by calling on totally unfamiliar organizations.
Spotters	Salesperson pays someone for lead information.
Telemarketing	Salesperson uses phone and/or telemarketing staff to generate leads.
Sales letters	Salesperson writes personal letters to potential leads.
Other sources	Salesperson uses noncompeting salespeople (people in his or her own firm, friends, and so on) to secure information.

probably be best to wait until the new customer has had a chance to use the product and experience both the product's benefits and the level of salesperson service.

Satisfied customers not only provide leads but also are usually prospects for additional sales. This situation is sometimes referred to as **selling deeper** to a current customer. Salespeople should never overlook this profitable opportunity. Sales to existing customers often result in more profits than do sales to new customers. For example, if a midsized company increased its customer retention by just 5 percent, its profits would double in only 10 years. Chapter 13 explores this topic more fully.

ENDLESS-CHAIN METHOD

In the **endless-chain method,** sales representatives attempt to get at least one additional lead from each person they interview. This method works best when the source is a satisfied customer and partner; however, it may also be used even when a prospect does not buy.

For example, at the conclusion of a meeting, the following conversation might ensue:

SELLER: Jim, you told me that you belong to several professional trade associations. Since you said you liked what I'm offering you, maybe you know of some other members who could use my services?

BUYER: Well, you know, maybe Sarah Harkins, and even Josh Smyth, could use this service, too.

SELLER: You know a lot more about these people than I do. If you were me, whom would you call first?

BUYER: Harkins, I guess.

SELLER: When I call Ms. Harkins, may I mention that we are doing some work with you?

Some people object to having their names used as a means of opening the door to friends or business acquaintances. Others, particularly those who trust the salesperson and/or are enthusiastic about the products or services, will not hesitate to provide the names of additional prospects and may even write a letter or card of introduction for the sales representative. The name of a lead provided by either a customer or a prospect, known as a **referred lead,** is generally considered to be the most successful type of lead.[6] Exhibit 7.3 illustrates how a sales representative successfully used the endless-chain method.

CENTER-OF-INFLUENCE METHOD

In the **center-of-influence method,** the salesperson cultivates a relationship with well-known, influential people in the territory who are willing to supply the names of leads. A friend of one of the authors likes to call centers of influence "bell cows" because the rest of the herd follow their lead.

This method, like the endless-chain method, works best if the center of influence is already a satisfied customer of the salesperson. Here is the way an indus-

---

EXHIBIT 7.3   Example of the Endless-Chain Method of Prospecting

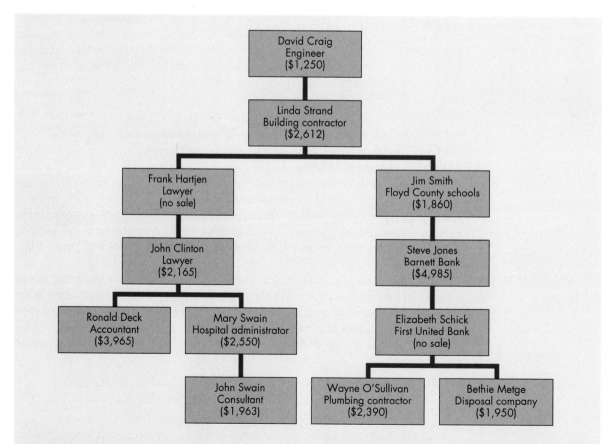

The sales representative used the endless-chain method to produce $25,690 in business (selling fax machines) within a 30-day period. All the sales resulted directly or indirectly from the first referral from an engineer to whom the sales rep had sold a mere $1,250 worth of equipment.

trial cleaning service salesperson used the center-of-influence method when meeting with a well-known and respected maintenance engineer:

> Now I've had the chance to explain my service, and you've had the opportunity to meet my cleaning crew. I wonder if you will do me a favor? You mentioned that it was probably the best-designed package you've ever seen. I know that as an engineer you wouldn't personally need my services, but can you think of any of your business associates who could benefit from such a plan? Does one come to mind?

In industrial sales situations the centers of influence are frequently people in important departments not directly involved in the purchase decision, such as quality control, equipment maintenance, and receiving. The salesperson keeps in close touch with these people over an extended period, solicits their help in a straightforward manner, and keeps them informed about sales that result from their aid.

The Roper Organization, which has studied centers of influence for more than 45 years, states that they are consistent in one aspect: their degree of activity. Centers of influence tend to be those who enjoy being very socially involved in their communities. And people in the community not only trust these individuals but also seek out their advice.

One true story illustrates the method's use. A Xerox representative found that decision makers from several companies would get together from time to time. These accounts formed a **buying community:** a small, informal group of people in similar positions, often from several companies, who communicate regularly, both socially and professionally. The salesperson also found that one particular decision maker in that group, or community, would share the results of any sales call with the other members of the community. Thus a call on that account had the power of seven calls. By working carefully with this center of influence, the salesperson closed nine orders from the seven accounts, with sales that totaled more than $450,000.

Centers of influence may never buy. One church furnishings representative told of a pastor who suggested that the rep call on two other churches, both of which were in the market for pews. The pastor who made the referral has not purchased pews in more than 10 years and probably will not for many more. But the salesperson continues to spend time with that pastor, who is an important center of influence in the pastoral community.

How do you find centers of influence? Try asking customers and prospects whom they consider to be the most influential person in their industry or association. Then actively cultivate a relationship with the center of influence.

NETWORKING

Networking is the utilization of personal relationships by connected and cooperating individuals for the purpose of achieving goals. In selling, networking simply means establishing connections to other people and then using those networks to generate leads, gather information, generate sales, and so on. Note that networking can, and often does, include centers of influence and satisfied customers.

Networking is crucial in many selling situations. For example, trying to sell in China without successful networking (called *guanxi* in China) would be disastrous.[7] Almost everyone can benefit by networking more actively.

Successful networkers offer a number of practical suggestions.[8] First, call at least two people per day and go to at least one networking event every week to increase your exposure and time with your contacts. You must make a special effort to move outside your own "comfort zone" in a social setting. Learn to mingle with people you don't already know. One expert calls this behavior acting like a host instead of like a guest. Second, spend most of your initial conversation with a new contact talking about his or her business, not yours, and don't forget to learn about the person's nonbusiness interests. Third, follow up with your new contact on a regular basis with cards, notes of congratulations about awards or promotions and articles and information that might help her or him. Whenever you receive a lead from your contact, send a handwritten, personal note thanking the person for the information, regardless of whether the lead buys from you. Whenever possible, send your new contact lead information as well.

THE INTERNET

Probably the fastest-growing method of generating leads is through the Internet. Successful salespeople are using websites, e-mail, Listservs®, bulletin boards, forums, roundtables, and newsgroups to connect to individuals and companies that may be interested in their products or services. New technologies, which are unfolding at a dizzying pace, allow a selling firm to use various methods, including audio, video (such as showing product demonstrations or plant tours), and text (letters of reference, product specifications, specials, lists of contacts) to provide information to prospects. For example, T/R Systems, which sells printing systems, uses its website to give leads information about products, show them where the nearest dealers are located, and gather their names and addresses if they desire more information.[9] The result is about 20 new leads directly from the website each week, of which about one-third are actually prospects. One advantage of Web-based promotions is the number of international leads that can be secured, and T/R realizes this benefit as well. It is very important for firms to plan ways to respond quickly to prospects' requests from websites.[10]

Firms use the Web to solicit leads in a number of ways.[11] Foremost, firms make sure their sites are listed on the major and important **search engines,** the tools that individuals use to locate sites. Search engine placement can be one of the most difficult areas of marketing on the Web because many times a search engine does not have a proper category for the products that the firm sells. These

A company's Web pages help solicit leads for its salespeople.

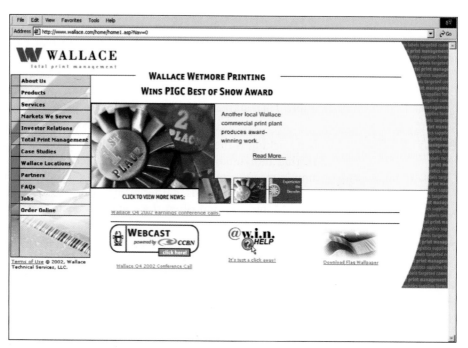

© Wallace Computer Services, Inc.

have to be continually monitored and updated because the search engines change their criteria regularly. Firms also use banner advertising on other websites, either for a fee or on a barter basis. **Banner advertising** consists of ads placed at the top, sides, or bottom of a Web page, encouraging the viewer to visit a different website. For example, Marketing Logistics, a firm that sells teaching aids to the early childhood industry, placed banner ads on the CNN Parent Network and CareGuide websites. Another way to gather leads on the Internet is to post a message on user group sites or via e-mail to a list the company has purchased.

Firms increasingly take advantage of new software that helps them utilize the Web more effectively in prospecting. For example, Resonate, a Sunnyvale, California, firm, uses ProspectMiner software. ProspectMiner automates a search process (using keywords supplied by Resonate) of multiple search engines and online databases. When it thinks it has found a good prospect for Resonate, the software searches the prospect firm's website, gathering key data like financial information, contact information, names of company officers, and important news items. This prospect information is then provided to Resonate salespeople for action.[12]

Firms are also developing extranets, Internet sites that are customized for specific targets. Extranets are usually used to build relationships with current customers, but some companies are also using these sites to generate leads. For example, Turner Broadcasting System (TBS), owner of CNN, TBS Superstation, and TNT, set up an extranet that's accessible only to media buyers.[13] Buyers are able to access programming information, cable research data, and Turner's salespeople from the site.

Some potential problems exist with using the Web to generate leads. Because not everyone has Internet access, some potential customers will be missed. Also, Internet access speeds, although improving, are still often very slow, a frustration for many busy executives. In fact, it has been estimated that more than $4 billion in e-commerce sales are lost each year because of slow download times.[14]

Some salespeople have learned how to successfully utilize e-mail to generate leads, a technique called **e-selling.** For example, Kendra Lee decided to use both e-mail and a traditional mailing to a list she secured.[15] The result was not a single lead from the mailing, but 26 leads from her e-mail messages. There are potential drawbacks to using e-mail, however. **Spam,** a term used for unwanted and unsolicited junk e-mail, is causing concern and frustration among Internet users. Although careful marketers target their recipients and the messages they send, some people may still get angry at receiving an unsolicited message. Also, dealing with the replies can be quite time-consuming. For example, Joe Davis receives and answers about 100 e-mail messages a day in connection with his consulting business. Finally, because of the "casual" nature of e-mail, salespeople can make mistakes in its application for generating and responding to leads. As one writer put it, "E-mail allows us to act before we can think."[16] Responding without thinking carefully can do more damage than good, which may be why more than 60 percent of salespeople aren't using e-mail for prospecting.[17]

ADS, DIRECT MAIL, CATALOGS, AND PUBLICITY

Firms have developed sophisticated systems to generate inquiries from leads by using advertising and direct mail. For example, Hewlett-Packard (HP) sends out direct mail to potential customers for its color copiers. The firm also places advertisements in trade publications, such as *Presentations.* A reader of the ad can request additional information by calling a toll-free number or by returning the reader service card at the back of the magazine.

HP also participates in **postcard packs.** A postcard pack is a group of postcards (usually between 15 and 50 different cards) that provide information from many firms. Each firm has one card, usually describing one product or service. One side of HP's postcard contains information about a specific product or service (such as HP's Praesidium Internet security system). The other side, which is prestamped, carries HP's address. A company interested in learning more about HP's product simply fills in its name and address and drops the card in the mail.

Anyone who inquires about HP's products receives a cover letter, information about the advertised product, and a follow-up inquiry card. A copy of the inquiry goes to the appropriate salesperson. Based on knowledge of the territory, the salesperson decides whether a personal follow-up is appropriate. If the inquirer returns the second inquiry card (frequently called a **bounce-back card**), HP again notifies the salesperson. Then the salesperson can follow up on the lead with a visit or a phone call.

Many marketing promotions are tied to a toll-free number and the inquirer's fax machine. The prospect calls the toll-free number, talks to a salesperson (or voice mail), and is then asked to supply his or her fax number. The requested information is sent within seconds, often while the salesperson is still on the phone with the prospect.

Salespeople sometimes discount the value of leads generated by inquiries. That's not a good practice, according to M.H. McIntosh, who has researched and tracked more than 40,000 sales inquiries. He found that 24 percent who inquire will buy from someone in 6 months; by 12 months the buy rate rises to 45 percent.[18]

SHOWS

Many companies display or demonstrate their products at trade shows, conventions, and fairs. Sales representatives are present to demonstrate products to visitors, many of whom salespeople have not called on before.

Often the primary function of salespeople at shows is to qualify leads for future follow-up. Typically having only 5 to 10 minutes with a prospect, they need to get down to business and qualify the visitor quickly. At other trade shows (such as furniture shows), salespeople actually sell and therefore generally spend more time with the buyer. Chapter 15 provides more information on how to close sales at shows.

Successful salespeople practice adaptive selling (discussed in Chapter 6) when interacting with prospects who stop by their booths.[19] Thus instead of mechanically asking, Are you enjoying the show? or Can I help you with something today? sharp salespeople try to discover whether the lead has a need or a want that they can meet. The seller then provides the lead with helpful information and gathers

Participating in trade shows and holding seminars are two activities that help salespeople discover and qualify leads.

Einzig Photographers

Einzig Photographers

CAN'T GET SOMEONE TO DRIVE TO YOUR PROSPECTING SEMINAR?
TRY ONLINE, INSTEAD

Prospects are increasingly busy and have less and less time to drive to seminars that sellers put on for their benefit. What are some possible solutions? How about paying the prospects to attend, or giving them something of real economic value? While those solutions have promise, some progressive firms are trying a new approach: Web-based seminars.

Oracle Corporation has been using Web-based seminars for several years. All of the seminars are live and are designed specifically for prospective clients of Oracle's high-tech systems. Prospects can choose from a list of seminars that are displayed on Oracle's Web page and dial in at the appropriate date and time. Oracle pays for

any costs prospects might incur in dialing into the system. Around 125 prospects have "attended" each seminar. After experiencing the show, prospects are directed to appropriate Oracle Web pages to learn more about products and order if they so desire.

"It costs our clients nothing but time," claims Nat Robinson, Oracle's Internet marketing program senior manager, "and we're reaching a much wider audience than we would have if we were doing in-person seminars." Oh, and what about sales revenues? They're up, too.

Source: Melinda Ligos, "Point, Click & Sell," *Sales and Marketing Management*, May 1999, p. 54.

---

information that will be used later in further qualifying the lead and preparing for a sales call. Timely follow-up of leads is critical if sales are to follow a show.

SEMINARS

Today many firms use seminars to generate leads and to provide information to prospective customers.[20] For example, a local pharmaceutical representative for Bristol-Myers Squibb will set up a seminar for 8 to 10 oncologists and invite a nationally known research oncologist to make a presentation. The research specialist usually discusses some new technique or treatment being developed. During or after the presentation, the pharmaceutical representative for Bristol-Myers Squibb will describe how Squibb's drug Taxol® helps in the treatment of ovarian and breast cancer. Selling Scenario 7.1 explains how one company uses on-line seminars to generate prospects.

What are some key things to keep in mind when planning a seminar? Make sure your seminar appeals to a specialized market and invite good prospects, especially those prospects who might not be willing to see you one-on-one. The subject should be something your attendees have a strong interest in, while your speaker must be considered an authority on the topic. Try to go as high-quality as possible (remember, you're building an image) and consider having food. Finally, you should take an active role before, during, and after the seminar.

LISTS AND DIRECTORIES

Individual sales representatives can develop prospect lists from sources such as public records, telephone directories, chamber of commerce directories, newspapers, trade publications, club membership lists, and professional or trade membership lists. Secondary sources of information from public libraries also can be useful. For example, industrial trade directories are available for all states. Exhibit 7.4 lists some useful secondary sources for leads.

It is often useful to know the **standard industrial classification (SIC)** code for an industry when researching for leads, since many publications are indexed by SIC codes. The SIC system is being replaced by the new **North America industry classification system (NAICS)**, which is a uniform classification for all countries in North America.[21]

EXHIBIT 7.4   Partial List of Secondary Sources of Lead Information*

Source	Description	Website
Annual reports for firms in Europe and Asia	Links to annual reports and Web home pages for firms in Asia and Europe	www.carol.co.uk/carol.html
Annual reports for U.S. firms	Links to most annual reports, as well as home pages	www.reportgallery.com
IndustryLink	Directory of links to industry websites	www.industrylink.com
Current Industrial Reports	Measures of industrial activity	www.census.gov/ftp/pub/cir/www/
Thomas Register of American Manufacturers	Lists manufacturers by product classifications, company profits, and specific product information	www.thomasregister.com/loggedin.cgi
Fortune 500 Information	Details on *Fortune 500* firms	www.fortune.com
Inc. 500 Information	Details on the fastest growing small businesses in America, the *Inc. 500* list	www.inc.com/inc500/
Encyclopedia of Associations**	Lists 23,000 national associations; more than 20,000 international organizations; 295,000 nonprofit organizations; and more than 92,000 regional, state, and local organizations	www.gale.com
Web Yellow Pages	Contains more than 11 million U.S. business listings	www.bigyellow.com
Business Lists (InfoUSA)**	Contains a complete database on millions of U.S. businesses	www.infousa.com
Middle Market Directory** (Dun & Bradstreet)	Lists 14,000 firms worth between $500, 000 and $1 million	www.dnb.com
Hoover's Online	Provides an excellent search tool for information on businesses	www.hoovers.com
Moody's Industrial Directory**	Contains an annual listing of names, type of business, and a brief financial statement for more than 10,000 publicly held corporations	www.moodys.com
Databases of articles in journals, newspapers, and magazines from search banks like ABI Inform, First Search, and Lexis-Nexis**	Allow you to find articles that have been written about firms and individuals	www.proquest.com www.lexis-nexis.com

*Most libraries own hard copies of some of these resources.

**Must purchase or pay a fee to use.

Salespeople can purchase a number of prospecting directories and lead-generating publications. You can purchase, by geographical area, mailing lists for all gerontologists (specialists in geriatrics), Lions clubs, T-shirt retailers, yacht owners, antique dealers, Catholic high schools, motel supply houses, nudists, multimillionaires, pump wholesalers, and thousands of other classifications. These lists can be delivered as printed mailing labels or on a CD-ROM. Some lists can be secured directly from the Web.

Salespeople should keep in mind that purchased lists can have several drawbacks. The lists may not be current. They may contain some inaccurate information regardless of the guarantee of accuracy. People who are on lists may be targeted by many, many firms and thus be less open to hearing from yet another salesperson. Finally, because lists are easy to obtain and use, some salespeople tend to rely on them exclusively when other methods of prospecting might result in better leads.

Most lists are simply names and telephone numbers. However, prospecting systems can be much more elaborate. For example, construction firms in some large cities can pay to access computerized databases of planned construction projects that meet the user's criteria (type of work to be performed, amount budgeted for the project, method of payment, and so on). Such lists obviously include much more than just names and phone numbers of leads.

In international selling situations, procuring lists can be much more difficult. One of the biggest problems in selling in Mexico under the North American Free Trade Agreement (NAFTA) is that mailing lists and databases simply do not exist. Nor is this phenomenon unique to Mexico; many firms dealing in international selling environments face similar problems.

DATA MINING AND CRM SYSTEMS

Sophisticated firms are developing interactive **databases** that contain information on leads, prospects, and customers. For example, Pioneer, one of the country's largest producers of seed corn, has a dynamic database of 600,000 farm operators in the United States and Canada that everyone in the firm can access. The system has resulted in better sales prospecting and more tailored sales presentations. Chapter 16 more fully examines the issue of databases.

Progressive firms are using **data mining**, artificial intelligence and statistical tools to discover insights hidden in the volumes of data in their databases.[22] For example, Eagle Equipment of Norton, Massachusetts, uses iMarket software to target its sales calls to the best prospects. Using the company's database, the software identifies prospects most likely to buy something and then matches that profile against a database of 12 million businesses. The resulting prospect lists are sorted by SIC codes, size, and target categories, ready for the sales force to use in generating new business.[23]

CRM systems are also being tapped to help locate the best prospects to call upon. For example, AMD, the $4.6 billion computer chip maker that competes primarily against Intel, used the CRM system called One-to-One Lead Management to discover the profile of the best prospect. The results so far have been outstanding, with one sale paying for the entire development cost of the system.[24]

COLD CALLING

Before learning about other prospecting methods, college students often assume salespeople spend most of their time making cold calls. In using the **cold canvass method,** or **cold calls** (by call we usually mean a personal visit, not a telemarketing call), a sales representative tries to generate leads for new business by calling on totally unfamiliar organizations. Historically, this method was used extensively. However, cold canvassing can waste a salesperson's time, since many companies have neither a need for the product nor the ability to pay for it. This fact stresses the importance of qualifying the lead quickly in a cold call so as not to waste time. Also, today cold calling is considered rude by many purchasing agents and other professionals.

Salespeople often rate making cold calls as the part of the job they like least.[25] Thus, as mentioned earlier, most firms now encourage their salespeople to qualify leads instead of relying on the cold call. In fact, American Express (Amex) Financial Advisors banned cold calling for its 8,000 salespeople nationwide in late 1995. This policy has forced the reps to use other methods, such as networking and referrals.

Still, some companies use cold calling.[26] And some companies use a selective type of cold canvass they refer to as a **blitz:** A large group of salespeople attempts to call on all of the prospective businesses in a given geographical territory on a specified day. For example, an office machine firm may target a specific four-block area in Guadalajara, Mexico; bring in all of the salespeople from the surrounding areas; and then have them, in one day, call on every business located in that four-block area. The purpose is to generate leads for the local sales representative as well as to build camaraderie and a sense of unity among the salespeople.

SPOTTERS

Some salespeople use **spotters,** also called **bird dogs.** These individuals will, for a fee, provide leads for the salesperson. The sales rep sometimes pays the fee simply for the name of the lead but more often pays only if the lead ends up buying the product or service. Spotters are usually in a position to find out when someone is ready to make a purchase decision. For example, a janitorial service firm employee who notices that the heating system for a client is antiquated and hears people complaining about it can turn this information over to a heating contractor.

A more recent development is the use of outside paid consultants to locate and qualify leads. Small firms attempting to secure business with very large organizations are most likely to use this approach. For example, Synesis Corporation, a small firm specializing in computerized training, used the services of a consultant to identify and develop leads. The result of one lead was a major contract with AT&T.

Beware, however, when offering a fee to a customer.[27] Your action may be misconstrued by the customer as exploiting the relationship. Also, some customers' firms may prohibit such behavior. Sometimes it is better to send a personal thank-you note or small gift to the customer instead.

TELEMARKETING

Increasingly, firms are relying on telemarketing to perform many functions sales representatives used to perform. **Telemarketing** is a systematic and continuous program of communicating with customers and prospects via telephone. Telemarketing is not limited to consumer sales; in fact, all the examples in this section involve business-to-business companies. Telemarketing is now used to sell everything from 25-cent supplies to $10 million airplanes.

In **outbound telemarketing** telephones are used to generate and then qualify leads. These calls may be initiated directly by the salesperson or by inside sales representatives (inside sales reps were discussed in Chapter 1).[28] **Inbound telemarketing** uses a telephone number (usually a toll-free number) that leads and/or customers can call for additional information. Again, the call may be answered by several types of persons: the salesperson, an inside salesperson, or a customer service representative. For example, Motorola Corporation's Land Mobile Products Sector, which sells mobile communication systems to such diverse entities as contractors, hotels, and police stations, uses outbound telemarketing to generate and then qualify leads for its sales force. Qualified leads are turned over to field sales representatives if the order is large enough to warrant a personal visit to the company. If the prospect needs a smaller system, a separate telemarketing salesperson will handle the account. Motorola also uses inbound telemarketing by providing

Earl Kogler/International Stock

a toll-free number for people who want more information about a product or service Motorola offers. Because of this excellent telemarketing organization, Motorola's field reps have more time to spend with qualified prospects and more time to develop long-term customer relations.

LIMITATIONS OF TELEPHONE PROSPECTING

Although the telephone is a wonderful tool that can enhance productivity, it also has some limitations. First, customers may find telephone calls an annoying inconvenience. Did you know that the average executive in 1998 received 190 voice mail messages per day, and that by 2000 it was up to 201 messages per day via fax, cell phone, and e-mail?[29] In fact, the Federal Trade Commission (FTC) enforces a number of laws and rules (such as the Telephone Consumer Protection Act and the Telemarketing Sales Rule) that, among other things, require significant disclosures before a telemarketer can even begin selling to consumers.[30] Unexpected calls may interrupt customers involved in meetings or concentrating on their work. When telephoning customers—in fact, at all times—salespeople need to respect the customers' privacy and not abuse the privilege.

Second, telephones limit communications to verbal messages. For this reason, the telephone may be a poor choice when salespeople need to show the product to determine whether someone is a prospect. Also, salespeople cannot read customers' nonverbal cues in a telephone conversation and thus may miss or misunderstand a customer's message.

Third, attracting and maintaining the customer's attention and interest is harder over the telephone than it is in person. During face-to-face encounters, people are generally more polite and will concentrate on the person with whom they are talking. But customers talking on the telephone can engage in other activities; they may even continue to work or read a report or magazine.

Fourth, outbound telemarketers sometimes call firms without knowing anything about them. This process can lead to embarrassing mistakes, as Beth Cocchiarella found when she made a telemarketing call to the competition. "I was mortified," she said.[31] Can you imagine asking your competitor to look at your new product? Since then her firm has invested in a system that provides the telemarketer with more information about the company he or she is calling so as to avoid similar embarrassing situations.

Fifth, it can be very hard to actually connect with the prospect on the phone today. Many prospects use caller ID to screen calls. As one rep put it, "How many times a day do I sit there thinking that people are *not* taking my calls—on purpose?"[32] Add to that voice mail, which also intercepts salespeople's calls. A recent estimate is that you must call 40 telephone numbers to make 10 complete calls.[33]

Finally, saying no is much easier over the phone than in person. Because they cannot see the salesperson, customers may even be rude during telephone conversations. To end a phone conversation by hanging up is easy; to walk away from a face-to-face conversation with a salesperson is harder.

TIE-IN WITH OTHER TOOLS

Firms are learning to tie together direct mail, e-mail, and registrations at the company's website with inbound and outbound telemarketing to reach potential prospects effectively. For example, one firm offers a catalog to interested parties. After receiving a request, the firm sends out a catalog and has a salesperson follow up with a phone call about a week after the mailing. This phone call allows the salesperson to gauge the strength of the lead as a prospect.

SALES LETTERS

Prospecting sales letters should be integrated into an overall prospecting plan. For example, Xerox salespeople who handle smaller businesses send prospecting sales letters every day. They follow up three days later with a telephone prospecting call and ask for an appointment for a personal visit. The telephone call begins with a question about the letter.

Like the telephone, sales letters have limitations. Once the message is sent, it cannot be modified to fit the prospect's style. The sender also has no chance to alter the message on the basis of feedback. Blanket mailings, then, can seem impersonal. And the recent anthrax scare has caused many to be wary of any unsolicited mail they might receive, resulting in much mail being thrown away without consideration.[34]

Because people in business receive so much mail, sales letters should be written with care. Think about the amount of junk mail and junk e-mail you receive and how much you throw away or delete without a second glance. It's not surprising that the rate of response from mailings is often as low as 2 percent.[35] Sales letters must stand out to be successful.

One way to make sales letters stand out is to include a promotional item with the mailer. First National Bank of Shreveport, Louisiana, targeted certified public accountants (CPAs) for one mailer. The bank timed the mailers to arrive on April 16, the day after the federal income tax filing deadline. Included in each mailer was a small bottle of wine, a glass, and cheese and crackers—a party kit designed to celebrate the end of tax season. The bank followed up with telephone calls two days later and ultimately gained 21 percent of the CPAs as new customers.

The salesperson must first consider the objective of any written communication (like a sales letter or e-mail message) and the audience. What action does the salesperson desire from the reader? Why would the reader want to undertake that action? Why would the reader not want to undertake the action? These questions help guide the salesperson in writing the letter.

The opening paragraph must grab the reader's attention, just as a salesperson's approach must get a prospect's attention in a face-to-face call. The opening gives the readers a reason to continue reading, drawing them into the rest of the letter.

Another way to gain attention is to have a loyal client whom the prospect respects write the introduction (or even the entire letter) for the salesperson. Here's an example of an opening paragraph:

> Thanks for stopping by the Datasource booth at the Strictly Business Computer Expo. I hope you enjoyed the show and had some fun shooting hoops with us! Were you there when one highly energetic attendee shot the basketball clear over into the Microsoft booth and knocked the presenter's Palm™ handheld right out of his hand? You won't believe what he did next! I'll fill you in on the details in a moment, but first I'd like to invite you to something I know you're not going to want to miss.

The next paragraph or two, the body of the letter, considers why the reader would and would not want to take the desired action. Benefits of taking the action should be presented clearly, without jargon, and briefly. The best-presented benefits are tailored to the specific individual, especially when the salesperson can refer to a recent conversation with the reader. A reference such as the following example can truly personalize the letter:

> As you said during our visit at the show, you're looking for a software firm that can work with a small business like yours, without making you feel like a second-class citizen. At Datasource, we've committed ourselves to working exclusively with small to midsized firms like yours.

If the salesperson and the buyer do not know each other, part of the body of the letter should be used to increase credibility. References to satisfied customers, market research data, and other independent sources can be used to improve credibility. For example:

> You may have heard that last year we won the prestigious Youcon Achievement Award, presented by the Tennessee Small Business Development Center in recognition for outstanding service specifically to small businesses. In fact, the small businesses themselves are the voters for the award. We're proud of that award because it tangibly reflects the commitment we've shown. And we have dedicated ourselves to continue in that tradition.

The final paragraph should seek commitment to the desired course of action. Whatever the action desired, the letter must specifically ask that it take place. The writer should leave no doubt in the prospect's mind as to what he or she is supposed to do. The writer should make the action for the prospect easy to accomplish, fully explain why it should be done now, and end with a positive picture. Here's an example:

> So I want to personally invite you to a free lunch seminar at Datasource. You'll hear from our partners on the very latest solutions to your technology challenges. The food promises to be great, and the information will be presented in a casual, small group setting. Please take a moment to reserve your spot at the lunch by visiting our website, www.datasource.com, or call 800-343-8764. You'll be glad you did.

A postscript (or PS) can also be effective. Postscripts stand out because of their location and should be used to make an important selling point. Alternatively, they can be used to emphasize the requested action, such as pointing out a deadline.

Thinking It Through

What do you hate most of all about junk mail (e-mail or regular mail)? Can you see any patterns in the way junk mailings present their sales messages? Could a field salesperson adapt some of their ideas to an industrial or trade selling situation?

THE "STRANDED AT THE AIRPORT" PROSPECTING METHOD

Jeff Multz knows the importance of prospecting wherever you go. Recently he was traveling home from visiting a customer in Virginia and got stranded in the Dulles airport. Sitting at the gate, he wondered how he should spend his time. Jeff noticed that a number of other travelers were stranded as well, among them about 190 sales reps just leaving a sales convention.

Now what you have to understand is that Jeff Multz works for Emerging Market Technologies and sells customer relationship management software for salespeople. And what was he surrounded by? Salespeople. Enough said.

Before long, Multz had 25 salespeople surrounding his laptop watching a demo of the software, 10 of which

worked for *Fortune* 100 firms. "I had a little trade show right in the airport, complete with business cards and information kits. I presented the product for about four hours to all of those sales and marketing executives."

The results? He's already landed two new accounts from the group, and he has six hot prospects worth millions in sales. All just from realizing that prospecting is a never-ending activity that can occur anywhere—even in a busy airport terminal with travel-frustrated leads.

Source: Christine Galea, "The Boldest Thing I Did to Make a Sale," *Sales and Marketing Management*, March 2000, p. 63.

OTHER SOURCES OF LEADS

Many salespeople find leads through personal observation. For example, by reading trade journals carefully, salespeople can learn the names of the most important leaders (and hence decision makers) in the industry. Sellers also read general business publications (such as *Business Week* and *The Wall Street Journal*) and local newspapers. It's easier now since so much of this is available free online. Also, a number of fee-based publications provide the same type of current information.[36] Sometimes you'll find prospects at the least likely times and places, as Building Partnerships 7.1 illustrates.

Nonsales employees within the salesperson's firm can also provide leads. Some companies strongly encourage this practice. For example, Computer Specialists Inc., a computer service firm, pays its nonsales employees a bonus of up to $1,000 for any names of prospective customers they pass along. In one year the program resulted in 75 leads and nine new accounts.

Government agencies can also supply lead information. For example, the Commerce Department identifies some of the hottest prospects for aircraft and aircraft parts, construction materials, computers and home electronics, and so forth around the world. The *Commerce Business Daily* provides information about federal government bid opportunities and can be viewed at http://cbdnet.gpo.gov.

Leads can be found in many other places as well. Salespeople for noncompeting but related products can often provide leads, as can members of trade associations. Good friends can also provide leads. Of course, one of the best ways to learn about new business opportunities is to keep up with regional, national, and world trends from sources such as *American Demographics* and *World Watch* magazines and industry surveys (Manufacturing USA, Service USA, Standard & Poor's Industry Surveys, U.S. Industrial Outlook, and the like).

LEAD QUALIFICATION AND MANAGEMENT SYSTEMS

Salespeople need to develop a process for qualifying leads, often called a **lead qualification system.** As mentioned early in this chapter, salespeople must ensure that their leads meet the five basic criteria of a prospect. Let's look more closely at this process.

Many firms view prospecting as a funneling process in which a large number of leads are funneled (or narrowed down) into prospects and some, finally, into customers.[37] To help salespeople use their time wisely, firms will often engage in **prequalification** of leads before turning them over to the field sales force. Sometimes the prequalification process is as simple as purchasing a prequalified list. For example, Street Fighter, Inc., a firm specializing in training small businesses to thrive on tight budgets, asked its list vendor to prequalify the leads supplied with the following characteristics: the contact name must be vice president or higher, the organization must have a minimum of 50 locations, and the organization must have sales in excess of $25 million.[38] At other times a firm will use the resources of telemarketers to prequalify leads. For example, telemarketers at Accrue Software identify the appropriate decision makers and further prequalify leads before passing them on to the outside sales force.[39]

Even though leads may appear to be good prospects, sometimes a salesperson can still waste his/her time. It is imperative that all prospects meet the selling company's parameters for what constitutes a good prospect. How does a "real" prospect differ from an "unreal" prospect, one who is not as worthy of time and effort? Brian Jeffrey, a sales trainer and consultant, notes the following characteristics of "unreal" prospects: They often try to create the impression that they are more important than they are, they resent your asking questions, they give vague or incomplete answers to your specific questions, they try to evade questions regarding budgets, and they try to get you to change your standard procedures (such as price, terms).[40] Real prospects, on the other hand, don't object to your questions, value your time, and are realistic about money and when they want to buy.

Salespeople must not only qualify leads but also carefully analyze the relative value of each lead. This part of the process is called a **lead management system.** Grading prospects and establishing a priority list results in increased sales and the most efficient use of time and energy. The following examples demonstrate the variety of factors considered. Belden Wire & Cable bases its lead-ranking matrix on issues such as whether the lead has a project that includes Belden's products, whether that project is going to happen in the next six months, and whether the lead currently purchases wire or cable. All leads are sent to the field sales force, with "hot" or "warm" leads given preference over "cold" ones. Steve Anderson, a top producer at Cadenhead Shreffler Insurance, grades leads on the basis of how they contacted the firm. Anderson ranks phone calls to his firm ahead of reader response cards because the calls exhibit an attitude that seems to say, "I don't mind being sold."

Beth Rounds, of CRI, uses six questions to rank prospects:[41]

1. How did you hear about us? (Leads from the Yellow Pages get a lower ranking than referrals from a colleague.)

2. What kind of work is it? (CRI wants to make sure that the prospect isn't just pricing a one-time project or one that the company can't handle well.)

3. What's your budget? (CRI wants to make sure that the prospect is realistic in terms of the costs involved.)

4. What are your decision criteria? (CRI doesn't usually do well in bid situations or drawn-out buying-committee types of decisions.)

5. Whom are we competing against for your business? (CRI wants to make sure that it is going up against its primary competitors. If primary competitors are not involved, that sends up a red flag.)

6. Why are you thinking of switching? (CRI wants to hear the prospect voice a legitimate need for a new supplier.)

The judicious use of technology makes lead qualification and management more efficient and effective. For example, Private Business, Inc., which develops and markets software for banks, uses software to analyze its current database and to create a demographic profile.[42] It then matches this profile against a listing of 10 million businesses to identify leads that are similar to its existing customers. The result is better management of the most important leads, the ones most likely to turn into customers.

Most salespeople now use laptops, PCs, personal wireless mobile tools like Palm™ handhelds, and software packages to keep track of leads. For example, Chad Stinchfield, national sales manager for Apprise Technologies, tracks his leads with software called ACT. (This is the same software that came shrink-wrapped with this textbook.) All of his records of calls and to-do lists are in his ACT database, which can be quickly retrieved with the click of a mouse.

A salesperson's use of software and hardware to track leads and prospects is often tied into a large, complete corporate system for managing prospects and salespeople's time and territories (Chapter 16 discusses this issue more fully). For example, software company Macromedia uses a comprehensive lead management system to keep track of leads from beginning to end.[43] All leads are centrally managed and prequalified by phone, fax, or the Internet. Based on additional information gleaned, each lead is graded and given a priority status before being directed to the appropriate salesperson. The system continues to monitor the lead as it moves through the sales cycle, and the information is used to prepare revenue and manufacturing forecasts. Macromedia's lead management system not only keeps the sales force happy but also has improved the company's profitability. As another example, IBM has tied its lead generation and management system into its CRM system. The results have been better tracking and prioritization of leads and prospects.[44]

Any good lead management system, like Macromedia's, should evaluate the profitability of sales resulting from various lead-generating activities instead of just counting the number of names a particular method yields. Analysis may show that the present system does not produce enough prospects or the right kinds of prospects. Salespeople may, for example, depend entirely on referred names from company advertising or from the service department. If these two sources do not supply enough names to produce the sales volume desired, other prospecting methods should be considered. A salesperson should not hesitate to

Although it is acceptable to socialize, this salesperson must learn not to waste so much time in the office.

SuperStock

scrap time-honored prospecting systems even if they have been used for years in the firm or industry or even by the salesperson's own sales manager. One of the key tenets of the learning organization (see Chapter 1) is to actively "unlearn" traditional but detrimental practices.[45] If a prospecting method that used to be excellent is no longer producing solid, profitable leads, it should be discarded for a more appropriate method. Salespeople should learn to study the methods that the most successful salespeople in their firm use because salespeople differ greatly in their ability to judge the strength of leads.

OVERCOMING A RELUCTANCE TO PROSPECT

People often stereotype salespeople as bold, adventurous, and somewhat abrasive. This view that salespeople are fearless is more fiction than fact.[46] Salespeople often struggle with a reluctance to prospect that persists no matter how well they have been trained and how much they believe in the products they sell. Many people are uncomfortable when they initially contact other people, but for salespeople reluctance to call can be a career-threatening condition.

Research shows a number of reasons for reluctance to call. Reasons include worrying about worst-case scenarios; spending too much time preparing; being overly concerned with looking successful; being fearful of making group presentations, of appearing too pushy, of losing friends or losing family approval, and of using the phone for prospecting; feeling intimidated by people with prestige or power, or feeling guilt at having a career in selling; and having a compulsive need to argue, make excuses, or blame others.

A recent study investigated sales call anxiety, of which sales prospecting would be one component. The authors discovered four dimensions of sales call anxiety: a negative self-evaluation by the salesperson ("I will be nervous and forget what I want to say"), imagined negative evaluations from customers ("If I don't know the answers to all of her questions, she's going to think I'm stupid"), a salesperson's physiological symptoms ("I'm sweating and blushing and my hands are cold"), and a desire to perform safety-seeking behaviors (avoiding eye contact, speaking quickly, fiddling with the hands, and ultimately withdrawing from contact with the prospect at all).[47]

Reluctance to call can and must be overcome to sell successfully. Several activities can help:

- Start by listening to the excuses other salespeople give to justify their call-reluctance behavior. Evaluate their validity. Then identify the excuses you use to avoid making calls and evaluate the validity of those excuses. You'll usually be surprised to find that most excuses really aren't valid.

- Engage in sales training and role-playing activity to improve your prospecting skills and your ability to handle questions and rejections that arise.

- Make prospecting contacts with a supporting partner or sales manager. Just their presence will often provide additional needed confidence (you won't feel so alone).

- Set specific goals for all of your prospecting activity. Chapter 16 will provide more direction in this activity.

- Realize the economic value of most prospecting activities. For example, if you keep good records, you may discover that every phone call you make (regardless of whether that particular prospect buys) results in an *average* of $22 commission in the long run.

- Stop negative self-evaluations from ruling your behavior. Learn to think positively about the future instead of focusing on your past blunders.

- Remember that you are calling on prospects to solve their needs, not just so you can line your pocket with money. You are performing a vital, helpful, important service to your prospects by calling on them. (If that isn't true, maybe you should find another sales job!)

- Control your perceptions of what prospects might say about you, your company, or your products. You don't *know* what their reactions will be until you meet with the prospects. Leads do buy from salespeople. One estimate is that 63 percent of all leads actually end up buying from someone within a year.[48]

- Learn and apply relaxation and stress-reducing techniques that you can implement before and during prospecting.

- Recount your own prospecting successes, or those of others. Read books by people who have prospected successfully or creatively. Realize that persistence pays off in the long run.

Summary

Locating prospective customers is the first step in the sales process. New prospects are needed to replace old customers lost for a variety of reasons and to replace contacts lost in existing customers because of plant relocations, turnover, mergers, downsizing, and other factors.

Not all sales leads qualify as good prospects. A qualified prospect has a need that can be satisfied by the salesperson's product, has the ability and authority to buy the product, can be approached by the salesperson, and is eligible to buy.

Many methods can be used to locate prospects. The best source is a satisfied customer. Salespeople sometimes obtain leads through their customers by using the endless-chain and center-of-influence methods. Companies provide leads to salespeople through promotional activities such as the Internet, inquiries from advertising and direct mail, telemarketing, trade shows, and seminars. Salespeople can also use networking, lists and directories, cold canvassing (including blitzes), spotters, and other helpful sources to generate leads.

Effective prospecting requires a strong plan that hinges on developing a lead qualification and management system and overcoming reluctance to prospect.

KEY TERMS

banner advertising   189
bird dog   194
blitz   193
bounce-back card   190
buying community   187
center-of-influence method   186
cold call   193
cold canvass method   193
databases   193
data mining   193
endless-chain method   185
e-selling   189
exclusive sales territories   183
house accounts   183
inbound telemarketing   194
lead   180
lead management system   199
lead qualification system   198

networking   187
North America industry classification system (NAICS)   191
outbound telemarketing   194
postcard pack   189
prequalification   199
prospect   180
prospecting   180
qualifying a lead   180
referred lead   186
search engines   188
selling deeper   185
spam   189
spotter   194
standard industrial classification (SIC)   191
systems integrator   182
telemarketing   194

Questions and Problems

1. Suppose your sales manager says the following to you: "Look, I know how to prospect effectively! After all, I've been selling for 25 years, haven't I? And you're just starting to sell. Okay, here's what I expect you to do. I want you to make 10 cold calls every day. That's all. Just start knocking on doors. Oh yeah, and report them on this call sheet." As you reflect on what he said, you are confused and anxious. You feel there are much better ways of prospecting than just relying on cold calling. What will you do? What, if anything, will you say to your sales manager?

2. How would you develop a prospect list under the following situations?
   a. You belong to a social organization on campus that needs to recruit new members.
   b. You are a marketing student about to graduate from college, and you want to find a full-time sales position.
   c. You are a veteran salesperson for Dell computers and are being transferred to Dell's new office in Leverkusen, Germany.

3. What information do you need to qualify the leads generated in each part of question 2?

4. What information should a salesperson collect to qualify leads for the following?

   a. A commercial printer that specializes in printing elaborate four-color books.

   b. Sponsorship of the local community theater.

   c. Hospital gowns.

5. "Salespeople should focus their energy on leads that are small firms, firms that may not yet qualify as prospects for our larger competitors. We'll let our competitors go after the larger prospects." Comment on this statement.

6. Assume you are starting a career as a stockbroker. Develop a system for rating prospects. The system should contain several important factors for qualifying prospects and scales with which to rate the prospects on these factors. Use the system to rate five of your friends.

7. In industrial sales situations several people influence the purchase decision. Suppose you have just completed an interview with an industrial prospect and believe you should contact other people in the company. How will you raise the subject with the prospect?

8. Salespeople are often reluctant to prospect for new customers. What advice would you give to help a new salesperson overcome reluctance to prospect?

9. How can you engage in networking now to increase your odds of landing a good job after you graduate?

10. If you were a salesperson for the following companies, how would you develop a prospect list?

    a. A manufacturer of relatively small farm equipment.

    b. A travel agency specializing in Austrian vacations.

    c. A manufacturer of an antitheft alarm device for bicycles.

Case Problems

CASE 7.1

3M's Digital Library Assistant

3M is a diversified international company with a wide portfolio of businesses. The company enjoys leading market shares for its products and services, most of which are focused on technical differentiation. Products include everything from touch screen displays, high-speed computing interconnects, and medical products to Scotch® tape and PostIt® notes.

One of 3M's latest products is called a Digital Library Assistant (DLA), a small hand-held unit that is designed for public libraries but could be used by anyone with a collection of books or materials. The DLA, using mobile scanner technology, helps manage the collection in terms of shelving, sorting, and searching for books quickly and easily. For example, it can quickly and easily:

- Find lost or missing items in the collection.

- Electronically "read" the collection and give guidance as to how to put it back in order so future users can retrieve the books easily.

- Weed out the collection of materials to be discarded.

- Reshelve items with 100 percent accuracy.

- Confirm that items on a book cart are in proper order before they are taken to the stacks for reshelving.

- Spot errors in the catalog and in the spine labels of books.

- Do all of this by using the existing electromagnetic security system and without any need to retag or mark the entire collection.

Information about more than 1 million items can be downloaded from a library's automation system into the DLA's memory card. The interface between the library's current system and the DLA is seamless and flawless. And of course, the DLA has a comfortable ergonomic design with a swivel antenna that aids in reading books at all levels and in all positions.

3M is ready to market the system to Israel. You have been assigned to prospect for new accounts in that country.

Source: 3M 2000 annual report, and 3M website (www.3m.com), accessed on March 10, 2002.

QUESTIONS

1. Which prospecting methods will you use?
2. How will you qualify the leads you find? Which qualifying factors will be most important?
3. How will you organize your prospecting activities? How will you keep good records?

CASE 7.2

Identifying Actual Leads

This exercise is designed to improve your skill at identifying actual leads. Consider the following list of products and services:

A new herbicide for soybeans.

Transport services (you are a trucking company) for transporting milk.

A software package for accountants that has been on the market two years.

A newly designed walking shoe.

A new 12-gauge shotgun.

Security systems for small businesses.

A new line of canoes.

A new mountain bike.

Office furniture that is made out of recycled plastic.

Used computer printers.

A new breed of laying hens.

Window-washing services for tall buildings.

Used costumes from movies.

A new line of stuffed collectible dolls.

A new *Principles of Marketing* textbook that focuses on e-commerce.

Choose two products and/or services from the preceding list and answer the following questions.

QUESTIONS

1. Provide a list of company names and addresses for 10 leads. Make any assumptions necessary. You don't have to know whether the leads already use the product or service. Explain where you got the list of names.
2. Briefly describe how you could qualify each lead (as to whether it is a prospect).
3. What other sources of leads could you use for each product or service you chose? Which sources would probably be the best?

Additional References

Bishop, Bill. "The 7 Deadly Sins of Referrals." *Advisor Today* 96, June 2001, p. 92.

Bosik, Darren. "So Many Customers, So Little Time." *1to1 Magazine*, May/June 2002, pp. 39–43.

Cecil, Jim. "Patient, Professional, Persistent." *Rough Notes* 9, September 2001, pp. 124–26.

Frook, John Evan. "How One Manufacturer Converts Leads into Sales." *B to B Magazine* 87, January 14, 2002, pp. 21–23.

Greco, Susan. "Sales: What Works Now." *Inc. Magazine*, February 2002, pp. 52–59.

Kaydo, Chad. "How to Find New Customers." *Sales and Marketing Management* 152, February 2000, p. 100.

Kaydo, Chad. "You've Got Sales." *Sales & Marketing Management*, October 1999, pp. 28–39.

Macintosh, Gerrard, and James W. Gentry. "Decision Making in Personal Selling: Testing the K.I.S.S. Principle." *Psychology & Marketing*, August 1999, pp. 393–408.

Marchetti, Michele. "Want Big Sales? Think Small: How Companies Are Tapping the Lucrative Small and Medium-Size Business Market." *Sales and Marketing Management*, June 2000, p. 15.

McCall, Kimberly L. "Follow the Lead." *Inc. Magazine*, May 2002, pp. 83–84.

Nemac, John. "How to Use Referrals to Generate Greater Sales." *The American Salesman* 45, January 2000, pp. 10–13.

"New E-mail Prospecting Drives Customer Acquisition." *Direct Marketing*, June 2000, p. 79.

Spinks, Nelda; Barron Wells; and Melanie Meche. "Netiquette: A Behavioral Guide to Electronic Business Communication." *Corporate Communications* 4:3 (1999), pp. 145–55.

Stevens, Ruth P. "CRM: It's about Prospecting, Too." *1to1 Magazine*, February 2002, as accessed on 3/13/02 at http://www.1to1.com.

Urbaniak, Anthony J. "Prospecting Systems That Work." *American Salesman*, March 1999, pp. 26–30.

Verbeke, Willem, and Richard P. Bagozzi. "Sales Call Anxiety: Exploring What It Means When Fear Rules a Sales Encounter." *Journal of Marketing* 64, July 2000, pp. 88–101.

Yoder, Eric. "Is Outbound Telemarketing Dead?" *1to1 Magazine*, April 2002, pp. 20–24.

Chapter

8 *Planning the Sales Call*

SOME QUESTIONS ANSWERED IN THIS CHAPTER ARE:

■ Why should salespeople plan their sales calls?

■ What precall information is needed about the individual prospect and the prospect's organization?

■ How can this information be obtained?

■ What is involved in setting call objectives?

■ Should more than one objective be set for each call?

■ How can appointments be made effectively and efficiently?

Salespeople are vulnerable to the great temptation to call on a prospect or customer without planning what to say and how to say it. Depending on spur-of-the-moment thinking is easy. However, all salespeople benefit from planning their calls in advance. This chapter discusses the kind of precall information you will need to gather and suggests where you can gather it, how to plan the sales call, and how to make appointments.

"The pharmaceutical industry has increasingly become more competitive. Some statistics indicate that there are well over 50,000 pharmaceutical representatives in the industry. This makes being a successful planner a must."

Brian Cobb, GlaxoSmithKline Pharmaceuticals

PROFILE

Brian Cobb, a marketing major with a sales concentration, graduated from Butler University in 1998. During college he participated in a sales internship with Purcell Agricultural.

"Throughout my life, I have come to realize that planning makes the difference between success and failure. This not only relates to the sales call, but to the career as well. Upon graduation from college, I worked hard to find a decent first job. As I reflect on this activity, I realize how misguided I was. Many of my professors in college gave me positive guidance as to performing a job search, yet I never grasped the idea of having a plan. My experiences have taught me that having a plan truly helps you to 'work smarter, not harder,' just as the saying goes.

"After all the job interviews I completed upon graduation, I finally landed a sales position with ADT, a home security company. Each day, I went out cold calling. I went everywhere I possibly could. I figured the more people I talked to, the more sales I could earn. How wrong I was! This effort represented and still represents, in my opinion, the perfect ingredient for burnout. What I needed was a plan, yet due to my lack of one, I left this company in six months.

"That departure led me to a new industry and new job with Cellular One, a cellular phone company. It was at this point I realized that if I was going to be successful in sales, I was going to have to do a much better job of planning. I began to set sales goals. I also began to set career goals. I laid out in my mind plans to reach and exceed the sales quotas and goals given to me by my firm. The experience that I gained in the cellular industry taught me how to be productive in a highly competitive industry. I would attribute this primarily to successful planning. After nearly a year and a half, this positive experience led me to my current career as a sales representative with GlaxoSmithKline Pharmaceuticals.

"The pharmaceutical industry has increasingly become more competitive. Some statistics indicate that there are well over 50,000 pharmaceutical representatives in the industry. This makes being a successful planner a must. Each representative competes for the medical practitioner's time, a very limited and precious commodity. When this time is granted by the doctor, the rep must be extremely well prepared.

"In my occupation, the plan includes determining exactly what message to present to the medical practitioner. It is this message that aids in increasing market share. Personally, I tailor my messages to each physician by the information I receive via my company reports. For example, one doctor may need information about once-a-day dosing. Another may need information on combination therapy with other drugs. Yet another doctor may need specific information on drug interactions.

"Naturally, all of this planning requires me to keep up-to-date with new information introduced and any new studies that would be beneficial to physicians I see. That takes time. By doing so, however, I know I am presenting current and relevant information, which adds to my credibility and helps to build stronger relationships.

"Planning is definitely the most important step for any salesperson. Without a plan, there is no direction. Yet with a plan, success awaits."

Visit Our Website @ www.gsk.com.

WHY PLAN THE SALES CALL?

Successful salespeople know that advance planning of the sales interview is essential to achieve in selling. The salesperson should remember that the buyer's time is valuable. Without planning the sales call, a salesperson quite easily may cover material in which the buyer has no interest, try to obtain an order even though that is an unrealistic expectation for this sales call, or strike off into areas that veer from what the buyer actually needs to hear. The result is wasted time and an annoyed prospect. However, by having a clear plan for the call, the salesperson more likely will not only obtain commitment but also win the buyer's respect and confidence.

Salespeople should also remember the value of their own time. Proper planning helps them meet their call objectives efficiently as well as effectively. They then have more time to make additional calls, conduct research on the target customer or other customers, fill out company reports, and complete other necessary tasks. The result is better territory management. (See Chapter 16 for more discussion about time and territory management.)

Of course, planning must fit into the salesperson's goals for the account. Some accounts will have greater strategic importance and thus will require more planning. (See Chapter 16 for a discussion about classifying accounts and prospects.) Those accounts with which a firm is partnering will obviously need the most planning, whereas smaller accounts may warrant less planning. Also, salespeople must not make planning an end unto itself and a way to avoid actually making calls. Exhibit 8.1 provides a flow diagram that shows how the concepts in this chapter are related.

OBTAINING PRECALL INFORMATION

Often the difference between making and not making a sale depends on the amount of homework the salesperson does before making a call. The more information the salesperson has about the prospect, the higher the probability of meeting the prospect's needs and developing a long-term relationship. However, the salesperson must be aware of the costs involved in collecting information. At some point, the time and effort put into collecting information become greater than the benefits obtained.

The following dialogue shows what can happen in a sales call made with inadequate precall information:

SALESPERSON: Good morning, Mr. White. I'm Mary Thompson, the new sales rep for McNeil Clothing.

CUSTOMER: My name is Wasits, not White.

SALESPERSON: Oh! I'm sorry. I should have asked your secretary to spell your name when I called to make an appointment. I want to show you our new fall line that's just perfect for the growing teen market.

CUSTOMER: Most of our customers are middle-aged. I don't really want to attract teens to my store. They make a lot of noise, and they bother the older customers. To be honest, some of them even kind of scare me!

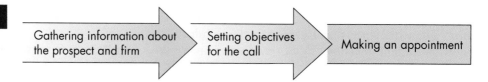

EXHIBIT 8.1

A Flow Diagram of the Planning Process

Gathering information about the prospect and firm → Setting objectives for the call → Making an appointment

Gathering information from individuals in the prospect's firm before making a call on the prospect is often a wise investment of time.

© Tom Tracy

SALESPERSON: Well, we also have a line for the middle-aged market. Here's some photographs of the items in the line [reaches into her purse for a package of cigarettes and puts one to her lips]. Would you like a cigarette?

CUSTOMER [looking at the cigarettes more than the photos]: If you don't mind . . . well, cigarette smoke gets into the clothes in our store. Please don't smoke.

By not obtaining precall information, this salesperson immediately encountered several embarrassing situations. With such a poor start, the salesperson is unlikely to attain her call objective.

Clearly, a salesperson who has been calling regularly on a prospect or customer may not need to collect a lot of additional information; records and notes from prior calls may be adequate to prepare for the sales call. The same holds true for a new salesperson if the previous one kept good records. But beware! In this fast-paced world, things are changing every day. Consider the following dialogue:

SALESPERSON [walking up to the receptionist of one of his best customers]: Hello, Jim. I'm here to see Toby. I have some information I promised to share with her about our new manufacturing process. She was pretty excited about seeing it!

RECEPTIONIST [looking tired]: Sorry, Jeff. Toby was transferred last week to our Toronto plant. Haven't you heard about our latest reorganization? Just went into effect two weeks ago. I'm still trying to figure it out. It seems that all of our engineering people are moving to the Toronto site.

SALESPERSON [looking confused and worried]: No, I hadn't heard! Well, who took Toby's job? That person really needs to see this information.

RECEPTIONIST: No one took her place. I think they're going to outsource a lot of what she did [starting to pick up the phone for an incoming call]. It's just not going to be the same around here anymore.

The key: Don't assume that your knowledge about the account is automatically up-to-date.

Of course, before you make an initial call on an important prospect, you will often expend considerable effort on collecting precall information about both the individual prospect and the prospect's company. Don't expect this information gathering to be quick, easy, or cheap. For example, Tom Carnes, owner of a printing firm in Las Vegas, wanted to increase his sales in the legal market. He learned that paralegals usually control the flow of paper in law offices and that a professional association of paralegals existed. He decided to meet with the leader of that organization for two hours twice a month for two or three months to learn about the legal market, paying her $500 for each meeting. The efforts in gaining precall information paid off with sales of $600,000 in the first year alone.[1]

It is important to learn and maintain current knowledge about both the prospect as an individual and his or her firm. The sections that follow examine these areas more closely.

THE PROSPECT/ CUSTOMER AS AN INDIVIDUAL

Salespeople should attempt to learn the following types of information about a prospect or a customer:

Personal
- Name (including pronunciation).
- Family status.
- Education.
- Aspirations.
- Interests (such as hobbies) and disinterests.

Attitudes
- Toward salespeople.
- Toward your company.
- Toward your product.

Relationships
- Formal reporting relationships.
- Important reference groups and group norms.

Styles
- Social style (driver or another category—see Chapter 6).
- Decision-making style[2] (entrepreneurial, planning, bureaucratic).

Evaluation of Products/Services
- Product attributes that are important.
- Product evaluation process (see Chapter 4 for details).

If this list seems long, consider the fact that Harvey Mackay, one of the leading business writers, actually lists 66 questions (the "Mackay 66") that a seller should ask about a customer.[3] Most firms have developed their own unique lists of questions that salespeople need to consider to call on a prospect successfully.

THE PROSPECT'S/ CUSTOMER'S ORGANIZATION

Information about the prospect's/customer's company obviously helps the salesperson understand the customer's environment. This type of information enables the salesperson to more quickly identify problem areas and respond accordingly. For example, in a modified rebuy situation, it would not be necessary to educate the prospect about general features common to the product class as a whole. Using the prospect's valuable time by covering material he or she already knows is minimized. Information like the following about the prospect's organization would be helpful:

Demographics
- Type of organization (manufacturing, wholesaling, retailing).
- Size, number of locations.
- Products/services offered.
- Financial position and its future.
- Culture of the organization.[4]

Prospect's Customers
- Types.[5]
- Benefits they seek from the prospect's products/services.

Prospect's Competitors
- Who they are.
- How they differ in their business approaches.
- Prospect's strategic position in the industry[6] (dominant, strong, weak, tenable).

Historical Buying Patterns
- Amount purchased in the product category.
- Sole supplier or multiple suppliers. Why?
- Reason for buying from present suppliers.
- Level of satisfaction with suppliers.
- Reasons for any dissatisfaction with suppliers or products currently purchased.

Current Buying Situation
- Type of buying process (new task, straight rebuy, or modified rebuy—see Chapter 4).
- Strengths and weaknesses of potential competitors.

People Involved in the Purchase Decision
- How they fit into the formal and informal organizational structure.
- Their roles in this decision (gatekeeper, influencer, or the like).
- Who is most influential.
- Any **influential adversaries** (carry great influence but are opposed to us)?
- Current problems the organization faces.
- Stage in the buying cycle.

Policies and Procedures
- About salespeople.
- About sales visits.
- About purchasing and contracts.

PRIVACY CONCERNS

While you're gathering all this information, you must be aware of privacy laws and policies. **Privacy laws** limit the amount of information that a firm can obtain about a consumer or business and specify how that information can be used or shared with others. For example, the Gramm-Leach-Bliley Act requires financial institutions to give its customers written notification of its privacy policies and practices and outlaws sharing private information with third parties without the customers having an opportunity to opt out of such sharing. Many related laws are working their way through Congress as well.

For business-to-business salespeople, the concern is primarily that the information gathered is of important financial and strategic importance. So salespeople have to be careful how they use that information and with whom they share it. To make matters worse, some salespeople don't have sophisticated systems for maintaining the information they retrieve, making it easier for that information to fall into the wrong hands. And even reps that use sophisticated databases and software to track information and make it available to their firm (such as those who use ACT) are at risk because they can be found liable if that information is used incorrectly by a third party later.

Some individuals don't like information to be collected about them at all. A recent study of U.S. citizens found that 57 percent are totally against allowing companies to obtain information about them without their consent, while 20 percent were mildly against such practices.[7] And firms don't forgive salespeople or the seller's employers who misuse information.

Here are some recommendations:

- Know the laws and keep current. Chances are laws have changed even as this book has gone to press. Remember that ignorance of a law is no excuse.

- Learn what your firm's privacy policy is. Then follow it carefully. Not to do so is considered fraud.

- Think about the information you wish to collect and ask yourself, "Is it necessary that I learn this? It is necessary that I write this down?"

Thinking It Through

It's your first week on the job as a new salesperson. You were given a laptop computer and time and territory management software that the regional manager has tailored specifically for your sales region. Your district sales manager instructs you to fill in *all* the fields (name, company name, title, who currently buying from, and so on) completely for each new prospect. Most of the information you are asked for seems to make a lot of sense. However, you notice that you are asked to find out each prospect's political party affiliation and the names of each prospect's children. You don't feel comfortable asking for this kind of personal information. What are you going to do?

SOURCES OF INFORMATION

Gathering all the information listed in the preceding sections for every prospect and organization is initially impossible. The goal is to gather what is both possible and profitable. Remember, your time is valuable! Also, you don't want to fall into the trap sometimes referred to as **analysis paralysis,** which is when you prefer to spend practically all of your time analyzing the situation and finding information instead of making sales calls. Salespeople must strike a proper balance between time spent in acquiring information and time spent making calls.

RESOURCES WITHIN YOUR COMPANY

One of the best sources of information can be the records in your own company, especially if your firm has developed a sophisticated database, as described in Chapter 7. The most useful databases include, in addition to standard demographic information, information on any direct inquiries made by the prospect (from direct mail inquiries, through the telemarketing division of your firm, or the like), a sales history on the firm, whether anyone from your company has called on the prospect, and the results of any sales meetings.

Firms are devising many ways to keep the field sales force well informed. For example, D. A. Stuart Company has developed an intranet to keep its salespeople up-to-date on everything that the marketing department is doing.[8] Lotus has developed a database to enable its sales force to gather precall information.[9] The company has a Sales Enablement Team whose only responsibility is to gather and package information into databases for the sales force. Lotus also plans to link directly to external sources of information, such as Dun & Bradstreet data, so that salespeople can properly qualify and pursue prospects. Lotus is even installing high-speed ISDN lines in its salespeople's homes to maximize productivity.

Even if your firm doesn't have such a database, you should try to gather information about your prospect. For example, wouldn't it be nice to find out *before*, as opposed to *during* a sales call, that the prospect used to be a big customer of your firm but quit for some reason?

For important sales, you may well be working with a sales team that interacts with a prospect (a topic more fully addressed in Chapter 17). This team, sometimes called a **selling center,** consists of all people in the selling organization who participate in a selling opportunity.[10] Members of the team may be able to provide or help you secure needed information.

THE INTERNET

Twenty years ago, it took a great deal of time to research and discover information about a prospect. Now, as we mentioned in Chapter 7, a salesperson can learn a wealth of information in a very short time with the Internet. For example, Conectiv, a large energy and telecommunication company in Delaware, secured the multimillion-dollar business of one of its largest prospects ever. "They chose us to be their energy supplier, and most of the information I got for a report used by the salesperson was from the Internet," claims Alan Kappauf, market intelligence analyst for the firm.[11] Such stories are not uncommon. And using the Web can increase sales by a great factor; one study found that sales rise an average of 37 percent when salespeople use it to find and follow up on leads.[12]

A first place to look for information would be the prospect company's own Web page. It is amazing what one can find there. A recent study of *Fortune* 100 firms discovered that a large percentage had each of the following pieces of information: link to the annual report (100 percent), information about the firm's products and service (99 percent), latest news about the firm (99 percent), a summary about the firm (95 percent), and a statement of values (87 percent).[13]

The sources listed in Exhibit 7.4 would be a good place to start to find information. For example, a salesperson would be able to learn many things about a prospect at www.hoovers.com, Hoover's free website. The salesperson could easily search by company name, ticker symbol, keywords, or a person's last name for each of the 14,000 public and private organizations listed, including U.S. and international firms. For each company, there is a brief overview, a company profile, stock quotes, a list of officers, financials, links to its website(s), links to press releases, and a listing and automatic link to its major competitors. The seller could also peruse news (from Hoover's own files, plus automatic links to all major news services) or easily link to any other major Web search engine to find out more about the company, the market, or specific industries. News articles often include information about the firm's strategy, new product launches, plans for division changes, lawsuits, new investments, competitive challenges, and so on. To learn more about the prospect's industry, the seller can read an analysis of industry sectors (18 to choose from), including industry snapshots, key players, trends, definitions, and links to other industry views. There are even online prospecting tools (including databases of leads, requests for proposals from firms, and industry-specific contact information). Finally, the seller may want to subscribe to one of Hoover's six free weekly newsletters which can be sent to the seller's e-mail account. The newsletters include the most current company information, news reports, and so on.

Keep in mind that most of this information is free (for a fee you can get even more information from Hoover's online) and comes from just one source. Now multiply that by the thousands of online sources for information that a salesperson can access, and you can see that a new problem for salespeople is deciding how to manage all of that information. One reason that firms are starting to build databases is to centralize the information that's important to their field sales force.

You can also set up personalized Web pages from many servers that will scan sources for the information you seek and provide periodic updates that can assist your selling and planning efforts. For example, you can set up a personal Web page directly from Netscape that will keep you abreast of the topics you are most interested in.

In addition to checking the Web sources noted in Chapter 7, you may also want to visit the JustSell.com site (www.justsell.com). It contains many helpful links for salespeople, including several that offer free company and industry profiles.

Sources like Hoover's website are excellent for providing information.

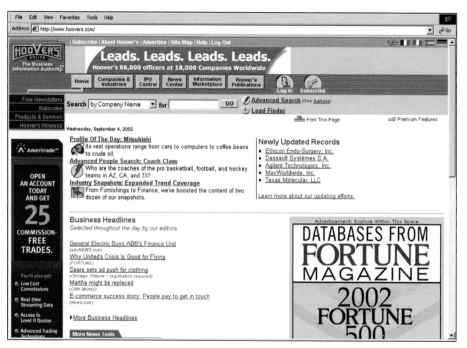

Courtesy of Hoover's Online (www.hoovers.com).

SECRETARIES AND RECEPTIONISTS

Secretaries and receptionists in the prospect's firm usually are a rich source of information. Consider for example, Sam Roth, an office supplies salesperson, who arrived at a prospect's office only to learn he had been called away to an important meeting. In talking to the prospect's secretary, however, Roth learned that the prospect was indeed the sole decision maker and exactly what the firm's needs were with regard to the products Sam was selling. He even went so far as to explain to the secretary how his product could meet the firm's needs. Gathering this precall information paid off. The next day the secretary called to set up a meeting between Sam and her boss. The result was a very large order.

Be courteous, however, because secretaries and receptionists are accustomed to having salespeople pry for all sorts of free information. Prioritize your questions and provide justification for asking them. Above all, treat secretaries and receptionists with genuine respect.

NONCOMPETING SALESPEOPLE

Another source for precall information is noncompeting salespeople. In fact, one of the best sources of information is the prospect's own salespeople because they empathize with your situation.

TRADITIONAL SECONDARY SOURCES

Traditional secondary data sources can also be helpful (we described many of them in Chapter 7, when we discussed sources of prospects). Firms such as Standard & Poor's, Hoover's, Wards, and Moody's publish a number of manuals and directories that are available in many public libraries. These sources can help answer questions about brand names, key contacts, historical information, the current situation and outlook for the firm and the industry, location of plants and distribution centers, market shares, and so on.

THE PROSPECT

Much information can be gleaned directly from the prospect. However, don't expect prospects to sit down and answer any and all questions you might have, especially for topics where the information is fairly easy to get (like what products the prospect makes or sells). Prospects don't have time to fill you in on all the details of their business. If you don't know the basics, many prospects will just refuse to deal with you.

To demonstrate the creativity possible in gathering information, Harvey Mackay relates how his first boss taught him to learn about competitor activity. MacKay and his boss "drove to our arch competitor's plant. We parked about 50 yards away from the shipping department and waited until the trucks began to exit to make the day's deliveries. The rest of the day, we followed those trucks. By the end of the day, we had a good idea of our competition's local customer base, obtained in record time and at no cost."[15]

It is also worth mentioning that, just as you are gathering information about the prospect prior to a meeting, the prospect can and often does collect information about you. Even before the sale your prospect can request price quotes via e-mail. He or she can also view your Web page, as well as your competitors' Web pages. Plus the prospect can easily chat with colleagues via newsgroups and Listservs to learn about you or your firm. As one writer puts it, "The Internet arms them to the teeth with product information."[16] Any salesperson who doesn't understand that point won't be as prepared for the kinds of questions that a prospect might ask or for comments that a prospect might make.

OTHER SOURCES

Many other sources can provide information. Some information may have been gleaned at a trade show the prospect attended. Much information will be in the lists and directories from which the prospect's name came. A center of influence will often be able to provide some information. Occasionally a prospect will be important enough to warrant hiring an outside consultant to collect information, especially if you are gathering precall information for international selling. Although some information about foreign companies is available, much will not be obtainable. As the editor of *Business Geographics* magazine put it, "U.S. marketers are spoiled by the breadth and depth of data that is available in the U.S."[17]

SETTING CALL OBJECTIVES

A most important step in planning is to set objectives for the call.[18] Merely stating the objective "I want to make a sale" will not suffice. The customer's decision-making process (see Chapter 4) involves many steps, and salespeople need to undertake many activities as they guide customers through the process.

Yet, as Neil Rackham, an internationally respected sales researcher, notes, "It's astonishing how rarely salespeople set themselves call objectives of any kind—let alone effective ones. Although most books on selling emphasize the importance of clear call objectives, it's rare to see these exhortations turned into practice."[19] Why? Probably because many salespeople want to start doing something, instead of "wasting time" planning. But without a plan, they actually increase their chances of wasting time.

As a first step in setting objectives, the salesperson should review what has been learned from precall information gathering. Any call objectives should be based on the results of this review. Also, the seller must keep in mind the relationship the firm wishes to have with the prospect. Not all prospects will or should become partners with the seller's firm.[20]

Call objectives should not be created in a vacuum. They should be developed while taking into account the firm's goals, the sales team's goals, and the salesperson's goals.[21] Some experts have even argued for the importance of salespeople maintaining consistency between their personal goals and selling objectives. Regardless of the type of goal you are referring to, the old adage is true: If you don't know where you're going, you may wind up somewhere else.

In their well-received sales training book *Strategic Selling*, Miller and Heiman[22] stress the importance that sales call planning be related to the firm's strategic goals for the account. Four basic steps must occur in this strategic analysis:

1. Compare your current position with the account against your sales objective.
2. Develop various alternative positions you could take.
3. Determine which position would best obtain your objective and create an action plan to achieve it.
4. Implement your new action plan.

For this strategic analysis to occur, it is critical that a salesperson know what his or her current position with the account is. This is perhaps easier when dealing with a brand new prospect than for a customer you have done business with for years. Notice that the strategic analysis builds heavily on feedback and review of what's happening in an account. For now, realize that call objectives are set not only for that first call to a brand new prospect, but also for each call to existing customers.

CRITERIA FOR EFFECTIVE OBJECTIVES

All objectives should be specific, realistic, and measurable. A call objective that meets only one or two of these criteria will be an ineffective guide for the salesperson. We will now examine each criterion in more detail.

An objective must be *specific* to be effective. It should state precisely what the salesperson hopes to accomplish, who the objective targets are, and any other details (suggested order quantity, suggested dates for future meetings, length of time needed for a follow-up survey, or the like). Specific objectives help the salesperson avoid "shooting from the hip" during the presentation and perhaps moving the prospect along too rapidly or too slowly.

Objectives must also be *realistic*. Inexperienced salespeople often have unrealistic expectations about the prospect's or customer's response in the sales call. For example, if Ford Motor Company currently uses Sony radios on all of its models, a Phillips salesperson who expects Ford to change over to Phillips radios in the first few sales calls has an unrealistic objective. It is important for sellers to plan objectives for a call that can be accomplished within the time allocated for that sales call. For objectives to be realistic, the salesperson needs to consider factors such as cultural influences. For example, some firms have a corporate culture of being extremely conservative. Creating change in such a culture is very time-consuming and often frustrating for the seller. The national culture is very important in selling to international prospects. When selling to Arab or Japanese businesses, salespeople should plan to spend at least several meetings getting to know the other party. Developing relationships with Chinese businesspeople requires a great deal of entertaining.[23] Selling in Russia is often slowed because of bureaucracy and incredible amounts of red tape. As these examples illustrate, culture is an important consideration in attempts to set realistic call objectives.

Finally, call objectives must be *measurable* so that salespeople can objectively evaluate each sales call at its conclusion and determine whether the objectives were met. This suggests they should be written down. If a salesperson's stated

Even a salesperson who fails to achieve the primary call objective will be encouraged to at least achieve the minimum call objective.

Larry Williams/Masterfile

objective is to get acquainted with the prospect or to establish rapport, how can the salesperson assess whether this goal was achieved? How can someone measure "getting acquainted"? To what extent would the salesperson have to be acquainted with the prospect to know that he or she achieved the sales call objective? A more measurable sales call objective (as well as a more specific and realistic one) is something like the following: To get acquainted with the prospect by learning which clubs or organizations she or he belongs to, which sports the prospect follows, what his or her professional background is, and how long the prospect has held the current position. With this revised call objective, a salesperson can very simply determine whether the objective was reached.

An easy way to help ensure that objectives are measurable is to set objectives that require a buyer's response. For example, achievement of the following objective is easy to measure: to make a follow-up appointment with the buyer.

Successful salespeople in almost every industry have learned the importance of setting proper call objectives. Pharmaceutical salespeople for Novartis set very clear objectives for each sales call they make to a physician. Then they lay out a series of objectives for subsequent calls so that they know exactly what they hope to accomplish over the next several visits. One industrial products sales manager recommends that her salespeople keep their call objectives in view while they are on the sales call, helping them to focus on the true goals of the sales call. Both of these examples share a common theme: The salesperson needs to set specific, realistic, measurable call objectives. Exhibit 8.2 lists examples of call objectives that meet these criteria.

SETTING MORE THAN ONE CALL OBJECTIVE

Salespeople have learned the importance of setting multiple objectives for a sales call. Not only do they set a **primary call objective** (the actual goal they hope to achieve) before each sales call; they also set a **minimum call objective** (the minimum they hope to achieve) because they realize the call may not go exactly as

---

EXHIBIT 8.2
Examples of Call Objectives

Objectives Related to the Process Leading up to the Sale

- To have the prospect agree to come to the Atlanta branch office sometime during the next two weeks for a hands-on demonstration of the copier.
- To set up another appointment for one week from now at which time the buyer will allow me to do a complete survey of her printing needs.
- To inform the doctor of the revolutionary anticlotting mechanism that has been incorporated into our new drug and have her agree to read the pamphlet I will leave.
- To have the buyer agree to pass my information along to the buying committee with his endorsement of my proposal.
- To have the prospect agree to call several references that I will provide to develop further confidence and trust in my office-cleaning business.
- To have the prospect agree on the first point (of our four-point program) and schedule another meeting in two days to discuss the second point.
- To have the prospect initiate the necessary paperwork to allow us to be considered as a future vendor.

Objectives Related to Consummating the Sale

- To have the prospect sign an order for 100 pairs of Levi's jeans.
- To schedule a co-op newspaper advertising program to be implemented in the next month.
- To have the prospect agree to use our brand of computer paper for a trial period of one month.
- To have the retailer agree to allow us space for an end-of-aisle display for the summer promotion of Raid insect repellent.

planned (the prospect may be called away or the salesperson may not have all the necessary facts). On the other hand, the call may go better than the salesperson originally thought it would. Thus, although rarely achieved, an **optimistic call objective** (the most optimistic outcome the salesperson thinks could occur) is also set. The optimistic call objective will probably relate to what the salesperson hopes to accomplish for the account over the long term (that is, the account objectives— see Chapter 16).

The primary call objective, for example, of a Nestlé Foods rep might be to secure an order from a grocer for 10 cases of Nestlé Morsels for an upcoming coupon promotion. That is what the seller realistically hopes to accomplish in the call. A minimum call objective could be to sell at least 5 cases of Morsels, whereas an optimistic call objective would be to sell 20 cases plus set up an end-of-aisle display plus secure a retail promotional price of $2.89.

It is possible to have more than one primary call objective for a single call. For example, several primary objectives a salesperson might hope to accomplish in a single meeting are to sell one unit, be introduced to one other member of the buying center, and have the prospect agree to send along a packet of information to an executive. In this example, if the salesperson genuinely hopes and expects to achieve all three objectives in the next meeting, they will all be considered primary call objectives. To aid in planning the call, some trainers suggest that the salesperson further prioritize these primary objectives into two groups: The most important primary objective is called the primary objective, whereas the remaining ones become **secondary call objectives.** So, in this example, if selling the product is the most important thing to accomplish in the next meeting, the objectives will be as follows:

Primary call objective: Sell one unit.

Secondary call objectives: Be introduced to one other member of the buying center.

Have the prospect agree to send along a packet of information to an executive.

Multiple call objectives have many benefits. First, they help take away the salesperson's fear of failure because most salespeople can achieve at least their stated minimum objective. Second, multiple objectives tend to be self-correcting. Salespeople who always reach their optimum objective realize they are probably setting their sights too low. On the other hand, if they rarely meet even their minimum objective, they probably are setting their goals too high.

SETTING OBJECTIVES FOR SEVERAL CALLS

By developing a series of very specific objectives for future calls, the salesperson can develop a comprehensive strategy for the prospect or customer. This approach is especially important in a partnering relationship. To illustrate the use of multiple call objectives, Exhibit 8.3 gives a set of call objectives for visits over a period of time. The left side of the exhibit contains the long-term plan and each call objective that the Panasonic salesperson developed for Johnson Electronics. Note the logical strategy for introducing the new product, the V500. The right side of Exhibit 8.3 shows the actual call results.

The salesperson was not always 100 percent successful in achieving the call objectives. Thus several subsequent objectives needed to be modified. For example, because the meeting on October 10 resulted in the buyer dropping K555 CD players, the call objectives on November 10 and November 17 need to reflect that Johnson Electronics no longer carries the K555. The seller may also want to add a call objective for October 17: to discuss more about the situation with

Overall Plan Developed on Oct. 1		Actual Call Results	
Expected Date of the Call	Call Objective	Date of Call	Call Results
Oct. 10	Secure normal repeat orders on K33 and K555 CDs. Increase normal repeat order of K431 CD player from three to five units. Provide product information for new DVD product V500.	Oct. 10	Obtained normal order of K33. Steve decided to drop K555 (refused to give a good reason). Purchased only four K431 players. Seemed responsive to V500 but needs a point-of-purchase (POP) display.
Oct. 17	Erect a front-counter POP display for V500 and secure a trial order of two units.	Oct. 18	Steve was out. His assistant didn't like the POP (thought it was too large!). Refused to use POP. Did order one V500. Told me about several complaints with K431.
Nov. 10	Secure normal repeat orders for K33, K555, and K431. Schedule one co-op newspaper ad for the next 30 days featuring V500. Secure an order for 10 V500s.	Nov. 8	Obtained normal orders. Steve agreed to co-op ad but bought only five V500s. Thinks the margins are too low.
Nov. 17	Secure normal repeat orders of K33, K555, and K431. Secure an order for 20 V500s.	Nov. 18	Obtained normal order on K33, but Steve refused to reorder K431. Claimed the competitor product (Sony) is selling much better. Obtained an order of 15 units of V500.

K555 (because of the outcome of the October 10 meeting) and perhaps try to reintroduce it. This example illustrates the importance of keeping good records, making any necessary adjustments in the long-term call objectives, and then preparing for the next sales call.

One sales vice president for a large sales force has some specific advice about setting multiple call objectives:

> The primary objective of the first session is to have another chance to visit. What this allows you to do is have your standards relatively low because you are trying to build a long-term relationship. You should be very sensitive to an opportunity to establish a second visit. What you want to do is identify aspects of the business conversation that require follow-up and make note of them. . . The key is not the first visit . . . it is the second, the third, the twenty-second visit.[24]

Some industries typically have a very long interval between when a prospect is first visited and when an actual sale is consummated. If so, this factor needs to be considered when setting up multiple call objectives and may imply that others get involved in the selling cycle. For example, Kodak's Motion Analysis Systems, which sell high-speed cameras that can photograph things too fast for the human eye to see, estimates that the typical sale can take anywhere from 9 to 18 months to close.[25] Kodak has its field sales force give a demonstration of the cameras and then uses telemarketers to keep the prospects updated in a fashion that is consistent with the prospects' buying time frames. Kodak also sends out newsletters several times a year to prospects. These tools give salespeople time to make calls on other accounts until the prospect is ready to buy. It is important for salespeople to consider the company's other promotional efforts when developing multiple call objectives for a prospect.

When setting multiple call objectives, the salesperson should obviously consider whom to call on in upcoming meetings. Although it seems obvious that the decision maker (who is often a middle manager for many products and services) should be included in those calls, visiting briefly with senior-level managers may also make sense. But what information would you share with the CEO, for example? The answer is the **value proposition,** a written statement (usually one or two sentences) that clearly states how purchasing your product or service can help add shareholder value. The value proposition should be specific and measurable and should be tied to the prospect's mission statement. Meetings to share the value proposition with senior managers probably should include middle managers from the prospect's firm and take no more than 30 minutes.

BUYERS MAY BE SETTING GOALS ALSO

It's important that salespeople understand that buyers may very well also be setting objectives for the salesperson's sales call.[26] These objectives are based on perceptions of how the salesperson's product or service can add value. **Customer value** has been defined as "the customer's perception of what they want to have happen in a specific use situation, with the help of a product or service offering, in order to accomplish a desired purpose or goal."[27] Salespeople's job is to discover what customers value and then find ways to improve customer value relative to their own products or services.

What are some things that buyers are looking for in order to increase value? Recent research found that 8 out of 10 purchasing managers plan to continually increase expectations in the following areas: on-time delivery, to-spec quality of products, competitive pricing, proper packaging/paperwork, technical support/service, quality of sales calls, level of technological innovation, and emergency response.[28] Thus sellers can expect that buyers may be setting goals for sales calls in these areas.

MAKING AN APPOINTMENT

After gathering precall information and setting objectives, the salesperson's next step is generally to make an appointment. Many sales managers insist that their salespeople make appointments before calling on prospects or customers. Sales managers have found from experience that working by appointment saves valuable selling time. One large sales organization estimates that advance appointments increase the effectiveness of its sales force by at least one-third.

Appointments dignify the salesperson. They help get the sales process off to a good start by putting the salesperson and the prospect on the same level—equal participants in a legitimate sales interview. Appointments also increase the chances of seeing the right person and having uninterrupted time with the prospect. This section describes how to see the right person at the right time and the right place, how to interact with gatekeepers, and how to phone for an appointment.

HOW TO MAKE APPOINTMENTS

Experienced sales representatives use different contact methods for different customers. They have found through trial and error that a certain method of making an appointment works well with a regular customer but may be entirely ineffective with a new prospect. (Keep in mind that in multiple-call situations, an appointment for the next call is usually made at the conclusion of the visit.) They have also found that knowledge of many different methods and techniques for making appointments is extremely helpful in obtaining sales interviews. Building Partnerships 8.1 provides some examples of creative ways to get in and see the prospect.

Since the salesperson is now moving into that part of the sales cycle in which contact with the prospect is beginning to occur, it's important to point out that attitude (and the salesperson's mood) can have a tremendously important impact on suc-

TRYING TO GET IN? CREATIVITY MAY BE THE ANSWER

What should you do when a prospect, who you know has a need for your product, refuses to meet with you? Maybe creativity is the answer. Here are two examples.

Randy Rosler set up a meeting to sell his greeting card company's products to UPS, but UPS's director of marketing had to cancel the meeting and never returned Rosler's calls to set up another meeting. From conversations with the receptionist, Rosler found that the director loved golf. So he bought some golf balls and sent them to the director with a card attached that read "Thought I'd take another swing at it . . ." on the outside, with ". . . as I've been unable to reach you. I'm looking forward to speaking with you soon." on the inside of the card. His next phone call was successful. Rosler got the appointment and UPS's business.

A Wallace rep really wanted to see Steve, an important prospect, but Steve always had an excuse for why he couldn't meet with the rep. In desperation the rep used his creative juices. He decided to send Steve a fresh pineapple every Monday morning. The card attached simply read "From the Pineapple Guy." For seven weeks he sent a pineapple. On Monday of the eighth week, the rep showed up in person at Steve's reception area. When asked who wished to see Steve, the rep said simply, "The Pineapple Guy." Needless to say, the rep was ushered right in.

Sources: Personal contact; Christine Galea, "The Boldest Thing I Did to Make a Sale," *Sales & Marketing Management*, March 2000, p. 64.

---

cess.[29] A positive mood has been found to promote helping behavior, something very important for salespeople attempting to develop partnerships with their customers. Let's now look at some basic principles and techniques for making appointments.

THE RIGHT PERSON

Appointments increase the chances of seeing the right person and having uninterrupted time with the prospect.

Some experts emphasize the importance of going right to the top. "Start at the top," proclaims John O'Hearn, director of sales and marketing at the Westin La Cantera Resort in San Antonio, Texas. "It's called cutting to the chase. A lot of times the people at the bottom don't really know [what's going on]." Michael Hausman, VP of sales for a group of luxury hotels and resorts, agrees: "You're dealing with egos. You're definitely better off if you can reach someone higher up."[30]

Ariel Skelley/The Stock Market

After carefully studying more than 35,000 sales calls, Neil Rackham offers a radically different view from those just mentioned.[31] His research suggests that a salesperson should initially try to call on the **focus of receptivity**, the person who will listen receptively and provide the seller with needed valuable information. Note that this person may not be the decision maker or the one who understands all of the firm's problems. As Michael Hausman, vice president of Associated Luxury Hotels International, says, "Lower-level people, including administrative employees or junior managers, can provide valuable information about the company's culture and needs. That knowledge can help the salesperson deliver a more customized sales pitch when [he or she] finally speaks to the higher-ranking decision maker."[32]

The focus of receptivity, according to the research, will then lead the salesperson to the **focus of dissatisfaction,** the person who is most likely to perceive problems and dissatisfactions. Finally, the focus of dissatisfaction leads to the **focus of power,** the person who can approve action, prevent action, and/or influence action. Getting to the focus of power too quickly can lead to disaster because the seller has not yet built a relationship and does not really know the buyer's needs. In summary Rackham notes, "There's a superstition in selling that the sooner you can get to the decision maker the better. Effective selling, so it's said, is going straight to the focus of power. That's a questionable belief."[33]

Finally, the salesperson might want to consider the effects of downsizing on organizational buying behavior. A recent study suggests that salespeople direct efforts at upper-level managers in firms that are experiencing high degrees of downsizing, so as not to rely too heavily on current buying group participants (who might lose their jobs soon).[34]

Of course, nothing is more frustrating than thinking you are making a final presentation only to realize you are not talking to the decision maker. To illustrate, for years a Nekoosa paper salesperson called mainly on printers. After a careful analysis of sales records and the sales potential, the salesperson concluded that the territory was not producing maximum sales volume. Many sales were lost because the printers lacked the authority to specify the brand of paper their clients used. The sales representative solved this problem by contacting the printers' sales reps and finding out from them which clients normally specified a certain brand of paper when placing printing orders. The paper sales rep then contacted those printers' clients directly and explained the merits of the company's products to them.

Buying companies frequently want to manage all interactions between their firms and the salesperson and have set up policies, procedures, and channels to do so. Is it acceptable to bypass these "normal channels" and use a backdoor approach (see Chapter 4) when making calls? In other words, do firms frown on salespeople who bypass the traditional routine? The answer depends on many factors. Cultural norms always play a part. When asked whether it is generally acceptable to bypass hierarchical lines, 75 percent of the Italian respondents said no, whereas only 22 percent of the Swedish respondents said no (in the United States 32 percent said no).[35]

Whether to actually go over the buyer's head depends on many factors. How important is the account? What are the chances of securing the business? What will the company's reaction be? What damage will be done to the long-term relationship? Salesperson Joe Cousineau had to ask himself these very questions after being rudely brushed off by the purchasing agent of one of his biggest potential clients.[36] Figuring he really had nothing to lose, Cousineau's response was to call the company president. The president asked whether anyone else had witnessed the purchasing agent's rude behavior. Fortunately, the receptionist had seen it all. After verifying Cousineau's story with the receptionist, the president not only offered to see Cousineau but also ended up buying Cousineau's full-blown program. What happened to the rude purchasing agent? His company forced him to take a position as a salesperson, perhaps to have him experience firsthand the rejection he had been doling out to salespeople who called on him.

Frequently in industrial selling situations, no one person has the sole authority to buy a product. The salesperson may first be required to obtain the approval of a line organization representative or of an operating committee. For example, a forklift sales representative for Clarke had to see the safety engineer, the methods engineer, the materials-handling engineer, and the general superintendent before he could sell the product to a certain manufacturing company. In this case the salesperson should try to arrange a meeting with the entire group as well as with each individual.

THE RIGHT TIME

Much has been written about the best time of day for sales interviews. Certain salespeople claim the best time to see prospects is right after lunch, when they are likely to be in a pleasant mood. Others try to get as many appointments as they can during the early morning hours because they believe the prospects or customers will be in a better frame of mind then. There is little agreement on this subject, for obviously the most opportune time to call will vary by customer and type of selling. The salesperson who calls on wholesale grocers, for example, may find from experience that the best time to call is from 9 A.M. to 11 A.M. and from 1:30 P.M. to 3:30 P.M. A hospital rep, on the other hand, may discover that the most productive calls on surgeons are made between 8:30 A.M. and 10 A.M. and after 4 P.M.

For most types of selling, the best hours of the day are from approximately 9 A.M. to 11:30 A.M. and from 1:30 P.M. to 4 P.M. This schedule is particularly true for business executives, who like to have the first part of the day free to read their mail and answer correspondence and the latter part of the day free to read and sign their letters. (Chapter 16 provides more information about the proper time to make calls.)

Although these hours may be the most favorable, salespeople need not restrict appointments to these times. Each salesperson soon learns the most favorable hours and days for each customer. For example, Islamic religious custom calls for its followers to stop five times a day for prayers, and you might want to time your call accordingly.[37] Certainly for those customers with which the firm is partnering, extra care should be taken to make calls at times that are favorable for both buyer and seller.

THE RIGHT PLACE

The sales call must take place in an environment conducive to doing business. Often the salesperson has no say in where the call will take place. When possible, however, the salesperson should choose a place free of distraction for all parties. Such is not always the case, however. For example, studies have shown that nearly half of all salespeople have been to a topless bar with a customer, usually (72 percent of the time) because the customer asked for it.[38] In addition to distractions, topless bars present a number of problems for the salesperson who uses them to achieve sales. For example, is it ethical to gain business by using such exploitative tactics? Also, once a buyer has purchased on the basis of this entertainment, chances are the seller will have to keep it up or lose the customer.

Some sales calls may also make use of the latest technology. For example, **videoconferencing**, meetings in which people are not physically present in one location but are connected via voice and video, seems to be growing in usage.[39] British Petroleum, Bristol-Myers Squibb, and HQ Global are several firms that are relying on videoconferening much more. Markel Corporation has a new travel policy: Hotel and airfare costs will only be authorized if the seller can show that a videoconference meeting wouldn't be appropriate.[40] In a variant on videoconferencing, called **webcasting** or **virtual sales calls**, the meeting is broadcast over the Internet.[41] For example, due to downsizing, emWare, Inc. has only eight salespeople. According to Michael Nelson, CEO of emWare, "Virtual sales calls have become a necessity. And they've turned out to be enormously successful."[42] Salespeople should learn how to plan for such meetings. One key is to carefully plan all technical elements of the presentation and to rehearse them as much as possible (Chapter 10 provides more insight into practicing and avoiding problems). Experts also suggest that it makes sense to form new relationships in person, then use videoconferencing and virtual sales calls to maintain and build the relationships.

If one does choose to schedule the meeting within a meal, which one should you choose? Breakfast tends to be less expensive than other meals and avoids breaking up the workday, but not everyone eats breakfast, and some have early morning activities they don't want to alter (like sleeping or exercising). Lunch occurs during the working business day and seems to be particularly appropriate for discussing business, but the prospect might have to cut the meal short due to an emergency or problem at work (cell phones seem to have made this an even more real probability). Dinners generally offer more time to develop relationships, including relationships with spouses and others, but are more expensive; and not everyone likes to be away from family at night. One additional difficulty is to choose a place to eat that ". . . is interesting to the client, but not inconsistent with his or her tastes."[43] This can be tricky, given the diversity in the workplace.

Meetings can occur just about anywhere—even in a hospital operating room, as Selling Scenario 8.1 illustrates.

CULTIVATING RELATIONSHIPS WITH SUBORDINATES

Busy executives usually have one or more subordinates who plan and schedule interviews for them. These **gatekeepers** (or **barriers** or **screens,** as salespeople sometimes call them) often make seeing the boss rather difficult. For example, a secretary, who usually feels responsible for conserving his or her superior's time, tries to discover the true purpose of each salesperson's visit before granting an interview with the boss. According to one study, decision makers receive over 200 selling contacts per day from business-to-business marketers, so the screen's behavior should not seem unreasonable![44]

Salespeople should go out of their way to treat all subordinates with respect and courtesy. First, it is the right thing to do. Second, subordinates can be the true key to the salesperson's success or failure with an organization. They may not be able to buy the salesperson's product, but they can often kill his or her chances for a sale.

Sales strategists have identified three basic ways to interact with the screen. The salesperson can go "over the screen." This occurs when the seller, while talking to the screen, drops names of people higher up in the organization. As a result, the

Videoconferencing makes it easy for a U.S. salesperson to make a presentation in São Paulo, Brazil.

John Maier, Jr./The Image Works

IF YOU'RE FINISHED WITH YOUR PRESENTATION, COULD YOU PASS THE SCALPEL, PLEASE?

Sales presentations can and often do occur in some rather unusual places. But maybe you didn't know that they sometimes happen in an operating room of a hospital. That's right. During surgery salespeople are sometimes present, answering questions about equipment and providing insights into how their product or service might benefit the surgeon. For some salespeople it happens rather frequently, as much as six surgeries in a single morning.

Each hospital has its own rules governing salespeople in the operating room. Most concur that a salesperson is never to touch a patient. Unfortunately that's exactly what did allegedly happen a few years ago, and the patient died. David Myers, a sales rep for a division of Johnson & Johnson, allegedly participated in the surgery of a young woman with a non–life-threatening tumor. He had

been trying for some time to get the hospital to buy a new tool for removing tumors. During surgery, he operated some of the controls because the nurses hadn't been trained in the tool's proper use.

A statement by Myer's firm said, "The actions of our representative were in compliance with our longstanding policies," and Myers didn't lose his job. The hospital did change some of its own policies with regard to salespeople in surgery and required more informed consent by the patient.

The patient's husband has filed suit in the case. The moral: Be careful that you follow all the rules in force at the place you hold a sales meeting.

Source: Sarah Lorge, "Do Salespeople Belong Here?" *Sales and Marketing Management,* February 1999, p. 16.

screen may allow the seller in to see the boss right away for fear of getting into trouble. Or the salesperson can go "under the screen" by trying to make contact with the prospect before or after the screen gets to work (or while the screen is taking a coffee break). For example, one salesperson related the following:

> There was one secretary I could not get past to save my soul . . . I kept calling at odd times: early in the morning, late at night, lunchtime—whenever she might be gone. Finally, her boss answered. I explained why I was calling, and he said OK to a meeting. It just took persistence.[45]

Finally, the salesperson can work "through the screen" by simply involving the screen in the process. In this scenario the seller would have to convince the gatekeeper that a meeting with the boss was in the boss's best interests.

Salespeople should work to achieve a friendly relationship with the prospect's subordinates.

Thinking It Through

Do you see problems in working over the screen? How about working under the screen? What might these tactics do to long-term relationship development?

TELEPHONING FOR APPOINTMENTS

There are several ways to make an appointment, including in person, by mail, or by phone. Making an initial appointment in person is desirable (the salesperson can gather more precall information) but is usually too time-consuming for the salesperson. Using the mail (e-mail or postal mail) requires more lead time and may languish unread in the "junk mail" clutter. Therefore, the phone is most often used to make the initial appointment. Salespeople can save many hours by phoning to make appointments.

Salespeople need to use the phone correctly and effectively. All of us have used telephones since childhood; many of us have developed bad habits that reduce our effectiveness when talking over the phone. Perfect your phone style by practicing alone before making any calls. Make sure you know what you want to say before placing the call. Many would argue that it is a polite gesture to start by asking, "Is this a good time to talk?"[46] Don't be too rushed to be nice; it is never acceptable to be rude. And don't forget to smile as you talk. Even though the prospect won't see it, she or he will hear it in your enthusiastic tone of voice.

Active listening (see Chapter 5) is as important when conversing over the phone as when conversing in person. Take notes and restate the message or any action you have agreed to undertake. In addition, you will need to encourage two-way communication. If you have ever talked with two-year-olds over the phone, you know that if you ask them a yes-or-no question, they tend to shake their heads yes or no rather than verbalize a response. Similarly, you cannot nod your head to encourage someone to continue talking on the phone. Instead, you must encourage conversations with verbal cues such as Uh-huh, I see, or That's interesting. Finally, just as in face-to-face conversation, you must be able to tolerate silences so that customers have an opportunity to ask questions, agree or disagree, or relate a point to their circumstances.

What if in trying to reach the prospect you reach his or her voice mail instead? Here are some tips from experts. If you are making a cold call to set up an appointment, it is usually best not to leave a message. Instead, go to the operator and try to reach the prospect's secretary and find a good time to call back. If you have a referral or have talked to the person before, leave a clear, concise message that includes a suggested time for the person to return your call (so you will know when to expect the call and can be prepared). When leaving a message, don't just talk and talk until the tape runs out. A little casual conversation is fine, but remember that the prospect's time is important. Also, make your message compelling—for example, "Alan, I just fell into a terrific opportunity, but it's an offer I can only pass along to a few customers. Timing is tight. If you want to hear the details, call me at (phone number) before the close of business Thursday." Be yourself and don't be afraid to use humor. For example, Sue Yellin, head of a training firm in New York, leaves this message: "Hello. This is your mother. I'm at Sue Yellin's office. Could you give me a call at 212-555-2721?"[47] Slowly repeat your name and phone number at the end of your message. And remember, never leave bad news on voice mail.

A salesperson should use techniques that feel comfortable and discard any that do not feel natural. It is also important to set objectives for your phone call and strategize what you're going to say and why. Here is an example for using the phone to make an appointment:[48]

1. [State customer's name.] Hello, Mr. Walker? (pause)
2. [State your name.] This is Glen Scott, with Gamma Industries.
3. [Politely check time.] I hope I didn't catch you in the middle of something urgent or pressing? (Pause)
4. [State purpose and make presentation.] I'm calling to let you know about our new color laser copier. I've shown it to several other designers in town, and they found it to be a real money saver with more features than any copier on the market right now.
5. [Close.] I'd like to meet with you and share some feedback from your business associates. Could you put me on your calendar for 30 minutes next Monday or Tuesday?
6. [Show appreciation and restate time, or keep door open.] Thank you, Mr. Walker. I'll be at your office at 9 A.M. on Tuesday.

[or]

I appreciate your frankness, Mr. Walker. I'd like to get back to you in a couple of months. Would that be all right?

A potential customer may have objections, or reasons for not granting an interview. The goal of the telephone call, however, is to make an appointment, not to sell the product or service. Exhibit 8.4 shows appropriate responses to common objections Xerox copier salespeople encounter when making appointments. Salespeople need to anticipate objections and decide exactly how to respond. The planned responses should be developed with the prospect's perspective in mind. In other words, ask yourself, as though you were the prospect, what you would like to hear in response to each objection.[49]

When salespeople call for appointments, prospects frequently ask questions about the product or service. The salesperson should not be drawn into giving a sales presentation over the telephone. Remember, the purpose of the call is to obtain an appointment, not to make a sale. In fact, some firms use their telemarketing staff to set appointments for salespeople to avoid being drawn into a complete sales presentation. Telemarketers can also save the sellers much valuable time. For example, Shachihata, an office supplies company, found that its 30 reps were spending 70 percent of their time setting up appointments. The company employed 10 part-time employees to take over this task, which resulted in a 15 percent increase in sales. The sales manager summarized, "I don't know why more companies don't do this."[50]

Some salespeople have their secretaries make telephone appointments for them. This approach often gives them greater prestige in the mind of the prospect or customer. If the secretary cannot obtain an appointment, the salesperson may make a second call, using a different approach.

Sometimes it takes creativity to get an appointment with a difficult-to-reach prospect. Carol Davidson, salesperson for a small trade publication on the West Coast, was having trouble getting an appointment with a buyer on the East Coast. After trying all of the "normal" methods, here's what she did:

> I went to a local shoe store that displays shoes by putting one on a rack, with the mate in the back room. They always end up losing shoes and usually have a box full of strays to dump at the end of the week. I was able to get an expensive Italian shoe at no cost, which I then mailed to my client with a note that began, "Now that I

EXHIBIT 8.4

Responses to Objections
Concerning
Appointments

Objection from a Secretary	Response
I'm sorry, but Mr. Wilkes is busy now.	What I have to say will take only a few minutes. Should I call back in a half-hour, or would you suggest I set up an appointment?
We already have a copier.	That's fine. I want to talk to Mr. Wilkes about our new paper-flow system design for companies like yours.
I take care of all the copying.	That's fine, but I'm here to present what Xerox has to offer for a complete paper-flow system that integrates data transmission, report generation, and copiers. I'd like to speak to Mr. Wilkes about this total service.

Objection from the Prospect	Response
Can't you mail the information to me?	Yes, I could. But everyone's situation is different, Mr. Wilkes, and our systems are individually tailored to meet the needs of each customer. Now . . . [benefit statement and repeat request for appointment].
Well, what is it you want to talk about?	It's difficult to explain the system over the telephone. In 15 minutes, I can demonstrate the savings you get from the system.
You'd just be wasting your time. I'm not interested.	The general objection is hiding a specific objection. The salesperson needs to probe for the specific objection: Do you say that because you don't copy many documents?
We had a Xerox copier once and didn't like it.	Probe for the specific reason of dissatisfaction and have a reply, but don't go too far. The objective is to get an appointment, not sell a copier.

Source: Courtesy of Xerox Corporation. Used by permission.

have my foot in the door . . ." Though it may seem like a silly gimmick, it worked and turned into my first order from this prospect—the first of many, I might add.[51]

At times salespeople may have to use determination, persistence, and ingenuity (as Carol did) to obtain interviews, but they should never resort to deceitful or dishonest tactics. The use of subterfuge to obtain appointments has no place in professional selling. Salespeople who select prospects carefully in terms of product needs should not have to conceal the purpose of the visit.

ADDITIONAL PLANNING

In addition to the activities described in this chapter, a successful salesperson thinks ahead to the meeting that will occur and plans accordingly. For example, salespeople should plan how they intend to make a good first impression and build credibility during the call. It is also important to plan how to further uncover the customer's needs and strengthen the presentation. Salespeople should anticipate the questions and concerns the prospect may raise and plan to answer them helpfully. These issues are discussed in detail in the next several chapters. For now, be aware that these activities should be planned before the meeting begins.

Before making the sales call it is important to practice.[52] How long should a rep spend practicing? Longer than many would think. As Mark Twain once said, "It usually takes more than three weeks to prepare a good impromptu speech." One rule of thumb for very important presentations is that the seller spend 30 minutes preparing and practicing for each one minute of presentation time.[53] While that rule is often broken, it does indicate the importance of planning and practicing the presentation. Of course the time spent in practicing would depend on how much time the seller has plus what the goals of the presentation are. Some firms are helping their salespeople prepare, and hence have more time to practice, by offering them easy-to-access information and presentation templates. For example, Keebler gives its sales reps an online database of trends, information, and presentation templates.[54] This system greatly reduces the time the salesperson has to spend searching internal and external sources.

One other thing that some salespeople do before making the actual sales call is called **seeding:** that is, sending the customer important and useful things prior to the meeting. For example, one company constantly searches newspapers, magazines, and other sources for material that may be useful for a prospect.[55] This material is sent to the prospect, at intervals, prior to the call, each time with a note saying something like "Jim, I thought you would find this article useful!" This material does *not* include the selling firm's catalogs, brochures, pricing, and so on. Rather, it is just good, useful information that will help the prospect's business. The result? The prospect views the seller as someone trying to truly be helpful and as someone who really understands the prospect's business.

Summary

This chapter stressed the importance of planning the sales call. Developing a clear plan saves time for both salespeople and customers. In addition, it helps salespeople increase their confidence and reduce their stress.

As part of the planning process, salespeople need to gather as much information about the prospect as possible before the first call. They need information about both the individual prospect and the prospect's organization. Sources of this information include lists and directories, secretaries and receptionists, noncompeting salespeople, and direct inquiries made by the prospect.

To be effective, a call objective should be specific, realistic, and measurable. In situations requiring several calls, the salesperson should develop a plan with call objectives for each future call. Also, many salespeople benefit from setting multiple levels of objectives—primary, minimum, and optimum—for each call.

As a general rule, salespeople should make appointments before calling on customers. This approach enables the salesperson to talk to the right person at the customer's site.

A number of methods can be used to make appointments. Perhaps the most effective is the straightforward telephone approach: stating the salesperson's name, establishing a link with the prospect or customer, stating the purpose of the call, and asking for an appointment.

KEY TERMS

analysis paralysis   214
barriers   227
customer value   223
focus of dissatisfaction   225
focus of power   225
focus of receptivity   224
gatekeepers   227
influential adversaries   213
minimum call objective   220
optimistic call objective   221

primary call objective   220
privacy laws   214
screens   227
secondary call objectives   221
seeding   232
selling center   215
value proposition   223
videoconferencing   226
virtual sales call   226
webcasting   226

Questions and Problems

1. Suppose that during your information-gathering phase you identify a very hostile influential adversary named Mike. You know that Mike will do everything possible to see your competitor get the business. In talking about this with your sales manager, she suggests that you find some way to covertly strip Mike of his credibility and thus cause him to be a nonissue. Would you follow your manager's advice? What kinds of things would you be willing to do? What would you be uncomfortable doing?

2. Setting call objectives takes time and effort on the part of the salesperson. Are there any situations in which it would not make sense for a salesperson to set a call objective? If so, what are they?

3. Respond to the following statement: Setting call objectives reduces my ability to be adaptable during the call.

4. Evaluate the following objectives for a sales call:
   a. Show and demonstrate the entire line of 10 color inkjet printers.
   b. Find out more about competitors' services under consideration.
   c. Increase the buyer's trust in my company.
   d. Determine which service the prospect is currently using and how much it costs.
   e. Have the buyer agree to hold our next meeting at some third location (other than either party's office).

    f. Get an order for 15 AV-8B Harrier II Plus combat jets.

    g. Make the buyer more comfortable with the fact that our firm has been in business only three months.

5. Think for a moment about trying to secure a job. Assume you are going to have your second job interview next week with Kimberly Clark for a sales position. Most candidates go through a set of four interviews. List your primary objective, minimum objective, and optimistic objective.

6. Why is making appointments before visiting a customer desirable? Under which circumstances might the salesperson not need to make appointments?

7. Assume you are trying to sell several new styles of couches to a furniture store. Your boss listed three possible objectives for your next call: sell 2 new styles, sell 10 new styles, and have the prospect watch a demonstration that shows the wearability of the couches. Identify the primary objective, the minimum objective, and the optimistic objective.

8. Evaluate the following approach for getting an appointment: Ms. Thompson, I'm going to be working in your area next week. When can I come by to tell you about our new product?

9. Much attention is given to the best time of day for sales interviews. List the best time of day to call on the following individuals:

    a. A college professor (to sell textbooks).

    b. A lawyer (to sell investigative services).

    c. A product manager (to sell magazine ad space).

    d. A janitor (to sell janitorial supplies).

    e. A senior buyer at a grocery store's corporate headquarters (to sell a new food product).

    f. A computer operations supervisor (to sell repair services).

    g. An accountant (to sell fax machines).

10. Review the list of prospects in question 9 and identify

    a. The worst time of day to call on each individual.

    b. The worst time of year to call on each individual.

11. Suppose you belong to Friends of the Library, an organization that plans to hold a dinner to raise funds for new book acquisitions. To be a success, the event will need a great deal of community support, especially from local businesses.

    a. Which sources will you use to identify potential sponsors?

    b. What information do you need to qualify them properly?

Case Problems

CASE 8.1

Caterpillar Wheel Loaders

Caterpillar is number one in the world in heavy construction, helping companies move millions of tons of earth every day. Caterpillar machines are used to build tunnels, dams, highways, bridges, airports, and railroads. Their machines are state-of-the-art in terms of fuel economy, operator comfort and safety, productivity, reliability, and they comply with all of the latest tough emissions requirements.

Last week the new Caterpillar salesperson, John Vandergriff, had his first meeting with Skelly Joresog, a buyer from United States Steel (USS) at their MinnTac plant in Virginia, Minnesota. The meeting was brief, with John just wanting to introduce himself to the buyer. During the meeting, John was excited to learn that USS was considering buying several new wheel loaders within the next year. Wheel loaders are the machines that can scoop up large amounts of material in their buckets and then dump it where needed (into a pile, into a dump truck, onto a conveyor belt, and so forth).

Skelly seemed to think that the MinnTac plant hadn't bought any new wheel loaders for quite some time. Skelly is a new buyer who just arrived at MinnTac from a USS assignment in Pittsburg. Although John was new to Caterpillar sales, he didn't remember hearing about any Caterpillar sales of wheel loaders to MinnTac in the last five years.

John asked if he could give a presentation in a month to lay out what Caterpillar had to offer. Skelly agreed, limiting the meeting to one hour.

Caterpillar offers a number of different wheel loaders from compact (45–82 horsepower) to small (90–125 horsepower) to medium (160–311 horsepower) to large (520–1,370 horsepower). John imagines that since MinnTac is a large mine, they will probably be needing the largest wheel loaders made by Caterpillar.

Sources: Caterpillar 2000 annual report, and caterpillar.com website (viewed on 3/2/02).

Questions

1. What kind of information should John gather about Skelly before his next meeting with him?
2. What kind of information should John gather about MinnTac before his next meeting there?
3. Which sources can John use to gather the needed information?

CASE 8.2
XanEdu Online Course-Specific Content

"Look, I've seen a lot of dot-coms come and go," Dr. Crystal Longview exclaimed. "You're here today, with lots of fancy charts and graphs, but tomorrow you'll be gone. And I'll be left to start all over again in developing my course packet of material." She waved the air as if to indicate the meeting was over.

But Connie Faggerty, salesperson for XanEdu, a division of the ProQuest Corporation, wasn't so easily removed. "Look, I hear what you're saying," Connie acknowledged. "I know there have been tons of upsets with dot-coms. But that's not what we are. We have been in business for many, many years. I'm sure you've heard of our former name: Bell & Howell, a well-respected name in higher education."

Dr. Longview sat up a little straighter. "Yes, of course I've heart of B&H. But you're not in here selling movie projectors or slide projectors."

"Right. Because I'm here to sell you what *you* need. You don't need movie projectors. What I think I heard you say is that you need a way to make it easier for yourself and your distance education students to get the very latest business information available."

After a few more minutes of discussion, Dr. Longview asked Connie to return in a week and meet with a group of three staff people that work in the distance education program of the business school at the university. "To be honest with you, I had never heard of your company before you walked in today. I don't know if my staff members are more up-to-date on this than I am," Dr. Longview said, shaking Connie's hand. "Now that you've piqued my curiosity, I'm going to start checking to see what else is available like this. Well, we'll see you in a week."

XanEdu is a division of the Information and Learning sector of ProQuest. XanEdu provides online access to thousands of periodicals, dissertations, books, and newspapers. All materials are cleared for copyright, thus greatly reducing the time and effort on the part of the instructor. XanEdu offers course packs that are customized for each specific course, making it easier for the professor to ensure that his or her students have access to the latest work in the field. And the course packs are very up-to-date, being developed by some of the strongest Web search engines available.

Many XanEdu course packs have been sold to undergraduate students, professors, graduate programs, and distance education programs. The U.S. college student market is expected to grow by 1 million students over the next five years. And close to 70 percent of college students already own PCs, with 95 percent having Web access.

Source: ProQuest 2000 annual report and proquestcompany.com.

Questions

1. Assume you are Connie Faggerty. List your call objectives for your next call with the group. Develop a three-call follow-up schedule and list the objectives for each call.
2. What kind of information would you like to have before your next meeting? How could you obtain that information?

Additional References

Cohen, Andy. "Best Ways to Get Calls Returned." *Sales and Marketing Management* 154, March 2002, p. 16.

Cummings, Betsy. "Do Customers Hate Salespeople? Only If They Commit One of These Deadly Sins of Selling." *Sales and Marketing Management,* June 2001, pp. 44–51.

Graham, John R. "Sales Strategies for a Changed World." *The American Salesman* 46, January 2001, pp. 16–22.

Hunt, Kenneth A., and R. Edward Bashaw. "Using Buyer's Information Processing to Formulate Selling Strategies." *Industrial Marketing Management* 28, January 1999, pp. 99–107.

Lewin, Jeffrey E. "The Effects of Downsizing on Organizational Buying Behavior: An Empirical Investigation." *Journal of the Academy of Marketing Science* 29:2 (2001), pp. 151–64.

Millar, Bill. "Pitching In: Medical Suppliers Are Shifting Emphasis from Selling Products to Becoming Value-Added Service Partners to Physicians." *1to1 Magazine,* April 2002, pp. 34–38.

Ottinger, William F. "Sales Calls in a Multi-Call Environment." *Trusts and Estates,* May 1999, p. 22+.

Overholt, Alison. "Virtually There." *Fast Company,* March 2002, pp. 109–14.

Philadelphia, Desa. "Video Traveler." *Time: Time Bonus Section Inside Business,* February 2001, pp. Y2–Y4.

"SMM's Best of Sales & Marketing." *Sales and Marketing Management,* September 2001, pp. 26–32.

Sullivan, Robert. "Out to Lunch." *Sales and Marketing Management,* April 2000, pp. 110–11.

Walle, Don Vande; Steven P. Brown; Willliam L. Cron; and John W. Slocum Jr. "The Influence of Goal Orientation and Self-Regulation Tactics on Sales Performance: A Longitudinal Field Test." *Journal of Applied Psychology,* April 1999, pp. 249–59.

Woodruff, Robert B., and Sarah Fisher Gardial. *Know Your Customer: New Approaches to Understanding Customer Value and Satisfaction.* Cambridge, MA: Blackwell Publishers, 1996.

Zielinski, Dave. "Thinking Strategically." *Presentations,* September 1999, pp. 37–46.

Chapter

9 *Making the Sales Call*

SOME QUESTIONS ANSWERED IN THIS CHAPTER ARE:

■ How should the salesperson make the initial approach to make a good impression and gain the prospect's attention?

■ How can the salesperson develop rapport and increase source credibility?

■ Why is discovering the prospect's needs important, and how can a salesperson get this information?

■ How can the salesperson most effectively relate the product or service features to the prospect's needs?

■ Why is it important for the salesperson to make adjustments during the call?

■ How does the salesperson recognize that adjustments are needed?

■ How can a salesperson effectively sell to groups?

At this point in the sales process, we assume that an appointment has been made, sufficient information about the prospect and his or her organization has been gathered, and the salesperson has developed strong objectives for the call. In this chapter we discuss how to make the actual sales call. Exhibit 9.1 provides an organizing framework for our discussion.

EXHIBIT 9.1   Essential Elements of the Sales Call

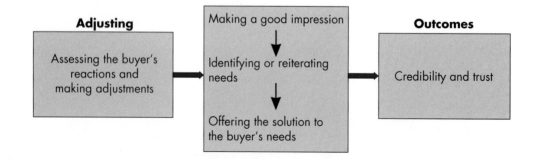

Adjusting

Assessing the buyer's reactions and making adjustments

Making a good impression

↓

Identifying or reiterating needs

↓

Offering the solution to the buyer's needs

Outcomes

Credibility and trust

"I focus on the prospect, who wants to spend more time talking about herself or himself, instead of what I have to sell."

Alexander Marquette, PartStock Computer Solutions

PROFILE

After graduating from the University of Minnesota—Duluth with a BBA Marketing degree in 1996, Alexander Marquette started his sales career in the technology industry, selling computer hardware, software, and services to medium and large businesses. He started in inside sales, supporting existing accounts and learning how to satisfy the client and how to adapt to the fast pace of the technology industry. A few years ago he moved into outside sales, developing new business. Alex is currently working for PartStock Computer Solutions as an account executive, showing businesses and schools how to make a tight technology budget work.

"Today's buyers are sharper, more savvy, and focused on saving time and money," says Alex. "They can smell a poorly prepared salesperson a mile away. Salespeople get only one chance to make a solid first impression. When making a cold call, the first 8 to 10 seconds will make or break the relationship. The prospect has hundreds of items on his/her plate and you're not one of them.

"Recently I spent three weeks developing a solid sales presentation for an important client. I talked with my existing clients, learning why they buy from me, asking what specific benefits we offer that fit their needs. I also talked with our sales staff to develop needs identification questions, a list of possible sales objections, and a fine-tuned list of features and benefits.

"From these meetings I now have a comprehensive sales presentation planned. It's really quite simple. I spend most of my time asking questions. I make sure I have benefits for each feature that are specifically targeted for my prospect. After discussing a benefit, I immediately ask a probing question to gauge the situation. My hope is to spot a 'Hot Button,' a feature/ benefit that is really important to the prospect, sometimes important enough to instantly close a deal.

"The main portion of my presentation is laid out on 10 pages. For the first seven, each page has one feature with three bulleted specific benefits for this client. The last three pages talk about my company and product offerings. Usually I don't get through all of my pages. In an average sales call, I spend less than 20 percent of the time talking about our product or company. Usually I need to schedule another meeting to continue the conversation. In my experience, it takes from four to six sales calls or meetings to close a deal.

"I focus on the prospect, who wants to spend more time talking about herself or himself instead of what I have to sell. By attentively listening and asking good open questions I can develop rapport with the prospect. I recently attended a seminar by Brian Tracy, who said, 'Today's buyers all listen to the same radio station, WIIFM (What's In It For Me).'

"Being prepared with open questions and a presentation that shows the prospect I care about his/her needs proves I am genuinely interested in partnering to solve problems. Brian Tracy said that this approach '. . . separates the top-performing salespeople from the rookies.' I have found that my success is directly proportionate to the level of planning I have done prior to making the initial cold call and meeting."

By the way, after four sales calls on the prospect mentioned in his profile, Alex did get the business.

Visit Our Website @ www.partstockpc.com.

MAKING A GOOD IMPRESSION

This chapter begins by considering how to make a good impression and begin to develop a long-term relationship. We then examine the initial needs assessment phase of a relationship and how to relate solutions to those needs. Finally, we discuss the relationship between adaptability and successful sales calls.

There are, of course, many conceptualizations of the selling process. For example, Karl Sooder at the University of Central Florida finds value is describing the selling process as the Four A's (**a**cknowledge, **a**cquire, **a**dvise, and **a**ssure).[1] First the seller acknowledges the buyer by greeting/welcoming/honoring and building trust. Next the rep acquires information via needs analysis and a summary of that analysis outlining the agreement between buyer and seller about the current situation and the desired solution. Advising comes next, during which the seller narrows the possible choices to specific options, sells benefits of those options (not just features), watches for buying signals, and asks for the order. Finally, the seller assures the buyer after the sale by enhancing satisfaction with the buying decision and giving proper follow-up and referrals.

The content of an actual sales call depends on the specific situation the salesperson encounters as well as the extent of the relationship the salesperson has already established with the other party.[2] In this chapter we discuss the important elements of sales calls in general. However, keep in mind that some activities, such as making a good first impression, are less of an issue for existing partnering customers than they are for leads on whom you are making a first call.

Successful salespeople have learned the importance of making a good impression. When salespeople fail to arrive on time, make a poor entrance, fail to gain the buyer's interest, or lack rapport-building skills, it is difficult for them to secure commitment and build partnerships.[3] This section discusses how salespeople can manage the buyer's impression of them, a process often termed **impression management**. Most of the information presented here assumes that the salesperson is making a first call on a prospect. However, impression management continues throughout calls.

One of the most important ways to ensure a good first impression is to be well prepared (as we discussed in Chapter 8). Some salespeople prepare a checklist of things to take to the presentation so they won't forget anything.

WAITING FOR THE PROSPECT

Being on time for a scheduled sales call is critical to avoid giving the buyer a negative impression. With the advent of cell phones, there is practically no good reason for not calling if you're going to be a few minutes late to the appointment. Because of the importance of arriving on time, salespeople usually arrive a few minutes early and have to wait to see the prospect. Further, the prospect occasionally is running behind and lets the salesperson wait beyond the appointment time. Either scenario can result in salespeople sitting and waiting, sometimes for long periods, for their prospects to see them.

Every salesperson must expect to spend a certain portion of each working day waiting for sales interviews. Successful salespeople make the best possible use of this time by working on reports, studying new product information, planning and preparing for their next calls, and obtaining additional information about the prospect. Thankfully, laptops and palm PCs, especially with satellite links, make this activity easier to accomplish in a prospect's waiting room. (Chapter 16 covers time management more fully.)

Some sales managers instruct their sales representatives not to wait for any prospect, under normal circumstances, more than 15 minutes after the appointment time. Why? To demonstrate that the seller's time is also very important. Exceptions are necessary, of course, depending on the importance of the customer and the distance the salesperson has traveled. In all cases salespeople should keep the sales call in perspective, realizing that their time is also valuable. Chapter 16 discusses just how valuable that time really is!

When the salesperson arrives, the receptionist may merely say, "I'll tell Mr. Jones that you are here." After the receptionist has spoken with Mr. Jones, the salesperson should ask approximately how long the wait will be. When the wait will be excessive and/or the salesperson has another appointment, it may be advisable to explain this tactfully and to ask for another appointment. Usually the secretary either will try to get the salesperson in to see the prospect more quickly or will make arrangements for a later appointment.

THE ENTRANCE

In the first meeting between a salesperson and a prospect or customer, the first two or three minutes can be very important.[4] Making a favorable first impression usually results in a prospect who is willing to listen. A negative first impression, on the other hand, sets up a barrier that may never be hurdled. Note that one advantage of an existing partnering relationship is that the salesperson has already established a bond and has built a reputation based on his or her prior actions.

The entrance, like the presentation itself, can occur anywhere. For someone selling cellular telephones, for example, it can occur in a traditional office setting, while a farmer is sitting on his or her combine or tractor, or in the yard of a tow truck operator. The key is for the salesperson to be adaptable (review Chapter 6 on how a salesperson can adapt) to the situation and make an effective entrance for that particular scenario.

VERY FIRST IMPRESSIONS

Salespeople may make a poor impression without realizing it. They may know their customer's needs and their own product, but overlook seemingly insignificant things that can create negative impressions. As Chapter 5 related, how you dress can affect the message you send to the buyer.[5] Also, studies have shown that the physical attractiveness of salespeople can influence purchase intentions of buyers.[6] Exploratory research even suggests that gender can make a difference. Salespeople who sold to members of the opposite sex had higher performance than those selling to buyers of the same sex.[7] Further, evidence suggests that women often have to work harder to be taken as seriously in their sales presentations (even with female buyers) as men.[8] And don't forget that according to generation gap experts, it is often quite difficult for a Generation X (born 1965–1978) salesperson to relate to a Baby Boomer (born 1946–1964) buyer, and even harder to relate to a Traditionalist (born 1922–1946) buyer.[9]

Sales calls can occur in practically every location.

Courtesy Bristol-Myers Squibb Pharmaceutical

Mark Tuschman/The Stock Market

Mark Tuschman/The Stock Market

So what should a seller do to create a good first impression? You should be well groomed; enter confidently (but not cocky) by using erect posture, lengthy stride, and a lively pace; and among the first words out of your mouth should be something like "Thanks for seeing me." And don't forget to smile. Watch what happens when you look at someone and smile. In 99 out of 100 times, you will receive a smile in return.

It is also important to remember prospects' names and how to pronounce them. There are many ways to try to remember someone's name (such as giving your full attention when you hear it and then repeating the name immediately, associating it with someone else you know with the same name, associating it with the person's most prominent feature or trait, using it during the conversation, and writing it down phonetically). Whatever you do, make sure to pronounce the prospect's name correctly.

HANDSHAKING

Salespeople should not automatically extend their hand to a prospect, particularly if the prospect is seated.[10] Shaking hands should be the prospect's choice. If the prospect offers a hand, the salesperson should respond with a firm but not overpowering handshake while maintaining good eye contact. Chances are that you have experienced both a limpid handshake—a hand with little or no grip— and a bone-crunching grip. Either impression is often lasting and negative. Also, if you tend to have sweaty hands, carry a handkerchief.

Women should shake hands in the same manner men do.[11] They should avoid offering their hand for a social handshake (palm facing down and level with the ground, with fingers drooping and pointing to the ground). Likewise, a man should not force a social handshake from a woman in a business setting.

The salesperson selling in an international context needs to carefully consider cultural norms regarding the appropriateness of handshaking, bowing, and other forms of greeting. For example, the Chinese prefer no more than a slight bow in their greeting, whereas an Arab businessperson may not only shake hands vigorously but also keep holding your hand for several seconds. A hug in Mexico communicates a trusting relationship, but in Germany such a gesture would be offensive because it suggests an inappropriate level of intimacy. Germans tend to pump the hand only once during a handshake. Some African cultures snap their fingers after shaking hands, but other Africans would see this act as tasteless. And some Eastern cultures also use the left hand for hygienic purposes, so offering a left hand to them would insult them. In some cultures it is important to offer a business card at both the beginning and the end of a meeting.[12]

SELECTING A SEAT

When selecting a seat, it is a good idea to look around and start to identify the prospect's social style and status (see Chapter 6). For example, in the United States important decision makers usually have large, well-appointed, private offices. But be careful. In Kuwait, a high-ranking businessperson may have a small office

Women should shake hands in the same manner as men do.

E. Metter/The Image Bank

and lots of interruptions. Don't take that environment to mean he or she is a low-ranking employee or is not interested.

Asking permission to sit down is usually unnecessary. The salesperson should read the prospect's nonverbal cues to determine the right time to be seated. And note that many calls will not involve sitting down at all (such as talking to a store manager in a grocery store aisle, conversing with a supervisor in a warehouse, asking questions of a surgeon in a post-op ward).

GETTING THE CUSTOMER'S ATTENTION

Recall from Chapter 6 that there are several types of sales presentations, including standard memorized, outlined, and customized. In this chapter we assume that the salesperson has chosen a customized presentation.

Getting the customer's attention is not a new concept. It is also the goal of many other activities you are familiar with (advertising, making new friends, writing an English composition, giving a speech, writing a letter to a friend).

Time is very valuable to prospects, and prospects concentrate their attention on the first few minutes with a salesperson to determine whether they will benefit from the interaction. The first few words the salesperson says often set the tone of the entire sales call. The **halo effect** (how and what you do in one thing changes a person's perceptions about other things you do) seems to operate in many sales calls. If the salesperson is perceived by the prospect as effective at the beginning of the call, he will be perceived as effective during the rest of the call, and vice versa.

Some experts argue that the customer's name should be used in the opening statement. Dale Carnegie, a master at developing relationships, said a person's name is "the sweetest and most important sound" to that person. Using a person's name often indicates respect and a recognition of the person's unique qualities. Others disagree with this logic, claiming that using the person's name, especially more than once in any short length of time, sounds phony and insincere. A compromise is to use the prospect's name in the opening and then to use it sparingly during the rest of the call.

Some approaches to opening a sales call are described next. An **approach** is a method designed to get the prospect's attention and interest quickly and to make a smooth transition into the next part of the presentation (which is usually to more fully discover the prospect's needs). Because each prospect and sales situation is unique, salespeople should be adaptable and be able to use any or a combination of openings. Again, keep in mind that approaches are generally less important with partnering customers whom the salesperson has already met.

INTRODUCTION APPROACH

In the **introduction approach** salespeople state their names and the names of their companies and may hand the prospect a business card. Handing the prospect a business card helps the prospect remember the salesperson's name and firm. Prospects may not hear the name because they are busy sizing up the salesperson. Some salespeople think a business card can be distracting and find that giving their card at the end of the interview is more effective. Progressive salespeople are starting to use business cards that are also CD-ROMs. These CD business cards, which can hold between 30 MB and 50 MB of information and may include video clips and HTML links, cost from $1.30 to $2 per card.[13]

The introduction approach is the simplest way to open a sales call. However, it is perhaps the least effective way because it is unlikely to generate much interest. It is used most often in conjunction with other methods.

Here is a basic introduction approach:

> Ms. Fontaine, thank you for seeing me today. My name is John Locklear, and I'm with Best Foods.

REFERRAL APPROACH

Using the name of a satisfied customer or a friend of the prospect can begin a sales call effectively. Salespeople frequently present letters of introduction or testimonials. The **referral approach** is often effective with amiables and expressives (see Chapter 6) because they like to focus on relationships.

Because prospects often will contact these references, salespeople should use only the names of individuals and companies to whom they would like the prospect to talk. Successful salespeople always gain permission from references prior to using them. Dropping names and stretching the truth concerning third parties will almost always backfire. Also, remember this advice: "The right contact may get you in the door, but it's knowledge that gets and keeps the business."

Here are some examples of referral approaches:

> Mr. Lewis, I appreciate your seeing me today. I'm here at the suggestion of Ms. McQueen of Brock Control Systems, Inc. She thought you would be interested in our new marketing and sales productivity system.

> Mr. Braden, several of the other CPAs in town are now using our database management software package. Here are some letters they have written about what our service has meant to them.

BENEFIT APPROACH

Perhaps the most widely used sales call opening is the **benefit approach,** which focuses the prospect's attention on a product benefit. For this approach to be effective, the benefit must be of real interest to the prospect. Unless the salesperson knows the prospect's needs (either from good precall information gathering

Sharing letters from satisfied customers helps a salesperson establish credibility.

© SuperStock

or from other visits), this approach cannot succeed. In addition, the benefit should be specific, something the prospect can actually realize and something that can be substantiated during the presentation. The benefit approach is effective for drivers and analyticals (who like to get down to business rather quickly) because it gets right to the point. For example:

> Mr. Scofield, I would like to tell you about a copier that can reduce your copying costs by 15 percent.

> Your secretary can save one hour per day by using the spelling checker and automerge features of this new version of WordPerfect (word processing package).

> Ms. Twombly, AT&T can save your firm at least $100,000 by transmitting voice, data, and images all at the same time, over one line, using our new ISDN network.

PRODUCT APPROACH

The **product approach** involves actually demonstrating a product feature and benefit as soon as the salesperson walks up to the prospect. Its advantage is that it appeals to the prospect visually as well as verbally. Handing the product to prospects for their examination adds even more involvement. This approach can be very effective for expressives. Here are several examples:

> [Carrying a palm PC into an office] Ms. Joyner, you spend a lot of time on the road as an investigative lawyer. Let me show you how this little handheld PC can transform your car (or any place you go) into an efficient, effective office.

> [Handing the buyer a scarf made out of a new synthetic material] Is it silk?

> [Handing a photograph of a computer-controlled milling machine to a production manager] How would you like to have this machine in your shop?

One pharmaceutical salesperson uses an interesting approach that resembles a product approach for the service features of her product, a prescription drug:

> [Playing a recording of a telephone ringing] That call could be one of your patients calling to complain about her estrogen replacement therapy. But not if she is on our drug.

COMPLIMENT APPROACH

Most people enjoy being praised or complimented, but such an approach poses a danger. Insincere flattery is often obvious and offensive to prospects. In using the

compliment approach, the compliment must be both sincere and specific. Sincerity relates directly to specificity. For example, the compliment "Mr. Smith, congratulations on the cost savings you achieved through the recent reorganization" is far more effective than "Mr. Smith, you are a really good businessperson."

Also, complimenting the obvious will not be effective. Chances are that others have already complimented the prospect about obviously noteworthy things (like a golf tournament trophy in the office or a much publicized and unusual fourth-quarter profit for the prospect's firm).

The compliment approach can also backfire. One salesperson, when calling on a 55-year-old man, noticed a picture of a beautiful 25-year-old woman on the buyer's desk. The seller said, "You certainly have a beautiful daughter," to which the buyer replied, "That's my wife!" It is generally best to stick to neutral topics unless you are sure of your information.

The compliment approach can be effective for all personality types. Here are two examples:

> I noticed as I walked in that you are carrying the new INX15 machines. They're going to set a new standard of excellence in your industry. You're the first dealer I've called on who is displaying them. It's perfect evidence of your innovativeness and quest for quality!

> I was calling on one of your customers, Jackson Street Books, last week, and the owner just couldn't say enough good things about your service. It sure says a lot about your operation to have a customer just start praising you out of the blue.

QUESTION APPROACH

Beginning the conversation with a question or by stating an interesting fact in the form of a question is the **question approach.** It gets the customer's attention, motivates a response, and initiates two-way communication. The following questions illustrate this approach:

> Ms. Garnett, what is your reaction to the brochure I sent you on our new telemarketing service?

> Mr. Ledford, if I can show you a way to reduce your turnover, would you be interested?

> Ms. Stiles, have you heard of the new free delivery service our firm is offering to doctors' offices such as yours?

DEVELOPING RAPPORT

Rapport in selling is a close, harmonious relationship founded on mutual trust. Ultimately the goal of every salesperson should be to establish rapport with each customer. Often salespeople can accomplish this with some friendly conversation early in the call. Part of this process involves identifying the prospect's social style and making necessary adjustments (see Chapter 6).

The talk about current news, hobbies, mutual friends, and the like that usually breaks the ice for the actual presentation is often referred to as **small talk.** Studies show that one of the top 10 traits of successful salespeople is the ability to be sociable.[14] Examples include the following:

> I understand you went to Ohio State? I graduated from there with a BBA in 1999.

> Did you happen to see the Cowboys game on TV last night?

> I was just talking to Sarah DiPuma, the controller, downstairs. She and I are on the same softball team, and wow, can she ever pitch a fastball!

Customers are more receptive to salespeople with whom they can identify—that is, with whom they have something in common. Thus salespeople will be more effective with customers with whom they establish such links as mutual friends, common hobbies, or attendance at the same schools. Successful salespeople engage in small talk more effectively by first performing **office scanning,** looking around the prospect's environment for relevant topics to talk about.

Be careful, however, when engaging in small talk, or it can be to your detriment. Stephanie Briggs tells of a client who asked her opinion of the economic outlook. "I foolishly told him my view of the economy, which was that it was going down. He was so put out that I would disagree with him. It took me months to repair our relationship." It is generally best to avoid controversial topics. Also, especially for first calls on prospects, you want to avoid using trite phrases like How are you doing today? because they don't sound sincere.

 Of course, salespeople should consider cultural and personality differences and adapt the extent of their nonbusiness conversation accordingly. For example, an AT&T rep would probably spend considerably less time in friendly conversation with a New York City office manager than with, say, a manager in a rural Texas town. Businesspeople in Africa place such high value on establishing friendships that the norm calls for a great deal of friendly conversation before getting down to business. Chinese customers want a lot of rapport building before they get down to business. Amiables and expressives tend to enjoy such conversations, whereas drivers and analyticals may be less receptive to spending much time in nonbusiness conversation. Also, there would not be much of a need for small talk if the salesperson had utilized the question or product approach when getting the customer's attention.

At this point in the sales call (after gaining the prospect's attention and establishing some rapport), a salesperson will often share his or her goals for the meeting with the prospect. This step can help build further rapport and trust. For example:

> Just so you know, my goal today is simply to verify what your needs might be and then, as I promised in the phone call, to share with you the results of the lab test we conducted last fall. I'm not going to ask you to buy anything!

WHEN THINGS GO WRONG

Making and maintaining a good impression is important. How nice it would be if the beginning of every call went as smoothly as we have described here. Actually, things do go wrong sometimes. (Question 4 in the "Questions and Problems" section at the end of this chapter allows you to think about what you would do in some rather awkward situations. You should read the questions even if your professor doesn't assign them.)

The best line of defense when something goes wrong is to maintain the proper perspective and a sense of humor. It's probably not the first thing you have done wrong and probably will not be your last. A good example of a call going downhill fast is the following experience, related by a salesperson:

> I pulled my right hand out of the pocket and stuck it forward enthusiastically to shake. Unfortunately, a ball of lint, about the size of a pea, had stuck to the tip of my fingers and was now drifting slowly down onto the document he had been reading. We both watched it descend, as compelling as the ball on New Year's Eve. We shook hands, anyway. I said, "Excuse me," and bent forward to blow the ball of lint off the document. As I did so, I put a dent in the front edge of his desk with my briefcase.[15]

The worst response by this salesperson would be to faint, scream, or totally lose control. A better response would include a sincere apology for the dent and an offer to pay for any repairs. Further, proper planning might have prevented this situation in the first place. If the salesperson had walked into the room with his hands out of his pockets, he would not have picked up the lint.

What if you say something that is truly embarrassing?[16] (According to Mark Twain, "Man is the only animal that blushes, or needs to.") The first thing you should do is to apologize sincerely. Then change the subject or move on in your presentation. Try to relax and put the incident behind you. And learn this lesson: Next time think before you speak!

Of course, you can get into trouble without even saying a word. Be careful when using gestures in other cultures because they often take on different meanings. For example, the OK sign (touching your thumb to your index finger) actually means "worthless" in France, "can I have small change?" in Japan, and "the bird" in Brazil.[17] Imagine the reactions you would get by giving the OK sign at the conclusion of signing a contract in each of these cultures!

Here's one final story about a blunder, which makes an important point. Barbara Geraghty, who runs a speaking and training firm, was making a first call on an executive. She walked into his office and, mistaking it for her intended seat, sat right down in his chair. She was so embarrassed and felt out of control. How did she make it come out all right? She didn't. The prospect did, in his graciousness. He just laughed and said, "You sure know how to take control." He didn't make fun of her or try to get any mileage out of her mistake. Barbara summed up the lesson she learned: "While we expect executives to be demanding—to have no tolerance for even small mistakes—that wasn't so in this case and, in fact, has rarely been so in my experience. . . They know that they make mistakes, and they will accept your mistakes, too."[18] That thought should be comforting to salespeople who will, at some point, certainly make mistakes.

IDENTIFYING THE PROSPECT'S NEEDS: THE POWER OF ASKING QUESTIONS

Once the salesperson has entered and captured the buyer's attention, it is time to identify the buyer's needs.[19] To begin this process, a salesperson might use transition sentences like the following (assuming a product approach was used to gain attention):

> Well, I'm glad you find this little model interesting. And I want to tell you all about it. But first I need to ask you a few questions to make sure I understand what your specific needs are. Is that OK?

If the buyer gives permission, the salesperson then begins to ask questions about the buyer's needs.

Occasionally, a salesperson makes the mistake of starting with product information rather than with a discussion of the prospect's needs. The experienced salesperson, however, attempts to uncover the prospect's needs and problems at the start of the relationship. In reality, discovering needs is still a part of qualifying the prospect. Selling Scenario 9.1 describes the importance of differentiating your product in the buyer's mind, and how discovering needs is a part of this process.

Research continually demonstrates the importance of needs discovery. An analysis by Huthwaite, Inc., of more than 35,000 sales calls in 23 countries over a 12-year period revealed that the distinguishing feature of successful salespeople was their ability to discover the prospect's needs.[20] Discovering needs was more important than opening the call strategically, handling objections, or using closing techniques effectively.

There is an underlying reason for every customer need, and the salesperson must continue probing until he or she uncovers the root problem or need. This

This salesperson needs to discover the customer's problems with their current rental of earth-moving equipment before describing the rental equipment he is selling.

©Mark Richards/PhotoEdit

process has been termed "finding the need behind the need"[21] and is graphically illustrated in Exhibit 9.2.

Given the importance of needs discovery, it is not surprising that most sales training programs now teach salespeople how to discover the prospect's needs. Yet author Joseph Mancuso made the following observation: "Most children ask about 60 questions a day. After they graduate from college, they're asking two questions a day and one of them is, When do we eat?"[22] All of us need to ask more questions and let the prospect talk more.

As you discover needs, keep in mind that this process can be very uncomfortable for the prospect. The prospect may resent your suggesting that there could be a problem or a better way to do things. When faced with direct evidence that things could be better, the prospect may express fear (fear of losing her or his job if things are not corrected, or of things changing and the situation getting worse than it is now). Also, remember that the amount of time and effort needed to discuss needs varies greatly depending on the type of industry, the nature of the

EXHIBIT 9.2

Finding the Need behind the Need

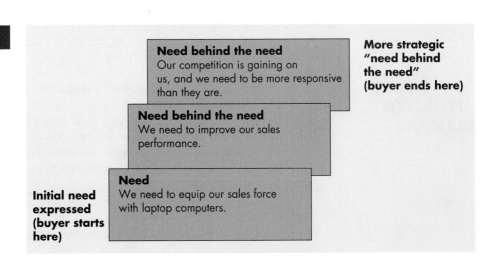

Need behind the need
Our competition is gaining on us, and we need to be more responsive than they are.

More strategic "need behind the need" (buyer ends here)

Need behind the need
We need to improve our sales performance.

Need
We need to equip our sales force with laptop computers.

Initial need expressed (buyer starts here)

DIFFERENTIATE OR DIE

Your goal as a salesperson is to identify the prospect's needs and satisfy those needs. But what if several competitors can also satisfy those needs? How can you get the business? The key is differentiation. You have to help the prospect see that your product is truly different from the competitors' products.

For example, what if you're selling rocks? How can you differentiate that product? Graniterock Company salespeople do so by talking, not about their rocks, but about the services associated with buying rocks from their company. One of the biggest inconveniences for rock customers is the lost time of entering the pit, loading the stone, "checking out," and exiting the pit. Salespeople for Graniterock can differentiate their company by talking about their GranitXpress system, which allows customers' trucks to roll into the quarry and be out more quickly. The system works like an industrial ATM machine and is different from anything the competitors offer. The president notes that the company

has doubled its market share in the last 10 years, thanks to its salespeople selling the differentiating service that goes with the rock.

Suppose you're selling elevators? How can you differentiate that? Salespeople for Otis Elevator Company do so by talking about their Remote Elevator Monitoring system, which allows Otis to keep track of elevators in customers' buildings. By doing so they are able to spot potential problems and have them fixed before a major shutdown occurs.

Salespeople sometimes want to talk about a long list of their product's features. Instead, they should talk about features that offer benefits that are truly needed by their customers, benefits that differentiate them from their competitors. When a salesperson doesn't do that, those customers really have no reason to buy.

Source: Chad Kado, "A Position of Power," *Sales and Marketing Management,* June 2000, pp. 105–14.

product, how well the salesperson and buyer know each other, and so forth. We will come back to this issue after we examine methods of identifying needs.

REMEMBER TO COMMUNICATE EFFECTIVELY

Chapter 5 covered most of the important communication principles regarding how to effectively ask questions of the prospect and be a better listener. Remember to speak naturally while asking questions. You don't want to sound like a computer asking a set of rote questions. Nor do you want to appear to be following a strict word-for-word outline that you learned in your sales training classes.

Remember, it is a good idea to gain permission before beginning to ask questions. For example, you might say something like, Do you mind if I ask you a few questions so I can learn more about ways to serve your needs?

We will now briefly describe two of the most widely used systems of needs identification taught to salespeople today.

ASKING OPEN AND CLOSED QUESTIONS

In the first method of needs discovery, salespeople are taught to distinguish between open and closed questions and then encouraged to utilize more open questions. Many highly respected sales training organizations, such as Wilson Learning Corporation and Learning International, use this type of approach. **Open questions** require the prospect to go beyond a simple yes-or-no response. They encourage the prospect to open up and share a great deal of useful information. For example:

What kinds of problems have the new federal guidelines caused for your division?

What do you know about our firm?

When you think of a quality sound system, what comes to mind?

Closed questions require the prospect to simply answer yes or no or to offer a short, fill-in-the-blank type of response. Examples include the following questions:

Have you ever experienced computer downtime as a result of an electrical storm?

Is fast delivery important for your firm?

Customers have expressed a desire to have many features, including four channels, AC/DC power, a four-year warranty, and easily upgradable equipment. Which of these are important to you?

In most cases salespeople need to ask both open and closed questions. Open questions help to paint the broad strokes of the situation, whereas closed questions help to zero in on very specific problems and attitudes. Some trainers believe simple, closed questions are best at first. Prospects become accustomed to talking and start to open up. After a few closed questions, the salesperson moves to a series of open questions. At some point he or she may revert back to closed questions.

What are some good (and bad) questions that salespeople ask? A group of certified purchasing managers gave their perspectives and examples of good questions, which include the following:

What kind of value-added components are you looking for?

How can we help improve your product or process?

If you're interested in my product, how do you plan to use it?

What can I do to make your job easier?

Here are some of the panel's examples of bad questions:

What does your company do?

Can we do something for you?

Are you the person who is going to make the buying decision?

Whom are you buying from now?

What will it take to get your business?[23]

Angie Main, a radio advertising salesperson, likes to ask her prospects the following two open questions to discover their needs:

What misconceptions do people have about your business?

If you could tell people one thing about your business, what would you want to tell them?

Notice how the questions focus on the needs of the prospect rather than the solution (how her radio station can meet those needs).

Exhibit 9.3 contains an illustrative dialogue of a bank selling a commercial checking account to a business. In this sales presentation the salesperson's questions follow a logical flow. Note that follow-up probes are often necessary to clarify the prospect's responses. At the conclusion of asking open and closed questions, the salesperson should have a good feel for the needs and wants of the prospect.

One final suggestion is to summarize the prospect's needs. For example:

So, let me see if I have this right. You are looking for a checking account that pays interest on your unused balance and has a monthly statement . . . Is that correct?

Summarizing helps to solidify the needs in the prospect's mind and ensure that the prospect has no other hidden needs or wants.

EXHIBIT 9.3

Using Open and
Closed Questions
to Discover Needs

Salesperson's Probe	Prospect's Response
Have you ever done business with our bank before? [closed]	No, our firm has always used First of America Bank.
I assume, then, that your checking account is currently with First of America? [closed]	Yes.
If you could design an ideal checking account for your business, what would it look like? [open]	Well, it would pay interest on all idle money, have no service charges, and supply a good statement.
When you say "good statement" what exactly do you mean? [open]	It should come to us once a month, be easy to follow, and help us reconcile our books quickly.
Uh-huh. Anything else in an ideal checking account? [open]	No, I guess that's about it.
What things, if any, about your checking account have dissatisfied you in the past? [open]	Having to pay so much for our checks! Also, sometimes when we have a question, the bank can't answer it quickly because the computers are down. That's frustrating!
Sure! Anything else dissatisfy you? [open]	Well, I really don't like the layout of the monthly statement we get now. It doesn't list checks in order; it has them listed by the date they cleared the bank.
Normally, what balance do you have on hand in your account? What minimum balance can you maintain? [closed]	About $8,500 now. We could keep a minimum of around $5,000, I guess.
Are you earning interest in your account now? [closed]	Yes, 3 percent of the average monthly balance if we maintain at least a $5,000 balance.
What kind of service charges are you paying now? [closed] [more questions]	$25 per month, $.25 per check, $.10 per deposit.
Is there anything else that I need to know before I begin telling you about our account? [open]	No, I think that just about covers it all.

SPIN® TECHNIQUE

The SPIN® method of discovering needs was developed by Huthwaite, Inc., an international research and training organization, after analyzing thousands of actual sales calls.[24] The results indicated that successful salespeople go through a logical needs identification sequence, which Huthwaite labeled **SPIN:** situation questions, problem questions, implication questions, and need payoff questions. SPIN® works for those salespeople involved in a **major sale,** one that involves a long selling cycle, a large customer commitment, an ongoing relationship, and large risks for the prospect if a bad decision is made. Major sales can occur anywhere but often involve large or national accounts. For example, both Johnson Wax and Firestone use SPIN® for their major accounts but use other techniques for smaller accounts.

SPIN® actually helps the prospect identify unrecognized problem areas. Often, when a salesperson simply asks an open question such as "What problems are you having?" the prospect replies, "None!" The prospect isn't lying; he or she just may not realize that a problem exists. SPIN® excels at helping prospects test their current opinions or perceptions of the situation. Also, SPIN® questions may be asked over the course of several sales calls, especially for large or important buyers. An abbreviated needs identification dialogue appears in Exhibit 9.4; it demonstrates all components of SPIN® for a salesperson selling desktop publishing programs.

EXHIBIT 9.4

Using the SPIN®
Technique to Sell
Desktop Publishing

Salesperson: Do you ever send work out for typesetting? [situation question]

Prospect: Yes, about once a month we have to send work out because we are swamped.

Salesperson: Is the cost of sending work out a burden? [problem question]

Prospect: Not really. It costs only about 5 percent more, and we just add that to the customer's bill.

Salesperson: Do you get fast turnaround? [problem question]

Prospect: Well, now that you mention it, at times the turnaround is kind of slow. You see, we aren't given very high priority, since we aren't big customers for the printer. We use them only when we have to, you know.

Salesperson: What happens if you miss a deadline for your customer because the turnaround is slow? [implication question]

Prospect: That happened only once, but it was disastrous. John, the customer, really chewed me out, and we lost a lot of our credibility. As I say, it happened only once, and I wouldn't like it to happen again to John—or any of our customers, for that matter!

Salesperson: If I can show you a way to eliminate outside typesetting without having to increase your staff, would you be interested? [need payoff question]

Prospect: Sure. The more I think about it, the more I realize I have something of a time bomb here. Sooner or later, it's going to go off!

SITUATION QUESTIONS

Early in the sales call, salespeople ask **situation questions,** general data-gathering questions about background and current facts. Because these questions are very broad, successful salespeople learn to limit them; prospects quickly become bored or impatient if they hear too many of them. Inexperienced and unsuccessful salespeople tend to ask too many situation questions. In fact, many situation-type questions can be answered through precall information gathering and planning. If a salesperson asks too many situation questions, the prospect will think the salesperson is unprepared. Here are some examples of situation questions:

What's your position? How long have you been here?

How many people do you employ? Is the number growing or shrinking?

What kind of handling equipment are you using at present? How long have you had it? Did you buy or lease it?

PROBLEM QUESTIONS

When salespeople ask about specific difficulties, problems, or dissatisfactions the prospect has, they are asking **problem questions.** Experienced salespeople tend to ask many such questions. In smaller sales, the use of problem questions is strongly related to success. In major sales, however, the salesperson must ask additional kinds of questions to discover needs and obtain commitment. Here are some examples of problem questions:

Is your current machine difficult to repair?

Have you experienced any problems with the overall quality of your forklifts?

Do your operators ever complain that the noise level is too high?

IMPLICATION QUESTIONS

Questions that logically follow one or more problem questions and are designed to help the prospect recognize the true ramifications of the problem are **implication questions.** Implication questions cannot be asked until some problem area has been identified (through problem questions). They attempt to motivate the prospect to search for a solution to the problem. Ultimately implication questions set the stage so that the seriousness of the problem outweighs the cost of the solution (which the salesperson will offer later). Successful salespeople in major sales tend to ask lots of implication questions, such as these:

What happens if you ship your customer a product that doesn't meet specs?

Does paying overtime for your operators increase your costs?

What does that do to your price as compared to your competitors'?

Does the slowness of your present system create any bottlenecks in other parts of the process?

NEED PAYOFF QUESTIONS

When salespeople ask questions about the usefulness of solving a problem, they are asking **need payoff questions.** They want the prospect to focus on solving the problem rather than continually thinking about the problem itself. In contrast to implication questions, which are problem centered, need payoff questions are solution centered:

If I can show you a way to eliminate paying overtime for your operators and therefore reduce your cost, would you be interested?

Would you like to see a reduction in the number of products that don't meet quality specifications?

Would an increase in the speed of your present system by 5 percent resolve the bottlenecks you currently experience?

If the prospect responds negatively to a need payoff question, the salesperson has not identified a problem serious enough for the prospect to take action. The salesperson should probe further by asking additional problem questions, implication questions, and then a new need payoff question.

CONCLUSIONS ABOUT SPIN®

One critical advantage of SPIN® is that it encourages the prospect to define the need. At no time during the questioning phase does the salesperson ever talk about his product. As a result, the prospect views the salesperson more as a consultant trying to help than as someone trying to push a product.

SPIN® selling has been taught to thousands of salespeople in *Fortune* 500 firms. Many salespeople quickly learn to master the technique, whereas others have more difficulty. The best advice is to practice each component and to plan implication and need payoff questions before each sales call. Also SPIN® works very well for buyers that have a real problem (like inventory piling up). It is perhaps more difficult to use when the seller is only discussing an opportunity (no real problems, but my solution could help you make *more* money). Chapter 17 will provide another example of SPIN® in the context of selling within the salesperson's own firm.

REITERATING NEEDS YOU IDENTIFIED BEFORE THE MEETING

The extent to which one has to identify needs during any call depends on the success of precall information gathering. The salesperson may fully identify the needs of the prospect before making the sales call. In that case reiterating the needs early in the sales call is advisable so that both parties agree about the problem they are trying to solve. For example:

Mr. Jonesboro, based on our several phone conversations, it appears that you are looking for an advertising campaign that will position your product for the rapidly growing senior citizen market, at a cost under $100,000, using humor and a well-known older personality, and delivered in less than one month. Is that an accurate summary of your needs? Has anything changed since we talked last?

Likewise, in multiple-call situations, going through a complete needs identification at every call is unnecessary. But it is still best to briefly reiterate the needs identified to that point:

In my last call we pretty much agreed that your number one concern is customer satisfaction with your inventory system. Is that correct? Has anything changed since we met last time, or is there anything else I need to know?

ADDITIONAL CONSIDERATIONS

How many questions can a salesperson ask to discover needs? It depends on the situation. Generally, as the buyer's risk of making the wrong decision goes up, so does the amount of time the salesperson can spend asking the prospect questions. For example, a Boeing salesperson could address an almost unlimited number of questions to United Air Lines because the airline realizes the importance of having Boeing propose the right configuration of airplane. A salesperson for Johnson Wax calling on a local grocery store, on the other hand, has very little time to probe about needs before discussing an upcoming promotion and requesting an end-of-aisle display. Regardless of the situation, the salesperson should carefully prepare a set of questions that maximize the use of available time. Exhibit 9.5 provides one trainer's opinion of the 12 best questions to ask a prospect.

Occasionally the prospect will refuse to answer important questions because the information is confidential or proprietary. The salesperson can do little except emphasize the reason for asking the questions. Ultimately, the prospect needs to trust the salesperson enough to divulge sensitive data. (Chapters 2 and 13 discuss trust-building strategies.)

At times buyers do not answer questions because they honestly don't know the answer. The salesperson should then ask whether the prospect can get the information. If the prospect cannot do so, the salesperson can often ask the buyer's permission to probe further within the prospect's firm.

On the other hand, some buyers not only will answer questions but also will appear to want to talk indefinitely. In general, the advice is to let them talk, particularly in many cultures. For example, people in French-speaking countries tend to love rhetoric (the act and art of speaking); attempts to cut them off will only frustrate and anger them.

EXHIBIT 9.5

Twelve Good Questions to Ask a Prospect: One Trainer's Opinion

1. Tell me about your business.
2. Describe the people in your organization.
3. What are your responsibilities?
4. What are the biggest challenges you face in growing business?
5. What are your priorities?
6. [Ask a relationship question.]
7. What do you like most about your current supplier?
8. If you could change anything about your current supplier, what would you change?
9. What are your criteria for making a decision?
10. Describe your decision-making process.
11. How will you measure success when using our products?
12. What are your expectations for working with a new supplier?

Source: Jim Meisenheimer, "The 12 Best Questions to Ask Potential Customers," *Cintermex*, March/April 1999, pp. 22–27.

DEVELOPING A STRATEGY FOR THE PRESENTATION

Based on the needs identified, the salesperson should develop a strategy for how best to meet those needs. This process includes sorting through the various options available to the seller to see what is best for this prospect. To do so, the salesperson usually must sort out the needs of the buyer and prioritize them. Decisions have to be made about the exact product or service to recommend, the optimal payment terms to present for consideration, service levels to suggest, product or service features to stress during the presentation, and so on. (Chapter 8 also talks about developing a strategy.)

Products have many, many features, and one product may possess a large number of features that are unique and exciting when compared to competitive offerings. Rather than overload the customer with all of the great features, successful salespeople discuss only those that specifically address the needs of the prospect. For example, suppose that a Panasonic salesperson learns (from SPIN® questioning) that a prospect is looking for a VCR to use only as a playback device for training tapes. In this situation the Panasonic representative should not discuss, or even mention, that one feature of the VCR is that it is cable ready. The buyer has absolutely no need for this feature. To talk about features of little interest to the customer is a waste of time.

OFFERING THE SOLUTION TO THE BUYER'S NEEDS

After the salesperson discovers the buyer's needs and develops a strategy to effectively communicate a solution to those needs, it is time to make a presentation that shows how they can be addressed. This step includes relating product or service features that are meaningful to the buyer, assessing the buyer's reaction to what is being said, resolving objections (covered in Chapter 11), and obtaining commitment (the topic of Chapter 12).

The salesperson usually begins offering the solution by making a transition sentence, something like the following: Now that I know what your needs are, I would like to talk to you about how our product can meet those needs. The seller's job is to translate product features into benefits for solving the buyer's needs.

RELATING FEATURES TO BENEFITS

A **feature** is a quality or characteristic of the product or service. Every product has many features designed to help potential customers. A **benefit** is the way in which a specific feature will help a particular buyer and is tied directly to the buying motives of the prospect. A benefit helps the prospect more fully answer the question What's in it for me? (Exhibit 9.6 lists examples of features and

EXHIBIT 9.6   An Example of Features and Benefits

Introducing the Grand L Series.

Features	Benefits
The transmission allows you to shift-on-the-go between the four main gears and forward to reverse.	You can work more quickly and efficiently.
A larger-diameter clutch disc improves operating efficiency and has a longer life.	You won't spend as much on maintenance costs.
The independent PTO can be switched on and off without stopping.	You can work without being interrupted.
The low-noise, low-emission, E-TVCS diesel engine delivers more power with higher torque rise.	You can get more work done in less time.
A full-floating ISO-mounted flat deck provides ample legroom and minimal vibration.	You'll be more comfortable.
The quick-attach front loader has high lift height and powerful lift capacity.	You can move larger loads with less effort.

Now all you have left to complain about is the weather.

KUBOTA TRACTOR CORPORATION

© 1996 Kubota Tractor Corporation

For more information, write to: Kubota Tractor Corporation, P.O. Box 2992-GCM, Torrance, CA 90509-2992. Financing available through Kubota Credit Corporation.

Source: © Kubota Tractor Corporation.

sample benefits for a tractor.) The salesperson usually includes a word or a phrase to make a smooth transition from features to benefits:

> This china is fired at 2,600° F, and what that means to you is that it will last longer. Because it is so sturdy, you will be able to hand this china down to your children as an heirloom, which was one of your biggest concerns.

> This set of golf clubs has shallow-faced fairway woods, which means that you'll be able to get the ball into the air easier. That will certainly help give you the distance you said you were looking for.

> Our service hot line is open 24 hours a day, which means that even your third-shift operators can call if they have any questions. That should be a real help to you, since you said your third-shift supervisor was very inexperienced in dealing with problems.

Some trainers suggest going beyond just mentioning features and benefits. One variation, **FAB,** has salespeople discussing features, **advantages** (why that feature would be important to anyone), and benefits. For example:

> This car has antilock brakes (feature), which help the car stop quickly (advantage), which provides the safety you said you were looking for (benefit).

In another variation, **FEBA,** salespeople mention the feature, provide evidence that the feature actually does exist, explain the benefit (why that feature is important to the buyer), and then ask whether the buyer agrees with the value of the feature and benefit. For example:

> This car has the highest-quality antilock brakes on the market today (feature) as proven by this test by the federal government (evidence). They will provide the safety you said you were looking for (benefit); don't you agree (agreement)?

Buyers are not interested in facts about the product or the seller's company unless those facts help solve their wants or needs. The salesperson's job is to supply the facts and then point out what those features mean to the buyer in terms of benefits. Chapter 10 more fully discusses how to offer proof of assertions.

Buyers typically consider two or more competitive products when making a purchase decision. Thus salespeople need to know more than just the benefits their products provide. They need to know how the benefits of their products are superior or inferior to the benefits of competitive products. Of course, as you explain the benefits of your service, you must make sure that the prospect is looking for those benefits. That's a lesson Millard Choate, CEO of Choate Construction, discovered the hard way.[25] In meeting with one prospect, Choate explained how his company usually completed projects in record time. "Normally, that's how we get jobs," he explained later. However, the prospect rejected his proposal. Why? "The company wanted to go at a slower pace. The prospect said our company was more powerful than his company wanted." The moral: Always sell to the needs of your customer.

Sometimes, when selling certain commodities, it is important to sell the features and benefits of the seller's firm instead of the product. For example, Ray Hanson sells fasteners such as bolts and nuts. He states, "In the fastener industry I have found that a generic product, such as a nut or bolt, doesn't have too many features and benefits. We talk to our potential customers about the features our company has and how these features could benefit them as our customers."[26]

When selling to resellers, salespeople have two sets of benefits to discuss with the prospect: what the features of the product will do for the reseller and what the product features will do for the ultimate consumer of the product. Covering both sets of features and benefits is important. Exhibit 9.7 illustrates the two sets of features.

Features	Benefits
Of Importance to the Final Consumer	
Trusted name brand.	Because you trust the Jello brand name, you know that this is a high-quality product.
Only 60 calories per bar.	You can enjoy a treat without worrying about its effect on your weight.
Real fruit in every bite.	You are getting needed nutrition from a snack.
Only fruit and cream brand that comes in a variety pack.	You will be able to meet the various flavor preferences of your family members.
Each pack has 12 bars.	You get a better value by purchasing in this family-size pack. Also, you won't run out of snacks as quickly and have to make a trip back to the grocery store.
Of Importance to the Grocery Store	
Test marketed for three years.	Because of this research, you are assured of a successful product and effective promotion; thus your risk is greatly reduced.
$10 million will be spent for consumer advertising in the next 18 months.	Your customers will come to your store looking for the product.
40-cent coupon with front positioning in the national Sunday insert section.	Your customers will want to take advantage of the coupon and will be looking in your freezer for the product.
At the suggested retail price of $3.39, your profit margin will be 20 percent.	This product has a 5 percent higher profit margin than other fruit and cream bars you sell, so you'll make more profit each time you sell a box.
All advertising will feature Bill Cosby.	Both parents and children trust and enjoy Bill Cosby. His appearance in the advertising will increase desire to purchase the product. As a result, customers will come to your store looking for the product.
Trusted name brand, 60 calories per bar, real fruit filling, comes in a variety pack, 12 bars in each pack (list of features important to final consumers).	Your customers will like the product and continue to purchase it. This will create fast turnover of the product and result in higher overall sales and profits.

ASSESSING REACTIONS

While making a presentation, salespeople need to continually assess the reactions of their prospects. The prospect needs to agree that the benefits described would actually help his or her company. By listening (see Chapter 5 to review how to be a better listener[27]) to what buyers say and observing their body language, salespeople can determine whether prospects are interested in the product. If buyers react favorably to the presentation and seem able to grasp the benefits of the proposed solution, the salesperson will have less need to make alterations or adjustments. But if a prospect does not develop enthusiasm for the product, the salesperson will need to make some changes in the presentation.

USING NONVERBAL CUES

An important aspect of making adjustments is interpreting a prospect's reactions to the sales presentation. By observing the prospect's five channels of nonverbal communication, salespeople can determine how to proceed with their presentations. Exhibit 9.8 lists signals, or nonverbal cues, that salespeople who are sensitive to a prospect's body language can read. (Chapter 5 provides more detailed information about nonverbal cues.)

Channel	Positive	Mixed	Negative
Body angle	Upright, direct to salesperson	Leaning away from salesperson	Leaning far back or thrusting toward salesperson
Face	Friendly, smiling, enthusiastic	Tense, displeased, superior	Angry, determined, shaking head
Arms	Relaxed, open	Closed, tense	Tightly crossed or thrusting out
Hands	Relaxed, open	Clasped, fidgeting with objects	Fist, pointed finger
Legs	Uncrossed, crossed toward salesperson	Crossed away from salesperson	Tightly crossed away from salesperson

Positive nonverbal cues are encouraging for the salesperson, and he or she should send the same cues to the prospect. If the prospect gives mixed signals, the salesperson needs to ask open questions to draw out the prospect's reasons for caution. Negative nonverbal signals indicate a serious problem, and the salesperson should refocus the discussion completely after probing for concerns. The best way to avoid negative signals is to deal effectively with mixed signals when they appear. One of the biggest causes of negative signals is the use of an overly aggressive sales pitch.

VERBAL PROBING

As salespeople move through a presentation, they must take the pulse of the situation. This process is often called a **trial close.** For example, after discussing a particularly important feature that helps to meet the prospect's needs, the salesperson should say something like the following:

How does that sound to you?

Can you see how that feature helps solve the problem you have?

Have I clearly explained this feature to you?

You now know a little more about our service. Do you foresee any initial limitations to the service?

The use of such probing questions helps to achieve several things. First, it allows the salesperson to stop talking and encourages two-way conversations. Without such probing, a salesperson can turn into a rambling talker while the buyer becomes a passive listener. Second, probing lets the salesperson see whether the buyer is listening and understanding what is being said. Third, the probe may show that the prospect is uninterested in what the salesperson is talking about. This response allows the salesperson to redirect the conversation to areas of interest to the buyer. This kind of adjustment is necessary in almost every presentation and underscores the fact that the salesperson should not simply memorize a canned presentation that unfolds in a particular sequence.

Salespeople must listen. Often we hear only what we want to hear. This behavior is called **selective perception,** and everyone is guilty of it at times. For example, read the following sentence:[28]

Finished files are the result of years of scientific study combined with the experience of years.

Now go back and quickly count the number of Fs in that sentence. Most non-native English speakers see all six Fs, whereas native English speakers see only three (they don't count the Fs in of because it is not considered an important word).

Nonverbal cues help salespeople know when to make adjustments. In this picture, even though all members of the buying team are looking at the salesperson, they seem to be giving different nonverbal cues. Can you interpret the cues?

Garry Conner/Index Stock Imagery/PictureQuest

The point is that once salespeople stop actively listening, they miss many things the buyer is trying to communicate.

MAKING ADJUSTMENTS

Salespeople can alter their presentations in many ways to obtain a favorable reaction. For example, salespeople may discover during the sales presentation that the prospect simply does not believe they have the appropriate product knowledge. Rather than continue with the presentation, they should redirect their efforts toward establishing credibility in the eyes of the prospect. Salespeople need to continually adapt to the situation at hand.

Other adjustments might require collecting additional information about the prospect, developing a new sales strategy, or altering the style of presentation. For example, a salesperson may believe a prospect is interested in buying an economical, low-cost motor. While presenting the benefits of the lowest-cost motor, the salesperson discovers the prospect is interested in the motor's operating costs. At this point the salesperson should ask some questions to find out whether the prospect would be interested in paying a higher price for a more efficient motor with lower operating costs. On the basis of the prospect's response, the salesperson can adopt a new sales strategy, one that emphasizes operating efficiency rather than the motor's initial price. In this way the sales presentation is shifted from features and benefits based on a low initial cost to features and benefits related to low operating costs.

BUILDING CREDIBILITY DURING THE CALL

To develop a close and harmonious relationship, the salesperson must be perceived as having **credibility;** that is, he or she must be believable and reliable. A salesperson can take many actions during a sales call to develop such a perception.[29]

To establish credibility early in the sales call, the salesperson should clearly delineate the time she or he thinks the call will take and then stop when the time is up. How many times has a salesperson said, "This will take only five minutes!" and 30 minutes later you still can't get rid of him? No doubt you would have perceived the salesperson as more credible if, after five minutes, he or she stated, "Well, I promised to take no more than five minutes, and I see our time is up. How would you like to proceed from here?" One very successful salesperson likes to ask for half an hour and take only 25 minutes.[30] Salespeople who learn how to accurately calculate the time needed for a call and then stand by their promises will be much more successful in establishing credibility.

Another way to establish credibility is to offer concrete evidence to back up verbal statements. If a salesperson states, "It is estimated that more than 80 percent of the households in America will own DVD players by 2010," he or she should be prepared to offer proof of this assertion (for instance, hand the prospect a letter or an article from a credible source). Ways to establish credibility are discussed in greater detail in Chapter 10.

Of course, one way to establish credibility is to avoid making statements that do not have the ring of truth to them. Jerry Vass, chairman of an executive sales training company, suggests that sellers should avoid claiming, "'We're the best' or 'we're number one.' You see it everywhere. Just how many #1's are there in the world anyway? These words, spoken or printed, launch an obvious assault on the buyer's intelligence and are the easiest way possible to break trust. The buyers roll their eyes when you use these words."[31] Salespeople should also remember that, in addition to damaging credibility, truth-stretching comments can come back to haunt them in the form of legal liability (see Chapter 3 for a review of legal issues).

Many salespeople have found that the most effective way to establish credibility is to make a **balanced presentation** that shows all sides of the situation—that is, to be totally honest. Thus a salesperson might mention some things about the product that make it less than perfect or may speak positively about some exclusive feature of a competitor's product. Will this approach defeat the seller's chances of a sale? No. In fact, it may increase the chances of building long-term commitment and rapport.[32] Building Partnerships 9.1 provides an example of using a balanced presentation. Salespeople can keep customers happy and dedicated by helping them form correct, realistic expectations about the product or service.

 Salespeople can build credibility by recognizing subcultural differences, not only in foreign markets but in North America as well. How? By demonstrating sensitivity to the needs and wants of specific subcultures and avoiding biased or racist language.

In selling complex products, sales representatives often must demonstrate product expertise at the beginning of the sales process—for example, by telling the customer, without bragging, about their special training or education. They can also strengthen credibility with well-conceived, insightful questions or comments.

When selling complicated technical products and services, Todd Graf notes, "You have to keep it simple. Teach as you go. Keep it simple. Make transitions slow and smooth and always ask if they understand (half the time they don't). This is key because they may have to go back and explain some of your features to the decision maker who isn't present in this meeting."[33]

 Salespeople (especially those who look young or are inexperienced) who establish their expertise will improve their credibility when they make their presentations. Tracey Brill, a young salesperson, notes that a seller should never use a word if he or she doesn't know the exact definition. Some buyers may even test the salesperson. She relates an example of a call on one doctor:[34]

BRILL: Because product X acts as an agonist at the Kappa receptor, miosis will occur.

DOCTOR: What does *miosis* mean?

BRILL: It means the "stage of disease during which intensity of signs and symptoms diminishes."

DOCTOR: No! *Miosis* means "contraction of the pupils."

BRILL: I did look it up in the 1989 edition of *Taber's Encyclopedic Medical Dictionary*. I would be happy to bring it next time I come in because I wouldn't want you to think I would use a phrase without knowing what it means.

BE HONEST . . . THE ORDERS WILL SURELY FOLLOW

You are always selling yourself. If you do that exceptionally well, the orders will surely follow. In today's highly competitive economy, where every product or service is viewed as a commodity, the relationship that you build with the customer is the most critical element in the selling process.

I personally learned early in my sales career that a focus on the customer's needs was my most powerful sales tool. I learned this lesson more than 20 years ago, almost by accident, from an experience with a medical school professor. At that time I sold microscopes for the instrument division of the American Optical Company. The company was highly ethical and customer focused, so it always stressed that we must sell only what our customers really needed for their application. The goal of both the company and its salespeople was to always sell the best products that served our customers' needs and the medical community.

I was making one of my twice-yearly trips to a large medical school in one of the western states. I met a professor in the hall who asked me into his office to discuss a special application for a microscope. We had a long discussion in which he explained and then showed me in detail what he had to do in applying this new procedure. We had built a good relationship over several years. It was obvious that he wanted to buy now, and from me. That was great, except for one problem: My microscope might work, but only with a great deal of difficulty, whereas our competitor, B&L, had a scope that seemed like it was specifically designed for his application.

After a lot of soul searching, I did what I thought was right. I told him about the B&L scope and told him how to reach the company to place an order. He was almost speechless and thanked me over and over again for my advice. As the days passed, I missed that order. I felt the empty spot in my wallet where that commission should have been.

I visited the professor on my next trip and again he thanked me for my recommendation of the competitive microscope. He said it worked perfectly.

Two years later I bumped into that same professor in a corridor, and he asked me to stop by his office to discuss a specialized microscope. When I arrived, the professor told me the specifications of the scope he needed, and it turned out that we had a perfect fit. What he needed was a very expensive industry-standard microscope for his application. This type of microscope could be supplied by all my competitors.

"When will you need the scope delivered?" It was a good thing I was sitting down when he replied, "I have the budget approved, and we will need all of them when the remodeling of the classroom is completed." I don't remember exactly what I said, but I think I stuttered out something like, "Them?" "Yes," he replied, "We will need 25 scopes to equip the entire classroom." This order was the largest the company had ever received for this model. It was sold without a demonstration or a sample or a competitive bid. When I offered to send him a sample to look over, his reply made my day; no, no—it made my year: "I don't need to see it, I know you would only recommend what I really need, only the best."

That experience taught me a lot; it gave me an understanding of the selling process that has served me well over many years, in many different industries, with all sorts of customers and products. What I am always selling is myself. What I mean is, I'm always selling my relationship with the customer, my credibility, my honesty, my expertise, my concern for my customer. Once I sell me . . . the rest is just a logical process of understanding my customers' needs, their goals, and what will create a true win–win relationship. If you can't create a win–win sale with your customer, never, never accept anything else . . . since the ultimate loser will only be you.

Source: Bob Newzell is host and moderator of *Sales Talk,* a one-hour talk/interview show on the Business Radio Network, which is heard on 85 stations around the United States. He is a speaker and sales trainer and designs special sales training programs for companies across the country.

At this point the doctor walked out of the room, and Brill thought she had lost all credibility. Actually, he had just gone out and grabbed a dictionary. The first definition was the contraction of the pupils, and the second was Brill's definition. Brill's definition, not the doctor's, fit the use of the term for this medication. The doctor then shook Brill's hand and thanked her for teaching him a new definition of the word! The salesperson's credibility certainly increased.

SELLING TO GROUPS

Selling to groups can be both rewarding and very frustrating. On the plus side, if you make an effective presentation, every member of the prospect group becomes your ally. On the down side, groups behave like groups, with group standards and norms and issues of status and group leadership.

When selling to groups, the salesperson must gather information about the needs and concerns of each individual who will attend. Jim Farmer, an executive vice president of PDP Inc., relates a meeting he was involved with when the seller didn't do this:

> There were five people on the committee, and instead of finding out something about their individual concepts ahead of time, the rep went in with the conventional stacks of material and the idea of laying it all out in gruesome detail. It was painful. He spent an hour explaining our R&D, another hour on implementing options, half an hour doing a demo—on and on, with no sense of how anything related to the people in the room.[35]

To avoid this problem, salespeople should discover (for each prospect group member) member status within the group, authority, perceptions about the urgency of the problem, receptivity to ideas, knowledge of the subject matter, attitude toward the salesperson, major areas of interest and concern, key benefits sought, likely resistance, and ways to handle this resistance. To follow up with the story by Farmer, contrary to his fears, the group allowed the seller to make a second visit. But this time, the seller was prepared. He had discovered the specific needs of the individuals in the buying group:

> With so much less to talk about, the entire presentation took only 30 minutes. What's more, the salesperson didn't even have to ask for the sale. After a successful presentation, the vice president of the prospect company quickly asked, "What steps do we need to take for implementation?"[36]

The salesperson should also discover the ego involvement and issue involvement of each group member.[37] An **ego-involved** audience member perceives the subject

Selling to groups requires special skills in monitoring several individuals at once, as well as being able to respond to customers with occasionally conflicting needs.

IT International Ltd/e-Stock Photo

matter to be important to his or her own well-being. For example, a person whose job might be eliminated by the introduction of a new computer system would be highly ego involved with regard to the computer system. An **issue-involved** person considers the subject important even though it may not affect him or her personally. For example, an accountant might be interested in what type of new production equipment will be purchased even though the use of that equipment will not affect the accountant in any direct way. Learning the ego involvement and issue involvement of each member in the audience allows the salesperson to adapt portions of the presentation to the specific needs of particular people.

It is important to develop not only objectives for the meeting but also objectives for what the seller hopes to accomplish with each prospect present at the meeting. Planning may include the development of special visual aids for specific individuals present. The seller must expect many more objections and interruptions in a group setting compared to selling to an individual.

An informal atmosphere in which group members are encouraged to speak freely and the salesperson feels free to join the group's discussion usually works best in these situations. Thus an informal location (such as a corner of a large room as opposed to a formal conference room) is preferred. Formal presentation methods, such as speeches, that separate buyers and sellers into them-versus-us sides should be avoided. If the group members decide that the meeting is over, the salesperson should not try to hold them.

Of course, most things you have learned about selling to individuals apply equally to groups. You should learn the names of group members and use them when appropriate. You should listen carefully and observe all nonverbal cues. When one member of the buying team is talking, it is especially important to observe the cues being transmitted by the other members of the buying team to see whether they are, in effect, agreeing or disagreeing with the speaker.

In many cases the selling firm will utilize a selling team when meeting with a group of buyers. In fact, the use of teams is becoming more widespread in learning organizations (see Chapter 1 for a discussion of learning organizations).[38]

There are several types of group selling situations. If the group meeting is actually a negotiation session, many more things must be considered. As a result, we devote an entire chapter (Chapter 14) to the topic of formal negotiations. Also, sometimes a salesperson makes a call on a prospect with his or her sales manager, someone from technical support, someone from customer support, a sales executive from the firm, or a group from the selling firm. These situations require coordination and teamwork. Because of the importance of the various selling team scenarios, the issue of selling teams is more fully discussed in Chapter 17.[39]

Summary

Salespeople need to make every possible effort to create a good impression during a sales call. The first few minutes with the prospect are important, and care should be taken to make an effective entrance by giving a good first impression, expressing confidence while standing and shaking hands, and selecting an appropriate seat.

The salesperson can use any of several methods to gain the prospect's attention. Salespeople should adopt the approach that is most effective for the prospect's personality style. Also critical is the development of rapport with the prospect, which can often be enhanced by engaging in friendly conversation.

Before beginning any discussion of product information, the salesperson must establish the prospect's needs by using open and closed questions. The SPIN technique is very effective for discovering needs in the major sale. In subsequent calls the salesperson should reiterate the prospect's needs.

When moving into a discussion of the proposed solution or alternatives, the salesperson translates features into benefits for the buyer. The salesperson also makes any necessary adjustments in the presentation based on feedback provided by the buyer's nonverbal cues and by verbal probing.

A close, harmonious relationship will enhance the whole selling process. The salesperson can build credibility by adhering to stated appointment lengths, backing up statements with proof, offering a balanced presentation, and establishing his or her credentials.

When selling to groups, the salesperson must gather information about the needs and concerns of each individual who will attend. The seller should also uncover the ego involvement and issue involvement of each group member. It is important to develop objectives not only for the meeting but also for what the seller hopes to accomplish with each prospect present at the meeting.

Now that you know how to start the sale, discover needs, relate features to specific benefits for the buyer, and build credibility, it is time to look more closely at how to communicate your ideas more effectively. That's the topic of the next chapter, "Strengthening the Presentation."

KEY TERMS

advantages   258
approach   244
balanced presentation   262
benefit   256
benefit approach   244
closed questions   251
compliment approach   246
credibility   261
ego-involved   264
FAB   258
feature   256
FEBA   258
halo effect   243
implication questions   253
impression management   240
introduction approach   244

issue-involved   265
major sale   252
need payoff questions   254
office scanning   247
open questions   250
problem questions   253
product approach   245
question approach   246
rapport   246
referral approach   244
selective perception   260
situation questions   253
small talk   246
SPIN®   252
trial close   260

Questions and Problems

1. Suppose you are calling on a prospect who hands you a brochure illustrating the features and benefits of a competitor's product. You look it over and notice that the brochure is six months old. Since that brochure was printed, your competitor has added some new features that make it much more competitive with what you're offering today. Should you be candid and tell the prospect what you know, even though it will put the competitor's product in a much better light?

2. Assume that you are selling computer software packages to certified public accountants (CPAs). How long beyond the agreed-on appointment time would you be willing to wait in each of the following situations? Why?

   a. This is your first call on a very important CPA. She is the president of the local CPA organization. You have never met her, and you do not know anything about her.

   b. This is your first call on one CPA partner of a two-partner firm. The other partner has already heard your presentation and was somewhat impressed.

   c. This is your first call on a small, sole-proprietorship CPA in a small town. You just started selling two weeks ago and have not yet closed any sales. The CPA is an expressive.

   d. You have achieved great success in your territory. This is your fifth call on one of the big CPAs in your city. You have a lot of software installation work to do this afternoon for other clients. This CPA is a driver and rarely has more than five minutes of time to talk to you on a visit.

3. Which approach method would you use for each prospect listed in question 2 to get his or her attention? Explain the reasons for your choices.

4. Occasionally things don't go according to your plan. Describe what you would do in each of the following situations:

   a. You offer your hand for a handshake, and the prospect just looks at you, not offering her hand.

   b. The seat your prospect offers you is uncomfortable, too low, or in direct sunlight.

   c. You use the referral approach, and the prospect says, "I've never trusted that man anyway."

   d. You use the product approach, and the prospect just keeps playing with the product. You are afraid to move on to your presentation without her attention.

   e. You state, "This will take only 15 minutes"; then the prospect rambles and uses up most of your time in trivial chitchat. At the end of 15 minutes, you haven't accomplished your call objectives.

   f. In the middle of your presentation, the secretary rings in to inform your prospect that her next appointment has arrived at the front desk.

   g. Your hands start to tremble just before you go into the prospect's office.

   h. You are presenting your product. As you lean over to get something out of your briefcase, your pants split open in the back with a loud tearing sound.

   i. You are at dinner with a prospect, and you accidentally spill soup on your tie or scarf.

5. Think for a moment about trying to secure a sales job. Assume you are going to have an interview with a district manager at Wallace, Inc., next week for a sales position. What can you do to develop rapport and build credibility with her?

6. "I don't need to discover my prospect's needs. I sell toothpaste to grocery stores. I know what their needs are: a high profit margin and fast turnover of products!" Comment.

7. Assume that you are selling automobile tires to a customer. Develop a series of open and closed questions to discover the prospect's needs.

8. Assume that you represent your school's placement service. You are calling on a large business nearby that never hires college graduates from your school. Generate a list of SPIN® questions, making any additional assumptions necessary.

9. Prepare a list of features and benefits that could be used in a presentation to other students at your college. The objective of the presentation is to encourage them to enroll in the selling course you are taking.

10. In a selling situation between a salesperson and a prospect, much of what is said is really never heard, and part of what is heard is often misinterpreted by one or both of the parties. Which techniques can a salesperson use to improve communication with a prospect?

11. "I always shake hands with anyone I call on. If I didn't shake hands, people would not trust me. Besides, it's common knowledge that you're supposed to shake hands in business settings. It makes you seem more friendly." Comment.

12. In which situations should a salesperson use the prospect's first name? When should a more formal salutation be used?

Case Problems

CASE 9.1

Sony Handycam Camcorders

Robert Heimann is a salesperson for Sony. Today he called on the corporate headquarters of Circuit City to introduce a new line of very small Handycam camcorders. Here is the dialogue that occurred between Robert and Janet Saunders, a senior buyer at Circuit City.

ROBERT [walking up to Janet, handing her a Handycam camcorder]: Have you ever seen anything like that?

JANET [tossing a report she was reading on her desk and looking at the camcorder a little before putting it on her desk]: I don't know. What is it? There are so many little gadgets available today, we can't carry them all. [Looking at her appointment book carefully, then looking up at Robert.] Weren't you going to tell me about a new inkjet printer?

ROBERT: No, I don't sell inkjet printers. You must have me mixed up with someone else. I'm Robert Heimann from Sony.

JANET: Oh. Well, what can I do for you?

ROBERT: I'm trying to sell you a new product that's hot on the market today: It's the brand new Sony MICROMV Handycam Camcorder Model DCR-IP5, the smallest and lighest in the world.

JANET [looking confused]: What?

ROBERT: Let me ask you a few questions. What do you look for when trying to decide on a new product?

JANET [regaining her composure and picking up a notepad and pen to take notes on]: I look for a product that has broad appeal to a wide range of customer types. Also, one that will supply Circuit City with a good profit margin. Of course, the product must complement what we already sell. It should result in cross-selling opportunities.

ROBERT: What is your buying budget for digital imaging products this year?

JANET [dropping her pad on the desk in frustration]: That's confidential information.

ROBERT: That's OK. It won't make much difference in my presentation anyway. These new camcorders are so hot I know you'll want them regardless of how much you have budgeted to spend.

JANET [with a smirk on her face]: You sound awfully sure of yourself!

ROBERT [mirroring Janet's smirk]: I am! These babies have 1/6" advanced HAD CCD, 680 Pixels; up to 500 lines of horizontal resolution; Carl Zeiss Vario-Sonnar Lens; a 10X Optical/120X Precision Digital Zoom; a 2.5" Precision SwivelScreen Hybrid LCD Display of 211 K, . . .

JANET [interrupting]: So you've got lots of features! But how are these things selling?

ROBERT: Great! Well, they just came on the market. [Waving his hand to the side to indicate it's not something to worry about.] But our research says they are going to sell like hotcakes. Say, did I tell you they have an InfoLithium Battery with AccuPower Meter System and an i.LINK MICROMV Interface that is IEEE 1394?

JANET [laughing out loud]: I don't really know if you told me or not. What is our cost?

ROBERT: The retail selling price is $1,299.99.

JANET: Yeah, but what will they cost me?

ROBERT: Oh, sorry. Your cost is $715.50 if you buy more than 1,000 units, which shouldn't be too much to buy given the number of stores you have.

JANET [picking up her pad and pen again]: I wonder what our profit margin would be.

ROBERT: It's great, of course. You can price it whatever you want. That's up to you. These are a must buy this year, Janet. Can I sign you up for 1,000 units?

JANET: I don't know. I don't know how they would fit in with our current products. I'm also worried about our profit margin.

ROBERT: If you buy today, we could have them delivered in four weeks. OK?

JANET: I need to think about it. Maybe you can come back in a few months if you're in the area.

ROBERT: Well, I think you should . . .

JANET [interrupting]: I'm sorry, but I have a meeting upstairs in five minutes. Have a nice day.

Sources: Sony's 2001 annual report and www.sony.com (viewed 3/22/02).

QUESTIONS

1. Identify and evaluate the attention-getting approach Robert used. Discuss any ways in which it could be improved.
2. In what ways did Robert develop rapport and build credibility? What else could he have done in this area?
3. Evaluate Robert's attempt at discovering needs. Provide recommendations for improvement.
4. How well did Robert relate product features to Janet's needs? How could he have improved?
5. Was Robert sensitive enough to recognize when adjustments were necessary in his presentation? Suggest ways he could improve.

Lexington Medical Supply Company has been in the medical equipment and supplies industry for more than 20 years. Until recently, the staple of its business has been laboratory chemicals and glassware.

Lexington has just introduced its first piece of automated equipment: a slide processor. The slide processor is a fully automated device that dramatically increases the speed at which slides for microscopic analysis can be prepared. As a result of carefully dispensing expensive processing chemicals, the unit can save laboratories considerable money on the use of these chemicals; the unit also saves on the labor overtime that is often incurred where a high volume of processing is required or when laboratories are understaffed.

In the video segment, you will watch Fred Hernandez, a rep for Lexington Medical Supply Company, calling on Dr. Charlotte Walters, chief of pathology at Memorial Medical Center, the city's largest and most comprehensive health care facility. Fred has been speaking regularly with the laboratory supervisor, Curtis Mathews, and, with Curtis's support, has arranged for Dr. Walters to see a demonstration of the slide processor.

Fred knows that both Curtis and Dr. Walters would like to modernize the operation of the laboratory, and Fred thinks the purchase of the processor is a good place to start. Fred also knows that Dr. Walters will probably need the hospital administrator's approval for a purchase of this size.

Following are important features and benefits of the new slide processor:

Features	Benefits
Fully automated	Reduces need for human contact during processing procedures
	Frees technologists to do more challenging and interesting work, reducing boredom and turnover
	Ensures consistent and easily readable slides, which speeds slide analysis
High-speed operation	Completes an average day's workload in half the time it takes to process manually, thus reducing overtime expenses
	Eases processing backlogs
Precision chemical dispensing	Reduces significantly the use of expensive chemicals, thus cutting lab costs (savings on chemicals typically provide a payback on equipment in two years)

QUESTIONS

To help you think through how Fred could discover Dr. Walters's needs, do the following:

1. Develop a set of open and closed questions to fully discover Dr. Walters's needs.
2. Develop a set of SPIN® questions to discover Dr. Walters's needs.
3. Reread the preceding material and be prepared to watch the videotape in class. Watch how Fred actually discovered Dr. Walters's needs.

Additional References

Anderson, James C. "Relationships in Business Markets: Exchange Episodes, Value Creation, and Their Empirical Assessment." *Journal of the Academy of Marketing Science* 23: 4 (1995), pp. 346–50.

Burgoon, Judee K.; David B. Buller; and W. Gill Woodall. *Nonverbal Communication: The Unspoken Dialogue*. Boston: McGraw Hill, 1996.

Castleberry, Stephen B., and C. David Shepherd. "Effective Interpersonal Listening and Personal Selling." *Journal of Personal Selling and Sales Management,* Winter 1993, pp. 35–50.

Castleberry, Stephen B.; C. David Shepherd; and Rick Ridnour. "Effective Interpersonal Listening in the Personal Selling Environment: Conceptualization, Measurement, and Nomological Validity." *Journal of Marketing Theory and Practice,* Winter 1999, pp. 30–38.

Dixon, Andrea L.; Rosann L. Spiro; and Maqbul Jamil. "Successful and Unsuccessful Sales Calls: Measuring Salesperson Attributions and Behavioral Intentions." *Journal of Marketing,* July 2001, pp. 64–78.

Donoho, Casey L., and Michael J. Swenson. "Top-Down versus Bottom-Up Sales Tactics Effects on the Presentation of a Product Line." *Journal of Business Research* 37, 1996, pp. 51–61.

Evans, Kenneth R.; Robert E. Kleine, III; Timothy D. Landry; and Lawrence A. Crosby. "How First Impressions of a Customer Impact Effectiveness in an Initial Sales Encounter." *Journal of the Academy of Marketing Science* 28: 4 (2000), pp. 512–26.

George, Jennifer M. "Salesperson Mood at Work: Implication for Helping Customers." *Journal of Personal Selling and Sales Management,* Summer 1998, pp. 23–30.

Goldner, Paul. "Six Questions to Ask Customers." *Executive Excellence* 18, November 2001, p. 20.

Gwinner, Kevin P.; Dwayne D. Gremier; and Mary Jo Bitner. "Relational Benefits in Services Industries: The Customer's Perspective." *Journal of the Academy of Marketing Science* 26: 2 (1998), pp. 101–14.

Hanan, Mack. *Consultative Selling: The Hanan Formula for High-Margin Sales at High Levels.* New York: AMACOM, 1990.

Hart, Michael. "A Compelling Introduction Leads to a Good Presentation." *Presentations,* August 2000, p. 82.

Meisenheimer, Jim. "The 12 Best Questions to Ask Potential Customers." *Cintermax,* March–April 1999, pp. 22–27.

Mowatt, Jeff. "Making Connections: How to Create Rapport with Anyone in under 30 Seconds." *The Canadian Manager* 25, Fall 2000, pp. 26, 29.

Napolitano, Lisa. "Customer-Supplier Partnering: A Strategy Whose Time Has Come." *Journal of Personal Selling and Sales Management,* Fall 1997, pp. 1–8.

Neuborne, Ellen. "Tag-Team Pitches." *Sales and Marketing Management* 154, March 2002, p. 57.

Patton, W. E., III. "Use of Human Judgment Models in Industrial Buyers' Vendor Selection Decisions." *Industrial Marketing Management* 25, 1996, pp. 135–49.

Peppers, Don, and Martha Rogers. "Needs Differentiation: The Critical Benchmark in Customer Marketing." *1to1 Magazine,* April 2002, pp. 52–53.

Peterson, Robert A.; Michael P. Cannito; and Steven P. Brown. "An Exploratory Investigation of Voice Characteristics and Selling Effectiveness." *Journal of Personal Selling and Sales Management,* Winter 1995, pp. 1–15.

Peterson, Robert A.; George H. Lucas, and Patrick L. Schul. "Forming Consultative Trade Alliances: Walking the Walk in the New Selling Environment." *NAMA Journal,* Spring 1998, pp. 10–15.

Reilly, Tom. "You're Not Alone." *Industrial Distribution* 90, September 2001, p. 60.

Sparks, John R., and Charles S. Areni. "The Effects of Sales Presentation Quality and Initial Perceptions on Persuasion: A Multiple Role Perspective." *Journal of Business Research* 55: 6 (2002), pp. 517–28.

Strutton, David; Lou E. Pelton; and John F. Tanner Jr. "Shall We Gather in the Garden: The Effect of Ingratiatory Behaviors on Buyer Trust in Salespeople." *Industrial Marketing Management* 25, 1996, pp. 151–62.

Szymanski, David M. "Modality and Offering Effects in Sales Presentations for a Good versus a Service." *Journal of the Academy of Marketing Science* 29: 2 (2001), pp. 179–89.

Test, Alan. "Asking Questions." *The American Salesman* 46, January 2001, pp. 8–10.

Wagner, Judy A.; Noreen M. Klein; and Janet E. Keith. "Selling Strategies: The Effects of Suggesting a Decision Structure to Novice and Expert Buyers." *Journal of the Academy of Marketing Science* 29: 3 (2001), pp. 289–306.

Waldrop, Dawn E. "What You Wear Is Almost as Important as What You Say." *Presentations*, July 2000, p. 74.

Warner, Fara. "How Fitch Makes Its (Fast) Pitch." *Fast Company*, March 2002, pp. 126–30.

Weilbaker, Dan C., and William Weeks. "The Evolution of National Account Management: A Literature Perspective." *Journal of Personal Selling and Sales Management*, Fall 1997, pp. 49–59.

10 Strengthening the Presentation

SOME QUESTIONS ANSWERED IN THIS CHAPTER ARE:

■ How can salespeople use verbal tools to strengthen the presentation?

■ Why do salespeople need to augment their oral communication through tools such as visual aids, samples, testimonials, and demonstrations?

■ What methods are available to strengthen the presentation?

■ How can salespeople utilize visual aids and technology most effectively?

■ What are the ingredients of a good demonstration?

■ Is there a way to quantify the salesperson's solution to the buyer's problem?

■ How can salespeople reduce presentation jitters?

Whereas Chapter 9 outlined the mechanics of what to present (that is, features and benefits), this chapter teaches how to present the material effectively. After studying this chapter, you should be able to bring your presentations "alive," keeping your prospects awake and interested as well as helping them remember what you said.

"Your audience is looking to you for information."

Rhonda Killen, Quaker Tropicana Gatorade

PROFILE

Shortly after graduating with a Marketing/ Management BBA in 1998, Rhonda Killen began a sales position within the food service division at Quaker Tropicana Gatorade (formerly Quaker Oats). Her specific sales territory is central and southwestern Ontario in Canada.

"My position with Quaker Tropicana Gatorade requires me to prepare and execute presentations to groups and individuals of various positions, on a regular basis. It is important to make the most of the time that I have in front of my buyers. Implementing a few key elements helps ensure an effective sales presentation, and achieves my presentation objectives.

"The very first step in meeting my customers' needs is uncovering what those needs are. When I entered this industry and began to learn about the company and my competition, I assumed that a low price would be the most predominant need of my customer. I quickly learned that this assumption was wrong. Many customer needs came into play. For example, sales support, marketing support, and product innovation are key customer priorities within the food service industry. In order to uncover the needs of my buyers, I will often ask them what they like and dislike about their current supplier (who is most often a competitor of mine). Their answer will outline the agenda for the remainder of the sales presentation. Obviously, knowing my competition is essential when using this sales technique. If my potential customers are frustrated by the lack of marketing and sales support they receive from their current supplier, the support that I and my company can offer (and more specifically the benefits that it would provide to the customer) should be the primary focus of my presentation. This focus will create a true sense of value to my customer.

"I make product demonstrations a part of my presentation whenever possible. I make it a point to have the customer work with the product, involving them in the presentation. This keeps the buyers' interest, and it also helps my buyer to experience the benefits of the product or service firsthand.

"I deal with some buyers who get straight to the point of business, are focused on their own objectives, and are very direct. Some of my other buyers are more personable and not as direct. Mindfully adapting my selling techniques to meet the needs of various buyers makes them feel confident and comfortable in dealing with me. This is a key element in developing a positive business relationship.

"As a sales representative, I recognize that my customers have preferred learning styles: Some are visually oriented, some are verbally oriented. Therefore it is important that I know how to use both verbal and visual tools to captivate my buyers' interest. Having an agenda as a visual aid at the beginning of your presentation often helps attract my buyers' attention, while outlining the focus of my meeting. I always provide an agenda for the people to whom I am presenting. I also tell them exactly what I want them to take away from the presentation (for example, two key benefits of the product). In order to help the buyer remember what I have covered in my presentation, I will recap my key points at the end of my presentation, both verbally and visually (most often via a Powerpoint slide).

"If I could offer one piece of advice on how to 'deal with sales presentation jitters' it would be to remember that you are the expert. Your audience is looking to you for information. I act as a consultant to my buyers, being able to provide them with information that will help their businesses flourish. Over time I have become familiar with frequently asked questions and concerns of my potential customer/audience. This experience and expectation of questions have provided me with confidence that I'll be able to answer my customer, which demonstrates my expertise. I have found that if you are confident in yourself, your company, and your product . . . it will show."

Visit Our Website @ www.qtgcanada.com.

CHARACTER- ISTICS OF A STRONG PRESENTATION

Communication tools such as visual aids, samples, testimonials, demonstrations, and the use of humor are an important ingredient in most sales calls. Use of such tools focuses the buyer's attention, improves the buyer's understanding, helps the buyer remember what the salesperson said, offers concrete proof of the salesperson's statements, and creates a sense of value.

KEEPS THE BUYER'S ATTENTION

Naturally, you want to keep the prospect's attention. If you do nothing but talk about your solution, buyers will easily get bored and stop paying attention. How many times has your mind wandered during classroom lectures while the instructor earnestly discussed some topic? What happened? The instructor lost your attention. In contrast, your attention probably remains higher in a class when the instructor uses visuals and humor effectively, brings in guest speakers, and finds ways to get you actively involved in the discussion.

The same is true of buyer–seller interactions. Unless you can get the buyer actively involved in the communication process and doing more than just passively hearing you talk, the buyer's attention will probably turn to other topics.

The buyer's personality can also affect his or her attention span. For example, one would expect an amiable to listen more attentively to a long presentation than, say, a driver would. Thus an effective salesperson should consider the personality of the prospect and adapt the use of communication aids accordingly (see Chapter 6 for more on personality styles).

IMPROVES THE BUYER'S UNDERSTANDING

Many buyers have difficulty forming clear images from the written or spoken word. Salespeople need to utilize all available communication tools to help such people understand the solution to their problem or the opportunity being presented. An old Chinese proverb says, Tell me—I'll forget. Show me—I may remember. But involve me, and I'll understand.

Some product benefits may not easily be explained in nontechnical language. In such cases only buyers with a technical background may understand a verbal explanation. But a simple demonstration may show non–technically oriented buyers exactly which benefits they can expect.

To help the prospect better understand, five basic channels may be used: the senses of hearing, sight, touch, taste, and smell. Appeals should be made to as many of these senses as possible. Studies show that appealing to more than one sense, called **multiple-sense appeals**, increases understanding dramatically, as Exhibit 10.1 illustrates. For example, a recent study found that presentations using visuals are 43 percent more persuasive than those without visuals.[1]

Sellers of some products use appeals to all five senses; others appeal to just two or three. In selling Ben & Jerry's ice cream novelties to a grocery store manager, the salesperson may describe the product's merits—an appeal to the sense of hearing—or show the product and invite the merchant to taste it—appeals to sight, touch, and taste. Appeals to the grocer's fifth sense, smell, are also possible. On the other hand, salespeople who sell machinery are limited to appeals that will affect the buyers' senses of hearing, sight, and touch.

HELPS THE BUYER REMEMBER WHAT WAS SAID

A salesperson may be such an effective orator that the buyer's attention is retained and the buyer fully understands what the seller is saying. Nevertheless, a truly successful call must achieve one other element: The buyer must remember what was said. Recall that, on average, people immediately forget 50 percent of what they hear; after 48 hours they have forgotten 75 percent of the message!

EXHIBIT 10.1

How We Learn and
Remember

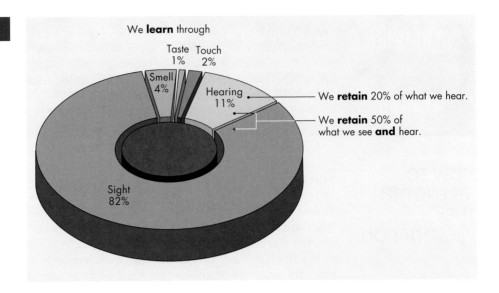

We **learn** through

Taste 1% Touch 2%

Smell 4%

Hearing 11% — We **retain** 20% of what we hear.

— We **retain** 50% of what we see **and** hear.

Sight 82%

Securing an order often requires multiple visits, and in many situations the prospect must relay to other people information learned in a sales call. In these circumstances it becomes even more critical for the seller to help the buyer remember what was said.

Even selling situations involving one call or one decision maker will be more profitable if the buyer remembers what was said. Vividly communicated features create such a strong impression that the buyer remembers the seller's claims and is more likely to tell others about them.

Lasting impressions can be created in many ways. One salesperson swallows some of the industrial cleanser to show that it is nontoxic; another kicks the protective glass in the control panel of a piece of machinery to show that it is virtually unbreakable under even the roughest conditions; still another invites prospects to make an error when using a word processor and then shows how the program spots the error and corrects it automatically. A salesperson may demonstrate a weight-sensored alarm system by using the pressure of a feather to activate it. Whatever the method used, the prospect is more likely to remember a sales feature if it is presented skillfully in a well-timed demonstration.

OFFERS PROOF OF THE SALESPERSON'S ASSERTIONS

Let's face it: Most people just won't believe everything a salesperson tells them. Creating trust is very important.[2] Many of the communication tools we discuss in this chapter provide solid proof to back up the salesperson's claims. For example, a salesperson can easily claim that a liquid is nontoxic, but the claim is much more convincing if the salesperson drinks some of the liquid in front of the prospect.

CREATES A SENSE OF VALUE

The manner in which a product is handled suggests value. Careful handling gives the impression of value even if no words are spoken. Careless handling implies that the product has little value. In contrast, a rare painting, an expensive piece of jewelry, or a delicate piece of china will be perceived as more valuable than it is if the salesperson uses appropriate props, words, and care in handling it.

The use of communication tools can also make a statement about the importance of the buyer. The prospect should rightfully reflect, "If the seller went to all of this trouble to help me understand, I must be important. I must be worth the attention."

HOW TO STRENGTHEN THE PRESENTATION

Salespeople should ask themselves the following questions: How can I use my imagination and creativity to make a vivid impression on my prospect or customer? How can I make my presentation a little different and a little stronger? With this frame of mind, salespeople will always try to do a better and more effective job of meeting their customers' needs.

A seller has many communication tools available to strengthen the presentation. We will explore the use of word pictures, stories, humor, charts, models, samples, gifts, catalogs, brochures, pictures, ads, maps, and illustrations; the best way to utilize testimonials and test results; how to effectively use various media; how to give powerful demonstrations; how to create useful handouts; how to write effective proposals; and how to quantify the solution. Salespeople often keep a journal of ideas and examples of what works well in presentations.[3]

Before we describe the various methods, however, it is important to reiterate a point made in the preceding chapter. A seller should not just grab a method because it sounds trendy or because it worked in a previous sales call or just because it is highly entertaining (a great "dog and pony show"). Rather, a seller should strategically select methods and media that will helpfully address the needs of the buyer.[4] This process includes responding to the buyer's unique style (see Chapter 6 to review social styles). For example, expressives like to see strong, intense colors and lots of photos, cartoons, fancy fonts, and positive images (smiles); analyticals prefer visuals that are clean and simple, a list of references, and lots of details; amiables prefer visuals with people in them and a relatively slow-moving presentation; in contrast, drivers want crisp, professional visuals with bold lettering to highlight important points. Strategizing also includes considering elements such as how many people will attend the presentation, which stage of the buying process they are in, what information they need, what type of situation this is (new task, modified rebuy, straight rebuy), and so on (see Chapter 4 for more buying factors to consider).

VERBAL TOOLS

WORD PICTURES AND STORIES

The power of the spoken word can be phenomenal. To be successful, the salesperson needs to remember all the hints on communicating effectively (see Chapter 5).[5] Chapter 5 also describes the use of word pictures to make your point. Stories of all types can be effective. Here are some points to keep in mind when using stories:[6]

- If at all possible, use stories from your own life, not those that are borrowed or made up. If you do borrow one, don't try to act like it is your personal story.
- Make sure you have a reason for telling the story.
- Use the "hook" of the story to tie back directly into your presentation.
- Be accurate and vivid with the words you choose. Learn to paint a clear picture.
- Pace the story. Watch your audience carefully for cues. Use silence and pauses effectively.

- Choose stories that fit your own style. Don't try to be someone you're not.
- Stories can be quite short—even a few sentences.

Here's an example of a story, adapted from the book *The Age of Unreason* by Charles Handy:

> At precisely 0513 on the morning of April 18, 1906, a cow was standing somewhere between the main barn and the milking shed on the old Shafter ranch on the outskirts of San Francisco. Suddenly the earth shook and the cow disappeared; all that remained was a small section of tail.
>
> Now why on earth would I tell you a story about a cow? The Shafter cow story symbolizes the dangers of the turbulent marketing environment of today. Suddenly, without warning, the forces struck, changing the configuration of the earth, destroying a city, and swallowing a cow.
>
> Just as swiftly, a major client can disappear to a competitor, a major market can dry up, or a new technology can make your service obsolete.[7]

HUMOR

Another way a salesperson can help keep the buyer's attention is through the use of humor. The wonderful effects of laughter will put everyone more at ease, including the salesperson. You can use humorous stories from your own experience, borrowed humor, or humor adapted from another source. Here are some things to keep in mind:

- Don't oversell the joke (Here's one that'll really break you up!).
- Don't apologize before telling a joke (I never was good at telling a joke, but I'll try to get through this.)
- Identify any facts that are absolutely necessary for the punch line of the story to make sense (Jerry Joyner, my next door neighbor who was always sticking his nose in other people's business, . . .).
- Use humor from your own life. That way you don't have to worry that your joke is circulating widely on the Web.
- Enjoy yourself while you're relating the humor by smiling and animating your voice and nonverbals.
- Practice telling the joke different ways to see which exact wording works best.
- Make sure your punch line is clear.

But beware of overdoing humor or using off-the-wall humor. Both can backfire, as one presenter found out when he used the following opening line about

Salespeople should use humor to get and keep the customer's attention.

an overweight attendee: Pull up two chairs and have a seat. The presenter knew right away that it was a big mistake. Or as another presenter, who addressed a group of lawyers and decided to use humor, found:

> I launched into the Internet lawyer joke which, even as I uttered it, sounded cold and mean-spirited—it had to do with burying 20 lawyers alive. I had expected this gang of upholstered rogues to laugh raffishly. A barrister friend had assured me that lawyers love lawyer jokes; he set me up big time. I looked out and I could see the twinges on their faces as they realized that this was how outsiders viewed their profession.[8]

Be cautious about using insider jokes, especially if you're still considered an outsider.

Also, understand that what is funny to one person or group may not be funny to others. Several examples will help you see this point. A foreigner from Egypt may not appreciate someone from America making fun of Egyptian culture—but someone from Egypt can tell that same joke and get plenty of laughs. In recent research involving more than 100,000 people from 70 countries, it was found that men prefer humor about aggression or sexual innuendo, while women prefer humor that involves word play. The same study found that Canadians seem the least likely to laugh at jokes, while Germans laugh the most.[9]

VISUAL TOOLS

A salesperson can use various visually oriented tools to strengthen the presentation, including charts, models, samples, gifts, catalogs, brochures, pictures, advertisements, maps, illustrations, testimonials, and test results. This section explores the content and use of those tools, followed by a discussion of the various media (portfolios, slides, projectors, whiteboards, and so on) available to display the results.

CHARTS

Charts help illustrate relationships and clearly communicate large amounts of information. Charts may show, for example, advertising schedules, a breakdown of typical customer profiles, details of product manufacture, or profit margins at various pricing points.

Charts can easily be customized by including the name of the prospect's company in one corner or by some other form of personalization. Customization helps to project the impression that the presentation is fresh and tailor-made for this prospect.

Salespeople also use charts to illustrate the investment nature of purchasing a product. This topic is discussed, and an example provided, later in this chapter.

Following are several important hints for developing charts and related visuals:

- Know the single point the visual should make and then ensure that it accomplishes that point.

- Use current and accurate information.

- Don't place too much information on a visual; on a textual visual, don't use more than seven words per line or more than seven lines per visual. Don't use complete sentences; the speaker should verbally provide the missing details.

- Use bullets (dots or symbols before each line) to more easily differentiate issues and to emphasize key points.

- Don't overload the buyer with numbers. Use no more than five or six columns and drop all unnecessary zeros.

- Clearly label each visual with a title. Label all columns and rows.

- Recognize the emotional impact of colors and choose appropriate ones. Be careful, especially in international settings. An abundance of green connected to a humorous graph might be offensive in Islamic countries, since green is a religious color. In Brazil and Mexico, purple indicates death.[10]

- If possible, use graphics (like diagrams, pie charts, and bar charts) instead of tables. Tables are often needed if actual raw numbers are important; graphics are better for displaying trends and relationships.

- Use consistent art styles, layouts, and scales for your collection of charts and figures. Consistency makes it easier for the buyer to follow along.

- Check your visuals closely for typographical errors, misspelled words, and other errors.

MODELS, SAMPLES, AND GIFTS

Visual selling aids such as models, samples, and gifts may be a good answer to the problem of getting and keeping buyer interest. Miniature models go to the interview as substitutes for products too large or bulky to transport easily. For example, Brink Locking Systems salespeople carry along a miniature working model of the company's electronic door locks when calling on prison security systems buyers. The model allows the salespeople to show how the various components work together to form a fail-safe security network.

Other salespeople use cross-sectional models to communicate with the buyer. For example, salespeople for Dixie Bearings use a cutaway model of a power transmission friction reduction product. This model helps the buyer, usually an industrial engineer, to clearly see how the product is constructed, resulting in greater confidence that the product will perform as described.

Some sales representatives even carry samples of large and bulky products. Fax machine salespeople for Ambassador Office Equipment have found it pays to bring along the types of machines they plan to sell. When the prospect wants a demonstration, the fax machine is available immediately. Experience has shown that anything can happen if the salesperson gets the interest of the prospect and then must return to the office to get a sample fax machine. Several more calls may be needed to secure an appointment for a demonstration.

Depending on the service or product, samples can make excellent sales aids. Food, office supplies, paper products, and long-distance services exemplify the many products or services that may be sold through the use of samples. Bristol-Myers Squibb pharmaceutical salespeople almost always leave drug samples for doctors to distribute to their patients. If the samples perform effectively, the doctors will begin prescribing the drugs for other patients.

Samples and gifts frequently help to maintain the prospect's interest after the call and serve as a reminder for prospects or customers who either buy or do not buy during the presentation. In a Johnson Wax sales campaign, salespeople called on buyers of major chains to describe the promotion. Salespeople walked into each buyer's office with a solid oak briefcase containing cans of aerosol Pledge, the product to be highlighted during the promotion. During the call the sales representative demonstrated the Pledge furniture polish on the oak briefcase. At the conclusion of the visit, the rep gave the buyer not only the cans of Pledge but also the briefcase. Of course, gift giving must be done with care (see Chapter 3 for a discussion of the ethics of gift giving).

CATALOGS AND BROCHURES

Catalogs and brochures can help salespeople communicate information to the buyer effectively. The salesperson can use them during presentations and then leave them with the buyer as a reminder of the issues covered. Brochures often summarize key points and contain answers to the usual questions buyers pose.

Firms often spend a great deal of money to develop visually attractive brochures for salespeople. Exhibit 10.2 shows an example of a brochure used by salespeople. Creatively designed brochures usually unfold in a way that enables the salesperson to create and maintain great interest while showing them.

PICTURES, ADS, MAPS, AND ILLUSTRATIONS

Pictures are easy to prepare, are relatively inexpensive, and permit a realistic portrayal of the product and its benefits. Photographs of people may be particularly effective. For example, leisure made possible through savings can be communicated via photographs of retired people at a ranch, a mountain resort, or the seashore. Illustrations drawn, painted, or prepared in other ways also help to dramatize needs or benefits. Copies of recent or upcoming ads may contribute visual appeal. Detailed maps can be easily developed, for example, to show how a magazine's circulation matches the needs of potential advertisers.

TESTIMONIALS AND TEST RESULTS

Testimonials are statements, usually letters, written by satisfied users of a product or service. These letters commend the product or service and attest that the writer believes it to be a good buy. For example, company representatives who sell air travel for major airlines have found case histories helpful in communicating sales points. Canadian Airlines recounts actual experiences of business firms, showing the variety of problems that air travel can solve.

The effectiveness of a testimonial hinges on the skill with which it is used and a careful matching of satisfied user and prospect. In some situations the testi-

EXHIBIT 10.2

A brochure with great visual appeal.

Courtesy Raleigh

mony of a rival or a competitor of the prospective buyer would end all chance of closing the sale; in other cases this type of testimony may be a strong factor in obtaining commitment. As much as possible, the person who writes the testimonial should be above reproach, well respected by his or her peers, and perhaps a center of influence (see Chapter 7). For example, when selling to certified public accountants (CPAs), a good source for a testimonial would be the president of the state's CPA association.

Before using a testimonial, the salesperson needs to check with the person who wrote it and frequently reaffirm that he or she is still a happy, satisfied customer. One salesperson for Unisys routinely handed all prospects a testimonial from a satisfied customer of a new software package. But, unknown to the salesperson, the "satisfied customer" became an unsatisfied one and actually returned the software. The salesperson kept handing out the letter until one of his prospects alerted him to the situation. He will never know how many other prospects lost interest after contacting that customer.

Salespeople should not just hand out a testimonial to every prospect; such letters should be used only if they help to address the buyer's needs or concerns. For example, with a buyer concerned about service, the salesperson could use a testimonial that specifically mentions service. Also, be aware that prospects may discount testimonials. (I'll bet you used your only satisfied customer, probably a relative, to write this letter. Besides, it talks about things only in very general terms.) This kind of thinking highlights the importance of using testimonials strategically rather than routinely.

Salespeople can also use test results to strengthen the presentation. Tests on the product or service may have been conducted by the seller's firm or some third-party organization (such as Consumer Reports or Underwriters Laboratories). Generally, tests conducted by independent, recognized authorities have more credibility for the prospect than tests done by the seller.

MEDIA USED TO DISPLAY VISUAL TOOLS

Many media are available to display the types of items just mentioned. New media, and improvements to existing media, are being introduced almost every week. Salespeople are encouraged to choose media that are appropriate for the exact situation, and not merely choose a tool because it is new or exciting. Time-honored media, such as portfolios or overhead projectors, may sometimes be appropriate; at other times it may be important to use the most high-tech media available.

If you do choose high-tech media, you should consider the results of a recent study of presenters: 96 percent agreed that technology, in general, enhances presentations; however, 54 percent of the same group also felt that technology can detract from a presentation.[11] Choose and use your media carefully. Popular media include portfolios, 35mm slides, VCRs, computers, and visual projectors. Exhibit 10.3 summarizes some of the strengths and weaknesses of these products.

SALES PORTFOLIOS Most salespeople have developed a **portfolio,** which is simply a paper-based collection of visual aids, often placed in some sort of binder or container, that can be used to enhance communication during a sales call. Salespeople do not intend to use everything in the portfolio in a single call; rather, the portfolio should contain a broad spectrum of visual aids the salesperson can find quickly should the need arise. In international selling situations where the buyer does not speak the seller's language, visuals are particularly important.

EXHIBIT 10.3   Visual Aids: A Comparison

Type of Visual	Relative Cost	Difficulty in Transporting	Complexity in Operating	Effective with Large Groups?
Portfolio	Low	No	Easy	Yes, if you use an easel type
35mm slides	Medium	Medium	Medium	Yes
VCRs	Medium–high	Medium–high	Medium–high	Yes
Computers	High	Low–medium	High	No, unless hooked up to a projector
Projectors				
Overhead projectors	Medium	Medium	Easy	Yes
Document cameras	High	Medium	Medium	Yes
Whiteboards	High	High	Medium	Yes
Color video projectors	High	Medium–high	Medium–high	Yes
Videowalls	Very high	Very high	Medium–high	Yes

The easel type of portfolio can stand by itself on the prospect's desk or counter. A **flip chart,** a large easel type of portfolio placed on the floor, is used in making presentations to a group. All such easel portfolios are arranged to aid in the anticipated flow of the conversation; the salesperson turns each page after it has been read or used for illustration. Here are a few tips for using flip charts:

- Use a gridded pad, not a plain one. Grids help you to draw straight lines and align your notes.
- Use special flip-chart markers because they won't bleed through the paper.
- Avoid using yellow, pink, or orange markers because they can be hard to see.
- You can lightly write in any notes to yourself in pencil next to the key points.
- Take care of your flip charts. Tattered ones look unprofessional.

Portfolios can also be carried in a binder. The contents may be labeled by tabs and punched to fit rings in a binder. Binders make the material easy to find and are convenient to carry and use. For example, Toledo Scale Company sales representatives use binder portfolios that contain detailed illustrative material indexed and tabbed for all the items Toledo sells.

A large commercial building contractor improved selling efforts by preparing a visual presentation of important facts concerning the business. The spiral-bound portfolio contained thumbnail sketches of the company's key employees; a financial statement; a list of special equipment; copies of letters from satisfied owners of various types of buildings; and pictures of completed industrial plants, apartment houses, stores, supermarkets, and shopping centers. This appeal to the prospect's eye tells a story many words and many minutes cannot equal.

When showing visuals in your portfolio, make sure the portfolio is turned so the buyer can see it easily. Also, don't let the visual interfere with your interaction. It should not be placed, like a wall, between you and the buyer. Remember to look at the buyer, not at your visual; maintaining eye contact is always important.

Maintain proper control of the visuals during the presentation. Without control, buyers may thumb through catalogs or look ahead at visuals before the salesperson has adequately covered the current visual. One technique is to remove the visual after it has been used. This approach also cuts down on desk clutter and helps you to be more organized. But be careful about removing visuals too quickly. Remember, you are there to meet the buyer's needs.

35MM SLIDES Slides have been effective selling aids for years. One structural timber firm used slides to convince buyers that laminated wood treated with waterproof glue was a good substitute for steel. Pictures of construction jobs that were actually using laminated arches were converted into a powerful slide show to communicate to architects and builders exactly how and where the company's product was used.

An advantage of slides has always been the relatively low cost of producing them. Also, salespeople can easily tailor the show to any buyer simply by removing and/or reordering the slides. Slide shows for large groups often utilize multiple projectors and multiple screens along with a stereo sound track. Computers can also be used to give slide presentations, as will be discussed shortly.

VCRS Today's sophisticated buyers are accustomed to watching high-definition cable TV and movies that include outstanding graphics, sound, and production. Effective salespeople can respond to this trend by using professionally developed video clips during the presentation. VCRs improve on slides in that the former portray action. Salespeople use VCRs to help the buyer see how quality is manufactured into the product (as in a tape showing the production process at the manufacturing plant), how others use the product or service (a tape showing a group of seniors enjoying the golf course at a retirement resort), promotional support offered with the product (a tape of the actual upcoming TV commercial for the product), and even testimonials from satisfied users. VCRs are used not only by salespeople in one-on-one and group presentations but also at trade shows and for training the buyer's employees after the sale.

When using VCRs, make sure the video is fast-paced and relatively short. Don't show more than four minutes of a video at one time. In the past one of the greatest complaints against VCRs was that they were bulky and impossible to use in office settings. Technology, however, has alleviated these concerns.

COMPUTER HARDWARE AND SOFTWARE More and more salespeople have adopted laptop computers, notebook computers, tablet computers,[12] and palm PCs for use in sales calls. The beauty of these devices is their ability to store large amounts of easily retrievable information, including text, audio, video, and still images. Inputting all of this data is made much easier with the increasing sophistication of scanners, digital cameras, and software (such as Onyx EnCyc or PowerPoint). For example, Merck pharmaceutical salespeople carry laptops with a database of technical information, as well as complete copies of articles from medical journals. This technology enables the salespeople to create completely unique presentations for each physician based on the doctor's need for specific kinds of information. Progressive firms, like Aetna, are investing in **digital asset management** software systems to archive, catalog, and retrieve digital media and text. Salespeople access the software system when preparing their presentations to easily call up photos, videos, audio files, PowerPoint templates, Web pages, legal documents, streaming media, and just about anything else that has been digitally entered into the system.

A phrase has been coined, **digital sales assistant (DSA)**, to indicate any software tool that is designed to help salespeople get their message across. PowerPoint and Astound are two examples of DSAs. As you utilize DSAs there are several things to consider. Do you want to create a "canned" presentation, which forces the seller to follow a predetermined path through the slides and information? (This is termed a **linear DSA**.) The advantage is that you can develop a very logical flow of information and can easily master its execution through practice. The disadvantages are the same as for standard memorized presentations (see Chapter 6): primarily a lack of customization to the buyer's needs. A linear DSA might be most appropriate for a presentation to a large group where customization at a moment's notice may not be important. For example, a software vendor used a linear DSA when giving a presentation to a group of 150 business owners because the number of people present and the time restrictions didn't really allow for questions and answers during the presentation. You've probably witnessed a number of linear DSAs in classroom presentations when students used PowerPoint.

In contrast, a **nonlinear DSA** allows the flexibility of choosing the order of presentation. Thus it is an interactive tool, and you're not forced to show all the slides. Instead, the seller can easily respond to a buyer's concerns, discovered with verbal probing (see Chapter 9) or through buyer's objections (covered in Chapter 11). This flexibility is accomplished by the use of branches and buttons embedded in the presentation software, which cause the program to skip to other topics. On the negative side, compared to a linear DSA, a nonlinear DSA is harder to craft because each section must be able to make sense on its own. Some experts advise a combination approach, where the introduction of the presentation is a linear DSA, followed by a nonlinear DSA to address specific needs or questions raised during the presentation.

Use DSAs with the same care you would any other media. Don't let the technology itself become the reason for your presentation. You're there to help satisfy needs, not wow the prospect with the latest high-tech gadgets. Also, keep in mind the following (in addition to the comments earlier about developing charts):

- Don't develop so many slides that you are going to drown your prospect. Thirty slides or so should be plenty.

- Don't get carried away by using every tool in the DSA. When Lufthansa first gave its salespeople laptops with PowerPoint, they were including all sorts of unnecessary and distracting items like animations, pink backgrounds, and confetti. Use special effects sparingly.

- Don't cram too much information on a slide. Some experts suggest that computer presentation slide shows should never have more than four points per slide and four or five words per point. If your buyer is busy reading your slides, she or he probably isn't listening to you.

- Keep the text big. And use colors strategically. Remember that some people don't have great eyesight and some are color-blind.

- Recognize times when old-fashioned overheads might be preferred—for example, when using high-tech material makes you look too trendy or flashy to a very conservative buyer.

- If you're going to showcase Web pages as a part of your presentation, it may be wise to download the pages into your presentation software instead of using a live Internet connection (to avoid slow connect times, Web congestion, or network congestion; or to avoid finding the site suddenly under construction or unavailable).

- Know and obey copyright laws. You can't just grab images off the Web and use them.[13]

Computers not only offer excellent visuals and graphics but also allow the salesperson to perform what-if analyses (What will happen to your profits if you resell our product at $1.15 each instead of the $1.01 you suggested?) much more easily and graphically, thanks to spreadsheet programs like Lotus and Excel. For example, a Procter & Gamble (P&G) key account salesperson was using the computer to demonstrate how a new P&G product would deliver more profit than would a competitor's product in the same shelf space. When the buyer asked what would happen if the P&G product sold for $1.69 instead of the $1.75 suggested price, the salesperson was able to easily change this number in the spreadsheet program. Instantly all charts and graphs were corrected to illustrate the new pricing point, and comparisons with the competitor's product were generated.

Here are some tips for effectively using computers:

- Be prepared. Have backup batteries, adapters, and copies of disks or CDs. Some experts even suggest that traveling presenters call several rental companies in cities where they will be presenting to learn about the kinds of equipment they can secure in case of a catastrophe.

- To avoid embarrassing downtime, get to really know your hardware and software so you can recover if the system crashes. High-tech equipment can be difficult to operate and prone to malfunction at the most inopportune times.

- Make sure both you and your customer can comfortably view the output.

- Don't let the computer presentation replace you, the salesperson, in the meeting.

- You're there to help your prospect solve a need, so make sure that your audience has ample opportunity to ask questions.

- After every computer presentation, ask yourself what worked well and what did not. Make adjustments accordingly.

Thinking It Through

You turn the lights down for a PowerPoint computer slide presentation. As you begin flipping through the slides, adding your own stories and examples, you get a sense of pride in this excellent, well-designed slide show. It's the best you've ever created. And to top it off, your manager and regional manager are with you during this presentation. You couldn't be happier . . . until the 13th slide, when your eye catches an unusual jerking movement made by the buyer. As you nervously watch more closely, you realize the prospect is falling asleep! Panic sets in. Your entire presentation is on these stupid PowerPoint slides. You have no hard copy of the slides, and your portfolio is back at your office. What's more, if you turn the lights up, the prospect certainly won't be able to view the slides. You wish you had chosen some background color other than dark brown for your slides. What do you do now?

VISUAL PROJECTORS Traditional overhead projectors can be an effective visual medium. The image projected on a wall can be up to 25 times larger than that on a written page, drawing more attention and creating greater impact. Such projectors are noiseless and simple to operate. Overhead transparencies can be made quickly and inexpensively on a copier or computer printer. Here are a few tips on using overhead projectors effectively:

- Face your audience, not the screen. And don't block anyone's view with your body or the projector itself.

- Change your transparencies smoothly and never leave an empty screen.

- Tape the power cord to the floor to keep yourself from tripping over it!

- Have a spare bulb. If you have no light, you have no presentation.

Document cameras, also called **visual presenters,** are similar to traditional overhead projectors in their ability to display transparencies. However, since they are essentially cameras, they are also capable of displaying any three-dimensional object without the use of a transparency. For example, you can easily display a cut-away model of a product or the pages of an open book. Sophisticated document cameras can also be connected to your PC for display of computer images (such as JPEG files). Exhibit 10.4 shows what a document camera looks like.

Electronic whiteboards, or digital easels, are used by salespeople, especially when working with customers who prefer to brainstorm an issue or problem.[14] These devices come in various configurations. A simple **electronic copyboard** can scan and print whatever is written on its surface and is not connected to a computer. A **computer-peripheral whiteboard,** always connected to a computer, can do what an electronic copyboard can do, plus it can save the session as a computer file. A **computer-interactive whiteboard,** the most sophisticated type, allows users to access and control software applications on the computer, utilizing interactive meeting software tools. For example, a salesperson using a computer-interactive whiteboard could pull up images or files from a computer's hard drive (word processing files, spreadsheet files, video clips, graphs, diagrams, hand-drawn images), the firm's network, or the Web, and display and manipulate them directly on the whiteboard. Hewlett-Packard executives use these to make electronic presentations to remote offices in the United States and Europe with their teleconferencing system. Exhibit 10.5 displays an example of a common whiteboard.

Salespeople use other projection systems as well. Color video projectors connect to a VCR or computer and are better than a TV for projecting images to a

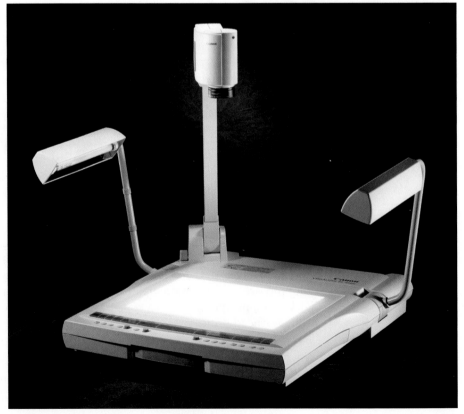

RE-450X Video Visualizer. Courtesy of CanonUSA, Inc.

Courtesy SMART Technologies, Inc.

large group of people. Videowalls are capable of high-resolution imaging of computer graphics and video.

PRODUCT DEMONSTRA-TIONS

One of the most effective methods of appealing to the buyer's senses is through product demonstrations or performance tests.[15] Customers and prospects have a natural desire to prove the product's claims for themselves. Obviously, the proof is much more satisfying and convincing to anyone who is a party to it. The following examples illustrate effective methods of demonstration for each specific situation encountered.

Paper sales representatives use demonstrations to sell quality. Having prospects hold two sheets of paper to the light, the reps point out that in a good grade of paper the fibers are evenly distributed, whereas in a poor grade of paper uneven distribution produces a mottled effect. To show opacity, they have the customer place a material with black lines on it under the sheet and check for show-through.

One enterprising sales representative was having trouble convincing the buyer for a national retailer that the salesperson's company could provide service at all of the retailer's scattered outlets. On the next trip to the buyer, the sales representative brought along a bag of darts and a map marked with the chain's hundreds of stores and service locations. The buyer was invited to throw darts at the map and then find the nearest stores. The test pointed out that the nearest location for service was always within 50 miles. This "service demonstration" helped win the representative's company a multimillion-dollar order.

Some products can be sold most successfully by getting the prospect into the showroom for a hands-on product demonstration. Showrooms can be quite elaborate and effective. For example, Hewlett-Packard (HP) operates a medical marketing center in Germany. Prospects from across Europe can try all of HP's medical products. Patient responses are electronically simulated, which allows medical personnel to test the equipment in mock-emergency situations.

Here are a number of helpful hints for developing and engaging in effective demonstrations:

- Be prepared. Practice the demonstration until you become an expert. Plan for everything that could possibly go wrong.

- Secure a proper place for the demonstration, one free of distractions for both you and the buyer. If the demonstration is at the buyer's office, make sure you have everything you need (power supply, lighting, and so on).

- Check the equipment again to make sure it is in good working order prior to beginning the presentation. Have necessary backup parts and supplies (like paper or bulbs).

- Get the prospect involved in a meaningful way. For example, if you are selling a tractor to a farmer, don't just drive it for him or her; let the farmer drive the tractor. In a group situation, plan which group members need to participate.

- Always relate product features to the buyer's unique needs.

- Make the demonstration an integral part of the overall presentation, not a separate, unrelated activity.

- Keep the demonstration simple, concise, and clear. Long, complicated demonstrations add to the possibility that the buyer will miss the point. Limit technical jargon to technically advanced buyers who you know will understand technical terms.

- Plan what you will do during any dead time—that is, time in which the machine is processing on its own. You can use these intervals to ask the buyer questions and have the buyer ask you questions.

- Find out whether the prospect has already seen a competitor's product demonstration. If so, strategically include a demonstration of features the buyer liked about the competitor's product. Also, plan to show how your product can meet the prospect's desires and do what the competitor's product will not do.

- Find out whether any buyers present at your demonstration have used your product before. Having them assist in the demonstration may be advantageous if they view your product favorably.

- Probe during and after the demonstration. Make sure buyers understand the features and see how the product can help them. Also, probe to see whether buyers are interested in securing the product.

Remember Murphy's law: What can go wrong will go wrong! And occasionally things do go wrong during a demonstration, like when Bill Gates, CEO of Microsoft, was giving the big launch demonstration of Windows 98 and his com-

Getting the buyer actively involved during the call is important.

Bill Bachman/e-Stock/PictureQuest

puter froze. If a demonstration "blows up" for any reason, your best strategy usually is to appeal to fate with a humorous tone of voice: Wow, have you ever seen anything get so messed up? I should run for Congress! Don't let technical glitches embarrass or frustrate you. Life is not perfect, and sometimes things just don't work out the way you plan them. If it will help, remember that prospects also are not perfect and sometimes they mess things up as well.

WOW, IS THAT GUY EVER RUDE!

"I don't guess you really know what you're talking about, do you?! No, you don't even have a clue!" Charged words. Fighting words. They are hard enough to accept if you're in a private meeting with another person. They are much harder to deal with when you are in a group. And yet salespeople can expect to have such statements thrust upon them during sales calls, often in meetings that involve a number of members of a buying committee or team. How should a seller respond to rude buyers?

First, do your homework. Know who is planning on attending and what their personality styles are like. Second, sometimes the rudeness is because of a previous bad experience with your firm. If so, get it out on the table and deal with it. Don't try to hide from the issue or postpone it. Get the facts, acknowledge that you sense the anger, and ask the audience for possible solutions. Third, don't be afraid to empathize with the statement

made by the buyer. By doing so, you're not condoning the exhibited socially reckless behavior, you're just admitting that he or she may have a point worth addressing. Fourth, sometimes you just have to take control of the situation. One trainer suggests saying something like this: "Hey, Larry," said with a big grin, "I've heard you're a tough nut to crack— am I right?" By grinning you hope to defuse the severity of your statement and make it seem a little like a joke. However, you just made it clear that enough is enough. Lastly, if all else fails, go watch stand-up comedians at work. Since they have some of the toughest audiences to deal with, your job as a salesperson will seem easy.

Sources: Personal experience; John Wareham, "Executive Intelligence: From the Podium," *Across the Board,* March/April 2001, p. 67–68; Erin Strout, "Warming Up to an Icy Audience," *Sales and Marketing Management,* June 1999, p. 70.

Maintaining a cool and level head will probably impress the prospect with your ability to deal with a difficult situation. It may even increase your chances of a sale, since you are demonstrating your ability to handle stress (something that often occurs during the after-sale servicing of an account). Selling Scenario 10.1 provides some guidance on how to handle a rude or unruly person from the prospect's firm.

HANDOUTS

Handouts are written documents provided to help buyers remember what was said. A well-prepared set of handouts can be one of the best ways to increase buyer retention of information, especially over longer periods. A common practice is to make a printed copy of the overheads and give that to the buyers at the conclusion of the presentation. Some programs (like PowerPoint) allow you to print several slides on each page.

Others would argue that your use of handouts should be more strategically focused.[16] Thus handouts are not just a last-minute thought, but rather are a tool that needs to be carefully planned at the same time you are preparing your presentation. For example, you could draw a line on a piece of planning paper and on the left side list the things you will do and say during the presentation, while on the right side listing the items that should go into the handout. In that way the two will work together and be complementary.

What things can go into a handout? Complex charts and diagrams can be included. Because you want to keep your presentation visuals relatively simple (see the preceding hints), your handouts can supply more complete, detailed information. You may also want to include some company reports or literature. However, to avoid making the buyer wade through a lot of nonrelevant information, include only important sections. You may even want to highlight sections of the reports. Other items to include are Web addresses with a description of each site, case studies, magazine articles, and yes, even a copy of your presentation slides themselves (with room to take notes if you're going to give the buyer your handout during the presentation). Whatever you choose, here are some tips:

- Don't forget the goal of your meeting. That should drive all of your decisions about what to include in your handouts.

- Make sure the handouts look professional. And use graphics, instead of text, whenever possible.

- Don't cram too much information on a page. White space is fine. Try not to fill more than two-thirds of any page with information.

- Don't drown your prospect in information. Include only helpful information in your handouts.

Handouts are even more important for foreign buyers, especially those who are nonnative English speakers. You might even consider giving them a copy of your handouts before your meeting so they can become more comfortable and familiar with concepts and phrases. Including a glossary, with definitions, will also be appreciated by foreign buyers.

WRITTEN PROPOSALS

In some industries written proposals are an important part of the selling process. Some proposals are simple adaptations of brochures developed by a corporate marketing department. But in industries that sell customized products or require competitive bidding[17] (such as many state and local governments do), a written proposal may be necessary for the buyer to organize and compare various offerings.

Proposals are also useful when the salesperson cannot see the decision maker. If, for example, the salesperson is calling on the Tamaulipas, Mexico, office and the final decision will be made in the corporate office in Mexico City, a proposal can be used to sell that home office decision maker.

THE RFP PROCESS

A document issued by a prospective buyer asking for a proposal may be called a **request for proposal (RFP)**, request for quote (RFQ), or request for bid (RFB). For brevity's sake, we will refer to all of these as RFPs.

The RFP should contain the customer's specifications for the desired product, including delivery schedules. RFPs are used when the customer has a firm idea of the product needed. From the salesperson's perspective, being a part of the specifying process makes sense. Using the needs identification process, the salesperson can assist the customer in identifying needs and specifying product characteristics. The result may be that the only product that can meet the specifications is the one sold by that salesperson; when the resulting product truly meets the needs of the customer, that outcome is fair.

Buyers do not want stacks of material that make them search for answers; bids priced low in the expectation that the vendor can make it up later in add-ons, changes, and upgrades; and glossy marketing hype.

WRITING PROPOSALS

Proposals do the selling job when the salesperson cannot be present. A key issue is keeping the customer's needs in mind. Always write down what the customer needs during the initial meeting. If not, two days later the salesperson will have forgotten some details she or he wanted to cover in the proposal.

Proposals, then, have three parts: an executive summary, a description of the current situation in relation to the proposed solution, and a budget (which details costs). When preparing proposals, salespeople can use the checklist that appears in Exhibit 10.6 to ensure that the proposal proves how the product will satisfy the buyer's needs. Some firms have even developed computer programs to automatically generate sales proposals in response to a set of questions the salesperson answers about a particular customer. This is especially helpful because sometimes buyers use RFPs just to keep their current suppliers in check. In such a case, a seller might want to minimize the amount of time spent responding to an RFP. (A familiar saying in sales is "You can't cash an RFP.")

The **executive summary** provides, in one or two pages, the total cost minus the total savings, a brief description of the problem to be solved, and a brief description of the proposed solution. The summary should satisfy the concerns of an executive who is too busy or unwilling to read the entire proposal. The executive summary also serves to pique the interest of all readers by allowing a quick glance at the benefits of the purchase.

Many salespeople actually compare the current situation with the proposed solution on the same sheet. They do so by listing problems with the current product or service in one column and describing how the proposed solution resolves those problems in a second column. The format resembles the Ben Franklin approach to gaining commitment, described in Chapter 12. Such an approach has several advantages: It reminds the customer of the needs actually described in an earlier conversation or an RFP, and it can directly link the benefits of the proposed solution to satisfying those needs. Exhibit 10.7 provides a short example of such a format. If this proposal will be sent to the home office, the salesperson should make it clear that the present situation was identified by the customer's local personnel.

Some proposals are too complicated for such a simple approach. Discussion of the current situation and a description of the proposed solution may each require

EXHIBIT 10.6 A Proposal Checklist	A proposal must answer the following questions convincingly: ✔ *What Problem Are You Going to Solve?* Show that you understand the problem and the organization's needs. Define the problem as the audience sees it, even if you believe that the presented problem is part of a larger problem that must first be solved. ✔ *How Are You Going to Solve It?* Prove that your methods are feasible. Show that a solution can be found in the time available. Specify the topics you'll investigate. Explain how you'll gather data. ✔ *What Exactly Will You Provide for Us?* Specify the tangible products you'll produce; explain how you'll evaluate them. ✔ *Can You Deliver on What You Promise?* Show that you have the knowledge, the staff, and the facilities to do what you say you will. Describe your previous work in this area, your other qualifications, and the qualifications of any people who will be helping you. ✔ *What Benefits Can You Offer?* In a sales proposal, several vendors may be able to supply the equipment needed. Show why the company should hire you. Discuss the benefits—direct and indirect—that your firm can provide. ✔ *When Will You Complete the Work?* Provide a detailed schedule showing when each phase of the work will be completed. ✔ *How Much Will You Charge?* Provide a detailed budget that includes costs for materials, salaries, and overhead costs. Source: Kitty Locker, *Business and Administrative Communication,* (Burr Ridge, IL: Irwin, 1989), pp. 401–2.

EXHIBIT 10.7

An Example of the
Ben Franklin Format

Your Current Vendor (Quick Print)	Our Proposed Solution (Quickie Printers)
No delivery: You must bring it in, using 30 minutes per round trip.	Free pickup and delivery: No time is lost driving to or from the copying store; receptionist can stay and do her job, with no more overtime.
Open 8 A.M. to 6 P.M.	Open 24 hours per day: Overnight turnaround, which you need for most proposals and bids, now possible on all jobs at no extra cost; gives your marketing staff more time to prepare proposals and bids, resulting in more professional and more profitable bids.
No special discounts	Preferred customer plan: Saves you 5 percent on every order, 10 percent on certain types of jobs; your workers are more productive, and you pay less for copying!

a separate section. Still, readers must be able to quickly relate characteristics of the proposed solution to the needs being met. In fact, don't just assume that a bigger proposal is a better one. One study found that shorter proposals (those with fewer graphics and other elements) actually resulted in more sales.[18]

PRESENTING THE PROPOSAL

Prospects use proposals in many different ways. Proposals can be used to convince the home office that the local office needs the product, or proposals may be used to compare the product and terms of sale with those of competitors. As we mentioned earlier, the intended use will influence the design of the proposal; it will also influence how the salesperson presents the proposal.

When the proposal is going to be sent to the home office, it is wise to secure the support of the local decision maker. Although that person is not the ultimate decision maker, the decision may rest on how much effort that person puts into getting the proposal accepted. Salespeople often use a "team effort" approach by asking the local recommending person how to assist in getting the proposal accepted. The salesperson may want to ask for permission to follow up with a phone call directly to the home office, offer to help write a recommendation letter, or ask for permission to have a national account representative or senior executive call on the prospect's home office.

Buying centers often use proposals to compare competitive offerings. The salesperson is asked to present the proposal to the buying committee. The challenge is that, as you learned in Chapter 4, buying center members play different roles and have different needs. Therefore, some parts of the presentation and the proposal will be of particular interest to each individual. Larry Boyd, sales representative for Quantum Medical, a manufacturer of sonogram equipment, solves this challenge by preparing a separate proposal for each member of the buying committee. Financial information, for example, is usually in the copy the hospital administrator receives.

There are several options if you are going to give an oral presentation of your proposal. First, you can give the buyers a copy of the complete proposal before your presentation. During the meeting you would spend about 5 to 10 minutes summarizing the proposal and then ask for questions. Second, if you choose to give the written proposal to the buyers during the oral presentation, you may want to distribute the proposal a section at a time, as you are talking about that section. In that way you might avoid having them read ahead instead of listening to your oral presentation.

VALUE ANALYSIS: QUANTIFYING THE SOLUTION

As mentioned in Chapter 2, one of the trends in buying is more sophisticated analyses by buyers. This section explores methods available to help the buyer conduct these types of analyses.

Salespeople can strengthen the presentation by showing the prospect that the cost of the proposal is offset by added value; this process is often called **quantifying the solution** or **value analysis.** Some of the most common ways to quantify the solution are simple cost–benefit analysis, comparative cost–benefit analysis, return on investment, payback period, net present value, and opportunity cost.

Quantifying the solution is more important in some situations than in others. Some products or services (like replacement parts or repairs) pose very little risk for the prospect. These products are so necessary for the continuation of the prospect's business that very little quantifying of the solution is usually needed. Other products pose moderate risk (such as expanding the production capacity of a plant for an existing successful product) or high risk (like programs designed to reduce costs or increase sales; these present higher risk because it is hard to calculate the exact magnitude of the potential savings or sales). For moderate- and high-risk situations, quantifying the solution becomes increasingly important. Finally, certain products pose super-high risk (brand-new products or services, which are riskier because no one can calculate costs or revenues with certainty). Attempts at quantifying the solution are imperative in super-high-risk situations. In summary, the higher the risk to the prospect, the more attention the salesperson should pay to quantifying the solution.

SIMPLE COST–BENEFIT ANALYSIS

Perhaps the simplest method of quantifying the solution is to list the costs to the buyer and the savings the buyer can expect from the investment, often called the **simple cost–benefit analysis.** For this analysis to be realistic and meaningful, information needed to calculate savings must be supplied by the buyer. Exhibit 10.8 shows how one salesperson used a chart to compare the costs and benefits of purchasing a two-way radio system.

COMPARATIVE COST–BENEFIT ANALYSIS

In many situations the salesperson also compares the present situation's costs with the value of the proposed solution. Or the salesperson compares his or her product with a competitor's product. For example, a company with a premium-priced product may justify the higher price on the basis of offsetting costs in other areas. Or, if productivity is enhanced, the increased productivity has economic value. In the example in Exhibit 10.9, the current washer must be changed three times as often as the new washer, but the new washer costs much more. If a prospect heard that you want $150 for a washer and he has been paying $25, he may say no immediately. Even if you explain that the new washer lasts longer than the old one, the new washer still appears to be twice as expensive ($15,000 per year versus $7,500). But if you can identify other costs associated with changing the washer, such as overtime or lost production time, and you can quantify those costs (as Exhibit 10.9 shows), you may be able to prove that the more expensive washer actually saves money. When you quantify costs, it is important to get the prospect to determine how much is lost dollarwise in production time or how much that overtime costs. Prospects will have greater faith in the numbers they provide.

When we examine the proposal in Exhibit 10.9, we see that because the proposed washer is changed less often than the existing washer, the total costs per year are only $27,000 compared with current costs of $43,500. This leads to a proposed savings of $16,500 per year!

EXHIBIT 10.8

Cost–Benefit Analysis
for a Mobile Radio

Monthly Cost

Monthly equipment payment (five-year lease/purchase)*	$1,352.18
Monthly service agreement	295.00
Monthly broadcast fee	464.00
Total monthly cost for entire fleet	$2,111.18

Monthly Savings

Cost savings (per truck) by eliminating backtracking, unnecessary trips (based on $.21/mile × 20 miles × 22 days/month)	$92.40
Labor cost savings (per driver) by eliminating wasted time in backtracking, etc. ($6.50/hour × 25 minutes/day × 22 days/month)	59.58
Total cost savings per vehicle	151.98
Times number of vehicles	× 32
Total monthly cost savings for entire fleet	$4,863.36

	Years 1–5	Year 6+
Monthly savings	$4,863.36	$4,863.36
Less: monthly cost	2,111.18	759.00*
Monthly benefit	2,752.18	4,104.36
Times months per year	× 12	× 12
Annual benefit	$33,026.16	$49,252.32

*Payment reflects ongoing cost of service agreement and broadcast fees.

EXHIBIT 10.9

An Example of a
Comparative
Cost–Benefit Analysis

	Your Current Washer			Our Proposal (The Maxi-Seal Washer)		
	Quantity	Cost	Total	Quantity	Cost	Total
Initial cost	300	$25	$7,500	100	$150	$15,000
Changing cost*	300	120	36,000	100	120	12,000
Total costs per year			$43,500			$27,000
		Proposed savings	$16,500			

*Changing cost per unit = 8 hours × $15 labor = $120.

RETURN ON INVESTMENT

The **return on investment** (ROI) is simply the net profits (or savings) expected from a given investment, expressed as a percentage of the investment:

$$\text{ROI} = \text{Net profits (or savings)} \div \text{Investment}$$

Thus if a new product costs $4,000 but saves the firm $5,000, the ROI is 25 percent ($5,000 ÷ $4,000 = 1.25). Many firms set a minimum ROI for any new products, services, or cost-saving programs. Salespeople need to discover the firm's minimum ROI or ROI expectations and then show that the proposal's ROI meets or exceeds those requirements.[19] In the washer example, ROI would be calculated by taking the savings in labor hours ($36,000 – $12,000 = $24,000) and dividing by the investment. In this case you would use the incremental cost of $7,500, and ROI equals 320 percent.

PAYBACK PERIOD

The **payback period** is the length of time it takes for the investment cash outflow to be returned in the form of cash inflows or savings. To calculate the payback period, you simply add up estimated future cash inflows and divide into the investment cost. If expressed in years, the formula is

$$\text{Payback period} = \text{Investment} \div \text{Savings (or profits) per year}$$

Of course, the payback period could be expressed in days, weeks, months, or any other period.

As an example, suppose a new machine costs $865,000 but will save the firm $120,000 per year in labor costs. The payback period is 7.2 years ($865,000 ÷ $120,000 per year = 7.2 years).

In the washer example (Exhibit 10.9), payback would be calculated by dividing $7,500 (incremental cost of the new washers per year) by $24,000 (savings in labor hours per year), which is .31 years. So in less than four months, the extra cost of the new washers is covered by the savings.

Thus, for the buyer, the payback period indicates how quickly the investment money will come back to him or her and can be a good measure of personal risk. When a buyer makes a decision, his or her neck is "on the line," so to speak, until the investment money is at least recovered. Hence it's not surprising that buyers like to see short payback periods.

We have kept the discussion simple to help you understand the concept. In reality the calculation of the payback period would take into account many other factors, such as investment tax credits and depreciation.

NET PRESENT VALUE

As you may have learned in finance courses, money left idle loses value over time (a dollar today is worth more than a dollar next week) because of inflation and the firm's cost of capital. Thus firms recalculate the value of future cash inflows into today's dollars (this process is called *discounting the cash flows*). One tool to assess the validity of an opportunity is to calculate the **net present value (NPV)**, which is simply the net value today of future cash inflows (discounted back to their present value today at the firm's cost of capital) minus the investment. The actual method of calculating NPV is beyond the scope of this book, but many computer programs and calculators can calculate NPV quickly and easily.

$$\text{Net present value} = \frac{\text{Future cash inflows discounted}}{\text{into today's dollars}} - \text{Investment}$$

For large capital outlays, the prospect usually needs to see the return on investment, payback period, and/or net present value.

© Mary Messenger

As an example of the preceding formula, let's assume that a $50 million investment will provide annual cash inflows over the next five years of $15 million per year. The cash inflows are discounted (at the firm's cost of capital), and the result is that they are actually worth $59 million in today's dollars. The NPV is thus $9 million ($59 million – $50 million).

As with ROI and payback period, many firms set a minimum NPV. In no case should the NPV be less than $0. Again, we have kept this discussion quite simple to help you understand the basic concept.

OPPORTUNITY COST

The **opportunity cost** is the return a buyer would have earned from a different use of the same investment capital. Thus a buyer could spend $100 million to buy any of the following: a new computer system, a new production machine, or a controlling interest in another firm.

Successful salespeople identify other realistic investment opportunities and then help the prospect compare the returns of the various options. These comparisons can be made by using any of the techniques we have already discussed (simple cost–benefit analysis, ROI, payback period, NPV). For example, a salesperson might help the buyer determine the following information about the options identified:

	NPV	Payback Period
Buying a new telecommunications system	$1.6 million	3.6 years
Upgrading the current telecommunications system	0.4 million	4.0 years

Salespeople should never forget that prospects have a multitude of ways to invest their money.

OTHER METHODS OF QUANTIFYING THE SOLUTION

Among the many ways to quantify the solution are turnover, contribution margin, accounting rate of return, and after-tax cash flows. Salespeople should use methods that are understandable to the prospect and reflect the prospect's unique needs and concerns.

When you are selling to resellers, there are additional ways to quantify the solution. We discuss these methods fully in Chapter 15.

DEALING WITH THE JITTERS

Let's face it. For many people giving a presentation is a frightening experience. Even seasoned salespeople can get the jitters when the presentation is for a very important client or when the prospect has been rude in an earlier meeting. It all comes down to fear: "fear of failure, embarrassment, losing control, being judged, not being perfect, disappointing our superiors, showing our weaknesses, exposing our ignorance, looking like idiots, being laughed at, and going blank."[20] The reasons don't even have to be valid. If you have the jitters, you need to help resolve them.

Here are some tips from the experts on how to reduce presentation jitters:[21]

- Know your audience well. Building Partnerships 10.1 shows how one salesperson used knowledge of her audience to successfully plan for and strengthen a presentation to law enforcement trainers.

KNOW YOUR AUDIENCE WELL

Let's say you represent a small town of 32,000 in Texas (whose claim to fame is that it has a big airport), and you're trying to convince a 1,000-member organization to hold its meeting there. Other cities the group is considering include Chicago and Orlando. What would you do? How would you plan? What would you say and do in your presentation? As Marcy Roitman, national sales manager for Grapevine, Texas, knows, the most important thing is to really know your audience.

Marcy did her homework. Among other things, she

- Contacted cities that had hosted past conferences for this group, the American Society of Law Enforcement Trainers.

- Learned that police officers are tough on the outside but much softer on the inside and have strong ties to patriotism and fellow police officers.

- Practiced her presentation over and over and over.

- Requested to be among the last cities to give her presentation to the buying committee.

So what did she do during the presentation? Lots! She

- Started with humor: Where in the world is Grapevine, Texas?

- Involved actual police training officers from her own town to explain the firing ranges, driving tracks, and other pertinent things that Grapevine offers.

- Sold features that benefited her particular audience: a hotel that can accommodate the entire conference group, 80 nearby restaurants, the ability to close down the town's main street for a group function, and possible side trips, such as a day on a ranch.

- Gave a six-projector multimedia presentation of what she had to offer. This included patriotic images of police officers, fireworks, and other "small town" images.

- Ended with an emotional appeal: a moving rendition of Lee Greenwood's song "Proud to Be an American."

When the lights came on, some of the officers were in tears. Did she get the business? Are you kidding? Of course she did.

Source: John F. Yarbrough, "Toughing It Out," *Sales & Marketing Management,* June 1996, pp. 82–83.

- Know what you're talking about. Keep up to date.[22]

- Prepare professional, helpful visuals. These not only help your audience understand the presentation, but also can help you remember some important points.

- Be yourself. Don't try to present like someone else.

- Get a good night's sleep.

- For presentations to groups, feed off the energy and enthusiasm of several friendly, happy-looking people in your audience. (Note: That's what professors often do!)

- Recognize the effect of fear on your body and reduce the accompanying stress manifestations by stretching, taking deep breaths to relax breathing, and so on.

- Visualize your audience as your friends—people who are interested and eager to hear what you have to say.

- Psych yourself up for the presentation. Think of the successes you have had in your life (previous presentations that went well or other things you have done well).

- Realize that everyone gets nervous before a presentation at times. It is natural. In fact, it can help you keep from being cocky.

- PRACTICE, PRACTICE, PRACTICE!! And finally, practice.

Summary

Strengthening communication with the buyer is important. It helps to focus the buyer's attention, improves the buyer's understanding, helps the buyer remember what was said, and can create a sense of value.

Many methods of strengthening communication are available. These include such items as word pictures, stories, humor, charts, models, samples, gifts, catalogs, brochures, pictures, ads, maps, illustrations, testimonials, and test results. Media available include portfolios, 35mm slides, VCRs, computers, and visual projectors.

A backbone of many sales presentations is the product demonstration. It allows the buyer to get hands-on experience with the product, something most other communication methods do not offer. Handouts and written proposals can also strengthen presentations.

It is often important to quantify the solution so the buyer can evaluate the costs in relation to the benefits he or she can derive from the proposal. Some of the more common methods of quantifying the solution include simple cost–benefit analysis, comparative cost–benefit analysis, return on investment, payback period, net present value, and a calculation of opportunity cost.

All communication tools require skill and practice to be used effectively. Outstanding salespeople follow a number of guidelines to improve their use of visuals, demonstrate their products more effectively, and reduce their nervousness.

KEY TERMS

computer-interactive whiteboard   288
computer-peripheral whiteboard   288
digital asset management   285
digital sales assistant (DSA)   285
document cameras   288
electronic copyboard   288
electronic whiteboard   288
executive summary   294
flip chart   284
handouts   292
linear DSA   286
multiple-sense appeals   276

net present value (NPV)   298
nonlinear DSA   286
opportunity cost   299
payback period   298
portfolio   283
quantifying the solution   296
request for proposal (RFP)   293
return on investment (ROI)   297
simple cost–benefit analysis   296
testimonials   282
value analysis   296
visual presenters   288

Questions and Problems

1. Men tend to respond more to jokes involving sexual innuendo than women do. Assume this statement is true for a male buyer you are going to call on next Tuesday. You learn that he loves jokes with a sexual bent. Is there any reason you should *avoid* using a joke with a sexual theme when calling on him?

2. J. H. Patterson of National Cash Register fame trained sales representatives to "talk with their pencils." What advantages does the use of this type of sales aid offer?

3. A Herman Miller salesperson has planned a sales call to sell the Aeron office chair to a large insurance firm's corporate headquarters. She has developed a presentation around visual illustrations in a desktop easel portfolio. After placing the easel in front of her prospect, she seats herself on the right side and begins her presentation. As she gets to the second page of the portfolio, the prospect picks it up and starts thumbing through it, looking at the pictures and illustrations. The prospect says, "Go ahead with your presentation. I can hear you while I glance through your portfolio."

   a. What should the salesperson do? Explain the reasons for the action you recommend.

   b. How can she effectively communicate product features of office chairs in a portfolio?

4. When it comes to making substantial outlays for hospital surgical equipment, hospital administrators understandably like to be shown the machines. Obviously, however, even the most enterprising sales representative cannot bring an oxygenator (which performs the work of lungs during open heart surgery) to the hospital. The conventional sales rep relies on the power of words to convince administrators to visit the demonstration center or another hospital that is currently using this product. Can you think of a better way to make a presentation to the prospect?

5. Assume you plan a flight demonstration to prove some of the claims you have made for a new-model Piper, Cessna, or Beechcraft airplane. Would the demonstration be the same for each of these three individuals: a nervous person, an economy-minded person, and a performance-minded person? Explain.

6. How could you demonstrate the following products?
   a. A stereo speaker in a showroom.
   b. A word processor in an office.
   c. Shatterproof plate glass in a factory.
   d. Air conditioning in an industrial warehouse.
   e. A water purifier to a potential reseller.

7. Which communication tools would you use to provide solid proof for the following concerns expressed by prospects?
   a. No one has asked me to carry the product.
   b. I think the costs are higher than my benefit from it.
   c. I don't believe I could ever learn how to use that product feature.
   d. I don't have time to go see your plant in New York. Further, I don't think your plant has the most modern equipment, which you'd need to order to produce a product of the quality we are looking for.
   e. You look too young to service my account.
   f. I'm not sure how your product compares to the competitor's product.

8. This chapter generally described visual aids as positive, useful tools for salespeople. When should visual aids not be used? Are there any times when they could actually be detrimental to communication effectiveness? Explain.

9. Sometimes things don't go the way you plan them. What would you do in each of the following situations?
   a. The power goes off in the middle of a computer demonstration, and you lose all of the data you have been inputting for the last eight minutes.
   b. The buyer says, "Look, I don't want to see a bunch of pictures and charts! Just tell me how you'll save me money."
   c. You involve the prospect by having her help you calculate the savings she will enjoy with your machine. While putting the last number in the calculator, she apparently hits the wrong key. As a result, she calculates the time needed to recoup her investment as 258 years instead of the actual 14 years.
   d. You hand the prospect a page from your price book. He takes it, looks at it, opens his desk drawer, and tosses it in. Because your industry has severe price competition, your company's policy forbids you to leave your price sheet with anyone.
   e. You are showing your buyer some items in the portfolio, and you accidentally knock it off the desk. The rings open up, and the pages scatter all over the floor.
   f. You offer the prospect a sample of your new food product. He tastes it, makes a face, and says, "That's really pretty awful tasting!"

g. You are in the middle of using a computer to demonstrate returns on investment at various pricing points. Suddenly you forget how to call up the next screen. No matter how hard you try, you just can't remember what to do next!

h. You are in the middle of painting a word picture when the buyer is interrupted by a phone call. The call lasts about five minutes. The buyer turns back to you and says, "Now, where were we?"

10. Which communication tools would you use to communicate the following facts?

a. We have been in business for over 100 years.

b. I am dependable.

c. Even though I've been selling this product for only two months, I do possess the necessary product knowledge.

d. I know our last product was a flop, but this product was developed with extensive test marketing.

e. Unlike our competitors, my company has never been sued by a customer.

11. Assume that you are selling a new sound system to a movie theater in your town. The system will cost $350,000. It is estimated that the new system will improve sound quality so much that more patrons will watch movies. You expect revenues to increase by $39,000 each year over the next 20 years. At the movie theater's cost of capital, the discounted cash inflows have a value today of $400,000. Use this information to calculate the following:

a. Return on investment.

b. Payback period.

c. Net present value.

Case Problems

CASE 10.1

Boeing 717 Jets

The Boeing Company, after merging with McDonnell Douglas, is the world's largest aerospace company. It is the world's largest producer of commercial jetliners and military aircraft and is the largest NASA contractor. The firm has annual revenues of more than $56 billion and has customers in 145 countries. Boeing employs 210,000 people worldwide.

The Boeing 717-200 commercial airplane was launched in October 1995 to serve the growing market for planes that accommodate about 100 passengers. The Boeing 717 is designed to operate supereconomically on high-frequency, short-to-medium-range routes. Its basic configuration consists of five-across coach class seating. All-new interiors include illuminated handrails, the largest windows of any 100-seat jetliner, vacuum lavatories, and larger-than-average overhead baggage racks. The Boeing 717 is environmentally sensitive with reduced fuel consumption, reduced exhaust emissions, and significantly lower sound levels compared to competing aircraft now in service. The plane was designed by a global team of supplier–partners in North America, Europe, and Asia. Their goal was to create the highest-quality new airplane at the lowest possible acquisition cost.

Two BMW/Rolls-Royce BR715 engines deliver an estimated 18,500 to 21,000 pounds of thrust each. The plane is 124 feet long and 29.3 feet high, and has a total wingspan of 93.3 feet. The Boeing 717 has a range of 1,781 statute miles in the basic configuration. With optional auxiliary fuel tanks, the plane can travel 2,304 statute miles. The first delivery of the new design went to AirTran Airways in summer 1999.

Source: Information for this case came from the Boeing website (www.boeing.com) and the 1995 annual report of McDonnell Douglas.

1. Describe how you would use the communication tools described in this chapter to sell the Boeing 717 to one of the major U.S. airlines (such as Delta, United, or American). Assume that not one of the major U.S. airlines has purchased a Boeing 717 in the past. You are giving a presentation to three members of the airline: the VP of purchasing (an analytical, who is most concerned about acquisition costs), the VP of operations (a driver, who is most concerned about operating costs such as maintenance and fuel consumption), and the VP of marketing (an expressive, who is most concerned about how the airline's customers will like the plane). The airline you are selling to has a variety of makes and models of jets in its fleet, including Boeing jets.

2. Develop a short (five-minute) linear digital sales assistant (DSA) slide show that you can use to introduce the Boeing 717-200 to potential buyers at a trade show.

CASE 10.2

Strengthening the Presentation: A Prevideo Exercise

Consolidated Employee Benefits is a national provider of medical and hospital insurance programs to large and medium-size corporations. Consolidated has set the industry standard for progressive benefits administration. A sophisticated, computerized communications system links all 64 of its regional branch offices. Consolidated is proud of its record of offering policyholders fast and accurate claims processing and customized benefits programs.

In the video segment you will watch, Dennis Savage, an account executive for Consolidated, is meeting with Tom Hong, vice president of personnel for Arrow Computers, and the benefits administrator, Pat Olsen. Savage has had several meetings with Olsen and has learned that Arrow intends to change its insurance carrier. Savage also knows that two other companies are vying for the account. Savage knows that the final decision on a new carrier will be made by Tom Hong and the company treasurer, Jordon Gates. Savage's objective is to get Hong to arrange for him to present a proposal to Gates.

The package Savage is selling has four main features:

Features	Benefits
Fully automated claims processing provides a standard turnaround of 7 to 10 days and, by special arrangement, a 3-to-5-day turnaround.	Accelerates claims payments.
Highly trained claims administrators review all claims rejected by system.	Ensures reliable claims settlement; reduces employee complaints about settlements.
Sixty-four regional claims offices are located throughout the country.	Meets a growing company's need for conveniently located offices to ensure efficient service; maintains local focus on available medical services; provides quick, informed aid to employees from nearby offices.
A computerized communications system links all regional offices with computer terminals in client offices.	Minimizes settlement problems by providing online reports.

QUESTIONS

To help you think about how Savage could strengthen the presentation to Hong and Olsen, answer the following questions:

1. For each of the four features, list several ways that Savage can strengthen the presentation (such as charts, samples, letters, demonstrations). Make sure your suggestions will provide concrete proof of each asserted feature and benefit.
2. Describe any special tactics you would utilize with regard to strengthening the presentation under the following scenarios:
   a. Hong is a driver; Olsen is an analytical.
   b. Hong is an expressive; Olsen is an expressive.
3. Reread the case and be prepared to watch the videotape in class. Watch how Savage actually strengthened the presentation. Make notes about what Savage had to do before the meeting to prepare to use the tools he employed.

Additional References

Anderson, Rolph E. "Personal Selling and Sales Management in the New Millennium." *Journal of Personal Selling and Sales Management*, Fall 1996, pp. 17–32.

Chalmers, Sophie. "Winning Pitches." *Director* 53, May 2000, p. 17.

Chronister, Tom. "Technology Should Not Keep Audiences in the Dark." *Presentations*, May 2002, p. 62.

Deeter-Schmelz, Dawn R., and Rosemary Ramsey. "A Conceptualization of the Functions and Roles of Formalized Selling and Buying Teams." *Journal of Personal Selling and Sales Management*, Spring 1995, pp. 47–60.

Duman, Jill. "Presentation Prowess: Presenter Helps Companies Get the Message Out the Right Way." *Customer Relationship Management*, December 2001, pp. 63–64.

Gaulke, Sue. *101 Ways to Captivate a Business Audience*. New York: AMACOM, 1997.

Gilyard, Burl. "Speaking Volumes." *Presentations*, March 2002, pp. 38–43.

Hill, Julie. "The Big Cheese." *Presentations*, May 2002, pp. 29–34.

Hill, Julie. "The Charting Game." *Presentations*, March 2001, pp. 51–54.

Hill, Julie. "Must the Show Go On?" *Presentations*, April 2000, pp. 37–41.

Holcombe, Marya W., and Judith Stein. *Presentations for Decision Makers*. New York: Van Nostrand Reinhold, 1996.

Jeary, Tony. *Inspire an Audience: Proven Secrets of the Pros for Powerful Presentations*. Dallas: Trophy Publishing, 1997.

Jennings, Richard G., and Richard E. Plank. "When the Purchasing Agent Is a Committee." *Industrial Marketing Management* 24 (1995), pp. 411–19.

Kushner, Malcolm. *Successful Presentations for Dummies*. Foster City, CA: IDG Books Worldwide, 1996.

McIlhenny, David. "Listeners Come for Content, So Be Sure It Reaches Them." *Presentations*, March 2001, p. 80.

Merritt, Mark. "The Great White Way: What's New in Electronic Whiteboards." *Presentations*, September 2001, pp. 55–60.

Presentations magazine. Much information is available at its website: www.presentations.com.

Rasmusson, Erika. "Making a Presentation? Break a Leg!" *Sales and Marketing Management*, January 2000, p. 73.

Regenold, Stephen. "Crop, Resize, Touch Up, Print: A Buyers Guide to the Latest Digital-Imaging Software." *Presentations*, October 2001, pp. 75–79.

Richardson, Priscilla. "Use These Tricks to Speak All Day without Growing Hoarse." *Presentations,* May 2000, p. 90.

Rotondo, Jennifer. "Learn to Use Colors That Reinforce Your Message." *Presentations,* April 2001, pp. 28–29.

Strout, Erin. "A Decent Proposal." *Sales and Marketing Management,* March 1999, p. 85.

Strout, Erin. "The Show Must Go On." *Sales and Marketing Management,* November 2001, pp. 52–59.

Strout, Erin. "Throwing the Right Pitch." *Sales and Marketing Management,* April 2001, pp. 61–64.

"The Pros and Cons of High-Tech Presenting: Four Experts Debate the Challenges of Communicating in the Gizmoed Age." *Presentations,* April 1999, pp. 33–41.

Venkatesh, R.; Ajay K. Kohli; and Gerald Zaltman. "Influence Strategies in Buying Centers." *Journal of Marketing,* October 1995, pp. 71–82.

Weiss, Wendy. "Do You Have Sales Stage Fright?" *Working Woman,* October 1999, pp. S14–15.

Whittler, Tommy E. "Smooth Operators: Reflections on Sales Representatives' Influence Expressions." *Journal of Personal Selling and Sales Management,* Spring 1996, pp. 53–56.

Zielinski, Dave. "Motivating the Masses." *Presentations,* May 2001, pp. 41–48.

Zielinski, Dave. "Stop Joking and Start Using Humor to Communicate Better." *Presentations,* January 2000, pp. 35–42.

11 Responding to Objections

SOME QUESTIONS ANSWERED IN THIS CHAPTER ARE:

- When do buyers object?
- What objections can be expected?
- How should salespeople prepare to respond to objections?
- Which methods and techniques are effective when you are responding to objections?
- How do you deal with tough customers?

All salespeople encounter objections during the selling process. All buyers, at some time or other, voice an objection to something the salesperson says or does. In fact, some customers may raise irrational or irrelevant objections that have nothing to do with the product, the company, or the salesperson. Of course, buyers also raise valid concerns and questions.

Skill in responding to objections is just as necessary as skill in making appointments, conducting interviews, demonstrating products, and obtaining commitment. When new salespeople realize buyers' objections are a normal and natural part of the sales process, they can treat such objections as sales opportunities.

"As my training and experience progressed, I learned that precall planning and organization are essential to effectively addressing client objections. Since the majority of objections are quite common, it's crucial to plan what my responses will be."

Virginia Wichern, 3M

PROFILE

Upon graduating in May 2000 with a major in professional sales from the College of St. Catherine's, Virginia Wichern moved directly into a sales position with 3M in the Occupational Health and Environmental Safety Division. One of the first things her trainer told her was the importance of recognizing objections as a valuable selling tool. "Up to that point the salesperson and the customer are just talking. If you don't have some objections, you don't really have the customer's interest." Instead of feeling defensive or intimidated by client objections, Virginia learned to look at them in a more constructive light. She feels that "objections really secure my job" and that "without objections, there wouldn't be a need for me."

"As my training and experience progressed, I learned that precall planning and organization are essential to effectively addressing client objections. Since the majority of objections are quite common, it is crucial to plan what my responses will be. Plus, by anticipating objections, I'm able to incorporate a discussion about the issue into the presentation, addressing some of the concerns before they even come up. The more I get to know my customers and build relationships with them, the more I try to tailor my presentations to the type of objections they may bring up.

"A common objection that I've learned to address is price. Like most salespeople, I compete in a market with some very solid competitors, and for some product segments these are generally considered commodity markets. Adding to the dilemma, 3M is known for innovative and high-quality products that are rarely the least expensive. This gives me the opportunity to come up with other creative ways to sell 3M products against less expensive alternatives."

To understand Virginia's approach to overcoming the price objection, consider an actual challenge that she faced. "I worked with a company that required respiratory protection for some welding conditions.

The minimum protection required by OSHA for most welding applications is a filtering face piece that cost from $1.50 to $8.00 per employee. I was proposing a powered air system that cost approximately $1,500 per employee, so price objections were significant. I used a CD-ROM program that calculates the hidden costs of eye injuries and workers' compensation–related expenses. I explained to the safety director that by choosing a powered air respiratory system, which is significantly more expensive than the minimum required protection, the company would be able to increase overall productivity. I reasoned that because 3M's face shield would eliminate eye injuries, employees would not be interrupted with trips to a clinic or need eye-related breaks. The cost of sending a worker to a clinic because of an eye injury is large. Eye injuries mean lost production time and increased insurance costs. An extra benefit would be the added comfort the respirator would provide the employees, allowing them to work at a longer, steadier pace than with an alternative system. By using a computer program to quantify lost time and production from eye injuries into a dollar figure for the customer, I was able to encourage the costomer to consider the larger picture. By selection of a higher-quality product, savings could be realized from a system that not only met compliance standards but also cut down on workers' compensation costs. I've found this to be an effective way of addressing the price objection. It encourages the customer not only to think of the cost of the product itself, but also to consider the many hidden costs surrounding the issue."

As Virginia has learned, "if you can make the customer understand the long-term cost savings derived through other benefits, the customer will realize how the price of the product is recovered, and buy that product."

Visit Our Website @ www.3m.com/occsafety.

WHEN DO BUYERS RAISE OBJECTIONS?

An **objection** is a concern or a question raised by the buyer. Salespeople should do everything they can to encourage buyers to voice concerns or questions. The worst type of objection is the one the buyer refuses to disclose because a hidden objection cannot be dealt with. Many sales have been lost because salespeople didn't find out the objections or didn't helpfully respond to them.

Salespeople can expect to hear objections at any time during the buyer–seller relationship (see Chapter 4 for a review of the buying process). Objections are raised when the salesperson attempts to secure an appointment, during the approach, during the presentation, when the salesperson attempts to obtain commitment, and during the after-sale follow-up. Objections can also be made during formal negotiation sessions (see Chapter 14).

SETTING UP AN INITIAL APPOINTMENT

Prospects may object to setting the appointment times or dates that salespeople request to introduce the product. This type of objection happens especially when products, services, or concepts are unfamiliar to the buyer. For example, a commercial benefits salesperson for Prudential might hear the buyer make the following statement when asked to meet and learn more about a cafeteria-style benefits package: No, I don't need to see you. I've not heard much about what you're selling, so it must not be too good. The same types of objections can also occur during the approach.

THE PRESENTATION

Buyers can offer objections during the approach to the presentation (see Chapter 9). They may not like or believe the salesperson's attention-getting opening statement. They may not wish to engage in small talk or may not agree with statements made by the seller attempting to build rapport. Buyers may object to the salesperson's stated goals for the meeting.

Objections often come up to points made in the presentation. For example, a computer disaster recovery salesperson for XL DATACOMP might hear this objection: We've never had a flood before! Why should I pay so much money for a service I may never use?

Such objections usually show the prospect's interest; thus they can actually be desirable. Compared to a prospect who just says, No thanks, and never raises his or her concerns, selling is easier when buyers voice their concerns because the salesperson knows where the buyers stand and that they are paying attention.

Buyers sometimes let the salesperson deliver the entire presentation without showing any reaction. Judging the effectiveness of the presentation is difficult in such circumstances.

ATTEMPTING TO OBTAIN COMMITMENT

Objections may be voiced when the salesperson attempts to obtain commitment. For example, a Ryerson Steel salesperson who has just asked the buyer permission to talk to the buyer's chief engineer may hear this objection: No, I don't want you talking to our engineers. My job is to keep vendors from bugging our employees.

Skill in uncovering and responding to objections is very important at this stage of the sales call. Also, knowing the objections that are likely to occur helps the salesperson prepare supporting documentation (letters of reference, copies of studies, and so on).

Salespeople who hear a large number of objections at this point in the sales call probably need to further develop their skills. An excessive number of objections may indicate a poor job at needs identification and the omission of significant selling points in the presentation. It may also reveal ineffective probing during the presentation to see whether the buyer understands or has any questions about what is being discussed.

Some buyers need extensive information before committing themselves because they have to justify their decision to others.

Jon Feingersh/The Stock Market

AFTER THE SALE

Even buyers who have agreed to purchase the product or service can still raise objections. During the installation, for example, the buyer may raise concerns about the time it is taking to install the equipment, the quality of the product or service, the customer service department's lack of friendliness, or the credit department's refusal to grant the terms the salesperson promised. To develop long-term relationships and partnerships with buyers, salespeople must carefully respond to these objections. After-sale service is more fully discussed in Chapter 13.

COMMON OBJECTIONS

Prospects raise many types of objections. Although listing every objection is impossible, this section attempts to outline the most common buyer objections.

It should be noted that some buyers like to raise objections just to watch salespeople squirm uncomfortably. (Fortunately, most buyers aren't like that!) Seasoned buyers, especially, sometimes like to make life difficult for sellers, particularly for young, nervous sellers. For example, Peggy, a manufacturer's salesperson for Walker Muffler, used to call on a large auto parts store in an attempt to have the store carry her line of mufflers. Jackie, the store's buyer, gave Peggy a tough time on her first two calls. At the end of her second call, Peggy was so frustrated with the way she was being treated that she decided never to call there again. However, as she was walking out of the store, she ran into a Goodyear rep who also called on Jackie to sell belts and hoses. Because the two salespeople were on somewhat friendly terms, Peggy admitted her frustrations to the Goodyear rep. He replied, "Oh, that's just the way Jackie operates. On the third call he is always a nice guy. Just wait and see." Sure enough, Peggy's next call on Jackie was not only pleasant but also productive! Buyers like Jackie usually just want to see the sales rep work hard for the order.

The following sections examine the five major types of objections (objections related to needs, product, source, price, and time), which are summarized in Exhibit 11.1, as well as several other objections that salespeople sometimes hear.

OBJECTIONS RELATED TO NEEDS

I DO NOT NEED THE PRODUCT OR SERVICE

A prospect may validly state that the company has no need for what the salesperson is selling. A manufacturer that operates on a small scale, for example, may have no use for expensive machinery designed to handle large volumes of work. Similarly, a salesperson who is selling an accounts receivable collection service will find that a retailer that sells for cash does not require a collection service.

Objections Related to Needs

I do not need the product or service.

I've never done it that way before.

Objections Related to the Product

I don't like the product or service features.

I don't understand.

I need more information.

Objections Related to the Source

I don't like your company.

I don't like you.

Objections Related to the Price

I have no money.

The value does not exceed the cost.

Objections Related to Time

I'm just not interested today.

I need time to think about it.

Salespeople may encounter objections such as "My business is different" or "I have no use for your service." These objections, when made by an accurately qualified buyer, show that the buyer is not convinced that a need exists. This problem could have been prevented with better implication and need payoff questions (see Chapter 9).

If the salesperson cannot establish a need in the buyer's mind, that buyer can logically be expected to object. In **pioneer selling**—selling a new and different product, service, or idea—the salesperson has more difficulty establishing a need in the buyer's mind. For example, salespeople for Alpine Paper Company often hear "I don't think we need it" when the buyer is asked to carry a line of recycled paper products.

I'VE NEVER DONE IT THAT WAY BEFORE

Most human beings are creatures of habit. Once they develop a routine or establish a custom, they tend to resist change. Fear or ignorance may be the basis for not wanting to try anything new or different. The buyer's natural tendency to resist buying a new product or changing from a satisfactory brand to a new one can be found behind many objections.

Habits and customs also help to insulate the prospect from certain risks to some degree. For example, suppose you are selling a new line of office chairs to Harry, a newly promoted assistant buyer. If Jane, the previous assistant buyer and now the senior buyer, bought your competitor's product, Harry would appear to take less risk by continuing to buy from your competitor. If Harry buys from you, Jane may think, I've been doing business with the other firm for 15 years. Now, Harry, you come in and tell me I've been doing it wrong all these years? I'm not sure you're going to be a good assistant buyer.

OBJECTIONS RELATED TO THE PRODUCT

I DON'T LIKE THE PRODUCT OR SERVICE FEATURES

Often the product or service has features that do not satisfy the buyer. At other times the prospect will request features currently not available. Customers may say,

I don't like the design.

It doesn't taste good to me!

I wish you included free maintenance.

We prefer printed circuits.

I was looking for a lighter shade of red.

I can't get my machines repaired quickly by your service technicians.

It took a month for us to receive our last order.

I DON'T UNDERSTAND

Sometimes objections arise because customers do not understand the salesperson's presentation. Because these objections may never be verbalized, the seller must carefully observe the buyer's nonverbal cues. (See Chapter 5 for a discussion of nonverbal communication.) Misunderstandings frequently occur with customers who are unfamiliar with technical terms, unaware of the unique capabilities of a product, or uncertain about benefits arising from services provided with the product, such as warranties. Unfortunately, buyers often will not admit that they do not understand something.

For example, when desktop publishing programs were introduced for personal computers, a salesperson for an IBM distributor gave a presentation to a very busy plant manager of a consumer products firm. The new software would allow the manager to create and produce the plant's monthly newsletter to plant employees in-house, instead of sending the work out to be typeset and run off. The manager, however, did not understand the new product's concept. He thought that the software would create the newsletter but that the firm would still have to send the work out to be typeset and run off. However, he did not want to appear ignorant and simply told the salesperson that he was not interested. The rep never knew that the manager simply had not understood the product until later, when the manager bought a competitor's desktop publishing program.

I NEED MORE INFORMATION

Some buyers offer objections in an attempt to get more information. They may have already decided that they want the product or service but wish to fortify themselves with logical reasons they can use to justify the purchase to others. Also, the salesperson may not have provided enough credible proof about a particular benefit.

Conflict may also exist in the buyer's mind. One conflict could be a struggle taking place between the dictates of emotion and reason. Or the buyer may be concerned about the risk, and the seller hasn't sufficiently sold value. The buyer may be trying to decide between two competitive products or between buying and not buying. Whatever the struggle, buyers who object to get more information are usually interested, and the possibility of obtaining commitment is good.

OBJECTIONS RELATED TO THE SOURCE

I DON'T LIKE YOUR COMPANY

Most buyers, especially industrial buyers, are interested in the sales representative's company because the buyer is put at risk if the seller's firm is not financially sound, cannot continually produce the product, and so forth. These buyers need to be satisfied with the selling company's financial standing, personnel, and business policies. Buyers may ask questions such as these:

Isn't your company a new one in the field?

Is it true your company lost money last year?

OK, I'M SMALL: SO WHAT'S THE BIG DEAL?

Small isn't always beautiful, at least in the eyes of some companies who are looking for a supplier. Buyers can fear that a small supplier might not be able to meet their needs or might not even be in business next month. Suppose you're a seller for a small firm. What can you do to help buyers feel better about your company's small size?

For starters, how about reducing the risk with a money-back guarantee? That's what MTS-Group Inc., a small recruiting firm, does. If its clients aren't totally satisfied in the first 60 days, they not only get their money back but they also get free job-posting advertising. But suppose your firm doesn't offer such a guarantee. Now what?

Stephen Paliska of PPS Parking, Inc., suggests sampling. Let prospects sample what you are selling and see whether they like it. Stephen does it for his valet parking services to prospective hotels. Sure, he is giving the hotels a free week of valet parking services. But so far, every hotel has signed up for either a one-year or two-year contract. Not bad, huh?

What else can a seller do? How about using your company's small size to your advantage by giving prospects a sense of the personalized attention you can offer? Providing your home phone number in case they need to reach you after hours, making yourself available for the buyer's community outreach activities, and offering other personal services can demonstrate the kind of one-on-one attention they may not get from a larger firm. In fact, these activities might help prospects visualize the entrepreneurial spirit your firm possesses, something that can be very attractive to companies looking for new solutions to old problems.

It may take creativity. It may take time and extra energy. But there's no reason small firms can't find a niche in the ultracompetitive world of selling today.

Sources: Personal correspondence and experience; Susan Greco, "When Small Isn't Beautiful: You Can Overcome Fears about Your Company's Size," *Inc.*, March 1998, pp. 97–99.

How do I know that you'll be in business next year?

Isn't your firm the one that was indicted by a federal grand jury for price fixing?

Your company is a little too small to meet our needs, don't you agree? (See Building Partnerships 11.1 for a discussion about how a seller can respond to this objection and build a partnering relationship with the concerned buyer.)

Your company isn't very well known, is it?

Who does your designing?

Can your company give us the credit we have been receiving from other companies?

How do I know you can deliver on time?

Why does your company have a bad image in the industry?

Of course, buyers who don't want to be rude may not actually voice these concerns. But unvoiced questions about the sales rep's company may affect their decisions and the long-term partnerships the sales rep is trying to establish.

I DON'T LIKE YOU

Sometimes a salesperson's personality clashes with a prospect's. Effective salespeople know that they must do everything possible to adjust their manner to please the prospect. At times, however, doing business with some people appears impossible.

Prospects may object to a presentation or an appointment because they have taken a dislike to the salesperson or because they feel they cannot trust the salesperson. Candid prospects may say,

You seem too young to be selling these.

You've never worked in my industry. How can you be trained to know what I need?

I don't like to do business with you.

You're a pest! I don't have any time for you.

You and I will never be able to do business.

More commonly, the prospect shields the real reason and says something like this:

We don't need any.

Sorry, we're stocked up.

I haven't any time today to discuss your proposition.

In some situations, the buyer may honestly have difficulty dealing with a particular salesperson. If the concern is real (not just an excuse), the seller's firm sometimes institutes a **turnover (TO)**, which simply means the account is given to a different salesperson. Unfortunately, TOs occasionally occur because the buyer has gender, racial, or other prejudices or because the salesperson is failing to practice adaptive selling behaviors.

Thinking It Through	Assume that you have worked as a salesperson for an industrial chemical firm for six months. You have attended a two-week basic selling skills course but have not yet attended any product knowledge training classes. You are making a sales call with your sales manager. The buyer says, "Gee, you look too young to be selling chemicals. Do you have a chemistry degree?" Before you get a chance to respond, your manager says, "Oh, he [meaning you] has already completed our one-month intensive product knowledge course. I guarantee he knows it all!" What would you say or do? What would you do if the buyer later asked you a technical question?

OBJECTIONS RELATED TO THE PRICE

I HAVE NO MONEY

Companies that lack the resources to buy the product may have been classified as prospects. As indicated in Chapter 7, the ability to pay is an important factor in lead qualification. An incomplete or poor job of qualifying may cause this objection to arise.

When leads say they cannot afford a product, they may have a valid objection. If so, the salesperson should not waste time; new prospects should be contacted.

THE VALUE DOES NOT EXCEED THE COST

Most buyers must sacrifice something (called *opportunity costs*—see Chapter 10) to buy a product. The money spent for the product is not available for other things. When we buy as individuals, the choice may be between the down payment on a new car and a vacation trip; for businesses, it may be between expanding the plant and distributing a dividend to stockholders.

EXHIBIT 11.2

Value: The Relationship between Costs and Benefits

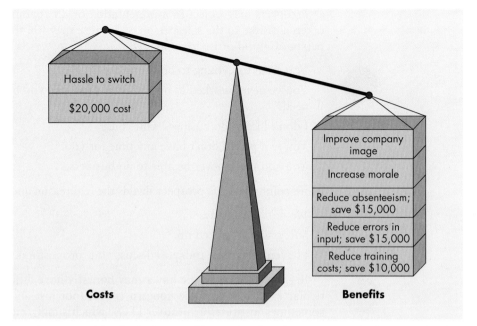

Costs	Benefits
Hassle to switch	Improve company image
$20,000 cost	Increase morale
	Reduce absenteeism; save $15,000
	Reduce errors in input; save $15,000
	Reduce training costs; save $10,000

Note: If costs outweigh benefits, the decision will be not to buy. If benefits outweigh costs, the decision will be to buy.

Buyers usually object until they are sure that the value of the product or service being acquired more than offsets the sacrifice. Exhibit 11.2 illustrates this concept. The question of value received often underlies customers' objections.

Whatever the price of a product or service, somebody will object that it is too high or out of line with the competition. Here are some other common price objections:

I can't afford it.

I can't afford to spend that much right now.

I never accept the first price quoted by a salesperson.

I was looking for a cheaper model.

I don't care to invest that much; I'll use it only a short while.

I can beat your price on these items.

We can't make a reasonable profit if we have to pay that much for the merchandise.

We always get a special discount.

I'm going to wait for prices to come down.

Although objections about price occur more often than any other kind of objection, they may be just masks to hide the real reason for the buyer's reluctance. (A more complete discussion of dealing with price objections appears later in this chapter.) Implicit in many price objections is the notion of product or service quality. Thus the buyer who states that your price is too high may actually be thinking, The quality is too low for such a high price.

OBJECTIONS RELATED TO TIME

I'M JUST NOT INTERESTED TODAY

Some prospects voice objections simply to dismiss the salesperson. The prospect may not have enough time to devote to the interview, may not be interested in the particular product or service, may not be in the mood to listen, or may have decided because of some unhappy experiences not to face further unpleasant interviews.

These objections occur when salespeople are cold calling (see Chapter 7) or try to make an appointment. Particularly aggressive, rude, impolite, or pesky salespeople can expect prospects to use numerous excuses to keep from listening to a presentation.

I NEED TIME TO THINK ABOUT IT

Buyers often object to making a decision "now." Many, in fact, believe that postponing an action is an effective way to say no. Salespeople can expect to hear objections such as the following, especially from analyticals and amiables (see Chapter 6):

I haven't made up my mind.

I want to think it over.

I'd like to talk it over with my partner.

See me on your next trip.

I'm not ready to buy.

I don't want to commit myself.

I think I'll wait awhile.

I want to look around.

I'm waiting until my inventory goes down.

I want to turn in the old unit at the end of the season.

Just leave me your literature. I'll study it and then let you know what we decide.

OTHER OBJECTIONS

Listing every possible objection that could occur under any situation would be impossible. However, following are a number of additional objections that salespeople often hear:

I'm satisfied with the company we use now.

We have a reciprocity agreement with your competitor.

We are all stocked up.

We have no room for your line.

This buyer is providing the nonverbal cues that may say "I don't want to commit myself."

Francisco Cruz/SuperStock

There is no demand for your product.

You'll have to see Mr. X.

Sorry, but I just don't do business with blacks or women.

My brother-in-law is in the business.

Your competitor just came out with a brand-new product that seems superior to yours.

I've heard complaints from my friends who use your product.

I prefer to do business with Arab-owned firms.

Sure, we can do business. But I need a little kickback to make it worth my time and trouble.

I believe we might be able to do business if you are willing to start seeing me socially.

It's a lot of hassle in paperwork and time to switch suppliers.

PREPARING TO RESPOND

DEVELOP A POSITIVE ATTITUDE

Responding to objections in a helpful manner requires careful thought and preparation. Exhibit 11.3 summarizes the activities of successful salespeople in this regard. To respond to objections effectively, nothing can substitute for having a positive attitude. Proper attitude is shown by answering sincerely, refraining from arguing or contradicting, and welcoming—even inviting—objections. Objections should be expected and never taken personally.

Simply pretending to be empathetic is useless; buyers can easily see through such pretense. Also, once the buyer gets the idea that the salesperson is talking for effect, regaining that buyer's confidence and respect will be almost impossible. Empathy shows as much in the tone of voice and facial expressions as in the actual words spoken.

The greatest evidence of sincerity, however, comes from the salesperson's actions. One successful advertising agency owner states, "I have always tried to sit on the same side of the table as my clients, to see problems through their eyes." Buyers want valid objections to be treated seriously; they want their ideas to be respected, not belittled. They look for empathetic understanding of their problems. Real objections are logical to the prospect regardless of how irrational they may appear to the salesperson. Salespeople must assume the attitude of helper, counselor, and adviser and act accordingly. To do so, they must treat the prospect as a friend, not a foe. In fact, buyers will feel more comfortable about raising objections and will be much more honest the more they trust the salesperson, the better the rapport, and the stronger the partnering relationship.

The temptation to prove the prospect wrong, to say "I told you so" or "I'm right and you're wrong," is always strong. This kind of attitude invites debate,

---

EXHIBIT 11.3

Responding to Objections: Traits and Behaviors of Successful Salespeople

- They develop and maintain a positive attitude about objections.
- They commit to always tell the truth.
- They anticipate objections and prepare helpful responses.
- They relax and listen and never interrupt the buyer.
- They address known problems before the prospect does; that is, they forestall known concerns.
- They make sure that the objection is not just an excuse.
- They are sincerely empathetic to the buyer's objections.

encouraging—perhaps even forcing—the prospect to defend a position regardless of its merits. Egos get involved when prospects find their positions bluntly challenged. Most will try to defend their own opinions under these circumstances because they do not want to lose face. The sales presentation may then degenerate into a personal duel that the salesperson cannot possibly win. Arguing with, contradicting, and showing belligerence toward a prospect are negative, unwise actions.

The reality is that salespeople run into more rejection in a day than most people have to absorb in weeks or months. Because of the emotional strain, many see selling as a tough way to make a living. However, salespeople must remember that objections present sales opportunities. People who object have at least some level of interest in what the salesperson is saying. Further, objections provide feedback as to what is really on the prospect's mind. Only when this openness exists can a true partnering relationship form. To capitalize on these opportunities, salespeople must show that they welcome any and all objections. Salespeople have to make the prospect believe they are sincerely glad the objection has been raised. This attitude shows in remarks such as the following:

I can see just what you mean. I'd probably feel the same way.

I'm glad you mentioned that, Mr. Atkinson.

That certainly is a wise comment, Ms. Smith, and I can see your problem.

If I were purchasing this product, I'd want an answer to that same question.

Tell me about it.

Maintaining a positive attitude toward objections will go a long way toward building goodwill.

COMMIT TO ALWAYS TELL THE TRUTH

In dealing with prospects and customers, truthfulness is an absolute necessity for dignity, confidence, and continued relations.[1] Lying and deception are not a part of a successful long-term relationship. Over time it will be hard to remember which lie you told to which customer. Salespeople should avoid even white lies and half-truths when they answer objections.

Salespeople who tell lies, even small ones, need to recognize they have a problem and then find ways to change. One way to avoid lies is to spend more time gaining knowledge about their products and the products of their competitors. Sellers who do so aren't as tempted to lie to cover up the fact that they don't know some information requested by the prospect. Sellers also should commit to tell the truth, even if competitors don't follow suit.[2] It is simply the right thing to do.

ANTICIPATE OBJECTIONS

Salespeople must know that at some time, objections will be made to almost everything concerning their products, their companies, or themselves. Common sense dictates that they prepare answers to objections that are certain to be raised (probably 80 percent or more can be anticipated) because few salespeople can answer objections effectively on the spur of the moment.[3]

Many companies draw up lists of common objections and effective answers and encourage salespeople to become familiar with these lists. Some firms also videotape practice role-plays to help salespeople become more proficient in anticipating objections and responding effectively in each situation.

Successful sales representatives may keep a notebook and record new objections they encounter, along with any new ideas for responses; they also pick up helpful suggestions at sales meetings. They recognize that different personality types may require different types of responses or proof, and plan accordingly.

When salespeople know an objection will be raised, they should have good answers ready. The ability to respond readily to objections helps to build confidence. Unanticipated or unanswerable objections can easily cause embarrassment and lost sales.

RELAX AND LISTEN—DO NOT INTERRUPT

When responding to an objection, listen first and then answer the objection. Allow the prospect to state a position completely. Do not interrupt with an answer, even if the objection to be stated is already apparent to you. Listen as though you have never heard that objection before. Unfortunately, too many salespeople conduct conversations somewhat like the following:

> SALESPERSON: Mr. Clark, from a survey of your operations, I'm convinced you're now spending more money repairing your own motors than you would by having us do the job for you—and really do it right!
>
> CUSTOMER: I wonder if we are not doing it right ourselves. Your repair service may be good. But after all, you don't have to be exactly an electrical genius to be able to . . .
>
> SALESPERSON: Just a minute now! Pardon me for interrupting, but there's a point I'd like to make right there! It isn't a matter of anyone being a genius. It's a matter of having a heavy investment in special motor repair equipment and supplies like vacuum impregnating tanks and lathes for banding armatures, boring bearings, and turning new shafts.
>
> CUSTOMER: Yeah, but you don't understand my point. What I'm driving at . . .
>
> SALESPERSON: I know what you're driving at. And I assure you you're wrong! You forget that even if your own workers are smart cookies, they just can't do high-quality work without a lot of special equipment.
>
> CUSTOMER: But you still don't get my point! The idea I'm trying to get across—if I can make myself clear on this third attempt—is this: The maintenance workers that we now have doing motor repair work . . .
>
> SALESPERSON: Could more profitably spend their time on plant troubleshooting! Right?
>
> CUSTOMER: That isn't what I was going to say! I was trying to say that between their troubleshooting jobs, instead of just sitting around and shooting the bull . . .
>
> SALESPERSON: Now wait a minute, Mr. Clark. Wait jus-s-t a minute! Let me get a word in here! If you've got any notion that a good motor rewinding job can be done with somebody's left hand on an odd-moment basis, you've got another think coming. And my survey here will prove it! Listen![4]

Obviously, this type of attitude and interruption is likely to bring the interview to a quick end.

Salespeople should plan to relax as buyers offer objections. It's even OK to plan on using humor in your answers to objections. For example, if the buyer objects to the standard payments and asks how low your company could go, you could respond as follows:

> Well, if I could get the bank to send *you* money each month, would you buy it?

After laughing, the seller could talk about the various payment options. Using humor, as in this example, may help defuse the nervousness that both buyer and seller are feeling during this part of the process. For more insight into the use of humor, see Chapter 10.

FORESTALL KNOWN CONCERNS

Good salespeople, after a period of experience and training, know that certain features of their products or services are vulnerable, are likely to be misunderstood, or are materially different from competitors' products. The salesperson may have products with limited features, may have to quote a price that seems high, may be unable to offer cash discounts, may have no service representatives in the immediate area, or may represent a new company in the field.

In these situations, salespeople often forestall the objection.[5] To **forestall** is to prevent by doing something ahead of time. In selling, this means salespeople raise objections before buyers have a chance to raise them. For example, one salesperson forestalled a concern about the different "feel" of a split computer keyboard (the ones that are split down the middle to relieve stress and strain on the hands and wrists):

> I know you'll find the feel to be different from your old keyboard. You're going to like that, though, because your hands won't get as tired. In almost every split keyboard I've sold, typists have taken only one day to get accustomed to the new feel, and then they swear that they would never go back to their old-fashioned keyboards again!

A salesperson might bring up a potential price problem by saying, You know, other buyers have been concerned that this product is expensive. Well, let me show you how little it will really cost you to get the best.

Some salespeople do such a good job of forestalling that buyers change their minds without ever going on record as objecting to the feature and then having to reverse themselves. Buyers are more willing to change their thinking when they do not feel constrained to defend a position they have already stated.

Although not all objections can be preempted, the major ones can be spotted and forestalled during the presentation. Buyers have no need to raise an objection already stated—and answered—by the salesperson.

Forestalling can be even more important in written proposals (see Chapter 10), since immediate feedback between buyer and seller is not possible. Such forestalled objections can be addressed throughout the proposal. For example, on the page describing delivery terms, the seller could insert a paragraph that begins this way: "You may be wondering how we can promise an eight-day delivery even though we have such a small production capacity. Actually, we are able to . . . because . . .

Another option for forestalling objections in written proposals is to have a separate page or section titled something like "Concerns You May Have with This Proposal." The section could then list the potential concerns and provide responses to them.

EVALUATE OBJECTIONS

Objections may be classified as unsatisfied needs (that is, real objections) or excuses. **Excuses** are concerns expressed by the buyer that mask the buyer's true objections. Thus the comment "I can't afford it now" would simply be an excuse if the buyer honestly could afford it now but did not want to buy for some other reason.

A buyer seldom says, "I don't have any reason. I just don't want to buy." More commonly, the buyer gives a reason that appears at first to be a real objection but is really an excuse: "I don't have the money" or "I can't use your product." The tone of voice or the nature of the reason may provide evidence that the prospect is not offering a sincere objection.

Salespeople need to develop skill in evaluating objections. No exact formula has been devised to separate excuses from real objections. Sometimes it is best to follow up with a question:

BUYER: I wish it came in red.

SELLER: If I can get it in red, will you buy it?

If the buyer says yes, you know the concern is real. If the buyer says no, you know the buyer is just offering the objection about color as an excuse.

Circumstances can also provide a clue as to whether the objection is a valid concern. In cold calling, when the prospect says, "I'm sorry, I don't have any money," the salesperson may conclude that the prospect does not want to hear the presentation. However, the same reason offered after a complete presentation has been made and data on the prospect have been gathered through observation and questioning may be valid. Salespeople must rely on observation, questioning, knowledge of why people buy (see Chapter 4), and experience to determine the validity of reasons offered for objections.

Usually buyers are serious about their jobs, are qualified to buy, and deal professionally. When they are not, however, they may offer objections that are hard to deal with and hard to evaluate. For example, some buyers will act in ways that serve their own interests to the detriment of the firm they work for. Some buyers do not like their jobs or their firms. Some buyers are so egotistical they think they know it all. Some are doing their job to the best of their ability, but that ability just isn't too great. Separating excuses from valid objections might be difficult in these types of situations.[6]

EFFECTIVE RESPONSE METHODS

Any discussion of specific methods and techniques for responding to objections needs to emphasize that no one perfect method or technique exists for answering all objections completely. Some prospects, no matter what you do, will never believe their objections have been adequately addressed.

In some instances spending a lot of time trying to convince the prospect may not be wise. For example, when an industrial recycling salesperson contacts a prospect who says, "I don't believe in recycling," the salesperson may better spend available time calling on some of the vast number of people who do.

Salespeople should develop a procedure for responding to objections. The following steps can be applied and adapted to most selling situations:

1. Listen carefully; don't interrupt. Let the prospect talk; don't get angry! Remember, we stated earlier that the salesperson should plan on not interrupting. Now, in the heat of the presentation it is important to follow through on that promise and actually not interrupt. A wise man said, "He that answereth a matter before he heareth it, it is folly and shame unto him."[7]

2. Confirm the objection by repeating what the prospect said. Make sure you understand the objection. Ask questions to permit the prospect to clarify objections.

3. Acknowledge the apparent soundness of the prospect's opinion. In other words, agree as far as possible with the prospect's thinking before providing an answer.

4. Evaluate the objection. Determine whether the stated objection is real or just an excuse.

5. Decide on the method(s) to use in answering the objection. Some factors to be considered are the phase of the sales process in which the prospect raises the objection; the mood, or frame of mind, evidenced by the prospect; the reason for the objection; the personality type of the prospect; and the number of times the reason is advanced. Flexibility is critical.

6. Get a commitment from the prospect. The answer to any objection must satisfy the prospect if a sale is to result. Get the prospect to agree that the objection has been answered.

This section describes seven common methods for responding to objections. As Exhibit 11.4 indicates, the first two, direct denial and indirect denial, are used only when the prospect makes an untrue statement. The next five methods—compensation, feel–felt–found, boomerang, pass-up, and postpone—are useful when the buyer raises a valid point or offers an opinion.

Before using the methods described in this section, salespeople almost always need to probe to help the prospect clarify the concerns and to make sure they understand the objection. This technique is often called the **probing method.** If the prospect says, "Your service is not too good," the salesperson can probe by saying, "I'm not sure I understand," or by asking a question. For example:

Not too good?

What do you mean by not too good? Exactly what service are you referring to?

Is service very important to you?

Can you explain what you mean?

While this probing is usually verbal, it can also include nonverbal probing. For example, Professor Donoho, at Northern Arizona University, teaches a technique called FSQS, the friendly silent questioning stare, to encourage buyers to elaborate or explain more fully what their concern is.

Many serious blunders have occurred because the salesperson did not understand the question, answered the wrong question, or failed to answer the objection fully. For example, a sales training manager was listening to a representative for a consulting firm talk about her services. At one point in the conversation, the manager asked, "Has anyone in our industry, the electrical products industry specifically, ever used this training package before?" The consultant answered, "Sure, we have sold this package to several firms. Why, just last week I received a nice letter from Colgate that had nothing but good things to say . . ." The manager did not buy the training package; he figured that if the consultant did not even know how to listen, the sales training package she was selling could not be very good either. (Chapter 5 provides many helpful suggestions regarding the art of questioning and probing.)

EXHIBIT 11.4

Common Methods for Responding to Objections

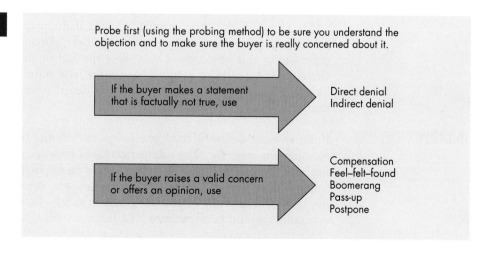

Probe first (using the probing method) to be sure you understand the objection and to make sure the buyer is really concerned about it.

If the buyer makes a statement that is factually not true, use → Direct denial / Indirect denial

If the buyer raises a valid concern or offers an opinion, use → Compensation / Feel–felt–found / Boomerang / Pass-up / Postpone

A salesperson who doesn't know the answer to the buyer's objection might say, I don't know the answer to that question. But I'll find out and get the answer to you. The seller should paraphrase the question, write it down (this step helps jog the seller's memory as well as demonstrate to the buyer that the seller really intends to follow up), gather the information, and follow up quickly and exactly as promised. If you call the customer with the information and he or she is not available, leave the information on voice mail and then call later to verify that the prospect got the information. And don't forget that it is your responsibility to know most facts, so be prepared the next time for similar and additional questions and concerns. You can be sure your competitor is going to try to have complete answers ready.

Thinking It Through	How can the use of technology (such as databases, computers, communication technology) help prevent a seller from having to answer, "I don't know the answer to that question. But I'll find out and call you with the information as soon as I can get it!"?

DIRECT DENIAL

At times salespeople face objections based on incomplete or inaccurate information by the buyer. They should respond by providing information or correcting facts. When using **direct denial**, the salesperson makes a relatively strong statement to indicate the error the prospect has made. For example:

> BUYER: I am not interested in hearing about your guidance systems. Your firm was one of the companies recently indicted for fraud, conspiracy, and price fixing by a federal grand jury. I don't want to do business with such a firm.
>
> SALESPERSON: I'm not sure where you heard that, but it simply is not true. Our firm has never been involved in such activity, and our record is clean. If you would care to tell me the source of your information, I'm sure we can clear this up. Maybe you're confusing us with another firm.

No one likes to be told that he or she is wrong, so the direct denial must be used with caution. It is appropriate only when the objection is blatantly inaccurate and potentially devastating to the presentation. The salesperson must also possess facts to back up such a denial.

The direct denial should never be used if the prospect is merely stating an opinion or if the objection is true. For example, the direct denial would be inappropriate to this objection: I don't like the feel of simulated leather products. Direct denial should be avoided even for a false statement if the objection is of little importance to the buyer. An indirect denial would be more appropriate in that case.

INDIRECT DENIAL

In the **indirect denial** method, the salesperson denies the objection but attempts to soften the response. The salesperson takes the edge off the response by agreeing with the prospect that the objection is an important one. Prospects expect salespeople to disagree; instead, a salesperson who recognizes the sincerity of the objection will carefully respect the prospect's view. This approach avoids a direct contradiction and confrontation. To begin an answer, a salesperson would do well to agree with the prospect, but only to the extent that the agreement does not weaken the validity of the salesperson's later denial. For example:

> BUYER: Your machines break down more often than those of most of your major competitors.
>
> SALESPERSON: I can see why you would feel that way. Just 10 years ago that statement would have been right on target. However, things have changed with our new quality assurance program. In fact, just last year Syncos Ratings, a well-respected independent evaluator of quality in our industry, rated us as number one for fewest breakdowns.

The important features of indirect denial are that salespeople recognize the position of the customer who makes the objection and then continue by introducing substantial evidence. The beginning statement should always be true and assure the prospect that the question is a good one. Examples of opening statements follow:

> There is some truth to what you are saying.
>
> With the market the way it is today, I can certainly see why you're concerned about that.
>
> I'll bet 90 percent of the people I call on voice the same concern.
>
> That's really an excellent question, and it allows me to clear up a misconception that perhaps I've given you.

Indirect denial should never be used if the prospect has raised a valid point or is merely expressing an opinion. It can be used for all personality types and is especially effective for amiables and analyticals because they like less assertive salespeople.

COMPENSATION METHOD

Every product has some advantages and some disadvantages compared to competing products. Also, an absolutely perfect product or service has never been developed; the firm always has to make cost–benefit decisions about what features to include.

Buyers note these trade-offs and often object because the salesperson's product is less than perfect. The wise salesperson will admit that such objections are valid and then proceed to show any compensating advantages. This approach is called the **compensation method** of responding to objections. Here is an example:

> PROSPECT: This machine has only four filling nozzles. Your competitor's has six nozzles.
>
> SALESPERSON: You're absolutely right. It has only four nozzles, but it costs $4,000 less than the competitor's models, and you said you needed a model that is priced in the lower range. Also, our nozzles are designed for easy maintenance. You have to remove only four screws to get to the filter screens. Most other models have at least 10 screws. Fewer screws will reduce downtime considerably, which is something else you said you were very concerned about.

The compensation method is an explicit use of the multiattribute model discussed in Chapter 4. A low score on one attribute can be compensated for by a high score on another attribute. In fact, the compensation method is often referred to as the **superior benefit method** because the benefit of one attribute overcomes a concern about a less important attribute. The method can be effective for many objections and concerns. It seems most appropriate for analyticals, who are accustomed to conducting trade-off analyses. However, it is useful for all other personality types as well.

Of course, the buyer may not value the compensating advantages or may really need the features at issue (perhaps the machine must have six nozzles to work with another piece of the prospect's equipment). In such cases salespeople can recommend a different product (from their own line, if available, or from a competitor) or search for other prospects.

Another time that the compensation method may be used is when the prospect says, "I'm just going to think about it. I'll be in touch with you later." The seller can show how acting today more than compensates for the "pain" of making a decision today. These reasons usually include explaining the hidden costs of delaying the decision (it will go off sale, you will be saving money over your current system each month that you have our proposed system, our product may be out of stock when you need it, summer is a particularly good time to install a new system, or the like).

FEEL–FELT–FOUND METHOD

When buyers' objections reflect their own attitudes or opinions, the salesperson can show how others held similar views before trying the product or service. In this method, called the **feel–felt–found method,** the salesperson goes on to relate that others actually found their initial opinions to be unfounded after they tried the product:

> PROSPECT: I don't think my customers will want to buy a DVD player with all of these fancy features.
>
> SALESPERSON: I can certainly see how you feel. Bob Scott, down the road in Houston, felt the same way when I first proposed that he sell these. However, after he agreed to display them next to his current DVD line, he found that his customers were very interested. In fact, he called me four days later to order more.

The sequence of the feel–felt–found method is important, as is the person or persons identified in each stage. The sequence should be as follows: I can see how *you feel . . . others felt* the same way . . . yet *they found . . .* Inexperienced salespeople often mix up the order or the parties identified (for example, by saying "yet you will find").

Although the feel–felt–found technique is sound in principle, it should probably be used sparingly. Anyone with knowledge about selling (such as professional buyers) can easily spot this method, and it may appear to be phony or canned.

A buyer may question the credibility and knowledge of a salesperson. In this situation the salesperson can use the feel–felt–found method to help resolve those concerns.

Color Day Production/The Image Bank

Proof of the salesperson's assertion in the form of a testimonial letter strengthens the method; in fact, some trainers refer to this approach as the **third-party-testimony method**. If a letter is not available, the salesperson might be able to supply the name and phone number of the third party. The salesperson should always secure the third party's permission first, however. (See Chapter 10 for suggestions for references.)

Although the feel–felt–found method can be used for all personality types, it seems most appropriate for expressives and amiables. Both types tend to care about what other people think and are doing.

BOOMERANG METHOD

When using the **boomerang method** of responding to objections, the salesperson turns the objection into a reason for acting now. This method can be used in many situations (when making an appointment, during the presentation, when attempting to secure commitment, and in postsale situations):

PROSPECT: I'm too busy to see you right now.

SALESPERSON: I know you are busy, and that's the reason I would like to take 30 minutes of your time. I operate a service designed to save busy executives like yourself up to two hours every day.

The boomerang method requires care. It can appear very pushy and "salesy." It sounds like a high-pressure sales tactic you would have heard from someone selling patent medicine in the 1800s (You can't afford not to buy this amazing little bottle of Dr. Bob's Elixir!).

This method does have useful applications, however. Often the product or service is actually designed to save the buyer substantial amounts of time or money. If the buyer objects to spending either the time to listen or the money, the boomerang method may be a powerful tool to help the buyer see the benefit of investing these resources.

This method works with most personality types. Drivers may require the boomerang technique more often than other buyers because drivers tend to erect time constraints and other barriers and are less willing to listen to just any salesperson's presentation.

PASS-UP METHOD

At times the buyer voices opinions or concerns more to vent frustration than anything else. When this occurs, the best strategy may be to use the **pass-up method:** Simply let the buyer talk, acknowledge that you heard the concern, pause, and then move on to another topic.

BUYER: Hey, you use Britney Spears in your commercials, don't you? Sure you do. Now I want to tell you that I don't like her style or what she stands for! Kids today need a role model they can look up to. What happened to the kind of role models we used to have?

SALESPERSON: I certainly understand your concern. I remember my dad talking about some of his role models and the respect he had for them. [Pause] What were we talking about? Oh, yes, I was telling you about the coupon drop we are planning.

In this example the salesperson used the pass-up method because the buyer apparently was just blowing off steam. A buyer who really wanted some response from the salesperson would have used the salesperson's pause to ask a direct question (Can't you change your commercials?) or make a statement (I refuse to do business with companies that use stars like Britney Spears in their commercials!).

In reality, a salesperson often can do little about some prospects' opinions. What are the chances that this salesperson's firm will pull a $5 million ad campaign just because one buyer objects? It is doubtful that a firm would take such action unless the buyer had tremendous power in the relationship.

Sometimes the salesperson can use the pass-up method by simply agreeing with the prospect and then moving on, which suggests to the buyer that the concern really should not be much of an issue. For example:

BUYER: You want $25 for this little plastic bottle?!

SELLER: Uh-huh. That's what they cost . . .[pause] Now do you see the switch on this side? It's used if you ever need to . . .

The pass-up method should not be used if the objection raised is factually false. Also, it should not be used if the salesperson, through probing, could help clarify the buyer's thinking on the topic. Experience is the key to making such a determination. In general, though, the pass-up method should be used very sparingly.

POSTPONE METHOD

In the early part of a sales interview, the prospect may raise objections that the salesperson would prefer to answer later in the presentation, after discovering the prospect's needs. Using the **postpone method,** the salesperson would ask permission to answer the question at a later time:

BUYER [very early in the call]: How much does the air compressor cost?

SALESPERSON: If you don't mind, I would prefer to answer that question in a few minutes. I really can't tell you how much it will cost until I learn more about your air compressor needs and know what kinds of features you are looking for.

The prospect will seldom refuse the request if the sales representative appears to be acting in good faith. The sales representative then proceeds with the presentation until the point at which the objection can best be answered.

Some objections are best answered when they occur; others can be responded to most effectively by delaying the answer. Experience should guide the sales representative. The salesperson should take care not to treat an objection lightly or let it appear that he or she does not want to answer the question. Another danger in postponing is that the buyer will be unable to focus on what the salesperson is saying until the concern is addressed. On the other hand, the salesperson is responsible for helping the buyer to critically evaluate the solution offered, and often the buyer can process information effectively only after learning preliminary facts.

Salespeople make the most use of the postponement technique when a price objection occurs early in the presentation. However, this technique can be utilized for almost any type of objection or question. For example, postponing discussions about guarantees, delivery schedules, implementation time frames, and certain unique product features until later in the presentation is often preferable.

What if the buyer is convinced that he or she deserves the answer right now? Then the salesperson should answer the objection now. Salespeople usually have more to lose by demanding that the buyer wait for information than by simply providing the answer when the buyer strongly requests it. For example:

PROSPECT: What are the delivery schedules for this new product?

SALESPERSON: I would really prefer to discuss that after we talk about our unique production process and extensive quality control measures.

PROSPECT: No, I want to know now!

SALESPERSON: Well, keep in mind that my later discussion about the production process will shed new light on the topic. We anticipate a four-to-five-month delivery time after the contract reaches our corporate headquarters.

USING THE METHODS

The seven methods just discussed appear in sales training courses across all industries and geographic boundaries. To help you more easily distinguish the differences among the various techniques, Exhibit 11.5 provides an example of the use of each method for the objection "Your product's quality is too low."

Salespeople often combine methods when answering an objection. For example, a price objection may initially be postponed and then be discussed later, using the compensation method. At other times several methods can be used in one answer. Here is an example:

BUYER: I don't think this product will last as long as some of the other, more expensive competitive products.

SALESPERSON: That's probably the very reason you should buy it [boomerang method]. It may not last quite as long, but it is less than half the cost of competitive products [compensation method]. I can certainly understand your concern, though. You know, Mark Hancock felt the way you do. He was concerned about the product's life. But after he used our product for one year, he found that its life expectancy didn't create any problems for his production staff [feel–felt–found method].

Before moving on with the presentation, the salesperson needs to make sure that the buyer agrees that all objections have been completely answered. Without this commitment, the salesperson does not know whether the buyer understands the

---

EXHIBIT 11.5

Responding to Objections: Using Each Method

Objection: Your product's quality is too low.

Responses*

Direct denial: That simply is not true. Our product has been rated as the highest in the industry for the last three years.

Indirect denial: I can certainly see why you would be concerned about quality. Actually, though, our product has been rated as the highest in the industry for the last three years.

Compensation: I agree that our quality is not as high as that of some of our competitors. However, it was designed that way for consumers who are looking for a lower-priced alternative, perhaps just to use in a weekend cottage. So you see, our somewhat lower quality is actually offset by our much lower price.

Feel–felt–found: I can certainly understand how you feel. Mortimer Jiggs felt the same way before he bought the product. But after using it, he found that the quality was actually equal to that of other products.

Boomerang: The fact that the quality is lower than in other products is probably the very reason you should buy it. You said that some of your customers are looking for a low-priced product to buy for their grandchildren. This product fills that need.

Pass-up: I understand your concern. You know one of the things I always look for is how a product's quality stacks up against its cost. [Pause] Now, we were talking about . . .

Postpone: That's an interesting point. Before discussing it fully, I would like to cover just two things that I think will help you better understand the product from a different perspective. OK?

*These are not necessarily good answers to the stated objection. Also, the choice of method would depend on whether the objection is factual or not. Thus the replies given in this table are designed simply to differentiate the various methods.

answer or whether the buyer's concerns have been fully addressed. To achieve this commitment, the salesperson can use one or more of the following types of phrases:

Did I answer your question?

Does that make sense?

Do you see why that issue is not as important as you originally thought?

I hope I haven't confused you.

Do you have any more questions?

OBJECTIONS WHEN SELLING TO A GROUP OF BUYERS

Selling to a group of buyers (see Chapter 9) requires some extra care.[8] If one person offers an objection, the seller should rephrase the question and try to get a sense of whether other buyers share the concern. At times it may make sense to throw the issue back to the group. For example, if a buyer says that the people in his or her department won't attend the type of training sessions being proposed, the seller might respond as follows: Does anyone else have that same problem in their department? You all know your organizational climate better than I do. Have any of you found a way to deal with that issue that you would like to share with us? Any response from the seller should usually be directed to all buyers, not just the one who asked the question. After responding, the seller needs to make sure that all buyers are satisfied with the answer before moving on.

THE PRICE OBJECTION

Sales managers continually hear from salespeople that price is the most frequently mentioned obstacle to obtaining commitment. In fact, about 20 percent of buyers are thought to buy purely on the basis of price (which means that a full 80 percent buy for reasons other than price). As a result, all salespeople need to prepare for price objections. This section relates the concepts covered in this chapter to this common objection. Selling Scenario 11.1 describes how one salesperson deals with price objections.

Price is still an issue even between partnering firms. One leading firm in its industry has estimated that only 3 percent of its orders are sold at list price; the rest are price discounted.[9]

Before moving on with the presentation, the salesperson needs to make sure the buyer agrees that all objections have been completely answered.

Larry Williams/Masterfile

HOW LOW DO YOU THINK WE SHOULD LOWER OUR PRICE?

Jason Higgins sells display creations for trade show events and exhibits. Price objections are common in his industry, but one prospect went a little too far. The prospect—we'll call him George—was asking for a price that was below even Jason's cost to produce. George even claimed that he had found a lower price from a competitor. Now the only problem is that Jason was friends with this competitor and was well aware of the competitor's prices and costs as well. In short, there was no way George had actually gotten such a low quote from the competitor.

Jason decided a different tactic was needed to help George look at prices objectively. "At your company, what's an acceptable, not optimal, markup?" Jason asked his buyer. After some reluctance, George replied, "I suppose 30 percent or thereabouts."

Jason turned to a page in his portfolio that displayed his company's actual costs to produce the product, and highlighted all the applicable items. He wrote down the

actual shipping and labor charges that this sale would produce. Finally, he asked George to add up all the costs and calculate Jason's markup.

George looked over the list and started adding up the numbers. He shook his head and did it again. He seemed to be shocked by what the calculator was telling him.

"At *your* company, an acceptable markup, not an ideal markup, is at least 30 percent," Jason concluded. "*Our* actual profit is likely 12–14 percent. How reasonable is this?"

Needless to say, Jason made his point. George placed the order, and Jason secured a longtime customer.

Source: Jason Higgins, "Integrity Pays: Opening the Books," *Track Selling Times: The Voice of the Sales Profession* 132, November 1, 2000, as seen at http://www.MaxSacks.com/tstimes.html. Page viewed on November 1, 2000.

When faced with a price objection, salespeople should ensure that they have up-to-date information, establish the value of the product, and use communication tools effectively.

USE UP-TO-DATE INFORMATION

Successful salespeople make sure they have the most current pricing information available to them. They know not only their prices, but competitors' prices as well. Firms are helping salespeople in this regard. For example, Cisco Systems, maker of networking products for the Internet and most corporate intranets, has developed an intranet site for its salespeople called the Sales Dashboard.[10] If a Cisco salesperson finds that the company's price points are a little higher than the competition, the salesperson can use the Sales Dashboard to look for some sales or trade-in program that she or he can leverage to get the deal. It is important for sellers to have correct pricing facts.

ESTABLISH THE VALUE

The product's value must be established before the salesperson spends time discussing price.[11] The value expected determines the price a prospect is willing to pay. Unless the salesperson can build value to a point at which it is greater than the price asked, a sale will not occur. As a rule, value cannot be established during the early stages of the presentation.

Price objections are best handled with a two-step approach. First, the salesperson should try to look at the objection from the customer's viewpoint, asking questions to clarify the customer's perspective:

Too high in what respect, Mr. Jones?

Would you mind telling me why you think my price is too high?

Could you tell me how much we are out of line?

We are usually quite competitive on this model, so I am surprised you find our price high. Are the other quotes you have for the same size engine?

What do you feel would be a fair price for this service?

After learning more about the customer's perspective, the next step is to sell value and quality rather than price. Most customers prefer to buy less expensive products if they believe they will receive the same benefits. However, many customers will pay more for higher quality when the quality benefits and features are pointed out to them. Many high-quality products appear similar to lower-quality products; thus salespeople need to emphasize the features that justify a price difference.

For example, a Premier Industrial salesperson who sells industrial fasteners and supplies may hear this objection: That bolt costs $750! I could buy it elsewhere for $75. The salesperson should reply, "Yes, but that bolt is inside the inner workings of your most important piece of production equipment. Let's say you buy that $75 bolt. How much employee time and production downtime would it take to disassemble the machine again and replace that one bolt?" The salesperson can then engage in a complete cost–benefit analysis (see Chapter 10) to solidify the point.

USE COMMUNICATION TOOLS EFFECTIVELY

One pharmaceutical salesperson often hears that her company's drug for migraines is too expensive. Her response is to paint a word picture:[12]

DOCTOR: How much does this product cost?

SALESPERSON: It costs about $45. . . There are 15 doses per bottle, so it ends up about $3 per dose.

DOCTOR: That's too much money!

SALESPERSON: Consider your patients who have to lie in the dark because their headaches are so bad they can't see straight, can't think straight, and are nauseated by migraine pain. A price of $3 is really inexpensive to relieve these patients' pain, wouldn't you agree?

Just telling customers about quality and value is not enough; they must be shown. Top salespeople use the communication tools discussed in Chapter 10 to describe more clearly the quality and value of their products. This process includes activities such as demonstrating the product, showing test results and quality control procedures, using case histories, and offering testimonials.

Intangible features can also provide value that offsets price. Some of these features are services, company reputation, and the salesperson.

SERVICES

Good service in the form of faster deliveries, technical advice, and field assistance is but one of the many intangibles that can spell value, savings, and profits to a customer. For example, one company cut its prices in response to buyers' demands. However, the company later found that what the customers really wanted was technical support. As the company cut its prices, it had only reinforced its image as low-priced with little technical support.

COMPANY REPUTATION

For a customer tempted to buy on price alone, salespeople can emphasize the importance of having a thoroughly reliable source of supply: the salesperson's company. It has been demonstrated time and again that quality is measured by the reputation of the company behind it.

THE SALESPERSON

Customers value sales representatives who go out of their way to help with problems and promotions—salespeople who keep their word and follow through when they start something. These services are very valuable to customers.

Unfortunately, the first response of many salespeople to a price objection is to lower the price. Inexperienced salespeople, desiring to gain business, often quote the lowest possible price as quickly as possible. They forget that for a mutually beneficial long-term relationship to exist, their firm must make a fair profit. Also, by cutting prices the salesperson has to sell more to maintain profit margins, as Exhibit 11.6 clearly illustrates.[13]

EXHIBIT 11.6

Look Before You Cut Prices! You Must Sell More to Break Even

A business truism says that you can cut, cut, cut until you cut yourself out of business. This can certainly apply to cutting prices in an effort to increase profits. The two don't necessarily go together. For example: Select the gross profit being earned at present from those shown at the top of the chart. Follow the left column down until you line up with the proposed price cut. The intersected figure represents the percentage of increase in unit sales required to earn the same gross profit realized before the price cut. Obviously, it helps to know this figure so you don't end up with a lot of work for nothing.

See for yourself: Assume that your present gross margin is 25 percent and that you cut your selling price 10 percent. Locate the 25 percent column under Present Gross Profit. Now follow the column down until you line up with the 10 percent cut in selling price in column 1. You will need to sell 66.7 percent more units to earn the same margin dollars as at the previous price.

	Present Gross Profit					
Cut Price	**5.0%**	**10.0%**	**15.0%**	**20.0%**	**25.0%**	**30.0%**
1%	25.0	11.1	7.1	5.3	4.2	3.4
2	66.6	25.0	15.4	11.1	8.7	7.1
3	150.0	42.8	25.0	17.6	13.6	11.1
4	400.0	66.6	36.4	25.0	19.0	15.4
5	—	100.0	50.0	33.3	25.0	20.0
6	—	150.0	66.7	42.9	31.6	25.0
7	—	233.3	87.5	53.8	38.9	30.4
8	—	400.0	114.3	66.7	47.1	36.4
9	—	1,000.0	150.0	81.8	56.3	42.9
10	—	—	200.0	100.0	66.7	50.0
11	—	—	275.0	122.2	78.6	57.9
12	—	—	400.0	150.0	92.3	66.7
13	—	—	650.0	185.7	108.3	76.5
14	—	—	1,400.0	233.3	127.3	87.5
15	—	—	—	300.0	150.0	100.0
16	—	—	—	400.0	177.8	114.3
17	—	—	—	566.7	212.5	130.8
18	—	—	—	900.0	257.1	150.0
19	—	—	—	1,900.0	316.7	172.7
20	—	—	—	—	400.0	200.0
21	—	—	—	—	525.0	233.3
22	—	—	—	—	733.3	275.0
23	—	—	—	—	1,115.0	328.6
24	—	—	—	—	2,400.0	400.0
25	—	—	—	—	—	500.0

Salespeople must learn to deal with tough prospects and customers.

Jeff Smith/The Image Bank

DEALING WITH TOUGH CUSTOMERS

A recent Dartnell study found that 51 percent of salespeople give up when faced with tough customers, rather than work with them to mutual benefit.[14] Instead, sellers need to maintain the positive attitude discussed earlier, even with rude, hard-to-get-along-with prospects. It's not easy, and it's not fun.

Sellers need to realize that we all have bad days. Maybe the buyer is just having one. If the rudeness is quite blatant and the seller believes that this behavior is just due to the timing of the visit, the seller might say, I'm sensing that this might not be the best time to talk. Should we reschedule for another time?

If the buyer continues to be unreasonably rude, you might want to kindly call attention to the fact. After all, to develop a long-term win–win relationship and partnership you both need to be on the same footing. Perhaps saying something like this will clear the air: I'm sorry, Joe. I don't know quite how to say this. But it seems to me that you wish to argue more than learn about my products. I'll gladly continue if you think we can both approach this problem with professionalism and courtesy. Of course, it is important to keep in mind the various personalities that buyers can have (see Chapter 6) and the adjustments suggested for each.

Also, remember that the buyer's culture often dictates the way he or she will respond to a seller. For example, Germans are known as being thorough, systematic, and well prepared, but they are also rather dogmatic and thus lack flexibility and the desire to compromise. As a result, sellers not accustomed to such a culture could have difficulty dealing with a German prospect who raises a price objection in a strong tone of voice.

Summary

Responding to objections is a vital part of a salesperson's responsibility. Objections may be offered at any time during the relationship between buyer and salesperson. They are to be expected, even welcomed, and they must be handled with skill and empathy.

Buyers object for many reasons. They may have no money, or they may not need the product. They may need more information or misunderstand some information already offered. They may be accustomed to another product, may not think the value exceeds the cost, or may not like the product's features. They may want to get rid of the salesperson or may not trust the salesperson or his or her company. They may want time to think or may object for many other reasons.

Successful salespeople carefully prepare effective responses to buyers' concerns. Salespeople need to develop a positive attitude, commit to always telling the truth, refrain from interrupting, anticipate and forestall known objections, and learn how to evaluate objections.

Effective methods of responding to objections are available, and their success has been proven. Methods exist both for concerns that are not true and for objections that either are true or are only the buyer's opinion. Sensitivity in choosing the right method is vital. Salespeople need to develop skill in responding to price objections and in dealing with tough customers. Nothing will substitute for developing skill in these areas.

KEY TERMS

boomerang method   327
compensation method   325
direct denial   324
excuses   321
feel–felt–found method   326
forestall   321
indirect denial   324
objection   310

pass-up method   327
pioneer selling   312
postpone method   328
probing method   323
superior benefit method   325
third-party-testimony method   327
turnover (TO)   315

Questions and Problems

1. A prospect has just raised an objection about the price of your product, a commercial DVD player. You know that the DVDs you are selling usually go on sale a couple of times each year, but you're not sure when the next time will be. It could be as soon as a few weeks. Should you tell the buyer about the possible sale?
2. When making cold calls, sales representatives often need to get through a "screen," such as a receptionist, secretary, or assistant, to reach the decision maker. How would you answer the following objections from a screen?
   a. I'm sorry, but Mr. Harris is too busy right now.
   b. We're cutting back on expenditures.
   c. Could you just leave some literature?
   d. A representative of your company was here recently.
   e. I really don't think we can afford your equipment.
3. Categorize each of the following responses into the five basic types of objections. Then illustrate one way to handle each.
   a. During a demonstration, the customer says, "You know, I really like your competitor's model."
   b. After a sales presentation, the doctor says, "You have a good drug there. Thanks for your time, and if I decide to prescribe it, I'm sure you'll find out."

c. After the salesperson answers an objection, the prospect remarks, "I guess your product is all right, but—well, I don't think I need one just now. Thanks a lot."

d. After a thorough presentation, the prospect answers, "No, I'm sorry, we just can't afford it."

e. The customer says, "Oh, no! That's really too much money. I've been looking at the same product in an industrial catalog, and I can buy the exact same product at a much lower price."

4. Mary Betando spent considerable time working with a prospective buyer. She thought a good order would be forthcoming on her next call. A portion of her conversation with the buyer went as follows:

BUYER: You know, I like your terms and the styling of your product. But how can I be sure the small parts will hold up and be available?

MARY: We've never had any complaints on the parts, and I'm sure they will be easily available.

BUYER: You are sure of that?

MARY: Well, I've never heard of any problems.

BUYER [appearing unconvinced and looking at some papers on his desk without glancing up]: I'll let you know later what I plan to do. Thanks for dropping by.

How can you improve on Mary's answer to the buyer's concern?

5. Describe the differences between postponing an objection and forestalling an objection.

6. Occasionally, a buyer will offer several objections at one time. How would you respond if a buyer made the following comments without pausing: Say, does this machine use 110 or 220 volts? What kind of service will you provide monthly? What is the estimated life of this equipment, and have you sold it to anyone else in the area?

7. Indicate the appropriate action for the sales representative who encounters the following customer attitudes:

a. I like the things this copier can do—if it really does them. It's kind of hard to believe it'll give me reliable service, though, with all these features that could go wrong.

b. Let me be plain. Your company's reputation precedes you in this office. I've had more trouble with your company than you would care to hear.

c. That sounds fine. But there's really no reason to get rid of the copier I have. It works well enough for my purposes.

d. I see what you're saying. This machine you're talking about could end up saving us some time and money.

8. You and your college admissions staff are planning to make calls to local high school students. Your objective is to help the students see the benefits of attending your college and then have them apply.

a. Make a list of objections you may expect to encounter.

b. What can you do to meet these objections effectively? List the answer you would propose and label the method used.

9. You expect to hear this objection on your next sales call: Your new product will have more service problems than your competitor's product. How would you attempt to answer the objection in each of the following situations?

a. You are calling on an amiable with whom you have been doing business for four years.

b. You are calling on an expressive for the first time.

    c. You are calling on an analytical who bought one of your products three years ago but has bought nothing since.

    d. You are calling on a driver who currently uses your competitor's product.

10. You have been describing to a secretary and her boss a new office chair that your firm just introduced. The chair is designed to relieve back strain while the sitter uses a personal computer. The secretary seems very interested and says, "I would really like that!" The boss says, "Well, if it's what you want, OK. How much does it cost?" At your reply, "This one is $498," the boss exclaims, "For that little thing?" What should you say or do?

11. For each of the following objections, provide answers that clearly demonstrate the direct denial and indirect denial methods. Assume each objection is not true.

    a. Fishers don't need a boat that goes this fast!

    b. The cost of replacing the air bag in the car will be too high.

    c. I've heard that your firm is a pyramid organization. Products sold in that manner are usually a scam!

    d. Land is inexpensive in this rural area. It would be much easier and more cost-effective to just develop a new landfill than to build this recycling operation you are discussing.

    e. I heard your particle board is manufactured with resins that can cause cancer.

    f. The scent of this L'Essence fragrance is not identical to the fragrance you say you are imitating.

12. For each of the following objections, provide answers that clearly demonstrate the compensation method, boomerang method, feel–felt–found method, postpone method, and pass-up method. Assume all the objections are either true or are the prospect's opinion.

    a. Midwest Express does not fly to all the destinations to which our team needs to fly.

    b. I don't think our customers will like the lighter tint of the lenses of your Revo sunglasses.

    c. Your water purification units are not approved by the Environmental Protection Agency.

    d. My customers have never asked for this new L'Oréal hair color product.

    e. Your prices are the absolute highest in the plumbing tool industry.

    f. I don't like the way you use female models in your Coors promotions at bars.

Case Problems

CASE 11.1
Calaway Park

Calaway Park, western Canada's largest outdoor family amusement park, is located just 10 kilometers west of the city limits of Calgary on the Trans Canada Highway. The park offers a wide variety of rides that appeal to the entire family. For the younger set, these include Boulder Bumpers bumper cars, the Calaway Express train, the Super Jet roller coaster, Red Baron planes, a carousel, Tot Yachts, and others. Older children and adults enjoy the Big Eli Ferris wheel, the Corkscrew roller coaster, bumper boats, the Flume log ride, Paratrooper, Tip Top, and other rides. The entire family can enjoy together the Turn Pike antique car ride and Rocky Mountain Rail train ride.

The park offers other amusements as well, including a kiddie corral (including a ball crawl and a swinging bridge), a fishing hole, mini golf, midway games, and live daily entertainment at the Showtime Theatre and the Celebration Square Stage. Plus street entertainment is available, and characters perform throughout the day.

Calaway offers a number of places to eat that appeal to a wide variety of tastes and styles. These include Sweet Toothe, Mini Donuts, Burger Bistro, Franks for the Memories, Burger Hut, Big Chill, Pretzels and Churros, Fingers & Fries, Cotton Candy/Sno Cones, Corn Dogs, Terrace Garden Restaurant, and Showtime Munchies.

The park is open daily in the summer from 10 A.M. to 8 P.M. and on Saturday and Sunday in the fall from 11 A.M. to 6 P.M. Regular admission is $21.00 (ages 7–49); seniors and juniors get a discount ($13.00 and $15.00, respectively). Children under age 2 are free.

You are calling on the Calgary Police Service, which has seven district offices and seven community police stations located throughout the Calgary, Alberta, area. Assume that the service has 450 employees. You are trying to convince the service to hold a catered picnic at Calaway Park.

The catered picnic has several features. Admission prices are reduced to $11.00 (all prices include sales tax) for a complete park day pass, which includes unlimited rides, attractions, and entertainment (children under age 2 as well as season pass holders are free). For every 30 guests, the Calgary Police Service will receive one free admission. Picnic menu packages include potato chips; soft drink; one side dish of potato salad, macaroni salad, coleslaw, baked beans, or corn-on-the-cob; and one of these entrees:

Superdog Delight barbecued hot dog—$6.75

The Big Beef Burger 1/4 pound barbecued burger—$7.00

Chicken Deluxe barbecued chicken breast—$9.00

Additional soft drinks are $1.25, milk is $1.00, coffee is $50.00 per urn, beer is $4.25, and wine coolers are $4.50 each. Desserts can be added: Brownies are $1.00, ice cream treats are $0.75, and a super sundae bar is $2.50 each.

The Calgary Police Service has several options for its annual picnic in the area. These include parks (Fort Calgary Historic Park, Heritage Park, Prehistoric Park, city and province parks), the zoo, Botanical Gardens, and other amusement providers.

Source: The Calaway Park Web pages (www.calawaypark.com) as well as other Web pages related to Calgary, viewed March 30, 2002.

Questions

1. What objections could the buyer raise? (Use any assumptions necessary to develop this list.)
2. Provide a response to each objection you listed in question 1 (make any assumptions necessary to create your response). Include the name of the method you recommend for each objection.

CASE 11.2

Responding to Objections: A Prevideo Exercise

Commercial Furniture Systems (CFS) is a manufacturer and importer of modular office furniture and accessories. CFS offers its clients traditional office furniture as well as its designer-influenced Lugano Line. The Lugano Line was created specifically to meet the requirements of ultramodern design applications and unusual office layout situations.

CFS has recently brought to market several new products, including System-Tech office workstations and a line of replaceable modular wall panels that are available in various materials.

CFS is very proud of its newly developed computerized inventory and truck-tracking system, an innovation it believes will place the firm way ahead of the competition.

In the office furniture industry, interior designers and furniture manufacturers (like CFS) often develop strong professional relationships. When these relationships exist, it is difficult for a competing manufacturer to gain recognition from a designer.

In this video segment Catherine Craig, an account executive for CFS, is meeting with Joyce Lee, vice president of special projects for Clinton Associates, a large architectural design firm. Craig was referred to Lee by one of Clinton's clients. Craig knows that Clinton designed the interiors of several buildings for the Miller & Huntsman organization and that in each case it specified furniture from Harrison Company. She also knows that Lee is very happy with Harrison Company.

Craig's objective is to convince Lee to review a proposal for the use of CFS products on a Miller & Huntsman project.

Questions

To help you think about the objections Joyce Lee might raise in this meeting and how you think Catherine Craig should respond, answer the following questions:

1. List objections you think might occur during this first meeting between Lee and Craig.
2. Describe how you would respond to each objection listed in question 1. Be sure to label the method you recommend.
3. Reread the case and be prepared to watch the videotape in class. Watch for Lee's actual objections and Craig's responses. Evaluate Craig's responses.

Additional References

Cohen, Andy. "Don't Succumb to Price Pressures." *Sales and Marketing Management*, March 2001, p. 14.

Goldner, Paul S. "Overcoming Price Objection." *Agency Sales* 30, February 2000, pp. 61–63.

Hunt, Kenneth A., and R. Edward Bashaw. "A New Classification of Sales Resistance." *Industrial Marketing Management* 28, 1999, pp. 109–18.

Jeffrey, Brian. "Handling the Dreaded Price Objection." *Canadian Manager*, Spring 1997, pp. 26–27.

Joseph, Kissan. "On the Optimality of Delegating Pricing Authority to the Sales Force." *Journal of Marketing* 65, January 2001, pp. 62–70.

Lorge, Sarah. "Turning Objections into Sales Opportunities." *Sales & Marketing Management*, March 1999, p. 88.

Rackham, Neil. "Winning the Price War." *Sales and Marketing Management*, November 2001, p. 26.

Chapter

12 Obtaining Commitment

SOME QUESTIONS ANSWERED IN THIS CHAPTER ARE:

■ How much emphasis should be placed on closing the sale?

■ Why is obtaining commitment important?

■ When is the best time to obtain commitment?

■ Which methods of securing commitment are appropriate for developing partnerships?

■ How should pricing be presented?

■ What should a salesperson do when the prospect says yes? When the prospect says no?

■ What causes difficulties in obtaining commitment, and how can these issues be overcome?

O btaining commitment occurs throughout the sales process, beginning with actions such as asking for an appointment and concluding with asking for the sale. In a partnership sales result only when the buyer is convinced that the decision to purchase is wise. Once needs are identified and satisfied, attempting to gain commitment is a logical part of the selling process. This chapter describes how to obtain commitment in an honest, straightforward way.

PROFILE

Asking for the sale, called *closing the sale,* is a moment of truth for a salesperson. For Victor Reiss, senior marketing specialist with FedEx, this moment of truth is really the easiest part of the sales call, "if and only if you have established a solid rapport with your prospective client and have addressed all problems presented in the earlier phases. Only then," Reiss believes, have "you earned the right to ask for the business."

Reiss graduated from Butler University and began his career as a territory manager for Kraft FoodService in Noblesville, Indiana. After a couple of years, he moved over to FedEx as a sales executive. He earned his MBA while working, and is now a senior marketing specialist in Memphis, developing sales strategies and working with salespeople.

His experience working with other salespeople has given Reiss a broad perspective on asking for the sale. "Sales professionals often refrain from asking for the business because they perceive they are placing the client in an awkward position or they just want to avoid being rejected," says Reiss. But as he says, "believe it or not, the client is expecting you to ask for the business." The client expects to gain something from the sale. "When you do your job well, the client expects a win–win situation, a situation in which both of you win. A win–win situation means that closing the sale is a positive and pleasant experience for both you and the prospect."

Every potential client faces a choice of whether or not to buy. It should be the aim of every sales professional to make it easy for the client to make a decision in his or her favor. As Reiss notes, though, "In some cases, a client may decide to buy in order to fulfill their emotional needs, not actual needs." He believes that it is important to understand the buyer's feelings and emotions to determine how to position the product or service. The potential for the close "is increased immeasurably by your ability to objectively and honestly put yourself in the client's shoes. In other words, a thorough understanding of the client's dilemma, or the client's psychological conflict." The client may fear buyer's

remorse, negative career implications, organizational impact, or just the unknown. Reiss believes that satisfying these concerns is as much a part of the salesperson's job as is meeting engineering specs or delivery times. "Your job is to increase the comfort zone and to align with the customer's needs."

Reiss believes that once the professional salesperson has eliminated personal closing fears, possesses an understanding of the customer, and has made a professional presentation of the benefits being offered, simple closing techniques are best. "Do your job right and you don't have to rely on manipulative closing techniques," states Reiss. He does ask the buyer's opinion often, though, and doesn't just wait until the end. "If you get a 'no,' at a minimum you have gained tremendous insight or have a barometer of the customer's likelihood to do business with your company."

Reiss also believes that there isn't just one way to close. "The appropriate closing question will depend on the sales environment and in most cases the personality of the client. Dominant clients will need to have control over the sale and may want to draw their own conclusions. On the other hand, a risk-averse client will need constant reassurance."

Closing is the pinnacle of selling achievement. As Reiss notes, "Closing the sale is when you get your return on your investment of time. It is simply the continuation and natural outgrowth of asking and is the simplest stage in the sales cycle. To put it bluntly, if you do not close the sale, you have not accomplished anything." Reiss has seen his share of what he calls "a professional visitor or professional presenter," someone who makes calls but doesn't make sales. "If you do not close the business, neither you nor your company has been remunerated for your time and efforts. Try closing on every sale in order to develop a habitual successful pattern." As Reiss exhorts, "Take a risk, what do you have to lose? When you fail to close for fear of hearing the client say no, in that same manner you have also eliminated the opportunity for the client to say yes."

Visit Our Website @ www.fedex.com.

OBTAINING COMMITMENT TODAY

Asking for the buyer's business, often called **closing,** has always received a great deal of emphasis in sales training. Hundreds of books, audiocassettes, videocassettes, and seminar speakers have touted the importance of closing. According to conventional wisdom, the key to success in any sale is to find a method or methods of closing that will make the decision maker say yes.

However, a more effective perspective on this topic has emerged. Tony Alessandra, a well-respected sales trainer, sums it up this way:

> Forget 150 ways to handle objections or 50 ways to close the sale. These are commando selling techniques or gimmicks that make up for not being good. . . The only way to develop a long-term relationship with a customer is to use a nonmanipulative, consultative selling technique. The key to nonmanipulative selling is trust. A good salesperson establishes trust by being candid, honest, forthright, and most of all a good listener.[1]

Other trainers also believe the traditional emphasis on the close damages trust, insults the buyer's intelligence, and raises the possibility of losing commitment altogether.[2] Tim Conner, president of an international sales training organization, states,

> The emphasis in sales for decades has been on the "close" of the sale. I believe that this selling strategy is no longer appropriate given present consumers' attitudes, intelligence, and their need for practical solutions and increased information about products and services available to them today from a wide variety of organizations.[3]

Solid research provides strong evidence that questions the value of closing techniques. The research, based on more than 35,000 sales calls over 12 years, has found that in a major sale, reliance on closing techniques actually reduces the chances of making a sale.[4] Further, salespeople who were specifically trained in closing actually closed fewer sales. For very low-priced products (as in door-to-door magazine sales), however, closing techniques may increase the chances of a sale.

So why even cover closing at all? Because there are nonmanipulative and trustworthy ways to gain commitment and because obtaining commitment is critical for the success of salespeople and their firms. Without a buyer's commitment, no sale takes place. Also, buyers will rarely volunteer to make the purchase, even when that decision is obviously the right thing to do. One company looks at a sale as "just another way of reaffirming the relationship," meaning that commitment to the relationship is more important than any single sale.[5] This chapter covers the topic of obtaining commitment in a manner that is consistent with the theme of the book: developing and building long-term partnerships.

PART OF THE PROCESS

The process of obtaining commitment occurs throughout the natural, logical progression of any sales call. Recall from Chapter 4 that creeping commitment occurs when a customer becomes committed to a particular course of action throughout the buying process. Salespeople actually gain commitment repeatedly: when asking for an appointment, when checking to see whether all of the customer's needs have been identified, and when asking whether the prospect would like to see a demonstration or receive a proposal. Commitment, of course, is more than just securing an order. As Exhibit 12.1 illustrates, salespeople will attempt to obtain a commitment that is consistent with the objectives of the particular sales call.

Obtaining commitment is also important in moving the account through the relationship process. Once a sale is made, salespeople begin to plan for the next

EXHIBIT 12.1

Examples of
Commitments
Salespeople May
Attempt to Obtain

Examples of Presale Commitments

- To have the prospect agree to come to the Atlanta branch office sometime during the next two weeks for a hands-on demonstration of the copier.
- To set up another appointment for one week from now at which time the buyer will allow me to do a complete survey of her printing needs.
- To inform the doctor of the revolutionary anticlotting mechanism that has been incorporated into our new drug and have her agree to read the pamphlet I will leave.
- To have the buyer agree to pass my information along to the buying committee with his endorsement of my proposal.
- To have the prospect agree to call several references that I will provide to develop further confidence and trust in my office-cleaning business.
- To have the prospect agree on the first point (of our four-point program) and schedule another meeting in two days to discuss the second point.
- To have the prospect initiate the necessary paperwork to allow us to be considered as a future vendor.

Examples of Commitments That Consummate the Sale

- To have the prospect sign an order for 100 pairs of Levi's jeans.
- To schedule a co-op newspaper advertising program to be implemented in the next month.
- To have the prospect agree to use our brand of computer paper for a trial period of one month.
- To have the retailer agree to allow us space for an end-of-aisle display for the summer presentation of Raid insect repellent.

sale or for the next level of commitment that indicates a deepening relationship. At the same time, commitment is a two-way street. Salespeople also make commitments to buyers when the sale is made.

THE IMPORTANCE OF SECURING COMMITMENT

Overall, gaining commitment tells the salesperson what to do next and defines the status of the client. For example, gaining a needs identification appointment may mean that you have a "suspect"; at the end of that call, gaining commitment for a demonstration means you have a prospect. Gain an order and you gain a customer. Without gaining commitment, the salesperson may waste time doing the wrong things.

Salespeople need to become proficient in obtaining commitment for several other good reasons. First, if they fail to obtain commitment, it will take longer (more sales calls) to obtain a sale, if at all. Taking more time with one sale means fewer sales because you lose time for prospecting and other important activities. Second, assuming the product truly satisfies the prospect's needs, the sooner the prospect buys, the sooner she or he can realize the benefits of the product or service. Third, the company's future success depends on goodwill and earning a profit. Finally, securing commitment results in financial rewards for the salesperson; in addition, meeting needs is also intrinsically rewarding for the seller.

One thing to remember is that if you have done your job well and you have a product that the buyer truly needs, then you deserve the sale. The buyer is not doing you a favor by buying, and expects you to ask for the sale if you've done your work professionally. Not only is gaining commitment important for you and your company, it is the professional thing to do. What is not professional is a high-pressure close; typically, high-pressure closing is necessary (and inappropriate) when the salesperson has *not* done a good job throughout the entire process.[6]

Thinking It Through

Think for a moment about a major purchase that you or a family member made, such as a stereo or a car. During the shopping process, what were some of the worst closes you experienced? What really angers you when you try to shop for major purchases? What made the difference between those experiences and the ones you found satisfying?

Before we get into how to obtain commitment, some time should be spent on the importance of terms and conditions of the sale and how these influence the total cost. Sometimes terms are an important need and may be presented early in the call. But we present the credit terms here because often a buyer decides what to buy and then explores the financial terms that are available.

FINANCIAL TERMS AND CONDITIONS

Price is often the last element of the deal to be presented and discussed. Yet it is often one of the most important factors when the buyer makes the decision. The final price is really a function of the terms and conditions of the sale and depends on several factors. For example, Paula Shelton, a salesperson for Cort Furniture in Washington, D.C., encountered a buyer who demanded a 15 percent price cut and several extra benefits or he would cancel a large order. She almost gave in to close the sale but then realized that getting the sale at that price and with the extra services meant that Cort would lose money. So by probing to understand what the buyer needed, she realized that more favorable payment terms would maintain the original price—and she kept the customer.

Factors that affect price are the use of quantity and other discounts, as well as credit and shipping terms. Figuring out the final actual price can be difficult, especially in situations with many options and packages rather than standardized products. Companies such as Norand Corporation (a manufacturer of pen-input computers and wireless networks) are giving their salespeople laptops and software to configure products and calculate pricing options.[7]

DISCOUNTS

Discounts are given for many reasons and may be based on the type of customer (such as wholesaler or retailer, senior citizen or younger adult), quantity purchased, or some other factor. (Discounts used in selling to resellers are discussed in Chapter 15.) The most common type of discount is the quantity discount.

Quantity discounts encourage large purchases by passing along savings resulting from reduced processing costs. Businesses offer two types of quantity discounts: (1) the single-order discount and (2) a cumulative discount. An office equipment company offering a 10 percent discount on a single order for five or more facsimile machines is an example of a single-order discount. When offering a **cumulative discount,** that same company might offer the 10 percent discount on all purchases over a one-year period, provided the customer purchases more than five fax machines. The customer may sign an agreement at the beginning of the year promising to buy five or more machines, in which case the customer will be billed for each order at the discounted price (10 percent off). If the customer fails to purchase five fax machines, a single bill will be sent at the end of the year for the amount of the discount (10 percent of the single-unit price times the number of fax machines actually purchased). Another method is to bill the customer at the full price and then rebate the discount at the end of the year, based on the actual number of fax machines purchased.

CREDIT TERMS

Most U.S. sales are made on a credit basis, with **cash discounts** allowed for early payment. These cash discounts are the last discount taken, meaning that if a quantity discount is also offered, the cash discount is calculated after the quantity discount is taken off. A common discount is 2/10, n/30, which means that the buyer can deduct 2 percent from the bill if it is paid within 10 days from the date of invoice. Otherwise, the full amount must be paid in 30 days. Another common discount is 2/10, EOM, which means that the 10-day period begins at the end of the month. For example, if the customer receives $1,000 worth of supplies on February 15 with terms of 2/10, EOM and pays the bill on March 5, the customer would pay $980 (that is, $1,000 × 2% = $20 discount for paying cash; $1,000 − $20 = $980). But if the customer pays on March 11, the bill would be the full $1,000.

SHIPPING COSTS

The terms and conditions of sale include shipping costs. The seller who quotes a **free on board (FOB)** price agrees to load the goods on board a truck, freight car, or other means of transportation.

A great many variations exist in the use of FOB, but the term is used to specify the point at which the buyer assumes responsibility for both the goods and the costs of shipping them. Thus FOB destination means that the buyer will take responsibility for the goods once they reach the buyer's location, and the seller will pay the freight.

Suppose Johnson Wax quotes an FOB origin price. It will load the truck at its Racine, Wisconsin, plant, but the buyer bears the responsibility for paying for shipping. If Johnson Wax sold a truckload of Raid to Tom Thumb (a grocery chain headquartered in Dallas) under terms of FOB destination, Johnson Wax would pay for shipping and would have the Raid delivered to Tom Thumb's Dallas warehouse, where warehouse personnel would unload the truck.

Another form of FOB is FOB installed, meaning that title and responsibility do not transfer until the equipment is installed and operating properly.[8] In some instances, FOB installed can also mean that operator training must be provided before title transfers. These are important terms because there are significant costs associated with the technical installation and operator training for many pieces of sophisticated equipment. Buyers want to know the total price and what it includes.

The terms and conditions of a sale, including but not limited to price, can often play as important a role as the product itself in determining what is purchased.

If Home Made Brands (Newburyport, Massachusetts) receives a shipment FOB origin, then Home Made Brands pays for shipping. FOB destination means that the seller pays for shipping.

©Erv Schowengerdt

Creative salespeople understand the terms and conditions they have to work with so that they can meet the needs of their buyers while also meeting the profit objectives of their own companies.

PRESENTING PRICE

Price is often discussed at the end of the presentation simply because the salesperson may not know what that price will be until the final solution is agreed on. Because price is so important to the buyer, it is worth considering how price should be presented.

Most firms set prices after careful study of the competitors' offerings, the value delivered by the product or service, and the cost of providing the product or service. For these reasons the price should represent a reasonable and fair picture of the product's or service's value. Therefore, never apologize for a price or present the price apologetically; rather, present it with confidence.

Russ Berry, known as Father Troll because his company made troll dolls popular, relates this story about when he began his business. He needed a warehouse because he worked out of his apartment in Manhattan, and there was no room to store inventory. So he knocked on the door of a house that had a sign in the window reading "Garage for rent." He expected to pay $75 a month for the garage, but when the owner of the house said the rent was $50, Berry's response was "$50!" The owner thought Berry was objecting to the price, so he responded, "OK, $35." Berry, as have many other astute businesspeople, learned to always respond with skepticism to the first price offered. Yet in his story, he believed the value of the garage was more than twice what he actually paid for it.[9]

In addition to presenting the price with confidence, remember that price is not the focus of your presentation. The real issue is satisfying the needs of the buyer, of which budget is only one. True, a budget limitation can halt progress toward a sale. The real issue, though, is the total cost of ownership, which means the buyer should also factor in the value of the benefits delivered.

WHEN TO ATTEMPT TO OBTAIN COMMITMENT

Novice salespeople frequently ask themselves these questions: Is there a right time to obtain commitment? How will customers let me know they are ready to buy? Should I make more than one attempt? What should I do if my first attempt fails?

The right time to attempt to gain commitment is when the buyer appears ready, as evidenced by buying signals. Some salespeople say that one psychological moment in each sales presentation affords the best opportunity to obtain commitment, and if this opportunity is bypassed, securing commitment will be difficult or impossible. This belief is not true, however. Seldom does one psychological moment govern the complete success or failure of a sales presentation.

Most buyers will commit themselves only when they clearly understand the benefits and costs of such a decision. At times this point occurs early in the call. A commitment to purchase a large system, however, usually will not occur until a complete presentation and several calls have been made and all questions have been answered.

Buying signals, or indications that the buyer is ready to buy, can be evidenced both in the buyer's comments and nonverbally. Buying signals are also called **closing cues.**

BUYER COMMENTS

A customer's comments often are the best indication that he or she is considering commitment. A prospect will seldom say, "All right, I'm ready to endorse this product to our buying committee." Questions about the product or terms of sale and comments in the form of requirements or benefit statements signal readiness to buy, as do responses to trial closes.

BUYER QUESTIONS

Here are some examples of questions that signal readiness to buy:

> If I do agree to go with this cooperative advertising program, do you have any ads already developed that I could use?

> Do you have any facilities for training our employees in the use of the product?

> How soon would you be able to deliver the equipment?

> What do we do next?

Not all questions signal a readiness to buy. But if the question concerns implementing the purchase and points toward when, not if, the purchase is implemented, the prospect is getting ready to buy.

REQUIREMENTS

Requirements are conditions that have to be satisfied before a purchase can take place. For example:

> We need a cash discount for a supply order like this.

> We need to get this in weekly shipments.

Requirements that are stated near the end of the presentation are need statements that reflect a readiness to buy when they relate to how the purchase will be consummated. As the examples illustrate, requirements relating to financial terms or shipping indicate that the decision to buy the product has been made and now it is time to work out the details.

BENEFIT STATEMENTS

Sometimes prospects offer their own benefit statements, such as these:

> Oh, I like the way this equipment is serviced—it will make it much easier on my staff.

> Good, that color will match our office decor.

Such positive statements reflect strong feelings in support of the purchase, a sign that the buyer is ready.

RESPONSES TO TRIAL CLOSES

Salespeople can solicit such comments by continually taking the pulse of the situation with **trial closes,** or questions regarding the prospect's readiness to buy. Throughout the presentation, the salesperson should be asking questions:

> How does this sound to you so far?

> Is there anything else you would like to know at this point?

> How does this compare with what you have seen of competing products?

Such questions are an important element of any sales process because trial closes serve several purposes, including identifying the customer's proximity to making the decision, gaining agreement on minor points, and creating a true dialogue in which the ultimate close is a natural conclusion.

Many of the little decisions that move a customer through the creeping commitment process are trial closes. The salesperson, by asking trial closes, can determine how close the buyer is to making the final decision. Understanding the customer's proximity to buying can give the salesperson direction; for example, is it time to begin filling out an order form?

Recognize that trial closes also play an important role in making the conversation a dialogue that naturally concludes with a decision. Trial closes can help break the decision down into manageable pieces for both the buyer and the seller. Asking someone to buy a corporate jet, for example, without first gaining agreement on size or range is asking the buyer to make a decision without knowing what it is.

When a seller asks a trial close question, the buyer responds, thus creating a dialogue. Issues can be raised as objections or questions by the buyer, which tell the seller what to cover. Then, because the salesperson has been asking closing questions all along, the final close is just a natural part of the ongoing dialogue, as it should be.

NONVERBAL CUES

As in every phase of the presentation, nonverbal cues serve as important indicators of the customer's state of mind. While attempting to gain commitment, the salesperson should use the buyer's nonverbal signals to better identify areas of concern and see whether the buyer is ready to commit. Facial expressions most often indicate how ready the buyer is to make a commitment. Positive signals include eyes that are open and relaxed, face and mouth not covered with hands, a natural smile, and a relaxed forehead. The reverses of these signals indicate that the buyer is not yet ready to commit to the proposal.

Customers' actions also often indicate readiness to buy or make a commitment. For example, the prospective buyer of a fax machine may get a document and operate the machine or place the machine on the table where it will be used. The industrial buyer may refer to a catalog to compare specifications with competing products. A doctor, when told of a new drug, may pick up the pamphlet and begin carefully reading the indications and contraindications. A retailer considering whether to allow an end-of-aisle display may move to the end of an aisle and scan the layout. Any such actions may be signals for obtaining commitment; they should be viewed in the context of all available verbal and nonverbal cues.

Do the two buyers on the right look like they are ready to commit to a purchase?

© SuperStock

HOW TO SUCCESSFULLY OBTAIN COMMITMENT

To obtain commitment in a nonmanipulative manner, salespeople need to follow several principles, including maintaining a positive attitude, letting the customer set the pace, being assertive instead of aggressive, and selling the right product in the right amounts.

MAINTAIN A POSITIVE ATTITUDE

Confidence is contagious. Customers like to deal with salespeople who have confidence in themselves, their products, and their companies. On the other hand, unnecessary fear can be a self-fulfilling prophecy. The typist who fears making errors will make many; the student who fears essay exams usually does poorly; golfers who believe they will miss short putts usually do. So it is with salespeople: If they fear the customer will not accept their proposal, the chances are good they will be right.

One manager related the example of a salesperson selling laundry detergent who unsuccessfully tried to convince a large discount chain to adopt a new liquid version of the product. When the rep's sales manager stopped by the account later in the week to follow up on a recent stockout problem, the buyer related his reasons for refusing the liquid Tide: "Listen, I know you guys are sharp. You probably wouldn't come out with a new product unless you had tons of data to back up your decision. But, honestly, the sales rep who calls on me is always so uptight and apprehensive that I was afraid to adopt the new product! Don't you guys teach them about having confidence?"

LET THE CUSTOMER SET THE PACE

Attempts to gain commitment must be geared to fit the varying reactions, needs, and personalities of each buyer. Thus the sales representative needs to practice adaptive selling. (See Chapter 6 for a complete discussion of adaptive selling.)

Some buyers who react very slowly may need plenty of time to assimilate the material presented. They may ask the same question several times or show they do not understand the importance of certain product features. In these circumstances the salesperson must deliver the presentation more slowly and may have to repeat certain parts. Trying to rush buyers is unwise when they show they are not yet ready to commit.

As we discussed earlier in the book, buyers' decision-making styles vary greatly. Japanese and Chinese buyers tend to move more slowly and cautiously when evaluating a proposition. In contrast, buyers working for *Fortune* 500 firms located in the largest U.S. cities often tend to move much more quickly. The successful salesperson recognizes such potential differences and acts accordingly.

BE ASSERTIVE, NOT AGGRESSIVE

Marvin Jolson has identified three types of salespeople: aggressive, submissive, and assertive.[10] **Aggressive** salespeople control the sales interaction but often fail to gain commitment because they prejudge the customer's needs and fail to probe for information. Too busy talking to do much listening, they tend to push the buyer too soon, too often, and too vigorously. They might say, I can't understand why you are hesitant, but they do not probe for reasons for the hesitancy.

Submissive salespeople often excel as socializers. With customers they spend a lot of time talking about families, restaurants, and movies. They establish rapport quite effectively. They accept the customers' statements of needs and problems but do not probe to uncover any latent needs or opportunities. Submissive salespeople rarely try to obtain commitment. Sometimes they may be too close to the customer to close, as discussed in Building Partnerships 12.1.

Assertive salespeople are self-confident and positive. They maintain the proper perspective by being responsive to customer needs. Rather than aggressively creating new "needs" in customers through persuasion, they look for buyers who

TOO CLOSE TO CLOSE?

Building relationships is an important part of selling. Yet making friends and making sales are sometimes two very different things.

Bill Boardman, of Lone Star Foods, says his salespeople sometimes spend too much time making calls on current accounts. "They'll go for the easy sale, instead of finding ways to expand the business in those current accounts, or instead of working with a new account that represents incremental sales. They [the salespeople] are afraid they'll hurt the relationship if they 'push too hard.' But as a consequence, they don't push at all and sales don't grow."

Barbara Bauer, vice president of sales for the Omnia Group, calls this type of salespeople "simulation salespeople." They "look and sound exactly like real salespeople but cannot close," she says. She says this type of salesperson believes that "because customers might not like him if he asks them to buy, he's often reluctant to pressure his new friend into making a decision now—or ever."

So how does one close and still keep the relationship? Trent Weaver of Spirit Graphics says, "Be direct and ask for a decision. You know they are going to buy something to meet that need, and if you believe your product fulfills it, then you do them a disservice by not asking." Richard Langlotz, branch manager for Minolta Business Systems, agrees. "Up front, know what time frame they want to work on; then list and define decision dates for all of the small decisions they need to make, like when they want a proposal, when they want a demonstration, etc. Then everyone knows up front when each decision will be made and no one is surprised or feels pushed."

Boardman says, "The customer knows you are a salesperson and that it is your job to ask for the order. It's not a question of if, but rather how, you ask that's important." That's why he agrees with Weaver—be direct, don't use tricks, and help them buy the way they want to.

Sources: Bauer quote is from Barbara Bauer, "Relationship Building: Too Much of a Good Thing?" *Promotional Products Business,* December 1999, pp. 78–80; the rest is from personal interviews.

truly need their products and then use questions to acquire information. Their presentations emphasize an exchange of information rather than a one-way presentation. Exhibit 12.2 summarizes the differences among assertive, aggressive, and submissive salespeople's handling of the sales interview.

SELL THE RIGHT ITEM IN THE RIGHT AMOUNTS

The chance of obtaining commitment improves when the right product is sold in the right amount. Although this principle sounds obvious, it often is not followed.

For example, before attempting to sell two copiers, the office equipment sales representative must be sure that these two copiers, instead of only one copier or

This salesperson is too aggressive; in handing the pen to the customer, the salesperson hopes that he will use it to sign the order. Such hokey tricks should be avoided.

Bill Avon/PhotoEdit

Selling Activity	Selling Style		
	Aggressive	Submissive	Assertive
Defining customer needs	Believe they are the best judge of customer's needs	Accept customer's definition of needs	Probe for need-related information that customer may not have volunteered
Controlling the presentation	Minimize participation by customer	Permit customer to control presentation	Encourage two-way communication and customer participation
Closing the sale	Overwhelm customer; respond to objections without understanding	Assume customers will buy when ready	Respond to objections, leading to somewhat automatic close

perhaps three, best fit the needs of the buyer's office. The chemical company sales representative selling to an industrial firm must know that one tank car of a chemical is more likely to fit the firm's needs than ten 55-gallon drums. The Johnson Wax sales rep who utilizes the firm's Sell to Potential program knows the importance of selling not too few units (the store will run out of stock during the promotion) and not too many units (the store will be stuck with excess inventory after the promotion). Customers have long memories; they will refuse to do business with someone who oversells, and they may also lack confidence in someone who undersells. The chances to obtain commitment diminish rapidly when the salesperson tries to sell too many or too few units or the wrong grade or style of product.

Also, salespeople should not rely solely on trial orders. A **trial order** is a small order placed by a buyer to use if the product will work, and should not be confused with a trial close. A trial order is no commitment, and all too often a buyer will agree to a trial just to get rid of the salesperson. Further, if any learning curve is necessary, a customer who agrees to a trial might be unwilling to invest the time necessary to fully learn the product and will not fully realize the benefits. The product will be rejected often because customers don't have time to give fair trials. Trial orders can work well when the product is easy to implement (such as selling a new product to a retailer for resale) or when the benefits can be realized only by seeing the product in use.

Salespeople are likely to sell the right product in the right amounts if they keep a service attitude. For example, Herb Burnap, sales representative for Moore Business Forms, recently figured out a way to save his account 35 percent of its annual business forms bill by combining information that was on two forms into one. Burnap rightly believes that, although the first sale may be smaller if the right product is sold in the right amounts, repeat sales and goodwill will always more than make up the difference.

EFFECTIVE METHODS

"If closing is seen by so many sales experts as manipulative and insulting, are effective methods those that are manipulative but not insulting?" asked one of our students. It is a fair question, and the answer has two elements. First, the salesperson's purpose is to sell the right product in the right amounts. If the prospect does not need what is being sold, the salesperson should walk to the next door and start again. Thus there should never be a need for manipulation. Second, in addition to selling only what the customer needs, the salesperson should also sell in a fashion consistent with the way the buyer prefers to buy. Therefore, the salesperson should gain commitment in a manner that will help the buyer make the choice. We use the word *choice* here to mean that the buyer can say no. Manipulative techniques are designed to reduce or eliminate choice; partnering methods are not.

Studying successful methods and techniques enables salespeople to help prospects buy a product or service they want or need. Buyers sometimes have a need or a want but still hesitate to buy the product or service that will satisfy it. For example, an industrial buyer for a candy manufacturer refused to commit to a change in sweeteners, even though she needed better raw material. Why? Because the sweetener rep had met with her on four separate occasions, and the buyer had difficulty remembering all that was said and agreed on. Had the salesperson used the appropriate method (the benefit summary method, discussed later in this section), commitment might have been obtained. This section describes several of the most important methods for gaining commitment.

DIRECT REQUEST

The most straightforward, effective method of obtaining commitment is simply to ask for it, called the **direct request method.** However, salespeople need to be wary of appearing overly aggressive when using this direct request method. It works best with decisive customers, such as drivers who appreciate getting down to business and not wasting time. Examples:

> Can I put you down for 100 pairs of model 63?
>
> Can we meet with your engineer next Thursday to further discuss this?
>
> Will you come to the home office for a hands-on demonstration?
>
> Can you call the meeting next week?

BENEFIT SUMMARY

Early in the interview salespeople discover or reiterate the needs and problems of the prospect. Then, throughout the presentation, they show how their product can meet those needs. They do this by turning product or service features into benefits specifically for that buyer. As they present each benefit, they ask if that benefit meets the need. When using this approach, called the **benefit summary method,** the salesperson simply reminds the prospect of the agreed-on benefits of the proposal. This nonmanipulative method helps the buyer to synthesize points covered in the presentation to make a wise decision. For example, the salesperson attempting to obtain the buyer's commitment to recommend a proposal to a buying committee might say:

> You stated early in my visit that you were looking for a product of the highest quality, a vendor that could provide quick delivery, and adequate engineering support. As I've mentioned, our fasteners have been rated by an independent laboratory as providing 20 percent higher tensile strength than the closest competitor, resulting in a life expectancy of more than four years. We also discussed the fact that my company can deliver fasteners to your location within 3 hours of your request and that this promise holds true 24 hours a day. Finally, I discussed the fact that we have four engineers on staff whose sole responsibility is to provide support and develop specifications for new fasteners for existing customers. Would you be willing to give the information we discussed to the buying committee along with your endorsement of the proposal?

One advantage of the benefit summary method over the direct request method is that the seller can help the buyer remember all the points discussed in the presentation. The summary becomes particularly important in long presentations and in selling situations involving several meetings prior to obtaining commitment. The salesperson cannot assume that the buyer will remember all the major points discussed in the presentation.

BALANCE SHEET METHOD

Sometimes referred to as the *Ben Franklin method* because Franklin described using it to make decisions, the **balance sheet method** aids prospects who cannot make a decision, even though no reason for their behavior is apparent. Such a prospect may be asked to join the salesperson in listing the pros and cons of buying now or buying later, of buying the salesperson's product or that of a competitor, or of buying the product or not buying it at all.

However, like many nonmanipulative sales techniques, this method can insult a buyer's intelligence if used inappropriately. The salesperson may start to obtain commitment with the following type of statement:

> You know, Mr. Thacker, Ben Franklin was like you, always anxious to reach the right decisions and avoid the wrong ones. I suppose that's how you feel. Well, he suggested taking a piece of paper and writing all the reasons for deciding yes in one column and then listing the reasons for deciding no in a second column. He said that when you make this kind of graphic comparison, the correct decision becomes much more apparent.

That close may seem manipulative; it certainly sounds silly. A more effective start may be to simply draw a T on a plain piece of paper, place captions on each side of the crossbar, and leave space below for the insertion of specific benefits or sales points. Then just ask the buyer to list pros and cons of making the purchase. For example, assume the product is National Adhesives's hot-melt adhesive used to attach paper labels to plastic Classic Coke bottles. Coca-Cola is currently using a liquid adhesive made by Ajax Corporation. The top of the T might look like this:

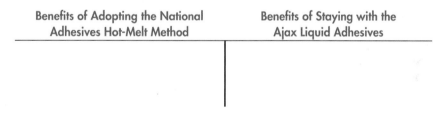

Benefits of Adopting the National Adhesives Hot-Melt Method	Benefits of Staying with the Ajax Liquid Adhesives

The salesperson may say something like, "Making a decision like this is difficult. Let's see how many reasons we can think of for your going with the National Adhesives system." The salesperson would write the benefits (not features) in which the customer has shown interest on the left side of the T. Next, the salesperson would ask the customer to list reasons to stay with the Ajax adhesive on the right side. When completed, the T lists should accurately reflect all the pros and cons of each possible decision. At that point the buyer is asked, "Which method do you think is the wisest?"

When used properly, the balance sheet method can help hesitant buyers express their feelings about the decision, which gives the salesperson an opportunity to deal with those feelings. It is especially appropriate for a buyer who is an analytical, but would make less sense for an expressive. However, the balance sheet approach takes time and may appear "salesy," particularly if relatively unimportant benefits are considered to be equal to more important reasons not to buy. Also, the list of benefits of the product being sold will not always outnumber the list on the other side of the T.

In the **probing method** sales representatives initially attempt to obtain commitment by another method, perhaps simply asking for it (the direct request method). If unsuccessful, the salesperson uses a series of probing questions designed to discover the reason for the hesitation. Once the reason(s) becomes apparent, the salesperson asks a what-if question. (What if I could successfully resolve this concern? Would you be willing to commit?) An illustrative dialogue follows:

SALESPERSON: Could we make an appointment for next week, at which time I would come in and do a complete survey of your needs? It shouldn't take more than three hours.

PROSPECT: No, I don't think I am quite ready to take that step yet.

SALESPERSON: There must be some reason why you are hesitating to go ahead now. Do you mind if I ask what it is?

PROSPECT: I'm just not convinced that your firm is large enough to handle a customer of our size.

SALESPERSON: In addition to that, is there any other reason why you would not be willing to go ahead?

PROSPECT: No.

SALESPERSON: If I can resolve the issue of our size, then you would allow me to conduct a survey?

PROSPECT: Well, I wouldn't exactly say that.

SALESPERSON: Then there must be some other reason. May I ask what it is?

PROSPECT: Well, a friend of mine who uses your services told me that often your billing department sends him invoices for material he didn't want and didn't receive.

SALESPERSON: In addition to that, is there any other reason for not going ahead now?

PROSPECT: No, those are my two concerns.

SALESPERSON: If I could resolve those issues right now, would you be willing to set up an appointment for a survey?

PROSPECT: Sure.

This dialogue illustrates the importance of probing in obtaining commitment. The method attempts to bring to the table all issues of concern to the prospect. The salesperson does not claim to be able to resolve the issues but simply attempts to find out what the issues are. When probing has identified all the issues, the salesperson should attempt to resolve them as soon as possible. After successfully dealing with the concerns of the buyer, the salesperson should then ask for a commitment.

There are many modifications of the probing method. One other way to achieve the same results is the following:

SALESPERSON: Are you willing to buy this product today?

PROSPECT: No, I don't think so.

SALESPERSON: I really would like to get a better feel of where you are. On a scale of 1 to 10, with 1 being absolutely no purchase and 10 being purchase, where would you say you are?

PROSPECT: I would say I'm about a 6.

SALESPERSON: If you don't mind my asking, what would it take to move you from a 6 to a 10?

Also, it is important to always keep cultural differences in mind. For example, if a Japanese businesswoman wants to tell an American salesperson that she is not interested, she might state, "Your proposal would be very difficult," just to be polite. If the seller attempts to use the probing method, the Japanese businesswoman may consider the seller to be pushy or a poor listener. In the same way, an Arab businessperson will never say no directly, a custom that helps both sides avoid losing face.[11]

ALTERNATIVE CHOICE

In many situations a salesperson may have multiple options to present to a buyer. For example, Teo Schaars sells diamonds directly from cutters in the Netherlands to consumers in the United States. When he started in sales, he would display several dozen diamonds on a purple damask–covered table. Sales were few until his father, a Dutch diamond broker, suggested that he limit his customers' choices; there were simply too many diamonds to choose from, overwhelming the buyer. Schaars found his father's comments to be wise advice. Now Schaars spends more time probing about budget and desires and then shows only two diamonds at a time, explaining the key characteristics of each. Then he allows the customer to express a preference. Schaars may have to show half a dozen or more diamonds before a customer makes the final decision, but he rarely shows more than two at a time.

OTHER METHODS

Literally hundreds of techniques and methods to obtain commitment have been tried. Exhibit 12.3 lists a number of traditional methods. Most of them, however, tend to be ineffective with sophisticated customers; nevertheless, all can be used in a nonmanipulative manner if appropriate. For example, the minor-point close can be appropriate if there really is a need to make a choice between two options; the factor that makes the method manipulative is the assumption that the minor choice is the equivalent to making the sale.

No method of obtaining commitment will work if the buyer does not trust the salesperson, the company, and the product. Gaining commitment should not require the use of tricky techniques or methods to force buyers to do something they do not want to do or to persuade them to buy something they do not need.

IF COMMITMENT IS OBTAINED

The salesperson's job is not over when commitment is obtained. In fact, in many ways the job is just beginning. This section describes the salesperson's responsibilities that accrue after the buyer says yes.

Selecting a method to gain commitment requires an understanding of the buyer's culture.

Derek Berwin

EXHIBIT 12.3   Some Traditional Closing Methods

Method	How It Works	Remark
Minor-point close	The seller assumes it is easier to get the prospect to decide on a very trivial point than on the whole proposition: What color do you like, blue or red?	This method can upset a prospect who feels he or she is being manipulated or tricked into making a commitment. Even unsophisticated buyers easily spot this technique.
Continuous *yes* close	Throughout the presentation, the seller constantly asks questions for which the prospect most logically would answer *yes*. By the end of the discussion, the buyer is so accustomed to saying *yes* that when the order is requested, the natural response is *yes*.	This method is based on self-perception theory. As the presentation progresses, the buyer begins to perceive himself or herself as being agreeable. At the close, the buyer wants to maintain this self-image and almost unthinkingly says *yes*. Use of this method can destroy long-term relationships if the buyer later feels manipulated.
Assumptive close	The seller, without asking for the order, simply begins to write it up. A variation is to fill out the order form as the prospect answers questions.	This method does not even give the buyer the courtesy of agreeing. It can be perceived as being very pushy and manipulative.
Standing-room-only close	The seller attempts to obtain commitment by describing the negative consequences of waiting. For example, the seller may state, "If you can't decide now, I'll have to offer it to another customer."	This method can be effective if the statement is true. However, if the prospect really does need to act quickly, this deadline should probably be discussed earlier in the presentation to reduce possible mistrust and the feeling of being pushed.
Benefit-in-reserve close	First, the seller attempts to obtain commitment by another method. If unsuccessful, the seller says, "Oh, I forgot to tell you that if you order today I can offer you an additional 5 percent for your trade-in."	This method can backfire easily. The buyer tends to think, "If I had agreed to your first attempt to obtain commitment, I would not have learned about this new enticement. If I wait longer, how much better will your offer be?" The buyer may then seek additional concessions in every future sale attempt.
Emotional close	The seller appeals to the buyer's emotions to close the sale. For example, the seller may say, "This really is a good deal. To be honest with you, I desperately need to secure an order today. As you know, I work on a straight commission basis. My wife is going to have surgery next week, and our insurance just won't cover. . ."	Many obvious problems arise with this method. It is an attempt to move away from focusing entirely on the buyer's personal needs. It does not develop trust or respect. Do not use this close!

NO SURPRISES

Customers do not like surprises, so now is the time to go over any important information they will need to fully enjoy the benefits of the product or service. For example, if you are selling life insurance and a physical is required, give the customer as much detail as possible to prepare him or her for that experience. Or if a company is going to lease a piece of heavy equipment, let the customer know that delivery will occur after a credit check and how long that credit check will take. No customer wants to be kept waiting in the dark, not knowing whether he or she will ever get the new product.

CONFIRM THE CUSTOMER'S CHOICE

Customers like to believe they have chosen intelligently when they make a decision. After important decisions, they may feel a little insecure about whether the sacrifice is worth it. Such feelings are called **buyer's remorse** or **postpurchase dissonance.**

Successful salespeople reassure customers that their choice was judicious. For example:

> I know you will enjoy using your new office machines. You can plan on many months of trouble-free service. I'll call on you in about two weeks to make sure everything is operating smoothly. Be sure to call me if you need any help before then.

Or:

> Congratulations, Mr. Jacobs. You are going to be glad you decided to use our service. There is no finer service available. Now let's make certain you get off to the right start. Your first bulletin will arrive on Tuesday, March 2.

One way to help customers feel good about their decision is to assure them that they have made an intelligent choice. Remarks such as the following may also be appropriate:

> You've made an excellent choice. Other stores won't have a product like this for at least 30 days.

> You've chosen an excellent model. Did you see it advertised in last week's *Time*?

> Your mechanics will thank you for ordering these tools. You will be able to get your work out much faster.

GET THE SIGNATURE

The buyer's signature often formalizes a commitment. Signing the order is a natural part of a well-planned procedure. The order blank should be accessible, and the signing should be treated as a routine matter. Ordinarily, the customer has decided to buy before being asked to sign the order. In other words, the signature on the order blank merely confirms that an agreement has already been reached. The decision to buy or not to buy should not focus on a signature.

The salesperson needs to remember several important points: (1) Make the actual signing an easy, routine procedure; (2) fill out the order blank accurately and promptly; and (3) be careful not to exhibit any excess eagerness or excitement when the prospect is about to sign.

SHOW APPRECIATION

All buyers like to think that their business is appreciated even if they purchase only small quantities. Customers like to do business with salespeople who show that they want the business.

Salespeople may show appreciation by writing the purchaser a letter. This practice especially develops goodwill after large purchases and with new customers. In some situations a small gift, such as a pen with the selling company's name on it, may also be an effective thank you. Salespeople should always thank the purchaser personally; the thanks should be genuine but not effusive.

When the president signs a piece of legislation, the signing is part of a formal celebration. But when you sign an order, make that step a normal part of the process and save the victory dance for later.

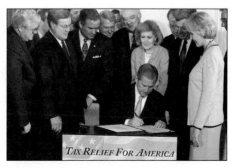

AFT/CORBIS

CULTIVATE FOR FUTURE CALLS

In most fields of selling, obtaining commitment is not the end of a business transaction; rather, it is only one part of a mutually profitable business relationship.[12] Obtaining commitment is successful only if it results in goodwill and future commitment. Harvey Mackay states:

> My definition of a great salesperson is not someone who can get the order. Anyone can get the order if he or she is willing to make enough promises about price or delivery. A great salesperson is someone who can get the order—and the reorder—from a prospect who is already doing business with someone else.[13]

Customers like to do business with salespeople who do not lose interest immediately after securing commitment. What a salesperson does after achieving commitment is called **follow-up.** As Frank DiCarlo, sales director for Calvin Klein, recognizes, "Making the sale is only the beginning." After making the sale, the salesperson must follow up to make sure the product is delivered when promised, set up appropriately, and so forth. We talk more about follow-up in later chapters. The point here is that the sale does not end with the customer's signature on the order form. Effective selling means building relationships with customers, not just going for the single sale.[14]

REVIEW THE ACTIONS TO BE TAKEN

An important step, particularly when commitment is next in the buying process, is to review what each party has agreed to do. In the case of a multiple-visit sales cycle, the salesperson must review not only what the client will do but also what the salesperson will do to prepare for the next meeting. To be welcomed on repeat calls, salespeople must be considerate of all of the parties involved in buying or using the product. They must pronounce and spell all names correctly, explain and review the terms of the purchase so no misunderstandings will occur, and be sociable and cordial to subordinates as well as those in key positions. In addition, the buyer or user must get the service promised. The importance of this point cannot be overemphasized. Chapter 13 provides detailed information about how to service the account and build a partnership.

IF COMMITMENT IS NOT OBTAINED

Naturally, the salesperson does not always obtain the desired commitment. The salesperson should never take this situation personally (which is easier said than done). Doing everything right does not guarantee a sale. Situations change, and customers who may have really needed the product when everything started may find that other priorities make a purchase impossible, such as illustrated in Selling Scenario 12.1.

Thinking It Through

Many students report that asking for the order is the hardest part of selling. Why is it difficult? Does the customer need you to ask for the sale? Have you ever needed a salesperson to ask you to buy? Why or why not?

This section describes some of the common reasons for failing to obtain commitment and offers practical suggestions for salespeople who encounter rejection.

WHAT DOES "NO" MEAN?

There's a saying in sales that when a buyer says "No," the real meaning is not no forever but no, not right now. The buyer may have a solution that's better now, but every buyer has to make similar purchases in the future, and you'll get your shot then.

Sometimes that future isn't so far off. Adriana Copaceanu started ABC Gifts and Baskets (her company fills baskets with gifts that companies give to their customers) and was looking for her first account. She heard of one business owner who made her own baskets, so Copaceanu called her, only to learn that the buyer had already made all she wanted for the year. So Copaceanu sent her a "thank-you" basket along with company information. The woman called two days later and purchased 150 baskets!

No can mean no forever, though, if the rep isn't listening and isn't sensitive to the buyer's needs. Sid Gottlieb, VP of sales and marketing for Corporate Sport, Inc., told a salesperson early in the conversation that he would not be buying anything for about six weeks. She ignored his cue to wrap things up and call back later by showing new items. After nearly 45 minutes, he asked her if she always took this long. Her reply was "I spend as much time as needed to get the order signed." As Gottlieb admits, "Don't assume that a delay or postponement is an automatic no." But that salesperson's lack of sensitivity and inability to listen cost her any future opportunities with Gottlieb.

A similar experience happened to Bill Kennedy, although at first he was on the losing end. "I had a customer who needed a front-end loader, but he felt ours was too expensive." Kennedy represents John Deere for a dealership in Texas. "He bought a competitive product, but after a little over a year, he was back on our lot, ready to get the Deere. Since I never slammed the competition and treated him like he was a valued customer, even though he bought the other product, he came back to see me when it didn't perform and needed replacing."

Copaceanu's first customer is still a customer, as is Kennedy's. A buyer who makes a decision to buy today will have to make that decision again; "No" doesn't have to be "No forever!"

Sources: Steve Atlas, "Warm and Fuzzy Tips from Buyers for Closing More Sales," *Selling Power*, October 2001, pp. 74–78; Adriana Copaceanu, "A Basketful of Sales," *Selling Power*, October 2001, p. 56; Bill Kennedy, personal correspondence.

SOME REASONS FOR LOST OPPORTUNITIES

WRONG ATTITUDES

As discussed earlier in the chapter, salespeople need to have a positive attitude. A fear that obtaining commitment will be difficult may be impossible to hide. Inexperienced salespeople naturally will be concerned about their ability to obtain commitment; most of us have an innate fear of asking someone else to do anything. Some salespeople even fail to ask for the sale because if they never ask, they will never hear no. As a result, they always have more prospects but fewer customers than everyone else. But all salespeople know they need to focus on obtaining commitment to keep their jobs.

Some salespeople display unwarranted excitement when they see that prospects are ready to commit. A salesperson who appears excited or overly eager may display nonverbal cues that suggest dishonesty or a lack of empathy.[15] At this point wary buyers may change their minds and refuse to commit.

One of the main reasons for salespeople's improper attitudes toward obtaining commitment is the historical importance placed on closing the sale. Closing has often been viewed as a win–lose situation (if I get the order, I win; if I don't get the order, I lose). Until salespeople see obtaining commitment as a positive occurrence for the buyer, these attitudes will persist.

POOR PRESENTATION

Prospects or customers who do not understand the presentation or see the benefits of the purchase cannot be expected to buy. The salesperson must use trial closes (see Chapter 9) and continually take the pulse of the interview.

A poor presentation can also be caused by haste. The salesperson who tries to deliver a 60-minute presentation in 20 minutes may skim over or omit important sales points. Forgoing the presentation may be better than delivering it hastily. Further, a sales presentation given at the wrong time or under unfavorable conditions is likely to be ineffective.

Another reason for not obtaining commitment is lack of product knowledge. One study of purchasing agents found that 80 percent were dissatisfied with the level of product knowledge salespeople displayed![16] If the salesperson does not know what the product does, you can be certain the buyer will not be able to figure it out either.

POOR HABITS AND SKILLS

Obtaining commitment requires proper habits and some measure of skill. The habit of talking too much rather than listening often causes otherwise good presentations to fail. Knowing when to quit talking is just as important as knowing what to say. Some salespeople become so fascinated by the sound of their own voices that they talk themselves out of sales they have already made. A presentation that turns into a monologue is not likely to retain the buyer's interest.

DISCOVERING THE CAUSE

The real reasons for not obtaining commitment must be uncovered. Only then can salespeople proceed intelligently to eliminate the barriers. Some firms have developed sophisticated systems to follow up on lost sales. The BCI Consulting Group, acting as an independent third party, will perform this service for a firm's sales force. Salespeople supply BCI with names and phone numbers of buyers who failed to buy. BCI then contacts these individuals to obtain objective feedback on both the client's company and its competitors. The consultant generates a report that identifies the reason(s) the buyer decided not to buy.[17]

SUGGESTIONS FOR DEALING WITH REJECTION

MAINTAIN THE PROPER PERSPECTIVE

Probably the inexperienced salesperson's most important lesson is that when a buyer says no, the sales process has not necessarily ended. A no may mean "Not now," "I need more information," "Don't hurry me," or "I don't understand." An answer of no should be a challenge to seek the reason behind the buyer's negative response.

In many fields of selling, most prospects do not buy. The ratio of orders achieved to sales presentations may be 1 to 3, 1 to 5, 1 to 10, or even 1 to 20. Salespeople may tend to eliminate nonbuyers from the prospect list after one unsuccessful call. This practice may be sound in some cases; however, many sales result on the second, third, fourth, or fifth call. When an earlier visit has not resulted in commitment, careful preparation for succeeding calls becomes more crucial.

Another perspective is that when a buyer says no it is because the buyer is not yet fully informed; otherwise, the buyer would have said yes. Consequently, if the buyer has given the salesperson the opportunity to make a presentation, the buyer recognizes that a need exists or is going to exist. What has not happened yet is that match between the offering and the need. At the same time, however, no does not mean "Sell me again right now." It may mean "Sell me again later."

Marty Lile, sales manager at Ritchie Pharmacal, believes this perspective helps salespeople remember that these prospects are still future customers and that the rejection isn't personal.[18]

The salesperson should have a clear objective for each sales call. When commitment cannot be obtained to meet that objective, the salesperson will often attempt to obtain commitment for a reduced request (a secondary or minimum objective). For example, the salesperson may attempt to gain a trial order instead of an actual order, although, as we discussed earlier, this opportunity should be offered as a last resort.

RECOMMEND OTHER SOURCES

A sales representative who uses the consultative selling philosophy (as described in Chapter 6) may recommend a competitor's product to solve the prospect's needs. When recommending other sources, the sales rep should explain why his or her product does not meet the prospect's needs and then provide the name of the competitive product. One salesperson for a welding supply company keeps a current list of competitive products. When a customer requests an item that the salesperson can't supply, he volunteers the name of a competitor who can. No one need feel sorry for the salesperson, though; he is extremely successful. "I haven't been squeezed out by a competitor in more than three years," he reports.[19]

After recommending other sources, the salesperson usually should ask the prospect for names of people who might be able to buy the seller's product. Also, the salesperson should emphasize the desire to maintain contact with the prospect in the event the seller's firm develops a competitive offering.

GOOD MANNERS ARE IMPORTANT

If obtaining commitment fails for any reason, the salesperson should react good-naturedly. Salespeople have to learn to accept no if they expect to call on prospects again. Even if salespeople do not obtain commitment, they should thank prospects for their time. Arguing or showing disappointment gains nothing. The salesperson may plan to keep in contact with these prospects through an occasional phone call, a follow-up letter, or product literature mailings. One salesperson likes to make the following statement at the conclusion of any meeting that does not result in commitment: "I'll never annoy you, but if you don't mind, I'm going to keep in touch."

It is a good idea to leave something behind that will let the prospect contact the salesperson in the future. Vicki Whiteford, owner and salesperson for a courier service, leaves a Rolodex card with her name and number. "We figure that even if everything else goes in the trash, they'll save the Rolodex card . . . And if they get mad at their messenger [current courier service], they're likely to call us because our name is right in front of them."[20]

BRINGING THE INTERVIEW TO A CLOSE

Few buyers are interested in a prolonged visit after they commit. Obviously, the departure cannot be abrupt; the salesperson should complete the interview smoothly. Goodwill is never built by wasting the buyer's time after the business is concluded.

Remember that most sales take several calls to complete. If an order wasn't signed (and often getting an order isn't even the objective of the call; see Chapter 8) and the prospect wishes to continue considering the proposal, the salesperson should leave with a clear action plan for all parties. An example of the kind of dialogue the salesperson might pursue follows:

While taking their leave, these salespeople will confirm that the buyer understands what will happen next and when they will return.

© Masterfile

SALESPERSON: When will you have had a chance to look over this proposal?

BUYER: By the end of next week, probably.

SALESPERSON: Great, I'll call on you in about 10 days, OK?

BUYER: Sure, set up something with my secretary.

SALESPERSON: Is there anything else I need to do for you before that next meeting?

The salesperson should always make sure the next step is clear for both parties. Therefore, review what you will do next, what the customer will do next, and when you will meet again.[21]

Often it is important that you follow up promptly with a thank-you and reminder note after the sales call. Mark Prude, from Wallace, suggests writing a note by hand immediately after the meeting, again reviewing what was said, what is to be done, and confirming the next meeting. By taking this action immediately, he avoids memory lapses, and his follow-up does not pile up! Such letters can also present a professional image and help customers remember the important points of the meeting.[22]

Summary Commitment cannot be obtained by some magical or miraculous technique if the salesperson has failed to prepare the prospect to make this decision throughout the presentation. Salespeople should always attempt to gain commitment in a way that is consistent with the objectives of the meeting. Obtaining commitment begins with the salesperson's contact with the prospect. It can succeed only when all facets of the selling process fall into their proper place. All sellers need to keep in mind the old saying: "People don't buy products or services; they buy solutions to their problems!"

The process of obtaining commitment is the logical progression of any sales call. Commitment is important for the customer, the seller's firm, and the seller. Commitments should result in a win–win situation for all parties concerned.

Pricing is an important element of any sale and is usually presented at the time of closing. Quantity discounts, payment terms, and shipping terms can affect the final price charged to the buyer as well as influence the decision.

There is no one "right" time to obtain commitment. Salespeople should watch their prospects closely and recognize when to obtain commitment. Successful salespeople carefully monitor customer comments, their buyers' nonverbal cues and actions, and their responses to probes. Comments can be in the form of questions, requirements, benefits, and responses to trial closes.

To successfully obtain commitment, the salesperson needs to maintain a positive attitude, allow the customer to set the pace, be assertive rather than aggressive, and sell the right item in the right amounts. Engaging in these practices will result in a strong long-term relationship between buyer and seller.

No one method of obtaining commitment works best for all buyers. The direct request method is the simplest to use; however, the prospect often needs help in evaluating the proposal. In those instances other methods may be more appropriate, such as the alternative choice, the benefit summary, the balance sheet method, or the probing method. No method of obtaining commitment will work if a buyer does not trust the salesperson.

If commitment is obtained, the salesperson should immediately assure the buyer that the choice was judicious. The salesperson should show genuine appreciation as well as cultivate the relationship for future calls.

If commitment is not obtained, the salesperson should analyze the reasons. Difficulties in obtaining commitment can be directly traced to wrong attitudes, a poor presentation, and/or poor habits and skills. Even if no commitment is obtained, the salesperson should thank the prospect for his or her time.

KEY TERMS

aggressive   349
assertive   349
balance sheet method   353
benefit summary method   352
buyer's remorse   356
buying signals   346
cash discount   345
closing   342
closing cues   346
cumulative discount   344

direct request method   352
follow-up   358
free on board (FOB)   345
postpurchase dissonance   356
probing method   354
requirements   347
submissive   349
trial close   347
trial order   351

Questions and Problems

1. Review the closing methods in Exhibit 12.3 and write out a nonmanipulative and a manipulative version of each. What is the difference?

2. "The ABCs of closing are 'Always be closing.'" Another version is "Close early—close often." What is your reaction to these time-honored statements?

3. Harold Bumpurs, a professional purchasing agent, says he has never noticed any tricky closes. His perception is due not to the smooth closing skills of the salespeople who call on him but to the total skill set they have developed. Prioritize a list of selling skills, from most important to least. How much time should be spent improving commitment-gaining skills as opposed to developing other skills? Why?

4. You are selling institutional refrigerators for use in school cafeterias, restaurants, and so on. After making a presentation that you think went rather well, you request the order and get this reply: "What you say sounds interesting, but I want some time to think it over." You answer, "Well, OK. Would next Tuesday be a good day for me to come back?" How can you improve on your answer?

5. One sales manager who worked for a refrigeration equipment company taught his salespeople the following close: Ask questions that allow you to fill out the contract. Assume the sale is made and hand the contract to the buyer, along with a pen. If the buyer doesn't immediately take the pen, drop it and make the buyer pick it up. Once the buyer has the pen in hand, he or she is more likely to use it to sign the contract, so just wait silently until the buyer does.
   a. Would you label this seller as assertive or aggressive?
   b. Is this a trick or merely dramatization?
   c. How would you respond to this behavior if you were the buyer?

6. The buyer says, "No!" and you suspect it is because she doesn't trust you. You have a lot riding on this sale, and you also believe that you have the best solution for the buyer. What do you do?

7. What makes a Lexus worth more than a Honda? How would you convince someone that it is worth more if she or he knew nothing about the various brands of cars? How would the buyer's lack of knowledge influence how you try to gain commitment?

8. A sales manager once told a salesperson, "You know that when Ms. Jacobs told you no, she was saying no to your proposal; she was not rejecting you personally." Why is understanding that statement vital to all salespeople?

9. One buyer stated, "All closing methods are devious and self-serving! How can a salesperson use a technique but still keep my needs totally in mind?" Comment.

10. Most of us have a natural fear of asking someone else to do something. What can you, as a student, do now to reduce such fear?

11. What would you say to a friend to gain his or her commitment to go on a spring-break trip? Describe exactly what you would say to your friend, using each of the following methods (make any assumptions necessary):
   a. Alternative choice
   b. Direct request
   c. Benefit summary
   d. Balance sheet
   e. Probing

12. Which laws govern the obtaining-commitment portion of a sales presentation? (Refer to Chapter 3 if needed.) How can a salesperson stay within these laws while attempting to gain commitment?

13. A customer is willing to order 100 cases listed at $20 per case to get a 15 percent quantity discount. Terms are 2/10, n30. The customer pays five days after receiving the invoice. How much did the customer pay?

Case Problems

CASE 12.1

Ericsson

Ericsson, probably best known in the United States for its cell phones, is a major global telecommunication system supplier headquartered in Sweden. Mats Roos, a Swedish national who sells to U.S. telephone companies, was calling on Renita Davis, senior engineer for Verizon. His primary call objective was to have Renita agree to set up an appointment in the next several weeks for Mats to present to the engineering committee.

MATS: Our switching systems can support the digital standards of both the United States and Europe, which means that, with some engineering changes in your network, your customers can use their phones on both continents.

RENITA: Mats, I've really been thinking that the switches built by Nortel are industry standard. What has Ericsson done differently with these switches?

MATS: Quality is something we take very seriously at Ericsson, but having the best-built old product isn't enough, is it? So we've also built probably the finest engineering staff over the past five years that you'll find anywhere. The result is a product line that was just awarded the Sultan's Engineering Award for Innovation in Egypt only last month.

RENITA: That's impressive, and you're right. A well-built product using yesterday's technology is of no benefit to us. But how much demand is there for bicontinental use?

MATS: Not as much as there will be, but more than you think. Research from DataMark indicates that 25 percent of all American intercontinental business travelers already have a separate phone for each continent, and another 20 percent rent a phone when in Europe. They are also forecasting growth at 20 percent plus per year for the next three years. What have you heard about bicontinental demand?

RENITA: I've seen that data from DataMark, as well as an article in the last issue of *Telephony*. But we've had no plans for such phones.

MATS: Why is that?

RENITA: We don't know how many of our users would want it—we don't think we've got that many intercontinental travelers among our current users.

MATS: What would be considered a significant percentage—of your total user population, I mean?

RENITA: I would guess 5 percent would be acceptable. What are others experiencing?

MATS: We've got one carrier with just barely 5 percent and one with just less than 5 percent. How does that sound?

RENITA: Intriguing, though we're not the same as others.

MATS: I know. That's why I'd like to set up a meeting with your engineering team in the near future. But we'll probably also need someone there from marketing, right?

RENITA: Yes, I suppose we would.

MATS: Will I have your endorsement at the meeting?

RENITA: We'll have to wait and see. I'll need some documentation on the figures you've given me, and I'd like that before we set up the meeting.

Questions

1. What form of closing did Mats use to gain Renita's commitment to the idea? Was that appropriate? Why or why not?
2. List how you would attempt to obtain commitment using three other methods of your choice. Write out exactly what you would say for each method (and be sure to identify the method).
3. Although you have been shown only a portion of the conversation, evaluate Mats's performance in terms of the following:
   a. Selling benefits, not features.
   b. Using trial closes.
   c. Using communication aids to strengthen the presentation.
   d. Responding to objections.
   e. Attempting to gain commitment at the proper time.

CASE 12.2

Closing Styles at Emerald Cloud

Emerald Cloud is a large convention hotel in Quebec and home to many regional association meetings. Customers for the convention facilities include trade and professional associations, companies, and others who hold meetings and conferences. Two salespeople were talking with Jean Deleuze, a relatively new salesperson at Emerald Cloud, about their most recent sales. Jacque Dubois was describing his sales call with the Canadian Association of Exposition Management, which had just agreed to hold its annual meeting at the Emerald Cloud.

JACQUE: I knew we had the best solution for the association. I wasn't going to take no for an answer. Why, I saved the group 15 percent from its costs for last year. So when the committee seemed to be hesitating, I pulled out the contract and asked, "Now, will you need both ballrooms for the closing dinner, or just one?" And when the head guy said they would need only one, I began filling out the contract. After I asked a few more questions one woman asked, "What are you doing?" I said, "I'm filling out our agreement. I know your association is going to really enjoy meeting at the Emerald." She just swallowed but didn't say anything, and that's when I knew I had it.

CLAUDINE NATALE [interrupting]: Oh, that's nothing. You should have seen me close the Funeral Directors convention. I handed the buyer the contract, and she just sat there and stared at it. I wasn't going to say anything—I knew that if I did, I lost. I swear, it was dead silence for nearly five minutes. Then she signed it and handed it back to me. I just thanked her and got out of there as fast as I could, before she could change her mind!

In Jean's mind, he could hear his own feeble first attempts at closing. In fact, for Jean's first sale the buyer said, "Well, don't you have a contract or something?" He wondered whether he could get as good at closing as Jacque and Claudine.

Questions

1. Assess the styles of Jacque, Claudine, and Jean. Identify each style. What evidence supports your claim?
2. What would you suggest Jean do? Be as specific as possible and explain your recommendation.

Brunswick Financial Services is an internationally recognized provider of diversified financial services. Founded more than 50 years ago, Brunswick is now involved in stock brokerage, mutual fund portfolios, and corporate and individual retirement programs.

Brunswick offers 15 investment portfolios, ranging from low-risk and conservative to highly speculative. The more speculative the investment, the higher the risk and the greater the potential return on money invested. Sales charges are based on a percentage of the amount of funds invested, plus a fixed annual management fee.

Brunswick has built a reputation on the high quality of service it provides for clients and for its prompt payment of retirement benefits. Brunswick is particularly proud of a government-approved application form that it uses, which speeds the process of initiating a retirement program.

In this video segment Ann Clark, an account representative for Brunswick, is calling on David Johnson, founder and president of Johnson Foods, a manufacturer and distributor of gourmet food products. Prior to this meeting Clark met with the company's comptroller, Joe Stone, about developing a proposal for a retirement program for Johnson's employees. Stone was very interested. He told Clark that it was an opportune time to start a pension plan for the tax benefits and the much-needed employee goodwill the plan would generate. He also told her that Johnson would certainly have the last word and was obstinate about even discussing the matter. Johnson is a very detail oriented, somewhat distracted kind of person. On the basis of financial information received from Stone, Clark developed a written proposal that Stone reviewed. Johnson has repeatedly postponed meeting with Clark.

Following are the key features and benefits of Brunswick's proposal:

Features	Benefits
Fifteen investment funds with different levels of investment security and potential return	Allows investors to choose a fund that meets their investment criteria; helps to ensure superior return on investment
Simplified, government-approved form	Keeps setup time to a minimum, usually less than two hours; reduces government approval time
Forty years of pension experience	Eases pensioners' transition into retirement; provides needed information
Investment advisers who discuss with the client company its investment goals and objectives	Increases confidence that money is invested in appropriate investment vehicles
Flexicon (an adjustable contribution schedule that allows for contributions of up to 15% of annual earnings)	Prevents investors from being locked into a fixed contribution schedule
Computerized benefits payment system	Ensures that retirees receive their checks in a timely manner

Questions

To help you think about how Clark might attempt to obtain commitment from Johnson in this call (assume the primary call objective is to have Johnson agree to set up a meeting for a formal presentation of Brunswick's offering), answer the following questions.

1. Outline how you would attempt to obtain commitment, assuming you use the following methods (add any assumptions necessary to develop the outline):
   a. Direct request method.
   b. Benefit summary method.

c. Balance sheet method.

d. Probing method.

2. Based on the limited information you have, which method do you think would be most appropriate?

3. Reread the case and be prepared to watch the videotape in class. Watch for the actual method Clark uses to obtain commitment. Evaluate her attempts to obtain commitment.

Additional References

Badovick, Gordon J.; Farrand J. Hadaway; and Peter F. Kaminski. "Attributions and Emotions: The Effects on Salesperson Motivation after Successful vs. Unsuccessful Quota Performance." *Journal of Personal Selling & Sales Management,* Summer 1992, pp. 1–12.

DeCarlo, Thomas; Kenneth Teas; and James McElroy. "Salesperson Performance Attribution Processes and the Formation of Expectancy Estimates." *Journal of Personal Selling & Sales Management,* Summer 1997, pp. 1–18.

Jolson, Marvin, and Lucette B. Comer. "The Use of Instrumental and Expressive Personality Traits as Indicators of Salesperson Behavior." *Journal of Personal Selling & Sales Management,* Winter 1997, pp. 29–44.

Sollner, Albrecht. "Asymmetrical Commitment in Business Relationships." *Journal of Business Research,* November 1999, pp. 219–33.

Strutton, David, and James R. Lumpkin. "The Relationship between Optimism and Coping Styles of Salespeople." *Journal of Personal Selling & Sales Management,* Spring 1993, pp. 71–82.

Strutton, David; Lou Pelton; and John F. Tanner, Jr. "Shall We Gather in the Garden? The Effect of Ingratiatory Behaviors on Buyer Trust in Salespeople." *Industrial Marketing Management,* March 1996, pp. 151–62.

13 After the Sale: Building Long-Term Partnerships

SOME QUESTIONS ANSWERED IN THIS CHAPTER ARE:

- How important is service after the sale?
- How should salespeople stay in contact with customers?
- Which sales strategies stimulate repeat sales and new business in current accounts?
- Which techniques are important to use when handling complaints?

The relationship between a salesperson and a customer seldom ends when a sale has been made. In fact, salespeople are finding that building relationships and even partnerships with customers is increasingly important. Such relationships help to ensure that customers will select a salesperson's products and services the next time they buy. This chapter provides insights into building a partnership with the buyer.

Elements beyond the control of the company or its sales representatives can always affect future business. However, one sure way to decrease future uncertainties lies in building solid, progressive business relationships with customers. These relationships, the topic of this chapter, may be developed through sound customer relations and proper servicing of accounts. The result of such relationships is additional selling opportunities.

"My success in publishing is built on the principle of partnerships."

Ted Barnett, McGraw-Hill

PROFILE

Not everyone goes directly from college to sales; for some, sales positions are taken after a start in another career. Such was the case for Ted Barnett, who began teaching right after college. As he learned, however, teaching and sales require very similar skills. "Teaching in the public schools for nine years taught me many selling skills: listening, analyzing needs, gathering information, making effective presentations, relationship building, and managing time." When Barnett decided to leave the classroom, he didn't want to leave education altogether. As he says, "Strong commitments to education led me into the educational publishing industry," where he now combines his educational background with his sales expertise for McGraw-Hill, the publisher of this textbook.

"My teaching experience gave me a unique perspective on the problems and concerns faced by professors and instructors in the classroom." Because of that experience, he's been able to generate consistent revenue growth for 17 of his 19 years in sales. "My success in publishing is built on the principle of partnerships. Understanding that customers rely on me for information, academic trends, market activity, and most important, service," Barnett works hard to build partnerships with his customers.

Barnett believes that effective customer service is the distinguishing characteristic that turns his customers into partners. The service supplied may range from reliable delivery of product and support resources to seminars on academic trends or technology training programs, or from problem solving to future program strategy planning.

A feature of customer service is the advocacy that a salesperson takes back to the company on behalf of the customer. "Many times I found myself negotiating with the company [in departments such as] editorial, production, or sales management on the value of recognizing the customer priorities and changing our operations to meet those needs. In some cases it might take long-term operational or scheduling changes to meet the professor's planning needs, or it might mean pushing for consistent technology support and training or bringing new technology into the classroom. Each case is a matter of demonstrating the value of delivering the service to the customer. The revenue follows."

Barnett also believes that establishing a reputation as an advocate for customer service among clients is a two-way street. "When customers become partners, they are willing to help you out," notes Barnett. In 2001 Barnett had surgery and was on medical leave for over a month. When he returned, a paralyzed vocal cord made speech nearly impossible. "In my case, I built enough credit with clients to sustain a growing revenue base in spite of a period of absence due to spinal surgery and a paralyzed vocal cord that took months of therapy to overcome. Using technology, I was able to maintain contact with customers and growth opportunities. The decision makers granted me the leeway that kept me in the running until I could again deliver the service they relied on. It didn't guarantee that I would win, but gave me the opportunity to compete." Some of his customers had no idea he was out; the level of service they received didn't change due to his hard work and use of e-mail and other technology. "That was a tough year, but revenue goals were achieved," notes Barnett.

Barnett's relationships with his clients are perhaps his most satisfying reward. "Sales growth over a long period of time can only occur when all the pieces are in place: great customer service, great products, and great relationships."

Visit Our Website @ www.mhhe.com.

THE VALUE OF CUSTOMERS

Ross/Flex, a Troy, Michigan, air and gas control maker, has never lost a customer. It has also become the dominant supplier in most of its accounts. For example, when Knight Industries needed a triple balance valve quickly, it requested designs from two of its regular suppliers, Ross/Flex and another company. Ross/Flex engineers worked directly with Jim Zaguroli, president of Knight, trading designs, prototypes, and ideas while the competitor's engineers worked on their own. The result? The Ross/Flex product was smaller and cheaper. Ross/Flex now has 100 percent of Knight's custom business and 70 percent of its off-the-shelf business.[1]

Many people believe the emphasis in selling is on getting the initial sale. For most salespeople, however, sales increases from one year to the next are due to increasing the revenue from existing accounts, not from getting new accounts. Even in industries where purchase decisions are made infrequently, salespeople gain a competitive advantage by maintaining strong relationships with their customers. Eventually, when buying decisions need to be made, those customers look to people they know. For example, when Turner Broadcasting purchases satellite time for television broadcasting from Hughes Telecommunications, the contract is for the entire life of the satellite (15 years or longer). Hughes may launch only a couple of satellites each year, but it is important that the Hughes salesperson maintain a high-quality relationship with Turner so that revenue is optimized through maximum customer satisfaction.

This chapter integrates the knowledge you have already gained in selling to new prospects with the material covered in Chapter 2 on building partnerships

Building goodwill is always an important element in a relationship. These buyers are enjoying an afternoon Cubs game, courtesy of their salesperson.

Michael Newman/PhotoEdit

so that you can learn how to sell to the same accounts over the long term. The chapter also discusses how to handle unhappy customers.

Customers are, of course, the primary revenue source for companies. But many businesspeople do not fully understand the value of a customer. For example, if a company can retain only 2 to 5 percent more customers (instead of losing those customers to competition), the effect on the bottom line is the same as cutting costs by 10 percent.[2] Similarly, it takes an average of seven sales calls to close a first sale but only three to close a subsequent sale.[3] Thus selling to satisfied customers not only costs less than acquiring new customers but also is easier.

Customers are also worth more in terms of revenue than some salespeople recognize. For example, a car salesperson may think only of the immediate sale, but each customer is potentially worth hundreds of thousands of dollars in revenue over the salesperson's lifetime. Exhibit 13.1 illustrates the value of a small attorney's office over a 20-year period for just a few salespeople. For example, if an office equipment/supply salesperson sold all of the copiers and office supplies needed during that 20-year period, total revenue would be over $80,000! If the salesperson thinks in terms of just one sale, however, the customer is worth only about $5,000.

Thinking It Through	How much do you spend on clothing each month? Now multiply that figure by 12. Assuming that you shop in the same places during the four years you will be in college, multiply that result by 4. The total is the amount of your clothing purchases over your college career. Does anyone treat you like a $1,000 customer, or are you treated like a $20 customer?

Research shows that successfully retaining customers is important to all companies. Manufacturers that set explicit targets for customer retention and make extraordinary efforts to exceed these goals are 60 percent more profitable than those without such goals or that fail to track loyalty.[4] Yet another study finds that the average company loses 20–50 percent of its customer base every year.[5] Salespeople are critical to the process: Another study finds that it takes only a slight dip in attention from the salesperson to lead to a willingness to consider alternative sources.[6]

Some industries, especially those that are losing customers as rapidly as they are finding new ones, are only now beginning to recognize the value of retaining customers. The cellular phone industry, for example, is experiencing a disconnect rate of 30 to 45 percent per year. Those companies must replace one-third to one-half of their customers each year just to stay even![7]

EXHIBIT 13.1			
Selected Expenses for a Small Law Firm	**Item**	**Cost**	**Total**
	Copiers	5 @ $5,000	$25,000
	Copying supplies	$50 per month	12,000
	Fax machines	5 @ $2,000	10,000
	Fax supplies	$20 per month	4,800
	Telephone systems	3 @ $1,000	3,000
	Other office supplies	$100 per month	24,000
	Office furniture	$5,000	5,000
	Total over 20 years		$83,800

Courtesy Hunt-Wesson

Customer retention requires accurate product knowledge and good service, as this Hunt-Wesson salesperson demonstrates.

We have already discussed the importance of good service in generating referrals and of becoming a trusted member of the community in which your buyers operate so you can acquire more customers (see Chapter 7). The value of satisfied customers is so high that it makes good business sense to build the strongest possible relationships.

As we discussed in Chapter 2, relationships go through several stages, beginning with awareness and ending in dissolution. In this chapter we focus on the three stages between awareness and dissolution—exploration, expansion, and commitment—as illustrated in Exhibit 13.2. As you read the rest of the chapter, you will see how trust is built and maintained throughout the life of the partnership.

EXPLORATION

In the exploration stage, the relationship is defined through the development of expectations for each party. The buyer tests the seller's product, how the seller responds to requests, and other similar actions after the initial sale is made. A small percentage of the buyer's business is given to minimize the risk in case the

| **EXHIBIT 13.2** | Stages of Partnerships |

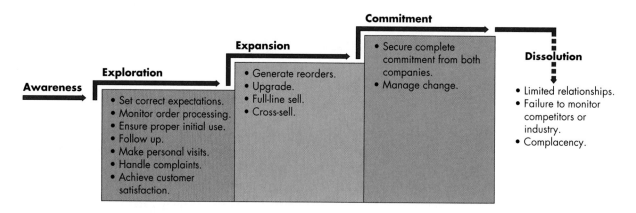

vendor cannot perform. When the vendor performs well, trust is developed, as is a personal relationship.

Beginning the relationship properly is important if the relationship is going to last a long time. Keep in mind that the customer is excited about receiving the benefits of the product as promised by the salesperson. An unfavorable initial experience with the product or with the company may be extremely difficult to overcome. Beginning the relationship properly requires that the salesperson set the right expectations, monitor order processing, ensure proper use of the product, and assist in servicing the product.

SET THE RIGHT EXPECTATIONS

The best way to begin a relationship is for each party to be aware of what the other expects. To a large degree, customers base their expectations on sales presentations.

Salespeople should make sure customers have reasonable expectations of product performance. If the salesperson exaggerates the capabilities of the product or the company, the customer will be disappointed. Admitting there has been a misunderstanding will not satisfy a customer who has registered a complaint. Avoiding complaints by setting proper expectations is best. Long-term relationships are begun by making an honest presentation of the product's capabilities and eliminating any misconceptions before the order is placed.

MONITOR ORDER PROCESSING

Although many people may work on an order before it is shipped, the salesperson is ultimately responsible, at least in the eyes of the customer, for seeing that the product is shipped when promised. Salespeople should keep track of impending orders and inform buyers when the paperwork is delayed in the customer's plant. Orders placed directly with a salesperson should be transmitted to the factory immediately. Also, progress on orders in process should be closely monitored. If problems arise in filling the order, the customer should be informed promptly; on the other hand, if the order can be filled sooner than promised, the customer should be notified so that the proper arrangements can be made.

Fortunately, computers have made the sales representative's job easier. Salespeople can use handheld terminals and laptop PCs to check on inventory and/or the status of an order. For example, Northeast Utilities account executives use customer relationship management software to monitor the billing cycle and ensure that sales are being processed properly.[8] Progressive firms have introduced automated order systems that allow the customer to sign a pad on the computer; the signature is sent to the company electronically, avoiding delays that might result if the contract were mailed.

This salesperson (in the tie) is working with the shipping department to make sure that his customer's order is delivered promptly.

Harry Sieplinga/HMS Images/The Image Bank

Some firms, such as GE and Baxter Healthcare, facilitate the automatic placement of orders by having their own computers talk to customers' computers. This technology, called **electronic data interchange (EDI)**, boosts the productivity of both the salespeople and the purchasing managers they call on. As a result, salespeople spend less time writing orders and more time solving problems; buyers save on ordering and inventory costs. Computerized communication for order placement is particularly useful when managing a customer's needs worldwide. Problems arising from elements such as time zones and language barriers are minimized.

Monitoring order processing and other after-sale activities is critical to developing a partnership. Studies continually show that buyers are displeased with most salespeople in this respect. One study indicated that failure to follow through after the sale was the buyers' second biggest complaint about salespeople (talking too much was first).[9] One example of superior after-sale follow-up is supply chain management, discussed in Selling Scenario 13.1.

ENSURE PROPER INITIAL USE OF THE PRODUCT OR SERVICE

Customer dissatisfaction can occur just after delivery of a new product, especially if the product is technical or requires special installation. Customers unfamiliar with the product may have problems installing or using it. They may even damage the product through improper use. Many salespeople visit new customers right after initial deliveries to ensure the correct use of the product. In this way they can also help the customer realize the full potential benefits of the product.

Some buyers may be knowledgeable about how to use the basic features of a product or service, but if it is not operating at maximum efficiency, the wise salesperson will show the buyer how to get more profitable use out of it. Many firms have staffed a customer service department to aid salespeople in this task. It is still the salesperson's responsibility, however, to make sure that the customer service department takes proper care of each new customer.

One former product manager for Olivetti reports that the company used to ship typewriters to the United States with a defective operator's manual. If the new owner followed the instructions exactly, there was no possible way to put in

In Bishop's Stortford, England, a Thermofrost representative trains a TESCO store manager in the proper maintenance of a Thermofrost display cooler. Getting customers off to the right start is essential to building long and satisfying relationships.

Courtesy Parker Hannifin Corporation

SUPPLY CHAIN MANAGEMENT

A current buzz term in business is *supply chain management,* but just what is it and how does it affect sales? Supply chain management is the combination of logistics with marketing to jointly manage the supply of products throughout the entire chain, from supplier to user. For Bose Corporation, supply chain management means having representatives from each of its top 10 suppliers working full-time at Bose. These salespeople have full access to all Bose information, including pricing and financial terms for all suppliers, even their competitors. They need that information to coordinate the detailed scheduling and other activities between their companies and Bose.

But supply chain management also includes delivering products with the right quality, codeveloping products to manage costs while meeting functionality requirements, and carrying out other similar activities. In a study of automakers, tier 1 suppliers were valued for their technological development ability, in addition to their contributions via logistics, more than for their price. These suppliers help automakers design cars that are cheaper to build while maintaining or improving their functionality. In this way these suppliers add value to the entire chain and, in most cases, are rewarded with greater profits.

The trust required to share such detailed information between companies is huge, and both companies can learn or develop important new technologies and products. As Vollman and Cordon wrote, "We know of a customer who developed an adhesive with a supplier that clearly made a major difference in the performance of the end products." The supplier then went on to sell that adhesive to the customer's competitors, which angered the original customer. But when Wal-Mart and Procter & Gamble developed cross docking (a shipping method that lowers costs), they did so knowing that Wal-Mart wanted other suppliers to cross dock while P&G had a competitive advantage to sell to other retailers. As one buyer said, "We don't expect Rockwool (the supplier) not to apply these newly learned competencies to its other major customers, we just want to stay one step ahead."

Sources: Thomas E. Vollmann and Carlos Cordon, "Building Successful Customer–Supplier Alliances," *Long Range Planning* 31 (1999), pp. 684–94; Jai-Beom Kim and Paul Michell, "Relationship Marketing in Japan: Buyer–Supplier Relationships of Four Automakers," *Journal of Business & Industrial Marketing* 14 (1999), pp. 118–29.

---

the ribbon. The manual was originally written in Italian and then poorly translated into English. To make matters worse, the product was redesigned, making the manual obsolete, but the company never changed it. In this situation salespeople had to ask customers to call when they received the product so the salespeople could demonstrate how to install the ribbon. In international sales companies often try to get by with manuals that use diagrams rather than words to avoid translation problems. In these situations salespeople should follow up with a personal visit to make sure the customer gets off to a good start.

To be most effective, the salesperson should not wait until the user has trouble with the product. The fewer the difficulties allowed to occur, the greater will be the customer's confidence in the salesperson and the product.

FOLLOW UP   The first follow-up a salesperson should perform after the sale is a call to say thank you and to check to see that the product is working appropriately. Some salespeople use specialty advertising, or gifts imprinted with their company's name, to say thanks. These items are generally small enough to avoid concerns about bribery and can include desk clocks, pens, and the like. But salespeople should also follow up regularly with their accounts to stay in touch with any changing needs or possible problems. In fact, failing to follow up is a major complaint that buyers have about salespeople.[10]

Joe Hunter, owner of Karr-Hunter Pontiac, told us that his dealership does several hundred dollars' worth of printing every month. He tried four printers before he finally found one who would call him every few weeks. Joe wanted that kind of follow-up to avoid running out of forms. Regular follow-up prompts Joe to check his stock and to order printing before he runs out. Regular follow-up with satisfied customers also promotes opportunities for securing references. Regular follow-up can be accomplished via a personal visit, the telephone, or even e-mail.

Iomega Corporation sells digital storage solutions and uses e-mail newsletters to keep in touch with customers.[11] These newsletters can be personalized with both the salesperson's and the customer's names, which helps maintain a sense of commitment to the relationship. Customers' replies to the e-mail go straight back to the rep.

MAKE PERSONAL VISITS

Personal visits can be the most expensive form of follow-up because of the time it takes to travel and because the sales call will last longer than one conducted through other means. A personal visit, though, can be extremely productive because the salesperson can check on inventories or the performance of the machine or other aspects that can be accomplished only at the customer's site. Plus, a customer may be more likely to disclose more information, such as a minor complaint or compliment, in a personal setting than over the phone. Regular personal visits can also build trust, a key component needed to move the relationship forward.

TELEPHONE

Between personal visits, it is often a good idea to make contact via telephone. A salesperson can make 12 or more such calls within an hour, efficiently checking on his or her clients. Telephone calls are two-way communication, giving the customer an opportunity to voice any concerns and minimizing intrusion. Contact management software, such as GoldMine, can help salespeople schedule telephone follow-ups. Ray Peters, with CBC Communications, has set GoldMine to give him 10 such follow-ups every day.

MAIL

Many companies provide form letters or thank-you cards to encourage their salespeople to follow up on new sales. Salespeople can also create their own form letters and use their contact management software to generate the most appropriate mailing list. The problem, though, is that these are still form letters. Creative use of certain fields in contact management software like GoldMine, however, enables salespeople to add a personalized paragraph, creating that special touch that can dramatically increase the impact of such a letter. E-mail is also becoming a common form of customer contact, with customers appreciating the opportunity to choose when to read and respond to the salesperson's contact.

Following up with customers signals that the salesperson is dependable and customer oriented. Although the objective may be to create a functional relationship rather than a strategic partnership, such follow-up is still necessary to remind the customer that you are the salesperson with whom they want to do business.

HANDLE CUSTOMER COMPLAINTS

Handling complaints is critical to developing goodwill and maintaining partnerships. Complaints can occur at any time in the partnering process, not just during the exploration stage. Handling complaints properly is always important, but perhaps even more so in the early stages of a partnership. Attempts to establish partnerships often collapse because of shortsightedness in handling customer complaints. Over 45 percent of buyers in one survey stop buying because of poor

This International Wood Products (IWP) salesperson is demonstrating the features of a new line of doors to a customer who already purchases other IWP products. Cross-selling opportunities like this leverage existing relationships to identify needs for additional products.

Daniel MacDonald/Stock, Boston

service, while another 20 percent stop because they are ignored.[12] Some firms spend thousands of dollars on advertising but make the mistake of insulting customers who attempt to secure a satisfactory adjustment.

Complaints normally arise when the company and its products do not live up to the customer's expectations. Assuming the proper expectations were set, customers can be disappointed for any of the following reasons: (1) the product performs poorly, (2) it is being used improperly, or (3) the terms of the sales contract were not met. Although salespeople usually cannot change the product or terms, they can affect these sources of complaints.

As we discussed earlier in this chapter, the cost of making the first sale is substantially higher than the cost of repeat sales, so making every reasonable effort to keep customers in whom the company has invested time and money is good business. Also, many customers don't go to the trouble of complaining, so when a customer does attempt to secure satisfaction because of disappointment with a product or service, the company should view the complaint as an opportunity to prove its reliability.

One study showed that when a company fails in its dealings with a complainant, the latter will tell 10 people, on average, about the bad experience; those who are satisfied tell only four to five others. Also, for every dissatisfied person who complains, an estimated 50 more simply stop buying the product.[13]

Despite all the care manufacturers take to produce good products, unsatisfactory items do find their way to the ultimate user or retailer. This inevitable situation becomes alarming if the unsatisfactory products become too numerous.

CAN YOU WIN THEM ALL?

To Kristen Robertson, a sales rep for Collier Electric, losing a customer is unthinkable. She hates to give up on an account. Sometimes, however, that is the best thing to do.

"We sell lighting systems, electrical products, conduit, and other such things to electricians who work on major construction projects. Construction projects are always behind schedule, and time is always critical," notes Robertson. "I had one account that had given me some business, but it seemed like very little considering how much I knew they were doing. Then they had a contract for a major sports arena, and I got the whole bid—nearly $200,000." Robertson adds that the order was not her largest, but close.

Many of the lighting system products were standard off-the-shelf items from a particular manufacturer, but there were several custom lighting products created for the executive suites (the offices for the facility) and for the private boxes. "We had quoted a bare-bones price on the entire deal in order to get the business." When the delivery arrived, the arena owner complained to the electrician that these custom lights were too small and didn't look right. "The electrician wanted us to replace them, overnight if possible, with larger lights! He tried to say we didn't have them built to spec but the lights were exactly as specified."

Robertson did all she could, finally shipping a similar but standard product completely free of charge. "The arena owner was satisfied, especially since we paid for the expedited delivery *and* the lights." To make matters worse, the electrician began bad-mouthing Collier with other electricians, complaining about being overcharged and other falsehoods.

"We finally had our attorney, our president, and me meet with this electrician. We literally had to catch him at a jobsite because he wouldn't see us. But it was the only way we could get him to stop complaining to others with nonfacts." What Robertson learned later was that several other vendors had the same experience, and that most of her customers ignored this person. "I hate losing an account, but that was one I was happy to let someone else have."

Most progressive companies have learned that an excellent way to handle customer complaints is through personal visits by sales representatives. Thus the salesperson may have total responsibility for this portion of the company's public relations. Salespeople who carry this burden must be prepared to do an effective job. Building Partnerships 13.1 illustrates how one salesperson with the responsibility and authority for customer service was able to turn around a customer's complaint.

Complaints cannot be eliminated; they can only be reduced in frequency. The salesperson who knows complaints are inevitable can learn to handle them as a normal part of the job. The following discussion presents some techniques for responding to complaints; Exhibit 13.3 provides an overview.

ENCOURAGE BUYERS TO TELL THEIR STORY

Some customers can become angry over real or imaginary grievances. They welcome the salesperson's visit as an opportunity to voice complaints. Other buyers are less emotional in expressing complaints and give little evidence of irritation or anger, but the complaint is no less important. In either case customers need to tell their stories without interruption. Interruptions add to the irritation of emotionally upset buyers, making it almost impossible to arrive at a settlement that is fair to all parties.

Customers want a sympathetic reaction to their problems, whether real or imagined. They want their feelings to be acknowledged, their business to be recognized as important, and their grievances handled in a friendly manner. An antagonistic attitude or an attitude that implies the customer is trying to cheat

EXHIBIT 13.3

Responding to
Complaints

- Encourage buyers to tell their story.
- Determine the facts.
- Offer a solution.
- Follow through with action.

the company seldom paves the way for a satisfactory adjustment. You can probably relate to this feeling if you have ever had to return a defective product or get some kind of adjustment made on a bill. Exhibit 13.4 suggests ways to handle irate customers.

Good salespeople show they are happy the grievance has been brought to their attention. After the customer describes the problem, the salesperson may express regret for any inconvenience. An attempt should then be made to talk about points of agreement. Agreeing with the customer as far as possible gets the process off to the right start.

DETERMINE THE FACTS

It is easy to be influenced by a customer who is honestly making a claim for an adjustment. An inexperienced salesperson might forget that many customers make their case for a claim as strong as possible. Emphasizing the points most likely to strengthen one's case is human nature. But the salesperson has a responsibility to his or her company, too. A satisfactory adjustment cannot be made until all the facts are known.

Whenever possible, the salesperson should examine, in the presence of the customer, the product claimed to be defective. Encouraging the customer to pinpoint the exact problem is a good idea. If the defect is evident, this step may be unnecessary. In other instances, make certain the complaint is understood. The purpose of getting the facts is to determine the cause of the problem so that the proper solution can be provided.

Experienced salespeople soon learn that products may appear defective when actually nothing is wrong with them. For example, a buyer may complain that paint was applied exactly as directed but repainting became necessary in a short time; therefore, the paint was no good. However, the paint may have been spread too

EXHIBIT 13.4

Handling Rude or Irate
Customers

1. Follow the Golden Rule—treat your customer the way you would like to be treated, no matter how difficult the client becomes.
2. Prove you listened—paraphrase the customer's concern, recognizing the customer's feelings along with the facts.
3. Don't justify, excuse, or blame others—be positive and thank the customer for bringing the problem to your attention so that you can resolve it.
4. Do the hard things first—the faster they get done, the more your customer will appreciate you and your efforts.
5. Do call back if the customer hangs up.
6. Give the customer someone else to call, but only in case you are not available— don't pass the buck!

Sources: Gary Dunn, "Irate Customers, What Can You Do?" *Promotional Products Business*, March 1999, pp. 72–75; Chad Kaydo, "How to Handle a Rude Customer," *Sales & Marketing Management*, April 1998, p. 88.

thin. Any good paint will cover just so much area. If the manufacturer recommends using a gallon of paint to cover 400 square feet with two coats and the user covers 600 square feet with two coats, the product is not at fault. Or if an office equipment salesperson sells a fax machine that requires special paper, the machine is not at fault if the customer gets unsatisfactory results from a low-grade substitute paper.

On the other hand, salespeople should not assume product or service failure is always the user's fault. They need an open mind to search for the facts in each case. Defective material may have found its way to the dealer's shelves, the wrong merchandise may have been shipped, the buyer may have been over-charged, or the buyer may have been billed for an invoice that was already paid. The facts may prove the company is at fault. Also, some companies have the policy that the customer is always right, in which case there is no need to establish responsibility. There is still a need, however, to determine what the cause was so the right solution can be offered.

In this phase of making an adjustment, salespeople must avoid giving the impression of stalling. The customer should know that the purpose of determining the facts is to permit a fair adjustment, that the inquiry is not being made to delay action or avoid resolution.

OFFER A SOLUTION

After the customer tells his or her story and the facts are determined, the next step is to offer a solution. At this time the company representative describes the process by which the company will resolve the complaint, and the rep should then gain agreement that the proposed solution is satisfactory.

Company policies vary, but many assign the responsibility for settling claims to the salesperson. Other companies require the salesperson to investigate claims and recommend a settlement to the home office. The proponents of both methods have good arguments to justify them. Some companies maintain that salespeople are in the best position to make adjustments fairly, promptly, and satisfactorily, especially if the customer and salesperson are geographically distant from the home office. Others believe that permitting salespeople to only recommend a course of action assures the customer of attention from a higher level of management. Therefore, the customer will be more likely to accept the action taken. Companies holding the latter view also claim that for many technical products, the salesperson is not qualified to make a technical analysis of product difficulties.

Whatever the company policy, the customer desires quick action and fair treatment and wants to know the reasons for the action. Most customers are satisfied if they quickly receive fair treatment. They must, however, be convinced of its fairness, and customers seldom are unless the reasoning behind the treatment is explained to them. Nothing discourages a customer more than having action postponed indefinitely or being offered vague promises. Although some decisions may take time, the salesperson should try to expedite action. The opportunity to develop a partnership may be lost if the time lapse is too great, even though action is taken in the customer's favor.

Some salespeople make disparaging remarks about their own companies or managers. Blaming someone else in the company is a poor practice because this behavior can cause the customer to lose faith in both the salesperson and the company. Moreover, if the customer does not like the proposed solution, the salesperson trusted to make an adjustment or recommendation should shoulder the responsibility. Any disagreement on the action taken should be ironed out between the salesperson and the home office staff. When reported to the customer, the action must be stated in a sound, convincing manner.

The action taken may vary with the circumstances. Some possible settlements when a product is unsatisfactory are

1. Replace the product without cost to the customer.
2. Replace the product and charge the customer for labor or transportation costs only.
3. Replace the product and share all costs with the customer.
4. Replace the product but require the customer to pay part of the cost of the new product.
5. Instruct the customer on how to proceed with a claim against a third party.
6. Send the product to the factory for a decision.

Occasionally customers make claims they know are unfair. Although they realize the company is not at fault, they still try to get a settlement. Fortunately, relatively few customers do this.

To assume that a customer is willfully trying to cheat the company would be unwise. He or she may honestly see a claim as legitimate even though the salesperson can clearly tell that the company is not at fault. The salesperson does well, then, to proceed cautiously and, if any doubt exists, to treat the claim as legitimate.

A salesperson convinced that a claim is dishonest has two ways to take action. First, he or she can give the buyer an opportunity to save face by suggesting that a third party may be to blame. For example, if a machine appears not to have been oiled for a long time, a salesperson may suggest, "Is it possible that your maintenance crew neglected to oil this machine?" Second, the salesperson can unmask the fraudulent claim and appeal to the customer's sense of fair play. This procedure may cause the loss of a customer. In some cases, however, the company may be better off without that customer.

Answers to the following questions often affect the action to be taken:

- What is the dollar value of the claim? Many firms have established standard procedures for what they classify as small claims. For example, one moving and storage firm considers any claim under $200 to be too insignificant to investigate fully; thus a refund check is issued automatically for a claim under this amount. Firms may also have a complete set of procedures and policies developed for every size of claim.

- How often has this customer made claims? If the buyer has instituted many claims in the past, the company may need to not only resolve the specific complaint but also conduct a more comprehensive investigation of all prior claims. Such a probe may reveal systematic flaws in the salesperson's company, product, or procedures. For example, Pinacor (a $5 billion technology distributor) identified a pattern of shipping complaints from one customer. By creating extra inventory, Pinacor was able to meet the customer's higher demands and then applied the same solution to other customers. The result was an overall increase in sales.[14]

- How will the action taken affect other customers? The salesperson should assume that the action taken will be communicated to other prospects and customers. If the complaining customer is part of a buying community (discussed in Chapter 7), chances are very good that others will learn about the resolution of the claim. Thus the salesperson must take actions necessary to maintain a positive presence in that community, possibly even providing a more generous solution than the merits of the case dictate.

The solution that will be provided must be clearly communicated to the customer. The customer must perceive the settlement as being fair. When describing the settlement, the salesperson should carefully monitor all verbal and nonverbal cues to determine the customer's level of satisfaction. If the customer does not agree with the proposed course of action, the salesperson should seek ways to change the settlement or provide additional information as to why the settlement is fair to all parties.

FOLLOW THROUGH WITH ACTION

A fair settlement made in the customer's favor helps to resell the company and its products or services. The salesperson has the chance to prove what the customer has been told for a long time: that the company will devote time and effort to keeping customers satisfied.

The salesperson who has authority only to recommend an adjustment must take care to report the facts of the case promptly and accurately to the home or branch office. The salesperson has the responsibility to act as a buffer between the customer and the company. After the claim is filed, contact must be maintained with the customer to see that the customer secures the promised settlement.

The salesperson also has a responsibility to educate the customer to forestall future claims. After a claim has been settled to the customer's satisfaction is a fine time to make some suggestions. For example, the industrial sales representative may provide a new set of directions on how to oil and clean a machine.

In two studies buyers were asked to name the characteristics of excellent salespeople. The seller's ability to go to bat for the buyer within the seller's firm was the most important characteristic in one study and the second most important in the other.[15] Mike Rose, sales representative for Menasha Corporation, sells packaging materials. He was named a top 10 sales representative by *Purchasing* magazine because of the way he represents his buyers to his company. For example, one customer had a problem with boxes popping open in shipment. Rose observed the problem and recognized that the dyes his company was using caused the adhesive to fail. He returned to his own company and persuaded it to invest in new dyes so that the adhesives would keep the boxes closed.[16]

Many businesses have built great names by following the slogan "The customer is always right." Yet the salesperson is often the person to make sure the company lives up to that slogan.

ACHIEVE CUSTOMER SATISFACTION

Although complaints always signal customer dissatisfaction, their absence does not necessarily mean customers are happy. Customers probably voice only 1 in 20 of their concerns. They may speak out only when highly dissatisfied, or a big corporation's buyer may not be aware of problems until the product's users vent their frustration. Lower levels of dissatisfaction still hurt sales. Salespeople should continuously monitor customers' levels of satisfaction and perceptions of product performance because customer satisfaction is the most important reason for reordering at this stage in the relationship, whereas dissatisfaction with the way they are treated is responsible for 84 percent of accounts leaving.[17]

When the customer is satisfied, an opportunity for further business exists. Complaints and dissatisfaction can occur at any time during the relationship, but handling complaints well during the exploration stage is one way to prove that the salesperson is committed to keeping the customer's business. When customers sense such commitment, whether through the handling of a complaint or through other forms of special attention, they may be ready to move to the expansion stage.

EXPANSION

The next phase of the buyer–seller relationship is expansion. When a salesperson does a good job of identifying and satisfying needs and the beginnings of a partnership are in place, the opportunity is ripe for additional sales. For example, as we discussed at the beginning of this chapter, Ross/Flex may have had only 10 percent of Knight's business at the start, but as trust developed, that percentage grew. With greater trust, the salesperson can focus on identifying additional needs and providing solutions. In this section we discuss how to increase sales from current customers to expand the relationship. Keep in mind, however, that the activities of the exploration stage (monitoring order processing, handling complaints, and so on) still apply.

There are several ways to maximize the selling opportunity each account represents. These include generating reorders, upgrading, full-line selling, and cross-selling.

GENERATING REPEAT ORDERS

In some situations the most appropriate strategy is to generate repeat orders. For example, Cargill provides salt and other cooking ingredients to Kelloggs. The best strategy for the Cargill salesperson may be to ensure that Kelloggs continues to buy those ingredients from Cargill. Several methods can be used to improve the likelihood of reorders. We will discuss each method in turn.

BE PRESENT AT BUYING TIME

One important method of ensuring reorders is to know how often and when the company makes decisions. For example, one salesperson uses contact management software like ACT! to track his customers' purchases. By simply sending them a letter a week before their usual purchases, he has been able to generate an 85 percent reorder rate—without making a personal visit.[18]

Buyers do not always have regular buying cycles, which can make it difficult for salespeople to be present at buying time. In these situations the seller still wants to be present in the buyer's mind. Two items that can help keep the seller present are catalogs and specialty advertising items. Catalogs are useful for buyers, who will usually refer to them when ready to buy. Specialty advertising items, such as pens or desk calendars, also aid buyers in reordering, especially if the toll-free number is easy to find. Florida Furniture Industries has used desk calendars for more than 60 years to remind furniture store buyers of whom to call when inventories are low.

HELP TO SERVICE THE PRODUCT

Most products need periodic maintenance and repair, and some mechanical and electronic products require routine adjustments. Such service requirements offer salespeople a chance to show buyers that the seller's interest did not end with the delivery of the product. Salespeople should be able to make minor adjustments or take care of minor repairs. If they cannot put the product back into working order, they must notify the proper company representative. They should then check to see that the repairs have been completed in a timely manner and to the customer's complete satisfaction.

As we discuss in Chapter 17, part of the salesperson's job is getting to know the company's maintenance and repair people. These repair people can act as the salesperson's eyes and ears when they make service calls. When a good relationship is established with service personnel, salespeople can learn of pending decisions or concerns and take the necessary action.

Salespeople should monitor parts shipments just as they would any order; in addition, they should supply up-to-date service manuals and place buyers' names on the service mailing list. In this way bulletins on maintenance and repair reach the proper people. If the customer's maintenance department in the plant is well informed about the product, user complaints fall off dramatically.

Helping to service the product is just as important—and maybe more so—when the product is a service, as Michael Maynard of Azimuth Partners discovered. With one account he kept trying to pitch new business after making a sale for a $20,000 research project, but wasn't getting anywhere. He found that more postsale follow-up was needed to make sure the project was going smoothly and the data were being used fully. Only then could the customer see the benefits of additional work.[19]

Larry Dorfman, president and CEO of Atlanta-based Automobile Protection Corporation (APCO), administers extended service contracts that pay for automobile breakdowns. The car dealer may be APCO's customer, but the service department of the dealership is the user of the service. Dorfman trains his salespeople to first visit the service department when visiting a current account because he believes that "until we service what we've already sold, we don't have the right to sell anything else."[20]

Thinking It Through	Some customers take advantage of salespeople by trying to have them perform almost all of the routine maintenance on a product for free. What can you as a salesperson do to curb such requests? How do you know where to draw the line?

PROVIDE EXPERT GUIDANCE

An industrial buyer or purchasing agent may need help in choosing a proper grade of oil or in selecting a suitable floor cleaner. A buyer for a retail store may want help developing sales promotion ideas. Whether the buyer needs help in advertising, selling, or managing, good salespeople are prepared to offer worthwhile suggestions or services.

The salesperson usually prospers only if the buyer prospers. Obviously, unless buyers can use a product or service profitably or resell it at a profit, they have no need to continue buying from that product's seller. One expert suggests finding non–selling-related ideas to offer your customers. When you use your industry expertise to solve problems or develop opportunities for your clients that do not involve the sale of your product, you add value to the relationship, which can ultimately help you expand your business within the account.[21]

Many firms have developed a team approach to providing guidance and suggestions. For example, Verizon uses a systems approach to help develop and maintain the communication systems of its major accounts. The major account service team (MAST) is composed of marketing (as chairperson), engineering, service, supply, and traffic representatives. This interdepartmental approach brings together all skills required to provide expert guidance and suggestions to meet the expanding, sophisticated needs of large customers.

Another salesperson named a top 10 sales representative by *Purchasing* magazine won the honor because of his expert guidance. John Paduch, now vice president of sales at American Supply Company of Gary, Indiana, saved one customer $1.4 million over five years through various ideas, such as showing how changing from stainless steel to cast iron pipes and valves saved $165,000 with no loss in quality. In addition, Paduch was able to assist the customer in reducing inventory by 47 percent. Such expert guidance led that customer to nominate John Paduch for *Purchasing*'s top 10 sales rep award.[22]

UARCO's philosophy for success in the highly competitive field of selling business forms includes expert advice. Its forms management program makes the company a business partner with, rather than merely a supplier to, its major accounts. Customers are shown how to control the costs of buying and using forms by such practices as redesigning existing forms, grouping forms for more economical ordering, keeping records of quantities on hand and on order, and keeping track of the dollar value of the inventory. UARCO's customers welcome such advice, and the result is a high reorder rate.

PROVIDE SPECIAL ASSISTANCE

Salespeople are in a unique position to offer many types of assistance to the buyer. This section briefly mentions a few of the types of assistance salespeople can give their customers.

Salespeople engage in many activities. For example, salespeople for Cott Beverages, a Canadian maker of private-label soft drinks for companies like Wal-Mart, work as consultants, offering advice on product design and store layout.[23] Salespeople at Simmons help set up mattress displays in furniture stores. Makita power-tool salespeople provide free demonstrations for customers of hardware stores. Most salespeople who sell to resellers will tidy up the shelves and physically restock them from the stockroom supplies. Salespeople also help train the reseller's employees in how to sell the products to the final consumers.

Gail Walker of Marquis Communications, a trade show and special events service agency, worked in the customer's booth at a trade show when one of the customer's salespeople got sick. She worked as hard as if she were one of the firm's employees. Providing such special assistance is one hallmark of excellence in selling. Good relationships are built faster and made more solid by the salesperson who does a little something extra for a customer, performing services over and above his or her normal responsibilities.

UPGRADING

Similar to generating reorders is the concept of upgrading. **Upgrading,** also called *upselling,* is convincing the customer to use a higher-quality product or a newer product. The salesperson seeks the upgrade because the new or better product serves the needs of the buyer more effectively than the old product did.

Upgrading is crucial to companies like Unisys. Unisys depends on current customers to upgrade to new products when they become available. But their customers were hearing more from the competition than from Unisys, so the company developed a direct mail and telemarketing program to support field salespeople. The result has been profit growth of 8 percent per year, compared to zero in 1997.[24]

When you upgrade, it is a good idea to emphasize during the needs identification phase that the initial decision was a good one. Now, however, needs or technology have changed, and the newer product fits the customer's requirements better. Otherwise, the buyer may believe that the seller is trying to take advantage of the relationship to foist a higher-priced product.

FULL-LINE SELLING

Full-line selling is selling the entire line of associated products. For example, a Xerox copier salesperson may sell the copier but also wants to sell the dry ink and paper the copier uses and a service contract. Or a Campbell Soup Company salesperson will ask a store to carry cream of potato soup as well as tomato soup.

The emphasis in full-line selling is on helping the buyer realize the synergy of owning or carrying all of the products in that line. For example, the Xerox salesperson may emphasize the security in using Xerox supplies, whereas the Campbell rep will point out that sales for all soups will increase if the assortment is broader.

CROSS-SELLING

Cross-selling is similar to full-line selling except the additional products sold are not directly associated with the initial products. For example, cross-selling occurs when the Xerox salesperson attempts to sell a fax machine to a copier customer or when a Campbell Soup Company rep sells spaghetti sauce to a soup buyer. Cross-selling involves leveraging the relationship with a buyer to identify needs for additional products. Again, trust in the selling organization and the salesperson already exist; therefore, the sale should not be as difficult as it would be with a new customer, provided the needs exist. One of the most unusual cross-selling situations is Moore Industries, which sells Filter Queen vacuum cleaners and Freedom Jet, a needleless insulin injector for diabetics. Salespeople try to sell Filter Queens to all Freedom Jet users and ask the Filter Queen users for leads on insulin-dependent diabetics.[25] Astra Pharmaceutical cross-sells through multiple reps. Because of the technical knowledge required to sell pharmaceuticals, a separate rep is needed for each product, but they use e-mail and other technology to leverage their knowledge about their doctor-customers.[26]

Cross-selling (and full-line selling) does require additional training, as illustrated in Exhibit 13.5. Some attempts at cross-selling, though, can resemble the initial sale, because the buying center may change. For example, the spaghetti sauce buyer may not be the same person who buys soups. If that is the case, the salesperson will have to begin a relationship with the new buyer, building trust and credibility.

TOTAL QUALITY MANAGEMENT AND ACCOUNT RELATIONSHIPS

Many companies review their purchasing habits when they implement total quality management (TQM). Originating in the United States but first fully implemented in Japan, TQM means many things, but one area with tremendous implications for salespeople is purchasing. Companies espousing a TQM philosophy are reducing the number of vendors with whom they do business in order to demand higher quality and other benefits from partnership-type relationships (recall the discussion of buying trends in Chapter 4). The result is that some

---

EXHIBIT 13.5

Seven Tips for Effective Cross-Selling

1. *Product knowledge:* Salespeople have to know all of their company's products. When companies introduce new cross-selling opportunities, training is needed to learn the new product lines.
2. *Cross-selling skills:* Salespeople must know how to identify the appropriate decision maker, how to leverage current relationships, and how to use other cross-selling skills. Cross-selling often requires additional training.
3. *Incentives:* Many salespeople are afraid of losing the first piece of business by asking for too much, so incentives can help make it worthwhile to ask.
4. *Reasonable quotas or goals:* The first goal when implementing a cross-selling strategy is to get salespeople to simply ask for the opportunity. Goals that are too tough encourage salespeople to force the cross-sale.
5. *Results tracking:* Effective organizations track results by individual and by sales team to identify cross-selling success. Many companies use contact management software like GoldMine or Microsoft Access for results tracking.
6. *Timing:* Creating a promotion campaign to support cross-selling efforts, particularly when seasonality is an issue, can make a cross-selling strategy very successful. Timing also refers to making sure that training occurs before the program starts.
7. *Performance appraisals:* Salespeople need feedback to identify where and how in the process to improve.

Source: Vicki West, PhD, and Jan Minifie, PhD. Used by permission.

salespeople are finding receptive ears for full-line selling and cross-selling proposals, whereas others are losing business. For example, Xerox, including Fuji Xerox and Rank Xerox in Europe, reduced its number of vendors from 5,000 worldwide to 500 over a period of 10 years.[27] Consequently, 4,500 salespeople lost what was probably their biggest account, and 500 salespeople increased their sales tremendously through full-line selling and cross-selling.

TQM also changes the way salespeople interact with their customers because customers are also demanding greater quality. In a study by the Quality Research Institute, only 15 percent of customers surveyed reported that their vendors had adequate quality management procedures, but 73 percent of executives believe their own companies have instituted effective quality procedures. TQM suggests that customers should set quality standards and participate in continuous improvement programs, which means that salespeople play an important role in ensuring that the voice of the customer is heard throughout the organization.

TQM and ISO 9000, a global quality standard, have increased global competition, making salespeople more important because of their role in satisfying customer needs. The TQM-driven trend to preferred-supplier programs is strong. In only two years the percentage of manufacturers with programs for developing preferred suppliers (and reducing the overall number of suppliers) grew from approximately 67 percent to almost 80 percent, and the number of ISO-certified companies rose from 3,000 to 15,500 over a four-year period.[28] The next section describes how companies become preferred suppliers in the commitment phase of the relationship.

COMMITMENT

When the buyer–seller relationship has reached the commitment stage, there is a stated or implied pledge to continue the relationship, as we discussed in Chapter 2. Formally, this pledge may begin with the seller becoming a **preferred supplier,** which is a much greater level of commitment than those levels discussed in Chapter 12. Although preferred-supplier status may mean different things in different companies, in general it means that the supplier is assured of a large percentage of the buyer's business and will get the first opportunity to earn new business.[29] For example, at Motorola only preferred suppliers are eligible to bid on new- product programs.[30] Thus *preferred supplier* is one term used for "partnership."

What does it take to become a preferred supplier? To become a preferred supplier for Bethlehem Steel, the supplier must pass several criteria (listed in Exhibit 13.6). In some cases a Bethlehem preferred supplier is a distributor, not a manufacturer. In these situations the supplier and Bethlehem Steel work in tandem to find the best

---

EXHIBIT 13.6

Preferred Supplier Criteria for Suppliers to Bethlehem Steel

- *Capability:* The purchasing team examines manufacturing, shipping, and administrative capabilities. Because Bethlehem requires significant monitoring by suppliers, even paperwork is scrutinized.
- *Organization:* Are employees dedicated? Is the company flexible or bureaucratic? Can it change as we change?
- *Financial health:* Bethlehem reviews audited financial statements to determine whether the supplier is well managed.
- *Culture:* Does the corporate culture fit with ours? Do we want the same things, and do we work in similar ways? Can we get along?
- *Willingness to commit:* Suppliers must be willing to commit the resources necessary to serve the account. For many suppliers, commitment means a full-time representative on Bethlehem's site.
- *Ethics:* Is the supplier trustworthy?

Source: Adapted from Jean Graham, "A Simple Idea Saves $8 Million a Year," *Purchasing,* May 21, 1992, pp. 47–49.

manufacturers at the lowest prices, with the result being increases in sales volume and better volume discounts. Bethlehem Steel gets the lowest price possible at the required service level, and the distributor makes more profit. Clearly this is a win–win opportunity.[31]

Note that upgrading, full-line selling, cross-selling, and handling complaints will continue to occur during the commitment stage. Because a commitment has been made by both parties to the partnership, however, expectations are greater. Handling complaints properly, appropriately upgrading or cross-selling, and fulfilling new needs are even more important because of the high level of commitment made to the partner.

Many buyers evaluate suppliers on criteria similar to those used by Bethlehem Steel.[32] Although the salesperson may not have the ability to influence corporate culture, she or he plays an important role in managing the relationship and leading both sides into commitment.

SECURING COMMITMENT TO A PARTNERSHIP

When firms reach the commitment stage, elements in addition to trust become important. Trust may be operationalized in the form of shared risk, such as Baxter International's agreements with some customers to share savings or expenses for joint programs. Along with the dimensions of trust such as competence and dependability (similar to Bethlehem's capability) and honesty (or ethics), there must be commitment to the partnership from the entire supplying organization, a culture that fits with the buyer's organizational culture, and channels of communication so open that the seller and buyer appear to be part of the same company. In fact, Mead and Pillsbury representatives asked each other, "If we were one company, what would we do differently?" The result was a level of commitment far greater and with more impact.[33]

COMMITMENT MUST BE COMPLETE

Commitment to the relationship should permeate both organizations, from top management to the secretary who answers the phone. This level of commitment means devoting the resources necessary to satisfy the customer's needs, even anticipating needs before the buyer does. As one buyer in the chemical industry says, "What we tend to find is that companies are out of synchronization between what they are selling and what (we) want . . . They try to sell you bulk chemicals when what you want is service, systems, and programs."[34] As other authors say, "There's a balance between giving and getting . . . When companies ask their customers for friendship, loyalty, and respect, too often they don't give those customers friendship, loyalty, and respect in return."[35] It is often the responsibility of the salesperson to secure commitment from his or her own company. Senior management must be convinced of the benefits of partnering with a specific account and be willing to allow the salesperson to direct the resources necessary to sustain the partnership. (Chapter 17 explores the process of building the internal partnerships the salesperson needs to coordinate those resources.)

Commitment also requires that all employees be empowered to handle the needs of the customer. For example, if the customer has a problem with a billing process, administration should be willing to work with the partner to develop a more satisfactory process. In a partnership the customer should not have to rely on only the salesperson to satisfy its needs.

COMMUNICATION

In the exploration stage, availability must be demonstrated (we already discussed the example of toll-free hot lines and voice mail to allow the seller's organization to respond quickly to customer calls). But in the commitment phase of a partnership, the seller must take a proactive communication stance. This approach means actively seeking opportunities to communicate at times other than when the salesperson has something to sell or the customer has a problem to resolve.

Partners are usually the first to learn of each other's new products, many times even codeveloping those products.[36] Part of the commitment between suppliers and their customer partners is the trust that such early knowledge will be kept confidential. Partners want to know what is coming out soon so they can make appropriate plans. But what happens if the new product is delayed or needs to have some bugs worked out? That happened to AlliedSignal when it introduced a 48-hour delivery plan to its major accounts. Just as the company was to begin taking orders, AlliedSignal realized that it wasn't ready to implement the plan. So top executives made joint calls with account reps, and together, AlliedSignal and its customers worked out solutions.[37]

Salespeople should also encourage direct communication among similar functional areas. In previous stages the two firms communicated through the buyer and the salesperson. If multilevel selling occurred, it occurred at even levels—that is, vice presidents talking to one another. But when two firms commit to a partnership, the boundaries between them, at least in terms of communication, should blur, as illustrated in Exhibit 13.7.

The buyer's production department, for example, should be able to communicate directly with the seller's engineering department rather than going through the salesperson, if production needs to work on a change in the product design. Although the salesperson would want to be aware of a product design change and ensure that engineering responded promptly to the customer's concern, direct communication means more accurate communication and a better understanding of the customer's needs. A better solution is more likely to result when there is direct communication.

CORPORATE CULTURE

Corporate culture is the values and beliefs held by senior management. A company's culture shapes the attitudes and actions of employees and influences the development of policies and programs.[38] For example, consider the following scene. In a large room with concrete floors are a number of cubicles built out of plywood. In each cubicle are a card table, two folding chairs, and a poster that says, "How low can you go?" Such is the scene in Bentonville, Arkansas, the corporate headquarters of Wal-Mart, where salespeople meet their buyers for Sam's Club and Wal-Mart. That room reflects Wal-Mart's culture of the lowest possible price.

A similar culture of constantly seeking ways to drive down costs is necessary for a seller to develop a partnership with Wal-Mart. A single salesperson will not change a company's corporate culture to secure a partnership with a buyer, but the salesperson must identify the type of culture both organizations hold and make an assessment of fit. Although a perfect match is not necessary, the salesperson must be ready to demonstrate that there is a fit. Offering lavish entertainment to a Wal-Mart buyer, for example, would not demonstrate a fit. Telling the buyer that you are staying at a Circle-6 Motel might.

 Companies have often sought international partners as a way to enter foreign markets. Wal-Mart partnered with Cifra when the U.S. retailer entered the Mexican market. Cifra provides distribution services and products to Wal-Mart for Sam's Club and Wal-Mart stores located in Mexico City, Monterrey, and Guadalajara. When partnering with companies from other countries, country culture differences as well as corporate culture differences can cause difficulties.

EXHIBIT 13.7

Direct Communication
between Partners

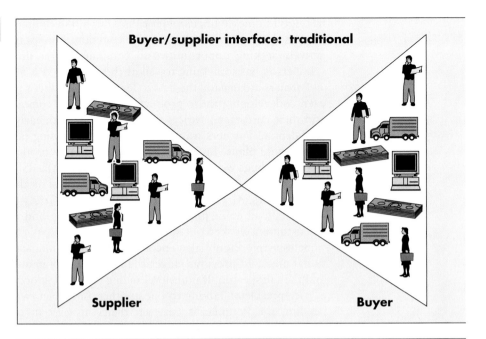

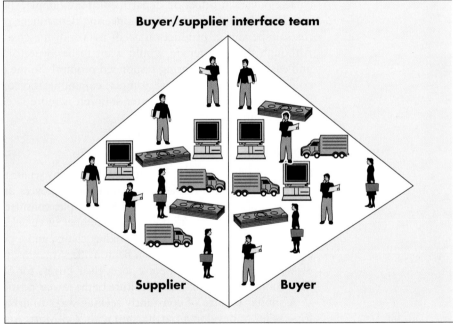

Source: Ginger Conlon, Lisa Napolitano, and Mike Pusateri, *Unlocking Profits: The Strategic Advantage of Key Account Management,* Chicago: National Account Management Association, 1997.

Though not attempting to change a company's culture, the salesperson who seeks a partnering relationship seeks change for both organizations. In the next section we discuss what types of changes salespeople manage and how they manage those changes.

THE SALESPERSON AS CHANGE AGENT

To achieve increasing revenue in an account over time, the salesperson acts as a **change agent,** or a cause of change in the organization. Each sale may involve some type of change, perhaps a change from a competitive product or simply a new version of the old one. Partnering, though, often requires changes in both the buying and selling organizations. For example, earlier we discussed John Paduch, who saved his customer $1.4 million. To achieve those savings, the buyer's company had to change the way it did business.

American Distribution Systems (ADS), a pharmaceutical distributor, and Ciba-Geigy, a pharmaceutical manufacturer, took six months to implement a joint operating plan that integrated systems of both companies. ADS created a cross-functional team that re-created ADS systems to function as part of Ciba-Geigy. At the same time, Ciba-Geigy had to share information and other resources to take full advantage of the benefits of the relationship. In this instance both buyer and seller had to change significantly for the partnership to work.

Change is not easy, even when it is obviously beneficial. The objective is to manage change, such as changing from steel to iron pipe, in the buyer's organization while giving the appearance of stability. Two critical elements to consider about change are its rate and scope. The **rate of change** refers to how quickly the change is made; the **scope of change** refers to the degree to which the change affects the organization. Broad changes affect many areas of the company, whereas narrow changes affect small areas. In general, the faster and broader the change, the more likely it will meet with resistance, as illustrated in Exhibit 13.8.[39]

To overcome resistance to change, the salesperson should consider several decisions. The first decision involves finding help in the buying organization for selling the proposal. Other important decisions are positioning the proposal, determining the necessary resources, and developing a time-based strategy.[40]

CHAMPIONS

First, the choice of one or more champions must be made. **Champions,** also called *advocates* or *internal salespeople,* work for the buying firm in the areas most affected by the proposed change and work with the salesperson to make the proposal successful. These champions can build momentum for the proposal by selling in arenas or during times that are off limits to the salesperson. For example, a champion may sell for the salesperson during a company picnic in a casual conversation with a coworker.

It is also important to recognize that one change is the change in status from preferred supplier to strategic partner. That change may also require a champion. Champions not only help persuade the firm to change but also help implement

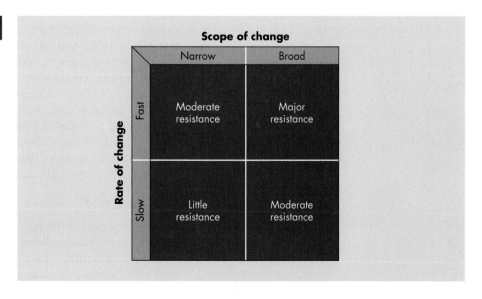

EXHIBIT 13.8

Change and Resistance
Resistance to change is greatest when the scope is broad and the rate of change is fast.

the change once the decision has been made.[41] Thus champions are very important to salespeople.

Salespeople can help potential champions by providing them with all of the knowledge they will need. Knowledge builds confidence; champions will have the courage to speak up when they are certain that they know what they are talking about. Salespeople can also motivate champions to participate fully in the decision process by showing how the decision meets their needs as well as the overall needs of the company.

POSITIONING THE CHANGE

Positioning the change is similar to positioning a product in mass marketing, as you may have learned in a principles of marketing course. In this case, however, the salesperson examines the specific needs and wants of the various constituencies in the account to position the change for the greatest likelihood of success. For example, Benson Bakery makes bread for restaurants. It was considering the purchase of equipment that would allow it to make bread and freeze it at the request of Steak and Ale, one of its major accounts. Hobart, which manufactures such equipment, could have positioned its equipment as delivering the best-quality product (marketing's concern) or as being the easiest to use and maintain (manufacturing's concern). Because manufacturing was not the key area in this decision, such a positioning may have been fatal.

Because salespeople are highly proactive in finding areas for improvement (or change) in their partners' organizations, positioning a change may determine who is involved in the decision. For example, suppose the IBM representative who calls on your school recognizes that the student computer labs are getting out-of-date. Is a proposal for new equipment primarily the domain of the computer services department, or is it the domain of faculty who teach computing classes? If the computer services department favors IBM but the users favor Apple, the IBM rep will be better served by positioning the change as the responsibility of the computer services department. Positioning the proposed change appropriately may spell success or failure for the proposal.

DETERMINING THE NECESSARY RESOURCES

The customer's needs may be beyond the salesperson's expertise. For example, Fram, a maker of auto parts, may be working with CarQuest, an auto parts retailer, to develop a major advertising program that will highlight their growing partnership. Such a change may require some selling to the advertising department at CarQuest. The Fram account representative will use the expert advice of Fram's own advertising department, its marketing research department, and probably its marketing management as well. These experts may visit CarQuest with the account rep and aid in securing that change in CarQuest's advertising focus.

The salesperson must assess the situation and determine what resources are needed to secure the buyer's commitment. Although the preceding example discusses allocation of personnel, salespeople must manage other resources as well, such as travel and entertainment budgets or sample supplies. (We discuss how to build internal partnerships to effectively coordinate company resources in Chapter 17.)

DEVELOPING A TIME-BASED STRATEGY

The salesperson must determine a strategy for the proposed change and set that strategy against a time line. This action accomplishes several objectives. First, the strategy is an outline of planned sales calls, with primary and minimum call objectives determined for each call. Second, the time line estimates when each

EXHIBIT 13.9   Time Line for Fram/CarQuest Strategy

Month 1	Month 2	Month 3	Month 4	Month 5	Month 6
Visit director of marketing. • **Primary objective:** Determine marketing needs. • **Minimum objective:** Secure permission to see merchandising manager and advertising manager	*Visit merchandising manager and advertising.* • **Primary objective:** Secure support in principle.	*Visit director of marketing.* • **Primary objective:** Specify objectives for new advertising plan and secure commitment in principle.	*Arrange tour of Fram facilities for VP of retail, marketing director, and advertising and merchandising managers.*	*Submit plan to director of marketing for approval.*	*Implement advertising program.*

call should occur. Of course, objectives and planned times will change depending on the results of each call, but this type of planning is necessary to give the salesperson guidance for each call, determine when resources are to be used, and make sure each call contributes to strategic account objectives.

For example, the Fram salesperson may determine that calls need to be made on five individuals at CarQuest. A time-based strategy would indicate which person should be visited first and what should be accomplished during that visit, as well as the order of visits to the remaining four members of the buying center. The strategy would also alert the salesperson as to when the advertising personnel were needed. Exhibit 13.9 illustrates such a time line.

CAUSES OF DISSOLUTION

Too often salespeople believe that once a customer has committed to a partnership, less work is needed to maintain that relationship. That belief, however, is untrue. One study found that 55 percent of all strategic partnerships dissolve within 3 to 5 years, and the rest have a further life expectancy of only 3.5 years.[42] Salespeople who subscribe to the belief that partnerships require less work fall victim to one or more common problems. As discussed in Chapter 2, the final stage for partnerships is dissolution, or breakup, but this stage can occur at any point, not just after commitment. Several potential problems, including maintaining few personal relationships, failing to monitor competitor actions or the industry, and falling into complacency, can lead to dissolution.

LIMITED PERSONAL RELATIONSHIPS

Salespeople tend to call on buyers they like; it is natural to want to spend time with friends. The result is that relationships are cultivated with only a few individuals in the account. Unfortunately for such salespeople, buyers may leave the organization, transfer to an unrelated area, or simply not participate in some decisions. Truly effective salespeople attempt to develop multiple relationships within an account.

Dun & Bradstreet calls this building customer relationships "high and wide." The company, which gathers and markets business data, believes it must be perceived as a value-added supplier, eventually becoming a strategic partner. The only way that Dun & Bradstreet believes it can reach the partnership level is to understand the senior executive's strategic perspective as well as that of the managers who implement programs. Dun & Bradstreet identified $26.5 million in additional sales in the first year of using the high-and-wide relationship strategy.[43]

One benefit of multiple relationships is that different champions can be selected for each proposal. Paul Kelly, a sales training consultant, suggests that after a proposal is decided on, the salesperson should review the process and identify the loudest opponent to the proposal in the buying organization. For the next proposal, the salesperson should solicit that person's support up front. The individual has already shown the courage and ability to fight for a position (even though it was against the salesperson's position)—ideal qualities for a champion.[44]

FAILING TO MONITOR COMPETITOR ACTIONS

No matter how strong the partnership is, competition will want a piece of the business. And no matter how good the salesperson is, there will still be times when the account is vulnerable to competitor action. Accounts are most vulnerable when a personnel change occurs (especially if the rep has developed relationships with a limited number of people in the account), when technology changes, or when major directional changes occur, such as a company starting a new division or entering a new market.

The successful salesperson, however, monitors competitor action even when the account seems invulnerable. For example, an insurance agency had all of the insurance business at a state university in Texas for more than 10 years but failed to monitor competitor action at the state capital and lost the account when another insurance agency found a sympathetic buyer in Austin. The loss of this one account cut annual earnings by more than 70 percent.

Monitoring competitor action can be as simple as checking the visitor's log at the front desk to see who has dropped by or keeping up with competitor actions and asking buyers for their opinions. Frequently, developing relationships with the many potential influencers in an account will also keep salespeople informed about competitor actions. As each person is visited, questions and comments about competitors will arise, indicating the activity level of competition.

Monitoring competition also means thinking about the benefits competitors offer, what their products do, and what their selling strategies are.[45] When salespeople understand what the competition offers, they can position their own company's unique capabilities more effectively. It is not enough to know where competitors have made calls; good salespeople also know what the competition is saying.

FAILING TO MONITOR THE INDUSTRY

Similar to failing to monitor competition is a failure to monitor the industry in which either the salesperson or the customer operates. Salespeople often assume that the responsibility of monitoring the industry lies with someone else, either higher-ups in their own company or with the customer. But salespeople who fail to monitor both industries stand to miss opportunities that change creates. As an extreme example, what would happen to the advertising agency's account executive if the Internet were ignored?

How does the professional salesperson monitor the industry? By reading trade magazines and by attending trade shows and conferences. The Wallace account manager who serves American Airlines reads airline and travel trade magazines, such as *Meetings & Conventions,* in order to understand the industry trends that will influence American's business. It's not enough to know your company's industry; with strategic partners, you must also know their industry.

FALLING INTO COMPLACENCY

Perhaps the most common thief of good accounts is complacency. In sales terms, **complacency** is assuming that the business is yours and will always be yours. It is failing to continue to work as hard to keep the business as you did initially to earn the business. For example, Coca-Cola was the sole supplier to El Volcan, the stadium for the professional soccer team, Los Tigres, in Monterrey, Mexico. After many years the stadium's concessions manager began to become annoyed with Coca-Cola, as service seemed lackadaisical. As a result, the contract was put out to bid; Pepsi responded with a significantly better offer and won the business.

Steven Berkey, sales manager at Victory Tube Company, identifies lost accounts by continually reviewing customer lists to see who is no longer placing orders. He also looks for significant drops in the amounts a customer orders, as this change signals an account that is trying other vendors.[46]

To avoid complacency, salespeople should regularly audit their own customer service. Some of the questions a salesperson may want to consider are as follows:

- Do I understand each individual's personal characteristics? Do I have these characteristics in my computer file on each account?

- Do I maintain a written or computerized record of promises made?

- Do I follow up on every customer request promptly, no matter how insignificant it may seem?

- Do I follow up on deliveries, make sure initial experiences are positive, and ensure that all paperwork is done correctly and quickly?

- Have I recently found something new that I can do better than the competition?

We opened this chapter by discussing the value of customers. But just as a reminder, research indicates that customers are five times more likely to stop doing business with a company because of poor service than any other reason.[47] Although striving for excellence in relationships with customers is important, one millionaire salesperson says, "You beat 50 percent of the people in America just by working hard. You beat another 40 percent by being a person of honesty and integrity . . . The last 10 percent is a dogfight in the free-enterprise system."[48] His words are a strong reminder of the importance of avoiding complacency in customer relationships.

CONFLICT

Not all dissolution is the result of conflict, as you can see from the types of reasons that most often lead to dissolution. But conflict between buyer and seller can occur, and when it does, the issues can be much more complex than the "usual" complaint.

Tom Bassett, corporate purchasing manager for Century Business Services (Independence, Ohio), notes that customer–supplier conflict is sometimes the result of conflicting policies within the customer's organization, and even conflict between parts of the organization.[49] A salesperson can moderate such conflict by helping the customer develop appropriate policies; one salesperson even brought in her own purchasing VP to consult with one of her clients.

Trust-destroying conflicts, though, can be avoided with several steps. First, start with a clear product description. If the product is a component part or critical for other reasons, and the potential for ambiguity exists, write out a clear description. Services providers are especially vulnerable to ambiguity in the sales process. Another important element is to define who has authority to do what—both for the customer and for the selling organization. For example, it has to be clearly understood who can authorize change orders if the product specs have to be modified. Both of these ideas require clear documentation, but good documentation is critical should such a dispute reach the courts.[50]

Recognize that complaints can be the beginning of major conflict. We discussed complaint handling as part of the exploration stage, but keep in mind that poor handling of complaints leads to the dissolution stage! Complaints in later stages are likely to lead to full-blown conflict if trust is not carefully salvaged. To repair damage to trust in a conflict, one consultant recommends the following seven steps (compare to the complaint-handling process discussed earlier):

1. Observe and acknowledge what has happened to lead to the loss of trust.
2. Allow your feelings to surface, but take responsibility for your actions.
3. Gain support—offer your peer a chance to save face and gain agreement on any mitigating circumstances.
4. Put the experience in the larger context to affirm your commitment to the relationship.
5. Shift the focus from assigning blame to problem solving.
6. Implement the solution.
7. Let go and move on.

Keep in mind that while the relationship may be between two organizations, even the deepest strategic partnership is ultimately the responsibility of two people.[51]

Summary

Developing partnerships has become increasingly important for salespeople and their firms. Salespeople can develop partnerships and generate goodwill by servicing accounts properly and by strategically building relationships. Both salespeople and buyers benefit from partnering.

Many specific activities are necessary to ensure customer satisfaction and to develop a partnering relationship. The salesperson must maintain the proper perspective, remember the customer between calls, build perceptions of trust, monitor order processing, ensure the proper initial use of the product or service, help to service the product, provide expert guidance and suggestions, and provide any necessary special assistance.

The best opportunities to develop goodwill are usually provided by the proper handling of customer complaints. Sales representatives should encourage unhappy customers to tell their stories completely, fully, and without interruption. A sympathetic attitude to a real or an imaginary product or service failure cannot be overemphasized. After determining the facts, the salesperson should implement the solution promptly and monitor it to ensure that proper action is taken.

The appropriate solution will depend on many factors, such as the seriousness of the problem, the dollar amount involved, and the value of the account. A routine should be developed to handle all complaints fairly and equitably.

In the expansion phase of the relationship, key sales activities are generating repeat orders, upgrading, cross-selling, and full-line selling. The goal is to achieve a partnership, in which case the seller is often designated a preferred supplier. At this level of relationship, it is important that both organizations commit to the relationship from top to bottom, and open communication directly between appropriate personnel in both organizations. At this point, salespeople become change agents as they work in both organizations to seamlessly integrate the partnership.

Sometimes, however, relationships break up. When partnerships dissolve, usually there are multiple reasons for the breakup. For example, when a salesperson leans too heavily on a few personal relationships and those people leave, or when the salesperson fails to monitor competitive actions, then the buying organization may feel less commitment to the relationship. Other reasons for dissolution include failing to monitor changes in the industry and just simply becoming complacent.

KEY TERMS

champion   393
change agent   392
complacency   396
corporate culture   391
cross-selling   388
electronic data interchange   376

full-line selling   387
preferred supplier   389
rate of change   393
scope of change   393
upgrading   387

Questions and Problems

1. How can a salesperson lose by overselling a customer?
2. Explain how the art of listening can be applied to a situation in which a customer makes a complaint. What can applying this art accomplish?
3. Your company has just introduced a new product. To determine whether the product could perform a customer's application, you asked the head of the service department, who said that it would. But after delivery, it is clear that the new product will not perform that application. What should you do? Does the stage of the buyer–seller relationship matter?
4. Should a salesperson handle all complaints so that customers are completely satisfied? Explain why or why not. Would your answer change if you were in the exploration stage versus the commitment stage?

5. The soundest philosophy for building partnerships may be summed up in these words: It's the little things that count. Identify six or eight "little things" a salesperson can do that will cost little or nothing but may be extremely valuable in building partnerships.

6. What is your reaction to the statement "The customer is always right"? Is it a sound basis for making adjustments and satisfying complaints? Can it be followed literally? Why or why not?

7. Your roommate or spouse complains that you don't do your share of the housework. Your friend complains that you never seem to have any free time anymore. What have you learned in this chapter that you could use to restore these relationships? If the answer is that you have learned nothing, justify that answer. If you have learned useful techniques, explain how they would apply to the two situations.

8. How do you know when full-line selling, upgrading, or cross-selling strategies are appropriate?

9. What are the various ways a salesperson can provide a potential champion with knowledge to build confidence? What types of knowledge will the champion need?

10. At the beginning of the chapter, we mentioned that cellular phone companies have a high disconnect rate. Why do they lose so many customers? What can the salesperson do to avoid these problems?

Case Problems

CASE 13.1

Ryder Truck Rental–Leasing

Ryder Truck Rental–Leasing is one of the largest truck-leasing companies in the United States, competing with Rollins for commercial rental and leasing. Unlike U-Haul, which rents primarily to consumers, Ryder's business comes from other businesses that either do not want to maintain their own fleets or use Ryder for periods when they need more trucking capacity.

A special analysis of truck usage has revealed that some business executives with a long history of using Ryder have not used Ryder in the past nine months. Ryder knows these executives must be using a competitor or other means of transportation. To win back as many of them as possible, Ryder's management has instructed sales representatives to call on all dormant accounts or those that have not done business with Ryder in the past nine months.

Scott Eccles, who has been with Ryder for three years as a sales representative, selected the owner of a small manufacturing company, Dan Kemp, as his first contact. Eccles made an appointment with Kemp, and the following interview took place:

ECCLES: Thought I'd stop around to see you, Mr. Kemp. Haven't heard your name mentioned lately.

KEMP: And you won't hear my name mentioned around your place again either. I'm through using Ryder. I'm sick and tired of being kicked around by your outfit. The last time I used your trucks, I had a driver sitting for two days waiting for either repair or replacement. And when he did get back on the road, the truck wouldn't go over 50 miles an hour.

ECCLES: How long ago did this happen?

KEMP: You oughta know; it was the last time I used your company—probably 10 or 12 months ago. You people advertise reliability. But if the truth were known, it's got to be the worst I've ever experienced.

ECCLES: Oh, it can't be as bad as all that!

KEMP: You don't think so, eh? You should have been the one to tell my best customer that her shipment was delayed. Her production line had to stop and wait for our parts to get there. They lost $30,000 in product. And you say, "It can't be as bad as all that."

ECCLES: Well, of course, we are terribly sorry about it, and we are trying to cut down on that sort of thing.

KEMP: I've heard that line before, but I haven't enough good customers to keep testing that statement. Moreover, you people just can't get a truck out here on time. I have two managers who ship by rental truck at least once a month. I've told them to use your competitor.

ECCLES: Say, those new Fords of ours can beat anything they have to offer.

KEMP: Says you, Mr. Eccles. My managers need trucks on time to get our products to our customers on time—oh, it's just not worth it.

ECCLES: Well, Mr. Kemp, we are trying to cut down on delays. We are learning more about maintaining our newer equipment, and we feel that we are making headway.

KEMP: I'm fed up with Ryder, and I'm not going to give you any more tries—not until you can really sell me that things are actually different. You haven't done a very good job so far.

Scott Eccles concluded the interview by saying he would certainly appreciate the opportunity to show that Ryder's service was all it was advertised to be.

Another Ryder sales representative, Jim Harris, was the luncheon speaker for a local Rotary Club when the club celebrated Transportation Day. He talked about the operations of Ryder in particular and about trucking problems in general. After the speech one of the Rotarians, Pam Pepper, congratulated Harris and said she enjoyed the talk. During the conversation, Harris learned that Pepper was a former Ryder customer but had become disgruntled and was no longer using Ryder.

Harris decided to call on Pepper. The following conversation took place about one week later:

HARRIS: Ms. Pepper, it's kind of you to give me a hearing on your complaints about Ryder.

PEPPER: Well, I felt I owed it to you after the way I criticized your company at our club the other day. You made a darn good speech, but when I thought about my experiences with Ryder, I got somewhat irritated.

HARRIS: Tell me about the experience that led you to use our competitor.

PEPPER: It wasn't one experience. It was a lot of the same old stuff over and over again. It was the repetition that got me down. I've used Ryder for nearly 20 years, and I've always thought the world of your management, to such an extent that I'm a stockholder. And I don't invest my money without thoroughly investigating and knowing the company.

HARRIS: I'm sorry that you feel the way you do about our company, Ms. Pepper. Specifically what did you experience?

PEPPER: Essentially, I use a company like you for special situations, such as when we have too many trucks down or at the end of our fiscal year to get out extra shipments. The last time I used Ryder, I had trouble getting enough trucks. Although a reservation was finally confirmed, when our drivers went to pick up the trucks, your agents said there was no record of a reservation. I'll bet I spent 20 to 30 minutes on the phone trying to get the reservation straightened out. They never did find any record of it and finally got us half of the trucks we needed about four hours later. But an hour with you people seems to be very unimportant. Also, your pricing plans are always changing.

I'm never sure whether our bills are accurate or whether we're paying too much or too little. And frankly, I can't take that risk.

HARRIS: You know, Ms. Pepper, if it weren't for the fact that we are getting those problems licked, I'd say you were justified in using other transportation.

PEPPER: Getting them licked? How?

HARRIS: In the first place, we have recently installed a new reservation system geared to our current needs. Under this setup we can usually confirm your trucks' availability immediately. You make only one call. One call does it all.

In addition, we've simplified our pricing plan, and it hasn't changed for six months. It is part of a new billing system designed to make it easier for everyone involved. The new system not only makes it easier for you to know whether your bill is accurate but also saves us money in handling our accounts. We've passed along these savings in the form of additional discounts for customers who use us regularly.

PEPPER: That discount idea sounds great, and your "one call" is an answer to a shipping manager's prayer—if only it works.

HARRIS: It works, all right. How about giving us a chance to prove it?

PEPPER [laughing]: How about those delays? My customers can't wait for their products. We are using your competitors whenever possible, and your competitors aren't having any problems.

HARRIS: Well, I'm not going to deny we've had delays with some of our equipment. The record isn't perfect yet, but we are way ahead of where we were only three months ago. How about giving us another try?

PEPPER: And then have another truck break down? All rental trucks are not as reliable as the ones we own, but Ryder seems to be the worst.

HARRIS: I'll admit we don't have an enviable record on that score. We have been putting on a campaign all over our system to improve our maintenance, which should increase reliability. Management is trying its best to clean up that problem. If you will try Ryder, I'm sure you will find an improvement on that point, too.

PEPPER: Well, you seem confident things are better. I'll tell you, I'll need a few trucks in about 10 days. I was going to use your competition, but I might try Ryder again. I'll call you as soon as I determine the exact date. But let me warn you, this is only a trial. I'm not going to use your company exclusively until I see some real results. You've told me a good yarn. Now we'll see.

HARRIS: Thank you. That's a fair arrangement. I'll call you early next week to learn whether you have set a definite date for your shipment.

QUESTIONS

1. What do you believe were the specific weaknesses and strengths of Eccles's interview?
2. What strengths and weaknesses did you observe in Harris's interview?
3. Did Eccles or Harris do the better job? Why?

CASE 13.2

Turning It Around

Sandy Garrett, manager of Personnel One Temporary and Permanent Placement in Tampa, Florida, held the phone away from her ear. The customer was shouting loud enough to be heard across the room.

"We deal with human beings; that's our product," notes Garrett. "And in this particular case, the people we sent to work for this account let us down. But as far as our client was concerned, it was Personnel One that let them down."

The client, a major insurance company headquartered in Tampa, had a data entry job that would take four temporary employees about three weeks to complete, including three days of training. Because of the training and the tight deadline, Garrett had asked for a three-week commitment from each person.

Unfortunately, one person's father died, and she quit to be with her family. Another found a permanent job and quit, leaving two people to finish the job in less than two weeks. The customer wasn't interested, though, in why they left; the only thing the customer knew was that there was a deadline and it wasn't going to be met.

Garrett offered to come to the customer's office and discuss alternatives, but the customer wanted none of that. "The last thing I heard before he hung up on me was, 'Sandy, we can't depend on Personnel One. We're going to another agency.'" But whether he wanted to see her or not, Garrett developed two possible solutions and drove straight to her client's office.

"He still didn't want to see me when I arrived," she said. "But I had two options and asked him to just look at them."

"Each option would take care of his biggest concern, which was getting people trained and productive in order to meet the deadline. And in each option we absorbed any additional cost." Garrett also reminded her client of everything that Personnel One had done right. But as she notes, "The biggest factor, though, was that I personally and immediately went to see him. He knew then how much his business meant to me."

QUESTIONS

1. Why was it so impressive to the buyer that Sandy personally and immediately went to see him? What did this action communicate?

2. Her decision to present two options was important and strategic. Why?

3. Write out exactly what you would plan to say in order to just get the buyer's permission to present the two options if you were Sandy and had to make this call. Be prepared to role-play.

Additional References

Brennan, Ross W., and Peter W. Turnbull. "Adaptive Behavior in Buyer–Supplier Relationships." *Industrial Marketing Management* 28 (1999), pp. 481–95.

Brown, Stephen. "The Moderating Effects of Insupplier–Outsupplier Status on Organizational Buyer Attitudes." *Journal of the Academy of Marketing Science,* Summer 1995, pp. 170–81.

Ford, David, and Raymond McDowell. "Managing Business Relationships by Analyzing the Effects and Value of Different Actions." *Industrial Marketing Management* 28 (1999), pp. 429–42.

Forenell, Claes; Michael Johnson; Eugene Anderson; Jaesung Cha; and Barbara Bryant. "The American Customer Satisfaction Index: Nature, Purpose and Findings." *Journal of Marketing,* October 1996, pp. 7–18.

Frankwick, Gary L.; Stephen S. Porter; and Lawrence A. Crosby. "Dynamics of Relationship Selling: A Longitudinal Examination of Changes in Salesperson–Customer Relationship Status." *Journal of Personal Selling & Sales Management* 21, Spring 2001, pp. 135–46.

Fredette, Michael. "Learning from the Other Side." *Purchasing Today,* April 2001, pp. 44–53. This article presents an interesting perspective of relationships and salespeople from the buyer's side.

Homburg, Christian, and Bettina Rudolph. "Customer Satisfaction in Industrial Markets: Dimensional and Multiple Role Issues." *Journal of Business Research* 52 (2001), pp. 15–33.

Jap, Sandy. "The Strategic Role of the Salesforce in Developing Customer Satisfaction across the Relationship Lifecycle." *Journal of Personal Selling & Sales Management* 21, Spring 2001, pp. 95–108.

Johnson, Julie; Hiram C. Barksdale, Jr.; and James S. Boles. "The Strategic Role of the Salesperson in Reducing Customer Defection in Business Relationships." *Journal of Personal Selling & Sales Management* 21, Spring 2001, pp. 123–34.

Keep, William; Stanley C. Hollander; and Roger Dickinson. "Forces Impinging on Long-Term Business-to-Business Relationships in the United States: An Historical Perspective." *Journal of Marketing* 52, April 1998, pp. 31–45.

Liu, Annie H., and Mark P. Leach. "Developing Loyal Customers with a Value-Adding Sales Force: Examining Customer Satisfaction and Perceived Credibility of Consultative Salespeople." *Journal of Personal Selling & Sales Management* 21, Spring 2001, pp. 147–56.

Medcof, John W. "Why Too Many Alliances End in Divorce." *Long Range Planning* 30, October 1997, pp. 718–32.

Menon, Anil; Sundar G. Bharadwaj; and Roy Howell. "The Quality and Effectiveness of Marketing Strategy: Effects of Functional and Dysfunctional Conflict in Intraorganizational Relationships." *Journal of the Academy of Marketing Science,* Fall 1996, pp. 299–313.

Pick, Polly. "Building Customer–Supplier Relationships in Electronics." *Long Range Planning* 32 (1999), pp. 263–72.

Qualls, William, and Jose Rosa. "Assessing Industrial Buyers' Perceptions of Quality and Their Effects on Satisfaction." *Industrial Marketing Management* 24 (1995), pp. 359–68.

Schultz, Roberta; Kenneth R. Evans; and David J. Good. "Intercultural Interaction Strategies and Relationship Selling in Industrial Markets." *Industrial Marketing Management* 28 (1999), pp. 589–99.

Sharma, Arun; Nikolas Tzokas; Michael Saren; and Panagiotis Kyziridis. "Antecedents and Consequences of Relationship Marketing." *Industrial Marketing Management* 28 (1999), pp. 601–11.

Thomke, Stefan, and Eric Von Hipple. "Customers as Innovators: A New Way to Create Value." *Harvard Business Review,* April 2002, pp. 74–81.

Ulwick, Anthony. "Turn Customer Input into Innovation." *Harvard Business Review,* January 2002, p. 91–97.

Wilson, David. "Deep Relationships: The Case of the Vanishing Salesperson." *Journal of Personal Selling & Sales Management* 20, Winter 2000, pp. 53–61.

Wilson, Timothy; Ulf Bostrom; and Rolf Lundin. "Communications and Expectations in After-Sales Service Provision: Experiences of an International Swedish Firm." *Industrial Marketing Management* 28 (1999), pp. 381–94.

4 Special Applications

Building on what you just learned in Part 3 about partnering, this section covers specific types of selling situations. In Chapter 14 you will learn about one form of selling that continues to grow in importance: formal negotiations. Topics include premeeting planning, opening the session, strategies and tactics, and effective ways to give and receive concessions.

Chapter 15 provides principles and guidance for the somewhat unique situation of selling to resellers. The chapter describes how salespeople aid resellers and discusses the role of supporting activities such as trade shows.

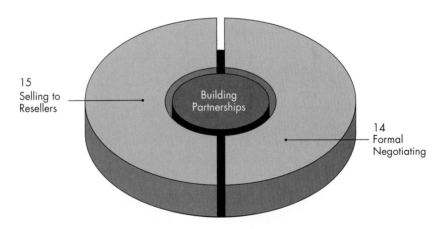

15
Selling to
Resellers

Building
Partnerships

14
Formal
Negotiating

14 *Formal Negotiating*

SOME QUESTIONS ANSWERED IN THIS CHAPTER ARE:

■ What is negotiation selling? How does it differ from nonnegotiation selling?

■ What items can be negotiated in selling?

■ What type of planning needs to occur prior to a negotiation meeting?

■ How should a seller set objectives?

■ How can the negotiation session be effectively opened? What role does friendly conversation play?

■ Which negotiation strategies and tactics do buyers use? How should negotiators respond?

■ What are the salesperson's guidelines for offering and requesting concessions?

We have all engaged in negotiations of some type. Most of these were informal (such as with your parents about attending a concert) and dealt with relatively minor issues, although they may have been intensely important to you at the time. This chapter discusses formal negotiations that occur between buyers and salespeople. The skills you will learn can also be used in your day-to-day negotiations with friends, parents, and people in authority positions.

"I think the most important ally you have in sales is trust and communication. If you have these two components, you will succeed—your customers will make sure of that."

Danielle Lord, US Foodservice

PROFILE

Shortly after graduating with a BBA degree, Danielle Lord began working at US Foodservice, one of the largest broad-line food service distributors in the United States. US Foodservice markets and distributes more than 43,000 brand items to over 300,000 food service customers, including hotels, restaurants, schools, and the like. Danielle became a National Account Executive in October 2000 and was given several large, high-maintenance accounts.

"I'm not much on titles . . . I do not 'fit the mold of a typical National Account Executive.' I am willing to do whatever it takes to get the job done. I deliver shorted groceries, speak to angry customers, take grocery orders, collect outstanding AR balances, make sure that sufficient inventories are brought in, pull invoices, create spreadsheets, present new product lines, represent the company at meetings—in short, I do whatever needs to be done. To my customers I am the company, and my integrity is on the line. I feel that my success is due to the strong connections I have made with my clientele as well as internal US Foodservice staff.

"The formal negotiations that I have been involved in are customer contract negotiations, either new contracts or renegotiating existing customer contracts. These negotiations take several months to finalize and can sometimes be very frustrating. New customer contracts are relatively 'easy' if I am prepared and know my company's capabilities. When I go into negotiations I know exactly what we can and cannot do . . . the bare-bones minimum it takes to be profitable. I know my business as well as their business, and what we need from the customer to have a successful partnership. If we are

able to reach an agreement, then it just takes a few more weeks to iron out the details and ship groceries. Most of the time we meet somewhere between bare-bones profitability and high profitability, which is a middle to mid-high profitable account. In a perfect world, negotiations would end there. However, the food service industry is not a perfect world, and negotiations are ongoing.

"Negotiations with existing customers are more difficult and can take up to six or eight months to complete. We may revise our amendments to the original contracts a dozen times before reaching an agreement, and then it looks nothing like the original proposal. Existing customers know our business very well and how we operate; they know our company's shortcomings as well as abilities. Bottom line: I better have done my homework and have the backup to show for it.

"Contract negotiations can be a time for you to really take an account to another level. If you are prepared and know your company's capabilities, as well as what type of business is profitable for your organization, a well-written contract can make a strong partnership between your company and the customer. Sure there are problems and bumps in the road, but my customers have confidence and trust that I will work it out. I think the most important ally you have in sales is trust and communication. If you have these two components, you will succeed—your customers will make sure of that. If you do not have trust and customer confidence you will not succeed; and in that case you may as well pack up your toys and go home."

Visit Our Website @ www.USFoodservice.com.

THE NATURE OF NEGOTIATION

The bargaining process through which buyers and sellers resolve areas of conflict and/or arrive at agreements is called **negotiation.** Areas of conflict may include minor issues (like who should attend future meetings) as well as major ones (such as cost per unit or exclusive purchase agreements). The ultimate goal of both parties should be to reduce or resolve the conflict.

Two radically different philosophies can guide negotiations. In **win–lose negotiating** the negotiator attempts to win all the important concessions and thus triumph over the opponent. This process resembles almost every competitive sport you have ever watched. In boxing, for example, one person is the winner, and the other is, by definition, the loser.

In the second negotiating philosophy, **win–win negotiating,** the negotiator attempts to secure an agreement that satisfies both parties.[1] You have probably experienced social situations similar to this. For example, if you want to attend a football game and your friend wants to attend a party, you may negotiate a mutual agreement that you both attend the first half of the game and still make it to the party. If this arrangement satisfies both you and your friend, you have engaged in win–win negotiating.

The discussion in this chapter assumes that your goal as the salesperson is to engage in win–win negotiating. In fact, this entire book has emphasized partnering, which is a win–win perspective. Partners attempt to find solutions that benefit both parties because each is concerned about the other party's welfare.

However, the buyer may be using a win–lose strategy, whereby the buyer hopes to win all major concessions and have the seller be the loser. To help you spot and prepare for such situations, we discuss many of these tactics as well.

NEGOTIATION VERSUS NON-NEGOTIATION SELLING

How does negotiation differ from the sales presentations we have discussed up to this point? This textbook has already covered many aspects of negotiating an agreement between buyer and seller. For example, in Chapter 11 we discussed the "negotiations" that occur as the seller is helping the buyer deal with objections. And in Chapter 12 we talked about obtaining commitment, which often requires negotiating on some key points. Importantly, however, we assumed that many, if not most, factors during a regular sales call are constrained, and not open to change or negotiation. For example, the price of an Allsteel Office chair model K316 has been set at $395. The Allsteel salesperson will not lower that price unless, of course, the buyer agrees to purchase large quantities. Even then the buyer will receive just a standard quantity discount as outlined in the seller's price manual. In essence, the salesperson's price book and procedure manual form an inflexible set of rules. If the buyer objects, an attempt to resolve the conflict will occur by using techniques discussed in Chapter 11 (such as the compensation method or the boomerang method).

In contrast, if the Allsteel seller enters formal negotiations with the same buyer, the price and delivery schedules will be subject to modification. The buyer neither expects nor wants the seller to come to the negotiation meeting with any standard price book. Instead, the buyer expects most policies, procedures, and prices to be truly negotiable.

Negotiations also differ from regular sales calls in that they generally involve more intensive planning and a larger number of people from the selling firm.

Prenegotiation planning may go on for six months or more before the actual meeting takes place. Planning participants usually cover a wide spectrum of functional areas of the firm, such as production, marketing, sales, human resources, accounting, purchasing, and executive officers.

Formal negotiations usually involve multiple buyers and multiple sellers.

Kaluzny & Thatcher/Stone

Finally, formal negotiations generally take place only for very large or important prospective buyers. For example, Quaker Oats might negotiate with some of the very large food chains, such as Jewel, Kroger, Safeway, and Cub Foods, but would not engage in a large, formal negotiation session with small local or mom-and-pop grocery stores. Negotiating is an expensive endeavor because it utilizes so much of so many important people's time. The firm wants to invest the time and costs involved in negotiating only if the long-term nature of the relationship and the importance of the customer justify the expense.

WHAT CAN BE NEGOTIATED?

If the customer is large or important enough, almost anything can be negotiated. Salespeople who have not been involved in negotiations before often find it hard to grasp the fact that so many areas are subject to discussion and change. Exhibit 14.1 lists some items that are often negotiated between buyers and sellers.

In reality, no single negotiation session covers all the areas listed. Each side comes to the bargaining table with a list of prioritized issues; only important points for which disagreement exists are discussed.

ARE YOU A GOOD NEGOTIATOR?

All of us are negotiators; some of us are better than others. We have negotiated with parents, friends, professors, and, yes, sometimes even with opponents. However, the fact that you have engaged in many negotiations in your lifetime does not mean you are good at negotiating.

The traits necessary to successfully negotiate vary somewhat, depending on the situation and the parties involved. Some characteristics, however, are almost universal. For example, a good negotiator must have patience and endurance; after two hours of discussing the same issue, the negotiator needs the stamina and willingness to continue until an agreement is reached. Also, a willingness to take risks and the ability to tolerate ambiguity become especially critical in business negotiations because it is necessary to both accept and offer concessions during the meeting without complete information.

EXHIBIT 14.1

Items That Are Often
Negotiated between
Buyers and Sellers*

Inventory levels the buyer must maintain.

Inventory levels the seller must keep on hand to be able to restock the buyer quickly.

Details about the design of the product or service.

How the product will be manufactured.

Display allowances for resellers.

Advertising allowances and the amount of advertising the seller does.

Sales promotion within the channel of distribution.

Delivery terms and conditions.

Retail and wholesale pricing points for resellers.

Prices and pricing allowances for volume purchases.

Amount and location of shelf positioning.

Special packaging and design features.

Service levels after the sale.

Disposing of unsold or obsolete merchandise.

Credit terms.

How complaints will be resolved.

Order entry and ease of monitoring orders.

Type and frequency of communication between the parties.

Performance guarantees and bonds.

*For a complete listing of potential issues to be negotiated, see William F. Morrison, *The Prenegotiation Handbook* (New York: Wiley, 1985), pp. 113–74.

Successful salespeople do not always make great negotiators.[2] In fact, negotiating could very well be the most difficult skill for any salesperson to develop. The unconscious reaction of most salespeople in negotiations often ends up being the opposite of the correct thing to do. For example, what if, in preparation for the upcoming negotiation session, the customer asks for very detailed specifications about your product? Most salespeople would gladly supply reams of technical data, full glossy pictures, an offer of plant tours, and the like. The problem with that approach lies in the possibility that the customer will pick several features that he or she does not need and then pressure for price concessions. (Look, I don't need that much memory capacity and don't want to pay for something I'm not going to use. So why don't you reduce your price? I shouldn't have to pay for something I'm not planning on ever using!) A salesperson who is a good negotiator would avoid this situation by supplying information to the customer only in exchange for the right to ask the customer more questions and thus gain more information.

People who fear conflict usually are poor negotiators. In fact, some negotiating strategies are actually designed to increase the level of conflict to bring all of the issues to the table and reach an equitable settlement. Along the same lines, people who have a strong need to be liked by all people at all times tend to make very poor negotiators. Other undesirable traits include being closed-minded, unorganized, dishonest, and downright belligerent.

Of course, cultural differences do exist.[3] For example, Brazilian managers may believe competitiveness is more important in a negotiator than integrity. Chinese managers in Taiwan may emphasize the negotiator's rational skills to a lesser extent than his or her interpersonal skills.

As this discussion indicates, being a truly excellent negotiator requires a very careful balance of traits and skills. Take a moment and complete the questionnaire in Exhibit 14.2 to rate your negotiating skills. Don't be discouraged by a

EXHIBIT 14.2

Negotiation Skills
Self-Inventory

Place a check by each item that accurately reflects your personality and traits on an average, normal day.

_____ 1. Helpful		_____ 20. Receptive
_____ 2. Risk taker		_____ 21. Easily influenced
_____ 3. Inconsistent		_____ 22. Enthusiastic
_____ 4. Persistent		_____ 23. Planner
_____ 5. Factual		_____ 24. Stingy
_____ 6. Use high pressure		_____ 25. Listener
_____ 7. Self-confident		_____ 26. Controlled
_____ 8. Practical		_____ 27. Think under pressure
_____ 9. Manipulative		_____ 28. Passive
_____ 10. Analytical		_____ 29. Economical
_____ 11. Arrogant		_____ 30. Gullible
_____ 12. Impatient		_____ 31. Afraid of conflict
_____ 13. Seek new approaches		_____ 32. Endurance
_____ 14. Tactful		_____ 33. Tolerate ambiguity
_____ 15. Perfectionist		_____ 34. Have strong need to be liked
_____ 16. Stubborn		_____ 35. Organized
_____ 17. Flexible		_____ 36. Honest
_____ 18. Competitive		_____ 37. Belligerent
_____ 19. Gambler		

How to score the checklist
All of the traits listed are positive except for the following negative traits: 3, 6, 9, 11, 12, 15, 16, 19, 21, 24, 28, 30, 31, 34, and 37. To arrive at a total score, give yourself one point for all positive traits and subtract one point for all negative traits. To interpret your total score: 19–22 = excellent; 15–18 = good; 11–14 = fair.

low score. You cannot easily change personality traits, but the rest of this chapter will suggest ways to improve your skills.

PLANNING FOR THE NEGOTIATION SESSION

Preparation and planning are the most important parts of negotiation, according to many expert sources. In Chapter 8 we discussed how to gather precall information and plan the sales call. All of that material is equally relevant when planning for an upcoming negotiation session—for example, learning everything possible about the buying team and the buyer's organization.

The meetings the salesperson will have with the buyer prior to the actual negotiation session facilitate this learning. The buyer may also be, or have been, a customer of the salesperson, with the upcoming negotiation session designed to review contracts or specify a new working relationship. Even in such scenarios, negotiators will want to carefully review the players and learn as many facts about the situation as possible.

LOCATION

Plan to hold the negotiation at a location free from distraction for both teams. A neutral site, one owned by neither party, is usually best; it removes both teams from interruptions by business associates, and no one has a psychological ("home court") advantage. Experienced negotiators find the middle of the workweek best for negotiations and prefer morning to afternoon or evening (because people are more focused on their jobs rather than after-hours and weekend activities).

In order not to be distracted, this seller should probably change the setting (more formal seating, seating arrangements where one isn't continually distracted by clothing, etc.).

© Masterfile

TIME ALLOTMENT

As you are probably aware, negotiations can take a tremendous amount of time. Some business negotiations take years. But how much time should be set aside for one negotiation session? The answer depends on the negotiation objectives and the extent to which both sides desire a win–win session. Studies have shown that high time pressure will produce nonagreements and poor outcomes when one or more sides take a win–lose perspective; but if both sides have a win–win perspective, high outcomes are achieved regardless of time pressure.

NEGOTIATION OBJECTIVES

Power is a critical element when developing objectives. The selling team must ask, Do we need them more than they need us? What part of our service is most valuable to them? Can they get similar products elsewhere? Optimally, both parties share balanced power, although this situation is rare in practice.

In developing objectives for the session, keep in mind that the seller will almost certainly have to make concessions in the negotiation meeting. Thus setting several objectives, or positions, is extremely important.

The **target position** is what your company hopes to achieve at the negotiation session. Your team should also establish a **minimum position,** the absolute minimum level you will accept. Finally, an **opening position**—the initial proposal—should be developed.

For example, for a Baxter salesperson negotiating the price for complete food service at a hospital, the target position could be $250,000, with a minimum position of $200,000 and an opening position of $300,000. In negotiations over service levels, the seller's opening position might be weekly delivery, the target position delivery twice a week, and the minimum position (the most the seller is willing to do) delivery three times a week.

To allow for concessions, the opening position should reflect higher expectations than the target position. However, the buyer team may consider a very high opening position to be unrealistic and may simply walk away. You have probably seen this happen in negotiations between countries that are at war. To avoid this problem, negotiators must be ready to support that opening position with solid information. Suppose the opening position for a Colgate-Palmolive negotiating team is to offer the grocer a display allowance of $1,000 (with a target position of offering $1,500). The team must be ready to prove that $1,000 is reasonable.

When developing objectives, negotiators need to sort out all issues that could arise in the meeting, prioritizing them by importance to the firm. It is critical to identify all issues, as Selling Scenario 14.1 demonstrates. Then the negotiators should develop a set of contingency plans to get a good idea, even

IT'S IMPORTANT TO IDENTIFY ALL ISSUES TO BE NEGOTIATED

How would you like to pay more than $15,000 for things like in-room videos that your meeting group didn't even use? That's what happened to a pharmaceutical company after it staged a conference at a Chicago hotel. The company had expected about 20 percent more attendees than actually showed up and was ready to pay for the hotel rooms that had been set aside for them. Imagine the company's surprise when it learned that the negotiated contract with the hotel also allowed the hotel to charge for things like meeting space, food and beverage pick-up, and in-room movies.

The pharmaceutical company's experience was not unique. In North Carolina a group's block of rooms was cut in half against its will. In Orlando a group was moved to another, less desirable hotel in town because Margaret Thatcher and Colin Powell (and their entourages) wanted to stay in the hotel the group had booked. And another pharmaceutical group was charged a cancellation fee for a small training session, even though the space it vacated was quickly booked with another group.

The moral of the story is this: Think of all issues that you need to include in your negotiation session. Plan for them in the agenda and then make sure the final written agreement is consistent with your verbally negotiated settlement.

Source: Melinda Ligos, "Killer Contracts," *Successful Meetings*, May 1999, pp. 50–63.

before the meeting begins, of their planned reactions and responses to the buyer's suggestions.

Talking over these issues beforehand helps the negotiation team avoid "giving away the store" during the heat of the negotiation session. It also allows the team to draw on the expertise of company experts who will not be present during the session.

The buyer team also develops positions for the meeting. Exhibit 14.3 presents a continuum that shows how the two sets of positions relate. With the positions illustrated, the parties can reach an agreement somewhere between the seller's minimum (S_M) and the buyer's maximum (B_M). However, if B_M falls to the left of S_M (has a lower maximum acceptable price), no agreement can be reached; attempts at negotiation will be futile. For example, if the buyer is not willing to pay more than $200 ($B_M$) and the seller will not accept less than $250 ($S_M$), agreement is impossible. In general, the seller desires to move as far to the right

EXHIBIT 14.3

Comparing Buyer and Seller Price Positions

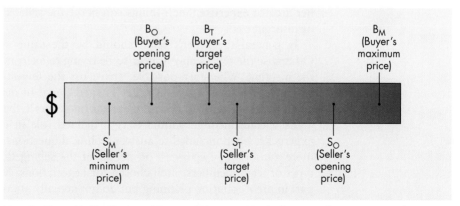

Note: See Howard Raiffa, *The Art and Science of Negotiation* (Cambridge, MA: Belknap Press, 1982) for a more complex discussion of the mathematical formulations designed to predict negotiation outcomes under various states.

of S_M (as high a price) as possible, and the buyer desires to move as far to the left of B_M (as low a price) as possible.

Negotiators need to try to anticipate these positions and evaluate them carefully. The more information collected about what the buyer hopes to accomplish, the better the negotiators will be able to manage the meeting and arrive at a win–win decision.

Negotiators create a plan to achieve their objectives. However, the chance of failure always exists. Thus planners need to consider strategy revisions if the original plan should fail. The development of alternative paths to the same goal is known as **adaptive planning.** For example, a firm may attempt to secure a premium shelf position by using any of the following strategies:

- In return for a 5 percent price discount.
- In return for credit terms of 3/10, net 30.
- In return for a 50–50 co-op ad campaign.

The firm would attempt to secure the premium shelf position by using, for example, the first strategy; if that failed, it would move to the second strategy; and so forth. Fortunately, with laptop computers and software such as Excel® and Lotus 123®, negotiators can quickly calculate the profitability of various package deals for their firms.

Many firms will engage in a brainstorming session to try to develop strategies that will meet the firm's objectives. A **brainstorming session** is a meeting in which people are allowed to creatively explore various methods of achieving goals.

Firms also use computer software, such as Negotiator Pro,[4] that is designed specifically to help salespeople prepare for negotiation sessions.

Once again, cultural differences exist. For example, Chinese and Russian businesspeople habitually use extreme initial offers, whereas Swedish businesspeople usually open with a price very close to their target position.

TEAM SELECTION AND MANAGEMENT

So far we have discussed negotiation as though it always involves a team of both buyers and sellers. Usually this is the case. However, negotiations do occur with only two people present: the buyer and the salesperson.

Teams offer both pros and cons.[5] Because of team members' different backgrounds, the group as a whole tends to be more creative than one individual could be. Also, team members can help one another and reduce the chances of making a "stupid" mistake. However, the more participants, the more time generally required to reach agreement. Also, team members may voice differing opinions among themselves, or one member may address a topic outside his or her area of expertise. Such things can make the seller's team appear unprepared or disorganized.

In general the seller's team should be the same size as the buyer's team. Otherwise the sellers may appear to be trying to exert more power or influence in the meeting. Whenever possible, strive for the fewest team members possible. Unnecessarily large teams can get bogged down in details; also, the larger the team, the more difficult reaching a decision generally becomes.

Each team member should have a defined role in the session. For example, experts are often included to answer technical questions; executives are present as more authoritative speakers on behalf of the selling firm. Exhibit 14.4 lists the types of team members often chosen for negotiations. Many of these people take part in prenegotiation planning but do not actually attend the negotiation session.

Team members should possess the traits of good negotiators, although it often does not work out that way. For example, many technical experts have no toler-

EXHIBIT 14.4

People Who May Serve
on the Selling
Negotiation Team

Title	Possible Role
Salesperson	Coordinates all functions.
Field sales manager (district manager, regional manager, etc.)	Provides additional local and regional information. Secures necessary local funding and support for planning and presentations. Offers information on competitors.
National sales manager/ vice president of sales	Serves as a liaison with corporate headquarters. Secures necessary corporate funding and staff support for planning and presentation. Offers competitor information.
National account salesperson/ national accounts sales managers	Provide expertise and support in dealing with issues for important customers. Offer information about competitors.
Marketing department senior executives, product managers, and staff	Provide suggestions for product/service applications. Supply market research information as well as information on packaging, new-product development, upcoming promotional campaigns, etc. Offer information about competitors.
Chief executive officer/president	Serves as an authority figure. Facilitates quicker decisions regarding changes in current policy and procedures. As a peer, can relate well with buyer's senior officers.
Manufacturing executives and staff	Provide information on current scheduled production as well as the possibility/cost of any modifications in the schedule.
Purchasing executives and staff	Provide information about raw materials inflows. Offer suggestions about possible quantity discounts from suppliers.
Accounting and finance executives and staff	Source of cost accounting information. Supply corporate target returns on investment; cost estimates for any needed changes in the firm under various buying scenarios; and information on order entry, billing, and credit systems.
Data processing executives and staff	Provide information on current data processing systems and anticipated changes needed under various buying scenarios. Help ensure that needed periodic reports for the buyers can be generated in a timely fashion.
Training executives and staff	Provide training for negotiation effectiveness and conduct practice role plays. Also provide information and suggestions on anticipated necessary buyer training.
Outside consultants	Provide any kind of assistance necessary. Especially helpful if the firm has limited experience in negotiations or has not negotiated with this type of buyer before.

ance for ambiguity and may fear conflict. As a result, the team leader needs to help them see clearly what their role is, as well as what they should not get involved in, during the session.

The team leader will manage the actual negotiation session. Because of their intimate knowledge of the buyers and their needs, salespeople often fill this post, rather than the executive on the team. When selecting a team leader, the seller's management needs to also consider the anticipated leader of the buyer team. It is unwise to choose a leader for the selling team who may be intimidated by the buyer's leader.

The team usually develops rules about who will answer what kinds of questions, who should be the first to respond to a concession offered by the buyers, who will offer concessions from the seller's standpoint, and so on. A set of nonverbal and verbal signals is also developed so team members can communicate with one another. For example, they may agree that when the salesperson takes out a breath mint, all team members are to stop talking and let the salesperson handle all issues; or when the executive places her red book inside her briefcase,

The salesperson's team must prepare for an upcoming negotiation session. Remember that the buyer's team is also planning.

Chuck Savage/The Stock Market

the team should move toward its target position, and the salesperson should say, "OK, let's look at some alternatives."

To ensure that team members really understand their respective roles and that all rules and signals are clearly grasped, the team should practice. This process usually involves a series of videotaped role-play situations. Many firms, such as Standard Register, involve their sales training department in this practice. Trainers, using detailed information supplied by the team, realistically play the roles of the buying team members.

INDIVIDUAL BEHAVIOR PATTERNS

The team leader needs to consider the personality style of each member of both teams to spot any problems and plan accordingly. Of course, one method would be to sort the members into analyticals, amiables, expressives, and drivers based on the dimensions of assertiveness and responsiveness (see Chapter 6 for a full discussion). Some researchers have developed personality profiles specifically for negotiations. This section presents one of the most widely used sets of negotiation profiles.

After studying actual conflict situations, a number of researchers arrived at a set of basic conflict-handling modes based on the dimensions of assertiveness and cooperativeness.[6] Exhibit 14.5 presents these five modes: competing, accommodating, avoiding, compromising, and collaborating. Note that these five styles are different from the social styles (drivers, amiables, expressives, and analyticals) that we have been using throughout the book. Because all negotiations involve some degree of conflict, this typology is appropriate for use by salespeople preparing for a negotiation session.

People who resolve conflict in a **competing mode** are assertive and uncooperative. They tend to pursue their own goals and objectives completely at the expense of the other party. Often power oriented, they usually surround themselves with subordinates (often called "yes-men") who go along with their ideas. Team members who use the competing mode look for a win–lose agreement: they win, the other party loses.

EXHIBIT 14.5

Conflict-Handling
Behavior Modes

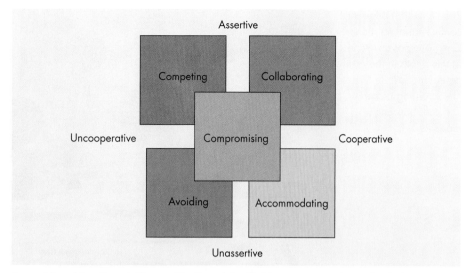

Source: Adapted from Kenneth Thomas, "Conflict and Conflict Management," in *The Handbook of Industrial and Organizational Psychology*, ed. Marvin Dunnett (Skokie, IL: Rand McNally, 1976).

Individuals in the **accommodating mode** are the exact opposite of competing people. Unassertive and highly cooperative, accommodators will neglect their own needs and desires to satisfy the concerns of the other party. In fact, they may seek a win–lose agreement, where they are the losers. Accommodators can be spotted by their excessive generosity; their constant, rapid yielding to another's point of view; and their obedience to someone else's order, even if it is obviously not something they desire to do.

Some people operate in the **avoiding mode,** an unassertive and uncooperative mode. These people do not attempt to fulfill their own needs or the needs of others. In essence, they simply refuse to address the conflict at all. They do not strive for a win–win agreement; in fact, they do not strive for any agreement.

The **compromising mode** applies to people "in the middle" in terms of cooperativeness and assertiveness. A compromiser attempts to find a quick, mutually acceptable solution that partially satisfies both parties. A compromiser gives up more than a competing person but less than an accommodating person. In many ways the compromiser attempts to arrive at a win–win solution. However, the agreement reached usually does not maximize the satisfaction of the parties. For example, a compromising person might quickly suggest, Let's just split the difference. Although this sounds fair, a better solution—one that would please both parties more—may be reached with further discussion.

Finally, people in the **collaborating mode** are both assertive and cooperative. They seek to maximize the satisfaction of both parties and hence to reach a truly win–win solution. Collaborators have the motivation, skill, and determination to really dig into an issue or a problem and explore all possible solutions. The best situation, from a negotiation standpoint, would be to have on both teams a number of people who generally use a collaborating mode.

As with the social style matrix described earlier, one person can exhibit different modes in different situations. For example, a buying team negotiator who perceives that his or her position on an issue extremely vital to the long-term welfare of the company is correct may revert from a collaborating mode to a competing mode. Likewise, when potentially heavy damage could occur from confronting an issue, that same buyer might move to an avoiding mode.

People exhibit different conflict-handling modes. Can you spot someone in this photo in the competing mode?
The avoiding mode?
The collaborating mode?

Mug Shots/The Stock Market

INFORMATION CONTROL

What do buyers do while selling teams engage in preparation? They prepare, too! Keep in mind that buyers have read as many books and attended as many seminars on negotiation as sellers have because this training is one of their best negotiating tools. Buyers try to learn as much as they can about the seller's team and plans, including the seller's opening, target, and minimum positions. Buyers also are interested in the seller's team membership and decision rules. As a result, the selling team leader needs to emphasize the need for security: Don't give everyone access to all information. In fact, many team members (such as technical support) do not need to have complete and exhaustive knowledge of all the facts surrounding the negotiation.

As an example, one *Fortune* 500 firm was negotiating a $15 million deal with one of its customers.[7] The selling team's leader had to leave the room for a few minutes, and while he was gone the plant manager for the selling firm came in. The plant manager, though intending to do no harm, bragged about how his company had already invested $2 million in a prototype and retooling just to prepare for the customer's expected commitment. Needless to say, when the seller's team leader returned to the room, the buyer said he had all the information he needed. Two days later, the buyer was a very tough negotiator, armed with the knowledge that the seller had already committed to the project. It pays to control the flow of information!

THE NEGOTIATION MEETING

Before discussing what occurs in the negotiation meeting, we should note that some buyers will attempt to engage in a win–lose tactic of beginning to negotiate when the other party does not expect it. This tactic has been called **ambush negotiating** or a **sneak attack**.[8] It can occur during meetings prior to the negotiation meeting or even during installation of the new product. For example, during the first week of installation of a new computer system, the buyer may state, "We're going to have to renegotiate the price of this system. Since we signed that contract, we have learned of a new system being introduced by one of your competitors." The seller should never negotiate in such a situation until prepared to deal with the issue completely.

At the negotiation meeting the buyer team and seller team physically come together and deliberate about topics important to both parties, with the goal of arriving at decisions. As mentioned earlier, this meeting usually has been preceded by one or more smaller buyer–seller meetings designed to uncover needs and explore options. Informal phone conversations probably were used to set some aspects of the agenda, learn about team members who will be present, and so on. Also, the negotiation itself may require a series of sessions to resolve all issues.

PRELIMINARIES

Engaging in friendly conversation to break the ice before getting down to business is usually a good idea. Use this time to learn and use the names of all members on the buyer team. This preliminary activity is especially important in many international negotiation meetings. For example, Japanese businesspeople usually want to spend time developing a personal relationship before beginning negotiations. In fact, researchers have found that before negotiations begin, both sides must develop a working relationship that permits them to focus on the task.

Every effort should be made to ensure a comfortable environment for all parties. Arranging ahead of time for refreshments, proper climate control, appropriate size of room, adequate lighting, and correct layout of furniture will go far to establish an environment conducive to negotiating.

Most negotiations occur at a rectangular table. Teams usually sit on opposite sides, with the team leaders at the heads of the table. If possible, try to arrange for a round table or at least a seating arrangement that mixes members from each team together. This seating plan helps the parties feel that they are facing a common task and fosters a win–win atmosphere.

If the buyer team has a win–lose philosophy, expect all kinds of ploys to be used. For example, the furniture may be too large or too small or may be uncomfortable to sit in. The buyers may sit in front of large windows to force you to stare directly into sunlight. You may discover that the sellers' seats are all placed beneath heat ducts and the heat is set too high. You should not continue with the meeting until all unfavorable physical arrangements have been set right.

As far as possible the selling team should establish a win–win environment. This environment can be facilitated by avoiding any verbal or nonverbal threatening gestures, remaining calm and courteous, and adopting an attitude of investigation and experimentation. The leader might even comment,

> I can speak for my team that our goal is to reach agreements today that we can all be proud of. We come to this meeting with an open mind and look forward to exploring many avenues toward agreement. I am confident that we will both prosper and be more profitable as a result of this session.

An **agenda,** a listing of what will be discussed and in what sequence, is important for every negotiation session. It helps to set boundaries and keeps everyone on track. Exhibit 14.6 offers an example of a negotiation agenda. The selling

EXHIBIT 14.6

Preliminary Negotiating
Session Agenda

Preliminary Agenda
Meeting between FiberCraft and Rome Industrial Inc.
Proposed New Spin Machine for 15 FiberCraft Plants
November 14, 2003

1. Introductions by participants.
2. Agree on the meeting agenda.
3. Issues:
   a. Who will design the new machine?
   b. Who will pay the costs of testing the machine?
   c. Who will have ownership rights to the new machine (if it is ever built for someone else)?
   d. Who will be responsible for maintaining and servicing the new machine during trial runs?
   e. Who will pay for any redesign work needed?
4. Coffee break.
5. Issues:
   a. How and when will the machines be set up in the 15 locations? Who will be responsible for installation?
   b. What percentage will be required for a down payment?
   c. What will the price be? Will there be any price escalation provisions? If not, how long is this price protected?
6. Summary of agreement.

team should come to the meeting with a preliminary typed agenda. Don't be surprised when the buyer team also comes with an agenda; in that case the first thing to be negotiated is the agenda itself. In general, putting key issues later in the agenda is advantageous. This approach allows time for each party to learn the other's bargaining style and concession routines. Moreover, agreement has already been reached on some minor issues, which, in a win–win situation, supports an atmosphere for reaching agreement on the major issues.

GENERAL GUIDELINES

To negotiate effectively, the seller team must put into practice the skills discussed throughout this book. For example, listening carefully is extremely important. Careful listening involves not only being silent when the buyer talks but also asking good probing questions to resolve confusion and misunderstanding.

The team leader must keep track of issues discussed or resolved. During complicated negotiations many items may be discussed simultaneously. Also, some issues may be raised but not fully addressed before someone raises a separate issue. The leader can provide great assistance by giving periodic status reports, including what has been resolved and the issues being discussed. More important, he or she can map out what still needs to be discussed. In essence this mapping establishes a new agenda for the remainder of the negotiation session.

Once again, cultural differences are important in negotiations. For example, most Canadians and Americans are uncomfortable with silence; most Japanese, on the other hand, are much more comfortable with extended periods of silence. North Americans negotiating with Japanese businesspeople usually find this silence very stressful. One study found that German negotiators tend to use a win–lose style, whereas the French use a win–win perspective.[9] Negotiators must prepare themselves for such probabilities and learn ways to reduce stress and cope in this situation.

If negotiations require an interpreter, carefully select someone well-qualified for the job. And don't expect everything you say to be translated correctly. Here are some items that have been translated into English from another language (so you can get a sense of the problem of translation errors):[10]

- In a family-style restaurant in Hong Kong: Come broil yourself at your own table.

- From an Italian hotel in the mountains: Standing among the savage scenery, the hotel offers stupendous revelations. There is a French window in every room. We offer commodious chambers, with balcony imminent to a romantic gorge. We hope you want to drop in. In the close village you can buy jolly memorials for when you pass away.

- In a Moscow newspaper under the heading "INTERPRETING": Let us you letter of business translation do. Every people in our staffing know English like the hand of their back. Up to the minute wise-street phrases, don't you know, old boy!

- In a Sarajevo hotel: Guests should announce abandonment of their rooms before 12 o'clock, emptying the rooms at the latest until 14 o'clock for the use of the room before 5 at the arrival or after the 16 o'clock at the departure will be billed as one more night.

Finally, keep in mind that during negotiations, people need to save **face**. Face is defined as the person's desire for a positive identity or self-concept. Of course, not all people strive for the same face (some want to appear "cool," some "macho," some "crass," and so on). Negotiators will at least try to maintain face and may even use the negotiation session to improve or strengthen this identity.[11]

DEALING WITH WIN–LOSE NEGOTIATORS

Many books have been written and many consultants have grown rich teaching both buyers and sellers strategies for effective negotiating. Unfortunately, many of these techniques are designed to achieve a win–lose situation. We will describe several to illustrate the types of tactics buyers might engage in during negotiations. This knowledge will help the negotiating team defend its position under such attacks.

Both buyers and sellers occasionally engage in the win–lose strategies described here. However, because we are assuming that sellers will adopt a win–win perspective, this section focuses on how to handle buyers who engage in these techniques. Exhibit 14.7 presents an effective overall strategy for dealing with win–lose negotiators.

GOOD GUY–BAD GUY ROUTINE

You have probably seen the **good guy–bad guy routine** if you watch many police movies or TV shows. A tough police detective interrogating the suspect gets a little rough. The detective uses bright lights and intimidation. After a few minutes a second officer (who has been watching) asks his companion to "go out and get some fresh air." While the tough detective (the "bad guy") is outside, the other detective (the "good guy") apologizes for his partner's actions. The good guy goes on to advise the crook to confess now and receive better treatment rather than wait and have the bad guy harass him or her some more.

Negotiators often try the same routine. One member of the buyer team (the bad guy) makes all sorts of outlandish statements and requests:

Look, we've got to buy these for no more than $15 each, and we must have credit terms of 2/10, net 60. After all the business we've given you in the past, I can't believe you won't agree to those terms!

EXHIBIT 14.7

What to Do When the
Buyer Turns to Win–Lose
Strategies

Detach yourself.	Don't respond right away. Instead, give yourself time to think about the issue. Say something like "Hold on, I'm not sure I follow you. Let's go back over what you just said again." Use the time you have gained to rethink your positions and what would be in the best interests of both parties.
Acknowledge their position and then respond.	In using this tool, you are trying to create a favorable climate for your response. You would start off by mentioning that you agree with them by saying something like "Yes, you have a good point there when you said . . ." After agreeing, you then make your point. For example, you might conclude by saying, "and I would like to make sure you continue to have minimal downtime. And for that to happen, you know, we really need to have someone from your firm attend the training." This tool is somewhat similar to the indirect denial and boomerang techniques discussed in Chapter 11.
Build them a bridge.	Come up with a solution that incorporates the buyer's suggestion. For example, "building on your idea, what if we . . ." or "I got this idea from something really neat you said at our meeting last Friday." This approach helps the buyer save face.
Warn, but don't threaten.	Sometimes you may have to help the buyer understand the consequences of his or her position. For example, if the buyer indicates that she or he must have a cheaper fabric for the furniture in an office building, you can say, "I know how important the choice of fabric is to your firm's image, but if you choose that fabric, you won't achieve the image you're really looking for. How much will that cost you in lost clients who might not get a sense that you are very successful?" A warning is not the same thing as a threat. A threat is what will happen if you don't get *your* way; a warning is what will happen if they do get *their* way.

Sources: Jeff Tanner, "Partnering-Based Negotiations," *Exhibitor Times*, August 1994, pp. 38–39; William Ury, *Getting Past No: Negotiating with Difficult People* (New York: Bantam Books, 1991).

Then another member of the buyer team (the good guy) takes over and appears to offer a win–win solution by presenting a lower demand:

> Hang on, Jack. These are our friends. Sure, we've given them a lot of business, but remember they've been good to us as well! I believe we should let them make a decent profit, so $15.50 would be more reasonable.

According to theory, the sellers are so relieved to find a friend that they jump on the good guy's suggestion.

As an effective defense against such tactics, the selling team must know its position clearly and not let the buyer's strategy weaken it. Obviously, the selling team needs the ability to spot a good guy–bad guy tactic. A good response might be

> We understand your concern. But based on all the facts of the situation, we still feel our proposal is a fair one for all parties involved.

LOWBALLING

You may also have experienced **lowballing.** Car dealers have used it for years. The salesperson says, "This car sells for $19,613." After you agree to purchase it, what happens? "Oh, I forgot to tell you that we have to charge you for dealer prep and destination charges, as well as an undercoating already applied to the car. So let's see, the total comes to $20,147. Gee, I'm sorry I didn't mention those expenses before!" Most people go ahead and buy. Why? They have already verbally committed themselves and do not want to go against their agreement. Also, they do not want to start the search process again.

The technique is also used in buyer–seller negotiations in industrial situations. For example, after the sellers have signed a final agreement with the buyer team, one of the buyer team members says, "Oh, I forgot to mention that all of our new contracts must specify FOB destination and the seller must assume all shipping insurance expenses."

The best response to lowballing is to just say no. Remind the buyer team that the agreement has been finalized. The threat of lowballing underscores the importance of getting signatures on contracts and agreements as soon as possible. If the buyers insist on the new items, the selling team will simply be forced to reopen the negotiations. (Try this tactic on car dealers, too!)

A variation of lowballing, **nibbling,** is a small extra, or add-on, the buyer requests after the deal has been closed. Compared to lowballing, a nibble is a much smaller request. For example, one of the buyers may state, "Say, could you give us a one-time 5 percent discount on our first order? That would sure make our boss happy and make us look like we negotiated hard for her." Nibbling often works because the request is so small compared to the entire agreement.

The selling team's response to the nibble depends on the situation. It may be advantageous to go ahead and grant a truly small request that could be easily met. On the other hand, if the buyer team uses nibbling often, granting these requests may need to be restricted. Again, the best strategy is to agree on the seller's position before the meeting begins and set guidelines for potential nibbles. Often the seller grants a nibble only if the buyer agrees to some small concession in return.

EMOTIONAL OUTBURSTS

How do you react when a close friend suddenly starts crying, gets angry, or looks very sad? Most of us think, What have I done to cause this? We tend to feel guilty, become uneasy, and try to find a way to make the person stop crying. That is simply human nature.

Occasionally buyer teams will appeal to your human nature by engaging in an **emotional outburst tactic.** For example, one of the buyers may look directly at you, shake his or her head sadly, slowly look down, and say softly,

> I can't believe it's come to this. You know we can't afford that price. And we've been good partners all these years. I don't know what to say.

This statement is followed by complete silence among the entire buyer team. Members hope that you will feel uncomfortable and give in to their demands. In an extreme case one or more buyers would actually walk out of the room or begin to shout or cry.

The selling team, once again, needs to recognize this behavior as the technique it is. Assuming no logical reason exists for the outburst, the negotiators should respond with a gentle but firm reminder of the merits of the offer and attempt to move the buyer group back into a win–win negotiating frame of mind.

BUDGET LIMITATION TACTIC

In the **budget limitation tactic,** also called a **budget bogey,** the buyer team states something like the following:

> The proposal looks great. We need every facet of the program you are proposing in order for it to work in our business. But our budget allows us only $250,000 total, including all costs. You'll have to come down from $300,000 to that number, or I'm afraid we can't afford it.

If a member of the buying team engages in an emotional outburst tactic, the seller should never respond in like fashion.

© Masterfile

This statement may be absolutely true. If so, at least you know what you have to work with. Of course, claims of budget ceilings are sometimes just a ploy to try to get a lower price.

The best defense against budget limitations is to do your homework before going into the negotiation session. Learn as much as you can about budgets and maximums allowed. Have alternative programs or proposals ready that incorporate cost reduction measures. After being told of a budget limitation during the negotiation session, probe to make sure that the claim is valid. Check the possibility of splitting the cost of the proposal over several fiscal years. Probe to find out whether the buyer would be willing to accept more risk for a lower price or to have some of the installation work done by the buyer's staff. You can also help to forestall this tactic by working closely with the buyer prior to the negotiation meeting, providing reasonable ballpark estimates of the cost of the proposal.

BROWBEATING

Sometimes buyers will attempt to alter the selling team's enthusiasm and self-respect by **browbeating** them. One buyer might make a comment like the following:

> Say, I've been reading some pretty unflattering things about your company in *The Wall Street Journal* lately. Seems like you can't keep your unions happy or your nonunion employees from organizing. It must be tough to get out of bed and go to work every day, huh?

If the selling team feels less secure and slightly inferior after such a comment, the tactic was successful.

You should not let browbeating comments influence you or your proposal. That's easier said than done, of course. Presumably you were able to identify in prenegotiation meetings that this buyer had this type of personality. If so, you could prepare by simply telling yourself that browbeating will occur but you will not let it affect your decisions. If you can make it through one such comment, buyers usually will not offer any more because they can see that browbeating will not help them achieve their goals.

One response to such a statement would be to practice **negotiation jujitsu**.[12] In negotiation jujitsu the salesperson steps away from the opponent's attack and then directs the opponent back to the issues being discussed. For example, the salesperson may say,

> We are concerned about our employees and are working to resolve all problems as quickly as we can. If you have any ideas that would help us in this regard, we would appreciate them. Now, we were discussing price . . .

MAKING CONCESSIONS

One of the most important activities in any negotiation is the granting and receiving of concessions from the other party. One party makes a **concession** when it agrees to change a position in some fashion. For example, if your opening price position was $500, you would be granting a concession if you agreed to lower the price to $450.

Based on many successful negotiations in a wide range of situations, a number of guidelines have been formulated to make concessions effectively:[13]

1. Never make concessions until you know all of the buyer's demands and opening position. Use probing to help reveal these.

2. Never make a concession unless you get one in return and don't feel guilty about receiving a concession.

3. Concessions should gradually decrease in size. At first you may be willing to offer "normal size" concessions. As time goes on, however, you should make much smaller ones. This approach helps the prospect see that you are approaching your target position and are becoming much less willing to concede.

4. If a requested concession does not meet your objectives, don't be afraid to simply say, "No. I'm sorry, but I just can't do that."

5. All concessions you offer are tentative until the final agreement is reached and signed. Remember that you may have to take back one of your concessions if the situation changes.

6. Be confident and secure in your position and don't give concessions carelessly. If you don't follow this advice, your buyers may lose respect for your negotiating and business skills. Everyone wants to conduct business with someone who is sharp and who will be in business in the future. Don't give the impression that you are not and will not.

7. Don't accept the buyer's first attempt at a concession. Chances are the buyer has built in some leeway and is simply testing the water.

8. Help the buyer to see the value of any concessions you agree to. Don't assume the buyer will understand the total magnitude of your "generosity."

9. Start the negotiation without preconceived notions. Even though the buyers may have demanded certain concessions in the past, they may not do so in this negotiation meeting.

10. If, after making a concession, you realize you made some sort of mistake, tell the buyer and begin negotiating that issue again. For example, if you made a concession of delivery every two weeks instead of every four weeks but then realize that your fleet of trucks cannot make that route every two weeks, put the issue back on the table for renegotiation.

11. Don't automatically agree to a "let's just split the difference" offer by the buyers. Check out the offer to see how it compares to your target position.

12. If the customer says, "Tell us what your best price is, and we'll tell you whether we are interested," remain noncommittal. Respond with, "In most cases, a price of $_ is the best we can do. However, if you want to make a proposal, we'll see what we can do."

13. Know when to stop. Don't keep trying to get and get and get even if you are able.

14. Use silence effectively. Studies have shown cultural differences in the negotiator's ability to use silence. For example, Brazilians make more initial concessions (use less silence early) than North Americans, who make more than the Japanese.

15. Plan the session well. In one study of successful negotiators, Neil Rackham found that "80 percent of the concessions obtained during negotiation resulted from things done before the negotiation started."[14]

The granting and receiving of concessions is often very complex and can result in the negotiations taking months or years to complete. Building Partnerships 14.1 describes some of the unusual concessions resulting from negotiations between Nike and the University of Michigan.

RECAP OF A SUCCESSFUL NEGOTIATION MEETING

Setting the proper environment early in the meeting puts you well on the way to a successful negotiation. Remember to develop an agenda and be aware of win–lose strategies that buyers may use. Offer concessions strategically.

This chapter discussed win–win and win–lose negotiation sessions. Seasoned veterans will note that, in some situations, the session could more accurately be classified as **win–win not yet negotiating**. In win–win not yet, the buying team achieves its goals while the selling team doesn't. However, the sellers expect to achieve their goals in the near future, thanks to the results of that negotiation session. For example, Antonio Willars in Monterrey, Mexico, relates the following:

I was working for the magazine *Revista Motor y Volante* and negotiating with Gonher, a lubricating oil company. At that time, no oil companies advertised in my magazine. So I negotiated an agreement with Gonher with a lower price than I had hoped to achieve, based on the belief that that sale would result in increased business over the long term. Although I didn't achieve my pricing goals in that session, I took a longer-term view. It paid off. That was the first of many, consistent sales to Gonher, all at our regular rates. Plus, many oil companies, such as Quaker State, now advertise in the magazine. So, although I had a "win not yet" outcome in that first meeting, we have now achieved a complete win–win situation.

When the session is over, be sure to get any negotiated agreements in writing. If no formal contract is possible, at least summarize the agreements reached. And don't forget to do postnegotiation evaluation and learn from your mistakes.[15]

Thinking It Through

How can the use of information technology help keep track of issues during a negotiation session and ensure that all agreements reached during a negotiation session are included in the final written agreement?

Studies have shown that more cooperation exists if both sides expect future interactions. Keep in mind that your goal is to develop a long-term partnership with your buyer. This process can be aided by being levelheaded, courteous, and, above all, honest. Also, do not try to get every concession possible out of your buyer. If you push too hard or too long, the buyer will get irritated and may even walk out. Never lose out on an agreement by being too greedy. Remember your goal: to reach a win–win settlement.

Summary

This chapter described how to engage in win–win negotiating. It also described how buyers may engage in win–lose negotiating.

Almost anything can be negotiated. The areas of negotiation will depend on the needs of both parties and the extent of disagreement on major issues.

A successful salesperson is not necessarily a good negotiator. Important negotiator traits include patience and endurance, willingness to take risks, a tolerance for ambiguity, the ability to deal with conflict, and the ability to engage in negotiation without worrying that every person present will not be on one's side.

As in regular sales calls, careful planning counts. This step involves choosing the location, setting objectives, and developing and managing the negotiating team. The salesperson does not act alone in these tasks, but instead draws on the full resources of the firm.

Preliminaries are important in sales negotiation sessions. Friendly conversation and small talk can help to reduce tensions and establish some degree of rapport. Agendas help to set boundaries and keep the negotiation on track. Win–lose strategies that buyers use include a good guy–bad guy routine, lowballing, emotional outbursts, budget limitation, and browbeating. As much as possible, the salesperson should respond to any win–lose maneuvers calmly and with the intent of bringing the other side back to a win–win stance.

Concessions, by definition, will occur in every negotiation. Many guidelines have been established to help negotiators avoid obvious problems. For example, no concession should be given unless the buyer gives a concession of equal value. Also, any concessions given are not formalized until the written agreement is signed; thus all concessions are subject to removal if appropriate.

KEY TERMS

accommodating mode   417
adaptive planning   414
agenda   419
ambush negotiating   418
avoiding mode   417
brainstorming session   414
browbeating   424
budget bogey   423
budget limitation tactic   423
collaborating mode   417
competing mode   416
compromising mode   417
concession   424
emotional outburst tactic   423

face   421
good guy–bad guy routine   421
lowballing   422
minimum position   412
negotiation   408
negotiation jujitsu   424
nibbling   423
opening position   412
sneak attack   418
target position   412
win–lose negotiating   408
win–win negotiating   408
win–win not yet negotiating   426

Questions and Problems

1. "Try to get a big concession from your opponent by giving away a small, insignificant concession yourself." Comment.
2. What are the advantages of having a sales job that involves only selling by negotiation? What disadvantages could such a job have?
3. Think about recent encounters you either have had or have witnessed that involved negotiations. Did each party use a win–win perspective or a win–lose perspective? What clues did you use to make that determination?
4. Salesperson Jim Keyes enjoys meeting people and helping them solve their problems. Although he is excited when he obtains commitment, he really

went into selling because he has a strong need to make friends and develop relationships. He is very patient and not averse to taking risks. Because his parents were in the military, he is accustomed to moving a lot and has developed a tolerance for ambiguity and new situations. Do you believe Jim will make a good negotiator? Why or why not?

5. "As a negotiator, solving your opponent's problem is your problem." Comment.

6. Assume you are going to have your fourth and final job interview with Camadon, an office equipment firm, next Friday. Knowledgeable friends have told you that because you "passed" the first three interviews, you will be offered the job during the fourth interview. Also, you know that Camadon likes to negotiate with its new hires.

   a. Think about your own needs and desires for your first job (such as salary, expense reimbursement, benefits, geographic location, promotion cycle).

   b. For each need and desire listed, establish your target position, opening position, and minimum position.

   c. Camadon has probably also developed positions that would meet each of your needs and desires. Describe how you might go about discovering these positions before next Friday's meeting.

7. Mary Joyner, a salesperson for Nabisco, is preparing for an important negotiation session with Kroger, a large, national food chain, regarding an upcoming promotional campaign. Her boss has strongly suggested that he attend the meeting with her. The problem is that her boss is not a good negotiator; he tends to get angry, is unorganized, and tries to resolve conflict by talking nonstop and thus wearing down the buyer team with fatigue. Her boss definitely has a win–lose negotiating philosophy. What should Mary do?

8. "You are the worst possible person to have negotiate for yourself. You care too much about the outcome. Always let someone else negotiate for you." State your reaction to this statement. What implications does it have in industrial sales negotiations?

9. During the negotiation session, buyers make all kinds of statements. What would be your response to the following, assuming each occurred early in the meeting?

   a. We refuse to pay more than $3.20 each. That's our bottom line—take it or leave it!

   b. Come on, you've got to do better than that!

   c. You know, we're going to have to get anything we decide here today approved by our corporate management before we can sign any kind of a contract.

   d. One of our buyers can't make it here for another hour. But let's go ahead and get started and see what progress we can make.

   e. Tell you what, we need to see a detailed cost breakdown for each individual item in your proposal.

10. Negotiators have been known to lie during an important meeting. How can you tell whether buyers are lying? What should you do if you catch them telling a lie?

11. "If your opponent begins to use an unethical tactic, walk out of the room." Comment.

Case Problems

FedEx is a 30-year-old worldwide company that offers a wide array of services, including express overnight delivery, small package ground delivery services, LTL (less than truckload) freight services for those with large shipments in one order, expedited door-to-door delivery services for those who need immediate delivery of time-sensitive material, and customs brokerage and trade facilitation solutions. It has total annual sales above $19.6 billion and more than 200,000 employees worldwide.

Marina Oels is a salesperson for FedEx in France. Oels sells primarily the FedEx overnight express services to her customers, but also tries to sell ground and customs brokerage services as well.

Bayer, a diversified, international health care and chemicals group with headquarters in Leverkusen, Germany, contacted Oels about four months ago to discuss its shipping needs for its newly opened facility in Sens, France. The new facility is designed to expedite the introduction of new pharmaceutical products worldwide, thanks to new high-throughput screening machines for evaluating substance efficacy. In six long meetings with the firm, Oels learned that Bayer would be shipping more than 500 express packages each month from the facility. Various meetings included the vice president of purchasing, the mail room manager, and a sizable group of operations center staff.

After carefully planning for a formal negotiation session, Oels and three other employees of FedEx (her sales manager, a regional vice president of sales, and the operation vice president) sat down to meet with negotiators from Bayer. Manfred Spinner, the vice president of purchasing for Bayer, was the chief negotiator for his team.

The meeting began cordially with both teams introducing their members and agreeing on an agenda for the meeting. After a few minutes of pleasant conversation, Manfred made the following statement: "I'm glad we are here today because I think this is a golden opportunity for both sides to win. I have been impressed with the service information that Marina has shared with me. Your services are top quality, which is something we demand. I've talked to several references that Marina gave me information about, and they are all happy with the services they receive from you. Let me start the ball rolling by saying that we are willing to purchase not only our overnight delivery services from you but also all of our expedited door-to-door services, customs brokerage services, and small package services. In fact, we would like to establish a partnership with FedEx by purchasing every service that you sell that we will have a need for in the European Union. This assumes, of course, that you will give us a large discount off your list price. We are willing to enter into this agreement with you if you will give us a 60 percent discount across the board on every service that you sell. What do you say to that?"

Oels was stunned. In all of her premeeting sessions with Manfred, he had never mentioned any arrangement like this. All of FedEx's planning had assumed her purchase of overnight shipping services at the new facility and nothing more. The situation was further compounded by the fact that FedEx is set up into different divisions across the EU, with each division having its own sales force. Manfred's offer would involve at least four other divisions of her corporation.

As she sat staring at her pencil, thinking hard, Manfred spoke again: "I see I've caught you a little off guard. No? Well, if we're going to come to any agreement, we need to do it today. I have to move ahead and start a new purchasing cycle for some new equipment that the facility needs. As you know, there are other firms that can supply these components." He paused, then smiled and continued. "I'll tell you what. We'll step out of the room and let your team discuss this. OK? We'll be back in, say, an hour. OK?"

Source: Information about the company was derived partly from annual reports and websites of FedEx and Bayer.

1. Evaluate the negotiation session to this point. How could Oels have better prepared for the meeting?
2. What should Oels do now? Be explicit and give reasons for your answers.

CASE 14.2
Identifying Conflict-Handling Modes

This chapter describes a number of basic conflict-handling modes that people use in negotiation. These include competing, collaborating, compromising, avoiding, and accommodating.

Carefully reread the section that describes these modes. For each mode, identify someone you know who falls into the mode and answer the following questions. It will probably help to think of a specific situation that you have observed or have experienced with the person.

QUESTIONS

1. How do you know this person has this conflict-handling mode? Identify specific behaviors that you have observed or heard about to support your assertion about this person.
2. How do you (and/or others) interact with this person during a conflict situation? (In other words, what do you do? How do you respond to this person's behavior?) Is your approach effective?
3. Would you like to have this person on your team during an important negotiation session? Why or why not?

Additional References

Alexander, Joe F.; Patrick L. Schul; and Denny E. McCorkle. "An Assessment of Selected Relationships in a Model of the Industrial Marketing Negotiation Process." *Journal of Personal Selling and Sales Management*, Summer 1994, pp. 25–39.

Busch, Karl R. "Increasing Your Power in a Single-Source Negotiation." *Inside Supply Chain Management*, January 2002, pp. 6–8.

Chang, K. "Purchasing Negotiating Outcomes: The Impact of National Character, Education Level, Job Function, Gender, and Negotiating Team Size." *Journal of International Selling and Sales Management* 4, Spring 1998, pp. 41–49.

Chang, Kuochung, and Cherng G. Ding. "The Influence of Culture on Industrial Buying Selection Criteria in Taiwan and Mainland China." *Industrial Marketing Management* 24 (1995), pp. 277–84.

DeShields, O.W., and G. de los Santos. "Salesperson's Accent as a Globalization Issue." *Thunderbird International Business Review* 42, January/February 2000, pp. 29–47.

Fisher, Roger, and William Ury. *Getting to Yes: Negotiating Agreement without Giving In*. 2nd ed. Boston: Houghton Mifflin, 1991.

Ghauri, Pervez N., and Jean-Claude Usunier, eds. *International Business Negotiations*. London: Elsevier Science, 1996.

Lewicki, Roy J.; John W. Minton; and David M. Saunders. *Negotiation*. 3rd ed. New York: Irwin McGraw-Hill, 1999.

Lewicki, Roy J.; David M. Saunders; and John W. Minton. *Negotiation*. New York: McGraw-Hill, 1999.

Lorge, Sarah. "Counterintuitive Selling." *Sales & Marketing Management*, August 1999, p. 78.

Luo, Yadong. "Partnering with Foreign Businesses: Perspectives from Chinese Firms." *Journal of Business Research* 55:6 (2002), pp. 481–93.

McRae, Brad. *Negotiating and Influencing Skills.* Thousand Oaks, CA: Sage Publications, 1997.

Mintu-Wimsatt, Alma, and Jule B. Gassenheimer. "The Moderating Effect of Cultural Context in Buyer–Seller Negotiation." *Journal of Personal Selling and Sales Management* 20, Winter 2000, pp. 1–9.

Money, Bruce. "International Multilateral Negotiations and Social Networks." *Journal of International Business Studies* 29:4 (1999), pp. 695–710.

Morris, Michael; Katherine Williams; Kwok Leung; Richard Larrick; M. Teresa Mondoza; Deepti Bhatnagar; Jianfeng Li; Mari Kondo; Jin-Lian Luo; and Jun-Chen Hu. "Conflict Management Style: Accounting for Cross-National Differences." *Journal of International Business Studies* 29:4 (1999), pp. 729–48.

Sharland, Alex. "The Negotiation Process as a Predictor of Relationship Outcomes in International Buyer–Supplier Arrangements." *Industrial Marketing Management* 30 (2001), pp. 551–59.

Volkema, Roger J. "A Comparison of Perceptions of Ethical Negotiation Behavior in Mexico and the United States." *International Journal of Conflict Management,* July 1998, pp. 218–33.

Volkema, Roger J. "Ethicality in Negotiations: An Analysis of Perceptual Similarities and Differences between Brazil and the United States." *Journal of Business Research* 45 (1999), pp. 59–67.

Waring, Becky. "Online Meeting Rooms." *Presentations,* March 2000, pp. 44–53.

Zhao, Jensen J. "The Chinese Approach to International Business Negotiation." *The Journal of Business Communication* 37, July 2002, pp. 209–37.

15 Selling to Resellers

SOME QUESTIONS ANSWERED IN THIS CHAPTER ARE:

- What is a reseller?

- How does the buying process of a reseller differ from the buying process of an end user?

- What common terms and conditions apply to such sales, and how do they affect sales?

- How do salespeople help resellers sell their products and services?

- How do salespeople build partnerships with resellers?

- What role do trade shows and markets play in the sale of goods to the trade?

Many salespeople work for companies that sell their products through resellers—retailers, wholesalers, and industrial distributors—rather than directly to end users. Salespeople who sell directly to end users present the benefits of their products to the people who will actually use them. However, salespeople who sell to resellers, the trade, must first convince the resellers that end users will want these specific products and then must help the reseller's salespeople sell the products.

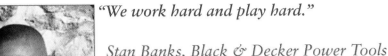

"We work hard and play hard."

Stan Banks, Black & Decker Power Tools

PROFILE

After Stan Banks graduated from the University of North Carolina, Chapel Hill, he went to work for Black & Decker as a district sales representative (DSR) on the Home Depot team. The Black & Decker account management team works with Home Depot buyers in its Atlanta corporate headquarters to get the company to stock Black & Decker products and develop merchandising programs to build sales. However, Home Depot store managers have considerable authority about what and how merchandise is displayed in their stores. Stan's first job was developing good working relationships with the store managers in his district to implement corporate initiatives.

To build these relationships, Stan started out showing the managers that he could help them sell more products. He volunteered to do demonstrations in front of the store—building a bird house or picnic table with Black & Decker tools. "I did not know anything about making things with power tools. But we have a great training program that prepared me in a lot of different areas."

Then he worked with sales associates in the store, training them on the features and benefits of Black & Decker's power tools. As store managers and sales associates recognized that Stan was helping them improve their performance, Stan started to propose merchandising programs for Black & Decker tools. For example, he showed managers how saw blades sales could be significantly increased if they were placed in the lumber section as well as in the power tool section.

Stan was promoted to be the manager for a SWARM team. Stan's team of seven salespeople generated interest and demand for Black & Decker tools in their territory by going to construction job sites and demonstrating new DeWalt tools. Stan's team also supported Black & Decker's event sponsorships, including NASCAR races and Skills USA competitions. Skills USA is a program in which young children compete in construction-related activities such as preparing architectural designs and woodworking.

Recently Stan was promoted to district sales manager. He has a team of salespeople responsible for 13 Lowe's home improvement centers in North Carolina and eastern Tennessee. One of the projects he and his team are working on is the introduction of a new DeWalt portable radio. "This radio has some great benefits for people on the job site. The heavy-duty construction and roll bars protect it from damage if it is dropped or hit. It can be used to charge our power tools. When we talk to workers on the job site, it draws a lot of attention.

"But when we're trying to get store managers to feature the radio on an end-aisle display during the Christmas season, we have to use a different approach. We need to show them how it's going to benefit them, how it's going to increase the inventory turns and profits of their store. Other companies are trying to get their products featured. So we have to demonstrate how the new radio is going to have a faster sell through and higher margin than our competitors' products. Then we have to help the sales associates build the display and keep it stocked.

"I really like my job and working for Black & Decker. We have a unique corporate culture. We are performance oriented. If you produce the sales, you get rewarded. The nice thing about working in sales is that it's easy for people to see how you are doing by looking at the sales figures. In four years I have more than doubled my compensation. We work hard and play hard. The people I work with are some of my best friends also."

Visit Our Website @ www.black&decker.com.

RESELLERS AND THE DISTRIBUTION CHANNEL

WHO ARE RESELLERS?

Resellers are firms in the distribution channel that link the manufacturer with the end user (see Exhibit 15.1). In the consumer products channel, the end users are consumers. These consumers buy products from retailers such as Wal-Mart, Home Depot, and Kroger. National retail chains typically operate their own warehouses and buy directly from manufacturers. But smaller retailers buy products from wholesalers rather than directly from manufacturers. Consumer-product trade salespeople work for manufacturers like Procter & Gamble, Kraft, Sony, and Black & Decker and sell products to wholesalers or directly to the retailers.

In the business-to-business, or industrial, channel, the end users are other businesses. For example, agricultural equipment is sold to farmers through dealers. Brazos Farm and Equipment is a John Deere dealer. In Brazos's showroom a John Deere salesperson sets up displays of John Deere tractors, lawn and garden equipment, and farm equipment parts and accessories. The sales representative teaches Brazos salespeople how to sell John Deere tractors and farm implements. The rep also assists Brazos with the local advertising of Deere products. Dealers do not have to carry all of Deere's products or participate in all of Deere's marketing programs, but seeing that they do participate is the job of the Deere rep.

Similarly, General Electric makes electrical switches for machinery. Its trade salespeople sell these switches to W. W. Grainger, an industrial distributor. When the switch on the drill press fails in a manufacturing plant, the person in charge of repairing the drill press buys the switch from the local W. W. Grainger distribution center.

Typically, business end users purchase goods (components, subassemblies, raw and processed materials) used in making their products both directly from the manufacturer and through a distributor. For example, Dell buys microprocessors from Intel and uses them in the Dell computers it produces. However, when Dell needs to purchase small quantities of Intel microprocessors to be used by design engineers, Dell will buy them from Arrow Electronics, a distributor with a local warehouse.

Trade sales is a great place to start a career because of the learning potential. The trade salesperson has to understand the consumer or final customer, as well as the entire distribution channel. The job has changed greatly in recent years, with trade salespeople working more closely with resellers to develop promotion and marketing plans, rather than simply taking inventory of the reseller's shelves and placing orders to restock. Thus all you have learned about building partnerships applies, making trade sales a strong career choice for many college graduates.

Selling to resellers may involve helping stores (left) or industrial distributors (right) take inventory or merchandize products.

Spencer Grant/PhotoEdit

John Boykin/PhotoEdit

EXHIBIT 15.1

Where Trade
Salespeople Fit in
Channels of Distribution

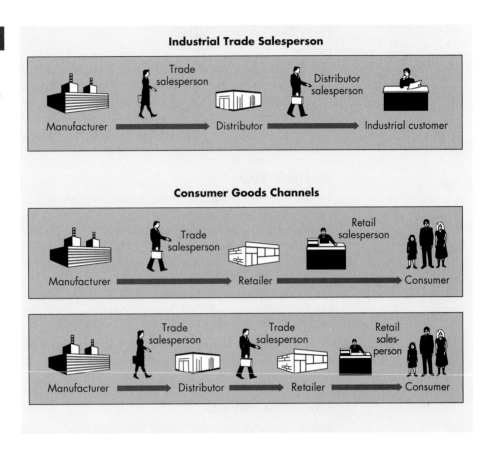

THE ROLE OF RESELLERS IN A DISTRIBUTION CHANNEL

Resellers undertake business activities and perform functions that increase the value of the products and services they sell to end users. These functions are

1. Providing an assortment of products and services.
2. Breaking bulk.
3. Holding inventory.
4. Providing services.

The Cutter and Buck salesperson is working with a dealer to train its salespeople and help the dealer market Cutter and Buck apparel.

David Young-Wolff/PhotoEdit

PROVIDING ASSORTMENTS

Industrial distributor W. W. Grainger carries 15,000 items made by more than 500 companies. Offering an assortment enables customers to buy a wide selection of parts from one company. Manufacturers specialize in producing specific types of products. For example, Aerovox makes capacitors, General Electric makes electrical components, and Intel makes microprocessors. If each manufacturer sold directly to end users, design engineers would have to contact many companies to buy components for new prototypes and projects.

BREAKING BULK

To reduce transportation costs, manufacturers and wholesalers typically ship cases of switches or frozen dinners to resellers. Resellers then offer the products in smaller quantities tailored to individual end users' usage patterns. This process is called **breaking bulk.**

HOLDING INVENTORY

A major function of industrial distributors and retailers is to keep inventory on hand so that products will be available when customers want them. Thus end users can keep a much smaller inventory of products on hand because they know that they can always get more from the resellers. By maintaining an inventory, resellers provide a benefit to consumers—that is, resellers reduce the end users' cost of storing products.

PROVIDING SERVICES

Resellers provide services that make it easier for customers to buy and use products. For example, resellers offer credit so customers can have a product now and pay for it later. In addition, resellers display products so consumers can see and test various items before buying. Some resellers have salespeople on hand to answer questions and provide additional information about products. Industrial distributors may even do some assembly of components to the end users' specifications.

INCREASING THE VALUE OF PRODUCTS AND SERVICES

By providing assortments, breaking bulk, holding inventory, and providing services, resellers increase the value customers receive from their products and services. To illustrate, consider a door in a shipping crate in an Iowa manufacturer's warehouse. That door won't satisfy the needs of a do-it-yourselfer (DIYer) or a home improvement contractor who wants to replace a closet door today. For the DIYer, a home improvement center like Home Depot or Lowe's sells one door that is available when the DIYer wants it at a conveniently located store. The home improvement center helps the customer select the door by displaying various doors so they can be examined before purchase. An employee is available to explain which door is best for closets and how the door should be hung. The center has an assortment of hardware, paint, and tools that the DIYer will need for the job. Thus resellers increase the value of products and services bought by their customers.

GETTING RESELLERS TO SELL YOUR PRODUCTS

To offer a broad assortment to their customers, resellers sell many different items. Each item is referred to as a **stock keeping unit (SKU).** For example, a blue, long-sleeve, button-down-collar Tommy Hilfiger men's dress shirt size 16/32 or a 5,000-watt Dayton professional-duty, portable, gasoline power generator is an SKU. A typical Wal-Mart store will have 25,000 SKUs, and a department store like JCPenney or Macy's will have more than 100,000 SKUs.

GETTING THE SHELF SPACE

Julie Autry is a ConAgra trade salesperson. Some of the brands that she sells to supermarkets are Hunts Ketchup, Wesson Oil, and Healthy Choice foods. Autry explains, "My number one priority is ensuring 100 percent distribution on all ConAgra products on every store call. We've found that more money is made when a product is displayed appropriately on the shelf and sold at the regular price than when the product is featured [in advertising] and displayed in a special endcap display. If the product is not available on the shelf, then the sale is lost."

Healthy Choice foods are a good example. Healthy Choice leads its category with a 53 percent market share in the Dallas/Fort Worth market. Therefore, Healthy Choice should have half or more of the freezer space, but may not lead the category's sales in a particular store. "From time to time, I enter a situation where the shelf space is not reflective of Healthy Choice's market share. This is where my job begins," Autry says. She knows that proper display of Healthy Choice will increase sales for the entire category. "Using data from IRI [an independent research company], I educate the

manager on the whole premium dinner category. I present the latest Dallas/Fort Worth market share information, which tells the manager that by making a merchandising change [changing the allocation of shelf space], the store and ConAgra will benefit."

Not all ConAgra products are category leaders. Autry would not use that strategy to sell the ConAgra brand of chili, for example, because a competitor leads that market. In that case Autry says, "I would make sure the product was in the store and in its proper location." She doesn't want that category leader taking her fair share of space for chili any more than she would allow Healthy Choice to have less than its fair share.

Autry recognizes the importance of building trust with her customers and always acting in their best interest: "Almost no other salespeople are in my customers' stores as frequently as I am. I am like another person on their staff, and they know that and trust me. That's one reason why I like working for ConAgra—we really work for our customers."

Most resellers sell products made by competing manufacturers. Kroger sells washing detergents made by Procter & Gamble and Unilever, and Arrow Electronics sells microprocessors made by Intel and AMC. Thus the trade salespeople working for manufacturers want to get resellers to spend more resources promoting the products made by their firms compared to competitor firms.

SHARE OF SPACE   When selling in consumer channels to retailers, trade salespeople are competing for space on the retailer's shelves and floor. Consumer purchases in supermarkets are greatly affected by the location of products on the shelves. Consumers tend to buy products that attract their attention—products that are at eye level and have a number of variations displayed on the shelf.[1]

Kraft, Lipton, and Rice-a-Roni all manufacture a noodles alfredo product. Each manufacturer's salesperson wants the most and best shelf space in the supermarket so consumers will buy more of his or her company's product. But only one product can have the best position, and the other products will have to make do with less space or an inferior position. The grocery store wants to assign shelf space in a way that will maximize total noodles alfredo sales, but the three salespeople are interested only in their own brands' sales. Building Partnerships 15.1 illustrates how a trade salesperson focuses on the returns from space.

Sometimes the battle is not ethical. One Noxell (Noxzema and Cover Girl cosmetics) rep described how she called on a pharmacy and discovered that her products were completely missing. A competitor had emptied the shelves of her products and moved them to the back room. The Noxell rep simply brought the lack of shelf space to the attention of the store manager and let him draw his own conclusions. The unethical competitor was later asked to remove its products.

In some cases the resellers are authorized dealers for a single company's products, and shelf space is not a concern. For example, Hallmark salespeople sell cards and gifts to Hallmark store owners, who can sell only Hallmark greeting cards and gift merchandise. When selling to the authorized dealers, the objective of the trade salespeople shifts from a battle for space to a partnering role to help the dealer sell more of the company's products. Al Summay, vice president of sales and service at Hallmark, says, "We're not selling to retailers, we're selling through retailers. We look at the retailer as the pipeline to the hands of the consumers." This perspective means that when retailers make money with Hallmark cards, Hallmark makes money.[2]

SHARE OF MIND

In selling to industrial distributors, the battle is not for space but for share of mind. **Mind share** is the degree to which a manufacturer's product receives attention from (occupies the mind of) the distributor's salespeople. The manufacturer wants the distributor's salespeople to demonstrate and recommend its products more than the competitor's products. For example, Panasonic manufactures electronic parts that other manufacturers use to make many types of products. Panasonic's distributors can recommend Panasonic or another product, and often there is little functional difference between the two. Panasonic wants to be the first brand recommended—that is, have the primary position in the mind of the distributor's salespeople. As you will see later in this chapter, Panasonic and other manufacturers seek to increase mind share by making it easier and more profitable for distributors' salespeople to sell that manufacturer's products.

RESELLER BUYING CONSIDERATIONS

Like all salespeople, trade salespeople must convince customers that their products and services will satisfy their needs. However, the criteria used by resellers and end users to evaluate products differ. End users focus on the benefits the product provides to them. When resellers purchase a product for resale, they are concerned with whether their customers will also buy the product. The reseller's profits are based not on how well the product performs (such as how the switch lasts), but on how well the product sells.

All firms want to get as high a return on investment (ROI) as possible. The critical investments that manufacturers make are in research and development, production facilities, and marketing. Resellers do not make investments to develop or produce products. Their critical investments are in inventory and space or real estate (warehouses and/or stores).

In the following sections we examine the different factors resellers consider in buying products from a supplier. In addition to the return on inventory and space, we also examine the impact of the reseller's and supplier's image.

RETURN ON INVENTORY—STRATEGIC PROFIT MODEL

The **strategic profit model** (SPM) breaks down the reseller costs and investments to illustrate the trade-offs resellers can make between profit margin and inventory turnover. Resellers often use the SPM to evaluate the financial performance of products they are selling or are considering selling.

The strategic profit model shown in Exhibit 15.2 illustrates the two critical factors affecting the financial performance of resellers. The top half of the diagram shows the components affecting net profits, and the bottom half shows the components affecting inventory turnover. As you can see from the following for-

EXHIBIT 15.2

The Strategic Profit
Model

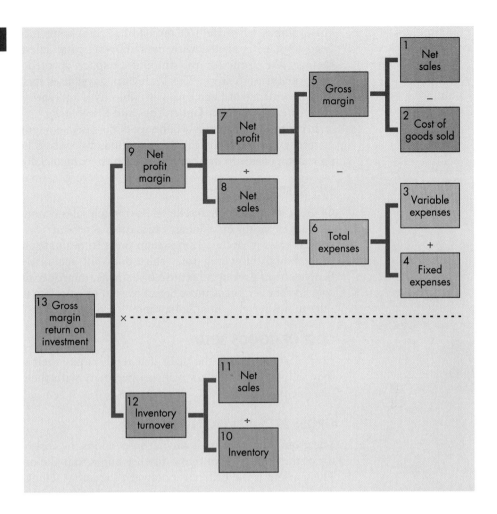

mula, these two factors determine the return the reseller gets on its inventory investment:

Net profit margin × Inventory turnover = Return on inventory investment

$$\frac{\text{Net profit}}{\text{Net sales}} \times \frac{\text{Net sales}}{\text{Inventory investment}} = \frac{\text{Net profit}}{\text{Inventory investment}}$$

These two factors illustrate two approaches that resellers can take to increase their ROI. They can either increase their net profit margin or increase their inventory turnover. Department stores typically have high net profit but low inventory turnover, whereas supermarkets produce the same ROI, as shown below, with low profit margins but high inventory turnover.

Type of Reseller	Net Profit Margin	Inventory Turnover	Return on Inventory Investment
Department store	10%	1.5	15%
Supermarket	1%	15	15%

Thus when evaluating a product or program, a reseller buyer focuses on three things: how many will be sold, at what profit, and how fast the product will sell.

For example, when Jim O'Connell of Lego Systems meets with Wal-Mart to sell Lego toys, he is armed with data showing total sales, gross margin return on footage (the profit for the amount of space devoted to Lego), and inventory turnover for each store. The Wal-Mart buyer uses this information to compare the performance of Lego toys with objectives and with other products sold in the same category, such as Tinker Toys and Brio blocks.[3]

In the remainder of this section we discuss each component in the reseller's strategic profit model. In the following sections we discuss how salespeople can affect these components to make their products more financially attractive to the reseller.

NET SALES

Of great interest to the reseller is how much sales revenue can be expected from a product or program. (When evaluating a product or program, reseller buyers express sales in dollars rather than units to evaluate the product's or program's profitability.) However, total sales does not accurately measure realized sales. People return products because of damage, improper fit, or for no apparent reason, and these returns must be subtracted to calculate net sales. **Net sales** is total sales minus returns, in dollars, represented by box 1 in Exhibit 15.2.

COST OF GOODS SOLD

Cost of goods sold is the price that resellers pay their suppliers for the products they sell. Clearly resellers want to negotiate with their suppliers for the lowest possible price.

GROSS PROFIT MARGIN

The **gross profit margin** is the net sales minus the cost of goods sold. One indicator of the gross margin that a reseller hopes to make on a product is its markup. The **markup** is the difference between the initial selling price and the cost of the product and is expressed as a percentage of the initial selling price. The formula for markup is

$$\text{Markup} = (\text{Initial price} - \text{Cost})/\text{Initial price}$$

Gross margin and markup are sometimes equal, but typically the gross margin is less than markup because it is based on the initial price and gross margin is based on what the product actually sold for.

The initial price is typically higher then the ultimate price because resellers often offer their customers discounts. This discount is referred to as a **markdown.** For example, if Linz Jewelers buys a diamond ring for $1,000, it may initially mark up the ring by 75 percent. A 75 percent markup means that the initial price of the ring is $4,000, using the following formula:

$$\text{Initial price} = \text{Cost}/(1 - \text{Markup}) = \$1,000/(1 - 0.75) = \$4,000$$

However, the customer may negotiate with the retail salesperson and buy the ring for $3,000. The gross margin that retailer gets is 67 percent: ($3,000 − $1,000)/$3,000. Industrial distributors often offer discounts if customers make large purchases (quantity discounts) or pay for merchandise quickly.

NET PROFIT MARGIN

Net profit margin is the profit the reseller makes, expressed as a percentage of sales. In mathematical terms:

$$\text{Net profit margin} = (\text{Gross profit margin} - \text{Total expenses})/\text{Net sales}$$

Net profit margin (box 9 in Exhibit 15.2) is influenced by the cost of goods sold (the price charged to the reseller, box 2 in the exhibit). Net profit margin is also influenced by the variable expenses (box 3), which can be affected by costs associated with reselling the product. Thus salespeople can influence net profit (box 7) in several ways, which can have a major impact on net profit margin.

For example, if Linz Jewelers sold 100 of those rings for an average price of $3,000, then Linz achieved total sales of $300,000. Assuming that Linz spent $10,000 advertising the rings and another $30,000 in salesperson commissions, and Linz allocated $5,000 in store rent and all other expenses to the rings, then net profit margin would be $300,000 minus $10,000, $30,000, and $5,000, or $255,000, or 85 percent of sales.

$300,000 sales

−10,000 advertising

−30,000 commissions

−5,000 rent and other expenses

$255,000 ÷ $300,000 = 85% net profit margin

INVENTORY TURNOVER

Inventory turnover (box 12 in Exhibit 15.2) is typically calculated by dividing the annual sales by the average retail price of the inventory on hand. Thus it measures how fast a product sells relative to how much inventory has to be carried—how efficiently a reseller manages its inventory. The reseller would like to have in the store only the amount needed for that day's sales because inventory represents an investment. Thus large retailers such as Wal-Mart receive daily delivery of some products. If the reseller is able to reduce its inventory level, it can invest this savings in stores or warehouses or in the stock market.

For example, if Linz Jewelers usually kept eight rings in stock, inventory turnover would be calculated by dividing total sales (remember, this was 100 rings) in units by average inventory. Thus inventory turnover would be 100/8 or 12.5 times. The answer represents the number of times that Linz sold the average inventory level.

Another way to calculate this is to divide total sales ($300,000 in the Linz example) by the average price of inventory (eight units × $3,000 or $24,000). The answer is the same, 12.5 times.

A reseller does not necessarily want to increase inventory turnover by reducing the amount of inventory carried. Several negative consequences can result. For example, sales may fall because stockouts occur more frequently and products are not available when customers want to buy them. Expenses can increase because the reseller has to order more frequently. Finally, the cost of goods sold may increase because the reseller pays higher shipping charges and does not get as big a quantity discount.

GROSS MARGIN ROI

When inventory turnover is multiplied by net profit margin, the buyer has determined the gross margin return on investment (box 13 in Exhibit 15.2). Note that we are using a simplified version of ROI to illustrate how a product is evaluated for purchase; overall ROI would include other assets and items not affected by a seller's program. To compare two products, the buyer can insert the projected sales of each, the costs of each, the costs associated with reselling the products (less any support from the manufacturer), and how much inventory must be kept on hand and then calculate the ROI. The choice would be made on the basis of which product had the better ROI.

For example, Kmart was offered a large discount from a vendor if the vendor could begin shipping in bulk to Kmart's warehouses instead of directly to the stores. At first glance the discount looked attractive because it lowered the cost of goods sold (box 2), which would improve gross margin (box 5) and thus improve net profit (box 7), net profit margin (box 9), and ultimately ROI (box 13). But Kmart would then incur other costs, such as increased shipping from its warehouses to the stores, increased handling to break down the vendor's large shipments into the amount needed for each store, and increased inventory. The first two costs would increase variable expenses (box 3), while increased inventory (box 10) would hurt inventory turnover (box 12). The overall result would be lower ROI (box 13). By forecasting these costs and applying the SPM, Kmart was able to avoid a costly mistake.

RETURN ON SPACE

As mentioned previously, the other key investment that resellers make is in space— retail store space and warehouse space. A measure that retailers use to assess the return on their space investment is sales per square foot or sales per shelf foot. The John Deere dealer would not use this measure because space is not at a great premium, but the dealer will compare alternative uses of display space. In a grocery store or a department store, however, shelf, or display, space is a finite asset that is used to capacity. Products therefore must be evaluated on how well they use the space allocated to them. For example, if a retailer generates $200 per square foot in sales with Tommy Hilfiger merchandise and only $150 selling Ralph Lauren merchandise, it will increase the space allocated to Tommy Hilfiger and reduce the space allocated to Ralph Lauren.

IMAGE

Image can mean many things, especially when selling to the trade. We will discuss the image consumers hold of the selling firm as well as the image buyers have of the salesperson. Both are important to the buyer in vendor selection.

IMAGE WITH CONSUMERS

Manufacturers invest considerable resources in developing an image of their brands in consumer minds. For example, Coca-Cola promoted an image of Tab, a diet cola, as the "diet cola for women" because it contained calcium, something Diet Coke does not have. Procter & Gamble has developed an image of Crest toothpaste as a cavity fighter, whereas Close-Up has an image of a whitening toothpaste that improves sex appeal. Those manufacturers want to preserve and build these images.

Therefore, the product's and the company's image in the marketplace must be consistent with the image the reseller wants to project. For example, a lawn and garden store that has an image of the lowest priced in town would not carry Snapper lawn mowers (premium-priced, high-quality products), but would carry Murray mowers (affordable, with fewer features). If the same store positioned itself on the basis of top quality and service, it would want to carry Snapper, not Murray.

IMAGE IN THE TRADE

The vendor also has an image in the trade. This image, based on how the company treats its distributors, is separate from the position the company strives for in the marketplace. In the Coca-Cola example, Tab has its image in the marketplace, and Coca-Cola Company has an image among grocery stores separate from that for Tab. For example, Coca-Cola strives for an image of strong marketing support with its grocery store buyers.

Vendor image can be very important. For example, John Deere has a reputation among dealers of providing excellent support. This reputation made it easier for Deere to extend its product lines into lawn and garden equipment when times got tight in the agricultural market. New dealers for the new products were willing to invest in Deere because of that company's reputation for support.

When buyers evaluate a potential supplier's reputation, they consider questions such as the following:

- Is this company ethical? Does it fulfill its promises?
- Will the supplier stand behind its offerings?
- Is the supplier financially healthy? Will it be around to supply me over a period of time?
- Is this supplier innovative or conservative?
- Will I be treated fairly—that is, given fair access to discounts, marketing support, delivery, and credit terms?

Salespeople play a big role in how the territory views their companies. Each salesperson has the opportunity to build a reputation or tear it down. Often the little things build a reputation, just as the little things build a relationship. As you review the preceding questions, you can see that being professional in the way you conduct yourself can have a very positive impact on the reputation of your company. Doing business with a reputable company reduces risk for the buyer. Companies want partners they can trust. Confidence in the selection of a partner is greatest when the buyer recognizes that the supplying company is reputable.

OTHER FACTORS TO CONSIDER

Unlike the hard financial aspects of reselling a product or evaluating the success of a marketing program, measuring the vendor's level of support is often not an objective process. Yet retailers and other resellers know that this element, the "soft" side of supplier selection, is as important as the hard, financial side. In fact, research shows that the two are often highly related.[4]

The dimensions on which vendors are evaluated include reliability, turnaround, facilitating functions, information, credit, and ethics. Other dimensions are risk and investment. Image represents the buyer's total perception of these factors.

Finally, trade salespeople need to recognize that resellers provide benefits, other than sales, to suppliers. Resellers not only promote the suppliers' products by advertising but also give manufacturers information about the market, what customers want, what the competition is doing, and other important data that help manufacturers respond to changing market conditions. Resellers also build displays, create special promotions, and perform other activities that help manufacturers achieve their goals. It is important that the salespeople who sell to resellers understand what resellers want so that mutual solutions can be achieved.

SELLING TO RESELLERS

How do salespeople use this knowledge of the factors that resellers consider in making buying decisions to do a more effective sales job? As a first step, salespeople understand that customers, the resellers, will be interested in ROI—a function of their total sales for the product, their profit margins, and how fast the product will sell. Professional salespeople also understand how their own performance will be evaluated by buyers and how the buying process will work. Then salespeople must prepare to answer customers' questions and prove benefits for the buyer, using methods similar to the proof methods we discussed in Chapter 10. Exhibit 15.3 lists the measures buyers use to consider their purchases and relates these factors to the proof processes salespeople use.

EXHIBIT 15.3

What Reseller Buyers Buy	How Salespeople Prove Benefits
Net sales	Selling history
	Market share
Net profit margin	Pricing terms
	Absorbing shipping costs
	Trade discounts
	Quantity discounts
	Promotional allowances
	Credit terms and financial discounts
	Marketing support
Inventory turnover	Selling history
	Market share
	Third-party proof
Image	Company history
	Turnaround

USING THE STRATEGIC PROFIT MODEL

Resellers evaluate many numbers and elements of marketing programs to make marketing and buying decisions. As you saw earlier, however, these evaluations boil down to three questions, often asked in this order:

- How quickly and easily will it sell (inventory turnover)?
- How much will sell (sales)?
- At what profit will it sell (profit margin)?

The salesperson must show how the product will meet the reseller's needs on these three dimensions.

Thinking It Through

How is the Internet changing the role and importance of trade salespeople?

IMPROVING TURNOVER

To improve inventory turnover and to manage their supply chain more efficiently, resellers are building partnerships with suppliers (see Chapter 4). **Efficient consumer response (ECR)**, **quick response (QR)**, **automatic replenishment (AR)**, and **just in time (JIT)** are inventory management systems designed to reduce the reseller's average inventory and transportation expenses but still make sure that products are available when end users want them. ECR describes systems that link packaged goods manufacturers and supermarkets. The term QR refers to systems connecting apparel manufacturers and retailers, and JIT and AR describe systems in business-to-business distribution channels.[5]

The September 11, 2001, tragedy created an outpouring of patriotic feelings among Americans. Within 24 hours there was a shortage of American flags, and there is only one major American flag manufacturer. The company had 80,000 flags in inventory on September 11. By the close of business September 12, both Target and Wal-Mart had completely sold out of flags—over 150,000 each. When the stores opened September 13, Wal-Mart had 80,000 more flags while

Target had none. How? Wal-Mart's QR system is updated every five minutes, whereas Target doesn't update its inventory system until the stores are closed in the evening. Wal-Mart had an order placed with expedited shipping *before* the stores closed and *before* Target knew it was out of flags! Similar situations occurred in other product categories, such as flashlights, batteries, battery-powered radios, bottled water, guns, ammunition, and other products that frightened Americans wanted.[6] As this example illustrates, EDI and ECR systems can give resellers significant competitive advantage.

Electronic data interchange (EDI) is a computer-to-computer transmission of data from a reseller, such as Wal-Mart, to vendors (such as American Flag Co.) and back. Resellers and vendors that have ECR or QR relationships use EDI to transmit purchase orders and shipping information.

Precision Fabric Group (PFG), an apparel manufacturer in North Carolina, even manufactures based on customer demand. If the retailer sells more of a certain color, it orders more of that color rather than a prepackaged combination, as is common in that industry. PFG can handle these orders because it developed several weaving technologies that allow it to speed up the manufacturing process. Hence it has a JIT manufacturing-through-retailing process.

For these systems to work effectively, suppliers and resellers need to have strong partnering relationships. They need to make considerable investment in learning each other's businesses and developing compatible electronic interfaces. In addition, the partners need to share sensitive information. Suppliers need to coordinate their production with special sales by resellers, and resellers need to prepare for new products being developed by suppliers.

Trade salespeople are responsible for managing these partnering relationships. They draw on the resources of their companies to make sure both parties benefit from the relationship.

PROVING SALES

An important point to remember when selling to resellers is that they deal with derived demand just as other organizational buyers do. Resellers are not interested in their own personal desire for the product, but instead care whether their customers will buy it. Students often forget this fact in practice presentations and spend too much time showing the buyer why the product is so wonderful, forgetting to tie those features to the buyer's need for strong sales.

For example, Wayne Cimperman sells accessories for skiing and in-line skating, such as a neck wallet that hangs around the skater's or skier's neck. In a meeting with one of the largest sports retailers in the Northeast, Cimperman

By communicating sales and inventory data electronically, resellers like Computerland can reduce the amount of inventory they need to keep in their warehouses.

Cindy Charles/PhotoEdit

Spenco's sales brochure includes sales data, providing proof to retailers that they will make more money if they stock Spenco products.

52 WEEKS ENDING 8/11/01
TOTAL US - DRUG STORES OVER 2MM

RANK		DOLLAR SALES	DOLLAR SHARE	SALES UNITS	UNIT SHARE	% STR SELLING	AVG UNIT PRICE
	TOTAL FIRST AID BANDAGES	127,397,129	100	43,925,692	100	100	2.9
1	TOTAL JOHNSON & JOHNSON BAND	48,413,047	38	15,729,534	35.8	100	3.08
2	TOTAL CTL BR	39,120,488	30.7	16,783,312	38.2	98	2.33
3	TOTAL CURAD	7,015,228	5.5	2,814,354	6.4	100	2.49
4	TOTAL 3M NEXCARE	6,234,823	4.9	1,786,998	4.1	99	3.49
5	TOTAL 3M NEXCARE ACTIVE STRIPS	5,496,196	4.3	1,767,886	4	99	3.11
6	TOTAL 3M NEXCARE COMFORT STR	5,204,520	4.1	1,651,182	3.8	98	3.15
7	**TOTAL SPENCO 2ND SKIN**	**4,557,856**	**3.6**	**569,526**	**1.2**	**91**	**7.5**
8	TOTAL CURITY TELFA	1,777,913	1.4	436,663	1	58	4.07
9	TOTAL 3M NEXCARE TEGADERM	1,675,962	1.3	231,699	0.5	83	7.23
10	TOTAL CURAD EXTREME LENGTHS	973,848	0.8	331,173	0.8	92	2.94
11	TOTAL 3M NEXCARE ACTIVE STRP E	850,213	0.7	290,252	0.7	92	2.93
12	TOTAL COVERLET	842,784	0.7	121,589	0.3	48	6.93
13	TOTAL 3M OPTICLUDE	793,689	0.6	139,337	0.3	48	5.7
14	TOTAL ADVANCED CURAD AQUA-PR	746,970	0.6	231,145	0.5	45	3.23
15	TOTAL JOHNSON & JOHNSON FIRST	619,517	0.5	130,287	0.3	64	4.76
16	TOTAL CURAD EXTREME SHAPES	482,400	0.4	165,384	0.4	28	2.92
17	TOTAL AMERICAN WHITE CROSS FIF	480,385	0.4	239,444	0.5	23	2.01
18	TOTAL NEW-SKIN	384,402	0.3	55,768	0.1	31	6.89
19	TOTAL SQUIBB CONVATEC STOMAH	341,550	0.3	14,767	0	1	23.13
20	TOTAL ADVANCED CURAD BLISTER-	334,823	0.3	62,431	0.1	29	5.36
21	TOTAL JOHNSON & JOHNSON BIOCL	219,081	0.2	30,053	0.1	34	7.29
22	TOTAL KID CARE	170,413	0.1	75,520	0.2	36	2.26
23	TOTAL KIDZ HEALTH	144,620	0.1	50,044	0.1	29	2.89
24	TOTAL SELECT BRAND	106,072	0.1	59,705	0.1	1	1.78
25	TOTAL 3M NEXCARE ULTRA SHEER	102,118	0.1	37,810	0.1	37	2.7
26	TOTAL SPYROFLEX	85,728	0.1	22,871	0.1	11	3.75
27	TOTAL CURAD FLEX-FABRIC	60,931	0	20,933	0	4	2.91
28	TOTAL GOOD SENSE	32,908	0	12,866	0	1	2.56
29	TOTAL QWIKSTRIP	32,533	0	8,175	0	14	3.98
30	TOTAL ASO CORPORATION-NBL	22,564	0	11,614	0	4	1.94
31	TOTAL CORALITE	15,140	0	15,019	0	0	1.01
32	TOTAL CURAD DESIGN ITS	11,341	0	4,881	0	2	2.32
33	TOTAL UNIVERSAL RAZOR INDUSTR	9,932	0	10,335	0	1	0.96
34	TOTAL ADVANCED CURAD COOL-WF	8,526	0	1,725	0	2	4.94
35	TOTAL ASO	7,016	0	2,852	0	3	2.46
36	TOTAL ADVANCED CURAD SOF-GEL	5,992	0	1,778	0	2	3.37
37	TOTAL NUTRAMAX PRODUCTS, INC.	5,061	0	2,116	0	1	2.39
38	TOTAL WILD HOT STRIPS	2,805	0	2,060	0	1	1.36
39	TOTAL JOHNSON & JOHNSON PROX	2,151	0	288	0	1	7.47
40	TOTAL DA GRINCH	1,431	0	518	0	0	2.76
41	TOTAL LISA FRANK FANTASY FRIEN	1,380	0	366	0	1	3.77
42	TOTAL COMPEED	930	0	204	0	0	4.56
43	TOTAL AMERICAN WHITE CROSS	928	0	745	0	2	1.25
44	TOTAL EBON-AIDE	420	0	183	0	0	2.29
45	TOTAL STAT-STRIP	232	0	130	0	0	1.79
46	TOTAL FAMOUS FIXINS INC-NBL	140	0	47	0	0	2.99
47	TOTAL STAR STRIPS	63	0	93	0	0	0.68
48	TOTAL TINKERBELL	59	0	31	0	0	1.95

Courtesy of Spenco Medical Co.

discovered that although the buyer liked Cimperman's neck wallet, the buyer already had thousands in stock from another supplier that were not selling. Cimperman diagnosed the problem as poor packaging; customers did not understand what the products were. Using data from similar chains, Cimperman showed how his neck wallets were outselling the competition five to one; but just as important, Cimperman showed how his packaging demonstrated product use to consumers. By proving that his product would sell, Cimperman became a major supplier to that chain of stores.[7]

When proving that the product will sell, the supplier is also addressing turnover. Suppliers provide marketing support so that their products will sell faster. Marketing support from the vendor improves the efficiency of the reseller. Vendor advertising, for example, should lead to greater product recognition by the consumer. The reseller has less selling to do because the vendor's advertising has already presold the consumer, thus improving turnover. Note that Spenco included its promotion plan featuring Paul Harvey as their spokesman on the brochure its salespeople use to sell the Spenco line. Buyers could rest assured that Spenco would help them sell the product, which should positively influence turnover.

USING SELLING HISTORY

Salespeople often use past sales experience to gain future sales. **Selling history** refers to how well the vendor's product or line sold during the same season in the previous year. Selling history is the most important factor in vendor selection to department store buyers choosing clothing and accessories as well as housewares and appliances.[8] It is also important in other types of selling to resellers. For example, Mott's USA uses FastTrack sales automation software, TIPS promotion expense software, and data on market share and sales history from IRI to show how well its apple juice products sold in the past and to project the impact of promotion plans on future sales.[9] An example of how selling history might be presented appears in Exhibit 15.4.

A sales representative trying to secure distribution through a new outlet has no selling history with that prospect to prove the selling power of the product or program, but success with similar dealers or retailers can be used, as Cimperman did with the neck wallet. Be careful in such situations, however; you do not want to give away confidential information, such as how much your prospect's competitor is making. For example, you should not tell Macy's that Foley's sells 200 cases of your product per week. That would be unethical and unfair to Foley's.

EXHIBIT 15.4	Proposal for Budget Box Grocery Stores	
Using Selling History to Sell Margin	**Last Spring's Off! Super Sales**	**This Spring's Deep Woods Off! Sell-Out**
		New Off! product
	50¢ coupon	50¢ coupon
	$1 million national ad campaign	$1.3 million TV ad campaign
		$8 million print ad campaign
	You sold <u>50 cases</u>	You sell <u>70 cases</u>
	Profit <u>$736</u>	Profit <u>$11,761</u>

USING MARKET SHARE

One common method of proving that a product will sell is to show market share. **Market share** is the percentage of total market sales accounted for by one product. In mathematical terms,

Market share = Brand sales/Total product category sales

For example, to say that General Electric switches have a 40 percent market share means that 40 percent of all switches sold are made by General Electric. Market share is most often used for consumer packaged goods because markets are easily defined by product categories and data concerning sales of various products are readily available. But market share may be less applicable in other industries, such as fashion goods and hardware, where markets may be poorly defined or data less readily available. The way salespeople present market share information depends on the type of buyer. For example, an amiable can be told that everyone loves this product—in fact, it is the leading product in the market; whereas an analytical will want to see the actual percentage. Such percentages are available from marketing research firms. In consumer packaged goods, BehaviorScan and Nielsen's Retail Index provide commonly used measures of market share. These services detail the percentage of products sold, by brand, in various categories. A salesperson selling copiers to office suppliers, however, would use data from companies such as Datapro to support claims for market share. Other market research companies collect similar market data for hardware, soft goods (linens, clothing, and so on), furniture, and other products. However, as previously noted, a salesperson in those markets may be less likely to use this type of data.

This part of the Spenco sales brochure provides market research to help salespeople demonstrate Spenco's brand equity.

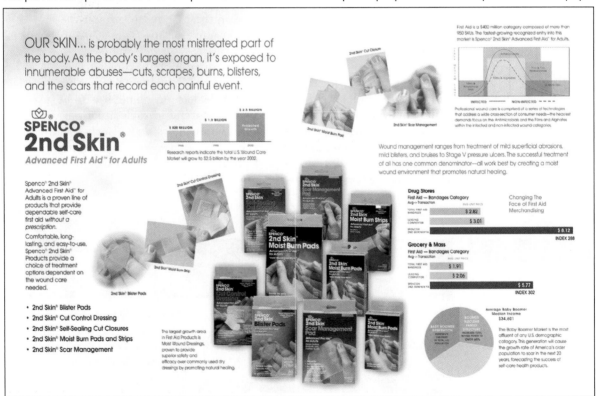

Courtesy of Spenco Medical Co.

Other proof sources of market share include test-market results; third-party sources such as articles in trade magazines; and company data that show sales growth, average volume per retailer, and other information. These sources can indicate that market share is increasing and that the product is selling, especially in the case of a new product. As you can see in the accompanying photo, Spenco also included data to prove growing market demand for its products.

SELLING PROFIT MARGIN

Net profit margin is the third factor that resellers consider. No matter how much a buyer for an industrial distributor likes a product, if he or she thinks it will not sell or cannot be marked up enough to make a profit, the distributor will not carry it.

The ultimate price that resellers pay for products and the subsequent margin they realize is complicated by a complex set of terms and conditions of which price is just one component. Other terms and conditions including discounts, promotional allowances, and credit terms can significantly affect the buyer's actual cost, profit margin, and ROI, as well as the profit made by the seller.

PRICING TERMS

Among the most common expressions used in quoting price are list price, net price, suggested retail price, guaranteed price, and FOB price. **List price** is the quoted or published price in a catalog or price list from which buyers may receive discounts. Because of the vast array of discount given in business-to-business channels, list price is often meaningless. **Net price** is the price buyers pay after all discounts and allowances have been subtracted. These would include quantity and other types of discounts that we will discuss shortly.

Suggested retail price is the price at which the manufacturer suggests the reseller should sell the product. The reseller, however, has no obligation to sell the product at that price. When presenting a product, the manufacturer's salesperson can suggest a retail price and base profit margin calculations on that price. However, to present margins and other sales-based information, the rep needs to use the price at which the reseller plans to sell the product.

Guaranteed prices are important to resellers during times of falling prices. For example, Apple may sell a computer model to Circuit City at $500. If Apple decreases wholesale prices to $400 before Circuit City can sell its inventory, Circuit City suffers an opportunity loss of $100 per computer. To encourage resellers to place larger orders, manufacturers may offer to protect the resellers' inventories with a guaranteed price. In our example, if Apple lowers its prices by $100, Circuit City is refunded the $100 for each computer still in inventory. It would be the salesperson's job to verify the inventory and initiate the refund request.

Other terms and conditions of sale affecting the reseller's cost are shipping charges. When a seller quotes an FOB (free on board—see Chapter 12) origin or factory price, the reseller pays for transportation. On the other hand, an FOB destination price means shipping is included in the price charged by the seller.

TRADE DISCOUNTS

Sometimes prices are stated in terms of discount off the suggested retail price given to different types of channel members. These discounts, referred to as **trade discounts** or **trade promotions**, recognize that wholesalers and retailers perform different activities and need to be given different margins to cover their costs. For example, a manufacturer may offer the wholesaler a trade discount of 35 percent off list price and a retailer only 20 percent off list price. The wholesaler's discount will then be taken off the resulting retailer's cost. Hence if the trade discounts are expressed as 20 and 35, the retailer pays 80 percent of suggested retail and the wholesaler pays 35 percent less. Note that the wholesaler does not pay 45 percent of retail; the wholesaler's discount is taken from the retailer's cost. Exhibit 15.5 illustrates how the trade discount works.

Most companies that use trade discounts classify their customers according to the trade discount allowed. However, in industries like supermarket retailing, the large chains are both retailers and wholesalers. In this situation manufacturers offer quantity discounts rather than trade discounts.

QUANTITY DISCOUNTS

Quantity discounts are based on the amount of merchandise bought. These discounts encourage large purchases by passing along savings resulting from reduced processing costs and should not be confused with trade discounts (which are designed to provide the reseller with profit). Quantity discounts are usually taken off the price after the trade discount is applied. Thus if a trade discount of 20 percent were applied to a retail price of $10, the quantity discount would be applied to the trade price of $8. A quantity discount of 10 percent means the final price to the reseller would be $7.20.

PROMOTIONAL ALLOWANCE

Manufacturers often offer special allowances if resellers agree to promote their products. Black & Decker may offer a special discount to Home Depot if Home Depot agrees to sell Black & Decker Dust Busters at a special price, advertise the special price in the local paper, and let a Black & Decker rep build an end-of-aisle display of Dust Busters. This allowance, usually offered as a discount off the regular price, is separate from any cooperative advertising allowance (which would be based on the cost of advertising, not the amount of product purchased) or any other discount. The supermarket industry refers to promotional allowances as a deal, the promotional discount offered to the retailer. The product is said to be "on deal." This promotional discount may be a quantity discount or may be in addition to regular quantity discounts. In the preceding example Black & Decker may have its products on deal, with an extra quantity discount for the retailer.

Salespeople play a major role in supporting these special promotions. The salesperson usually builds the display, sees that the retailer receives originals of any advertising, and ensures a proper inventory for the sale.

Deals can create problems. Sometimes retailers do not pass the savings on to their customers. Instead, because they can price the product for any amount, they keep the retail price at its regular level and pocket the extra earnings.

EXHIBIT 15.5

Trade Discount Example

Consumer pays retail price $10.00	←	Retailer pays wholesale price $10.00 −2.00 (20% trade discount) $ 8.00 Retailer's cost: $8.00 Retailer's price: $10.00	←	Wholesaler pays manufacturer's price $8.00 −2.80 (35% trade discount) $5.20 Wholesaler's cost: $5.20 Wholesaler's price: $8.00

Trade discounts are based on suggested retail price. Each discount is applied to the net price after previous discounts have been taken, beginning with the retail price and working back in the channel toward the manufacturer.

Resellers may also **forward buy**—buy a larger-than-normal amount to take advantage of the lower price. At first glance this action seems reasonable. But some resellers may purchase an entire year's inventory at the low price. Such a large order is much greater than the manufacturer anticipated for the special promotion period. Buying forward can disrupt the manufacturer's production plans in relation to real demand because the manufacturer expects orders to return to normal levels after the promotion period. But the reseller that bought forward places no more orders that year. Buying forward thus can create serious problems for manufacturers.

Salespeople can avoid the problem of buying forward if they resist the temptation to cut price to get the easy sale. Cumulative discounts can also help reduce buying forward because the buyer's lower price is based on total deliveries over a year. The motivation for buying more now is taken away because the lower price is not contingent on immediate delivery. Partnerships that include ECR can also limit the likelihood of forward buying because cost savings of ECR are lost. Those cost savings are based on low inventories, whereas buying forward raises the reseller's inventory levels.

CREDIT TERMS AND FINANCIAL DISCOUNTS

As discussed in Chapter 12, **cash discounts** are the last discount taken and, like the others, are not added to other discount percentages. The discounts are typically based on when the bill is paid, with higher discounts offered for earlier payments.

Resellers frequently request **deferred dating,** which allows them to pay after the selling season, as an extra form of discount. In the golfing industry, for example, the big selling season is early spring. Golf pro shops ask to be billed at the end of the season, when they have sold enough products to be able to pay the bill. Consignment and buyback are similar. **Consignment** means the retailer makes no payment until after the product is sold, no matter when the sale takes place. A **buyback** is a guarantee to buy back any unsold merchandise. Most salespeople are reluctant to use these terms because there is no financial commitment from the buyer (because the buyer has no financial risk) to ensure that the product sells. Consignment is used most often in the fashion business, and buybacks are used in many settings.

When selling to resellers in other countries, a company may ask customers to provide **letters of credit.** Letters of credit are like checks from a bank except that the company cannot collect cash from a customer's letter of credit unless it is able to prove that the customer did not pay for the merchandise. Letters of credit are the most common method of international payment.

In summary, we have seen the financial criteria on which product and marketing programs are evaluated. The financial needs of the reseller have been quantified to some degree, and you should have a better understanding of the ways to present a product's or program's financial capabilities. Notice too, however, how support needs interact with financial needs. For example, turnover is determined in part by the level of inventory that must be carried. Inventory levels are affected by the level of service, specifically how promptly and reliably the company can deliver. How fast and how much a product sells will also be affected by the job the salesperson does in assisting the dealer or retailer in merchandising the product and by the effectiveness of the marketing program the salesperson helps to create.

SELLING IMAGE

How can a salesperson build the image of her or his company? Salespeople also sell image and prove it with company history. For example, if a salesperson discovers that the buyer prefers carrying the products of innovative companies, the salesperson should remind the buyer of past innovations that the company developed.

CANON GOES INSIDE

Assisted selling is a strategy in which a manufacturer sends its own salespeople to work on the floor of a reseller in order to demonstrate the product, answer questions, and generally help the reseller make sales. When Canon launched its most recent line of BubbleJet printers, the company considered traditional approaches such as advertising to dealers, creating product brochures and other materials to go into dealers' stores, and other such tactics. But Canon felt that a different positioning strategy with its resellers was needed.

Canon decided to reposition itself with resellers as the company that educated consumers to make informed decisions. The first step was to place 100 salespeople in Best Buy stores during both high- and low-volume selling periods. These salespeople worked with consumers to help them make decisions concerning what most consumers feel is a sophisticated, relatively expensive product. Best Buy representatives could also learn from the Canon reps, so the reseller benefited long after the Canon reps were gone.

The test required significant planning. Key to the program's success was ensuring that sufficient inventory was on hand, and also preparing store management for the "invasion" of Canon salespeople. Appropriate brochures and other materials also had to be developed. The planning paid off, however: The test went so well that Canon expanded the program to other significant resellers.

Source: Kimberly Pollard, "Canon Goes Inside to Increase Sales," *Sales & Marketing Strategies and News*, September 2001, p. 42.

Then, when presented with the current innovation, the buyer sees this new product as part of an overall history of innovation. Selling Scenario 15.1 illustrates how Canon created an image as the consumer educator for sophisticated, expensive printers.

If possible, salespeople should carry copies of business or trade periodical articles about their company. Salespeople should also maintain a file of letters from satisfied customers. When a customer thanks a salesperson for service, the salesperson should ask for a letter. The letter will allow the salesperson not only to document the level of service with other accounts but also to prove his or her service skills to management if the need arises.

One word of caution: Many sellers get too wrapped up in discussing how wonderful their company is; they fail to make a connection to the buyer's needs, such as a concern about being treated fairly. Emphasizing one's company's reputation is most effective when buyers can relate that reputation to their needs.

TURNAROUND

Turnaround, an important aspect of image, is how quickly the seller delivers a product or service after the customer orders it. The term also describes how quickly a seller responds to a customer. Elsewhere in this book, you have read about the top salespeople as rated by their customers. Frequently these customers considered turnaround under difficult situations as one important criterion for performance.

Turnaround is often a function of salespeople's ability to plan and their relationships with others in the company. As we will discuss in Chapter 17, salespeople need to develop strong relationships with colleagues in their company's order entry, billing, credit, and shipping departments to provide the desired level of service to customers. At the same time, however, salespeople must plan their activities and sales calls to provide plenty of lead time. If normal delivery is two weeks, for example, a salesperson would not want to wait to tell retailers about a promotion until two days before it starts. Retailers will want to know at least two weeks in advance so they can receive sufficient inventories of the promoted product, build their displays, and so forth.

We have discussed throughout this text how salespeople build long-term partnerships and how important customer service and follow-up are in maintaining those partnerships. Turnaround can also apply to how quickly salespeople return phone calls and how promptly they handle credit requests and other problems. When customers know they can depend on the rep to turn their requests around on a timely basis, they will turn to that rep with more orders.

MERCHANDISE MARKETS, TRADE SHOWS, AND TRADE FAIRS

Another method of selling to resellers is to use trade shows (see Chapter 7 for a discussion of using trade shows for prospecting), trade fairs, and merchandise markets. In some cases a manufacturer lives or dies by how well it does in these special selling situations. Keith Clark, a company that manufactures office products such as calendars, depends heavily on the annual national office products association show. Its salespeople report that selling year-round is easier due to the impression the company makes on prospects at the show.

MERCHANDISE MARKETS

Merchandise markets are places where suppliers have sales offices and buyers from resellers visit to purchase merchandise. The Dallas Market Center, for example, hosts separate markets for children's wear, western apparel, linens, and other soft goods. The sellers are the manufacturers or distributors, and they sell only to resellers, not to the public. Sellers may lease showroom space permanently or only during market weeks. Sellers who lease space permanently usually bring in buyers during off-market periods or when no markets are being held.

Buyers visit many vendors during markets, selecting the products they will carry for the next season. In some industries, almost all sales to resellers occur during markets. These industries include hardware, clothing, toys, and furniture. The major furniture markets are held in San Francisco, Toronto, and High Point, North Carolina. The biggest toy show is held annually in New York City. Major clothing markets are held for each season (such as fall and spring) in New York City, Atlanta, Paris, Dallas, and Los Angeles.

TRADE SHOWS

Trade shows are short (usually less than a week), temporary exhibitions of products by manufacturers and resellers. Once the show is over, all vendors pack up and leave. Specialty Advertising Association International (SAAI), for example, holds its annual trade show in Dallas each year. Vendors at this show are all manufacturers looking for dealers for their products; the end users of the products are not admitted. Dealers make an entire year's worth of purchases at the SAAI show, so the show is a make-or-break situation for many manufacturers.

Comdex, the largest computer trade show in the world, is usually held in Las Vegas. Comdex differs from SAAI's show in that it has a dual audience: Vendors exhibit to end users (industrial consumers) as well as to resellers. Another show with a dual audience is Networld, a show for computer networking products. A recent survey of Networld exhibitors found that 40 percent of the vendors were promoting to dealers only, 40 percent were promoting to end users only, and 20 percent were looking for both dealers and end users. Successful trade shows reach qualified buyers who might not otherwise be reached, as illustrated in Exhibit 15.6.

Even firms that do not use resellers may have salespeople involved in trade shows. At many trade shows all attendees are customers. For example, the National Association of Legal Secretaries is a professional organization that promotes the welfare of legal secretaries. When it holds its annual convention, it also invites manufacturers of office equipment and other products to exhibit wares.

EXHIBIT 15.6   Usefulness of Trade Shows

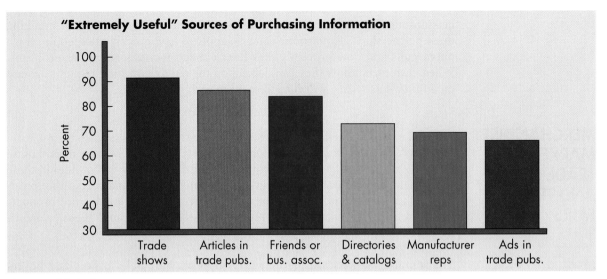

"Extremely Useful" Sources of Purchasing Information

The Power of Trade Shows
A Simmons MRB Study © Center for Exhibition Industry Research

The trade show is an adjunct of the convention, with the audience composed entirely of end users.

UMAX Technologies, a maker of computer scanners, exhibits at Comdex every year. UMAX looks for potential retailers and commercial accounts at the show. At Comdex the company hoped for 2,000 leads. It got 7,500 leads, balanced equally between resellers and users.[10]

 In Europe trade shows are called **trade fairs.** In Hanover, Germany, Europe's largest convention hall hosts many shows, including the Hanover fair, the European version of Comdex. This show attracts more than half a million visitors from around the world and displays the products of 4,500 manufacturers from more than 45 countries. Shows such as the Hanover fair can be extremely important for companies such as Microsoft and Novell when they are looking for local dealers and distributors in other countries.

Trade shows and markets, then, are two activities in which salespeople may engage, whether selling to resellers or to consumers. These shows provide excellent opportunities to locate prospects. Whereas the average number of calls needed to close a sale is 3.6 without trade shows, the average number of additional calls needed after exposure at a trade show is only 1.4. Thus closing a sale costs $997 without a trade show and only $550 with a trade show, on average.[11] A company that employs an effective system to track visitors to its booth and uses that system to encourage prompt follow-up by salespeople can maximize the sales opportunities that trade shows and markets offer.

SUPPORTING THE SALES EFFORTS OF RESELLERS

Some approaches that manufacturers use to support the sales effort of resellers are promotions to end users to build reseller sales, motivational programs directed toward reseller salespeople, and training efforts to increase the effectiveness of reseller salespeople.

Trade shows are an economical way for manufacturers to contact small business- to-business resellers.

© Einzig Photography

PROMOTIONS TO BUILD DEMAND

Some promotional programs that manufacturers use to build demand for their products are national advertising campaigns, contests and sweepstakes for end users, and special promotions, such as sponsoring a NASCAR racing team.

The importance of salespeople to a successful promotional campaign is illustrated by their actions when a manufacturer offers a coupon in a **freestanding insert (FSI)** (when you shake your Sunday paper, all those coupon ads that fall out are FSIs). Creative salespeople will tell retailers that FSIs are coming up to secure a special display and plan inventory. Then the retailer can maximize the sales of that product with the coupon without affecting the store's profit margin.

Manufacturers may have a co-op advertising program as part of their pull strategy. With **co-op advertising** (short for cooperative advertising), the manufacturer will pay some of the reseller's advertising costs. The manufacturer may provide the advertisement original, and the reseller will simply insert its name and address into the ad. Alternatively, the reseller may combine several co-op ads into one large ad. The reseller may be reimbursed for a percentage of the advertising costs or may be offered a discount off the price of the product.

Manufacturers in many businesses offer co-op advertising, but the consumer packaged goods industry is the heaviest user. Other users include the fashion industry, some hardware manufacturers, such as Stanley and Black & Decker, and home appliance manufacturers.

Manufacturers may also combine co-op advertising with a national promotional campaign. When you see a manufacturer's ad that says "at participating dealers," you are seeing a national promotional campaign that depends on the salespeople securing the participation of resellers. Those salespeople may also help participating dealers properly display the promoted products and use their in-store advertising to support the promotion. Free point-of-purchase displays may be a part of these trade promotions.

The Spenco promotion calendar helps resellers plan their orders for Spenco products and meet the additional demand created by company promotions.

2nd Skin® Advertising/Promotion Plan - 2002
Advertising and Promotion Plan for Calendar Year 2002

ADVERTISING BUDGET

Month/Year: 2002

Total Advertising Budget:

Percent of Sales: 19.9%

Dollar Amount $2,150,000

Medium	Specific Outlet (Name of Specific Newspaper or Magazine, etc.)	Frequency of Ads	Total Cost	% of Total Budget
Direct Mail	Pharm-Alert	Once	$ 45,000	2.1%
	American Podiatric Association	2X	$ 25,000	1.2%
Magazine	Modern Maturity	1X	$ 265,000	12.3%
	Prevention	3X	$ 237,000	11.0%
	Podiatry Managment	9x	$ 95,000	4.4%
Radio	ABC Radio/Syndicated Networks (Paul Harvey & Sean Hannity)	600 GRP	$1,198,000	55.7%
Internet	Banner Ads		$ 30,000	1.4%
Direct Response	Infomercial	TBA	$ 255,000	11.9%

Courtesy of Spenco Medical Co.

For example, Kiwi, a manufacturer of footwear accessories such as shoe polish and athletic-shoe cleaner, aids retailers in many ways, but the specific assistance given for a particular store depends on the store's needs. Merchandising materials that help display the product in the store are supported by ads in sports magazines, and if the retailer also needs local advertising help, Kiwi can provide it.[12]

Manufacturers use two major types of promotion strategies, often in tandem. The *pull strategy* is designed to stimulate demand among consumers for the manufacturer's product. The *push strategy* is used to stimulate sales efforts by the manufacturer's salespeople and/or the sales efforts by resellers.

MOTIVATING RESELLER SALESPEOPLE

Some approaches that manufacturers use to motivate reseller salespeople are contests and extra incentives for the reseller's salespeople, special display incentives, and special pricing incentives.

CONTESTS

Manufacturers frequently run **contests** for their resellers. Top dealers can win exotic trips or the opportunity to pick out merchandise from a catalog, paying with "dollars" earned through top sales performance. Other contests are directed toward the reseller's salespeople. While a student at Baylor University, Robert Wagner worked part-time for a local retailer selling computers and stereos. During the Christmas season, he sold enough IBM computers to place among IBM's top 10 retailer salespeople, earning him an all-expenses-paid trip to the Super Bowl. These types of trade promotions are used when the retailer requires a personal selling effort.

PUSH MONEY

Spiffs (sales promotion incentive funds), or **push money (PM),** are similar to offering resellers' salespeople a commission to sell the manufacturer's product. PM is paid directly to the retailer's salespeople by the manufacturer for selling the manufacturer's product. But the reseller's salespeople can earn PM only for a short period and for a specific product, unlike a regular commission. Spiffs work well only when the promotion requires a personal selling effort by the retailer's salespeople.

Some retailers discourage this practice because they do not want to push products on buyers and because the products may not be the best solutions for their customers. Other retailers frown on PM because they believe it diverts their sales staff's attention to products that may be less profitable to the store than other products. Salespeople, however, may appreciate the opportunity to earn extra money.

Thinking It Through	How would you feel if you knew the stereo salesperson you were buying from could receive a spiff for selling you a particular product? Would you feel any differently if you knew that the salesperson was paid straight commission, no matter which product was sold?

TRAINING RESELLERS

Training the reseller is necessary to enable a reseller's sales force to sell the product. The manufacturer's salespeople may be responsible for training the reseller's salespeople in how a product operates and how it should be sold.

For example, as mentioned earlier in this chapter, Kiwi has adopted a strategy of trade promotions involving advertising and merchandising. Its main competitor, SecondWind, uses an entirely different strategy, based primarily on training the trade. Part of the training is delivered through two free videos, one that trains the retailer on how to merchandise SecondWind products and one that focuses entirely on selling SecondWind shoe accessories at the time of a shoe sale (this approach is like asking whether you want fries with your hamburger). The company is planning another video, one that teaches retail salespeople how to sell any specific product in its line of shoe cleaners, deodorizers, laces, insoles, cleats, and replacement spikes.[13] In some situations the retail salesperson needs to learn general selling skills first (the purpose of SecondWind's first sales training video). Some companies have product specialists to assist salespeople with the training task, but the responsibility lies solely with the salesperson in many cases. Without such training, the reseller's salespeople will not have the knowledge or confidence to successfully sell the product, and the resellers do not have the expertise to conduct the training themselves.

Training resellers is more important in situations requiring personal selling by the reseller. For example, office supply stores often sell office equipment and furniture. These products require active prospecting and selling skills that focus on needs satisfaction. The stores' salespeople need training so that they can sell the office equipment and furniture appropriate to the buyer's needs. If customers require service, training may also be necessary. Sales clerks need to know the service procedures of the manufacturer so that the customer receives good service. Clerks may also be asked how something works or what is needed to solve a customer's problem (which is the purpose of the second sales training video from SecondWind). These situations may not require active selling, but a knowledgeable sales clerk can mean the difference between a satisfied customer and an irate ex-customer.

PARTNERING WITH RESELLERS

Throughout this book, we have emphasized developing strategic partnerships with buyers whenever possible. Just as in all other selling arenas, selling to resellers has been revolutionized by the concept of partnerships. And, as you have seen in this chapter, partnering is important to strategies such as efficient customer response (ECR) and quick response (QR) systems. In this section we take a closer look at another strategy related to partnering: category management.

CATEGORY MANAGEMENT

Category management is a process by which retailers and manufacturers jointly plan and implement marketing programs to improve the performance of an entire product category (including competitive products) for mutual benefit.[14] Category management strives to maximize profits for the entire category (for the retailer) by selecting the best assortment of merchandise and efficiently using pricing, promotion, point-of-purchase merchandising, and other techniques.

Some retailers turn to their best supplier in a category to help them manage the category. Known as **category captains,** these suppliers work as partners with the reseller to gain insight into customer needs and to develop a program for increasing category profits. A selling team from the supplier works with a team from the reseller to implement the category management program. The selling team, typically managed by the account representative, might include specialists in finance, production, marketing, and logistics.

The most important tool for effective category management is information. The supplier has information that was previously unavailable to the reseller through any other source. The reseller knew everything that went on in that store and therefore knew the impact of displays and special prices, but did not know the segmentation structure of the category's market; consumption trends; new product trends; and key influences on the category by region, market, or other division. Such information can be crucial to the success of a promotion strategy.

Category management has opened the communication channels. Sharing such information in the form of fact-based presentations that educate buyers enables salespeople and buyers to create joint marketing and promotion programs. These joint programs are more effective than the old method in which each party created an independent marketing program. But not just marketing programs are affected. Logistics, finance, and other phases of both companies' operations are affected by category management and partnership programs such as ECR.

One benefit of category management for the seller is that it can reduce forward buying for that salesperson's brand, but there is pressure to lower the usual price. With open communication an average price can be agreed on that is more than a deal price but less than the regular price. The manufacturer will still save money (because regular ordering allows for more efficient manufacturing) and can actually increase profits.

For example, a dried-fruit company examined market data (from IRI, a marketing research company) for Dallas and realized that one chain of stores accounted for 8.3 percent of all edible food sales but only 6.3 percent for dried fruits.[15] Closer examination revealed that raisins, the major component of the dried-fruit category, were selling at a rate half that of most other chains in the market. Further analysis indicated that raisin sales were actually decreasing at that chain, although increasing for the total market. What was the chain doing wrong?

By examining data from the retailer and comparing the information with its own data, the company learned that 34.4 percent of all Dallas raisin sales are produced through promotions, but that amount fell to 15.3 percent at that particular chain. Additional data showed that the chain promoted raisins fewer times and less heavily than did other stores in the market. A joint review between the company and the chain resulted in a promotion program to improve raisin sales. One event in the program was a baking promotion that did not involve a specific raisin company's brand, but was designed to simply increase raisin sales.

Category management began as a grocery store–consumer packaged goods strategy. This particular form of partnering, though, is spreading to other types of resellers such as discounters like Wal-Mart and sporting goods retailers.

Summary

Many students can easily picture how to sell a product to someone who will use it, but they have more difficulty understanding how to sell to resellers. Those who buy to resell, including wholesalers, distributors, and retailers, are called the trade. Resellers buy what sells, buy marketing support, and buy profits.

Industrial reseller salespeople speak of their battle as one for mind share. Each salesperson wants his or her product, rather than a competitor's, to be recommended whenever possible by the distributor's sales staff. Because the distributor's sales staff is key to selling the product to the user, mind share is more important than shelf space.

In evaluating products and vendors, resellers use the strategic profit model (SPM). This model evaluates a product or a store by examining net sales, net profit margin, and inventory turnover. When introducing a product or a program, salespeople can use selling history, market share, and similar products' results to prove how well a product can sell. Financial aspects such as the terms and conditions of the sale are also important.

Buyers also evaluate the product's image and the vendor's reputation. Reputation is often proven by taking care of the little things (as discussed in previous chapters).

Trade promotions are offered to resellers in an effort to stimulate sales. Pull strategies include advertising directly to the consumer, sponsoring contests, offering coupons, and the like. Push strategies include using push money, sponsoring contests for the retailer's salespeople, and building displays.

Merchandise markets, trade shows, and trade fairs can play a major role in a firm's sales efforts. In some industries most sales are gained at a market. Trade shows and trade fairs are important when selling to certain types of industrial users, as well as to resellers and end users.

Training the trade, an important dimension of service in many industries, may be needed to enable resellers' salespeople to sell the product well. The manufacturer's sales rep often performs this task.

Selling to resellers involves emphasizing different benefits such as gross margin and inventory turnover, but many of the same principles still apply. Many people find personal fulfillment in the challenges and rewards of selling to the trade.

KEY TERMS

automatic replenishment (AR)   446
breaking bulk   438
buyback   453
cash discounts   453
category captain   460
category management   460
consignment   453
contests   459
co-op advertising   457
deferred dating   453
efficient customer response (ECR)   446
electronic data interchange (EDI)   447
forward buy   453
freestanding insert (FSI)   457
gross profit margin   442
guaranteed price   451
inventory turnover   443
just in time inventory (JIT)   446
letters of credit   453
list price   451
markdown   442

market share   450
markup   442
merchandise markets   455
mind share   440
net price   451
net profit margin   442
net sales   442
push money (PM)   459
quick response (QR)   446
resellers   436
selling history   449
spiffs   459
stock keeping unit (SKU)   438
strategic profit model (SPM)   440
suggested retail price   451
trade discounts   451
trade fairs   456
trade promotions   451
trade shows   455
turnaround   454

Questions and Problems

1. Is encouraging buyers to order a large quantity so they can get a better quantity discount always a good idea? Why or why not?

2. Some students fail to see how anyone could get excited about selling frozen food products to resellers. But some people enjoy selling to supermarket chains. What differences in the attitudes of the two groups might account for their different perspectives?

3. The list price for a child's outfit is $20. Your company offers trade discounts of 40 percent and 30 percent to retailers and wholesalers, respectively. If outfits are ordered in quantities greater than five dozen, wholesalers receive an extra 3 percent discount. A wholesaler places an order for 10 dozen. What does the wholesaler pay? If terms are 2/10, n/30 and the wholesaler pays in five days, what price does the wholesaler pay?

4. Assume you sell laser printers. How would your presentation differ when selling to a business supply store like Office Depot versus selling to an industrial distributor?

5. The most common complaint of resellers is a lack of support by vendors. Give your opinion as to why this is true.

6. Most insecticides are sold in spring and early summer. If you were an Ortho rep selling pesticides to retailers, what effect would seasonality have on your activities? What effect would an upcoming national ad campaign by Ortho have on your activities?

7. What role do trade shows play in the overall marketing process? How does the role differ if one is selling through resellers rather than selling directly to users?

8. Discuss store loyalty versus brand loyalty. How would each affect the sales efforts of a manufacturer's salesperson? Would these concepts have any effect on a category management program?

9. How does category management differ from other forms of partnering? What impact do the buyer's customers have on any partnering relationship? How is technology used to manage categories and build partnerships?

Case Problems

CASE 15.1
Twin Peaks of the Baking Business

For Borden's baking goods division, the year is compressed between Thanksgiving and Christmas. These twin peaks comprise almost the entire year's worth of sales for Eagle Brand condensed milk, NoneSuch mincemeat, and other baking products, as well as dairy products such as Borden eggnog. But Americans are baking less, meaning that to boost sales Borden had to gain at the expense of competitors.

Borden realized, though, that when a consumer needs one baking ingredient, she or he probably needs all ingredients. With that concept Borden created a virtual company, a company called Premiere Partnership, that joined together the baking goods lines of Keebler Ready pie crust, Diamond walnuts, Sun Maid raisins, and Sunsweet dates—all brands owned by Borden. With each manufacturer paying about $500,000 for advertising, each gets the power of a $2 million ad campaign. The campaign includes a cosponsored freestanding insert (FSI) ad; an account-specific, in-store-distributed, 16-page recipe book; and temporary price reductions to drive sales at retail.

As a sales representative for Borden, you are planning tomorrow's activities. You want to call on the following stores:

Tusa Grocery. This small, family-owned grocery store is in a poor part of town. Tusa currently has only the 4-foot display, with no separate baking products area.

Big Savings Grocery. You will call on the grocery-item buyer for Big Savings, a four-store chain of midsize grocery stores. These stores have a display near the baking section available.

Brookshires. Brookshires, a regional discount chain, has 32 stores in a four-state area. Borden is an approved vendor. You are calling on the only store in your territory that carries no Borden products. The manager has told you he doesn't want Borden because he already carries Oak Farms (a competitor) and doesn't want the hassle of two vendors. You have collected data to show that Borden outsells Oak Farms in the other stores by an average of 10 percent.

Mac's Grocery. Mac's carries only Oak Farms in its 12 grocery stores. You called Mac's headquarters by phone because it isn't in your territory and found that all buying is done by local managers. They do not use an approved vendor list. When you visited this store last month, the manager did not have time to talk. She had no idea why they don't carry Borden but did say you could come back when she had more time. You set up an appointment for tomorrow.

QUESTIONS

1. Keeping in mind why resellers buy, what strategies will you use to introduce Premiere Partnership to these stores?
2. How will you maximize the shelf space for Borden in each store?
3. Assume the Tusa buyer is an analytical, the Big Savings buyer is an amiable, the Brookshires buyer is an expressive, and the Mac's buyer is a driver. How would you prove/dramatize the benefits for each buyer?
4. What disadvantages would you face if you tried a category management program with each of these stores? How would you go about presenting a category management program?
5. One problem with promotional discounts is that some resellers do not pass them on to their customers but pocket the extra profit. Another problem with promotions in general occurs when some resellers do not participate. Why would resellers not participate fully in a manufacturer's promotional programs? What effect would this behavior have on Borden's image? On the images of its partners? On the image of a nonparticipating grocery store?

CASE 15.2

Audio Warehouse

Bright and early on a Monday morning, Jill Cates found herself in the upstairs room at Cupp's, a local breakfast establishment. Cates is a salesperson for Audio Warehouse, a retail store that sells video and audio electronics. Recently, she closed a big sale with the psychology department of a local school with the help of Mario, her store manager. They sold more than $100,000 of Sony video equipment to the school.

This morning all the Audio Warehouse salespeople were at Cupp's, along with Mario and a rep from Sharp (a Sony competitor), for a rare Monday morning sales meeting. Breakfast was on Sharp, and Cates found herself enjoying the eggs and bacon that she never seemed to have time to make for herself.

Near the end of the meal, the Sharp rep stood up at the head of the table. "Thank you all for coming here so early in the morning," she began, and was interrupted by a chorus of "thank you for the breakfast" from the salespeople. "Oh, you are all very welcome. The reason I asked Mario to bring you all together is that Audio Warehouse has long been a strong retailer for me and for Sharp products, and I wanted to thank you for all of your hard work. In addition, I wanted to tell you of an exciting sales incentive campaign that we have for the next month."

She walked to an easel that had a large flipchart. As she pulled over the blank first page to reveal Sharp's slogan, "From Sharp minds come Sharp products," she said, "As you know, Sharp has kept new products coming that have really helped you make a lot of money." She flipped the page and pointed to several enlarged product photographs. "Here are several new products that will be arriving in your store around Thanksgiving, just in time for the Christmas season." She described each one, and each description was followed by applause.

"But as you know, we'll need room on the shelves for these new products. That's why my company has authorized the first direct incentive program ever for you, the Audio Warehouse salespeople." She flipped the page to uncover a large dollar sign. "For each of the products on the list that Mario is passing out that you sell, Sharp will pay you an extra $25 spiff." The salespeople broke out into wild clapping and a few cheers. "And every rep who earns $100 in spiffs will also earn 100 points that can be used to purchase merchandise in the prize catalog that Mario is passing out." She was interrupted again by cheers.

Flipping the page to a picture of a sunny tropical beach, she continued, "The top rep in my district as of December 1 wins—are you ready for this?—a trip to the Bahamas!" The reps went wild.

The rest of the meeting involved strategies to switch customers from other products to Sharp, how to present features and benefits of various Sharp products, and all of the details of the contest.

Three days later, Cates was in the store demonstrating two stereos, a Sharp and a Moyashita. Mario had priced the Sharp so that it was now only a few dollars more than the Moyashita to help the salespeople move the Sharp.

"Gee, Jill, I really like the looks of the Moyashita," said the customer. The Moyashita did have a more futuristic look than the Sharp's more traditional lines.

"That's true, Bill, but looks aren't everything. If I were you, I'd have the Sharp for the sound it produces."

"I just don't hear the difference."

"Well, it is your decision, Bill. So you want to take the Moyashita?" Cates asked. Bill nodded yes. Even with the sale, Cates was slightly disappointed. She was having some difficulty pushing those Sharps compared to some of the other salespeople.

A couple of weeks later, the Sony rep called Cates at home. After some small talk and questions about the new video center in the psychology department, he asked Cates why Sony's sales were down at Audio Warehouse.

"Have you talked to Mario about that?" Cates asked.

"Yes, but I don't get a straight answer. I get the feeling he's hiding something."

"Well, we're having a contest on some other products," admitted Cates.

"Hmm. I wonder what it would take to make Sony a player. Well, thanks, Jill. And sell a few Sonys, OK?"

"Sure thing," replied Cates. After she hung up, she thought about the contest. She got out the catalog and leafed through it, thinking about what she wanted to win.

QUESTIONS

1. Did Cates do anything unethical in the above scenario?
2. Strategically, why is Sharp using the promotion program? What other reasons would cause it to use a push program?
3. Why would Mario agree to the promotion? How would it affect his relationships with other vendors?
4. Based on the success with the psychology department, the Sony rep believed he was building a partnership with Mario and Audio Warehouse. Now he's not so sure. What should he do?

Additional References

Alvarado, Ursula Y., and Herbert Kotzab. "Supply Chain Management: The Integration of Logistics in Marketing." *Industrial Marketing Management* 30 (2001), pp. 183–98.

Blattberg, Robert C., and Edward J. Fox. *Category Management*. Washington, DC: Food Marketing Institute and the Center for Retail Management, Northwestern University, 1995.

Borders, Aberdeen Leila; Wesley J. Johnston; and Edward E. Rigdon. "Beyond the Dyad: Electronic Commerce and Network Perspectives in Industrial Marketing Management." *Industrial Marketing Management* 30 (2001), pp. 199–206.

Cohen, Andy. "6 Ways to Make Your Dealers Love You." *Sales & Marketing Management,* April 1998, pp. 53–55.

Evans, Joel R., and Barry Berman. "Conceptualizing and Operationalizing the Business-to-Business Value Chain." *Industrial Marketing Managhement* 30 (2001), pp. 135–48.

Fitzgerald, Kevin. "Purchasing Pros: Service Comes First." *Industrial Distribution,* February 1999, pp. D1–2.

Gaski, John F., and Nina M. Ray. "Measurement and Modeling of Alienation in the Distribution Channel: Implications for Supplier–Reseller Relations." *Industrial Marketing Management* 30 (2001), pp. 207–26.

Goodman, Lester E., and Paul A. Dion. "The Determinants of Commitment in the Distributor/Manufacturer Relationship." *Industrial Marketing Management* 30 (2001), pp. 287–300.

Koloszyc, Ginger. "Transforming the Store." *Stores,* May 1, 1999, pp. 22–26.

Lamons, Bob. "Involve Your Staff in Trade Shows for Better Results." *Marketing News,* March 1, 1999, pp. 9–11.

Lee, Don Y. "Power, Conflict, and Satisfaction in IJV Supplier–Chinese Distributor Channels." *Journal of Business Research* 52 (2001), pp. 149–60.

Levy, Michael, and Barton Weitz. *Retailing Management.* 4th ed. Burr Ridge, IL: Irwin/McGraw-Hill, 2001.

Marks, Steven. *EDI Purchasing: The Electronic Gateway to the Future.* New York: PT Publications, 1997.

McQuiston, Daniel. "A Conceptual Model for Building and Maintaining Relationships between Manufacturers' Representatives and Their Principals." *Industrial Marketing Management* 30 (2001), pp. 165–81.

Mirani, Robert; Deanne Moore; and Johna A. Weber. "Emerging Technologies for Enhancing Supplier–Reseller Partnerships." *Industrial Marketing Management* 30 (2001), pp. 101–14.

Mitchell, Tom. "Cisco Resellers Add Value." *Industrial Marketing Management* 30 (2001), pp. 115–18.

Simpson, Penny; Judy A. Siguaw; and Thomas L. Baker. "A Model of Value Creation: Supplier Behaviors and Their Impact on Reseller-Perceived Value." *Industrial Marketing Management* 30 (2001), pp. 119–34.

Skarmeas, Dionisis, and Constantine S. Katskikeas. "Drivers of Superior Importer Performance in Cross-Cultural Supplier–Reseller Relationships." *Industrial Marketing Management* 30 (2001), pp. 227–42.

Strutton, David; Neil Herndon; and Lou E. Pelton. "Competition, Collusion, and Confusion: The Impact of Current Antitrust Guidelines on Competition." *Industrial Marketing Management* 30 (2001), pp. 243–54.

Tepper, Bette. *Mathematics for Retail Buying.* 5th ed. New York: Fairchild Publications, 2000.

Tuten, Tracy, and David J. Urban. "An Expanded Model of Business-to-Business Partnership Formation and Success." *Industrial Marketing Management* 30 (2001), pp. 149–64.

Valero, Greg. "Reengineering the Distributor Salesforce." *U.S. Distribution Journal,* July–August 1997, pp. 24–28.

Weber, John A. "Partnering with Resellers in Business Markets." *Industrial Marketing Management* 30 (2001), pp. 87–100.

PART **5** The Salesperson
as Manager

This section discusses a little known but very important element of the profession of selling. Salespeople, by the very nature of their jobs, are managers, too. As you can see by the circle diagram, salespeople must manage their territory and their time, manage the resources within their companies, and manage their careers. In Chapter 16 we discuss techniques salespeople use to manage their time and other resources effectively. Chapter 17 presents many of the company resources that salespeople manage and discusses methods of building internal partnerships to deliver superior customer satisfaction. In Chapter 18 you will learn valuable lessons for managing your career, beginning with how to get your career started. Even if you choose a career or an initial job outside of sales, you will find the information in this section useful for improving your effectiveness.

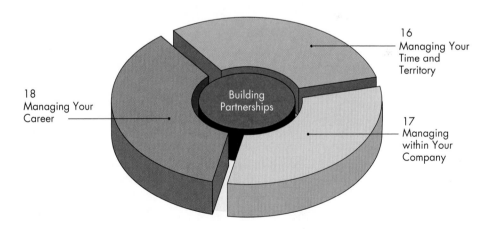

16
Managing Your
Time and
Territory

18
Managing Your
Career

Building
Partnerships

17
Managing
within Your
Company

16 Managing Your Time and Territory

SOME QUESTIONS ANSWERED IN THIS CHAPTER ARE:

- Why is time so valuable for salespeople?
- What can you do to "create" more selling time?
- What should you consider when devising a territory strategy?
- How does territory strategy relate to account strategy and building partnerships?
- How should you analyze your daily activities and sales calls?
- How can you evaluate your own performance so that you can improve?

Many salespeople work in the field, their only contact with the office by e-mail, telephone, or fax. Because no one tells them when to start working or when to quit for the day, they must be self-sufficient. Their success or failure depends on their own efforts to manage their time and their territory.

Salespeople have more individual freedom than almost any other type of employee. With that freedom comes the responsibility to manage themselves. Self-management involves using their scarcest resource, time, to make the most of their other resources: their customers and their skills.

"As our business grows, it is more important for me to remain focused on activities that increase business."

Justin Warner, Edward Jones

PROFILE

August in Phoenix—sounds like the title of a horror film. Unfortunately, that was the time and place I began my sales career. I had just graduated from college, moved my family to a new state, delivered our second child, and begun selling investments all about the same time. The goal: Build a new and profitable office for Edward Jones in a booming retirement community.

My early mornings began by my mapping out the streets in which I would knock on doors to introduce myself and ask the people to buy an investment. The goal was simple (or so I thought): 25 good presentations every day. Doors slammed in my face; people said no, some laughed, while others pitied me with a glass of water. My fears of failure, my young age, their wealth, and my obvious investment inadequacies only compounded the frustrations. After meeting several hundred people and getting virtually nowhere, I set out to visit them again. By using the contact logs, which I used to jot notes on the first visit, I planned and executed a return visit to all of my contacts. This I did two, three, four, and five times.

After several weeks of hard knocks, I began to notice something wrong in my presentations. I was leaving *me* out of the sale. Every broker in the world could get them the same product, so I had to be the difference. I set goals to find out more personal information about my prospects and also let them get to know me. I had five minutes, and trust had to be cultivated. Remarkably, I began building relationships!

Now, two and a half years later, business has changed from no accounts or assets to over 350 accounts and $25,000,000 in assets. I now have a full- and part-time associate and an office location. Managing the office has now become my biggest challenge. What tasks require my attention? Which might be handled by someone else?

A crucial factor to our business is that my associates and I are all working together. We set and review goals together. We establish, plan, and modify our action plans together. We each have specific duties, which allow us to stay focused on the tasks at hand. My full-time associate handles all the administrative work, while my part-time associate handles our marketing campaigns, seminars, and classes. I do the selling. We use a contact management computer program to coordinate activities between the three of us, as well as manage our proactive and reactive calls to clients and prospects.

I'm finding as our business grows it is more important for me to remain focused on those activities that will increase the business. I have contests with myself and other brokers to reward positive work—from ice cream cones to major vacations. Achievement merits a reward. Lastly, staying focused does not mean being isolated. In our business, our families come first. It is very easy to become so involved in your work that those who matter most become secondary. With this perspective and our desire to achieve, we expect continued success.

Visit Our Website @ www.EdwardJones.com.

THE VALUE OF TIME

The old axiom "Time is money" certainly applies to selling. If you work eight hours a day for 240 days out of a year, you will work 1,920 hours that year. If you earn $30,000, each of those hours will be worth $15.63. An hour of time would be worth $20.84 if your earnings climb to $40,000. Looking at your time another way, you would have to sell $208 worth of product per hour to earn $40,000 if you earned a 10 percent commission!

The typical salesperson spends only 920 hours a year in front of customers. The other 1,000 hours are spent waiting, traveling, doing paperwork, or attending sales meetings. Thus, as a typical salesperson, you really have to be twice as good, selling $434 worth of products every hour to earn that $40,000 commission.

The lesson from this analysis is clear: Salespeople must make every hour count to be successful. Time is a resource that cannot be replaced if wasted. But time is just one resource, albeit a critical resource, at the salesperson's disposal.

Managing time and territory is often a question of how to allocate resources. Allocating resources such as time is a difficult management process, but when done well, it often spells the difference between stellar and average performance. Many times it is difficult to know what is really important and what only seems important. In this chapter we discuss how to manage your time. Building on what you have learned about the many activities of salespeople, we also provide strategies for allocating resources among accounts—that is, managing your territory.

THE SELF-MANAGEMENT PROCESS

The self-management process in selling has four stages. The first stage is setting goals, or determining what is to be accomplished. The second stage is allocating resources and determining strategies to meet those goals. In the third stage the salesperson implements the time management strategies by making sales calls, sending direct mail pieces, or executing whatever action the strategy calls for. In the fourth and final stage, the salesperson evaluates performance to determine whether the goals will be reached and the strategies are effective or whether the goals cannot be reached and the strategies must change. This process is illustrated in Exhibit 16.1 and will serve as an outline for this chapter.

EXHIBIT 16.1

The Self-Management Process

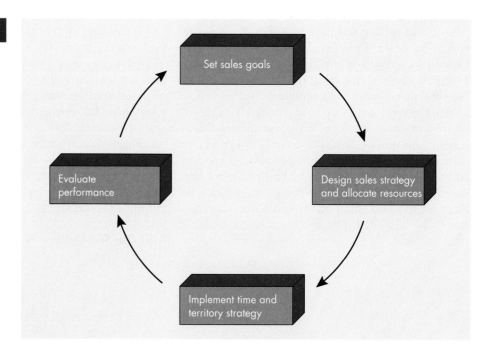

SETTING GOALS

THE NEED FOR GOALS

The first step in managing any worthwhile endeavor is to consider what makes it worthwhile and what you want to accomplish. Salespeople need to examine their careers in the same way. Career goals and objectives should reflect personal ambitions and desires so that the individual can create the desired lifestyle, as illustrated in Exhibit 16.2.[1] When career goals reflect personal ambitions, the salesperson is more committed to achieving those goals.

To achieve career objectives, salespeople must set sales goals. These sales goals provide some of the means for reaching personal objectives. Sales goals also guide the salesperson's decisions as to which activities to perform, when to perform those activities, whom to see, and how to sell.

The salesperson who lacks goals will drift around the territory, wasting time and energy. Sales calls will be unrelated to objectives and may be minimally productive or even harmful to the sales process. The result will be poor performance and, eventually, the need to find another job.

In Chapter 8 you learned that salespeople should set primary, secondary, and minimum call objectives so that the activities performed during the call will bring them closer to those objectives. The same can be said for setting sales goals: When sales goals are set properly and adhered to, the salesperson has a guide to direct his or her activities.

THE NATURE OF GOALS

As you read in Chapter 8, goals should be specific and measurable, reachable yet challenging, and time based. Goals should be specific and measurable so that the

EXHIBIT 16.2

The Relationship of Goals
Career goals are devised from lifestyle objectives. Sales goals should reflect career goals. While activities lead to sales, performance goals are usually set first. Then, using conversion goals, activity goals are set.

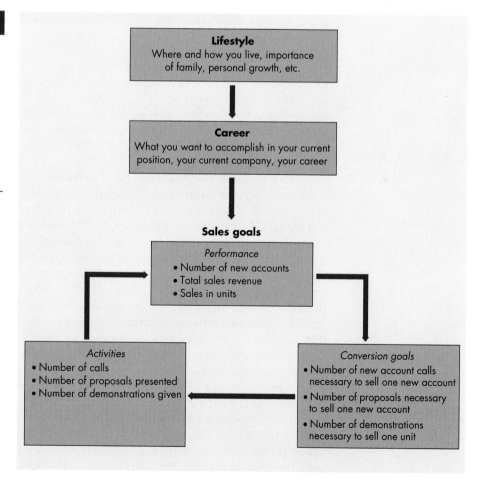

Sales managers often ask salespeople to state their goals publicly because these managers recognize the importance of setting personal objectives.

SuperStock

salesperson knows when they have been met. For example, setting a goal of making better presentations is laudable, but how would the salesperson know if the presentations were better or worse? A more helpful goal would be to increase the number of sales resulting from those presentations. The best goal would be a specific increase, such as 10 percent. Then there would be no question about the achievement of the goal.

Goals should also be reachable yet challenging. One purpose of setting personal goals is to motivate oneself. If goals are reached too easily, little has been accomplished. Challenging goals, then, are more motivating. But if the goals are too challenging, or if they are unreachable, the salesperson may give up.

Goals should also be time based; that is, goals should have deadlines. Putting a deadline on the goal provides more guidance for the salesperson and creates a sense of urgency that can be motivating. Without a deadline, the goal is not specific enough, and the salesperson may be able to drag on forever, never reaching the goal but thinking progress is being made. Imagine the motivational difference between setting a goal of a 10 percent increase in sales with no deadline and setting a goal of a 10 percent increase for the next month. The first instance lacks a sense of urgency, of needing to work toward that goal now. Without a deadline, the goal has little motivational value.

One problem some people have is periodically creating goals and then forgetting them. Goals should be written down and then posted. For example, each month Will Pinkham has a goal for selling five new accounts (Will sells office equipment for Ikon Office Solutions). At the start of each month, he puts a new list on the wall over his desk, and as he sells each new account, he adds it to the list starting at the bottom. He starts the list at the bottom to remind him that his goal is to sell five, so when he sells one, his goal becomes four, and so forth. Probably not all goals should be posted in highly public areas, but the idea is to keep the goal in front of you so that it continues to direct your activities.

Thinking It Through

What types of goals have you set for yourself in your college career? For specific classes? How would these goals meet the criteria of specific and measurable, reachable yet challenging, and time based? How do you keep these goals in front of you? What would you do differently now?

TYPES OF SALES GOALS

Salespeople need to set three types of sales goals: performance, activity, and conversions (refer back to Exhibit 16.2). Although many salespeople focus only on how many sales they get, setting all three types of goals is necessary to achieve the highest possible success.

PERFORMANCE GOALS

Goals relating to outcomes are **performance goals.** In sales, outcomes such as the size of a commission or bonus check, the amount of sales revenue generated or number of sales generated, and the number of prospects identified are common performance goals. For example, the salesperson in Exhibit 16.3 set a performance goal of $3,000 in commissions and another performance goal of eight sales. Revenue quotas are an example of goals set by the company, but each salesperson should also consider setting personally relevant goals. For example, you may want to set higher goals so that you can achieve higher earnings. People are more committed to achieving goals they set themselves; that commitment makes achieving them more likely. Performance goals should be set first because attaining certain performance levels is of primary importance to both the organization and the salesperson.

Performance goals do not always need to be quantifiable; for example, you might set a goal of improving your presentation skills. But even that type of goal should be measurable in terms of how many customers agree to buy. Personal development goals, such as improving presentation skills, are important to long-term professional growth. Every person, whether in sales or other fields, should have some personal development goals. Reaching those goals will not only improve overall job performance but also increase personal satisfaction. Like all

EXHIBIT 16.3 Goal Calculations		
Monthly earnings goal (performance goal):		$3,000
Commission per sale:		$375
$3,000 earnings ÷ $375 per sale = 8 sales		
Monthly sales goal (performance goal):		8
Closings goal (conversion goal):		10%
8 sales × 10 prospects per sale = 80 prospects		
Monthly prospect goal (performance goal):		80
Prospects per calls goal (conversion goal):		1 in 3
80 prospects × 3 calls per prospect = 240 calls		
Monthly sales calls goal (activity goal):		240
240 calls ÷ 20 working days per month = 12 calls		
Daily sales calls goal (activity goal):		12

performance goals, however, these goals should meet the criteria of being specific, challenging, and time based.

ACTIVITY GOALS

Salespeople also set activity goals. **Activity goals** are behavioral objectives: the number of calls made in a day, the number of demonstrations performed, and so on. Activity goals reflect how hard the salesperson wants to work. The company may set some activity goals for salespeople, such as a quota of sales calls to be made each week. Exhibit 16.3 lists two activity goals: 240 sales calls per month and 12 calls per day.

All activity goals are intermediate goals; that is, achieving them should ultimately translate into achievement of performance goals. As Times Mirror Cable Television discovered by auditing sales performance, activity goals such as 10 prospecting calls per day are needed for the salespeople to achieve the overall performance goals. Activity goals help salespeople decide what to do each day, but those goals must ultimately be related to making sales.[2]

However, activity goals and performance goals are not enough. For example, a salesperson may have goals of achieving 10 sales and making 160 calls in one month. The salesperson may get 10 sales but make 220 calls. That salesperson had to work much harder than someone who managed to get 10 sales in only 160 calls. That is why salespeople should also set conversion goals.

CONVERSION GOALS

Conversion goals are measures of a salesperson's efficiency. Conversion goals reflect how efficiently the salesperson would like to work, or work smarter. Unlike performance goals, conversion goals express relative accomplishments, such as the number of sales relative to the number of calls made or the number of customers divided by the number of prospects. The higher the ratio, the more efficient the salesperson. Exhibit 16.3 lists two conversion goals: closing 10 percent of all prospects and finding one prospect for every three calls. In the preceding example a rep who made 10 sales while making 160 calls could make 4 or 5 more sales by making 220 calls because that rep makes a sale every 16 calls.

Conversion goals are important because they reflect how efficiently the salesperson uses resources, such as time, to accomplish performance goals. For example, Freeman Exhibit Company builds custom trade show exhibits. Customers often ask for booth designs (called speculative designs) before making the purchase to evaluate the offerings of various competitors. Creating a custom booth design is a lot of work for a designer, and the cost can be high, but it does not guarantee a sale. If a salesperson has a low conversion rate for speculative designs, overall profits will be lower because the cost for the unsold designs must still be covered. If the rep can increase the conversion rate, the overall costs for unsold designs will be lower, hence increasing profits.

Working harder would show up in an increase in activity; working smarter should be reflected in conversion goals. For example, a salesperson may be performing at a conversion rate of 10 percent. Reaching a conversion goal of 12 percent (closing 1 out of 8 instead of 1 out of 10) would reflect some improvement in the way the salesperson operates—some method of working smarter.

Measuring conversions tells salespeople which activities work best. For example, suppose a salesperson has two sales strategies. If A generates 10 sales and B generates 8 sales, the salesperson may think A is the better strategy. But if A requires 30 sales calls and B only 20, the salesperson would be better off using strategy B. Thirty sales calls would have generated 12 sales with strategy B.

Comparing your performance with the best in your organization is a form of **benchmarking.**[3] Benchmarking can help you see where you are falling short. For example, if your conversion ratio of leads to appointments (the number of leads needed to get one appointment) is the same as that of the top seller but you are closing only half of your spec designs and that person is closing 80 percent, you know you are losing sales at the spec design stage. You can then examine what that person does to achieve the higher conversion ratio.

SETTING SALES GOALS

Performance and conversion goals are the basis for activity goals. Suppose a sale is worth $250 in commission. A person who wants to earn $2,000 per month (a performance goal) needs to make eight sales each month. If the salesperson sees closing 1 out of 10 prospects as a realistic conversion goal, a second performance goal results: The rep must identify 80 prospects to yield eight closings. If the rep can identify one prospect for every three sales calls (another conversion goal), 240 sales calls (an activity goal) must be made. Assuming 20 working days in a month, the rep must make 12 sales calls each day (another activity goal). Thus activity goals need to be the last type of goals set because they will be determined by the desired level of performance at a certain rate of conversion.

Even though the conversion analysis results in a goal of 12 calls each day, that conversion rate is affected by the strategy the salesperson employs. A better strategy results in a higher conversion rate and better allocation of time, one of many important resources that must be allocated properly to achieve sales goals. We discuss how to allocate resources in the next section.

ALLOCATING RESOURCES

The second stage of the time and territory management process is to develop a strategy that allocates resources properly. These resources are allocated to different sales strategies used with different types of accounts with the purpose of achieving sales goals in the most effective and efficient manner possible. The process of allocating resources is very important for Bill Arend, sales representative for SOS Technology, as Building Partnerships 16.1 illustrates.

RESOURCES TO BE ALLOCATED

Salespeople manage many resources. Some of these are physical resources, such as free samples, demonstration products, trial products, brochures, direct-mail budgets, and other marketing resources. Each of these physical resources represents a cost to the company, but to the salesperson they are investments. Salespeople consider physical resources as investments because resources must be managed wisely to generate the best possible return. Whereas financial investments may return dividends or price increases, the salesperson's investments should yield sales.

A key resource that salespeople manage is time. Time is limited, and not all of a salesperson's work time can be spent making sales calls. Some time must be spent attending meetings, learning new products, preparing reports for management, traveling to sales calls, and handling other nonselling duties; in fact, nonselling activities can take up to 70 percent of a salesperson's time. Thus being able to manage time wisely is important. As we discuss in the next chapter, salespeople also coordinate many of the company's other departments to serve customers well. Salespeople must learn how to allocate these resources in ways that generate the greatest level of sales.

WHERE TO ALLOCATE RESOURCES

For salespeople the allocation of resources is often a question of finding the customers or companies that are most likely to buy and then allocating selling resources to maximize the opportunities they offer. As you may have learned in your principles of marketing course, some market segments are more profitable

A MATTER OF LIFE AND DEATH

Selling is not usually a matter of life and death—even to Bill Arend, who sells emergency response training and equipment to companies for SOS Technology. Yet when Arend was working on the company's largest single sale, the prospect threw out an objection that seemed to kill the sale. OSHA requires companies to have trained CPR and first-aid personnel on site, and the prospect company had 59 locations around the country, with SOS units in only 6. So Arend walked in thinking he was going to easily add the other 53 when the customer said, "Bill, it appears from this Department of Labor memo that I don't have to have your equipment. In fact, it may be illegal. So I'd like to cancel all of our locations that have SOS."

Arend's first reaction was to sell. But when he saw that memo, he realized that trying to persuade the buyer that the memo was wrong was not the best approach. He recalls, "What I did was promise to find out more about it because I had never seen the memo before." So Arend went to the Houston Public Library to do some research. He was up until after 2 A.M., working on a 30-page proposal to document that the Department of Labor memo referred to a different product and to illustrate the need for SOS products and service in all of the customer's 59 locations. "I felt like I was back in school and about to take the hardest final exam of my life."

Arend's research convinced the buyer. But then came the task of getting all 59 locations trained and the equipment installed as soon as possible—a time management nightmare. "The day after we trained the staff at one location, a customer there had a heart attack. The staff was able to administer CPR and oxygen, saving his life," says Arend. "I hate to think what might have happened if I had put them off a day or two."

Yet that is the kind of total commitment it takes to prioritize activities. "My customers know that when I promise to act, I will act. At the same time, I don't make promises for my time that I don't think I can keep," Arend states. He knows, as well as his best customer knows, how important good time management is. In fact, it can be a matter of life or death.

than others. And just as the company's marketing executive tries to determine which segments are most profitable so that marketing plans can be directed toward those segments, salespeople examine their markets to allocate their selling resources.

Cable & Wireless, for example, has achieved success in the highly competitive market of long-distance services sold to businesses by consistently going the extra mile for its customers. However, Cable & Wireless carefully chooses small business customers for which it can add value and obtain more business. Each salesperson carefully quantifies the needs of the customer and then determines which accounts have sufficient potential to warrant building relationships with them.[4] Maximizing the opportunity means finding profitable ways to satisfy the greatest number of customers, but not necessarily everybody. In the following section we discuss how to analyze the market to identify potential customers who are most likely to buy so that resources will be allocated properly.

ACCOUNT CLASSIFICATION AND RESOURCE ALLOCATION

Not all customers have the same buying potential, just as not all sales activities produce the same results. The salesperson has to concentrate on the most profitable customers and minimize effort spent with customers that offer little opportunity for profitable sales. The proportion of unprofitable accounts is usually greater than one would think. As a rule, 80 percent of the sales in a territory come from only 20 percent of the customers. Therefore, salespeople should classify customers on the basis of their sales potential to avoid spending too much time and other resources with low-potential accounts, thus helping to achieve sales goals.

Customer management is not just a time management issue. Managing customers includes allocating all the resources at the salesperson's disposal in the

While this little store may appear smaller than Lowe's, the astute salesperson would determine each business's sales potential before classifying either as an A, B, or C account.

© Erv Schowengerdt

© Erv Schowengerdt

most productive manner. Time may be the most important of these resources, but salespeople also manage sample and demonstration inventories, direct mail budgets, printed materials, and other resources.

ABC ANALYSIS

The simplest classification scheme, called **ABC analysis,** ranks accounts by sales potential. The idea is that the accounts with the greatest sales potential deserve the most attention. Using the 80/20 rule, the salesperson identifies the 20 percent of accounts that (could) buy the most and calls those A accounts. The other 80 percent are B accounts, and noncustomers (or accounts with low potential for sales) are C accounts. Marion/Merrell Dow classifies physicians and Johnson Wax classifies retail stores this way. Federal Express studied buying habits of its customers and realized that 1 percent of its accounts generated 50 percent of revenue; it might call these A++ accounts! An example of an account analysis appears in Exhibit 16.4. As you can see, Sam Thompson has used estimated potential to classify accounts so that he can allocate sales calls to those accounts with the greatest potential.

Classification schemes can be used to generate call plans. Royal Bank of Canada segmented its customers into A, B, and C levels by looking at overall profitability, not total dollar activity. Then A accounts were assigned to specific account managers who had to make regular calls with specific product sales plans for each call. For B accounts, less frequent calls were made, but again, specific products were targeted for those calls. Royal Bank representatives did not call C accounts, though the same managers handled these accounts when they visited the bank. In the two-year period following implementation of this plan, average profit per A client grew 268 percent, while the number of A clients increased 292 percent.[5]

ABC classification schemes work well only in industries that require regular contact with the same accounts, such as consumer packaged goods and pharmaceuticals. Some industries (plant equipment, medical equipment, and other capital products) may require numerous sales calls until the product is sold. After that sale, another sale may be unlikely for several years, and the number of sales calls may diminish. Then the A, B, and C classification may not be very helpful.

Salespeople in some industries find grid and customer relationship analysis methods more useful than ABC analysis. They have learned that simply allocating

EXHIBIT 16.4   Account Classification

Salesperson: Sam Thompson   A. Analysis of Call Pattern: 2003

Customer Type	Number of Customers Contacted	Number of Calls	Average Calls per Customer	Sales Volume	Average Sales per Call
A	16	121	7.0	$212,516	$1,756
B	21	154	7.3	116,451	756
C	32	226	7.0	78,010	345
D	59	320	5.4	53,882	168
Total	128	821		$460,859	561

B. Annual Territory Sales Plan (dollars in thousands)

Account	Actual Sales 2001	Actual Sales 2002	Actual Sales 2003	Estimated Potential	2004 Forecast Sales	Number of Calls Allocated	Classification
Allied Foods	$100	$110	$160	$250	$160	48	A
Pic N-Save	75	75	90	300	115	48	A
Wright Grocers	40	50	60	175	90	24	B
H.E.B.	20	30	30	150	30	24	B
Piggly Wiggly	10	10	25	100	55	18	C
Sal's Superstore	0	0	30	100	80	18	C
Buy-Rite	0	0	0	80	75	18	C
Tom Thumb	0	10	20	75	70	18	C
Apple Tree	0	5	12	60	60	12	D
Buy Lo	0	0	10	60	50	12	D
Whyte's Family Foods	10	8	9	50	40	12	D

sales activities on the basis of sales potential may lead to inefficiencies. For example, satisfied customers may need fewer calls to maximize great potential than accounts of equal potential that are loyal to a competitor.

GRID ANALYSIS

The **sales call allocation grid** classifies accounts on the basis of the company's competitive position with an account, along with the account's sales potential. As with ABC analysis, the purpose of classifying accounts through grid analysis is to determine which accounts should receive more resources. Using this method, each account in a salesperson's territory falls into one of the four segments shown in Exhibit 16.5. The classification is determined by the salesperson's evaluation of the account on the following two dimensions.

First, the **account opportunity** dimension indicates how much the customer needs the product and whether the customer is able to buy the product. Some factors the salesperson can consider when determining account opportunity are the account's potential, growth rate, and financial condition. This rating is similar to the ABC analysis and is a measure of total sales potential. Again, the idea is that accounts with the greatest potential deserve the greatest resources.

Second, the **strength of position** dimension indicates how strong the salesperson and company are in selling the account. Some factors that determine strength

EXHIBIT 16.5

Sales Call
Allocation Grid

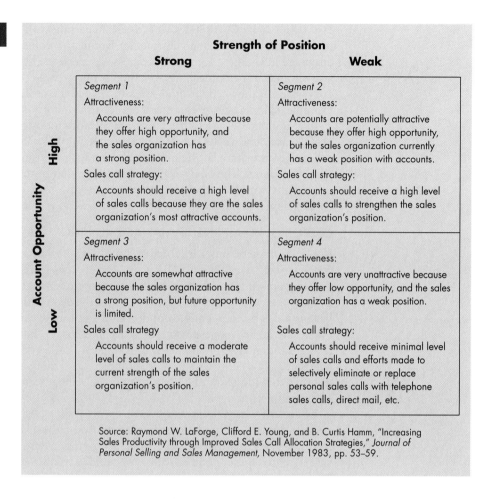

Strength of Position

	Strong	**Weak**

Account Opportunity — High / Low

Segment 1

Attractiveness:

Accounts are very attractive because they offer high opportunity, and the sales organization has a strong position.

Sales call strategy:

Accounts should receive a high level of sales calls because they are the sales organization's most attractive accounts.

Segment 2

Attractiveness:

Accounts are potentially attractive because they offer high opportunity, but the sales organization currently has a weak position with accounts.

Sales call strategy:

Accounts should receive a high level of sales calls to strengthen the sales organization's position.

Segment 3

Attractiveness:

Accounts are somewhat attractive because the sales organization has a strong position, but future opportunity is limited.

Sales call strategy

Accounts should receive a moderate level of sales calls to maintain the current strength of the sales organization's position.

Segment 4

Attractiveness:

Accounts are very unattractive because they offer low opportunity, and the sales organization has a weak position.

Sales call strategy:

Accounts should receive minimal level of sales calls and efforts made to selectively eliminate or replace personal sales calls with telephone sales calls, direct mail, etc.

Source: Raymond W. LaForge, Clifford E. Young, and B. Curtis Hamm, "Increasing Sales Productivity through Improved Sales Call Allocation Strategies," *Journal of Personal Selling and Sales Management,* November 1983, pp. 53–59.

of position are the present share of the account's purchases of the product, the attitude of the account toward the company and the salesperson, and the relationship between the salesperson and the key decision makers in the account. The strength of position helps the salesperson understand what level of sales is likely in the account. The account opportunity may be tremendous, say, $1 million. But if the account has always purchased another brand, the salesperson's strength of position is weak and his or her real potential is something much less than $1 million.

The appropriate sales call strategy depends on the grid segment into which the account falls. Accounts with high potential and a strong position are very attractive because the salesperson should be able to sell large amounts relatively easily. Thus these attractive accounts should receive the highest level of sales calls. For example, if you have an account that likes your product and has established a budget for it, and you know that the customer needs 300 units per year, you may consider that a segment 1 account (assuming 300 units is a high number) and plan to allocate more calls to that account. But if a competitor has a three-year contract with the account, you might be better off spending less time there. The account may buy 3,000 units per year, but you have little chance of getting any of that business. By classifying the account as a segment 2, you would recognize that the most appropriate strategy is to strengthen your position in the account. The sales call allocation grid, then, aids salespeople in determining where, by account, to spend time in order to meet sales goals.

THE GRID AND CURRENT CUSTOMERS The sales call allocation grid is a great tool for analyzing current customers. Recall the value of a customer that was discussed in Chapter 13; many businesses experience little or no profit in the first year of a customer's life. But over time profit grows if the salesperson is able to grow sales in the account, find ways to reduce the cost to serve the account (for example, shipping more can mean reduced shipping costs), and so on.

In a landmark study of the paper and plastics industry, the key to a company's profit was found to be customer share, not market share. **Customer share,** also called **account share,** is the average percentage of business received from a company's accounts. The analysis of companies in that industry indicated that even if a company was the dominant supplier to a group of buyers, another company could be more profitable if it served fewer customers but had all of their business.[6]

CUSTOMER RELATIONSHIP MANAGEMENT SOFTWARE

Use of computers and sales force automation software, such as ACT!, has grown tremendously over the past few years. Companies have found great productivity gains by creating one database of customers rather than separate databases used by salespeople, the credit department, and the service department. A single database enables the company to understand the buying history of an account that might use a field salesperson to place one order but order another product through the Internet. Using a form of software called customer relationship management (CRM) software, a more complete grid analysis can then be conducted in order to understand the account's needs. Selling Scenario 16.1 discusses CRM software in more detail.

Microsoft was able to apply such an analysis to its own customer base. The company was surprised to learn that many of the highest-spending small and medium-sized customers were actually giving Microsoft the lowest account share. Thus these good customers could actually become better customers because they had high potential for additional sales.[7]

Organizations use customer relationship management software, such as ACT! or Siebel Systems, to keep track of individual accounts. Companies can analyze that information to determine sales strategies, and they can also track the effectiveness of such strategies. For example, Bob Howell with Scarborough Company (a manufacturer of labels for clothing and furniture) was able to analyze his accounts. He learned that all but 100 accounts were either only marginally profitable or actually unprofitable. Howell was able to create a profile of his most profitable accounts to give to InfoUSA, a company that generates prospect lists (such as those we discussed in Chapter 7). Howell says, "I receive a disk of those kinds of accounts in my area codes (that define the sales territory). When I'm calling on customers, I can also call on suspects who have the same profiles as my A accounts."[8] Howell doesn't just want to make more sales, he wants to make more of the right kinds of sales, those that are most profitable. His CRM software helps him do that.

Another application for CRM software is *pipeline analysis.* Recall that in Chapter 7 we discussed how accounts can move through stages, from lead to suspect to prospect to customer. ACT!, for example, can complete a pipeline analysis, telling the salesperson how well she is moving accounts from one stage to the next.

Northwestern National Insurance used CRM software a little differently, though this example is fairly common. The company was processing about 27,000 applications for commercial insurance each year and declining half of them for a variety of reasons. For each of the 13,500 accepted applications, a personalized quote was prepared, and then only half of those would accept. Many sales were lost simply because competition could provide a quote more quickly. Northwestern automated the process with astounding results. Not only

MANAGING CUSTOMER RELATIONSHIPS

Over the past 20 years the average cost of a sales call has actually fallen, while at the same time compensation of salespeople has risen faster than the inflation rate. One very important reason for companies' ability to more efficiently utilize their salespeople has been technology advances that offer better customer management strategies.

First called *sales force automation (SFA)*, the class of software that now helps salespeople and their organizations manage customers is called *customer relationship management (CRM)*, and it has been integrated more fully into the overall company operations. Perhaps the earliest industry to adopt CRM software was the pharmaceutical industry, due to the heavy regulation that required close tracking of drug samples to doctors, which began with early SFA in the mid-1980s. In addition to these regulation needs, the pharmaceutical industry also has the largest sales forces of any industry. Managing the 37 million sales calls made in one year alone, combined with the intense service needs of doctors and hospitals, makes this industry a primary user of CRM solutions.

While pharmaceutical sales forces are big (the major firms employ over 6,000 each), IBM has a monstrous sales force with over 35,000 sales people. Add in 40,000 service and support personnel who need access to customer information, and the need for CRM solutions becomes incredible. "It's not just sharing information across the sales team, but the service team as well," says Cher de Rossiter, CRM project executive at IBM. Key to the CRM strategy is making sure the appropriate cost-to-serve channel, whether a field salesperson, a telephone salesperson, or a combination with the Internet, meets the needs of the customer.

So far, CRM solutions have not worked equally well for all salespeople. In a recent study of over 780 salespeople, only 60 percent of the respondents felt that their company's CRM solution was helpful for their job performance. Over 60 percent used the system daily, but only a third had integrated the software into their total sales process. At the same time, however, companies expect to quadruple the use of CRM solutions between 2002 and 2005. Companies like Silverline Technologies are finding that with CRM software, salespeople have more complete information available and can increase customer satisfaction, which increases retention and sales.

Sources: David Myron, "Big CRM Plans from Big Blue," *Customer Relationship Management*, April 2002, p. 13; Louise Yarmoff, "Healthy Sales," *Customer Relationship Management*, February 2001, pp. 64–72.

was the cost reduced significantly (previously it cost $50 to turn down an application and another $100 to produce a quote, averaging $400 to complete a sale), but the quicker turnaround improved the conversion ratio of quotes by 50 percent.[9]

Minolta Business Systems compiles data from its CRM database to create marketing campaigns that support the field sales force. For example, the company will create a profile of the organizations most likely to buy a specific product using the account records submitted by salespeople. Minolta uses that profile to generate a mailing list to introduce customers to the product. Salespeople are then given a prospecting list for making follow-up sales calls.

INVESTING IN ACCOUNTS

Planning based on customer analysis should result in more effective use of the opportunities presented by accounts. This improvement relates to the improved use of time, which is allocated to the appropriate accounts. But developing good strategies entails more than developing good time use plans; strategies require the use of other resources as well.

Salespeople invest time, free samples or trials, customer training, displays, and other resources in their customers. Dial, for example, often offers a free display to retailers who will carry a new Dial soap. Pharmaceutical reps receive a limited number of free samples to distribute; account analysis enables the salespeople to use their samples where they should result in the largest sales. Customer analysis helps salespeople determine where to invest resources—samples, training aids, displays, and so forth. Sales costs, or costs associated with the use of such resources, are not always costs in the traditional sense, but rather investments in the asset called customers. This asset generates nearly all of a firm's revenue. Viewed from this perspective, formulating a strategy to allocate resources to maintaining or developing customers becomes vitally important.

IMPLEMENTING THE TIME MANAGEMENT STRATEGY

Time is a limited resource. Once spent, it cannot be regained. How salespeople choose to use their time often means the difference between superstar success and average performance. As former pro baseball player turned salesperson Carl Warwick says, "In baseball, you've got someone setting a schedule for you and telling what time the plane leaves and when the bus leaves. But sales was self-discipline from the time you woke up in the morning till you went to bed at night."[10]

In this section we discuss the value of a salesperson's time and how to plan for its efficient use.

Remember that your time is worth $15 to $20 an hour, but only if you use it to sell. Use it to hone a golf game or spruce up the yard and opportunities to sell disappear. Although no manager really knows how a salesperson uses time, when the results are posted, accurate conclusions can be drawn.

Thinking It Through

How do you plan your time now? Do you use a computer to help you manage your time? How much of your time is planned by others, and how much of it are you free to allocate? What do you do to make sure you use your time wisely?

DAILY ACTIVITY PLANNING

To be effective time planners, salespeople must have a good understanding of their own work habits. For example, some people tend to procrastinate in getting the day started, whereas others may want to knock off early. If you are a late riser, you may want to schedule early appointments to force yourself to get started. On the other hand, if your problem is heading for home too early, schedule late appointments so that you work a full day. The salesperson in Exhibit 16.6 has scheduled an early appointment to get the day started.

Bob Dalaskey, director of sales for HHG Bekins Van Lines, teaches sales agents to take time at the end of the day and plan ahead for the next day. "It's important to take 5 or 10 minutes to organize yourself in your mind and set some priorities, rather than spending the first hour of the day getting your traction. If you wait until the start of the day, the next thing you know, it's 10:30."[11]

GUIDELINES

Salespeople need to include time for prospecting and customer care in their daily activities. Some minimize the time for such activities because they think sales do not occur on such calls, but prospects and happy customers feed future sales. IKON, an office equipment dealer, requires salespeople to handle customer care calls before 9 A.M. and after 4 P.M. and to schedule prospecting activities between 10 A.M. and noon and between 2 P.M. and 3 P.M. Scheduled appointments are worked in when customers require them. The company bases these guidelines on its experience with buyers and when they are available.

EXHIBIT 16.6   Sample Daily Plan

Scheduling Worksheet

Day: Wednesday   **Date:** June 2   **Location:** Cincinnati

Hours	Appointments and Events	Type of Activity	Deadline	Estimated Time Involvement	Results Anticipated or Required
8:30	Jones Int'l	Sales call		60 min.	Make presentation to Dave Carey, VP eng. Demonstrate x35 tester.
10:00	D. Squares Systems	Service		20 min.	Drop off new catalog to Sue Jabbar in purchasing.
10:45	Diamond Mfgr.	Sales call		15 min.	Deliver proposal to Jim O'Hara in purchasing. Pick up order.
11:15	Quad Distributor	Service		15 min.	Get OK to work with new salespeople from Jill Conner.
4:15	Write proposal for Wilkes Tool	Paperwork	Due 6/7	60 min.	Have manager review tomorrow morning.
5:15	Get sample for delivery tomorrow to Cube	Paperwork		5 min.	
5:20	Prepare schedule for tomorrow	Planning		10 min.	

Such planning guides are designed to maximize **prime selling time,** the time of day at which a salesperson is most likely to see a buyer. Prime selling time depends on the buyer's industry. For example, a good time to call on bankers is late afternoon, after the bank has closed to customers. However, late afternoon is a bad time to call on physicians, who are then making rounds at the hospital or trying to catch up on a full day's schedule of patients. Prime selling time should be devoted to sales calls, with the rest of the day used for nonselling activities such as servicing accounts, doing paperwork, or getting information from the home office.

Prime selling time can also vary from country to country. In the United States prime selling time is usually 9 A.M. to 4 P.M. with the noon hour off for lunch. In Mexico lunch starts and ends later, generally from 12:30 to 2:00 P.M.; offices may not close until 7 P.M. In Great Britain prime selling time starts later; a British Telecom rep may not begin making calls until 10 A.M.

PLANNING PROCESS

A process exists to help you plan your daily activities, with or without the aid of planning guides. This process can even help you now, as a student, take more control of your time and use it effectively.

As Exhibit 16.7 shows, you begin by making a to-do list. Then you determine the priority for each activity on your list. Many executives rank activities as A, B, or C, with A activities requiring immediate action, B activities being of secondary

EXHIBIT 16.7

Activities Planning
Process

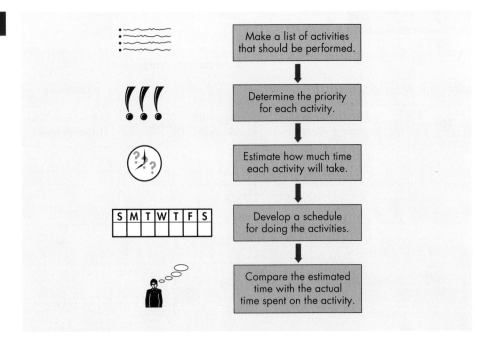

importance, and C activities being done only if time allows.[12] You can correlate these A, B, and C activities with the A, B, and C accounts discussed earlier, as well as activities such as paperwork and training. Prioritizing activities helps you choose which activities to perform first.

Note, however, the difference between activities that seem urgent and activities that truly are important. For example, when the phone rings, most people stop whatever they are doing to answer it. The ringing phone seems urgent. Activities such as requests from managers or even customers may have that same sense of urgency; the desire to drop everything else to handle the request is called the "tyranny of the urgent." And the "urgent" can get overwhelming: a study by Pitney-Bowes shows the average U.S. office worker sends and receives 52 phone messages, 36 e-mails, 36 pieces of mail, 14 faxes, and eight pager messages per day.[13] Yet, like most phone calls, even requests from customers may be less important than other tasks.[14] Successful businesspeople learn to recognize what is truly urgent and prioritize those activities first.

The next step in the planning process is to estimate the time required for each activity. In sales, as we mentioned earlier, time must be set aside for customer care and prospecting. The amount of time depends on the activity goals set earlier and on how long each call should take. However, salespeople often have unique activities, such as special sales calls, demonstrations, customer training, and sales meetings, to plan for as well. Time must also be set aside for planning and paperwork.

The next step, developing an effective schedule, requires estimating the amount of time such activities will require. As follow-up, be sure to compare how long an activity actually took with how long you thought it would take. Comparing actual time to planned time with the aid of planning devices such as a DayRunner or DayTimer (paper-based calendars and planners) or computer software can help you plan more accurately in the future.

USING THE COMPUTER FOR PLANNING

Many of the same customer management programs that salespeople use to identify and analyze accounts incorporate time-planning elements. This software can generate to-do lists and calendars through a tickler file or by listing certain customer types. A **tickler file** is a file or calendar that salespeople use to remember when to call specific accounts. For example, if customer A says to call back in 90 days, the computer will remind ("tickle") the salesperson in 90 days to call that customer. Or if the company just introduced a product that can knock out competitor B, the computer can generate a list of prospects with products from competitor B; the salesperson then has a list of prospects for the new product. As you can see in Selling Scenario 16.1, many companies have enlisted the computer to help salespeople manage their territories.

Platinum Technology equipped its salespeople with WisdomWare, a software package that creates knowledge bases. A *knowledge base* includes all the product knowledge that a salesperson needs to know, tips on what the competition is up to, and other pertinent information. As salespeople learn in the field, they add their findings to the knowledge base, which is then shared with all other salespeople at Platinum. Then each salesperson can use WisdomWare for account and territory planning.[15]

NEED FOR FLEXIBILITY

Although working out a daily plan is important, times will arise when the plan should be laid aside. You cannot accurately judge the time needed for each sales call, and hastily concluding a sales presentation just to stick to a schedule would be foolish. If more time at one account will mean better sales results, the schedule should be revised.

To plan for the unexpected, your first visit of the day should be to a prime prospect (in the terms discussed earlier, this would be an A account or activity); then the next best potential customer should be visited (provided the travel time is reasonable); and so forth. If an emergency causes a change of plans, at least the calls most likely to result in sales will have been made.

MAKING MORE CALLS

Making daily plans and developing efficient routes are important steps toward better time use. But suppose you could make just one more call per day. Using our analysis from the beginning of this chapter and Exhibit 16.3, this change would mean 240 more calls per year, which is like adding one month to the year!

Some salespeople develop an "out Tuesday, back Friday" complex. They can offer many reasons why they need to be back in the office or at home on Monday and Friday afternoons. Such a behavior pattern, however, means the salesperson makes 20 to 30 percent fewer calls than a salesperson who works a full week. Scott Woolford, national sales manager at M.D. Industries, a health care supply company, took a big account away from a competitor on a Friday afternoon. The buyer had a problem with the competitor's delivery schedule, and Woolford was able to guarantee delivery the next day—Saturday. Working a full week really paid off for Woolford.[16]

To get the most out of a territory, the sales representative must make full use of all available days. For example, the days before or after holidays are often seen as bad selling days. Hence, while the competition takes those extra days off, the salesperson can be working and making sales calls he or she would otherwise miss. The same reasoning applies to bad weather: Bad weather reduces competition and makes things easier for the salesperson who doesn't find excuses to take it easy. On the other hand, good weather can tempt the salesperson to the golf course, doing yard work, or otherwise avoiding the job. No matter the weather, the professional salesperson continues to work.

Salespeople can use certain techniques to increase the time they spend in front of customers selling instead of traveling. For example, Lisa Paolozzi found herself

Salespeople who make calls in bad weather often find that their competition has taken the day off, leaving the field wide open for those who want to succeed.

Steve Bly/Zephyr

working 16-hour days and was on the verge of quitting her sales job at FIND/SVP, a market research and consulting firm. One day, while flipping through her calendar, she realized, "I was all over the map. I was going on the number of appointments I needed, but I was so unorganized." Now she uses many time management techniques to organize herself and provide structure, with the result that she holds her company's record for the most sales in a year.[17] She uses routing and zoning techniques, as well as the computer. For example, mapping software can save her valuable time when traveling in an unfamiliar area. Rather than getting lost and calling the customer from the car for directions, she now relies on mapping software to help her find the account on the first try.

ROUTING

Routing is a method of planning sales calls in a specific order to minimize travel time. Two types of sales call patterns, routine and variable, can be more efficient with effective routing. Using **routine call patterns,** a salesperson sees the same customers regularly. For example, Marion/Merrell Dow pharmaceutical salespeople's call plans enable them to see all important doctors in their territory at least once each six weeks. Some doctors (those who see large numbers of certain types of patients) are visited every two weeks. The salesperson repeats the pattern every six weeks, ensuring the proper call level.

Variable call patterns occur when the salesperson must call on accounts in an irregular order. In this situation the salesperson would not routinely call on each account within a specified period. Routing techniques are useful, but the salesperson may not repeat the call plan on a cyclical basis.

The four types of routing plans, **circular routing, leapfrog routing, straight-line routing,** and **cloverleaf routing,** are illustrated in Exhibit 16.8. If a Marion/Merrell Dow salesperson used the cloverleaf method (with six leaves instead of four) for a routine call pattern, every sixth Tuesday would find that salesperson in the same spot. But a salesperson with variable call patterns could use the cloverleaf method to plan sales calls for an upcoming week and then use

| EXHIBIT 16.8 | Types of Routing Plans |

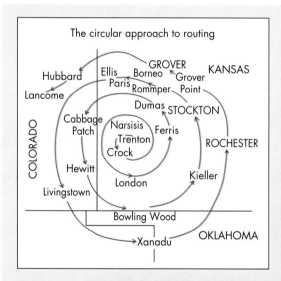

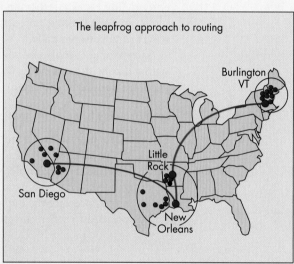

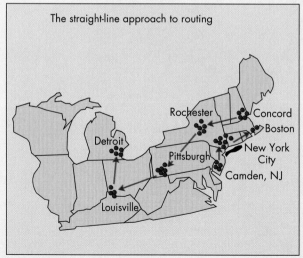

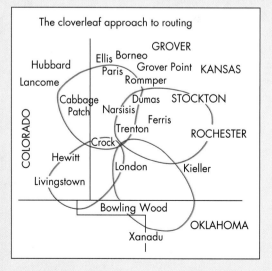

Source: Adapted from W. J. E. Crissy, H. Cunningham, and Isabella Cunningham, *Selling: The Personal Force in Marketing* (New York: John Wiley & Sons, 1977).

the straight-line method the next week. The pattern would vary depending on the demands of the customers and the salesperson's ability to schedule calls at convenient times.

ZONING

Zoning means dividing the territory into zones, based on ease of travel and concentration of customers, to minimize travel time. First the salesperson locates concentrations of accounts on a map. For example, an office supply salesperson may find that many accounts are located downtown, with other concentrations around the airport, in an industrial park, and in a part of town where two highways cross near a rail line. Each area is the center of a zone. The salesperson then plans to spend a day, for example, in each zone. In a territory zoned like the one in Exhibit 16.9, the salesperson might spend Monday in zone 1, Tuesday in zone 2, and so forth.

Zoning works best for compact territories or for situations in which salespeople do not call regularly on the same accounts. (In a large territory, such as the entire Midwest, a salesperson is more likely to use leapfrog routes, but the principle is similar.) Calling on customers that are in a relatively small area minimizes travel time between calls.

Salespeople can also combine zoning with routing, using a circular approach within a zone, for example. When zones are designed properly, travel time between accounts should be minimal.

USING E-MAIL AND TELEPHONE

Customer contacts should not always be in-person sales calls. As many companies have learned, some sales objectives can be accomplished over the phone or through e-mail. For example, some customer care calls can be handled by simply sending the customer an e-mail and asking whether everything is OK. The customer may appreciate the e-mail more than a personal visit because it can be read and responded to when the customer has time and doesn't take him or her away

EXHIBIT 16.9

Zoning a Sales Territory
A salesperson may work in zone 1 on Monday, zone 2 on Tuesday, and so forth.

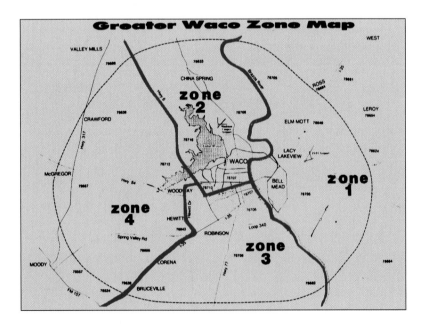

Source: *Waco Tribune Herald.*

from other pressing responsibilities. The salesperson may be able to make more customer care calls by e-mail, increasing the number of contacts with customers. Keep in mind, though, that not all customer care activities should be handled by e-mail or phone. Recall from Chapter 13 that there are many reasons, such as reorders and cross-selling, to continue to make sales calls in person to current customers.

Similarly, the telephone and direct mail can be used profitably for prospecting, as we discussed in Chapter 7. More calls, or customer contacts, can be made equally effectively with judicious use of the mail and telephone.

HANDLING PAPERWORK AND REPORTS

Every sales job requires preparing reports for management. All salespeople complain about such paperwork, but it is important. As we will discuss later, paperwork can provide information that helps a salesperson determine what should be improved. The information also helps management decide what types of marketing plans work and should be used again. Therefore, every salesperson should learn to handle paperwork efficiently.

Paperwork time is less productive than time spent selling to customers, so completing it quickly is important. Salespeople can do several things to minimize the impact of paperwork on their prime selling time.

First, salespeople should think positively about paperwork. Although less productive than selling, it can increase their productivity and the productivity of the company's marketing programs by facilitating a detailed review of selling activities and marketing programs.

Second, salespeople should not let paperwork accumulate. We once knew of a salesperson who never did expense reports. He finally offered a summer intern 10 percent if she would complete his expense reports for the previous 12 months. This deal cost him $600; in addition, he was essentially lending the company $500 per month, interest free.

Productive salespeople keep up with their paperwork at every opportunity, such as while waiting in a customer's lobby or in the car after a sales call.

Jeff Greenberg/PhotoEdit

David Young-Wolff/PhotoEdit

Routine reports should be completed daily. Nonproductive time (like time spent waiting for a customer) can be used for paperwork. Call reports and account records should be updated immediately after the call so that important points are remembered and any follow-up actions can be planned.

Finally, salespeople should set aside a block of nonselling time for paperwork. The quickest way to do this job is to concentrate on it and avoid interruptions. Setting aside a small amount of time at the beginning or end of each day for writing thank-you and follow-up notes and completing reports saves prime selling time for selling activities while ensuring that the salesperson keeps up with paperwork.

USING THE COMPUTER TO HANDLE PAPERWORK AND COMMUNICATIONS

Many companies, such as IBM, give their salespeople laptop computers. These computers can be hooked up to the company's network to access customer information and process other paperwork automatically. Salespeople who travel can then complete their paperwork while in a hotel, an airport waiting area, and other places. Salespeople calling on accounts overseas can also file reports or check the status of orders, even though the home office in another time zone may be closed for the night.

Computers can help international selling organizations operate smoothly by reducing communication barriers between the field and the home office. For example, Doug Loewe is the European marketing manager for CompuServe, managing a support staff in London and Munich, but his office is in New York. He answers about 50 e-mails a day from his overseas staff, whom he sees only about once every three months.[18] Tom Cole, senior buyer for Ranir Corporation in Grand Rapids, Michigan, uses e-mail to communicate with vendors from locations as scattered as Taiwan and England. "I talk to people all across the country that I may never meet, but I almost feel like they're friends," he says.[19] Computers and fax machines enable salespeople to communicate with colleagues and customers all around the world, despite significant time differences.

Some customer relationship management packages, like ACT!, include territory management capabilities. These packages allow salespeople to track their performance by calculating conversion rates, commissions, expenses, and other important figures. Such technology enables salespeople to file reports quickly. Owens-Corning's insulation division developed a system called Field Automation Sales Team, or FAST. This system not only tracks customer information and provides quick access to product information but also allows salespeople to track their performance and automate all of their reports to management.[20]

Joe Davis receives 100 e-mails per day and answers each one personally. He uses RadioMail, a service that allows him to receive or send e-mail to anyone, anytime, from any location, including the back seat of a cab. He admits that the main reason he began using wireless e-mail and other high-tech communication devices was for his own convenience, but now he believes he gains a competitive advantage by being able to communicate so quickly with any of his customers.[21]

To manage your time wisely, you must exploit a scarce resource in the most effective manner possible. Your objective is to make as many quality calls as possible by reserving prime selling time for selling activities. Routing, zoning, goal setting, and other methods of planning and scheduling time will help you maximize your prime selling time.

EVALUATING PERFORMANCE

Success in sales is a result of how hard and how smart a salesperson works. Unlike many other workers, however, salespeople have a great deal of control over both how hard and how smart they work. Evaluating performance is the component of self-management that provides direction for how hard the salesperson should be working as well as an opportunity to determine which strategies work best.

POSTCALL ANALYSIS

At the end of each call, many salespeople take a moment to write down what occurred and what needs to be done, perhaps using a printed form (see Exhibit 16.10) or entering the information into a territory management program. Information such as the customer's purchase volume, key people in the decision process, and current vendors is important to have, but so is personal information such as the fact that the buyer's three children play soccer. The salesperson can use that information when preparing for the next call.

Remember the plan you made for each sales call? That plan included one or more objectives. Postcall analysis should include reflecting on whether those objectives were reached. The professional salesperson not only looks for specific areas to improve but also evaluates the success of the overall sales call.

ACTIVITY ANALYSIS

When planning their time, salespeople set certain activity goals. They use these goals not only as guidelines but also to evaluate their own performance. At the end of each day, week, and month, salespeople should review their activities in relation to the goals they set. For example, the salesperson might use a form such as the one in Exhibit 16.11 to compare goals with actual performance. Goals would be written down at the time they are set—say, Sunday evening when planning the following week. Then, on Friday evening, the actual activities from each day would be tallied and totaled for the week and written next to the goals. The salesperson could then evaluate whether more calls of a certain type are needed in the following week.

EXHIBIT 16.10 Postcall Analysis Form

COMPANY NAME: _____

Contact name: _____
Decision maker's name: _____
Office address: _____
_____
Office phone: _____
First contact date: _____
Next contact date: _____
Ranking: (Hot) 5 4 3 2 1 (Cold)
Notes:

Date: _____
STATUS:
A—Current account
B—Current prospect
C—Competitor
D—Dormant
E—Not interested
INITIAL CONTACT:
D—Direct mail
T—Telephone
C—Cold call

COMPANY NAME: _____

Contact name: _____
Decision maker's name: _____
Office address: _____
_____
Office phone: _____
First contact date: _____
Next contact date: _____
Ranking: (Hot) 5 4 3 2 1 (Cold)
Notes:

Date: _____
STATUS:
A—Current account
B—Current prospect
C—Competitor
D—Dormant
E—Not interested
INITIAL CONTACT:
D—Direct mail
T—Telephone
C—Cold call

COMPANY NAME: _____

Contact name: _____
Decision maker's name: _____
Office address: _____
_____
Office phone: _____
First contact date: _____
Next contact date: _____
Ranking: (Hot) 5 4 3 2 1 (Cold)
Notes:

Date: _____
STATUS:
A—Current account
B—Current prospect
C—Competitor
D—Dormant
E—Not interested
INITIAL CONTACT:
D—Direct mail
T—Telephone
C—Cold call

COMPANY NAME: _____

Contact name: _____
Decision maker's name: _____
Office address: _____
_____
Office phone: _____
First contact date: _____
Next contact date: _____
Ranking: (Hot) 5 4 3 2 1 (Cold)
Notes:

Date: _____
STATUS:
A—Current account
B—Current prospect
C—Competitor
D—Dormant
E—Not interested
INITIAL CONTACT:
D—Direct mail
T—Telephone
C—Cold call

EXHIBIT 16.11 Postcall Analysis Form

	Goal / Actual	Goal / Actual	Goal / Actual	Goal / Actual	Goal / Actual	Goal / Actual	Goal / Actual	Goal / Actual
Rep Name: _____								
Date: _____								
Month: _____								
___to___								
___to___								
___to___								
___to___								
Total								

Remarks on this month's sales activities:

Action plan for next month:

Merrill Lynch, for example, recommends that new brokers make 100 telephone calls each day (calls count even if no one answers). Frank Baugh, a new broker in central Texas, made 7,544 calls in his first 92 working days, or 82 calls per day. His goal is now 120 calls per day to bring his average up to 100 in the next quarter.

PERFORMANCE ANALYSIS

Salespeople also need to evaluate performance relative to performance goals set earlier. For example, they often evaluate sales performance in terms of percentage of quota achieved. Of course, a commission or a bonus check also tells the salesperson if the earnings goal was met.

An earnings goal can be an effective check for overall performance, but salespeople also need to evaluate sales by product type, as outlined in Exhibit 16.12. Salespeople who sell only part of the product line may be missing opportunities for cross-selling or full-line selling, which means they have to work harder to achieve the same level of sales as the salesperson who successfully integrates cross-selling and full-line selling in the sales strategy.

PRODUCTIVITY ANALYSIS

Salespeople also need to identify which strategies work. For example, if using a certain strategy improved the ratio of appointments to cold calls made, that approach should be continued. Otherwise, the salesperson should change it or go

EXHIBIT 16.12

Sales Evaluation
Measures

Evaluation Measure	Calculation	How to Use It
Conversion rate 　For total performance 　By customer type 　By product type	$\dfrac{\text{Number of sales}}{\text{Number of calls}}$	Are your strategies effective? Do you need to improve by working smarter (i.e., a better strategy to improve your hit rate)? Compare yours to your company and/or industry average.
Sales achievement	$\dfrac{\$ \text{ actual sales}}{\$ \text{ sales goal}}$	Is your overall performance where you believe it should be? Are you meeting your goals? Your company's goals?
Commission	$\dfrac{\$ \text{ actual commission}}{\$ \text{ earnings goal}}$	
Sales volume (in dollars) 　By customer type		Where are you most effective? Do you need help with a customer type?
By product category		Are you selling the whole line?
By market share		How are you doing relative to your competition?
By new customers		Are you building new business?
By old customers		Are you servicing your accounts properly?
Sales calls 　Prospecting calls		Are your efforts in the right place?
Account calls 　Sales presentations 　Call frequency by 　customer type		

back to a previous approach. Frank Baugh, the Merrill Lynch broker, tried several approaches before settling on one that works well for him. Of course, Baugh keeps good records so he knows what works and what does not.

The **conversion ratio,** or number of sales per calls, is an important measure of effectiveness. Conversion ratios should also be calculated by account type; for example, a conversion ratio for type A accounts should be determined. Other conversion ratios can also pinpoint effective strategies and areas that need improvement.

Summary

A sales territory can be viewed as a small business. Territory salespeople have the freedom to establish programs and strategies. They manage a number of resources, including physical resources such as sample inventory, displays, demonstration equipment, and perhaps a company vehicle. More important, they manage their time, their customers, and their skills.

Managing a territory involves setting performance, activity, and conversion goals. Salespeople use these goals to allocate time to various activities and to manage customers.

To manage customers well, the salesperson must analyze their potential. Accounts can be classified using the ABC method or the sales call allocation grid. These analyses tell how much effort should be put into each account. Some organizations use CRM software to conduct these analyses on the entire customer database, which then helps to identify patterns within a territory. Salespeople can use these patterns to develop account sales strategies.

More calls (working harder) can be accomplished by moving nonselling activities, such as paperwork, to nonselling time. Also, selling time can be used more efficiently (working smarter). For example, routing and zoning techniques enable the salesperson to spend more prime selling time in front of customers instead of behind the steering wheel of a car.

Effective planning of the salesperson's day requires setting aside time for important activities such as prospecting and still making the appropriate number of sales appointments. Using the full workweek and employing technology such as telephones, computers, and fax machines can help the salesperson stay ahead of the competition.

Finally, salespeople must manage their skills. Managing skills involves choosing how to make sales calls and improving the way one sells. Improvement requires that salespeople first understand what they do well and what needs improvement. Evaluating their performance can provide them with that insight.

KEY TERMS

ABC analysis   477
account opportunity   478
account share   480
activity goals   474
benchmarking   475
circular routing   487
cloverleaf routing   487
conversion goals   474
conversion ratio   493
customer share   480
leapfrog routing   487

performance goals   473
prime selling time   483
routine call patterns   486
routing   486
sales call allocation grid   478
straight-line routing   487
strength of position   478
tickler file   485
variable call patterns   487
zoning   488

Questions and Problems

1. After reading this chapter, a salesperson protests, "That's no fun. I like to play golf every other afternoon. If I have to hustle every minute of every day, then forget it. I'll get another job!" What would you tell this salesperson?

2. Many companies call their salespeople "marketing representatives." Does this designation accurately describe the job? Why or why not? If not, when would it be an appropriate job title?

3. Compare and contrast the special problems of self-management for a computer salesperson who works in a computer store with those of a computer salesperson who calls on customers in their offices.

4. Shakespeare wrote, "To thine own self be true." How would you apply this statement to your planning and development activities?
5. Which factors are important for classifying customers? Why? How would these factors change depending on the industry?
6. Distinguish between routing and scheduling and between routing and zoning. Explain how routing and scheduling can interact to complement the planning of an efficient day's work.
7. How might a pharmaceutical salesperson increase the number of calls made per day? A construction equipment salesperson? A financial services representative? A representative who sells golf clubs to retailers and pro shops?
8. Sales managers know that making more sales calls results in more sales. Should sales managers encourage salespeople to continually increase the number of calls made each week? Explain your answer.
9. One recruiter told a class that students are used to getting feedback on how they are doing every couple of months, but salespeople do not get a "final grade" until a year has gone by. He claims that students have a hard time making that adjustment when they enter the work world. What do salespeople do to know where they stand at any given time? What do you do now that helps you know where you stand in your classes?
10. Do you ever find yourself "burning the midnight oil" to study or finish an assignment? What self-management principles could you use to avoid all-nighters? Is any software available to help you manage your time as a student?

Case Problems

CASE 16.1

Nortel

You sell ACT! software and have among your accounts Nortel's five Toronto-based divisions. One division (electronics parts) has 48 salespeople nationwide, and all are GoldMine users. Another division (telecommunications) allows salespeople to use whatever software they want, and of the 120 salespeople, 35 have GoldMine, 24 have ACT!, and 17 have Maximizer on their laptops; the rest have off-brand products or nothing. The other three divisions have not automated their sales forces, with 29 salespeople, 78 salespeople, and 425 salespeople. Each division operates autonomously.

You are calling on Leo Dunn, the vice president of sales for the controls division, the division with the largest sales force. Leo believes that sales force automation is an important element in enabling the division to reach its goals, but he hasn't been able to convince the executive committee to authorize the budget for buying laptops. He has asked you to provide a proposal for stand-alone computers, a proposal he will put with those from Compaq, Microsoft, and other vendors for a full package deal. He told you that ACT! is the most expensive contact management software package he's seen and that just because he's asking for the proposal doesn't mean yours is the one he'll go with if he gets the budget.

John Baskom, sales manager in telecommunications, is the brother-in-law of Judy Baskom, vice president of sales in electronics. Judy set up a meeting so that you can present ACT! to her and John. During the meeting you identified John's need to standardize contact management. He has a budget of $25,000 to put contact management on the reps' laptops and plans to implement the decision by December 31. Although John thanked Judy for setting up the meeting, he let you know that he wanted to look at all products. He is a GoldMine user. Next week, he'll visit with GoldMine and is still waiting to get the final Maximizer proposal. He will make the final decision alone but wants his sales managers' input after they view a demonstration.

Note: This case was created for class discussion and is not intended to represent anyone at Nortel or ACT!.

1. Assess the overall Nortel account in terms of the sales effort allocation grid.
2. Is the telecommunications division a suspect or prospect? Why? How would you assess that division in terms of the sales effort allocation grid?

"We sell a lot of farm equipment throughout this river bottom area," said Bob Hart, sales representative for Lang Implement Company, the Northern Farm Equipment Company dealer in Quincy, Illinois. Hart's territory lies on both sides of the Mississippi, in Illinois and Missouri. He covers it in a Northern pickup truck so he can go right out to his prospects when they are working in the field. Hart often meets his customers in an open-collar shirt, a leather jacket, and a felt hat that he rarely removes. In fact, Hart usually dresses more like one of his customers than a sales representative. He knows the problems of his customers, and he talks their language. He is proud of his ability to "run a tractor around a barnyard and tell pretty well by the sound whether or not the rear end is OK."

Hart has spelled out some of his ideas on selling farm equipment:

The first thing I do is get around to enough doors and barn lots to find a person interested in buying something. During this time of year, there may be weeks when I'm never in the office except in the morning before I start out on my calls. If you expect to sell farm equipment, you have to go out to the customer. And I usually have plenty of customers to call on. I do, however, want to spend some time in the store. A person who tends to business in the store can sell a lot of equipment and get a good many leads for future action.

When I drive from one customer's place to the next, I usually listen to the car radio. Doing so is very helpful, as I always pick up the community news and the market information everybody is talking about. Someone will tell you that the price of hogs or cattle dropped off yesterday and that he or she doesn't know whether to buy anything from you today. But if you catch that market news, maybe you can answer right back that hogs went up 50 cents today.

By putting selling techniques such as these into practice, Bob Hart has helped Lang Implement Company stay in the running with the best of its seven competitors in Quincy.

Hart drove 60 miles on March 4, spending the morning in Missouri and the afternoon in Illinois. He made eight calls and talked to two customers at the store. His efforts bore some fruit, but the day also produced its share of blind alleys and frustrations. At one stop he learned that the farmer had gone into Quincy to see him. Efforts to find another farmer at the grain elevator ended in failure. He found Harvey Ireland ringing pigs and had to talk business with him above the pigs' shrill, incessant squealing. Ireland finally decided not to deal.

Right after lunch Hart drove up to see Glenn Mugdalen (who was in partnership with his brother, Orville) about the possibility of trading for a baler. Glenn's wife, Martha, came out to meet Hart when she heard the dog bark. She sent him to talk with Orville at one of their fields, where he was sowing clover seed. Hart found Orville preparing to go into the fields with fertilizer. They passed the time of day before Hart got down to business.

BOB: I stopped over at Glenn's and talked with Martha. She said you had all the answers about the baler.

ORVILLE: Yes, sir. Well, I wish I did know all the answers about the baler.

BOB: If you go ahead and trade balers with us now, it'll help us to get rid of the used one.

ORVILLE: After thinking it over, we just kind of thought we'd be better off by having this one fixed.

BOB: You want us to pick it up, then?

ORVILLE: I believe so.

BOB: We can pick it up anytime. That's all right with us if you want to fix it and don't want to trade. And while we've got it down there fixing it, you might take a notion to go ahead and trade.

ORVILLE: That's right. I believe that's about as good a way as any to do it.

BOB: Another thing. I want to see what we can do on that tractor deal . . .

But 15 minutes of earnest talk in Orville's barnyard failed to bring the two men to terms on anything but repairing the baler (although a few days later, Orville did buy a new, fast hitch for his tractor).

Bob Hart's conversion rate was considerably less than eight for eight on March 4. But every minute he wasn't on the road, he was selling. He made two sales on March 4. Both were corn planters. One of the buyers came to him at the store after he made a pitch at the farm. He made the other sale because he went out after it.

Bill Adams owns 400 acres near LaGrange, Missouri, about 12 miles from Quincy. Hart had talked to him before about buying a new eight-row planter, using his old John Deere planter as a trade-in. Hart had also agreed to sell Adams's old crawler for him. On the morning of March 4, Hart crossed the river to LaGrange and found Adams at the wheel of his Case-IH tractor, hauling feed. The following conversation ended in a sale:

BOB: You know what I stopped for. We're going to trade that John Deere corn planter for that new Northern.

BILL: Just as soon as you sell that crawler.

BOB: They pick it up yet?

BILL: Nope.

BOB: Well, they're going to pick it up. Now listen. On that cash part of it, you know, we're not going to worry about that. But corn planting may be over before we get that crawler sold, and you know you want that new planter. What do you say we trade this morning?

BILL: I have to get some cash—that's all there is to it.

BOB: I know you haven't bought anything yet for which you haven't paid cash. But here's our point on the planter. What we're in a hurry for is to get the used one sold because you can wait too long and then you'll have to carry it over another year. That's when you lose money. How long would I have to carry you?

BILL: You might have to carry me till harvest.

BOB: Aw, I don't think so. You know you're going to buy that planter.

BILL: Oh, I can get by.

BOB: Doggone it, I'd sure like to trade with you. I want to look at that planter of yours again.

At this point Hart went into a shed to check the trade-in planter. When he came out, Adams waited while Hart returned to his pickup to do some figuring. The conversation began again when Hart finished.

BOB: Well, here's what I'll do. I'll bring that new planter over here for $9,300.

BILL: $9,300. Hmm. Let's see how you figured, Bob.

BOB: That's putting a lot of money in your planter.

BILL: You're taking that forage harvester in on that, aren't you, Bob—for $1,200?

BOB: No. Doggone it, I can't. [Short pause.]

BILL: You're still asking a lot of money, Bob.

BOB: But that's giving you an awfully good deal on the planter too, you must remember. If you keep yours, you're going to have to put runners on it. Six of them—that's $270. With this new one, you'd be getting a high-speed planter that will plant accurately.

BILL: Is that a good hill-drop planter?

BOB: It sure is. It'll hill drop 211 hills a minute. In other words, if you're spacing 40 inches apart, it'll hill drop at 6 miles an hour and put 95 percent of the grain in a hole the size of a silver dollar. Also, think of the productivity gain in upgrading from your current six-row unit to this eight-row model. You'll cover one-third more with each pass. [Long silence while Bill Adams thinks it over.]

BILL: That's a lot of money, Bob. It's a good trade, but . . . [Another long pause.]

BOB: You can see our point. Here it is, the fourth of March, and people are buying this equipment now. We don't want to wait around too long. [Another pause.]

BILL: Aw, I don't know. You always make me a good deal, Bob.

BOB: Sure I do. Why don't you let me write the order this morning? Let's see, that price is $14,500. I'm giving you $5,200 on your planter. That's $9,300 difference.

BILL: By the time this thaw is over, I'm liable to have to put all that money for a planter into gravel for these roads.

BOB: Well, you don't have to pay for that planter today. Tell me when you would pay for it.

BILL [pausing]: Reckon I can get the job done with that planter?

BOB: I know you can, because we'll come out and get it started for you.

BILL: Are you going to get somebody over here to get the fuel injectors on this tractor straightened out?

BOB: Sure, I'll get it fixed for you—get somebody out here right away. Can you pay me by April 15? That wouldn't crowd you any, would it?

BILL: Give me until the 15th of May. That'll give me a chance to sell some of the bred heifers.

BOB: OK, let me write it up. [At this point, Bob begins to write.]

BILL: Better give me $5,500 for my planter, Bob.

BOB: I'm giving you $5,200.

BILL: Well, I know, but it looks so much better.

BOB: Well, OK. You just sign here. And thanks a lot to you, Bill. I'm sure you'll be happy about it.

"The greatest thing we've got to sell is goodwill," Bob Hart says. "If we keep the customer's goodwill, we'll keep our fair share of the business. Courtesy calls pay real dividends in this business. About 80 percent of Lang Implement's sales are repeat business. The first sale to a person is a hard one to make. The next one comes easier, and the one after that even easier. By this time the customers come back because they like the way they've been treated."

1. How well do you think Bob Hart utilized his time on March 4? What, if any, suggestions would you make to Hart to improve his efforts?
2. If you were Bob Hart, what criteria would you use to evaluate the effectiveness of your sales efforts in that territory?
3. Assess Bob's position in his accounts, using the sales effort allocation grid.

CASE 16.3

McGraw-Hill

Pierce Totten is a salesperson for McGraw-Hill, the company that publishes this textbook. Pierce works from Minneapolis–St. Paul; his territory includes northern Minnesota and the following accounts:

Bemidji State, Bemidji: This school has 12 faculty members in the business administration program. It offers five majors: finance, generalist, management, marketing, and small business. It is a small school, with approximately 400 undergraduate business students.

Central Lakes College, Brainerd: There are 11 faculty members at the Brainerd campus of Central Lakes in the business department. The school offers eight majors: finance, management, marketing, accounting, information systems, insurance, economics, and entrepreneurship in a two- year associate program.

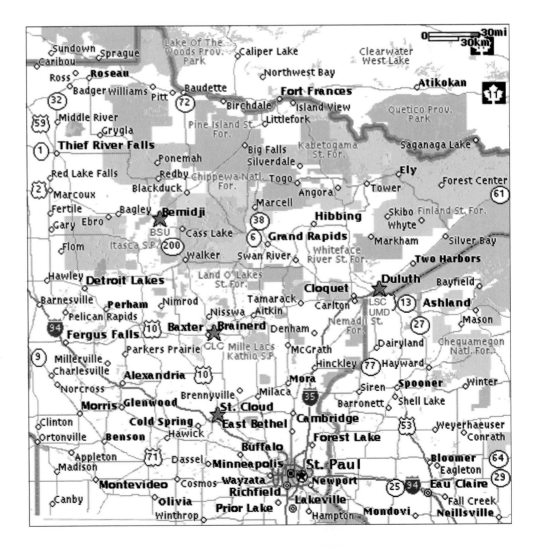

This pre-BBA program can be combined with programs at schools such as St. Scholastica. The school has 350 students at the Brainerd campus, and another 100 taking courses online.

Lake Superior College, Duluth: There are approximately 8,500 students at Lake Superior. The business department has 10 full-time faculty members and offers 19 majors in the bachelor's program. There are approximately 30 adjunct professors who teach one class each, but in almost all cases, the full-time faculty decide what books they use.

University of Minnesota–Duluth, Duluth: There are over 9,000 students total at UMD. The school of business and economics has over 40 faculty members (full-time) in four departments, and approximately 60 percent of all undergraduates are business majors.

St. Cloud University, St. Cloud: There are five departments offering 10 majors at St. Cloud. Over 70 faculty teach in the undergraduate program, serving approximately 3,500 students.

Source: Based on information and a scenario suggested by Dr. Jeff Totten, Southeastern Louisiana University, and a sales representative from another textbook publisher.

QUESTIONS

1. Plan an appropriate schedule for Pierce.
2. What are the three most important issues that Pierce needs to consider in scheduling his time? Why are these issues so important?

Additional References

Athaide, Gerard A., and Rodney L. Stump. "A Taxonomy of Relationship Approaches during Product Development in Technology-Based Industrial Markets." *Journal of Product Innovation Management* 16 (1999), pp. 469–82.

Buchwald, Art. "Selecting the Correct Sales Tool." *Customer Relationship Management,* November 2001, pp. 27–28. This is a good, short article on selecting a CRM software system.

Donaldson, Bill; Nikos Tzokas; and Mike Saren. "The Sale Never Closes: How Closer Relationships between Buyers and Sellers Change the Role of the Salesperson." *The Journal of Selling and Major Account Management* 3, Winter 2001, pp. 31–43.

Dwyer, Sean; Orlando Richard; and C. David Shepherd. "An Exploratory Study of Gender and Age Matching in the Salesperson–Prospective Customer Dyad: Testing Similarity–Performance Expectations." *Journal of Personal Selling and Sales Management* 18, Fall 1998, pp. 55–70.

Jolson, Marvin. "Broadening the Scope of Relationship Selling." *Journal of Personal Selling and Sales Management* 17, Fall 1997, pp. 75–88.

Lambe, C. Jay, and Robert Spekman. "National Account Management: Large Account Selling or Buyer–Supplier Alliance?" *Journal of Personal Selling and Sales Management* 17, Fall 1997, pp. 61–74.

Moon, Mark, and Susan F. Gupta. "Examining the Formation of Selling Centers: A Conceptual Framework." *Journal of Personal Selling and Sales Management* 17, Fall 1997, pp. 31–41.

Napolitano, Lisa. "Customer–Supplier Partnering: A Strategy Whose Time Has Come." *Journal of Personal Selling and Sales Management* 17, Fall 1997, pp. 1–8.

Managing within Your Company

SOME QUESTIONS ANSWERED IN THIS CHAPTER ARE:

■ Which areas of the company work with salespeople to satisfy customer needs?

■ How do salespeople coordinate the efforts of various functional areas of the company?

■ How do salespeople work with sales managers and sales executives?

■ How do company policies, such as compensation plans, influence salespeople?

■ How do salespeople work within the company to resolve ethical issues?

■ What is the organizational structure, and how does it influence salesperson activities?

Because salespeople manage and coordinate many elements of the firm's marketing mix, they are often called *territory managers.* And, of course, they work with and can themselves become sales managers. In this chapter we explore how salespeople manage their work within their companies to achieve their sales goals and create customer satisfaction.

As you read in the preceding chapter, successful salespeople learn to manage their time and their territory. But success also requires salespeople to manage their company's resources by coordinating the company's manufacturing, shipping, customer service—and even the sales managers—to fulfill customers' needs.

"I need people who understand the mission of driving growth through partnerships."

Shirley Hunter, Teradata

PROFILE

When asked where she works, Shirley Hunter mistakenly tells people sometimes that she works for EDS when she actually means EDS is her account. As global alliance manager for NCR's Teradata division, Hunter works with EDS to sell Teradata solutions to EDS customers. It's no wonder she occasionally gets confused, for as she puts it, "I find myself selling EDS's needs to our top management every day."

Hunter has worldwide responsibility for increasing Teradata's market share through building joint customer solutions with EDS. Together the firms identify opportunities in the market, develop solutions, and co-market. It may seem natural for Teradata to try to do whatever its customer wants, but sometimes what EDS wants conflicts with Teradata's goals. In that case, Hunter may have to prove to Teradata executives or engineers that what EDS wants is the right choice.

"We have a direct sales mentality," says Hunter, meaning that Teradata typically sells directly to the end user. But when EDS is involved, it is usually an EDS customer, not a Teradata customer, and "it is tough for Teradata people to give up control. It is especially difficult for our analysts, tech groups, and engineers to divulge information to a partner like EDS, because they aren't used to working with alliance partners." Hunter finds that she needs internal champions, "people who understand the mission of driving growth through partnerships; we bring those people to the table to help identify the current project, the components, and the process needed to achieve success."

At other times, Hunter has to convince EDS that Teradata is the right partner for a particular market. "There, too, we've identified champions within EDS who have embraced our solution and want to drive it across the other lines of business—what really drives success is a win—a customer where we can work together and we solve it with a combined solution. We work with these champions on how to work with EDS, politically." Hunter has to know how things work in EDS just as she does in Teradata. It is no wonder, then, that she occasionally says she works for EDS.

Visit Our Website @ www.teradata.com.

BUILDING INTERNAL PARTNERSHIPS

To effectively coordinate the efforts of various areas of a company, a salesperson must develop partnerships with the individuals in those areas. **Internal partnerships** are partnering relationships between a salesperson and another member of the same company. These partnerships should be dedicated to satisfying customer needs.

THE IMPORTANCE OF INTERNAL PARTNERSHIPS

By definition, a sales representative represents something. Students often think the title means that the salesperson represents only a company or a product, but at times the salesperson must represent the customer to the company. In fact, in a recent survey strategic account managers rated internal selling as their top concern.[1] For example, the salesperson may have to convince the warehouse manager to ship a customer's product next to meet a special deadline. The salesperson does not have the authority to order the manager to ship the product, but he or she must use persuasion. Or the rep may have to negotiate with production to get a product manufactured to a customer's specifications. Sometimes success in landing a sale may depend on the salesperson's ability to manage such company efforts.

This ability to work with groups inside the company can directly affect the rep's pocketbook. One of the authors, while selling for a major corporation, had an opportunity to earn a large bonus by making 30 sales. He had 31 orders, but a sale wasn't a sale until the product was delivered. Unfortunately, two orders were delivered after the deadline, and he did not get the bonus. In tracking down the slow deliveries, the hapless salesperson learned that the order entry clerk had delayed processing the orders. A little probing uncovered the reason: She was upset with the way he prepared his paperwork! Her performance was evaluated on how quickly an order was delivered, but his sloppy paperwork always slowed her down and got her into trouble. Delaying work on his orders was her way of getting his attention.

It worked! For several months after that, he enlisted her help in filling out the paperwork properly before he turned it in. After that, she never had a problem with his orders. And, when necessary to meet a customer's requirements, she would prioritize his orders.

THE ROLE OF SALES IN LEARNING ORGANIZATIONS

Salespeople not only sell a company, its products, and its services to customers but also sell their customers' needs to their companies. Carrying the customer's voice across a learning organization is one of the most important functions of the sales force. Although many learning organizations work to increase the customer contact time for support personnel so that they will understand customers, often the only person who really understands what the customer needs and why is the salesperson. The salesperson's ability to carry the voice of the customer across the learning organization is key to any firm.[2]

DHL, a Belgium-based global overnight express company, can attest to the importance of salespeople's voice of the customer role. A number of customers were seeking global sourcing contracts with DHL and its competitors. For example, Lucent Technologies was demanding 48-hour delivery time worldwide for Lucent's circuits, with similar demands on document shipping. Global contracts meant that DHL would need some form of centralization, a very different method of operating than the localized control that the company was used to. With salespeople driving the change, the organization was able to develop a process that involved operations, information technology, billing, and logistics

A TOP GLOBAL SUPPLIER

When you sell to automakers, your market is pretty small. Getting close to the customer isn't just an option, it's a necessity. But that doesn't mean that sales and marketing departments also have to be close, does it?

At Johnson Controls Automotive Systems Group (ASG), there is no choice there, either. Sales and marketing not only have to get along, they have to work closely together in order to win the customer's business. And they do work closely together, often taking training courses together and making sales calls together.

This close-knit relationship was a key factor in ASG's success with Ford's F series truck. Trying to win the seat business for the 2003 F series, three salespeople and two marketing people presented the ASG proposal. "We wanted to show Ford the demographics of who they and their competitors reach," says Rick Gunthner, ASG's director of seat systems marketing. "We don't want salespeople, when presenting, to just talk about products . . . we want our customers to see us as partners in this whole thing." The ASG presentation included so much research and knowledge about consumer desires that Ford was able to receive a lot of extra benefits by choosing ASG. Of course, it helps that salespeople, marketing people, and engineers all receive end-of-the-year bonuses when their accounts are profitable.

Not only has ASG won Ford's business, it has also won Ford's respect and two awards. Ford awarded ASG two major prizes—a Silver Award for top performance in quality and delivery in South America and a Recognition of Achievement Award for quality performance in the United States. Says Dana Lowell, director of product marketing, "Here, everybody is focused on one thing: making sure customers get what they want."

Sources: Andy Cohen, "In Control," *Sales & Marketing Management*, June 1999, pp. 32–38; William Dawson, "Johnson Controls Named One of Ford's Best Global Suppliers," company news release, April 29, 2002.

departments of regional offices around the globe. The result was that all heard the voice of the customer, and an effective strategy was created.[3]

In addition, salespeople must adapt to satisfy the needs and desires of those who influence sales performance. Salespeople who develop strong internal partnerships are successful because they meet the needs of their partners. Building Partnerships 17.1 describes how one company has been successful because of strong internal partnerships.

SELLING INTERNALLY

To service customers well, salespeople must often rely on personnel in other areas of the firm to do their respective jobs properly. But how well those other employees assist salespeople may be a function of the relationship the salesperson has already established with them. That relationship should be a partnership, just like the one the salesperson wants to establish with customers. To establish the appropriate partnership, the salesperson must invest time in understanding the customer's needs and then work to satisfy those needs.

> ## Thinking It Through
>
> Consider the impact electronic forms of communication have had on your life so far. How do such forms of communication help build internal partnerships, particularly when a salesperson is stationed far away from company headquarters? How can such forms of communication hinder a salesperson's efforts to build internal partnerships?

EXHIBIT 17.1

Seven Principles
of Selling Internally

1. Understand that it's your problem. **Accept responsibility** for gaining the support of the internal staff.
2. **Appeal to a higher objective.**
3. Probe to find out and **understand the personal and professional needs** of the internal customer.
4. Use arguments for support that adequately **address internal customer's needs** as well as your own.
5. Do not spend time or energy resenting the internal customers' inability to understand or accept your sense of urgency. Rather, spend this time fruitfully by trying to figure out how you can better communicate your needs in a manner that will **increase the internal customer's sense of urgency** to the level you need.
6. **Never personalize** any issues.
7. Be prepared to **negotiate.**

As summarized in Exhibit 17.1, the first step of selling laterally is to recognize that it is the salesperson's responsibility to develop relationships with other departments. Rarely do other departments have an incentive to take the initiative. Salespeople who expect other workers to serve them are frustrated by the lack of support they receive. The better perspective is, How can I serve them so we can serve the customer better?

Use questioning skills such as SPIN to understand the personal and professional needs of personnel in other departments. Salespeople have excellent communication skills but sometimes fail to use these skills when dealing with internal customers and support groups. SPIN and active listening are just as important to understanding the needs of colleagues as they are to satisfying customer needs. For example:

SALESPERSON: What do you do with these credit applications? (Situation)

CREDIT REP: We key the information into the computer system, and then it is processed by a credit company each night. The next morning we get a report that shows who has been approved and who hasn't. That's why it is so important to have a clean copy.

SALESPERSON: So the quality of the copy we give you is a problem? (Problem)

CREDIT REP: That's right.

SALESPERSON: What happens when you can't read the copy we give you? (Implication)

CREDIT REP: We put in incorrect information, which can result in a customer's credit application being rejected when it should have been accepted.

SALESPERSON: What happens when that happens? (Implication)

CREDIT REP: That's when we call you. Then we get the right information and reenter it. But we get in trouble because the approval cycle was made longer, and you know that the goal is to have a customer's order shipped in three days. We can't meet that goal if we're still working on their credit application.

SALESPERSON: So you need legible applications—and probably typewritten would be better than handwritten, right? (Needs payoff)

CREDIT REP: Yes, that would help a lot.

Keep in mind too that the salesperson cannot simply order a colleague to do what the salesperson wants, such as approving a customer's credit application. But if a salesperson can show that doing what he or she wants will also meet the needs of the colleague, the salesperson is more likely to receive the desired aid. Just as when selling to an external customer, persuasion requires the salesperson to meet the other person's needs as well. For example, if a salesperson can show a plant manager how an expedited order will result in a higher profit margin, thereby more than covering the plant manager's higher costs and helping that manager make production targets, both the plant manager's needs and the customer's needs will be met.

People from other departments, except for billing and customer service, do not have direct contact with the customer. Therefore, they do not feel the same sense of urgency the customer or the salesperson feels. Successful internal sellers can communicate that sense of urgency by relating to the needs of the internal customer. Just as they do with external customers, salespeople need to communicate the need to act now when they sell internally. They need to secure commitment to the desired course of action. Also, just as with external customers, the salesperson should be sure to say thank you when someone agrees to provide the support requested.

Selling to internal customers also means keeping issues professional. Personal relationships can and should be developed. But when conflicts arise, focus on the issue, not the person. Personalizing conflict makes it seem bigger and harder to resolve. For example, rather than saying, "Why won't you do this?" ask, "If you can't do this, how can we resolve the customer's concern?" This type of statement focuses the other individual on resolving the real problem rather than arguing about company policy or personal competence.

Be prepared to negotiate. Remember from Chapter 14 that negotiation is a set of techniques to resolve conflict. Conflicts between salespeople and members of the firm representing other areas will occur, and negotiation skills can be used to respond to conflicts professionally.

Salespeople must work with many elements of their organization. In fact, few jobs require the boundary-spanning coordination and management skill that the sales job needs. In the next section we examine the many areas of the company with which the salesperson works, what their needs are, and how they partner with the salesperson to deliver customer satisfaction.

COMPANY AREAS IMPORTANT TO SALESPEOPLE

The sales force interacts with many areas of the firm. Salespeople work with manufacturing, sales administration, customer service, and personnel. In some industries requiring customization of products, engineering is an important department for salespeople. Finance can get into the picture as well when that department determines which customers receive credit and what price is charged. In addition, salespeople work with members of their own department and the marketing department.

MANUFACTURING

Grafo Regia S.A. is a packaging and labeling firm in Monterrey, Mexico. Its clients include companies such as Kellogg, and it prints labels and boxes that are used around the world. A key competitive advantage for Grafo Regia is its ability to deliver small or large orders faster than its competitors. Because the primary competitive advantage is based on manufacturing, the sales managers and salespeople spend a great deal of time in the factory learning the manufacturing processes. More important, these salespeople have established personal relationships with workers at

Salespeople who develop internal partnerships with people in areas such as manufacturing and service can count on their internal partners for support.

SuperStock

Bill Lai/The Image Works

every level in the plant. Salespeople even play on manufacturing softball teams in a local corporate league, even though they may have to fly home from Kellogg's headquarters in Battle Creek, Michigan, to make a game.

These personal relationships help Grafo Regia respond quickly to customer needs. If Kellogg needs to change a Frosted Flakes package to include a promotion involving the San Antonio Spurs just for the San Antonio market, Grafo Regia can do it faster than anyone else. One main reason is that manufacturing and sales are on the same team and are not viewed as separate entities.

In general, manufacturing is concerned with producing product at the lowest possible cost. Thus in most cases manufacturing wants long production runs, little customization, and low inventories. Customers, however, want their purchases shipped immediately and custom-made to their exact specifications. Salespeople may have to negotiate compromises between manufacturing and the customer. Salespeople should also develop relationships with manufacturing so that they can make accurate promises and guarantees to customers.

ADMINISTRATION

The functions of order entry, billing, credit, and employee compensation require each company to have an administrative department. This department processes orders and sees that the salesperson gets paid for them. Employees in this area (as discussed earlier) are often evaluated on how quickly they process orders and how quickly the company receives customer payment. Salespeople can greatly influence both processes and realize substantial personal benefit for themselves.

The credit department is an important part of administration. Understanding the needs of the credit department and assisting it in collecting payments can better position the salesperson to help customers receive credit later. A credit representative who knows you will help collect a payment when a problem arises is more likely to grant credit to one of your customers. Some companies do not pay commission until after the customer has paid to ensure that salespeople sell to creditworthy accounts. These companies, such as Force Computers in San Jose, California, believe a close working relationship between sales and credit is critical to the financial health of the company.[4]

SHIPPING

The scheduling of product shipments may be part of sales administration or manufacturing, or it may stand alone. In any case salespeople need the help of the shipping department. When salespeople make special promises to expedite a delivery, they actually must depend on shipping to carry out the promise. Shipping managers focus on costs, and they often keep their costs under control by planning efficient shipping routes and moving products quickly through warehouses. Expedited or special-handling deliveries can interfere with plans for efficient shipping. Salespeople who make promises that shipping cannot or will not fulfill are left with egg on their faces. John Munn, a Coca-Cola key accounts representative, will help load and drive a delivery truck when one of his accounts needs an expedited shipment so that his promise is fulfilled with minimal interruption in the warehouse.

CUSTOMER SERVICE

Salespeople also need to interact with customer service. The need for this relationship should be obvious, but many salespeople arrogantly ignore the information obtained by customer service representatives. A technician who fixes the company's products often goes into more customers' offices or plants than the salesperson does. The technician often has early warning concerning a customer's switch to a competitor, a change in customer needs, or failure of a product to satisfy. For example, if an IBM technician spies a competitor's computer in the customer's office, the technician can ask whether the unit is on trial. If a good working relationship exists between the technician and the salesperson, the technician will warn the salesperson that the account is considering a competitive product. Close relationships and support of customer or technical service representatives mean not only better customer service but faster and more direct information flow to the salesperson. This information will help the salesperson gain and keep customers.

Salespeople, in turn, can help customer service by setting reasonable expectations for product performance with customers, training customers in the proper use of the product, and handling complaints promptly. Technicians are evaluated on the number of service calls they make each day and how long the product works between service calls, among other things. Salespeople can reduce some service calls by setting the right expectations for product performance. Salespeople can also extend the amount of time between calls by training customers in the proper use of the product and in preventive maintenance. An important by-product of such actions should be higher customer satisfaction.

MARKETING

Sales is part of marketing in some firms and separate from marketing in others. Marketing and sales should be highly coordinated because their functions are closely related.[5] Both are concerned with providing the right product to the customer in the most efficient and effective manner. Sales acts as the eyes and ears of marketing, while marketing develops the promotions and products that salespeople sell. Salespeople act as eyes and ears by informing the marketing department of competitor actions, customer trends, and other important market information. Marketing serves salespeople by using that information to create promotional programs or design new products. Marketing is also responsible for generating leads through trade show exhibiting, direct mail programs, advertising, and public relations.

Unfortunately, not all marketing and sales departments just naturally get along. In one survey one-third of the sales and marketing managers believed that the relationship between the two departments was average or poor.[6] In another study about two-thirds of the respondents (mostly from sales) rated their company's marketing programs as poor.[7] The biggest problem seems to be a lack of communication. In yet another study the lack of communication led to misunderstandings concerning responsibility and roles for each department. Neither sales nor marketing knew who was responsible for developing strategies, marketing and sales plans, and tactics.[8] Proactive salespeople, however, won't wait for marketing managers to make the first move. Rather than complain about poor marketing programs, these salespeople and sales managers prefer to participate in marketing decisions and keep communication lines open. When sales and marketing work together, salespeople have better programs with which to sell.

SALES

Within any sales force, there may be several types of salespeople. As you learned in earlier chapters, global account managers may work with the largest accounts while other representatives handle the rest of the customers, and the salesperson must interact with certain sales executives and sales managers. How these people work together is the subject of the next section.

PARTNERS IN THE SALES ORGANIZATION

The sales function may be organized in many different ways, but no matter how it is organized, it is rarely perfect. Usually some customer overlap exists among salespeople, meaning several salespeople have to work together to serve the needs of one account. Customer needs may require direct customer contact with the sales executive as well as the salesperson. At the same time, the salesperson must operate in an environment that is influenced by the policies and procedures created by that same sales executive and executed by the salesperson's immediate manager. In this section we examine how the activities of sales management affect salespeople.

SALES MANAGEMENT

Salespeople should understand the roles of both sales executives and field sales managers. Salespeople who are able to develop partnerships with their managers will have more resources available to perform at a higher level.

THE SALES EXECUTIVE

The sales executive is the manager at the top of the sales force hierarchy. This person is a policy maker, making decisions about how the sales force will accomplish corporate objectives. Sales executives play a vital role in determining the company's strategies with respect to new products, new markets, sales forecasts, prices, and competition. The executives determine the size and organization of the sales force, develop annual and long-range plans, and monitor and control sales efforts. Duties of the sales executive include forecasting overall sales, budgeting, setting sales quotas, and designing compensation programs.

SIZE AND ORGANIZATION OF THE SALES FORCE The sales executive determines how many salespeople are needed to achieve the company's sales and customer satisfaction targets. In addition, the sales executive must determine what types of salespeople are needed. For example, it is the sales executive who determines whether global account management is needed. Many other types of salespeople can be selected, which we will discuss later in this chapter. For now, keep in mind that the sales executive determines the level of customer satisfaction necessary to achieve sales objectives and then designs a sales force to achieve those goals. How that sales force is put together is important because salespeople often have to work together to deliver appropriate customer service and successfully accomplish sales goals.

FORECASTING Sales executives use a number of techniques to arrive at sales forecasts. One of the most widely used techniques is **bottom-up forecasting,** or simply adding each salesperson's own forecast into a forecast for total company sales. At each level of management, the forecast would normally be adjusted based on the manager's experience and broader perspective. This technique allows the information to come from the people closest to the market: the salespeople. Also, the forecast comes from the people with the responsibility for making those sales. But salespeople tend to be optimistic and may overestimate sales, or they may underestimate future sales if they know their bonuses depend on exceeding forecasts or if they think their quotas will be raised.

Salespeople are especially important to the forecasting process when the executive is attempting to forecast international sales.[9] Statistics used in the United States to forecast sales are often not available in other countries or, if available, may be unreliable. Therefore, the only reliable forecasting mechanism is the salesperson's own idea of what can be sold. For example, Harley-Davidson depends heavily on its salespeople in other countries for accurate forecasts of motorcycle sales. Harley-Davidson's international sales are more than 20 percent of total sales, making such forecasts important to its planning. Salespeople are the most important source of market information in international markets.

EXPENSE BUDGETS Managers sometimes use expense budgets to control costs. An expense budget may be expressed in dollars (for example, the salesperson may be allowed to spend up to $500) or as a percentage of sales volume (such as expenses cannot exceed 10 percent of sales). A regional manager or salesperson may be awarded a bonus for spending less than the budget allocates. However, such a bonus may encourage the salesperson to underspend, which could hurt sales performance. For example, if a salesperson refuses to give out samples, customers may not be able to visualize how the product will work; thus some may not buy. The salesperson has reduced expenses but hurt sales.

Although salespeople may have limited input into a budget, they do spend the money. Ultimately it is the salesperson's responsibility to manage the territorial budget. The salesperson not only has control over how much is spent and whether expenditures are over or under budget but also, and more important, decides where to place resources. Recall from Chapter 16 that these resources, such as samples and trial units or direct mailers, are investments in future sales. If they are used unwisely, the salesperson may still meet the expense budget but fail to meet his or her sales quota.

CONTROL AND QUOTA SETTING The sales executive faces the challenge of setting up a balanced control system that will encourage each sales manager and salesperson to maximize his or her individual results through effective self-control. As we have pointed out throughout this text, salespeople operate somewhat independently. However, the control system management devises can help salespeople manage themselves more effectively.

Quotas are a useful technique for controlling the sales force. A **quota** represents a quantitative minimum level of acceptable performance for a specific period. A **sales quota** is the minimum number of sales in units, and a **revenue quota** is the minimum sales revenue necessary for acceptable performance. Often sales quotas are simple breakdowns of the company's total sales forecast. Thus the total of all sales quotas equals the sales forecast. Other types of quotas can also be used. Understanding quotas is important to the salesperson because performance relative to quota is evaluated by management.

Profit quotas or **gross margin quotas** are minimum levels of acceptable profit or gross margin performance. These quotas motivate the sales force to sell more profitable products or to sell to more profitable customers. Some companies assign points to each product based on the product's gross margin. More points are assigned to higher-margin products. The salesperson can then meet a point quota by selling either a lot of low-margin products or fewer high-margin products. For example, assume an office equipment company sells fax machines and copiers. The profit margin (not including salesperson compensation) on copiers is 30 percent but only 20 percent on fax machines. Copiers may be worth three points each, whereas faxes are worth two. If the salesperson's quota is 12 points, the quota can be reached by selling four copiers, or six faxes, or some combination of both.

Activity quotas, similar to the activity goals we discussed in the preceding chapter, are minimal expectations of activities for each salesperson. The company sets these quotas to control the activities of the sales force. This type of quota is important in situations where the sales cycle is long and sales are few because activities can be observed more frequently than sales. For example, for some medical equipment, the sales cycle is longer than one year, and a salesperson may sell only one or two units each quarter. Having a monthly sales target in this case would be inappropriate, but requiring a certain minimum number of calls to be made is reasonable. The assumption made by management is that if the salesperson is performing the proper activities, sales will follow. Activities for which quotas may be established include number of demonstrations, total customer calls, number of calls on prospects, or number of displays set up.

COMPENSATION AND EVALUATION An important task of the sales executive is to establish the company's basic compensation and evaluation system. The compensation system must satisfy the needs of both the salespeople and the company. You, as a salesperson, need an equitable, stable, understandable system that motivates you to meet your objectives. The company, however, needs a system that encourages you to sell products at a profitable price and in the right amounts.

Salespeople want a system that bases rewards on effort and results. Compensation must also be uniform within the company and in line with what competitors' salespeople receive. If competitors' salespeople earn more, you will want to leave and work for that competitor. But your company expects the compensation system to attract and keep good salespeople and to encourage you to do specific things. The system should reward outstanding performance while achieving the proper balance between sales results and costs.

Compensation often relates to quotas. As with quotas, salespeople who perceive the system as unfair may give up or leave the firm. A stable compensation system ensures that salespeople can reap the benefits of their efforts, whereas a constantly changing system may lead them to constantly change their activities but never make any money. A system that is not understandable will be ignored.

The sales executive decides how much income will be based on salary or incentive pay. The salesperson may receive a **salary,** a regular payment regardless of performance, or **incentive pay,** which is tied to some level of performance. There are two types of incentives: commission and bonus. A **commission** is incentive pay for an individual sale, whereas a **bonus** is incentive pay for overall performance in one or more areas. For example, a bonus may be paid for acquiring a certain number of new customers, reaching a specified level of total sales in units, or selling a certain amount of a new product.

Sales executives can choose to pay salespeople a straight salary, a straight commission, or some combination of salary, commission, and/or bonus. Most firms

EXHIBIT 17.2

How Different Types of
Compensation Plans Pay

		Amount Paid to Salesperson			
Month	Sales Revenue	Straight Salary	Straight Commission*	Combination†	Point Plan**
January	$50,000 6 copiers 10 faxes	$3,500	$5,000	$1,500 (salary) 3,000 (commission) 4,500 (total)	$3,800
February	$60,000 6 copiers 15 faxes	3,500	6,000	1,500 (salary) 3,600 (commission) 5,100 (total)	4,800
March	$20,000 2 copiers 5 faxes	3,500	2,000	1,500 (salary) 1,200 (commission) 2,700 (total)	1,600

*Commission plan pays 10 percent of sales revenue.
†Commission portion pays 6 percent of sales revenue.
**Copiers are worth three points, faxes are worth two, and each point is worth $100 in commission.
Note: These commission rates are used only to illustrate how compensation schemes work. Point plans, for example, do not necessarily always yield the lowest compensation.

opt for some combination of salary and bonus or salary and commission. Fewer than 4 percent pay only commission, and slightly fewer than 5 percent pay only salary. Exhibit 17.2 illustrates how various types of compensation plans work.

Under the **straight salary** method, a salesperson receives a fixed amount of money for work during a specified time. The salesperson is assured of a steady income and can develop a sense of loyalty to customers. The company also has more control over the salesperson. Because income does not depend directly on results, the company can ask the salesperson to do things in the best interest of the company, even if those activities may not lead to immediate sales. Straight salary, however, provides little financial incentive for salespeople to sell more. For example, in Exhibit 17.2, the salesperson receives $3,500 per month, no matter how much is sold.

Straight salary plans are used when sales require long periods of negotiation, when a team of salespeople is involved and individual results cannot be measured, or when other aspects of the marketing mix (such as advertising) are more important than the salesperson's efforts in generating sales (as in trade selling of consumer products). Most sales trainees also receive a straight salary.

A **straight commission** plan pays a certain amount per sale and includes a base and a rate but not a salary. The **commission base,** the item from which commission is determined, is often unit sales, dollar sales, or gross margin. The **commission rate,** which determines the amount paid, is expressed as a percentage of the base (such as 10 percent of sales or 8 percent of gross margin) or as a dollar amount (like $100 per sale). Exhibit 17.2 illustrates two straight commission plans: One pays 10 percent of sales revenue, and the other is a point plan that pays $100 per point (using the copier and fax example we discussed previously).

Commission plans often include a draw. A **draw** is money paid to the salesperson against future commissions, in essence a loan that guarantees a stable cash flow. For example, in Exhibit 17.3 the salesperson receives a draw of $1,000 per month. No commissions were earned during January, but the salesperson still received $1,000. In February the rep earned $1,500, but $500 went to pay back

EXHIBIT 17.3

An Example of a Draw
Compensation Plan

Month	Draw	Commission Earned	Payment to Salesperson	Balance Owed to Company
January	$1,000	$ 0	$1,000	$1,000
February	1,000	1,500	1,000	500
March	1,000	2,000	1,500	

some of the draw from January, and the rep received only $1,000. In March the rep earned $2,000, of which $500 finished paying off the balance from January. Thus the rep was given $1,500 in March.

Straight commission plans have the advantage of tying the salesperson's compensation directly to performance, thus providing more financial incentive for the salesperson to work hard. However, salespeople on straight commission have little company loyalty and certainly are less willing to perform activities, such as paperwork, that do not directly lead to sales. Xerox experimented with such a plan but found that customer service suffered, as did company loyalty among salespeople.

Companies that do not emphasize service to customers or do not anticipate long-term customer relationships (like a company selling kitchen appliances directly to consumers) typically use commission plans. Such plans are also used when the sales force includes many part-timers because part-timers can earn more when their pay is tied to their performance. Also, part-timers may need the extra motivation straight commission can provide.

Under a bonus plan, salespeople receive a lump-sum payment for a certain level of performance over a specified time. Bonuses resemble commissions, but the amount paid depends on total performance, not on each individual sale. Bonuses, awarded monthly, quarterly, or annually, are always used with salary and/or commissions in **combination plans.** Metamor Technologies (a Chicago computer company) is like a growing number of companies that now pay salespeople a bonus for reaching customer service goals. For example, if a client agrees to serve as a reference and gives high marks on a customer satisfaction survey, the salesperson receives the maximum customer service bonus.[10]

Sales executives frequently combine two or three of the basic methods to form the compensation plan. Combination plans, also called salary-plus-commission plans, provide salary and commission and offer the greatest flexibility for motivating and controlling the activities of salespeople. The plans can incorporate the advantages and avoid the disadvantages of using any of the basic plans alone. Note in Exhibit 17.2 that the straight salary plan pays a higher salary than the combination plan, but the difference can be offset by the incentive portion.

The main disadvantage of combination plans lies in their complexity. Salespeople confused by this complexity could unknowingly perform the wrong activities, or sales managers could unintentionally design a program that rewards the wrong activities. Using the earlier office equipment example, if faxes and copiers were worth the same commission (for example, $100 per sale), the salesperson would sell whatever was easiest to sell. If faxes were easier to sell than copiers, the firm may make less money because salespeople would expend all of their effort selling a lower-profit product unless the volume sold made up for the lower margin. Even then, however, the firm may be stuck with a warehouse of unsold copiers.

Management uses salary-plus-commission plans to motivate salespeople (through commissions) to increase revenues while continuing to perform nonselling activities (paid for with salary) such as customer service. When management wants to develop long-term customer relations, salary-plus-bonus plans are used so that less emphasis is placed on getting new (and commissionable) sales. Bonus plans are also used when the sales effort involves a team of people.

Thinking It Through

As a buyer, under which plan would you prefer your salesperson to work? Which would you prefer if you were a salesperson? What conflicts might occur between buyer and seller because of the type of compensation plan?

FIELD SALES MANAGERS

Salespeople report directly not to a sales executive, but to a **field sales manager.** Field sales managers hire salespeople, evaluate their performance, train them, and perform other important tasks. Salespeople find it useful to partner with their managers because the managers often represent the salespeople to other parts of the organization. Also, the salesperson often has to sell the manager first on any new idea before the idea can be pitched to others in management. Building a partnering relationship with managers can go a long way toward getting ideas accepted.[11]

Sales managers can provide "curbside coaching" to their salespeople immediately after a sales call to help improve selling skills.

Michael Newman/PhotoEdit

EVALUATING PERFORMANCE

Field sales managers are responsible for evaluating the performance of their salespeople. The easiest method of evaluating performance is to simply add up the amount of sales that the salesperson makes. But sales managers must also rate their salespeople's customer service level, product knowledge, and other, less tangible qualities. Some companies, such as Federal Express, use customer satisfaction surveys to evaluate salespeople. In other companies the manager rates each salesperson, using evaluation forms that list the desired aspects. (An example of an evaluation form appears in Exhibit 17.4.) Such evaluations help managers determine training needs, promotions, and pay raises.

The records and reports salespeople submit also play an important role in communicating their activities to the sales manager. The manager then uses these reports to evaluate performance in a manner similar to the way the salesperson would. But these written reports are not enough; sales managers should also make calls with salespeople to directly observe their performance. These observations can be the basis for recommendations for improving individual performance or for commending outstanding performance. Other information, such as customer response to a new strategy, can be gained by making calls. This information should be shared with upper management to improve strategies.

TRAINING

The sales manager trains new hires and provides refresher training for experienced salespeople. To determine what refresher training they need, managers often use information gathered while observing salespeople making sales calls. Content of training for new salespeople may be determined by a sales executive, but the field sales manager is often responsible for carrying out the training.

Most experienced salespeople welcome training when they perceive that it will improve their sales. Unfortunately, salespeople often view training as an inconvenience that takes away from precious selling time. Steve Herzog, president of Herzog & Associates of Knoxville, Tennessee, says that ongoing skill training of experienced salespeople is part of a "trend toward creating an environment that consistently brings out the best in all personnel." Salespeople who take advantage of such training are far more likely to progress in their career.

EXHIBIT 17.4 Behavioral Observation Scale (BOS)		Almost Never						Almost Always
	1. Checks deliveries to see whether they have arrived on time.	1	2	3	4	5	6	7
	2. Files sales reports on time.	1	2	3	4	5	6	7
	3. Uses promotional brochures and correspondence with potential accounts.	1	2	3	4	5	6	7
	4. Monitors competitors' activities.	1	2	3	4	5	6	7
	5. Brushes up on selling techniques.	1	2	3	4	5	6	7
	6. Reads marketing research reports.	1	2	3	4	5	6	7
	7. Prospects for new accounts.	1	2	3	4	5	6	7
	8. Makes service calls.	1	2	3	4	5	6	7
	9. Answers customer inquiries when they occur.	1	2	3	4	5	6	7

Professional salespeople constantly seek to upgrade their skills; here, a group at Infocus Systems is reviewing a role play sales call.

Mark Richards/PhotoEdit

You should continue to welcome training, no matter how successful you are. It always offers the opportunity to improve your performance, or at least achieve the same level with less effort. Also, as you will see in Chapter 18, continuing to learn is important to the salesperson who is part of a learning organization.

MANAGING ETHICS IN SALES

Salespeople, particularly those within certain industries, have earned a reputation that is unfavorable. Most salespeople, though, want to act ethically. Because we have emphasized throughout this book methods of selling that help people solve problems and satisfy needs, we believe it is important to understand what companies do to encourage ethical behavior and how salespeople should work with their sales management partners to choose ethical options. First we discuss the sales executive's role in making ethics policy. Then we cover the roles of the field sales manager and the salesperson in implementing that policy.

ETHICS AND THE SALES EXECUTIVE

Part of a sales executive's job is to determine corporate policy concerning what is considered ethical and what is not and how unethical behavior will be investigated and punished. In addition, the sales executive must ensure that other policies, such as the performance measurement and compensation policies, also support the ethics of the organization. Performance measurement and compensation policies that reward only outcomes may inadvertently encourage salespeople to act unethically because of pressure to achieve and a culture supporting the credo "the end justifies the means." But when behavioral performance measurement systems are also in place, the compensation system can reward those who do things the right way.[12] Although unethical behaviors may result in short-term gain (and therefore may accidentally be rewarded in an outcome-only compensation scheme), they can have serious long-term effects, such as loss of customers, unhappy salespeople who quit, and other negative outcomes.[13]

Sales executives must therefore develop a culture that creates behavioral norms regarding how things should be done and what behaviors will not be tolerated. Such a culture can be enhanced through the development of formal policy, training courses on ethics, ethics review boards, and an open-door policy. **Open-door policies** are general management techniques that allow subordinates to bypass immediate managers and take concerns straight to upper management when the subordinates perceive a lack of support from the immediate manager. Open-door policies enhance an ethical culture because salespeople can feel free to discuss troublesome issues that involve their managers with someone in a position to respond. **Ethics review boards** may function in the same way, providing expert advice to salespeople who are unsure of the ethical consequences of an action. Ethics review boards may consist of experts inside and outside the company who are responsible for reviewing ethics policies, investigating allegations of unethical behavior, and acting as a sounding board for employees. Sales executives play an important role in determining how the corporate culture will support ethical activity by salespeople.

Salespeople also have the right to expect ethical treatment from their company. Fair treatment concerning compensation, promotion policies, territory allocation, and other actions should be delivered. Compensation is probably the area with the most common concerns, although problems can arise in all areas. Compensation problems can include slow payment, hidden caps, or compensation plan changes after the sale.

For example, one company paid its salespeople a straight commission of about 10 percent. When a salesperson sold one major account $11 million worth of product, the company changed her commission plan to a salary plus commission to cut her payment. In another example a company refused to pay a salesperson all of his commission because he earned more than the vice president of sales. The company claimed there was a **cap,** or limit, on earnings. Caps are not unethical; what was unethical was that the salesperson was not made aware of the cap prior to selling. Although some problems do occur, most companies want to hire and keep good salespeople, and most businesspeople are ethical.

Thinking It Through

Should schools have ethics review boards? What advantages would such boards have for the student? For the teacher? Would salespeople reap the same types of benefits if their companies had ethics review boards?

ETHICS AND THE FIELD SALES MANAGER

Salespeople often ask managers for direction on how to handle ethical problems, and the sales manager is usually the first person to investigate complaints of unethical behavior. Field sales managers can provide a role model for salespeople by demonstrating ethical behavior in role-plays during training or when conducting sales calls in the field. Sales managers should also avoid teaching high-pressure techniques and manipulative methods of selling.

RESPONDING TO UNETHICAL REQUESTS

Salespeople, however, may find themselves facing a sales manager who encourages them to engage in unethical behavior. When that situation occurs, a salesperson has several ways to avoid engaging in such behavior.[14] Perhaps the most obvious option is to find another job, but that is not always the best solution. If the organizational culture supports the unethical request, however, finding another job may be the only choice. Exhibit 17.5 lists choices available to the salesperson.

Another way to handle unethical requests is to blow the whistle, or report the behavior, if the salesperson has adequate evidence (if adequate evidence is not

Like Tiger Woods, sales managers are role models whether they want to be or not. As role models, it is imperative that they model ethical behavior at all times.

Michael Newman/PhotoEdit

available, sometimes simply threatening to blow the whistle may work). If this course of action is followed, the salesperson must be ready to accept a perception of disloyalty, retaliation by the manager, or other consequences. However, if senior management is sincere in efforts to promote ethical behavior, steps should be taken to minimize those negative outcomes. If an open-door policy or an ethics review board exists, the salesperson can take the concern to higher levels for review. For example, the salesperson could say, I'm not sure that is appropriate. I'd like to get the opinion of the ethics review board. If the action is unethical, the sales manager may back down at that point. It is also possible that the manager will try to coerce the salesperson into not applying to the ethics review board; if that is the case, another course of action may prove to be a better choice.

Another strategy is to negotiate an alternative. This response requires the salesperson to identify an alternative course of action with a high probability of

EXHIBIT 17.5

Strategies for Handling Unethical Requests from a Manager

- Leave the organization or ask for a transfer.
- Negotiate an alternative course of action.
- Blow the whistle, internally or externally.
- Threaten to blow the whistle.
- Appeal to a higher authority.
- Agree to the demand but fail to carry it out.
- Refuse to comply with the request.
- Ignore the request.

success. For example, if a sales manager tells the salesperson to offer a prospect a bribe, the salesperson should be prepared to prove that a price reduction would be just as effective. A similar tactic is to simply ignore the request. The salesperson may say to the manager that the request was carried out, when in fact it was not; the potential problem with this approach is that the salesperson has admitted to carrying out an unethical act (even though she or he did not), which can lead to future problems. Finally, the salesperson can simply deny the request. Denial can be a dangerous action in that it opens the salesperson to possible retaliation, particularly retaliation that is not obviously linked to the denial, such as denying access to training or reducing the size of the salesperson's territory.

The salesperson's choice of action will depend on how much proof is available, what alternative actions to the unethical action exist, and the type of relationship with the manager. Other factors to consider include the ethical climate of the organization and whether an open-door policy exists. The salesperson, however, is always in control of his or her behavior and should never rationalize a behavior by placing responsibility on the sales manager.

SALESPEOPLE AS PARTNERS

Many types of salespeople exist, including telemarketing representatives, field salespeople, product specialists, and account specialists. Often there is some overlap in responsibilities; when overlap occurs, companies should have policies that facilitate serving the customer.

GEOGRAPHIC SALESPEOPLE

Most sales departments are organized geographically. A **geographic salesperson** is assigned a specific geographic territory in which to sell the company's products and services. Companies often combine geographic territories into larger branches, zones, or regions. For example, Eli Lilly has geographic regions that include 50 or more salespeople. Each Lilly salesperson has responsibility for a specific geographic area. For example, one rep may call on physicians in a portion of Dallas, using ZIP code boundaries to determine the territory; that rep may have all physicians in ZIP codes 75212, 75213, 75218, 75239, 75240, and 75252. Geographic salespeople may also work with account managers, product specialists, inside salespeople, and other members of the company's sales team.

ACCOUNT SALESPEOPLE

Companies may organize salespeople by account in several ways. The most extreme example is to give a salesperson the responsibility to sell to only one company but at every location of that company in the country or the world. In another common form of specialization, some salespeople develop new accounts while others maintain existing accounts. Developing new accounts requires different skills than maintaining an already sold account. One RCA radio communications division uses field salespeople to develop new accounts and a telemarketing sales force to maintain the accounts. The field salespeople must identify prospects from noncustomers and sell the product. Once the RCA product has been installed, the account becomes the responsibility of the telemarketing sales force.

Similar customers often have similar needs, whereas different types of customers may have very different needs for the same product. In such cases salespeople may specialize in calling on only one or a few customer types, although they sell the same products. NCR has different sales forces for calling on manufacturing companies, retailers, and financial companies. Andritz, an international heavy machinery company, has salespeople who sell only to paper producers and other salespeople who sell only to wastewater treatment plants, even though the same product is being sold. Some Procter & Gamble salespeople call on central buying offices for grocery store chains; others call on food wholesalers.

Companies also divide their customers on the basis of size. Large customers, sometimes called **key accounts,** may have a salesperson assigned only to that account; in some cases a small sales force is assigned to one large account. Rockwell Automation has an account executive, a systems engineer, and a customer support representative assigned to each of certain large accounts. Steve Kelley, director of Rockwell Automation's Canadian division, says, "When our sales and service teams work together, we can optimize the solutions that we deliver to our customers."[15]

In other firms one company executive coordinates all the salespeople who call on an account throughout the nation or the world. These executives are called **national account managers (NAMs)** or **strategic account managers (SAMs).** These account managers are more than salespeople; they are business executives. As Unisource, a distribution company in Valley Forge, Pennsylvania, discovered, partnering with global accounts requires executive-level account management.[16]

Strategic account managers manage large teams of salespeople. John Slattery, for example, is Xerox's strategic account manager for the AT&T account. He works with more than 200 local Xerox people located in district offices around the world, as well as service specialists assigned to AT&T and other global accounts.[17] Xerox also assigns a senior executive to accounts like AT&T; account managers like Slattery can count on these senior executives for upper-level customer contact, internal politicking to support sales strategies, and other activities.[18]

The local geographic rep's responsibility may involve coordinating delivery with the local customer. This coordination may also require customer training on the product or working with a local store manager to set up displays, plan inventories, and so on. Local reps should also look for sales opportunities in the customer's location and provide this information to the SAM. They often become the eyes and ears of the SAM and provide early notice of opportunities or threats in the account, just as a service rep does for the geographic rep. IBM found that local reps did not want to work with SAMs because there was no compensation for servicing those accounts. So IBM completely revamped the compensation plan to encourage local reps' participation in strategic account selling and service.[19] SAMs often report directly to the vice president of sales or to a director of global sales, as illustrated in Exhibit 17.6, but work with geographic reps.

As described in Chapter 7, a **house account** is handled by a sales or marketing executive in addition to that executive's regular duties, and no commission is paid on any sales from that account. House accounts are often key accounts, but not all key accounts are house accounts. The main difference is that house accounts have no "true" salesperson. Wal-Mart has negotiated to be a house

EXHIBIT 17.6

SAMs in the Sales Force
Although SAMs and
geographic salespeople
have different
immediate managers,
they still work together.
SAMs coordinate the
efforts of geographic
reps within local buying
offices of global
accounts.

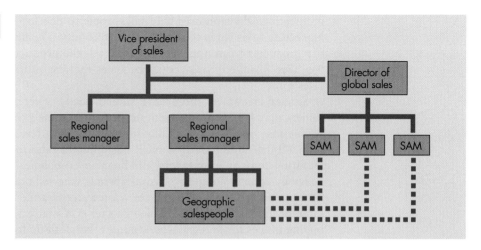

account with some suppliers with the expectation that those suppliers will pass on to Wal-Mart what they do not have to pay in commission or salary. General Dynamics attempted the same strategy when buying, but abandoned the plan upon realizing that lower costs also meant reduced service.

Somewhat different is the mega-account strategy used at Motorola. The top 20 international accounts are actually managed by Motorola's CEO, who works directly with the CEO in each account. These accounts are a form of house account, but the CEO does have sales responsibility and sales goals to achieve.

PRODUCT SPECIALISTS

When companies have diverse products, their salespeople often specialize by types of products. Johnson & Johnson, which sells baby products, has two specialized sales forces: the disposable products sales force and the toiletries sales force. Hewlett-Packard has separate sales forces that specialize in selling computers, electronic test instruments, electronic components, medical test equipment, or analytical test equipment. Each sales force has its own regional, district, and area sales managers. Insuror's of Texas has salespeople who specialize in auto insurance, others who specialize in homeowner's insurance, and still others who specialize in medical and disability insurance. However, all of Insuror's salespeople operate under the same sales management structure. Regardless of the management structure, sometimes the technical knowledge requirements are so great that organizing territories by product makes sense.

In addition to having management responsibilities similar to those for geographic reps, product salespeople must coordinate their activities with those of salespeople from other divisions. Success can be greater for all involved when leads and customer information are shared. For example, a Hewlett-Packard test instrument salesperson may have a customer who is also a prospect for electronic components. Sharing that information with the electronic components rep can help build a relationship that can pay off with leads for test instruments.

INSIDE VERSUS OUTSIDE

Our discussion to this point has focused on outside salespeople, called **field salespeople**—that is, salespeople who sell at the customer's location. **Inside salespeople** sell at their own company's location. Inside salespeople may handle walk-in customers or be telemarketing salespeople, or they may handle both duties. For example, a plumbing supply distributor may sell entirely to plumbers and employ inside salespeople who sell to those plumbers who come into the distributorship to buy products.

As we discussed in Chapter 7, the job of some telemarketing is to provide leads for field salespeople. Other types of telemarketing salespeople include account managers, field support reps, and customer service reps.[20] A telemarketer who is an account manager has the same responsibilities and duties a field salesperson does except that all business is conducted over the phone. Hewlett-Packard's test and measurement group, for example, has 40 account telemanagers, with accounts ranging from small electronics manufacturers to *Fortune* 100 companies.[21]

A **field support rep** is a telemarketer who works with field salespeople and does more than prospect for leads. For example, field support reps at RPG Digital Imaging do Web research, make phone calls to gather information and develop contacts, and build rapport with prospects. The field support rep may also cross-sell, upgrade, or seek reorders. Together with RPG field salespeople, field support reps develop account strategies, handle customer concerns, and perform similar duties.[22] We discuss these representatives further when we discuss team selling strategies shortly.

Customer service reps are inbound salespeople who handle customer concerns. **Inbound** means they respond to telephone calls placed by customers, rather than **outbound**, which means the telemarketer makes the phone call (prospectors, account managers, and field support telemarketers are outbound reps). For example, if you call the 800 telephone number on the back of a tube of Crest toothpaste, you will speak with an inbound customer service rep.

SALES TEAMS

A growing number of companies are adopting a team approach to sales.[23] Rockwell Automation's team approach to some key accounts is an example of a sales team. This concept is being used by companies that recognize they can best build partnerships by empowering one person, the account manager, to represent the organization. In **team selling** a group of salespeople support a single account. Each person on the team brings a different area of expertise or handles different responsibilities. As you see in Exhibit 17.7, each specialist can be called on to team up with the account managers.

EXHIBIT 17.7

Team Selling Organization
In team selling, product specialists work with account managers, who have total account responsibility. Product specialists are responsible for sales and service of only a limited portion of the product line and may work with several account managers.

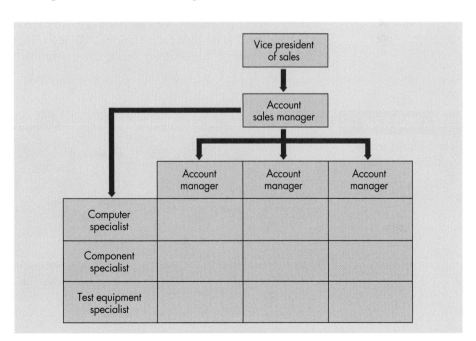

Before adopting team selling, companies may have had one salesperson for each product line. Xerox, for example, once had separate copier, duplicator, supplies, fax machine, printer, computer workstation, and communication network salespeople all calling on the same buyer. These reps would pass in customers' lobbies without recognizing one another. Customers grew tired of seeing as many as seven salespeople from Xerox. Now one account manager calls on the buyer and brings in product specialists as needed.

Xerox uses permanent teams, whereas Dendrite International, a software company, forms teams as needed. The company may involve as many as 50 employees over the 12-month cycle of any given sale. In both cases, though, salespeople are responsible for coordinating the efforts of the specialists and determining who is brought in and at what point in the sale.[24]

In an extension of team selling, **multilevel selling,** members at various levels of the sales organization call on their counterparts in the buying organization. (As charted in Exhibit 17.8, for example, the vice president of sales calls on the vice president of purchasing.) Multilevel selling can take place without a formal multilevel sales team if the account representative requests upper-level management's involvement in the sale. For example, you may ask your company's vice president of sales to call on the vice president of operations at a prospect's company to secure top-level support for your proposal.

Another type of sales team is made up of the field rep and the field support rep (see Exhibit 17.9). Some companies use one telemarketer for each field salesperson, whereas other companies have several salespeople working with a telemarketer. The telemarketer performs as many selling tasks as possible over the telephone. But when a sales call is needed at the customer's location, the field support rep makes the appointment for the field rep. Good communication and joint planning are necessary to avoid overbooking the field rep, as well as to prevent duplication of effort.

Maddocks Systems, a Vancouver, Canada–based logistics software firm, uses an approach to team selling that is somewhat similar to the Teradata–EDS relationship. "Our products go especially well with other companies' satellite communication systems that are attached to each truck to notify drivers of new jobs while they are on the road," says Sean Jennings, account manager for Maddocks. Jennings works frequently with account executives from the satellite company to share leads and give joint presentations. "When competing with other software vendors, I often get the contract because my customers also get the bonus of my

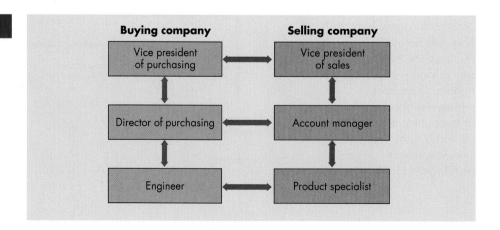

EXHIBIT 17.8

Forming Sales Teams for Multilevel Selling

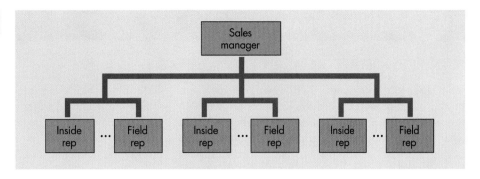

partner's satellite system." Not only does the sales team include someone from the satellite company, Maddocks also provides Jennings with representatives from marketing, inside sales, programming, and implementation departments.[25]

TECHNOLOGY AND TEAMWORK

Technology has greatly facilitated the growth of teams because it provides quick communication to anyone in the world. Technology also enables communication among people in different time zones, as conversations can be conducted via e-mail over a period of days, with none of the parties required to be in the office or on the phone at the same time. E-mail is used to keep the sales team informed, and some companies also communicate with customers via e-mail. IBM has taken its own technology and used it to develop methods of communicating and supporting field sales teams, as illustrated in Selling Scenario 17.1.

When Fallon McElligott, one of the country's fastest-growing advertising companies, made its pitch to win McDonald's Arch Deluxe advertising campaign, the company used a presentation that had been created by eight account supervisors from different areas of the firm. Moreover, most of the shared creative work was conducted electronically.[26] Each account manager would work on the presentation and then share the document with others. And yes, the company did win the Arch Deluxe account!

Many companies use sales teams to work with large accounts. Baxter, a hospital supply company, found that sales increased 50 percent faster in accounts handled by a team than by numerous salespeople acting independently.

SuperStock

IBM: TECHNOLOGY SUPPORTS TEAM SELLING

Team selling is most often used when customers are buying complex products or have significant information needs, when the account requires special treatment, and when a large number of people are involved in the buying process. Selling complex IBM computer systems fits that profile, and the company's team-selling strategy supports its sales. In fact, sometimes buyers make decisions with global implications, and salespeople in several countries may work on the same sale. Judicial use of its own technology has enabled IBM to build strategic account teams that serve global accounts efficiently and successfully.

One mechanism is comprehensive databases. Although IBM reps formerly had access to company files and knew which IBM computer systems each customer had, no records were available regarding competitive products that customers may also have. To obtain that information, the company purchased data from Dun & Bradstreet and Computer Intelligence. Further analysis of the data revealed a three-year buying cycle, so now IBM reps can target their accounts, knowing whom to call and about which system. As service technicians make calls, they can also use the same database and keep it up-to-date. The database is available to everyone in sales or service who works on the account.

IBM's direct marketing group also supports the field sales team. The field salespeople can, for example, use the company's intranet to integrate a direct marketing campaign to promote a seminar into their account strategy. As Kenton Erickson, IBM marketing manager, says, "Via the [IBM] intranet, they can download the invitation, personalize, and print a copy to deliver to their client." Also available on the intranet are Lotus Notes applications that enable members of the sales team to work on account projects together, even though they may never physically meet on the project. Individual team members can work on specific areas and then report on their work or even post it into the working document.

Technology is changing the nature of selling, particularly the way team selling is done. IBM is one company that has found many ways to use technology to support sales teams.

Sources: Kenton Erickson, "How IBM Marketers Capitalize on Their Intranet," *Direct Marketing to Business Report,* October 1996, pp. 15, 19; Donald Jackson, Scott Widmier, Ralph Giacobbe, and Janet Keith, "Examining the Use of Team Selling by Manufacturers' Representatives," *Industrial Marketing Management* 28 (1999), pp. 155–64; Laura Loro, "IBM Mends Marketing Using Databases," *Business Marketing,* February 1996, p. 24.

Conita Technologies uses a voice-activated system to help salespeople keep up with important information. While wireless Web applications are useful, until these applications can be integrated into cell phones, systems like the one Conita uses will make more sense. "The rep can access the system by cell phone in the back of a cab on the way to a client's office and obtain the latest trouble ticket or shipping information—whatever they need—through a voice interface," according to Conita's CEO, Jeff McElroy. International Computers Limited (ICL), of London, England, uses a similar system to enable its reps to access e-mail and calendars by phone. "Today's wireless handsets and pocket PCs will soon merge into a common set of technologies which will include voice as a must-have," according to Andy Irvine, ICL marketing manager. But until then, they'll make do with a voice-activated system.[27]

Summary

Successful salespeople manage resources and build internal partnerships—partnerships with people in order entry, credit, billing, and shipping, as well as sales and marketing. These partnerships allow salespeople to keep the promises they make to customers when someone else must carry out those promises.

Salespeople in learning organizations also have a responsibility to carry the voice of the customer to other areas of the organization. Successful learning organizations are more adept at adapting to changing customer needs and developing successful products when salespeople fulfill their role of speaking for the customer.

In the sales organization salespeople work with and for a sales executive and a field sales manager. The sales executive determines policy and maintains financial control over the sales organization. Salespeople participate in the development of forecasts that the sales executive uses in the planning process.

Another policy decision involves the method of compensation for the sales force. The four basic methods are straight salary, straight commission, bonus, and a combination plan. Straight commission plans provide strong financial incentive for salespeople but leave the company with little control over their activities. Salary plans give greater control to the company but offer less incentive for salespeople to work hard.

Sales executives are also responsible for creating a culture that supports ethical activities. Policies (such as open-door policies) can encourage salespeople to act ethically. Ethical review boards are also useful in reviewing ethics policies, investigating potential ethics violations, and counseling salespeople who have concerns about the ethics of possible actions. Sometimes, however, salespeople face unethical requests from their managers. If that occurs, salespeople can choose from several courses of actions, such as blowing the whistle or appealing to an ethics review board.

Partnerships must be built within the sales force, too. Some examples include team selling with product specialists, inside and outside teams, and multilevel selling.

KEY TERMS

activity quota   512
bonus   512
bottom-up forecasting   511
cap   518
combination plans   514
commission   512
commission base   513
commission rate   513
customer service rep   523
draw   513
ethics review board   518
field sales manager   515
field salespeople   522
field support rep   523
geographic salesperson   520
gross margin quota   512
house account   521
inbound   523
incentive pay   512

inside salespeople   522
internal partnerships   504
key accounts   521
multilevel selling   524
national account manager
   (NAM)   521
open-door policy   517
outbound   523
profit quota   512
quota   511
revenue quota   511
salary   512
sales quota   511
straight commission   513
straight salary   513
strategic account manager
   (SAM)   521
team selling   523

1. It took you four months to find a job, and you were almost out of money, when you finally landed your position. But today your boss asked you to do something unethical. You aren't sure what the corporate culture is yet because you are new at the company. How do you respond?

2. Your largest and most faithful customer wants its order shipped early. You could do that, but it would mean that a new, small account's order would be delayed. What will you do? In another situation you have an order from an account with the potential to be your biggest. But shipping tells you the product will be delayed one week, and credit refuses to allow the customer to pay COD on the first order, which is what the customer specifically requested. What will you do? What could you have done to prevent these problems?

3. A company that rents office equipment to businesses pays its salespeople a commission equal to the first month's rent. However, if the customer cancels or fails to pay its bills, the commission is taken back, even if the customer cancels 10 months later. Is this policy fair? Why or why not? Why would the company have this plan?

4. What is the role of the geographic salesperson in a national or strategic account? Assume that you are a NAM. What would you do to ensure the support of geographic reps? How would that support differ if you were a product specialist and worked in a team situation? How would you get the support of the account manager?

5. Consider your own experience in group work at school. What makes groups effective? How can you translate what you have learned about group work into managing a sales team? What difference would there be in your answer if you were a global account manager versus a sales manager?

6. To what extent should salespeople be allowed to manage themselves? What risks do you take as a sales manager when you allow self-management among salespeople? How can you minimize those risks?

7. Explain how compensation plans can create conflict among salespeople. How can companies alter compensation to influence customer care activities, increase prospecting activities, or increase prices?

8. Assume that your sales manager is working with you to evaluate your performance. As the sales call progresses, your manager begins to take over and ultimately dominates the call. Why might this situation occur? How would you handle it?

9. An experienced salesperson argues against salaries: "I don't like subsidizing poor performers. If you paid us straight commission, we'd know who could make it and who couldn't. Sure, it may take awhile to get rid of the deadwood; but after that, sales would skyrocket!" Explain why you agree or disagree with this statement.

10. How would you respond if you felt you were making as many calls as possible during the workweek, yet your manager demanded that you make more? The manager's reasoning is that if you make more, you will sell more. How would your response change if you were not meeting your sales quota? If you were selling twice your sales quota?

CASE 17.1

Flow Master Controls

Flow Master Controls, a manufacturer of heating and air conditioning control systems, has the following compensation program. Reps are paid a $1,500 draw per month, with straight commission paid on a point system and a bonus based on quota performance. The Digital Master, Flow Master's newest product, does much the same thing as the older Flow Master, but 30 percent faster and with greater accuracy. The point system is shown in Table 1:

TABLE 1

Product	Points/Sale	Quota
Digital Master	50	4 (units per month)
Flow Master	40	5
Hydrameter	35	6
Quadrameter	25	8
Triplex Scanner	5	45

Reps are paid $5 per point, or $5,175 plus a bonus of $500, if they sell quota for each product, for a total of $5,675. The total number of points to reach each month is 1,035, but reps have to reach quota for each product to get the bonus. Tables 2–4 show the performance of the district:

TABLE 2

Product	Quota	Number Sold
Digital Master	40	22
Flow Master	50	78
Hydrameter	60	63
Quadrameter	80	82
Triplex Scanner	450	479

TABLE 3

Name	Digital Master	Flow Master	Hydrameter	Quadrameter	Triplex Scanner	Total Points
McMahon	3	11	7	9	52	1,320
Davis	5	6	7	9	53	1,255
Foreman	2	9	7	11	46	1,210
Wu	4	8	6	8	48	1,170
Sanchez	3	8	7	6	48	1,105
Gruber	2	8	6	7	48	1,045
Sakamoto	1	8	6	8	48	1,020
Flora	1	7	7	8	47	1,010
Ricks	1	7	5	8	45	930
Dixon	0	6	5	8	44	835
Total	22	78	63	82	479	

TABLE 4

| Sales Call | Total Sales Calls | | | | | |
	Digital Master	Flow Master	Hydrameter	Quadrameter	Triplex Scanner	Total Calls
Quota	20	20	10	10	10	70
Foreman	28	17	11	9	10	75
Gruber	24	24	8	8	7	71
District average	27.2	18.6	9.5	10.4	9.7	75.4

Questions

1. Evaluate the district's sales performance. Draw conclusions (Just where are we doing well? Doing poorly?) but don't fix anything yet. Justify your conclusions.

2. Compare the performance of Foreman and Gruber. What are some possible explanations for the poor Digital Master sales?

3. The VP of sales says the problem is a compensation plan problem. How would you fix it?

4. The company is planning to create a new position called product specialist. This salesperson will work with territory salespeople and will have a sales quota for Digital Master only. The product specialist salesperson will work with one sales team (8 to 12 salespeople) and, once a territory rep has identified a Digital Master prospect, the rep will bring in the product specialist. How should the compensation plan be adjusted? Why?

5. The VP of sales managed to get the product specialist idea approved by the CEO, even though the CEO argued that the salespeople were just too lazy to make the effort to sell the Digital Master. Lower the compensation on it to the territory reps, and everyone will sell the Flow Master at its lower price, the CEO says. The best way to get more Digital Master sales is to cut compensation on the Flow Master to 20 points. What do you think should be done? Why?

CASE 17.2

Structural Steel Industries

It was nearly 5:00 on Friday afternoon when Charlie got the call from Laredo Construction. "Charlie, you gotta get someone out here now!" hollered Jack Belmont, owner of Laredo Construction. "You people tried to slip some foreign steel into our job, and now we gotta rip it all out. But we aren't going to do it. You are, and it better be done by Monday!"

Charlie could tell that Jack was furious, and he had every right to be. Jack's company was building a major complex at the naval base in San Diego. Because it was a job for the federal government, the specs called for all U.S. steel. Somehow steel from Structural Steel's Mexican supplier had been mixed with the domestic steel and sent to Laredo. If a navy inspector had seen it, Jack might even have had to forfeit a performance bond.

Structural Steel Industries (SSI) is a division of a larger steel fabricator. Steel fabricators take stock steel and make it into products. Miscellaneous steel fabricators, such as SSI, make custom steel components. SSI takes I-beams and other stock steel products and prepares them for assembly at a construction site. It cuts the steel to size, drills the holes for the rivets, and makes special beams and other steel products customized for specific buildings.

From the desk of Rose McPherson

University Book Source
407 Phyllis Avenue
Rochelle, IL 61068, USA

Dear Sir/Madam,

Thank you so much for your purchase. I hope you find everything to your satisfaction. Would you please let me know if there are any problems? I shall do my best to address them immediately.

As a small family business, I really care how customers think and I try very hard to make sure that each of my customers is happy. I would really appreciate it if you go back to the online market place where you placed your order and leave me positive feedback. And I'll be happy to do the same for you. To return this book for any reasons, please email me at *ubooksource@gmail.com* within 7 days of receiving it. I'll send you the return authorization to help ensure an accurate and speedy refund.

Yours truly,

Rose

P.S. Kindly consider visiting *www.ubooksource.com* for your future textbook needs.

Help make your college dream a little more affordable

The company, a small division, employs 45 welders and production workers (including a plant manager and four supervisors), 10 employees in shipping (including the shipping manager), two engineers, three salespeople, three project managers who work with salespeople and engineers to prepare bids, one controller, two secretaries, and Charlie (the chief executive officer).

Everyone from the plant supervisors on up (see Exhibit A) talks with customers directly. Because the jobs are custom, a lot of communication takes place among the contractor, the architect, and SSI to make sure everything is done just right.

In addition to a high degree of customer contact, each job requires a great deal of communication within SSI. As the flowchart in Exhibit B shows, all areas of the organization must interact throughout the project to ensure that SSI meets customer specifications.

After dealing with Jack, Charlie hung up the phone and buzzed Mary Longren, the project manager for Laredo's project. "Mary, who worked on the Laredo project?" Charlie queried.

"I did. Why?" she replied.

"I know you did. I meant who was the engineer and who inspected the goods before shipping? I just heard from Jack Belmont. Seems as though some of the steel was from a Mexican mill."

EXHIBIT A   SSI's Organization Chart

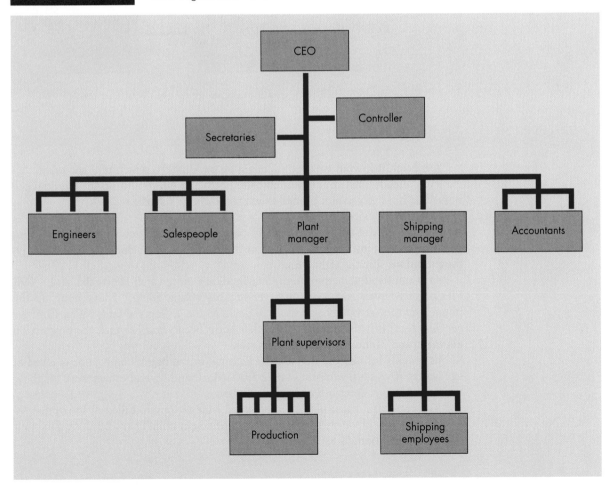

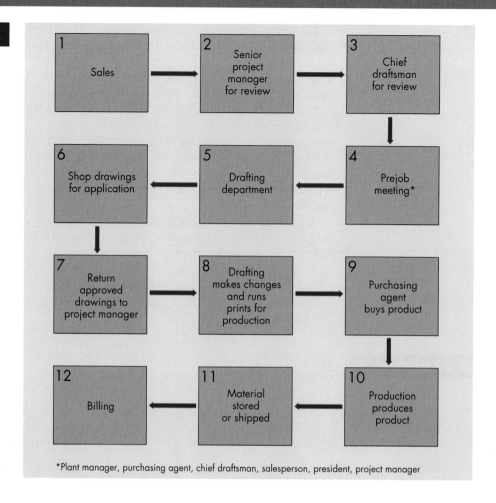

1 Sales	→	2 Senior project manager for review	→	3 Chief draftsman for review
6 Shop drawings for application	←	5 Drafting department	←	4 Prejob meeting*
7 Return approved drawings to project manager	→	8 Drafting makes changes and runs prints for production	→	9 Purchasing agent buys product
12 Billing	←	11 Material stored or shipped	←	10 Production produces product

*Plant manager, purchasing agent, chief draftsman, salesperson, president, project manager

"Oh great, just what we need! When is he building the structure?" she asked.

"He's already started. He wanted us to go to San Diego and rip the material out ourselves, but I've got him calmed down somewhat," Charlie replied.

"Was it all Mexican steel?"

Charlie sighed. "No, only about 40 percent. The good news is that only about half of that was installed before they realized the problem. But they can't do anything until we ship the right steel."

Mary muttered something that Charlie didn't quite catch. Then she said, "OK, I'll go get Manuel and Mark and get manufacturing going." Mary hung up the phone and then slapped her desk in disgust. To the ceiling she said, "Why can't we get this right? Is it that difficult?" She left her office to find Manuel, the production manager, and Mark, the shipping manager.

She quickly located the two among a crowd at the break lounge. She glanced at her watch; it was a few minutes after 5:00. Mark and several others were laughing loudly as Manuel described his weekend plans.

"You can forget those plans," interrupted Mary. "Laredo called. It seems that 40 percent of the steel we shipped was from a Mexican mill. That's a federal job, so it all has to be domestic steel."

"Well, we can get to it next week," Manuel replied, with his hands on his hips.

"'Fraid not, Manuel. Charlie wants it out this weekend."

"No way, Mary! We can't get all of that done this weekend. That was a full-week job." Manuel was almost shouting.

"Then we'll just have to get out what we can," she stated, noticing that Mark was smirking. "You can forget your weekend plans too, pal. You've got to get us domestic steel and get this shipped to San Diego as soon as a truckload is ready."

"Well, we'll just see about that," said Mark, slamming a Coke can into a trash container. "C'mon Manuel, let's go see Charlie." The two walked off, talking animatedly to each other. A few production workers got up and started to walk out.

"Hey, you guys can just wait right there!" yelled Mary. "You are going to get plenty of overtime today. And if you don't want it, Charlie will help you find another place to work." One worker acted as if he didn't hear and kept right on going. Two turned around and returned to the break area.

On Monday, Angela Davis, the salesperson who handled the Laredo account, called Charlie. "I got your message, boss. What's up?" she asked.

"Laredo got Mexican steel. We've managed to ship a little more than half of the stuff he had already installed, but it will be Wednesday before the final shipment goes out."

"That's just terrific. What's the matter with those people in manufacturing? Can't they read specs?" Angela asked. Laredo wasn't her largest customer, but it was one of her biggest, a class A account.

"Well, Angela," Charlie replied, pausing for effect, "it wasn't on the specs. Nothing manufacturing got said domestic only."

"But they should have known. It was a federal job!" she protested.

"Why should they have known? Anyway, you better call Jack Belmont and let him know what's happening. I'll let you talk to Mark next so you can get the full shipment schedule." Charlie transferred Angela to Mark. As Charlie hung up, he wondered where he was going to make up for the loss he was taking on the Laredo project.

Angela was in no mood for polite conversation when she finally reached Jack at the construction site. "Jack, this is Angela. Have you received the first emergency shipment yet?"

"No, we haven't. But it better get here soon. My guys are just sitting around." Jack sounded grim.

"You should get it any time now. I talked to Mark, and it went out about 5:00 this morning, so it should be there by 9:00."

"Look, Angela. If it isn't here by 9:00, you might as well keep it. I can't afford to do business with you people any longer." The line went dead as Jack hung up. Angela slumped against the wall of the pay phone booth, wondering what could go wrong next.

Questions

1. Who was primarily responsible for the Laredo project mistake? Who else was responsible? Why?
2. What can be done to prevent these problems in the future, and who should make those corrections?
3. Identify the managers who would be involved in a project and discuss what their priorities would be (such as the engineer would be most interested in the design itself).

Additional References

Bellizzi, Joseph A., and Ronald W. Hasty, "The Effects of a Stated Organizational Policy on Inconsistent Disciplinary Action Based on Salesperson Gender and Weight." *Journal of Personal Selling & Sales Management* 21, Summer 2001, pp. 189–98.

Boles, James; Wesley Johnson; and Alston Gardner. "The Selection and Organization of National Accounts: A North American Perspective." *Journal of Business and Industrial Marketing* 14:4 (1999), pp. 264–75.

Cravens, David. "The Changing Role of the Sales Force." *Marketing Management,* Fall 1995, pp. 49–57.

Darmon, Rene Y. "Optimal Salesforce Quota Plans under Salesperson Job Equity Constraints." *Revue Canadienne des Sciences de l'Administration* 18 (2001), pp. 87–101.

DeConinck, Jim; Ronald Stephens; and Richard Foster. "Variables That Influence Intentions to Discipline and Reward Ethical and Unethical Sales Behavior." *American Business Review,* January 1995, pp. 99–105.

Deeter-Schmelz, Dawn, and Rosemary Ramsey. "A Conceptualization of the Functions and Roles of Formalized Selling and Buying Teams." *Journal of Personal Selling and Sales Management,* Spring 1995, pp. 47–60.

Flaherty, Karen E., and James M. Pappas. "The Role of Trust in Salesperson–Sales Manager Relationships." *Journal of Personal Selling & Sales Management* 20, Fall 2000, pp. 271–78.

Good, David J., and Charles H. Schwepker, Jr. "Sales Quotas: Critical Interpretations and Implications." *Review of Business* 22 (2001), pp. 32–36.

Homburg, Christian; John P. Workman Jr.; and Harley Krohmer. "Marketing's Influence within the Firm." *Journal of Marketing* 63, April 1999, pp. 1–17.

Joshi, Ashwin W., and Sheila Randall. "The Indirect Effects of Organizational Controls on Salesperson Performance and Customer Orientation." *Journal of Business Research* 54 (2001), pp. 1–9.

Kahn, Kenneth, and John Mentzer. "Marketing's Integration with Other Departments." *Journal of Business Research* 42, May 1998, pp. 53–62.

Kurland, Nancy B. "Ethics, Incentives, and Conflicts of Interest." *Journal of Business Ethics* 14, 1995, pp. 465–75.

Larsen, T.; B. Rosenbloom; R. Anderson; and R. Mehta. "Global Sales Manager Leadership Styles: The Impact of National Culture." *Journal of Global Marketing* 13 (1999), pp. 31–49.

MacKenzie, Scott B.; Phillip Podsakoff; and Gregory A. Rich. "Transformational and Transactional Leadership and Salesperson Performance." *Journal of the Academy of Marketing Science* 29, Spring 2001, pp. 115–34.

McNeilly, Kevin, and Frederick A. Russ. "Does Relational Demography Matter in a Personal Selling Context?" *Journal of Personal Selling & Sales Management* 20, Fall 2000, pp. 279–88.

Millman, Tony. "How Well Does the Concept of Global Account Management Travel across Cultures?" *Journal of Selling and Major Account Management,* Spring 2001, pp. 31–46.

Moller, Kristian, and Arto Rajala. "Organizing Marketing in High-Tech Firms." *Industrial Marketing Management* 28, 1999, pp. 521–35.

Pardo, Catherine. "Key Account Management: The French Perspective." *Journal of Business and Industrial Marketing* 14:4 (1999), pp. 276–90.

Perry, Monica; Craig L. Pearce; and Henry P. Sims, Jr. "Empowered Selling Teams: How Shared Leadership Can Contribute to Selling Teams Outcomes." *Journal of Personal Selling & Selling Management* 19, Summer 1999, pp. 35–51.

Pettijohn, Charles; Linda S. Pettijohn; Albert Taylor; and Bruce Keillor. "Are Performance Appraisals a Bureaucratic Exercise or Can They Be Used to Enhance Sales Force Satisfaction and Commitment?" *Psychology & Marketing* 18, April 2001, pp. 337–64.

Pullig, Chris; James G. Maxham III; and Joseph F. Hair, Jr. "Salesforce Automation Systems: An Exploratory Examination of Organizational Factors Associated with Effective Implementation and Salesforce Productivity." *Journal of Business Research* 55 (2002), 410–15.

Rich, Gregory. "Salesperson Optimism: Can Sales Managers Enhance It, and So What If They Do?" *Journal of Marketing Theory & Practice*, Winter 1999, pp. 53–64.

Schultz, Roberta J., and Kenneth R. Evans. "Strategic Collaborative Communication by Key Account Representatives." *Journal of Personal Selling & Sales Management* 22, Winter 2002, pp. 23–31.

Sengupta, Sanjit; Robert Krapfel; and Michael A. Pusateri, "An Empirical Investigation of Key Account Salesperson Effectiveness." *Journal of Personal Selling & Sales Management* 20, Fall 2000, pp. 253–61.

Srivistava, Rajesh; David Strutton; and Lou Pelton. "The Will to Win: An Investigation of How Sales Managers Can Improve the Quantitative Aspects of Their Sales Force's Effort." *Journal of Marketing Theory & Practice* 9, Spring 2001, pp. 11–26.

Venkatesh, R.; Goutam Challagalla; and Ajay K. Kohli. "Heterogeneity in Sales Districts: Beyond Individual-Level Predictors of Satisfaction and Performance." *Journal of the Academy of Marketing Science* 29, Summer 2001, pp. 238–54.

18 Managing Your Career

SOME QUESTIONS ANSWERED IN THIS CHAPTER ARE:

- Which entry-level jobs are available to new college graduates?
- Where do I find these jobs?
- How should I go about getting interviews, and what should I do when I have an interview?
- Which selection procedures besides interviews might I go through?
- Which career paths are available in sales?
- How can I prepare myself for a promotion into management?

In this chapter you will find the answers to many questions concerning how to start and develop a successful career in sales and marketing. Your first sale will involve selling yourself to land that first position. But job searching is not always selling. As you will see, other activities are also necessary during the hiring process. That hiring process can be repeated each time you are considered for a promotion. Whether you enter sales as a career, use it as a launching pad for a career in marketing, or decide you are better suited for another career, this chapter will help you get started.

"I stayed with it, to get the job I wanted."

Lauren Johnston, Wallace

PROFILE

Sometimes it seems that the professional world is overwhelming with its demands. Yet only one trait was needed for Lauren Johnston to land the job she wanted most—persistence. Sales recruiters look for numerous traits, characteristics, and behaviors when hiring candidates. Being "self-motivated, a relationship builder, aggressive, sincere, genuine, persuasive, and customer focused" are all important, yet it was Lauren's persistence that got her a start.

Lauren Johnston is completing her second year with Wallace, working in the Jacksonville sales office, after graduating from Florida State University in the spring of 2000. Lauren finished her first year at 185 percent of quota, which consistently put her in the national top 20 among salespeople of her tenure. Lauren has been recognized for both her talent and presence in training classes, and she ably assisted Wallace with the recruiting of Florida college students for the last two hiring seasons. To cap all of these achievements, Lauren was the youngest member selected to participate in a national task force that was charged with analyzing and suggesting solutions to senior management regarding the retention and turnover of sales representatives. Lauren had been with Wallace for only eight months at the time of her selection for this task force—so she obviously made quite an impression during that short period!

Lauren went through her own recruiting process by doing all of the things that would be recommended for any college senior. She had two internships the summer before her senior year. She attended Seminole Futures (Florida State's career fair) in both of her senior semesters, focusing her efforts only on companies that had sales positions. She narrowed her list further, saying, "It really made a big impression on me, based upon the enthusiasm and confidence with which a company representative would discuss company opportunities with me. I wasn't interested in pursuing any company whose representatives weren't excited about their own jobs."

Lauren researched companies further and prepared questions regarding her wants for her upcoming interviews. She attended those companies' information sessions. She interviewed with 10 companies and spoke with 8 for second interviews. She went on office visits, narrowed down her finalists, and received an offer. However, she didn't get the offer that she truly wanted. She knew the job that she wanted based on "the overall feel I got from everyone I talked with at Wallace. Everyone seemed to like their job and the people they worked with. I thought I could see myself being happy and successful in that job. Those things were important to me."

Lauren attended Wallace's "College Day," or final interviews, just before graduation. She left that event confident that she had done her best to separate herself from the other candidates who wanted to go to Jacksonville, and immediately wrote a thank-you note to all the Wallace representatives that she had met. The only problem was that the Jacksonville office had only one position available, and was then full.

Lauren was very disappointed that she hadn't received a job offer from Wallace. She called Human Resources, expressed her disappointment, and asked, "What can I do to get the job that I *know* I'll be successful in doing?" She was instructed to remain in contact with Jeff Wright (Jacksonville's senior district manager) by any and all means available. She wrote and called several times over the next six weeks. No sales candidate had ever persisted to that degree to obtain a job offer with Wallace; Lauren essentially made it a necessity for Jeff to find a place for her! Jeff says,

"Based upon Lauren's persistence and tenacity in getting her job, it was obvious that she would approach her customers with the same intensity and would be successful!"

Today Lauren credits her persistence for "the appreciation that I have for my job." She states, "If I had originally received an offer, I would have only seen that as just another success. I stayed with it to get *the* job I wanted, and now see how important persistence is when the job gets difficult. I know I can make it now, because I had to fight to get this chance."

Visit Our Website @www.wallace.com.

Landing that first career position is an exciting moment! However, the job search is just the first task in managing your career. Like the chess player who is thinking two or three moves ahead, you too must think about subsequent opportunities. Also like the chess player, you must maintain some flexibility so that you do not checkmate your career if one strategy does not work.

Sales is a great place to begin a career. Just ask Carly Fiorina, CEO of Hewlett-Packard. During her college days, she worked for the company as a secretary. After graduation she gained sales experience with other companies, ultimately becoming president of the global services division of Lucent Technologies. Then Hewlett-Packard hired Fiorina for her sales and marketing expertise.[1] Or ask Jeffrey Immelt, CEO of General Electric. Immelt was competing with two other executives for the top spot when Jack Welch announced his retirement. Analysts and insiders alike say it was Immelt's sales experience and long history with customers that made him the top choice.[2] Like Fiorina, Immelt gained firsthand customer knowledge that he uses to succeed as a CEO. Because salespeople must represent the entire company, they learn about many aspects of the business and get to know people in various parts of the company. All of this knowledge can be put to use later in a career.

OPPORTUNITIES IN SELLING

Selling offers many opportunities. About 3.4 million people are engaged in non-retail sales, with nearly a million new jobs expected in the next decade.[3] In 2002 the *Occupational Outlook Quarterly* projected many jobs to open in manufacturing sales for the first decade of this century.[4]

Sales positions are growing faster than other types of positions, with 40 percent of companies expecting to add salespeople.[5] This fast-paced growth bodes well for marketing students because most marketing careers begin in sales. Corporate executives clearly recognize the importance of selling experience in any marketing career, as evidenced by people like Carly Fiorina and Jeffrey Immelt. Many people have also found career satisfaction by staying in sales throughout their working lives.

Whether the career is sales or any other field, similar questions apply when searching for a job. In this chapter the focus is on the search for a sales position and how to land the first job. We examine how companies make hiring decisions and offer tips on how to build selling and management skills while managing a career.

International opportunities are unlikely for most entry-level salespeople, but some entry-level marketing or sales positions can lead to international sales. Students who seek international opportunities may do well to begin with foreign companies doing business in the United States. International opportunities are also more likely with small companies already engaged in international business, especially for salespeople who have proven their abilities in a domestic sales position. Students who desire international sales should prepare themselves by learning the language of the people with whom they would like to do business and participating in exchange or foreign study programs. There is no substitute for living in a culture to learn it, and personal contacts made during those exchange programs can be useful later.[6]

MAKING A GOOD MATCH

The keys to being successful and happy lie in finding a good match between what you need and desire in a position and the positions companies offer. The first step, then, is to understand yourself, what you need, and what you have to offer. Then you must consider what each company needs and what each has to offer. As Exhibit 18.1 illustrates, a good match means that your needs are satisfied by what the company offers and that what you offer satisfies the company's needs.

UNDERSTANDING YOURSELF

Shakespeare said, "To thine own self be true," but to be true to yourself, you must know who you are, what you need, and what you can offer others.[7] Knowing these things about yourself requires substantial self-examination. We will pose some questions that can help you follow Shakespeare's suggestion.

UNDERSTANDING YOUR NEEDS

The first step in making a good match between what you have to offer and a company's position is to determine what you need. Important questions to consider include the following:

1. *Structure.* Can you work well when assignments are ambiguous, or do you need a lot of instruction? Do you need deadlines that others set, or do you set your own deadlines? If you are uncomfortable when left on your own, you may need structure in your work life. Many sales positions, such as missionary and trade sales, are in a structured environment with well-defined procedures and routines. Other positions require the salesperson to operate with little guidance or structure.

2. *Motivation.* Will financial incentives, personal recognition, or simply job satisfaction get you going? Probably it will be some combination of the three, but try to determine the relative value of each to you. Then you can weigh compensation plans, recognition programs, and other factors when considering which sales position is right for you. You may want to review

---

EXHIBIT 18.1

A Good Match between Salesperson and Company

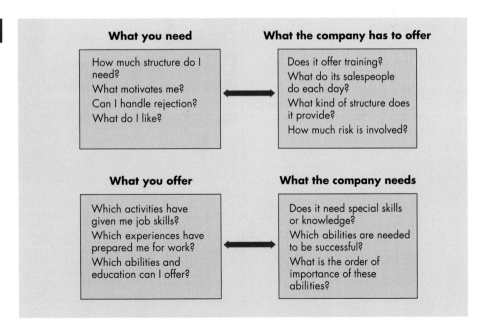

What you need
How much structure do I need?
What motivates me?
Can I handle rejection?
What do I like?

What the company has to offer
Does it offer training?
What do its salespeople do each day?
What kind of structure does it provide?
How much risk is involved?

What you offer
Which activities have given me job skills?
Which experiences have prepared me for work?
Which abilities and education can I offer?

What the company needs
Does it need special skills or knowledge?
Which abilities are needed to be successful?
What is the order of importance of these abilities?

the section on compensation plan types in Chapter 17 to aid in determining which plan best suits your needs.

3. *Stress and rejection.* How much stress can you handle? Are you a risk taker, or do you prefer more secure activities? What do you do when faced with stress? With rejection? These are important questions in understanding what you need from a sales position. For example, capital equipment sales jobs can be high-stress positions because sales are few and far between. Other jobs may require you to wade through many rejections before landing a sale. If you thrive on that kind of challenge, the rewards can be very gratifying. Some sales positions, though, involve working only with current customers, and salespeople incur little outright rejection. Every grocery store, for example, will carry at least some Procter & Gamble products.

4. *Interest.* What do you find interesting? Mechanical or technical topics? Merchandising? Art or fashion? You cannot sell something that bores you. You would just bore and annoy the customer.

UNDERSTANDING WHAT YOU HAVE TO OFFER

Other resources that can help you understand the person you are may be available through your college's placement center. You must also take inventory of what you bring to the job:

1. *Skills.* What activities and experiences taught you certain skills? What did you learn from those experiences and your education that you can apply to a career? Keep in mind that it is not the activities in which you participated that matter to hiring companies; it is what you learned by participating that counts.

Many companies, such as American Airlines, sell their products and services to other companies to be used to motivate superior sales performance. For example, every year Minolta Business Systems rewards its top salespeople with an exotic trip.

Courtesy American Airlines

2. *Knowledge.* College has provided you with many areas of knowledge, but you have also probably learned much by participating in hobbies and other interests. For example, you may have special computer knowledge that would be useful in selling software, or you may have participated in a particular sport that makes you well suited to sell equipment to sporting goods stores.

3. *Qualities and traits.* Every person has a unique personality. What part of your personality adds value for your potential employer? Are you detail oriented and systematic? Are you highly creative? In other words, what can you bring to the job that is uniquely you? Exhibit 18.2 lists traits of top salespeople, according to a study conducted for *Sales & Marketing Management* magazine.

Your answers to these questions will generate a list of what you have to offer companies. Then, when you are in an interview, you can present features that make you a desirable candidate.

WHEN TO ASK THESE QUESTIONS

Unfortunately, many students wait until just before graduation before seriously considering what type of career they desire. According to one career services director, students who start a search while in school will find a job three times faster than those who start after graduation. Although it is not always realistic to expect every student to map out a life plan prior to senior year, asking questions such as these as early as possible can guide a student to better course selection, better use of learning opportunities, and, ultimately, a better career decision. Then the student can begin actively searching for the job at the beginning of the senior year so that graduation signals the beginning of a career, not a career search.

UNDERSTANDING THE COMPANY

While developing a good feel for who you are and what you have to offer companies, you should also explore what is available and which companies offer positions that appeal to you. As you can see in Exhibit 18.3, numerous sources provide information regarding positions and growth opportunities in various industries and specific companies. Don't forget, though, that the best sources are personal; be sure to talk over job opportunities with your friends, friends of your parents, and your professors. Use term papers as an excuse to call professionals in a field that interests you. Join trade and professional associations now, as these offer great networking opportunities. As someone who has studied sales, you should use your prospecting skills, too. Let's discuss how to evaluate what you learn about the companies and their positions.

EXHIBIT 18.2

Traits of Top Salespeople

1. Strong ego: able to handle rejection with healthy self-esteem.
2. Sense of urgency: getting it done now.
3. Ego driven: obsessive about being successful.
4. Assertive: being firm without being aggressive (see the discussion in Chapter 12).
5. Willing to take risks: willing to innovate.
6. Sociable: good at building relationships.
7. Abstract reasoner: able to handle complex selling situations and ideas.
8. Skeptical: a healthy bit of suspicion, not counting on commission until the sale is really a sale.
9. Creative: able to set one's self apart from the competition.
10. Empathic: able to place oneself in the buyer's shoes.

Source: Adapted from Erika Rasmusson, "The Ten Traits of Top Salespeople," *Sales & Marketing Management*, August 1999, pp. 34–37.

EXHIBIT 18.3

Sources of Job
Information

Source	Example
Government	*U.S. Industrial Outlook*
Research services	*Standard & Poor's Industry Surveys*
Industry associations	Christian Booksellers' Association
Professional organizations	Sales and Marketing Executives International
General magazines	*Business Week, Money*
Trade magazines	*Sales & Marketing Management, SELLING*
Placement services	University placement office; nonfee private agencies such as Personnel One
Personal sources	Friends, relatives, industry association executives at trade shows, recruiters at career fairs
Websites	Sales.com, jobtrax.com

WHAT THE COMPANY HAS TO OFFER

When you meet a salesperson or sales manager, you should ask about compensation and recognition programs, training, career opportunities, and other information to determine whether the company truly offers benefits to satisfy your needs. You should also explore daily activities of the salesperson, likes and dislikes about the job, and what that person thinks it takes to succeed. This information will help you determine whether a match exists.

For example, if you need structure, you should look for a sales position in which your day is structured for you. Any industry that relies on repeated sales calls to the same accounts is likely to be highly structured. Industries with a structured sales day include consumer packaged goods sales (Procter & Gamble, Quaker Oats, and the like) and pharmaceutical sales (Novartis, Eli Lilly Company, and so forth). Even these sales positions, however, offer some flexibility and independence. Office and industrial equipment sales provide much less structure when the emphasis is on getting new accounts.

Knowing your comfort level with risk and your need for incentives should help you pick a company with a compensation program that is right for you. If you need the security of a salary, look for companies in trade sales, equipment sales, or missionary sales like pharmaceuticals or consumer package goods. But if you like the risk of straight commission, which can often be matched with greater financial rewards for success, explore careers in areas such as convention sales, financial services, and other straight-commission jobs.[8]

Other factors to consider include the size of the company and its promotion policies, particularly if the company is foreign. Many companies have a "promote from within" policy, which means that whenever possible they fill positions with people who already are employees. Such policies are very attractive if you seek career growth into management. A company that is foreign owned, however, may prefer to staff certain positions with people from its home country.

Take advantage of interests you already have. If you are intrigued by medical science, seek a medical sales position. If merchandising excites you, a position selling to the trade would be appropriate. A bar of soap by itself is not exciting, but helping customers find ways to market that bar of soap is.

WHAT THE COMPANY NEEDS

At this point in your job search, you may have narrowed your selection to a group of industries or companies. At a minimum you have a good picture of what a company should offer to land you as a salesperson. The next step is to

Career fairs, such as this one in Baltimore, can be a great opportunity to find sales positions.

Mark Richards/PhotoEdit

find a company that needs you. Finding out what a company needs will require some research, but you will find this step fun and rewarding.

In general, companies look for three qualities in salespeople: good communication skills, self-motivation, and a positive and enthusiastic attitude.[9] Al Lynch, CEO of JCPenney International, adds to this list quantitative skills and an ability to ask the right questions.

Companies in certain industries may also desire related technical skills or knowledge, such as medical knowledge for the field of pharmaceutical sales or insurance knowledge to enter that field. All companies need salespeople with computer skills because the computer is increasingly being used to track and manage accounts, communicate internally, and perform other important activities.[10] If you want to enter a field requiring specialized knowledge or skills, now is the time to begin acquiring that knowledge. Not only will you already have the knowledge when you begin to search for a position; you will also have demonstrated self-motivation and the right kind of attitude by taking on the task of acquiring that knowledge and skill.

THE RECRUITING PROCESS

Early in this book we discussed the buying process so that you would understand the purchase decision buyers make. Now we will look at the recruiting process so that you will understand how companies will view you as a candidate for a sales job or any other position.

SELECTING SALESPEOPLE

In recent years companies have made considerable progress in screening and selecting salespeople. Most have discarded the myth that there is a "sales type" who will be successful selling anything to anybody. Instead, they seek people who match the requirements of a specific position, using various methods to gain information and determine whether a good match will be made.

APPLICANT INFORMATION SOURCES

To determine whether a match exists between the job requirements and the applicant's abilities, information about the applicant must be collected. Companies use five important sources of information: application forms, references, tests, personal interviews, and assessment centers. We describe these five sources from the perspective of the company so you can understand how they are used to make hiring decisions. We also explain how you should use these sources of information so you can present yourself accurately and positively.

The **application form** is a preprinted form that the candidate completes. You have probably already filled these out for part-time jobs you have had. The form should include factual questions concerning the profile the company established for the position. Responses on the form are also useful for structuring the personal interview. Résumés provide much of the same information application forms do but are often too individualized for easy comparison. For this and other reasons, companies must supplement résumés with an application form (we discuss résumés in greater detail later in this chapter).

Contacting **references,** or people who know the applicant, is a good way to validate information on the application form. References can also supplement the information with personal observations. The most frequently contacted references are former employers. Other references are coworkers, leaders of social or religious organizations, and professors. You should be aware that some organizations try to develop relationships with faculty so they can receive leads on excellent candidates before visiting the placement office. Professors recommend students who have demonstrated the qualities the recruiting companies desire.

When you select references, keep in mind that companies want references that can validate information about you. Choose references that provide different information, such as one character reference, one educational reference, and one work-related reference.

Experienced sales managers expect to hear favorable comments from an applicant's references. More useful information may be contained in unusual comments, gestures, faint praise, or hesitant responses that may indicate a problem. Before you offer someone's name as a reference, ask that person for permission. At that time you should be able to tell whether the person is willing to give you a good recommendation.

Intelligence, ability, personality, and interest **tests** provide information about a potential salesperson that cannot be obtained readily from other sources. Tests can also correct misjudgments made by sales managers who tend to act on "gut feelings." Although tests were widely criticized in the early 1980s for failing to predict success better than other sources did, recent studies indicate that personality and interest tests are growing in popularity once more, in part because of their improved predictive power.[11]

Several types of tests may be given. H. R. Challey Inc. designs tests to determine a person's psychological aptitude for different sales situations. IBM requires sales candidates to demonstrate technical aptitude through a test. Many companies require candidates to pass a math test because of the importance of calculating price correctly. Still other tests indicate a candidate's ethical nature. Companies may require candidates to take tests in all of these categories.

The important point to remember about tests is to remain relaxed. If the test is a valid selection tool, you should be happy with the outcome no matter what it is. If you believe the test is not valid—that is, does not predict your ability to succeed in that job—you may want to present your feelings to the recruiter. Be prepared to back up your line of reasoning with facts and experiences that illustrate you are a good candidate for the position.

Interviews, or personal interaction between recruiter and candidate, are an important source of information for recruiters. Companies now give more attention to conducting multiple interviews in the selection process because sometimes candidates show only slight differences. Multiple interviews can improve a recruiter's chances of observing the differences and selecting the best candidate. We cover interviews in more detail later in the chapter.

Companies sometimes evaluate candidates at centrally located **assessment centers.** In addition to being used for testing and personal interviews, these locations may simulate portions of the job. Simulating the job serves two purposes. First, the simulation lets managers see candidates respond to a joblike situation. Second, candidates can experience the job and determine whether it fits them. For example, Merrill Lynch sometimes places broker candidates in an office and simulates two hours of customer telephone calls. As many as half of the candidates may then decide that being a stockbroker is not right for them, and Merrill Lynch can also evaluate the candidates' abilities in a lifelike setting.

Companies use many sources of information in making a hiring decision, perhaps even asking for a copy of a videotaped presentation you may make for this class. These sources are actually selling opportunities for you. You can present yourself and learn about the job at the same time, continuing your evaluation of the match.

SELLING YOUR CAPABILITIES

With an understanding of the recruiting process from the company's point of view, you can create a presentation that sells your capabilities and proves you have the skills and knowledge the company wants. Preparing the résumé, gaining an interview, and presenting your capabilities in the interview are important activities that require sound planning to present yourself effectively.

PREPARING THE RÉSUMÉ

The résumé is the brochure in your marketing plan. As such, it needs to tell the recruiter why you should be hired. Recruiters scan a résumé for only 20 seconds before deciding whether to study it more carefully.[12] Whether you choose the conventional style or the functional style of résumé, the purpose is to sell your skills and experience.

CONVENTIONAL RÉSUMÉS

Conventional résumés are a form of life history, organized by type of experience. The three categories of experience most often used are education, work, and activities/hobbies (see the example in Exhibit 18.4). Although it is easy to create conventional résumés, it is also easy to fail to emphasize important points. To avoid making this mistake, follow this simple procedure:

- List education, work experience, and activities.
- Write out what you gained in each experience that will help you prove you have the desired qualities.
- Emphasize what you learned and that you have the desired qualities under each heading.

For example, the résumé in Exhibit 18.4 is designed for a student interested in a sales career. Note how skills gained in this class are emphasized in addition to GPA and major. The candidate has also chosen to focus on customer service skills gained as a camp counselor, a job that a recruiter would otherwise overlook. Rather than just listing herself as a member of the soccer team, the candidate highlights the leadership skills she gained as captain.

FUNCTIONAL RÉSUMÉS Functional résumés reverse the content and titles of the conventional résumé, organizing by what the candidate can do or has learned rather than by types of experience. As you can see in Exhibit 18.5, an advantage of this type of résumé is that it highlights more forcefully what the candidate can do.

When preparing a functional résumé, begin by listing the qualities you have that you think will help you get the job. Narrow this list to three or four qualities and

EXHIBIT 18.4

Conventional Résumé
Example

Cheryl McSwain

After June 1:
435 Wayward View, Apt. B
State College, PA 10303
203/555-1289

Present Address:
612 Homer
Aurora, CO 86475
804/555-9183

Career Objective: Sales in the telecommunications industry

Education:
Colorado University, Boulder, Colorado
Bachelor of Business Administration, June 2003
Marketing
GPA: 3.25 on 4.0 scale

Major Subjects:
Personal Selling
Sales Management
Industrial Marketing

Other Subjects:
Microcomputing
Local Area Networks Management
Telecommunications

Emphasized selling and sales management in computing and telecommunications. Learned SPIN, social styles, and other adaptive selling techniques. Studied LANWORKS and Novell network management.

Work Experience: Sales representative, *The Lariat* (CU campus newspaper)
Practiced sales skills in making cold calls and selling advertising
Fall 2000 to present

Counselor, Camp Kanatcook
Learned customer service and leadership skills
Summers, 1999, 2000, 2001

Scholarships and Honors:
University Merit Scholar ($2,000/year, two years)
Top sales student, spring 2000
Dean's List, three semesters

Activities:
Member, Alpha Delta Pi Sorority
Rush chair, 2000
Motivated members to actively recruit; interviewed candidates for selection
Homecoming float chair, 1999
Managed float building; sorority awarded second in float competition
Women's soccer team, four years
Captain, 2002-2003
Led team to conference championship, fall 2002

then list activities and experiences to prove that you have those skills and abilities. The qualities are the headings for the résumé; the activities and experiences show that you have those qualities. One difficulty with this type of résumé is that one past job may relate to several qualities. If that is the case, emphasize the activity within the job that provided you with the experience for each specific quality.

THE CAREER OBJECTIVE As you have probably noticed, both sample résumés list a career objective. The career objective is important because it identifies immediately the desired position. One question many students ask is what to do when interviewing for several types of positions—for example, interviewing for retail management with one company and for sales with another. The solution is to create several résumés, each listing a different objective; then use whichever version is most appropriate for a particular company. The worst solution is to omit an objective; potential employers then have to guess what you want.

GAINING THE INTERVIEW

Students should begin examining different industries as early as possible, as we suggested earlier. As graduation looms closer and the time for serious job hunting

EXHIBIT 18.5

Functional Résumé
Example

Cheryl McSwain

After June 1:
435 Wayward View, Apt. B
State College, PA 10303
203/555-1289

Present Address:
612 Homer
Aurora, CO 86475
804/555-9183

Career Objective: Sales in the telecommunications industry

Sales and Customer Service Experience:
Studied SPIN and adaptive selling techniques in personal selling.
Sold advertising in *The Lariat,* campus newspaper. Responsibilities included
making cold calls, presenting advertising strategies, and closing sales.
Performed customer service tasks as camp counselor at Camp Kanatcook.
Served as the primary parent contact during drop-off and pick-up periods,
answering parent queries, resolving parental concerns, and handling similar
responsibilities.

Management and Leadership Experience:
Studied situational management in sales management.
Served as rush chair for sorority. Responsible for motivating members to
recruit new members and developed and implemented a sales training seminar
so members would present the sorority favorably within university guidelines.
Managed homecoming-float project Sorority awarded second place in float
competition.
Captained the women's varsity soccer team to a conference championship.

Telecommunications Skills and Experience:
Studied LANWORKS and Novell network management in
telecommunications.
Designed, as a term project, a Novell-based LAN for a small
manufacturing business.
Purchased and installed a six-computer network in a family-owned
wholesaling business.

Scholarships and Honors:
University Merit Scholar ($2,000/year, two years)
Top sales student, spring 2000
Dean's List, three semesters

arrives, your knowledge of the industries and companies that interest you will put you a step ahead. You will also understand the process the company will go through in searching for a new salesperson.

USING PERSONAL CONTACTS More important, you have already begun to make personal contacts in those fields— contacts you can now use to gain interviews. The same salespeople and sales managers who gave you information before to help you with term projects will usually be happy to introduce you to the person in charge of recruiting. Contacts you made at job fairs and trade shows can also be helpful.

Thinking It Through

Many students feel uncomfortable asking for favors from people they barely know. How can you overcome such feelings of discomfort? Why would someone want to help you find places to interview? What obligations do you have to people who provide you with the names of job contacts?

USING EMPLOYMENT POSTINGS Responding to Web postings or newspaper advertisements can also lead to job interviews. You will need to carefully interpret employment postings and then respond effectively to them.

All ads are designed to sell, and employment ads are no exception. But what sounds great may not be wonderful in reality. Here are some phrases often found in such ads and interpretations of them:[13]

Independent contractor: You will work on straight commission with no employee benefits. You will probably receive no training and little, if any, support.

Earn up to $___ (or *Unlimited income* or *Our top rep made $100,000 last year*): You need to know what the average person makes and what the average first-year earnings are, not what the top rep made or the upper limit. The job could still be desirable, but you need to find out what reality is before accepting a position.

Sales manager trainee: This is another title for sales representative. Don't be put off or overly encouraged by high-sounding titles.

Bonuses paid weekly, Daily commissions, or *Weekly commissions:* These are high-pressure jobs and probably involve high-pressure sales.

Ten salespeople needed now!: That's because everyone quit. This company uses salespeople and then discards them.

You should look for two things in an ad: what the company needs and what it has to offer. The company should provide concrete information concerning training, compensation plan (although not necessarily the amount), amount of travel to expect, and type of product or service you will sell. You should also expect to find the qualifications the company desires, including experience and education. If you do not have the experience now, call and ask how to get it. Be specific: What companies should I pursue that will give me the experience you are looking for?

The Internet can be a great source of leads for jobs; however, recruiters report receiving thousands of résumés for every job they post. If you really want a job with a particular company, approach it like a sales opportunity and use your networking or prospecting skills to make personal contact.

Courtesy of Monster®

RESPONDING TO POSTINGS Many postings and ads will ask you to write and may not list the company's name. A blind box number is given when the company name is not included in a newspaper ad; the box number is usually at the address of the newspaper. For example, the ad may say to send a résumé to Box 000, care of the *Dallas Morning News*. Don't be put off by the lack of company name; the posting or ad may be placed by a company such as IBM that would otherwise receive a large number of unqualified applicants. Companies use blind postings and blind box numbers for many legitimate reasons.

Many blind ads now ask you to e-mail your résumé. Similarly, when responding to Internet ads, like those on Monster.com, you may not know who the employer is. Do not let that put you off; however, if you already have a sales job and you are looking for a change, you may not want to reply to blind ads. One of our students did that; he was fired when it turned out the company in the ad was his own employer.

WRITING THE COVER LETTER

When you write in response to a posting, you are writing a sales letter. Like any sales letter, it should focus on what you can do for the company, not what you expect from it. The letter should start with an attention getter. Here is one example:

> In today's economy, you need someone who can become productive quickly as a territory representative. Based on your posting at Monster.com, I believe that I am that person.

This attention getter is direct, focuses on a probable need, and refers to the posting. The probability of getting a response to this cover letter is far greater than if you simply said,

> Please consider me for the territory representative position you posted at Monster.com.

The attention getter tells why you should be considered.

The body of the letter should center on two or three reasons you should be hired. For example, if you have the qualities of self-motivation and leadership, devote two paragraphs relating each to the position. Use your résumé as proof. For example:

> A territory representative position often requires self-motivation. As you can see from the attached résumé, I demonstrated self-motivation as a sales representative for the campus newspaper, as a volunteer for the local food bank, and as a member of the Dean's Honor Roll during two of the last four semesters.

The letter should close with a request for action. Ask for an interview and suggest times you are available. For example:

> Please call me to arrange an interview. My schedule allows me to meet with you on Tuesday or Thursday afternoon.

An alternative is to state that you will call:

> I will call you early next week to discuss my potential as a salesperson for XYZ Corporation.

No response does not necessarily mean you have been rejected; follow up with a phone call if you do not hear anything within a week. One student got a job because he called to verify that the sales manager had received his résumé. She had never seen it but was impressed enough with the student's phone call to arrange an appointment. Sometimes e-mail is lost or delayed, and you would not want a company to miss out on the opportunity to hire you because of a computer glitch!

One hiring manager, Ryan Donovan with Text 100 Corp., points out a few mistakes he sees far too often. For example, when applicants apply by e-mail, they change their address so quickly that Donovan can't reply. To make it worse, these candidates provide e-mail as their only contact method. Another beef he has is attaching your résumé or other documents in a format he can't open.[14]

THE INTERVIEW

Many students do not realize how much competition exists for the best entry-level sales positions, or perhaps they do not know what companies look for in new employees. Students often act as though they are shopping for a job. Job shoppers, however, are not seriously considered by recruiters, who are usually astute enough to quickly pick up on the student's lack of interest. If the job shopper does become interested, it is probably too late because the recruiter has already discounted this applicant. Like it or not, you are really competing for a job. As in any competition, success requires preparation and practice.

PREPARING FOR THE INTERVIEW Students who know something about the company and its industry lead the competition. You have already looked for company and industry information in the library, in business reference books, and in periodicals. You visited their website. You have also interviewed the company's customers, salespeople, and sales managers. You can use this knowledge to demonstrate your self-motivation and positive attitude, two of the top three characteristics sales managers look for in sales candidates. You will find it easier to demonstrate the third top characteristic, communication skills, with the confidence you gain from proper preparation.

In addition to building knowledge of the "customer," you must plan your responses to the questions you will be asked. Exhibit 18.6 lists standard interview questions.

Scenario questions are very popular with recruiters. These questions ask what the candidate would do in a certain situation involving actions of competitors (for example, what would you do if a customer told you something negative about your product that you knew to be untrue, and the customer's source of information was your competitor?). Such questions test ethics regarding competitors and the ability to handle a delicate situation. Scenario questions also test the candidate's response to rejection, ability to plan, and other characteristics. You can best prepare for these types of questions with this class and by placing yourself in the situations described in the cases and exercises in this book. You may also want to review the questions at the ends of the chapters.

EXHIBIT 18.6

Frequently Asked Interview Questions

1. What are your long-range and short-range goals and objectives? When and why did you establish these goals, and how are you preparing yourself to achieve them?
2. What do you consider to be your greatest strengths and weaknesses?
3. Why did you choose the career for which you are preparing?
4. How do you think a friend or professor who knows you well would describe you?
5. Why should I hire you?
6. In what ways do you think you can make a contribution to our company?
7. Do you think your grades are a good indication of your academic achievement?
8. What major problem have you encountered, and how did you deal with it?
9. What do you know about our company? Why are you seeking a position with us?
10. If you were hiring a graduate for this position, what qualities would you look for?

The sales field has several unusual characteristics, such as travel, that influence the type of questions asked. For example, if significant travel is part of the position, you may be asked, Travel is an important part of this job, and you may be away from home about three nights per week. Would you be able and willing to travel as the job requires? However, some questions are illegal, and you do not have to answer them—such as What is your marital status? Do you plan to have a family? Will that affect your ability to travel? Exhibit 18.7 lists some questions that are illegal, as well as legal questions that you may have to answer.

So what do you do when you are faced with an illegal question? One thing you should do is report the incident to your school's career services personnel if the interview is taking place on campus or as a result of the campus career services center. But when actually faced with the question, you have several choices. One is to ask, "Why do you ask? Is that important?" You may find that it is a question asked by an interviewer out of personal curiosity, and the interviewer may not have realized the question was inappropriate. Another response is to simply reply, "I'm sorry, I would prefer not to answer that question." If probed, then you can state that you believe the question is not legal, but you will check with career services later; if the question is legal; you will answer it later. If the interviewer is simply ignorant, you will probably get an apology, and then the interview will move on. Otherwise, you've identified a company where you may not wish to work. Your final option is, of course, to go ahead and answer the question.

At some point during the interview, the recruiter will ask whether you have any questions. In addition to using the standard questions concerning pay, training, and benefits, you should prepare questions that are unlikely to have been answered already. For example, suppose your research has uncovered the fact that the company was recently awarded the Malcolm Baldrige Award for Quality; you might plan to ask what the company did to win that award.

You may also want to plan questions about the interviewer's career, how it got started, and what positions he or she has held. These questions work best when

EXHIBIT 18.7

Examples of Legal and Illegal Questions

Subject	Legal Questions	Illegal Questions
Name	Have you ever used another name?	What is your maiden name?
Residence	Where do you live?	Do you own or rent your home?
Birthplace or national origin	Can you, after employment, verify your right to work in the United States?	Where were you born? Where were your parents born?
Marital or family status	Statement of company policy regarding assignment of work of employees who are related. Statement of company policy concerning travel: Can you accept this policy?	With whom do you reside? Are you married? Do you plan a family?
Arrest or criminal record	Have you ever been convicted of a felony? (Such a question must be accompanied by a statement that a conviction will not necessarily disqualify the applicant.)	Have you ever been arrested?

Source: Baylor University Career Services Center. See also Wayne Barlow, "Pre-Employment Interviews: What You Can and Cannot Ask," *Personnel Journal*, January 1996, p. 99.

you are truly interested in the response; otherwise, you might sound insincere. Answers to these questions can give you a personal insight into the company. Also, you may often find yourself working for the interviewer, so the answers to your questions may help you decide whether you like and can work with this person.

Other important subjects to ask about are career advancement opportunities, typical first-year responsibilities, and corporate personality. You also need to know how financially stable the company is, but you can find this information for public firms in the library. If the firm is privately owned, ask about its financial stability.

Finally, it may seem trivial, but shine your shoes! You are interviewing for a professional position, so look professional. A student once showed up for an interview dressed in cut-off shorts and a T-shirt. The interviewer assumed the student didn't care enough to dress for the interview and ended the interview before it began. If you do not look the part now, an interviewer will not see you in the part.

DURING THE INTERVIEW

The job interview is much like any other sales call. It includes an approach, needs identification, presentation, and gaining commitment. There are, however, several important differences because both parties are identifying needs and making presentations.

THE APPROACH Social amenities will begin the interview. You will not need the same type of attention getter that you would on a cold call. However, you may want to include an attention getter in your greeting. For example, use a compliment approach, such as "It must be very exciting to work for a Malcolm Baldrige Award winner."

NEEDS IDENTIFICATION One difference between sales calls and job interviews is that both parties have needs they have individually defined before the meeting (in a sales call, SPIN helps you to assist the buyer in defining needs). Questions such as Are you willing to relocate? are used not to define needs so much as to determine whether the company's needs will be met. You should prepare questions that will help you learn whether the company's offer will meet your needs.

Take notes during the interview, especially when asking about the company, so that you can evaluate whether your needs will be met. Carry a portfolio with extra résumés and blank paper and pen for note taking. You may want to ask,

Many colleges offer career and placement counseling, with companies coming to campus to recruit salespeople. This student is seeking advice from a career counselor at Farleigh Dickinson University.

Rhoda Sidney/PhotoEdit

Do you mind if I take notes? This information is important to me, and I don't want to forget anything.

Try to determine early whether your interviewer is a sales manager or a personnel manager. Personnel managers may have a difficult time telling you about the job itself, its daily activities, and so forth; they may be able to outline only things such as training and employee benefits. Sales managers, however, can tell you a lot about the job, perhaps to the point of describing the actual territory you will work in.

Personnel managers do not like being asked about salary; you will find that many people will advise you not to ask about money on the first interview. On the other hand, you are making an important decision. Why waste your time or theirs if the salary is much lower than your other alternatives? Sales managers are less likely to object; but just in case, you may want to preface a question about earnings by saying, Compensation is as important a consideration for me as training and other benefits when making a decision. Can you tell me the approximate earnings of a first-year salesperson? You will probably get a range rather than a specific figure. You could also wait until a later meeting to ask about earnings.

People who prefer security desire compensation plans with an emphasis on salary. Other people like the potential rewards of straight commission. If either is important to you, ask about the type of compensation plan in the first meeting. For example, you should ask, "What type of compensation plan do you offer: salary, straight commission, or a combination of salary plus commission or bonus?"

PRESENTATION Features alone are not persuasive in interviews, just as features alone do not persuade buyers to purchase products. The U.S. Army recruiting command uses a technique to sell the army that can be useful in interviewing. The technique is called **FEB,** which stands for feature, evidence, benefit. Cheryl McSwain (see Exhibit 18.4) might say, I was a camp counselor for two summers at Camp Kanatcook (feature), as you can see on my résumé (evidence). This experience taught me customer service skills that you will appreciate when I sell for you (benefit).

For example, Adam Caplan, a student at the Kellogg School (Northwestern University) was interviewing with Joseph Vansyckle of Drugstore.com and was asked how he handles stress in the work environment. Adam recounted his competitive tennis experience, saying, "During the point, I'm utterly focused and have a killer instinct, but when the point is over, it's very important for me to relax, to think about something else . . . before I get up again for the next point. Focused and relaxed—I apply that to my work and have found that it leads to success." He then related this experience to the job at Drugstore.com and how that characteristic would help him deal with work stress. Afterward, Vansyckle said that answer "was genius." The answer provided all three components: the feature (focus), evidence (tennis experience), and benefit (how he applies it to work stress).[15]

If asked to describe yourself, use features to prove benefits. Recruiters will appreciate specific evidence that can back up your claims. For example, if you say you like people and that is why you think you would be a good salesperson, be prepared to demonstrate how your love of people has translated into action.

Many students carry portfolios into interviews. A **portfolio** is an organized collection of evidence of one's career.[16] For example, a portfolio might contain letters of reference, a résumé, thank-you letters from customers, a paper on an internship, a strategic plan created for a business policy class, or even photographs of the homecoming float for which you were chairperson. Some of our students offer videos of their sales calls from this class as part of their portfolio. Portfolios are one method of offering proof that you can deliver benefits.

Keep in mind that the interviewer also will be taking notes. Writing down answers takes the interviewer longer than it takes for you to speak. Once the question is answered sufficiently, stop and allow the interviewer time to write. Many applicants believe they should continue talking; the silence of waiting is too much to bear. Stay silent, however; otherwise, you may talk yourself out of a sale.

GAINING COMMITMENT Because sales positions usually require skill at gaining commitment, sales managers will want to see whether the candidate has that skill. Be prepared to close the interview with some form of gaining commitment: I'm very excited about this opportunity. What is our next step?

Be sure to learn when you can expect to hear from the company, confirm that deadline, and write it down. You may want to say, So I'll receive a call or a letter within the next two weeks. Let's see, that would be the 21st, right?

Asking for commitment and confirming the information signal your professionalism and your organizational and selling skills.

SPECIAL TYPES OF INTERVIEWS

You can face many types of interviews: disguised interviews, stress interviews, and panel interviews, among others. **Disguised interviews,** or interviews in which the candidate is unaware that the interviewer is evaluating the candidate, are common at college placement offices. In the lobby you may meet a **greeter,** probably a recent graduate of your college, who will try to help you relax before a scheduled interview and offer you an opportunity to ask questions about the job and the company. Although you can obtain a lot of good information from a greeter, you may want to save some questions for the real interview. You may also want to repeat some questions in the interview to check for consistency. Keep in mind that the greeter is also interviewing you, even though the meeting seems like friendly conversation. Keep your enthusiasm high and your nerves low.

A **stress interview** is designed to place the candidate under severe stress to see how the candidate reacts. Stress interviews have been criticized as being unfair because the type of stress one experiences on a job interview often differs from the type of stress one would actually face on the job. Still, many reputable companies believe it appropriate to try to determine how a candidate reacts to stress because stress is a real part of just about every sales position. One tactic is to ask three questions at once and see how the candidate answers; another is to ask, "How are you going to lose money for me?" (translation: What mistakes have you made in the past and what might you do in the future?) or other reversed versions of appropriate questions.[17] While questionable in terms of measuring the appropriate form of stress, these methods are less questionable than the following: The interviewer asks the applicant to reveal something personal, such as a time when the person felt hurt. Once the situation has been described, the interviewer may mock the applicant, saying the situation wasn't that personal or that hurtful and surely the applicant can dig deeper. Another stress tactic is to ask the interviewee to sell something such as a pencil or a table.

You probably will not see stress interviews at a college placement office, but you could face one at some point in the job-hunting process. You may find it helpful to deal with a stress interview by treating it as a game (say to yourself, She's just trying to stress me out; I wonder how far she will go if I don't react). Of course, you may simply refuse to play the game, either by terminating the interview or by changing the subject. If you terminate the interview, you will probably not get the job.

In **panel interviews** you will encounter multiple interviewers. During a panel interview try to make eye contact with each interviewer. Focus on each person for at least three seconds at a time; anything less than that and you are simply sweeping the room. When asked a question, begin your answer by directing it to the questioner but then shift your attention to the group. By speaking to the group, you will keep all interviewers involved and avoid a two-person conversation.

Group interviews are similar to panel interviews, but include several candidates as well as several interviewers. Group interviews may take place in a conference room or around a dinner table. If you find yourself in a group interview, avoid trying to top the stories of the other candidates. Treat social occasions during office or plant visits as interviews and avoid alcohol or overeating. As with stress interviews, the key is to maintain your cool while being yourself. You cannot do that if you overindulge.

FOLLOW-UP

Regardless of the type of interview, you should send a thank-you note shortly afterward. Send one to the greeter, if possible (thus you will probably want to get this person's business card). If you had a panel interview, find out who the contact person is and write to that person. After thanking the person in the first paragraph, write a paragraph that summarizes the interview. Focus your summary on the reasons you should be hired. In the final paragraph reiterate your thanks and end with an assumptive statement, such as "I look forward to seeing you again."

Panel interviews require special tactics by the candidate to keep all interviewers involved.

Michael Newman/PhotoEdit

If you do not hear by the target date, contact the person. Call if the interviewer was a sales manager; write if a personnel manager spoke with you. Sales managers will appreciate the saleslike perseverance; personnel managers may not. Within another week, call the personnel manager also. Simply ask for the status of your application rather than whether you got the job. The process of deciding may have taken longer than expected, or other situations may have caused delays. You need to know where you stand, however, so that you can take advantage of alternatives, if possible.

INTERVIEWING NEVER ENDS

Even if you spend your entire career with one company, your job interviewing days are not over after you land that first job; you will interview for promotions as well. Some companies even interview candidates for admission to management development programs. The same techniques apply in all of these cases. You will still need to prepare properly, conduct the interview professionally, close for some level of commitment, and follow up.

MANAGING YOUR CAREER GOALS

An important aspect of career management is to set life-based objectives and then use them to determine your career objectives. Sharon and Greg Ross, for example, both sell for Holt Marketing and believe that their knowledge of each other's responsibilities helps them balance family and career needs.[18] Similarly, Ross Glatzer faced the conflicting loyalties of his career and family, deciding that a two-year sabbatical was needed to meet his family's needs. One survey reported that a lack of balance was one of the top reasons that managers resigned, were terminated, or were poorly evaluated.[19]

Balance, then, is important when setting career goals. Career decisions must be compatible with family and personal objectives. Keeping life goals in mind and remembering your reasons for setting those goals will help you map out a career with which you can be happy.

MAKING THE TRANSITION FROM COLLEGE TO CAREER

That first year after college is a unique and important time in anyone's life. How this transition is handled can have a big influence in whether you reach success or experience disappointment. Although a life's work is not created or ruined in the first months, a poor start can take years to overcome. It is not just a matter of giving up student attitudes and behaviors; making the transition also requires taking the time to understand and earn the rights, responsibilities, and credibility of being a sales professional.[20] You will make mistakes during that transition; everyone does (see Selling Scenario 18.1). But as many successful salespeople have learned, it isn't whether you make mistakes, but rather whether you learn from them.

Many new hires want to make a great first impression, so they charge ahead and fail to recognize that the organization was there long before they were and has already developed its own way of doing things. The first thing to do is learn the organization's culture, its values, and the way things are done there.

Another important aspect of the first year is that you are under a microscope. Your activities are watched closely as management and your peers try to decide whether you are someone on whom they can depend. Demonstrate a mature willingness to learn, plus respect for those with experience. Part of this mature willingness to learn means you hold your expectations in check and keep your promotion hopes realistic. Remember too that recruiters tend to engage in puffery when presenting the opportunities and benefits of a company. Although

SALES BLOOPERS

The first year in anyone's career can be exciting, but probably no career is as exciting when starting out as is sales. Closing those big deals can be thrilling. The first year, though, is also often filled with gaffes and bone-headed mistakes, things you wish had never happened.

Bill Maxwell was a new college graduate and a newlywed with little money when he got his first sales job. So he borrowed $1,000 from his parents to buy several business suits. "I found one that I liked and it fit really well, so I bought it in two different colors," he says. Getting dressed in the dark so as not to wake his wife, he didn't realize that the pants he put on didn't match the coat until he was at the customer's office. "I couldn't just reschedule, but it's hard to impress someone that you can handle the details of satisfying their needs when you can't dress yourself!" Still, Marwell says the customer laughed along with him, told stories of his own newlywed days, and is now one of Bill's best accounts.

Katie Washington entered sales straight out of college. Her position included taking clients to lunch, and she discovered an interesting restaurant that had just opened. "I had a client who really loved Indian food, and at the time, there weren't many Indian restaurants from which to choose. But this one looked great." So she set up a lunch meeting. When they arrived, they found out it was closed on Mondays, so they rescheduled for Thursday. On Thursday, she learned when she went to

pay the bill that the restaurant wouldn't accept Visa, only American Express. "I had to leave the customer there at the table while I went to an ATM." That customer wasn't too impressed.

Darren Jennings's biggest gaffe also involved an Indian restaurant. "My customer loves curry, and we went to a restaurant that he chose. He insisted on ordering the meal, one of his favorites, for both of us." But Jennings didn't realize the dish included cilantro, to which he is very allergic. "I saw it, and I knew I shouldn't eat it. But to be nice, I ate some, trying to avoid the cilantro." By the end of the meal, Darren's face and neck were red and blotchy, as well as very itchy. "It was obvious something was wrong; fortunately, it just looks bad, it isn't life-threatening." When he explained what happened in response to a question from the customer, the customer said, "You should have told me!"

Each of these salespeople achieved significant early success, but not without a mistake or two along the way. Washington says, "It didn't seem funny at the time," and my manager wasn't too happy when I tried to explain why I didn't land that account. But I've made other mistakes and still won the business." As Jennings says, "You realize you can relax and not worry about being perfect all of the time. The mark of a true professional is how you overcome mistakes, not whether you never make one."

the recruiter said it may be possible to earn a promotion in six months, the average may be much longer.

Seek a partnership with your manager. Although partnership implies a peer-level relationship and you do not have the experience to be a true peer with your manager, use the same partnering skills with him or her that you would use with customers. Find out what your manager needs and wants and then do it. Every workday is a test day except that you sometimes write the questions. Just like your professor, your manager wants the answers, not the problems. Give your boss solutions, and you will be well on the way to a partnership. Other salespeople can also help, as you can see in Building Partnerships 18.1.

MANAGING YOUR CAREER

Managing your career wisely will require conscious effort on your part. You are the person in your company to whom your career means the most. Many companies, such as 3M with its Assessment–Curriculum–Transfer of Learning program, have recognized that ownership of development belongs to the person, not to the company, and have turned training into self-directed development programs.[21] Even if your company has not formalized development into a self-directed program

MENTORING: A KEY TO CAREER SUCCESS

The sales job is unlike many others. For the most part, the salesperson operates alone, often miles away from any company office and without direct supervision or support. At best, a sales manager will work with a salesperson once or twice a month, perhaps for a half-day. One important element, though, in nearly every successful career is the presence of a mentor.

A mentor is an experienced salesperson who provides more than training: friendship, counseling, acceptance, and other forms of support. Most mentor/protégé relationships occur informally, but many companies now try to create mentoring programs because they've recognized the importance of good mentors. In fact, U.K. research suggests that both potential mentors and protégés find it difficult to create relationships on their own, and they want company-sponsored programs.

Bob Walker, who sells for a Quebec-based chemical distributor, says he found his own mentor through a shared interest in the Edmonton Oilers hockey team. But now that Bob is a mentor himself, he has organized a formal mentoring program for his company. "Mentoring is too important to leave to chance," he believes. Even though the company has a formal mentoring program, he offers these tips to would-be protégés: "First, in order to have a friend, you have to be a friend. Don't expect to only receive; you

have to be able to give to the relationship, too." Research supports Walker, as being able to build strong relationships is an important factor in mentor/protégé relationships.

"Second, keep your eyes open. I've seen some mentor/protégé relationships spiral downward because of the mentor's overall bad attitude, so choose your mentor wisely." Walker also believes that both the mentor and protégé can feed on each other's positive attitudes, with both becoming stronger.

As Walker believes, and research supports, an important benefit for the protégé is role clarity. "Realistically, no matter how good the company training is, no training program answers every question a young salesperson has. And sometimes the official answer may not make sense. A mentor can interpret things for the protégé and help make sense of confusing situations."

Sources: M. Lineham and J. S. Walsh, "Mentoring Relationships and the Female Managerial Career," *Career Development Journal* 4 (1999), pp. 348–54; Ellen B. Pullins, Leslie Fine, and Wendy Warren, "Identifying Peer Mentors in the Sales Force: An Exploratory Investigation of Willingness and Ability," *Journal of the Academy of Marketing Science* 24 (1996), pp. 125–36; Leslie Fine and Ellen B. Pullins, "Peer Mentoring in the Industrial Sales Force: An Exploratory Investigation of Men and Women in Developmental Positions," *Journal of Personal Selling and Sales Management*, Fall 1998, pp. 89–104.

or if the development program does not provide many options, take the time and effort to invest in yourself so that you can grow in your career. As the philosopher Eric Hoffer said, "In times of change, the learners inherit the earth, while the learned find themselves beautifully equipped to handle a world that no longer exists."[22]

Lifelong learning is important in today's learning organization. AT&T, for example, spends $1 billion annually on training.[23] Although many companies have downsized, it is the versatile, well-educated employee who not only keeps a job but also grows a career.

Lifelong learning can be an important factor in not only improving your position but also enjoying what you do. Once you have a position within an organization, your objective will be to develop yourself to get a promotion and then to be successful in that promotion. (To get the promotion after that, you will need to do well in the job you are seeking.) You should take several significant actions in each position along the way. The first action is to understand your options because sales can often lead to various positions.

DUAL CAREER PATH

When you start out in sales, many career options are open. Career paths can alternate between sales and marketing or follow a route entirely within sales or entirely within marketing. You may even wind up as chief executive officer of a major global corporation. Exemplifying how you might pursue various positions, Exhibit 18.8 depicts the career path for salespeople at Wallace Computer Services. Note that in addition to sales management opportunities, they have opportunities in marketing and product development that all begin in sales.

LEARN YOUR CURRENT JOB

Learn all you can about the job you have now. Many people want promotions as fast as they can get them, regardless of their readiness. But consider that you will probably be managing the people who will be holding your current job. To be truly effective as their manager, you should learn all you can about the job of the people you hope to manage while in the best position to do so: while you are one of them.

EXHIBIT 18.8

Career Path at Wallace

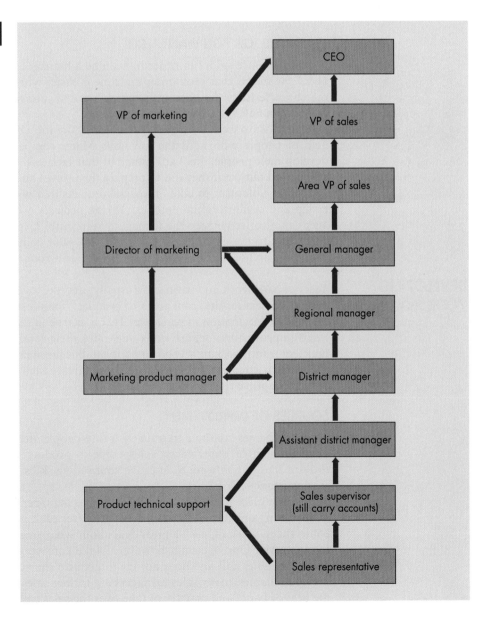

Learning doesn't end with college. Motorola employees, for example, regularly attend training classes at the Galvin Center, the company's training center in Chicago.

Reproduced with permission from Motorola, Inc. © 2002 Motorola, Inc.

LEARN THE JOB YOU WANT NEXT

A manager once said, "In order to become a manager, you must first be a manager." He meant that promoting someone is easier when that person already has the characteristics the position requires—that is, already acts like a manager—rather than having only potential.

Several ways exist for you to learn about the job you desire. First, solicit the help of people who hold the job now. Many companies expect managers to develop their people. Take advantage of that fact; ask for the help of such managers. Find out what they did to prepare themselves and what you should do.

Second, volunteer to take on special projects that will demonstrate your leadership and organizational abilities. Taking projects off the hands of your manager can also let you see the manager's responsibilities. Look for ways you can contribute to the overall sales team to show your commitment to the organization, your ability to lead and develop others, and your management skills.

DEVELOPING YOUR SKILLS

Years of hard work and frustration usually precede "overnight" success. For most people, success results from years of practice, limited success and unlimited failure, and determination to persevere. This is as true in sales as in any profession.

To improve their selling skills and raise their level of earnings, salespeople must constantly seek new ways to perform. But salespeople must also know what they do that already works! They need to evaluate their performance, looking for ways to improve their sales presentations.

SOURCES OF IMPROVEMENT

Most companies continue to train their salespeople after basic sales training, but most training of experienced salespeople is product related rather than sales skills related. If you want to improve your selling skills, you may have to actively seek assistance.

The first place to start is with the field sales manager. When that person works with you in your territory, solicit feedback after each call. During these curbside conferences, you can learn a great deal about what you are doing from an objective observer. One warning, however: Make sure your manager only observes during the sales call and does not try to get into the act! As we discussed in the previous chapter, many sales managers are former salespeople who get excited in the heat of battle and may try to take over the sales call.

Peers provide another source. Who is successful in the company? When gathered together for a sales meeting, many successful salespeople pick one another's brains for new ideas and strategies. Offer to work with them in their territories for a day or so in order to learn from them. In most situations they will be flattered and helpful. Clairol, for example, has a mentoring program that matches up successful salespeople with younger reps. Like many other companies, Clairol has found that this arrangement benefits both the mentor and the protégé.[24] Noncompeting salespeople in professional organizations such as Sales and Marketing Executives, an international organization of salespeople and marketing managers, will also be flattered to share their tips with you.

Bookstores offer a wealth of material for developing sales skills. Many good books remind salespeople of the basics of selling and present advanced methods of selling and negotiating. Be sure to save this book, too, as you will want to refer to it when you are in the field.

Sales seminars and cassette tapes are also available. Seminars, such as those offered by Dale Carnegie, Wilson Learning, and Tom Hopkins, can be very motivating. However, many experienced salespeople desire more than just motivation; they look for seminars that also teach new ways to present and gain commitment, as well as other sales skills. When they cannot attend the seminar, they purchase cassette tapes. They can listen while driving, using what would have been unproductive time to improve their skills.

Another source of improvement is an industry association. Many industries and professions offer certification programs, which not only require that you improve and update your knowledge and skills, but also offer proof to your customers that you have made that effort. In the promotional products industry, for example, one-third of buyers surveyed said that certification of the salespeople who sold to them was an important factor when choosing vendors.[25] Certification was one measure of service quality that these buyers used when comparing suppliers.

In this course you have begun to develop your interpersonal persuasion, or selling, skills. Whether or not you plan a career in sales, you owe it to yourself to continue to develop these skills.

MANAGING STRESS

Selling can be a stressful career. For example, with three days left in the month, Richard Langlotz, a sales manager at Minolta Business Systems, faced a sales team that lost $100,000 in business. One sale alone, worth $60,000, would have made the team's quota, but that account delayed its order for a few months. The other prospects decided to go with the competition. Suddenly it looked as though Langlotz was going to finish the month at only 50 percent of quota. To top it off, one of his salespeople quit. What did he do? "I took my sales team to a pizza place," Langlotz says. He thought about calling a meeting and getting tough with his team, but he realized they already had enough stress and didn't need any more from him. At the pizza parlor, without any prompting from him, each salesperson examined his or her prospect lists and determined how the team was going to move sales forecast for the next month into the current month. While they didn't recover the entire $100,000, they did sell enough to cover the team's quota.

Meeting quota is the most stressful part of the job, according to one survey. Phil Warnke, senior sales consultant at Achieve Global, says, "If I don't sell, I don't eat."[26] Many salespeople liken sales to a roller coaster ride, with great emotional highs when sales are good but emotional lows when sales are poor.

For some people, coping with stress results in changing jobs.[27] Changing jobs may be the right thing for some people to do. Others turn to less healthful releases, such as absenteeism, drugs, alcohol, and so forth.[28] All jobs have some

Regular exercise is an effective method of combating stress.

John Coletti/Stock, Boston

stress; managing that stress is important to leading a happy and healthy life. However, managing stress does not always mean removing the cause of stress. Sometimes, as with the loss of a loved one, most people find they must manage stress because they cannot remove or change its cause. Two types of stress common to salespeople because of the unique nature of sales positions are situational stress and felt stress.

SITUATIONAL STRESS

Situational stress is short-term anxiety caused by a situational factor.[29] You may face situational stress when waiting to make a sales presentation for your class, for example. The best strategy to deal with situational stress is to leave the situation or remove the situational factor causing the stress, but that approach is not always possible. You cannot, for example, simply tell your instructor that you are too stressed to sell in class today, so you are leaving! One technique for managing situational stress is to imagine that the situational factor has been removed (see Exhibit 18.9 for more ideas). In class, imagine that you have already finished your role-play. Mentally consider that feeling of relief you get when you know you have done a job well. Sometimes imaging success can reduce feelings of stress.

In sales situational stress may be caused by impending presentations, deadlines for closing orders (as in Richard Langlotz's case), and similar situations. Situational stress can cause stage fright in even the most experienced salespeople. One price of success is that situational stress will continue to occur, but successful salespeople learn to control their feelings of situational stress.

EXHIBIT 18.9	*Use imaging:* Close your eyes and imagine yourself past the source of stress. Try to feel the actual sensation of what it will be like when the stress is gone.

Coping with Situational Stress

Use imaging: Close your eyes and imagine yourself past the source of stress. Try to feel the actual sensation of what it will be like when the stress is gone.

Exercise: Exercise can moderate feelings of stress. When situational stress occurs over a period of time, set time aside for exercise breaks.

Take breaks: Take a walk, phone a friend, do something. If working on a stressful project, take regular stress breaks. Combine imaging techniques with breaks to increase the stress-reducing power of breaks.

Rest: In addition to breaks, be well rested when the situation arises. If you have a major presentation, get a good night's rest beforehand.

Prepare: If the situation involves future performance, prepare and practice. Prepare for every contingency, but don't let the tension build by thinking only of things going wrong.

Recover: Plan time for the postsituation recovery before you charge into the next high-stress situation. Doing two major presentations in one day, for example, may not provide you with the recovery time you need to do well in the second presentation.

FELT STRESS

Felt stress lasts longer than situational stress because the causes are more enduring. **Felt stress** is psychological distress brought about by job demands or constraints encountered in the work environment.[30] Perhaps the most common form of felt stress is role stress, or feelings of stress caused by a lack of role accuracy. **Role accuracy** refers to the degree to which the salesperson's perceptions of the sales role are correct.[31]

Role stress is brought about by role conflict and/or role ambiguity. **Role conflict** occurs when two partners demand incompatible actions of the salesperson. For example, Cameron Dube with Servall Packaging Industries once had a customer who was dissatisfied with a new machine. "While I was in [the customer's] office, I heard two sets of voices, my customer's and my boss's," he said. "The customer wanted something I knew the company wouldn't pay for."[32] Conflict occurred with the salesperson caught in the middle. **Role ambiguity** occurs when the salesperson is not sure what actions are required. The salesperson may not be sure what is expected, how to achieve it, or how performance will be evaluated and rewarded.

In general, the best way to handle role stress is to increase role accuracy (see Exhibit 18.10 for specific ideas). When the problem is role ambiguity, simply asking for further instruction or reviewing training materials may be helpful. Coaching and other management support can also be requested.

Role conflict and role ambiguity, however, require prioritizing activities. In the example of the salesperson who feels stress due to conflict between the customer's and the manager's demands, the salesperson must decide whose needs will be met. Once that decision is made, further stress can be avoided by refusing to dwell on the conflict. Note that the conflict is still there (both parties have conflicting demands), but the effect on the salesperson is minimized.

In either case a strong partnership with the sales manager can greatly aid in reducing stress. When a partnership is formed between a sales manager and a salesperson, the salesperson has a better understanding of the demands of the job, which activities should receive priority, and how the job should be performed. Partners also have access to more resources and more information, which can help remove some of the organizational constraints that can bring about stress.[33]

Strong sales skills can also reduce feelings of stress. Mastery of the job will reduce feelings of stress because the salesperson is in control of the situation.

EXHIBIT 18.10 Reducing Role Stress	*Prioritize:* Set your own priorities so that when different people place conflicting expectations on you, your preset priorities determine where your actions will go. *Seek support:* Enlist support of your priorities from your spouse, your manager, and other key people. By focusing on goals and priorities, you can reduce conflict over specific activities. *Reset expectations:* By prioritizing and seeking support, you can reset expectations of various constituencies so that they are in harmony. Communicate and gain agreement on what you are capable of doing so that others' expectations of you are realistic. *Act and move on:* Once you have made a decision to act, don't dwell on the conflict. Act and move on.

Summary

A sales career offers many opportunities for growth and personal development, but that career has to start somewhere. That is the purpose of the job search: to find a good match between what you need and have to offer and what a company needs and has to offer.

To achieve a match that results in mutual satisfaction, you must first understand who you are, specifically what you need and what you have to offer. You can ask yourself a number of questions to stimulate your thinking about the type of person you are and what you will need from a sales position. In addition, as you review your experiences in school, work, and other activities, you can identify the skills and characteristics that you have to offer.

Finding industries and companies with the characteristics you desire will require you to apply your marketing research skills. The library contains many sources of information that will help you. Personal sources can also be useful in providing information as well as leads for interviews, as can the Internet.

Sources for job interviews include the campus placement office, personal contacts, and advertisements. Résumés are personal brochures that help to sell a candidate. Writing effective cover letters will help you get interviews off campus, while the interview itself is similar to a sales call. Plan questions that demonstrate your knowledge of and interest in the company. Also, plan to ask for information that will help you make your decision. Follow up after the interview to demonstrate your desire and perseverance.

You are the person in the company to whom your career means the most. Therefore, you must actively manage your own career. Set career goals that are compatible with family and personal objectives. Keeping the reasons for these career goals in front of you will enable you to make better decisions.

Learn the job you have now. You may someday manage people who have this job; the better you know it, the better you will be at managing it. To become a manager, you must first be a manager. Learn the manager's job as well, and volunteer for activities and projects that will let you demonstrate your management ability.

Stress can occur in any job. Situational stress is short-term, whereas felt stress is longer-term. For many people, the key to managing stress is to reduce the influence stressors have because the causes of stress often cannot be eliminated.

Sales offers a challenging and exciting career. The opportunities are so varied that almost anyone can probably fit into some sales position. Even if you choose a career in another field, take advantage of the material in this chapter. You should find these job search and career management tips helpful in any field. Good luck!

KEY TERMS

application form   544
assessment center   544
conventional résumé   545
disguised interview   554
FEB   553
felt stress   563
functional résumé   545
greeter   554
group interview   555
interview   544

panel interview   555
portfolio   553
references   544
role accuracy   563
role ambiguity   563
role conflict   563
role stress   563
situational stress   562
stress interview   554
tests   544

1. You are interviewing for your dream job. Suddenly the interviewer notices your wedding ring and compliments you on it. But then he says, "You know, this job requires a lot of travel. What is your spouse going to say to that?" You answer the question, and he replies, "That's great, now, when you don't have kids. You don't have kids, do you? Because it is tough to be successful if you don't get the travel done." What do you do?

2. Some people recommend signing up for as many interviews as possible, reasoning that the experience will be helpful when you find a company with a job you really want. (And who knows? You might find a job you like.) Is this practice ethical? Why or why not? Are companies ethical when they come to campus and interview, even though a job is not available, just to maintain a presence on campus?

3. What would you do differently if you were being interviewed by an amiable, a driver, an analytical, or an expressive? What about a panel interview with one driver and one amiable? One analytical and one expressive?

4. Is a résumé the only document you should take into an interview? What other things might help document your capabilities?

5. Analyze yourself. List your strengths and weaknesses. What type of sales would best suit you? Why? Are you qualified for that job? If not, what do you need, and how would you go about getting it? How would you express your career objective in one sentence? If you are thinking of two or more industries, rewrite the career objective as you would for a résumé to be sent to recruiters in each industry.

6. The chapter suggests joining a trade or professional association now. How can the organization help you determine whether you are pursuing the right position? How could you network through the association?

7. Answer the questions in Exhibit 18.6 as you would in a sales job interview.

8. Your summer internship in a sales job was a very bad experience. Your biggest complaint was that the sales manager seemed incompetent. In spite of this negative experience, you like sales, so you are interviewing for a sales position. What would you say if asked why you do not seek full-time employment with the summer internship firm?

9. The chapter discusses finding successful salespeople and learning from them. Another important career tactic is to find a mentor. How would you find or select a mentor? What characteristics would you want to see in a mentor?

10. How does partnering reduce stress? Could multiple partnerships lead to role conflict? If so, what should the salesperson do when such conflict arises?

11. What stresses do you have now? How do you deal with stress? What healthy ways to handle stress do you use? What are some ways you respond to stress that may not be so healthy?

Case Problems

CASE 18.1

Becky Grounds's Interview

At 8:45 A.M. Becky Grounds arrived at her campus placement center for a 9:00 interview. She was surprised to be greeted by Matt Keepers, whom she had known in a marketing class. This conversation followed:

MATT: Becky, good to see you! I see that you are interviewing with us today. [Shakes Becky's hand and offers her a chair in the lobby.]

BECKY: Matt! Hi, how are you? I didn't know you were with HealthSouth. I've got the 9:00 spot.

MATT: Great! I started with HealthSouth right after graduation, and it has been a great six months. Tell me, are you interviewing with many medical firms or just with HealthSouth?

BECKY: I'm very interested in pharmaceuticals, but I know that HealthSouth is doing real well. So I thought that I should consider all medical companies. One of the physicians at a sports medicine center recommended HealthSouth. She said that your company does MRI scans for the NFL, as well as here at the university.

MATT: That's right, we do! I'm glad to hear that others agree we are one of the best. [Leans a little closer.] Look, just relax in the interview. HealthSouth really likes to get people from State, and I'm sure you will do well. [Looks up at the entrance of an older woman.] Oh, here's Jennifer Mayfield, my sales manager. She'll be interviewing you today. Jennifer, here's an old friend of mine, Becky Grounds.

JENNIFER [stepping forward and offering her hand]: Becky, it's nice to meet you.

BECKY [shaking her hand firmly]: It's nice to meet you, too, Ms. Mayfield. [Turning to Matt] Matt, it was good to see you again. Perhaps we'll talk some more later. [Becky and Jennifer seat themselves in the interviewing room; Jennifer opens a notebook.]

JENNIFER: Tell me about yourself, Becky.

BECKY: I'm the oldest of three children, and we were raised in a small town in the eastern part of the state. As a kid, I was very interested in soccer and wanted to be an Olympic soccer player. But an ankle injury ended my soccer career. Still, I learned a lot about self-discipline and the importance of hard work to achieve success, and I am still involved in soccer as a coach for a youth team. I chose State because it offers a strong marketing program. Marketing, and sales especially, seems to me to be a place where your success is directly related to your efforts. And I believe that more strongly now that I have taken the marketing courses here at State.

JENNIFER [writing furiously in her notebook]: I see. [Momentary silence as she finishes the notes, then looks up.] Tell me about a time when you were the leader of a group and things were not going your way. Perhaps it looked as if the group wasn't going to meet your objectives. What did you do?

BECKY: Let's see. There was the time when we were working on a group project for my marketing research class. Understand, though, that we had not elected a formal leader or anything. But no one in the group really wanted to do the project; everyone thought that research was boring. So at a group meeting, I suggested we talk about what we liked to do in marketing. After all, we were all marketing majors. Each person talked about why he or she had chosen marketing. Then I framed the project around what they wanted out of marketing. When they looked at it as a marketing project instead of a research project, it became something they wanted to do.

JENNIFER: Did you get an A?

BECKY: No, we got a B+. But more important, we were the only group that had fun, and I think we learned more as a result.

The interview went on for nearly 30 minutes. Becky thought she had done fairly well. She stopped in the lobby to write down her impressions and record Jennifer's answers to questions about the company. She smiled at Matt, who was talking to another applicant.

QUESTIONS

1. What did Becky do right? Why was that right? What did she do wrong? Why was that wrong?

2. What was Matt's purpose at the interview? What do you think Matt could tell Jennifer about Becky?

3. HealthSouth is a publicly traded company. What sources of information could Becky use to learn about the company? What information should she expect to get from those sources?

CASE 18.2

Help Wanted

You found these ads on Monster.com:

US—PA—Philadelphia—SALESPERSON
Local territory selling packaging products to manufacturers. Straight salary plus bonus, car allowance, full med & dent. No overnight. Exp. preferred, 3 mo. training. E-mail résumé to: Sales1@crummer.com.

US—Nationwide—SALES PROFESSIONAL
Selling network systems to small businesses. 20% travel. Opening new market. Sales exp. helpful, not nec. Must have some computer or telephone exp., college degree. 6 mo. tng. in NY. Co. car. Straight sal. first yr., sal. plus comm. after. E-mail résumé to Ms. R. Weinberg, RWein@wedocomputers.com.

QUESTIONS

1. What characteristics do you have that might work well in these positions? What characteristics do you think are necessary to be successful in these jobs? Why?
2. Tausha Aldridge from Crummer called and wants to interview you tomorrow. You never heard of the company until you saw the ad. How will you learn more about it?
3. It turns out that Crummer is a division of a U.S.–based *Fortune* 500 company, whereas Wedo is a distributor for several Japanese manufacturers. Crummer employs 535 salespeople; Wedo employs 47 salespeople. What are the advantages and disadvantages of working for Crummer? For Wedo?

CASE 18.3

Right First Job?

As a new college graduate from Western Carolina, Wendy Blackwell was excited to begin a job with LabSales Professionals. LabSales is a pharmaceutical firm that sells to cardiologists. But within six months Blackwell was looking for a new job and worried that her career was permanently damaged by leaving a job so quickly.

"I found the training really interesting, as I learned so much about cardiology and the drugs we sell," said Wendy. "But then I began making the calls." She quickly recognized that she had only a few minutes with a doctor, which was hardly any time for selling, and she felt that the only creativity required was what it took to get past the receptionist. "The other thing that really bothered me was that every six weeks I saw the same people in the same order. I never really knew who bought because of me, but I had to see them all, just the same."

Grabbing a burger at a restaurant in Knoxville, she ran into Ted Adams, a former classmate. Surprisingly, Ted, who had graduated a year ahead of Wendy, was also struggling with his job of 18 months. He had a double major in marketing and information systems and now sells computer software and hardware as a turnkey package. "I never really know what I'm going to run into—I just don't feel prepared," he said. "The company gave me a month's training, but I still don't know half of what my customers want and I have to get my manager to help. It takes months to get a sale, and the suspense is just killing me!"

QUESTIONS

1. What seems to be the problem for Wendy and Ted? What do you think they need in a job?
2. Using *Careers in Professional Selling* magazine, www.salescareers.com, or other websites, what types of sales positions do you think Wendy and Ted should pursue?

Additional References

Amin, Sammy; Abdalla Hayajneh; and Hudson Nwakanma. "College Students' Views of Sales Jobs as a Career: An Empirical Investigation." *American Business Review,* June 1995, pp. 54–60.

Brewer, Geoffrey. "Can You Teach People to Sell?" *Sales & Marketing Management,* March 1998, pp. 20–24.

Bush, Victoria, and Thomas N. Ingram. "Building and Assessing Cultural Diversity Skills: Implications for Sales Training." *Industrial Marketing Management* 30 (2001), pp. 65–76.

Castleberry, Stephen B., and Rick M. Ridnour. "Anticipatory Socialization: A Longitudinal Case Study of Salespeople Hired from College." *The Journal of Selling and Account Management* 4, Autumn 2001, pp. 53–69.

Cohen, Andy. "Sales Strikes Out on Campus." *Sales & Marketing Management,* November 1997, p. 13.

Fellman, Michelle. "We're in the Money! First Survey Says Sales Salaries Are Up." *Marketing News,* March 1998, pp. 1, 12.

"The 50 Best Companies to Sell For." *Selling Power,* October 2001, pp. 101–5.

Gurvis, Sandra. "Sales Degree: How America's Colleges and Universities Are Preparing the Salespeople of Tomorrow." *Selling Power,* May 2000, pp. 108–14.

Lysonski, Steven, and Srinivas Durvasula. "A Cross-National Investigation of Student Attitudes toward Personal Selling: Implications for Personal Selling." *Journal of Marketing Education* 20:2, August 1998, pp. 161–73.

McElroy, James, and Thomas DeCarlo. "Physical Attractiveness on Cognitive Evaluations of Saleswomen's Performance." *Journal of Marketing Theory and Practice* 9, Summer 2001, pp. 84–96.

Mount, Ian. "Gods of Sales." *Business 2.0,* October 2001, pp. 73–80.

Pitt, Leland F., and B. Rameseshan. "Realistic Job Information and Salesforce Turnover: An Investigative Study." *Journal of Managerial Psychology* 10 (1995), pp. 29–36.

Randall, James, and Cindy Randall. "A Current Review of Hiring Techniques for Sales Personnel: The First Step in the Sales Management Process." *Journal of Marketing Theory and Practice* 9, Spring 2001, pp. 80–93.

Richardson, Bradley. "Selling Sales to Students." *Sales & Marketing Management,* January 1998, p. 15.

Royal, Weld F. "Pleading Their Case (Salespeople's Top 5 Complaints about Selling)." *Sales & Marketing Management,* February 1995, pp. 50–57.

Stevens, Cynthia Kay, and Amy L. Kristof. "Making the Right Impression: A Field Study of Applicant Impression Management during Job Interviews." *Journal of Applied Psychology,* October 1995, pp. 587–606.

Verbeke, William, and Richard P. Bagozzi. "Sales Call Anxiety: Exploring What It Means When Fear Rules a Sales Encounter." *Journal of Marketing* 64, July 2000, pp. 88–101.

Role-Play Cases

This section provides a practical tool for developing your selling skills. Your professor will probably assign you a selling scenario to role-play in class. In this section you will find information on the role-plays. We have also included some helpful information on how to prepare for role-plays, as well as how to make constructive, helpful comments on the role-plays you will observe. Have fun!

HOW TO PREPARE FOR ROLE-PLAYS

Preparing for role-plays will depend somewhat on the topic of the role-play. Some of the role-plays will involve only part of the sales call. We will assume, however, that you are preparing for a complete sales call.

The first step is to organize your information. What do you know about this buyer? Do you know anything about his or her social style? What activity has there been in this account? What do you know about this type of customer? For example, if you are calling on a convenience store, what do you know about convenience stores in general as they relate to your product? Do they usually carry your product?

The next step is to write down your call objectives. Include primary, minimum, and optimistic objectives.

Next write a list of possible needs. Based on what you know about the person on whom you are calling, the account's buying history, and the type of account, what do you think he or she might need? How would he or she go about making the decision, and how would that person make the purchase (finance, pay cash, order by phone)?

Based on that information, you can begin to prepare for the content of the sales call. Develop open/closed or SPIN questions designed to develop those needs. Anticipate what aspects of that person's situation would create a problem that would lead to a need.

Examine your product and your promotions. What features will resolve those needs? What promotions will help the person buy? Then develop phrases that present benefits—that is, tie features to needs. Also, gather any material you may use; prepare testimonial letters, brochures, contracts, and any other support documents. You may also want to make a business card to have something to hand to the buyer.

Make a list of all the objections you can think of. Then develop responses to those objections. Plan how you will obtain commitment, based on your call objectives. Then memorize your approach. Many students tell us they are extremely nervous just before a role-play (we'll deal with that issue some more later). One way to handle your nerves is to memorize your opener, all the way up to SPIN. Once you get that far, you will forget about the camera and the class watching you, and you can settle down.

Now practice the rest of the role-play. You can practice your presentation out loud in front of the mirror or a friend. One word of caution, though: Not all of your presentation will be needed, because you will prepare for needs that may not exist. Don't go through the whole thing for the buyer during the actual sales call; just use the parts you need.

Mentally role-play, playing a constant "what if?" game. What if the buyer says this; how will you respond? What if the answer to a situation question is that; what will you do then? You won't cover every possibility, but you will be a lot better prepared for what actually does happen.

Now a word on nerves. We've already discussed one technique (memorizing the approach) for handling nerves. Another technique is designed to help you remain calm. Students often worry about the role-play, causing stress and nerves to build up. You can minimize this problem by imagining yourself being finished. Think about how good it will be to walk out of the classroom, done with the sales call. Or think about what you have planned for that evening, weekend, or whenever. Or think about one of your favorite places and what it must be like to be there right now. These thoughts will keep your mind off the role-play so that stress won't build up.

Be sure to get to the classroom early on the day of your role-play so you won't feel rushed. Also, remember to take all your material and blank videotape (if required) to class!

Just before you begin the role-play, take a deep breath, think about your opener, and smile. Aspiring concert pianists are taught to sit down, place their hands in their lap, and then begin. This sequence keeps them from rushing the beginning of the first piece. You don't want to rush, either.

Finally, if you are being videotaped, be sure to watch your tape after you're done and evaluate your performance. An unplayed videotape is of no value at all.

We wish you the greatest success, and remember to have fun.

HOW TO MAKE COMMENTS ON ROLE-PLAYS

As a student observer, you may be asked to evaluate your peers' performances, and your evaluations may become part of their grade. Whether or not your evaluation is averaged into their final grade, it is important for their development, and yours, that you do a good job.

As you watch role-plays for the purpose of providing feedback, you will find yourself learning more bout the art of selling. You will observe and think of ways to phrase ideas better, handle different types of customers, and develop strategies for persuading others. In order to do this you must observe carefully.

Identify what the person actually did. It is best if you can identify the technique used. For example, you recognize an objection-handling method as the feel–felt–found technique. Identifying what you saw serves two purposes: First, you have to learn the techniques (which will help you on exams and in your own role-plays); second, you can discuss the technique more appropriately after the role-play.

Then note whether the technique was appropriate. How did the buyer respond? How would you have responded if the technique had been used on you? Was the technique appropriate for the situation, for the buyer's social style, and for the product?

Finally, think about what you would have done if the technique was not appropriate. During the role-play, you'll have only enough time to write down what the person actually did. But in the moments afterward, you can contemplate alternative approaches.

Your comments to the seller, then, can be phrased in this manner. To comment on a technique or a phrase that you think could have been better, use this formula: First, identify what the person did and discuss why it was inappropriate or less than optimal. Then offer an alternative and explain why you think it is better. Finally, end with a comment about something the person did that was good. Even if you don't observe any problems, you can still comment on what was good.

Keep in mind that immediately after a presentation, the seller's emotions are strongest. The person is usually convinced that the presentation was awful and there was nothing good about it. Find something positive about which to comment. Everyone does something well in every role-play. You can really boost someone's confidence if you can find that one good thing and hold it up for the person to see. Then she or he will be more receptive to instructional comments.

ROLE-PLAY CASE 1   CALLAWAY BIG BERTHA C4 DRIVERS

Callaway Golf designs, creates, builds, and markets golf products that are superior and different from those of their competitors. Their commitment is that each new product must be a significant improvement not only in relation to their competitors, but also in relation to existing Callaway products. The company, founded by Ely Callaway, is the world's largest manufacturer of premium golf clubs and maker of golf balls and putters. It is listed on the New York Stock Exchange as ELY. Callaway products are designed and built in Carlsbad, California, and the firm employs some 2,500 employees.

Callaway makes many items for golfers. Their line of golf clubs includes Big Bertha (drivers and irons), Steelhead (woods and irons), ERC (drivers and fairway woods), and Hawk Eye (woods and irons). They also produce and market Odyssey Putters, Callaway golf balls, and a full range of accessories (headwear, gloves, golf bags, and so on).

For this role-play you'll be selling the C4 Driver. A driver is the club that the golfer usually uses to tee off at the start of each hole. Golfers want their drivers to help them hit long, straight shots. Over the past 15 years, a great deal of high-tech research has gone into making drivers that do just that. The C4 is one of the most sophisticated drivers on the market and is the result of years of research and development. The C4 is the largest and lightest head ever created by Callaway, without sacrificing durability. Students should visit www.callawaygolf.com for more details about the company and this particular golf club.

C4 stands for Compression Cured Carbon Composite, an aerospace high-tech material that is used in the face and the body of the club. This material results in a large, light, and extremely strong club head. The result for the golfer

is a very solid, pleasing sound on impact and outstanding performance. The larger head means the club has a larger face (the area that hits the golf ball), giving the golfer a bigger hitting area. This is sometimes called the "sweet spot," and the C4 has a huge sweet spot. The club's head is compression-molded in multiple layers using heat and extremely high pressure. The result is lightweight durability. Tungsten-loaded urethane weight strips distribute 55 grams of weight around the perimeter of the head, which results in explosive performance. The soleplate and leading edge are finished in aluminum, giving extreme durability and protection when the club brushes the ground. The C4 even has a new lightweight grip, which is made using a three-layer process, allowing the club to be soft and tacky but retain its durability. All of these features combined result in more club head speed, more forgiveness (when the golfer has a bad swing), and the potential for more distance off the tee.

Although the club is very high-tech, it conforms to all the USGA Rules of Golf and is legal for tournament play around the world. Both male and female professional golfers from all parts of the world use the C4 Driver. Here is a partial list (for a more current, complete list, see the Callaway golf Web page): Annika Sorenstam, Liselotte Neumann, Emilee Klein, Per-Ulrik Johansson, Paul Lawrie, Seve Ballesteros, and Niclas Fasth.

The C4 comes in a variety of configurations to suit the exact needs of each individual golfer. Golfers can choose from a host of lofts, both left- and right-hand heads, and a variety of shafts (ladies', light, regular, firm, strong, and custom).

On Callaway's website, golfers can locate the nearest stores, country clubs, and golf course pro shops that carry the new C4 Driver. The search can be by city name, state, or zip code, and provides the location's name, address, phone number, and approximate distance. Assume that all new vendors who decide to carry Callaway's clubs will be added to the database within 30 days.

Callaway has a touring trailer called the "Callaway Mobile Golf Performance Center." In this trailer, which travels around the country (see the Callaway Web page for locations), golfers are fit properly for the C4 or other Callaway clubs, fight bad shots, and learn how to follow a true swing. Callaway also has portable custom fitting units at more than 300 pro shops across the country.

Callaway has a number of competitors, which aren't exactly "asleep at the wheel" in terms of using high-tech components and extensive research. Some of the most well-known brands (with suggested retail prices) include Taylor Made (300 Series Steel Woods, $399), Wilson (Deep Red Driver, $389), Ping (TiSI Tec Driver, $459), Tommy Armour (Forged Titanium Driver, $260), Nike (Tour Accurary Ti Driver, $399), and Adams (Tight Lies ST Drivers, $329).

One of the strongest competitors for the Callaway C4 is the Ping TiSI Tec Driver. Ping combined a process called Chemical Milling Technology (CMT) with its proven TiSI technology. This driver was preferred by four of the top five at the 2001 World Long Drive Championships. Many pros use the new driver (see www.pinggolf.com for more details on this club and the pros who use it), including Kevin Sutherland, who won the PGA Accenture Match Play Championship.

For this role-play, assume that resellers can purchase the C4 Driver from Callaway at the following cumulative discount rates (cumulative discounts are based on actual purchases over 12 months):

1–25 units	25 percent off suggested retail selling price
26–99 units	35 percent off suggested retail selling price
More than 100 units	50 percent off suggested retail selling price

Assume that the suggested retail price for the C4 driver is $429.

Also assume that Callaway does not allow any returns for unsold merchandise. In terms of promotion, Callaway has lined up a strong program of advertisements in golf magazines, endorsements by major golf professionals on tour, and a full array of point-of-purchase materials.

Information for this case was derived from a number of sources: www.callawaygolf.com, www.gigagolf.com, www.bestvaluegolf.com, www.pinggolf.com, www.wilsonsports.com, www.taylormadegolf.com.

SELLING SITUATIONS

Situation 1

You are a new salesperson for Callaway calling on a small golf shop, Golf's Away. You have never called on this golf shop before (because you never seemed to have time to stop there), but you have sold to several larger golf shops and pro shops in the same town. You don't know anything about the shop or its primary market. Your objectives are to introduce yourself, tell the owner about the C4 Driver, and secure an order for one C4 Driver (to generate customer interest in the line of drivers).

Situation 2

You are a salesperson for Callaway who was just reassigned to a new territory. You've been with Callaway for five years and have had better-than-average success selling clubs. You were glad to get your new territory because it is the headquarters of Nevada Bob's, a national chain selling golf clubs and accessories. Nevada Bob's has purchased Callaway clubs in the past and, to the best of your knowledge, is happy with its sales. Nevada Bob's has also purchased Callaway balls and accessories. Your objective is to set up another meeting with Nevada Bob's buying committee to take place within the next two weeks. At that meeting you hope to sell Nevada Bob's 500 C4 Drivers for the upcoming golfing season.

Situation 3

You are a new salesperson for Callaway calling on the head pro at the Marty Irving Country Club in upstate New York. The country club offers a wide range of golf instruction by its pros, including one-week, two-week, and three-day camps. It also custom-fits and sells golf clubs made by most of the major golf club manufacturers. Although Marty Irving Country Club does carry some Callaway clubs, it is obvious that Ping is the dominant club there. Ping has the best "shelf position," and a number of Ping posters are displayed on the pro shop walls. This call will be your first to the head pro and to Marty Irving Country Club. Due to your schedule, you won't be able to walk through the pro shop before your appointment. You are new to the territory and the old rep didn't have many notes about the account. Your sales manager simply said, "For some reason, Marty Irving Country Club doesn't seem to like us." Your objective for the call is to introduce the C4 Driver to the pro and to secure an order for five units.

Situation 4

You are a salesperson for Callaway calling on a Web retailer called GolfGalore. GolfGalore sells many lines of golf clubs and accessories, often deeply discounted. You have called on GolfGalore before and get along well with the buyer. The buyer has always been interested in your latest lines but has never purchased as many units as you would have liked. Your objective for this call is to introduce the C4 line to the buyer and secure an initial order for 25 units.

Situation 5

You are a summer college intern for Callaway. You are on the golf team at your college and use the C4 Driver. During the summer Callaway is having you make calls on golf organizations in a five-county area. Today you'll be calling on the president of a local golf organization that caters to serious golfers who are also corporate executives. Your goal is to secure a day and time when you can make a short (20-minute) presentation to the organization's members about the C4 Driver. You know nothing about the organization or when its meetings (if any) are held.

ROLE-PLAY CASE 2 | ### ACT!

ACT! is an award-winning contact management software that integrates personal databases on accounts with calendar management, word processing, and other computer software applications. Sort of a combination between a card file and calendar, the software enables salespeople to quickly identify prospects for new products, search for prospects in a given area, and other similar applications. In addition, all call records are maintained in a manner that enables salespeople to instantly recall personal information about any individual inside any account.

The product sells for a suggested retail of $199 (check the home page [www.act.com] and use the most recent price) with a trade discount of 50 percent. ACT! wins a lot of awards (see the home page for a complete listing) for its ease of use and functionality. The home page also has a lot of reviews of ACT! and other packages, so read it to understand features and benefits more fully. You may also want to check out GoldMine's website (www.frontrange.com) because GoldMine is a major competitor to ACT!

ACT! offers retailers quantity discounts of 5 percent for orders of 100 or more sent to one location, as well as co-op advertising copayment. Essentially, the copayment is $100 for any ad that is at least 25 percent of a page devoted to ACT!, or 50 percent (whichever amount is smaller) for ads that are less than a quarter-page. Cash discounts are also offered at 2/10, n30.

ACT! offers network pricing, which can apply if all reps are using PCs at work and not using laptops. Laptops must use the nonnetwork version (and pay the appropriate pricing). Laptops can hook into a network and use ACT! when logged in, but not when not logged in. Here are the network prices:

5 units	$899
10	$1,695
25	$3,995
50+	$7,550

Volume discounts for multiple single-user copies are as follows:

25–50	15 percent
50–100	20 percent
100+	25 percent

RESELLER SITUATIONS

Miller Brokerage House

Today you are calling on the owner of Miller Brokerage House. Miller Brokerage is a small discount brokerage with about 50 brokers. The buyer is a very talented businessperson and known for being very tough on everybody. You had a mutual friend set up a meeting with the owner.

Simpson's Software

You are calling on the store manager for a mall location of Simpson's Software, an independent computer hardware/software outlet. This is the only such store in this mall. The buyer is responsible for determining products that the store will sell. The buyer has considered buying many different software packages that are similar to ACT! You would like for ACT! to be a big seller for this store, and you hope that the store will not sell other time management software. You made an appointment with the buyer from a cold call. You realize that you will make lower margins on units sold through a reseller, but your unit numbers could go up substantially.

Jim's Software Solutions

You are calling on the owner of Jim's Software Solutions, Jim's Software Solutions sells software packages primarily for small businesses. You met the owner while you were at college when you had to purchase some software for your boss. The owner has a small staff of about four people, and he makes all decisions regarding any purchases. You know that the store carries GoldMine, and you've seen as many as four facings of GoldMine in the store. Jim's sells GoldMine for $249. It also carries the PFS line, which includes a contact manager; but in the store you visited, you didn't see the PFS contact manager.

Northwest Office Supplies

You are calling on the owner of Northwest Office Supplies. Northwest Office Supplies provides a range of office supplies for small businesses (furniture, paper, pens, and so on). You met the owner because he went to high school with your father. The owner has about five outside salespeople and 10 inside salespeople. Most of the company's sales are delivered from its warehouse.

Henderson and Brock Bookstore

You are calling on the purchasing manager for Henderson and Brock Bookstore. Henderson and Brock Bookstore sells mostly books. It is a franchise of a national chain and has a good amount of leeway in the products that it offers for sale.

You thought that ACT! software would be a good product for this store to stock, and you cold-called the purchasing agent. The purchasing agent seemed genuinely interested in meeting you and discussing this software package.

INDUSTRIAL USER SITUATIONS

Oiler Realty

Today you are calling on the sales supervisor for Oiler Realty. This realty company has about 40 realtors. The company handles only residential real estate, and each realtor averages about 30 house showings per month. The buyer is afraid of becoming a "dinosaur" in this business and wishes to obtain a competitive edge over competitors. The buyer, who wishes to increase the number of house showings by about 10 percent, replied with an information card from the back of a software magazine and seems genuinely interested in ways to improve the company's market share.

Pine-Tar Roofing

You are calling on the president of Pine-Tar Roofing. Pine-Tar Roofing has about 25 estimators (they work a lot like salespeople) and 20 project managers. The company deals with mostly commercial buildings. Approximately 30 projects are "live" at any particular time. These projects generally last between two weeks and three months. The projects require several meetings with clients, suppliers, and municipal building inspectors. The buyer wishes to increase the number of projects that the company can handle without additional personnel. You met the buyer at a charity golf tournament about three weeks ago.

Safety Valve Company

You are calling on the sales supervisor for the local region of Safety Valve Company. The buyer has about 30 outside salespeople and 15 inside salespeople for the region. Safety Valve furnishes large valves for industrial (mostly refinery) applications. The sales supervisor called you after being told of your product by a friend of his.

Cougar Bank

You are calling on the regional director for Cougar Bank. The buyer has five managers, each of whom has about seven loan officers. The buyer's staff has a continuing client base, and the staff members need to keep in periodic contact with each of their clients. Each officer has about 200 clients. You spoke with the buyer while your church was playing the buyer's in a basketball tournament.

Jenkins Aerospace

You are calling on the engineering manager for Jenkins Aerospace. The buyer employs over 200 engineers. Each of these engineers, to varying degrees, has meetings with management, clients, and suppliers. Jenkins Aerospace has recently adopted the notion that "everyone is a salesperson at Jenkins." You met the prospect at a conference in Las Vegas about two months ago, and you scheduled an appointment to discuss your product.

Endnotes

CHAPTER 1

1. Wendell Berry , *The Unsettling of America.* 3rd edition. (San Francisco: Sierra Club Books, 1996). 2. Philip Kotler, *Marketing Management: Analysis, Planning, Implementation and Control,* 10th ed. (Upper Saddle River, NJ: Prentice Hall, 2000). 3. "The average cost of a sales call in industrial manufacturing in 2000 was $262.35, up from $202.19 in 1999," *The Controller's Report,* January 9, 2001, Institute of Management and Administration, from RDS Business and Management Practices, http://rdsweb2.rdsinc.com/texis/rds/suite. 4. Anders Gronstedt and Lisa Syracuse (eds.), *The ABC's of IMC: Building Blocks for Integrated Marketing Communications* (New York: Advertising Research Foundation, 1998). 5. Robert England, "Harnessing the Team," *Banking Strategies,* September/October 1998, pp. 61–62. 6. Marilyn Kennedy Melia, "The E-volving Salesman," *Chicago Tribune,* June 11, 2000; "Click First, Buy Later," *Marketing News,* May 21, 2001, p. 5. 7. Stanley Slater and John Narver, "Marketing Orientation and the Learning Organization," *Journal of Marketing,* July 1995, pp. 63–74; James Sinkula, "Market Information Processing and Organizational Learning," *Journal of Marketing,* January 1994, pp. 35–45; David Garvin, "Building a Learning Organization," *Harvard Business Review,* July/August 1993, pp. 78–90. 8. Troy Festervand, James Lumpkin, and Gerald Skelly, "Strategic Intelligence Systems and the Salesforce," in *Development in Marketing Science,* ed. Roger Gomer (Coral Gables, FL: Academy of Marketing Science, 1995), p. 155. 9. Ajay Kohli, Tasadduq Shervani, and Goutam Challagalla, "Learning and Performance Orientation of Salespeople: The Role of Supervisors," *Journal of Marketing Research,* Spring 1998, pp. 263–74. 10. Evert Gummesson, "Implementation Requires a Relationship Marketing Paradigm," *Journal of the Academy of Marketing Science,* 26, Summer 1998, pp. 242–49; Lisa Napolitano, "Customer–Supplier Partnering: A Strategy Whose Time Has Come," *Journal of Personal Selling and Sales Management* 17, Fall 1997, pp. 1–8; Atul Parvatiyar and Jagdish Sheth, "Paradigm Shift in Marketing Theory and Approach: The Emergence of Relationship Marketing," in *Relationship Marketing: Theory, Methods, and Applications,* ed. Jagdish Sheth and Atul Parvatiyar (Atlanta: Center for Relationship Marketing, Emory University, 1994), pp. 23–30; Shelby Hunt and Robert Morgan, "Relationship Marketing in the Era of Network Competition," *Marketing Management* 3:1 (1994), pp. 19–28. 11. Julie T. Johnson, Hiram C. Barksdale, Jr., and James S. Boles, "The Strategic Role of the Salesperson in Reducing Customer Defection in Business Relationships," *Journal of Personal Selling and Sales Management* 21, Spring 2001, pp. 123–34; Gerrard Macintosh and Lawrence Locksin, "Retail Relationships and Store Loyalty: A Multi-Level Perspective," *International Journal of Research in Marketing* 14 (1997), pp. 487–97; Erin Anderson and Thomas Robertson, "Inducing Multi-Line Salespeople to Adopt House Brands," *Journal of Marketing* 59, April 1995, pp. 16–31; Harold Biong and Fred Selnes, "The Strategic Role of the Salesperson in Established Buyer–Seller Relationships," working paper report no. 96–118 (Cambridge, MA: Marketing Science Institute, 1996). 12. The Alexander Group, Inc., SalesTime Maker, Software Services, February 8, 2002, http://tools.saleslobby.com/perfMgmt/2001 STM Presentation.pdf. 13. "How Firms in Mexico Reach Isolated Rural Villages," *Business Latin American,* September 9, 1991, pp. 289–95. 14. Dana Ray, "The Best of the Best," *Selling Power,* January/February 1999, p. 62. 15. Ginger Trumfio, "For the Love of the Laptop," *Sales & Marketing Management,* Part II, March 1995, pp. 31–32. 16. Geoffrey Brewer, "Selling an Intangible," *Sales & Marketing Management,* January 1998, pp. 52–55; Leonard Berry, "Relationship Marketing of Services—Growing Interest, Emerging Perspectives," *Journal of Academy of Marketing Science* 23 (1995), pp. 236–45. 17. "Deal of Fortune," *Sales & Marketing Management,* August 1997, p. 52. 18. Elizabeth Creyer and Ilias Hrsistodoulakis, "Marketing Pharmaceutical Products to Physicians," *Marketing Health Services,* Summer 1998, pp. 35–40. 19. James Champy, "The Road to Success: More than Any Other Factor, Your Ambition Leads to Greatness," *Sales and Marketing Management,* April 2000, pp. 42–43. 20. J. Brock Smith and Donald W. Barclay, "Selling Partner Relationships: The Role of Interdependence and Relative Influence," *Journal of Personal Selling and Sales Management* 19, Fall 1999, pp. 21–40. 21. "Death of the Pitch, by Barclays," *Marketing* (2001), p. 13; W. H. Weiss, "Demonstrating Creativity and Innovation," *Supervision* 63, March 2002, pp. 6–9; Susan A. Friedman, "Ten Steps to a Successful Trade Show," *Marketing Health Services* 22, Spring 2002, pp. 31–32; Julie Hill, "Genius at Work: How to Be More Creative in the World of Business," *Presentations,* November 2001, pp. 34–42. 22. Daniel Goleman, *Working with Emotional Intelligence* (New York: Bantam, 1999). 23. Andrew Vincher, Jeffery Schippmann, Fred Switzer, and Phillip Roth, "A Meta-Analytical Review of Predictors of Job Performance for Salespeople," *Journal of Applied Psychology* 83, August 1998, pp. 586–97; Michael Rega, "The Five Biggest Myths of Professional Selling," *American Salesman,* April 1998, pp. 11–15; Perri Capwell, "Are Good Salespeople Made or Born?" *American Demographics,* July 1993, pp. 12–13. 24. *Occupational Outlook Handbook,* 2002–2003 edition, U.S. Department of Labor, Bureau of Labor Statistics. 25. Susan DelVecchio, "The Salesperson's Operating Freedom," *Industrial*

Marketing Management 27, January 1998, pp. 31–40.
26. Nancy Arnott, "I'd Rather Be Selling," *Sales & Marketing Management,* July 1995, pp. 77–83.

CHAPTER 2

1. Jaclyn Fierman, "The Death and Rebirth of the Salesman," *Fortune,* July 25, 1994, p. 80. 2. Erika Rasmusson, "Driven to Sell," *Sales & Marketing Management,* August 1999, pp. 39–44. 3. This section draws heavily on Thomas Wotruba, "The Evolution of Personal Selling," *Journal of Personal Selling and Sales Management,* Summer 1991, pp. 1–12. 4. Sandy Jap and Barton Weitz, "A Taxonomy of Long-Term Relationships" (working paper, College of Business Administration, University of Florida, 1996); F. Robert Dwyer, Paul Schurr, and Sejo Oh, "Developing Buyer–Seller Relationships," *Journal of Marketing,* April 1987, pp. 11–27. 5. Ellen Garbarino and Mark S. Johnson, "The Different Roles of Satisfaction, Trust, and Commitment in Customer Relationships," *Journal of Marketing* 63, April 1999, pp. 70–87. 6. John Bowe, Marisa Bowe, and Sabin Streeter, "Doing Whatever It Takes," *Across the Board,* March/April 2001, pp. 56–61. 7. Robert W. Armstrong and Siew Min Yee, "Do Chinese Trust Chinese? A Study of Chinese Buyers and Sellers in Malaysia," *Journal of International Marketing* 9:3 (2001), pp. 63–86. 8. Felix T. Mavondo and Elaine M. Rodrigo, "The Effect of Relationship Dimensions on Interpersonal and Interorganizational Commitment in Organizations Conducting Business between Australia and China," *Journal of Business Research* 52 (2001), pp. 111–21. 9. Michelle Bell, "The Future of Selling Is Now: There's No Going Back," *ADvantages,* January/February 1999, pp. 7–13; T. Hendrick and L. M. Ellram, *Strategic Supplier Partnerships: An International Study,* (Tempe, AZ: Center for Advanced Purchasing Studies, 1993). 10. Robert Sharoff, "Starbucks Sells United a Special Blend," *Selling,* May 1996, p. 12. 11. Manohar U. Kalwani and Narakesari Narayandas, "Long-Term Manufacturer–Supplier Relationships: Do They Pay Off for Supplier Firms?" *Journal of Marketing,* Winter 1995, pp. 1–3; Robert Krapel, Deborah Salmond, and Robert Spekman, "A Strategic Approach to Managing Buyer–Seller Relationships," *European Journal of Marketing* 25 (1991), pp. 22–37; B. G. Yovonvich, "Do's and Don'ts of Partnering," *Business Marketing,* March 1992, pp. 38–39; "Smart Selling: How Companies Are Winning Over Today's Tough Customers," *Business Week,* August 3, 1992, pp. 46–52. 12. Barry Rehfeld, "How Large Companies Buy," *Personal Selling Power,* September 1993, pp. 31–32. 13. Company documents. 14. Lisa Ellram, "Partnering Pitfalls and Success Factors," *International Journal of Purchasing and Materials Management,* April 1995, pp. 36–44. 15. "Taking Aim at Tomorrow's Challenges," *Sales & Marketing Management,* September 1991, p. 80.
16. "Pritchett on Quick Response," *Discount Merchandiser,* April 1992, p. 64. 17. Daniel Fries, "Have Trust and Confidence," *Purchasing Today,* April 2001, p. 68. 18. John Swan and Johannah Nolan, "Gaining Customer Trust: A Conceptual Guide for the Salesperson," *Journal of Personal Selling & Sales Management,* November 1985, pp. 39–48; John Swan, I. Fred Trawick, David Rink, and Jenney Roberts, "Measuring Dimensions of Purchaser Trust of Industrial Salespeople," *Journal of Personal Selling and Sales Management,* May 1988, pp. 1–9. 19. John Hawes, "To Know Me Is to Trust Me," *Industrial Marketing Management,* July

1994, pp. 215–19; Frank Sonnenberg, "Trust Me . . . Trust Me Not," *Journal of Business Strategy,* January/February 1994, pp. 14–16; Dennis Bialeszewski and Michael Giallourakis, "Perceived Communication Skills and Resultant Trust Perceptions within the Channel of Distribution," *Journal of the Academy of Marketing Science,* Spring 1985, pp. 206–17; Christine Moorman, Gerald Zaltman, and Rohit Deshpande, "Relationships between Providers and Users of Market Research: The Dynamics of Trust within and between Organizations," *Journal of Marketing Research,* August 1992, pp. 314–28. 20. Thierry Volery, "The Role of Building Trust in Creating Effective Alliances: A Managerial Perspective," *Journal of Business Ethics,* July 1998, pp. 987–95. 21. "Eastman Kodak Brings Training into Sharper Focus," *Sales & Marketing Management,* September 1992, p. 62. 22. Nancy Arnott, "It's a Woman's World," *Sales & Marketing Management,* March 1995, pp. 54–59. 23. Philip Burger and Cynthia Cann, "Post-Purchase Strategy: A Key to Successful Industrial Marketing and Customer Satisfaction," *Industrial Marketing Management* 24 (1995), pp. 91–98. 24. Jon M. Hawes, Kenneth E. Mast, and John E. Swan, "Trust Earning Perceptions of Sellers and Buyers," *Journal of Personal Selling and Sales Management,* Spring 1989, pp. 1–8. 25. Edmund Lawler, "Building Relationships," *Business Marketing,* August 1992, p. 34. 26. Tracy L. Tuten and David J. Urban, "An Expanded Model of Business-to-Business Partnership Formation and Success," *Industrial Marketing Management* 30 (2001), pp. 149–64. 27. James Morgan and Susan Zimmerman, "Building World Class Supplier Relationships," *Purchasing,* August 16, 1990, p. 2. 28. Don McCreary, *Japanese–U.S. Business Negotiations* (New York: Praeger, 1986); Frank Acuff, "Negotiating in the Pacific Rim," *The International Executive,* May 1990, p. 21. 29. B. G. Yovovich, "Partnering at Its Best," *Business Marketing,* March 1992, p. 37. 30. Adam Fein and Erin Anderson, "Patterns of Credible Commitments: Territory and Brand Selectivity in Industrial Distribution Channels," *Journal of Marketing* 61:2, April 1997, pp. 19–35; Erin Anderson and Barton Weitz, "The Use of Pledges to Build and Sustain Commitment in Distribution Channels," *Journal of Marketing Research,* February 1992, pp. 18–34. 31. Rahul Jacob, "Struggling to Create an Organization for the 21st Century," *Fortune,* April 3, 1995, pp. 90–99. 32. Patricia Sellers, "How to Remake Your Sales Force," *Fortune,* May 4, 1992, p. 103. 33. Ibid. 34. Laura Litvan, "Increasing Revenues with Repeat Sales," *Nation's Business,* January 1996, pp. 36–37. 35. Alyson Hendrickson Wentz, "The Balancing Act: Working with Large and Small Accounts," *ADvantage,* July/August 1999, pp. 15–16.
36. Thomas Vollman and Carlos Cordon, "Building Successful Customer–Supplier Alliances," *Long Range Planning* 31:5, 1998, pp. 684–94. 37. Jennifer Myers, "Open Sesame!" *Profit: The Magazine for Canadian Entrepreneurs* 16:3, June 1997, pp. 38–40. 38. Alexandra J. Campbell and Robert G. Cooper, "Do Customer Partnerships Improve New Product Success Rates?" *Industrial Marketing and Management* 28 (1999), pp. 507–19. 39. Ira Sanger, "IBM Leans on Its Sales Force," *Business Week,* February 7, 1994, p. 110.

CHAPTER 3

1. Erin Strout, "Are Your Salespeople Ripping You Off?" *Sales & Marketing Management,* February 2001, pp. 57–62. 2. Frank Sonnenberg, "Trust Me . . .Trust Me Not," *Journal of Business*

Strategy, January/February 1994, pp. 14–16; Scott Kelley and Michael Dorsch, "Ethical Climate, Organizational Commitment, and Indebtedness among Purchasing Executives," *Journal of Personal Selling and Sales Management,* Fall 1991, pp. 55–65; I. Fredrick Trawick, John Swan, Gail McGee, and David Rink, "Influence of Buyer Ethics and Salesperson Behavior on Intention to Choose a Supplier," *Journal of the Academy of Marketing Science,* Winter 1991, pp. 17–23; Rosemary Lagace, Robert Dahlstrom, and Jule Assenheimer, "The Relevance of Ethical Salesperson Behavior on Relationship Quality: The Pharmaceutical Industry," *Journal of Personal Selling and Sales Management,* Fall 1991, pp. 39–47. 3. Willem Verbeke, Cok Ouwerkerk, and Ed Peelen, "Exploring the Contextual and Individual Factors on Ethical Decision Making of Salespeople," *Journal of Business Ethics* 15, Fall 1996, pp. 1175–87. 4. Ralph Clark and Alice Lattal, "The Ethics of Sales: Finding an Appropriate Balance," *Business Horizons,* July/August 1993, pp. 66–69. 5. Michele Marchetti, "Whatever It Takes," *Sales & Marketing Management,* December 1997, pp. 29–38. 6. Charles W. Schwepker, Jr., "Ethical Climate's Relationship to Job Satisfaction, Organizational Commitment and Turnover Intention in the Salesforce," *Journal of Business Research* 54 (2001), pp. 39–52. 7. Charles Schwepker, O. C. Ferrell, and Thomas Ingram, "The Influences of Ethical Climate and Ethical Conflict on Role Stress in the Sales Force," *Journal of the Academy of Marketing Sciences* 25, Spring 1997, pp. 106–16. 8. Ken Bass, Tim Barnett, and Gene Brown, "The Moral Philosophy of Sales Managers and Its Influence on Ethical Decision Making," *Journal of Personal Selling and Sales Management* 18, Spring 1998, pp. 1–17; Debra Haley, "Sales Management Students vs. Business Practitioners: Ethical Dilemmas and Perceptual Differences," *Journal of Personal Selling and Sales Management,* Spring 1992, pp. 60–63; Pratibha and James Kellaris, "Toward Understanding Marketing Students' Judgement of Controversial Personal Selling Practices," *Journal of Business Research* 23, June 1992, pp. 313–28. 9. S. J. Vitell and L. J. Grove, "Marketing Ethics and the Technique of Neutralization," *Journal of Business Ethics,* Summer 1988, pp. 433–38. 10. Thomas Dunfee, N. Craig Smith, and William Ross, "Social Contracts and Marketing Ethics," *Journal of Marketing* 63, July 1999, pp. 14–32; Thomas Wotruba, "A Comprehensive Framework for the Analysis of Ethical Behavior, with a Focus on Sales Organizations," *Journal of Personal Selling and Sales Management,* Spring 1990, pp. 29–42; Anusorn Singhapakdi and Scott Vitell, "Analyzing the Ethical Decision Making of Sales Professionals," *Journal of Personal Selling and Sales Management,* Fall 1991, pp. 2–12. 11. Bristol Voss, "Eat, Drink, and Be Wary," *Sales & Marketing Management,* January 1991, pp. 49–57; David Finn and William Moncrief, "Salesforce Entertainment Activities," *Industrial Marketing Management,* November 1985, p. 230. 12. Dawn Myers, "You Get What You Give So Make It Good," *Promotional Products Business,* June 1998, pp. 105–11. 13. Fiona Gibbs, "To Give or Not to Give," *Sales & Marketing Management,* September 1994, p. 136. 14. I. Fredrick Trawick, Fred Morgan, and Jeffery Stoltman, "Influence of Buyer Ethics and Salesperson Behavior on Intention to Choose a Supplier," *Journal of the Academy of Marketing Sciences,* Winter 1991, pp. 17–24. 15. Bill Kelley, "When a Key Person Leaves for a Competitor," *Sales & Marketing Management,* February 1988, pp. 48–50. 16. Leslie Fine, David Shepherd, and Sally Josephs, "Sexual Harassment in the Sales Force: The Customer Is NOT Always Right," *Journal of Personal Selling and Sales Management,* Fall 1994, pp. 15–30. 17. Debbie LeClair, O. C. Ferrell, and Linda Ferrell, "Federal Sentencing Guidelines for Organizations: Policy Issues for International Marketing," *Journal of Public Policy & Marketing* 16, Spring 1997, pp. 27–37; Terry Loie and John Tanner, "The Federal Sentencing Guidelines: Implications for Sales Management Courses," *Proceedings of National Conference on Sales Management,* April 1998; "Putting the Fear of Crime into Corporations," *Business Week,* March 12, 1990, p. 35; "Soon, Corporate Crime May Really Not Pay," *Business Week,* February 12, 1990, p. 36. 18. John Murray, "Is It Warranty or Just Puff?" *Purchasing,* March 20, 1997, pp. 21–24; Alexander Simonson and Morris Holbrook, "Permissible Puffery versus Actionable Warranty in Advertising and Sales Talk: An Empirical Investigation," *Journal of Public Policy & Marketing,* Fall 1993, pp. 216–33. 19. Robin Peterson, "Selling and Sales Management in Action: An Examination of Industrial Sales Representative Accuracy in Discriminating Selected Legal and Illegal Actions," *Journal of Personal Selling & Sales Management,* Spring 1994, pp. 67–72; Karl Boedecker, Fred Morgan, and Jeffrey Stoltman, "Legal Dimensions of Salespersons' Statements: A Review and Managerial Suggestions," *Journal of Marketing,* January 1991, pp. 70–80. 20. Meryl Davids, "Global Standards, Local Problems," *Journal of Business Strategy,* January/February 1999, pp. 22–35; Sak Onkvisit and John Shaw, "International Corporate Bribery: Some Legal, Cultural, Economic, and Ethical–Philosophical and Marketing Considerations," *Journal of Global Marketing* 42 (1991), pp. 5–20. 21. This section is drawn from Thomas Donaldson, "Values in Tension: Ethics Away from Home," *Harvard Business Review,* September/October 1996, pp. 48–62; Thomas Donaldson and Thomas Dunfee, "Toward a Unified Conception of Business Ethics: Integrative Social Contract Theory," *Academy of Management Review,* April 1996, pp. 123–56. 22. O. C. Ferrell, Thomas N. Ingram, and Raymond W. LaForge, "Initiating Structure for Legal and Ethical Decisions in a Global Sales Organization," *Industrial Marketing Management* 29 (2000), pp. 555–64. 23. Carolyn Hotchkiss, "The Sleeping Dog Stirs: New Signs of Life in Efforts to End Corruption in International Business," *Journal of Public Policy & Marketing* 17, Spring 1998, pp. 108–21.

CHAPTER 4

1. Michael Levy and Barton Weitz, *Retailing Management,* 4th ed. (New York: Irwin/McGraw-Hill, 2000), chapters 12–14. 2. Robert Sharoff, "For Service, Send in the Troops," *Selling,* November 1994, pp. 70–71. 3. U. S. Department of Commerce, *Statistical Abstract of the United States,* 119th ed. (Washington, DC: U.S. Government Printing Office, 1999), p. 115. 4. Mary Beth Marklein, "Selling to Uncle Sam," *Nation's Business,* March 1991, p. 29. 5. "The Biggest Customer: How to Sell State Governments on Buying Your Product or Service," *Selling Power,* October 1977, pp. 31–34; Erskine Bowles, "Uncle Sam on RAM," *Entrepreneur,* August 1993, p. 138. 6. See Scott Ward and Frederick E. Webster, Jr., "Organizational Buying Behavior," in *Handbook of Consumer Research and Theory,* ed. T. S. Robertson and H. Kassarjian (Englewood Cliffs, NJ: Prentice Hall, 1991), pp. 419–58. 7. Francy Blackwood, "Close, yet So Far Away," *Selling,* September 1994, pp. 24–26. 8. G. Tomas M. Hult, "The Effect of Global Leadership on Purchasing Process Outcomes," *European Journal of Marketing*

32, November/December 1998, pp. 1029–32; Shirley Cayer, "Low Key, but Savvy," *Purchasing,* October 1989, p. 54.
9. G. Tomas M. Hult, "Cultural Competitiveness in Global Sourcing," *Industrial Marketing Management* 31, January 2002, pp. 25–34. 10. Daniel Glick, "The Magic of 'Mr. Spud,'" *Newsweek,* November 27, 1989, p. 63. 11. The classic study of organizational buying is in Patrick Robinson, Charles Faris, and Yoram Wind, *Industrial Buying and Creative Marketing,* (Boston: Allyn & Bacon, 1967). For a description of how John Deere used an understanding of the buying process to build sales, see Norton Paley, "Cultivating Customers," *Sales & Marketing Management,* September 1994, pp. 31–32. For an interesting comparison of organizational buying in other countries, see Johan Roos, Ellen Veie, and Lawrence Welsch, "A Case Study of Equipment Purchasing in Czechoslovakia," *Industrial Marketing Management,* August 1992, pp. 257–63; and Tomasz Domanski and Elizabeth Guzek, "Industrial Buying Behavior: The Case of Poland," *Journal of Business Research,* January 1992, pp. 11–18. 12. John Sheridan, "Buying Globally Made Easier," *Industry Week,* February 2, 1998, pp. 63–64. 13. Julie Roberts, "Great Expectations: E-Procurement and Work Processes," *Purchasing Today,* October 2001, pp. 24–30. 14. Donald Barclay, "Organizational Buying Outcomes and Their Effects on Subsequent Decisions," *European Journal of Marketing* 4 (1992), pp. 48–64. 15. Philip Burger and Cynthia Cann, "Post-Purchase Strategy: A Key to Successful Industrial Marketing and Customer Satisfaction," *Industrial Marketing Management,* Summer 1995, pp. 60–65. 16. For a revised and expanded taxonomy of buying situations, see Michele Bunn, "Taxonomy of Buying Decision Approaches," *Journal of Marketing,* January 1993, pp. 38–56. See Scott Mitchell, "Buy-Phase and Buy-Class Effects on Organizational Risk Perception and Reduction in Purchasing Professional Services," *Journal of Business & Industrial Marketing* 13, Fall 1998, pp. 461–71, for another empirical study of buying decision types. 17. Barry Rehfeld, "How They Buy," *Personal Selling Power,* September 1993, p. 3. 18. Mark A. Moon and Susan Forquer Gupta, "Examining the Formation of Selling Centers: A Conceptual Framework," *Journal of Personal Selling and Sales Management* 17, Spring 1997, pp. 31–41; Philip Dawes, "Information Control and Influence in Emergent Buying Centers," *Journal of Marketing* 62, July 1998, pp. 55–69; Jerome Katrichis, "Exploring Departmental Level Interaction Patterns in Organizational Purchasing Decisions," *Industrial Marketing Management* 27, March 1998, pp. 135–47; Robert McWilliams, Earl Naumann, and Stan Scott, "Determining Buying Center Size," *Industrial Marketing Management,* February 1992, pp. 43–50. 19. Martin Everett, "This Is the Ultimate in Selling," *Sales & Marketing Management,* August 1989, pp. 32–37. 20. Stefan Stremersch, Stefan Wuyts, and Ruud T. Frambach, "The Purchasing of Full-Service Contracts: An Exploratory Study within the Industrial Maintenance Market," *Industrial Marketing Management* 30, January 2001, pp. 1–12. 21. Frank Bingham, Charles Quigley, and Povert Valvo, "Back-Door Selling: A Descriptive Model," in *Enriching Marketing Practice and Education,* ed. Elenora Stuart and Ellen Moore (Atlanta: Southern Marketing Association, 1997), pp. 244–48; I. Fredrick Trawick, John Swan, and David Rink, "Back-Door Selling: Violation of Cultural versus Professional Ethics by Salespeople and Purchaser Choice of Supplier," *Journal of Business Research,* Summer 1988, pp. 299–309. 22. "How to Use Chinese Culture to Your Advantage," *Personal Selling Power,* January/February 1994, p. 19.

23. Roland Rust, Anthony Zahorik, and Timothy Keiningham, "Return on Quality (ROQ): Making Service Quality Financially Accountable," *Journal of Marketing* 59, April 1995, pp. 58–70; D. Greising, "Quality: How to Make It Pay," *Business Week,* August 8, 1994, pp. 54–59; V. D. Hunt, *Managing for Quality: Integrating Quality and Business Strategy* (Burr Ridge, IL: Richard D. Irwin, 1993). 24. Elizabeth Ehrlich, "The Quality Management Checkpoint," *International Business,* May 1993, pp. 56–58. 25. "Ford Stresses Value Analysis to Lower Cost," *Purchasing,* March 7, 1996, pp. 54–55; David Sprague, "Adding Value and Value Analysis to TQM," *Journal for Quality and Participation,* January/ February 1996, pp. 70–72; James Carbone, "VA for Some More Important than Ever," *Purchasing,* June 20, 1996, p. 30. 26. Tony Henthorne, Michael LaTour, and Alvin Williams, "How Organizational Buyers Reduce Risk," *Industrial Marketing Management,* February 1993, pp. 41–48; Robert Settle and Pamela Alreck, "Risky Business," *Sales & Marketing Management,* January 1989, pp. 48–52. 27. David Gilliland, "Toward a Model of Business-to-Business Marketing Communications Effects," *Industrial Marketing Management* 26, January 1997, pp. 15–30. 28. Michael Morris, Ramone Avila, and Alvin Burns, "The Nature of Industrial Source Loyalty: An Attitudinal Perspective," in *Developments in Marketing Science,* Vol. II, ed. K. D. Bahns (Miami: Academy of Marketing Sciences, 1988), pp. 333–37. 29. Elizabeth Wilson, "The Relative Importance of Supplier Selection Criteria: A Review and Update," *International Journal of Purchasing and Materials Management,* June 22, 1994, pp. 35–42; John N. Pearson and Lisa M. Ellram, "Supplier Selection and Evaluation in Small versus Large Firms," *Journal of Small Business Management,* October 1995, pp. 53–58. 30. "Who's Making Purchasing Decisions?" *Sales & Marketing Management,* August 1998, p. 76. 31. Sarah Lorge, "Purchasing Power," *Sales & Marketing Management,* June 1998, pp. 43–46; Tim Minahan, "Purchasing Execs Take Shears to Corporate Costs," *Purchasing,* May 23, 1996, pp. 22–24; S. Tully, "Purchasing's New Muscle," *Fortune,* February 1995, pp. 75–83; Clarissa Cruz, "Buyers Take a Lead Role in Setting Corporate Strategies," *Purchasing,* May 9, 1996, pp. 31–33; Larry Smeltzer and Sanjay Goel, "Sources of Purchasing Managers' Influence within the Organization," *International Journal of Purchasing and Materials Management,* Fall 1995, pp. 2–11. 32. Andy Cohen, "Planning National Accounts to Get a National Footing," *Sales & Marketing Management,* April 1996, pp. 76–77. 33. Robert Reich, "The Myth of 'Made in the USA,'" *Wall Street Journal,* July 5, 1991, p. A6. 34. James Brian Quinn, "Strategic Outsourcing: Leveraging Knowledge Capabilities," *Sloan Management Review* 40, Summer 1999, pp. 9–18; Sana Siwolop, "Outsourcing: Savings Are Just the Start," *Business Week,* May 13, 1996, p. 40. 35. Kurt Salmon Associates, *Efficient Consumer Response: Enhancing Consumer Value in the Grocery Industry* (Washington, DC: Food Marketing Institute, Research Department, 1993). 36. Richard W. Oliver, "The End of Inventory?" *Journal of Business Strategy,* January/February 1999, pp. 65–78; Rhonda Lummus, "Defining Supply Chain Management: A Historical Perspective and Practical Guidelines," *Industrial Management & Data Systems,* January/February 1999, pp. 11–18; Charles Corbett, "Partnerships to Improve Supply Chains," *Sloan Management Review* 40 (Summer 1999), pp. 71–78. 37. Richard White, "JIT Manufacturing: A Survey of Implementations in Small and Large U.S. Manufacturers," *Management Science* 45, January

1999, pp. 1–14; Richard Germain, "The Context, Organizational Design, and Performance of JIT Buying versus Non-JIT Buying Firms," *International Journal of Purchasing and Materials Management* 34, Spring 1998, pp. 12–19; Claudia Pragman, "JIT II: A Purchasing Concept for Reducing Lead Times and Gaining Competitive Advantage," *Business Horizons,* July 1996, pp. 54–66. 38. Pauline Sullivan and Jikyeong Kang, "Quick Response Adoption in the Apparel Manufacturing Industry: Competitive Advantage of Innovation," *Journal of Small Business Management,* January 1999, pp. 1–18; Susan Fiorito, Eleanor May, and Katherine Straughn, "Quick Response in Retailing: Components and Implementation," *International Journal of Retail and Distribution Management,* May 1995, pp. 12–18. 39. Roberta Duffy, "Value through Integration," *Purchasing Today,* March 2001, pp. 36–40. 40. Elizabeth Baatz, "How Tools Unlock Supply Value," *Purchasing Magazine,* April 22, 1999, pp. 28–31; Dan Scheraga, "The New EDI," *Chain Store Age,* October 1, 1999, pp. 110–13. 41. Mark Brunelli, "Consultants See BIG Future for E-Commerce," *Purchasing Magazine,* October 21, 1999, pp. S83–S86. 42. James Carbone, "There's More to E-commerce than POS," *Purchasing Magazine,* December 10, 1998, pp. S14–S17; Ravi Kalakota, Ralph A. Oliva, and Bob Donath, "Move Over, E-commerce: Emerging Digital Marketplaces Promise the Next Wave of Business Competition," *Marketing Management,* Fall 1999, pp. 23–30; Chad Kaydo, "You've Got Sales," *Sales & Marketing Management,* October 1999, pp. 29–39; Robert Vogel, "The Evolution of B-to-B Selling on the Net," *Target Marketing,* August 1998, pp. 34–36; Andy Reinhardt, "Extranets: Log On, Link Up, Save Big," *Business Week,* June 23, 1998, p. 134. 43. Barry Lawrence and Anoop Varma, "Supply Chain Strategies: Distributors, Manufacturers and Customers Must Work Together to Create Efficient Relationships," *Industrial Distribution,* January 31, 1999, pp. 68–71; Barton Weitz and Kevin Bradford, "Personal Selling and Sales Management: A Relational Perspective," *Journal of the Academy of Marketing Science,* November 1999, pp. 378–97. 44. Simeon Chow and Reed Holden, "Toward an Understanding of Loyalty: The Moderating Role of Trust," *Journal of Managerial Issues* 9, Fall 2000, 275–98.

CHAPTER 5

1. See Robert Young, *Understanding Misunderstandings: A Practical Guide to More Successful Human Interaction* (Austin, TX: University of Texas Press, 1999). 2. Owen Hargie, *The Handbook of Communication Skills,* 2nd ed. (London: Routledge, 1997). 3. Matthew Budman, "Don't Neglect Face Time," *Across the Board* 38, September/October 2001, p. 79. 4. Kitty O. Locker and Stephen Kyo Kaczmarek, *Business Communication: Building Critical Skills* (New York: Irwin/McGraw-Hill, 2001), pp. 61–62. 5. "Abuse of the Language," *Online Learning,* January 2002, p. 8. 6. Melinda Ligos, "Does Image Matter?" *Sales and Marketing Management,* March 2001, p. 56. 7. Ibid., p. 56. 8. Patti Hathaway, "Building Rapport," *Executive Excellence* 18, July 2001, p. 13. 9. Kare Anderson, "For Ideas to Stick, Make Tasty Pictures with Words," *Presentations,* October 2000, p. 100. 10. Robert Peterson, Michael Cannito, and Steven Brown, "An Exploratory Investigation of Voice Characteristics and Selling Effectiveness," *Journal of Personal Selling and Sales Management,* Winter 1995, pp. 1–16. 11. Lucette Comer and

Tanya Drollinger, "Active Empathetic Listening and Selling Success: A Conceptual Framework," *Journal of Personal Selling and Sales Management* 9, Winter 1999, pp. 15–29; C. David Shepherd, Stephen Castleberry, and Rick Ridnour, "Linking Effective Listening with Salesperson Performance: An Exploratory Study," *Journal of Business & Industrial Marketing* 12 (1997), pp. 315–32; Stephen Castleberry and C. David Shepherd, "Effective Interpersonal Listening and Personal Selling," *Journal of Personal Selling & Sales Management,* Winter 1993, pp. 35–50; Stephen B. Castleberry, C. David Shepherd, and Rick E. Ridnour, "Effective Interpersonal Listening in the Personal Selling Environment: Conceptualization, Measurement, and Nomological Validity," *Journal of Marketing Theory and Practice,* Winter 1999, pp. 30–38. 12. Dave Zielinski, "Body Language Myths," *Presentations,* April 2001, p. 39. 13. Zielinski, "Body Language Myths," p. 42. 14. "The Eyes Have It!" in Philip Cateora, *International Marketing,* 9th ed. (New York: Irwin/McGraw-Hill, 1995), p. 541. 15. Zielinski, "Body Language Myths," p. 40. 16. Dana Ray, "Signals That Sell," *Selling Power,* July/August 1999, pp. 40–43. 17. John Perry, "Palm Power in the Workplace," *The American Salesman* 46, October 2001, p. 22. 18. Zielinski, "Body Language Myths," p. 42. 19. Zielinski, "Body Language Myths," p. 38. 20. Mark Selway, "Netiquette for Beginners: Minding Your Manners Is as Important in Cyberspace as It Is in More Conventional Spheres," *Accountancy,* April 1999, pp. 47–49; Nancy Woodward, "Do You Speak Internet?" *HRMagazine,* April 1999, pp. S12–S17. 21. Locker and Kaczmarek, *Business Communication: Building Critical Skills,* pp. 47–48. 22. "Training for International Sales," *Sales and Marketing Management,* June 1996, p. 72. 23. Locker and Kaczmarek, *Business Communication: Building Critical Skills,* pp. 49–50.

CHAPTER 6

1. Michael Boorom, "Relational Communication Traits and Their Effect on Adaptiveness and Sales Performance," *Journal of the Academy of Marketing Science* 26, Winter 1998, pp. 16–22; John Withey, "Face-to-Face Selling: Making It More Effective," *Industrial Marketing Management* 24, August 1995, pp. 239–47; Rosann Spiro and Barton Weitz, "Adaptive Selling: Conceptualization, Measurement, and Nomological Validity," *Journal of Marketing Research* 27, February 1990, pp. 61–70. 2. Ross Brennan and Peter W. Trunbull, "Adaptive Behavior in Buyer–Supplier Relationships," *Industrial Marketing Management* 28, September 1999, pp. 481–95. 3. See, for example, A. Tansu Barker, "Benchmarks of Successful Salesforce Performance," *Revue Canadienne des Sciences de l'Administration* 16, June 1999, pp. 95–104. 4. Stephen S. Porter and Lawrence W. Inks, "Cognitive Complexity and Salesperson Adaptability: An Exploratory Investigation," *Journal of Personal Selling and Sales Management* 20, Winter 2000, pp. 15–21; Barton Weitz, Harish Sujan, and Mita Sujan, "Knowledge, Motivation, and Adaptive Behavior: A Framework for Improving Selling Effectiveness," *Journal of Marketing,* October 1986, pp. 174–91; Harish Sujan, Mita Sujan, and James Bettman, "Knowledge Structure Differences between Effective and Less Effective Salespeople," *Journal of Marketing Research,* February 1988, pp. 81–86; David Szymanski, "Determinants of Selling Effectiveness: The Importance of Declarative Knowledge to the Personal Selling Concept," *Journal of Marketing,* January 1988, pp. 64–77;

Leslie Fine, "Refining the Concept of Salesperson Adaptability," in *Marketing Theory and Applications*, ed. Chris Allen et al. (Chicago, IL: American Marketing Association, 1992), pp. 42–49. 5. James Narus and James Anderson, "Business Marketing: Understand What Customers Value," *Harvard Business Review*, November/December 1998, pp. 53–58; Charles Genger, "A Personal Construct Analysis of Adaptive Selling and Sales Experience," *Psychology and Marketing*, July 1995, pp. 287–304; Harish Dsujan, Mita Sujan, and James Bettmen, "Knowledge Structure Differences between Effective and Less Effective Salespeople," *Journal of Marketing Research*, February 1988, pp. 81–86; David Syzmanski, "Determinants of Selling Effectiveness: The Importance of Declarative Knowledge to the Personal Selling Concept," *Journal of Marketing Research*, January 1988, pp. 64–77. 6. Marlane Miller, *What Color Is Your Brain?* (New York: Peridot Press, 2000); Dana Ray, "Work Your Brain," *Selling Power*, October 1999, pp. 119–23. 7. Henry Canady, "ESP at HP," *Selling Power*, September 1997, pp. 76–81. 8. Gregory Rich, "The Constructs of Sales Coaching: Supervisor Feedback, Role Modeling and Trust," *Journal of Personal Selling and Sales Management* 18, Winter 1998, pp. 53–63. 9. Thomas DeCarlo, R. Kenneth Teas, and James McElroy, "Salesperson Performance Attribution Processes and the Formation of Expectancy Estimates," *Journal of Personal Selling and Sales Management* 17, Summer 1997, pp. 1–17. 10. David Merrill and Roger Reid, *Personal Styles and Effective Performance* (Radnor, PA: Chilton, 1981); Robert Bolton and Dorothy Bolton, *Social Style/Management Style* (New York: AMACOM, 1984); Robert Bolton and Dorothy Bolton, *People Styles at Work: Making Bad Relationships Good and Good Relationships Better* (New York: AMACOM, 1996). 11. V. R. Buzzotta and R. E. Lefton, "What Makes a Sales Winner?" *Training and Development*, November 1981, pp. 70–73. 12. Gerald Manning and Barry Reece, *Selling Today: A Personal Approach*, 8th ed. (Upper Saddle River, NJ: Prentice Hall, 2001), pp. 350–368. 13. Anthony Alessandra and Michael O'Connor, *The Platinum Rule: Discover the Four Basic Business Personalities—And How They Can Lead You to Success* (New York: Warner, 1998). 14. Marlane Miller, *What Color Is Your Brain?* (New York: Peridot Press, 2000). 15. Lucette B. Comer and J. A. F. Nicholls, "Communication between Hispanic Salespeople and Their Customers: A First Look," *Journal of Personal Selling and Sales Management* 20, Summer 2000, pp. 121–27. 16. LuAlexis Laris, "Software Lets Users Evaluate Sales Strategy," *InformationWeek*, December 13, 1999, pp. 100–2; Berend Wierenga and Gerrit H. van Bruggen, "The Integration of Marketing Problem-Solving Modes and Marketing Management Support Systems," *Journal of Marketing* 61, Summer 1997, pp. 21–36; Paul Petach, "Picking the Pitch for the Prospect, by Computer," *Business Marketing*, October 1988, pp. 78–81; Robert Collins, "Artificial Intelligence in Personal Selling," *Journal of Personal Selling and Sales Management*, May 1984, pp. 58–66; Arlyn Rubash, Rawlie Sullivan, and Paul Herzog, "The Use of an 'Expert' to Train Salespeople," *Journal of Personal Selling and Sales Management*, August 1987, pp. 49–56. 17. Margaret McDonald, "Accessing the Virtual Mentor," *Knowledge Management*, May 1999, p. 21; Karen Starr, "How Sales Coaching Software Helps Reps Ace Sales Calls," *Selling Power*, April 1999, p. 32–35; Thomas Petzinger, Jr., "Bob Schmonsees Has a Tool for Better Sales," *Wall Street Journal*, March 26, 1999, pp. A1, A5.

CHAPTER 7

1. Bob Donath, "Quality Information Leads to Quality Leads," *Marketing News*, August 16, 1999, p. 11. 2. Mary Conners, "Referral Madness," *Working Woman*, July/August 1998, p. 68. 3. R. Bruce Money, Mary C. Gilly, and John L. Graham, "Explorations of National Culture and Word-of-Mouth Referral Behavior in the Purchase of Industrial Services in the United States and Japan," *Journal of Marketing*, October 1998, pp. 76–87. 4. George A. Norris, "We Asked Our Readers to Respond to This Question: How Do You Get Qualified Referrals?" *Advisor Today* 96, October 2001, p. 92. 5. Sarah Lorge, "The Best Way to Prospect," *Sales & Marketing Management*, January 1998, p. 80. 6. For more information on how to get good referrals, see John Nemac, "How to Use Referrals to Generate Greater Sales," *The American Salesman* 45, January 2000, pp. 10–13.; Bill Bishop, "The 7 Deadly Sins of Referrals," *Advisor Today* 96, June 2001, p. 92. 7. Howard Davies, Thomas K. P. Leung, Sherriff T. K. Luk, and Yiu-hing Wong, "The Benefits of 'Guanxi,'" *Industrial Marketing Management* 24 (1994), pp. 207–14. 8. Barry Farber, "Meet & Potatoes," *Entrepreneur*, February 2002, pp. 89–90. 9. Sarah Lorge, "Get More Customers Now," *Sales & Marketing Management*, November 1998, pp. 48–57. 10. See Mary E. Boone, "Is Your Site Too Successful?" *Sales & Marketing Management*, July 1999, p. 98. 11. Paul Estep and Stephen B. Castleberry, "eCommerce in the Early Childhood Industry: An Application," *The Arrowhead Journal of Business*, 1999, pp. 9–18. 12. Jason Compton, "Finding Gold on the Web," *Customer Relationship Management*, May 2000, pp. 107–8. 13. Brian Silverman, "Get 'Em While They're Hot," *Sales & Marketing Management*, February 1997, pp. 47–52. See also Mary E. Boone, "The Extranet Effect," *Sales & Marketing Management*, October 1997, p. 40. 14. Research conducted by Zona Research and reported on June 30, 1999, on their Web page: www.zonaresearch.com/info/press/99-jun30.htm. 15. Ginger Conlon, "Direct Mail Meets Its Match," *Sales & Marketing Management*, May 1999, p. 73. 16. Andrew Leonard, "We've Got Mail—Always," *Newsweek*, September 20, 1999, p. 60. 17. Stephan Schiffman, "Survey Says E-Mail Is a Big Zero with Salespeople," *American Salesman*, April 1999, p. 10. 18. Susan Greco, "Turning Leads into Sales," *Inc.*, April 1998, p. 117. 19. See John F. Tanner, Jr., "Adaptive Selling at Trade Shows," *Journal of Personal Selling and Sales Management*, Spring 1994, pp. 15–23. 20. See "Going for the No-Shows," *The Practical Accountant* 33 (July 2000), p. 10; "Seminars: What Are You Selling?" *The Practical Accountant* 33 (November 2000), p. 11; Marcy K. Furney, "The New Seminar Selling," *Advisor Today* 96 (2001), p. 102. 21. For information on SIC and NAICS codes, see the following: An excellent listing of Web resources is available at www.d.umn.edu/~jvileta/naics.html; 1997 NAICS codes are at http://www.census.gov/epcd/naics/naicscod.txt ; SIC codes are at www.osha.gov/oshstats/sicser.html. 22. "Virtual Prospecting," *Business Week, Industrial/Technology Edition*, Spring 2001, pp. 185–88. 23. Jill Duman, "Striking Gold," *Customer Relationship Management*, November 2001, pp. 59–60. 24. Ruth P. Stevens, "CRM: It's About Prospecting, Too," *1to1 Magazine*, February 2002, as accessed on 3/13/02 at http://www.1to1.com.. 25. Kevin Kelly, "Dialing for Dollars," *Business Week, Industrial/Technology Edition*, November 5, 2001, p. SB14. 26. For an interesting account of one salesperson who still cold-calls door to door, see Andy Cohen,

"Man about Town," *Sales and Marketing Management,* June 2000, p. 29. 27. See Bill Bishop, "The 7 Deadly Sins of Referrals," *Advisor Today* 96, June 2001, p. 92. 28. For an interesting discussion of outbound telemarketing, see "Fear of Phoning," *Bank Marketing* 34, January/February 2000, p. 8. 29. Kelly Beamon, "In the Loop: Facts and Stats to Keep You In-The-Know," *ADvantages,* September/October 1999, p. 47. 30. Interested readers can learn more about the rules and laws from the FTC home page at www.ftc.gov. 31. Michele Marchetti, "Prospecting: Finding Hot Leads," *Sales & Marketing Management,* March 1996, p. 44. 32. Robert Sullivan, "Getting Up the Gall to Call," *Sales and Marketing Management,* June 1999, p. 30. 33. Emily M. Akin, "The New Rules for Prospecting," *Advisor Today* 96, May 2001, p. 28. 34. Denny Hatch, "Anthrax: Sleeping with the Enemy: How Are Direct Marketers Coping?" *Target Marketing* 25, January 2002, pp. 15–20. 35. Emily M. Akin, "The New Rules for Prospecting," *Advisor Today* 96, May 2001, p. 28. 36. Chad Kaydo, "How to Find New Customers," *Sales and Marketing Management* 152, February 2000, p. 100. 37. For the classic treatment of the funneling process, see Robert B. Miller and Stephen E. Heiman, *Strategic Selling* (New York: William Morrow and Company, 1985). 38. Jeff and Marc Slutsky, "Prequalification 'Funnel' Yields Sales with Less Work," *Columbus Dispatch,* April 5, 1999, p. 6. 39. Sarah Lorge, "Get More Customers Now," *Sales & Marketing Management,* November 1998, pp. 48–57. 40. Brian Jeffrey, "Real or Unreal: Who's Who," *Agency Sales Magazine,* November 1996, pp. 54–55. 41. "Screening Prospects: Six Questions," *Inc.,* December 1998, p. 57. 42. "Cloning Your Customers," *Sales & Marketing Management,* March 1999, p. 88. 43. Robyn Griggs, "Give Us Leads! Give Us Leads!" *Sales & Marketing Management,* July 1997, pp. 67–72. 44. Ruth P. Stevens, "CRM: It's about Prospecting, Too," *1to1 Magazine* February 2002, as accessed on 3/13/02 at http://www.1to1.com. 45. Stanley F. Slater and John C. Narver, "Market Orientation and the Learning Organization," *Journal of Marketing,* July 1995, pp. 63–74. 46. Jim Cecil, "Patient, Professional, Persistent," *Rough Notes* 9, September 2001, pp. 124–26; Randy Schwantz, "Overcoming Call Reluctance," *American Agent & Broker* 72, August 2000, pp. 18–20. 47. Willem Verbeke and Richard P. Bagozzi, "Sales Call Anxiety: Exploring What It Means When Fear Rules a Sales Encounter," *Journal of Marketing* 64, July 2000, pp. 88–101. 48. Robyn Griggs, "Taking the Lead," *Sales & Marketing Management,* September 1995, pp. 40–48.

CHAPTER 8

1. Edward O. Welles, "Quick Study," *Inc.,* April 1992, pp. 67–76. 2. See Arun Sharma and Rajnandini Pillai, "Customers' Decision-Making Styles and Their Preference for Sales Strategies: Conceptual Examination and an Empirical Study," *Journal of Personal Selling and Sales Management,* Winter 1996, pp. 21–33. 3. See Harvey Mackay, *Swim with the Sharks without Being Eaten Alive* (New York: Morrow, 1988), pp. 25–34. 4. Roberta J. Schultz, Kenneth R. Evans, and David J. Good, "Intercultural Interaction Strategies and Relationship Selling in Industrial Markets," *Industrial Marketing Management,* November 1999, pp. 589–99. 5. See Daniel C. Smith and Jan P. Owens, "Knowledge of Customers' Customers as a Basis of Sales Force Differentiation," *Journal of Personal Selling and Sales Management,* Summer 1995, pp. 1–15. 6. John F. Monoky, "Know Your Customer's Risk Level," *Industrial Distribution,* February 1998, p. 88. 7. Mark McMaster, "Too Close For Comfort," *Sales and Marketing Management,* July 2001, pp. 42–48. 8. Andy Cohen, "Sales and Marketing: Separate but Equal?" *Sales & Marketing Management,* September 1998, p. 15. 9. Esther Shein, "Answering Machines," *Sales & Marketing Management,* March 1998, pp. 74–78. 10. Mark A. Moon and Susan Forquer Gupta, "Examining the Formation of Selling Centers: A Conceptual Framework," *Journal of Personal Selling & Sales Management* 17:2, Spring 1997, pp. 31–41. 11. "Knowledge Is Power," *Sales and Marketing Management,* May 1999, p. 75. 12. "Web Research Sends Sales Rising by 37," *The Arizona Republic,* August 14, 2000, Business and Money Section, p. D2. 13. Stephen B. Castleberry, "The Web as an Information Source for Sales Recruits: Its Effectiveness in Aiding Anticipatory Socialization of Salespeople," *Industrial Marketing Management,* in press (2002). 14. This description was accurate at the time the book went to press. One thing is obvious: The Web changes daily. Don't be surprised if this site has different offerings on the day you visit. 15. Harvey B. Mackay, "The CEO Hits the Road (and Other Sales Tales)," *Harvard Business Review,* March/April 1990, p. 32. 16. Beth Belton, "Technology Changes Sales Force," *USA Today,* February 9, 1999, as posted on the USA Today website at www.usatoday.com/news/acovtue.htm. 17. Sue Garrison, "Avoiding a Foreign Market Faux Pas," *Business Geographics,* July 1998, p. 8. 18. John R. Graham, "Sales Strategies for a Changed World," *The American Salesman* 46, January 2001, pp. 16–22; "SMM's Best of Sales & Marketing," *Sales and Marketing Management,* September 2001, p. 31. 19. Neil Rackham, *Major Account Sales Strategy* (New York: McGraw-Hill, 1989), p. 39. 20. See Brian Koon Huat Low, "Long-Term Relationships in Industrial Marketing," *Industrial Marketing Management* 25 (1996), pp. 23–35. 21. Robert McGarvey, "Ice Cubes to Eskimos," *Entrepreneur,* August 2000, pp. 68–72, 75–76. 22. Robert B. Miller and Stephen E. Heiman, *Strategic Selling* (Berkeley, CA: Miller Heiman & Associates, Inc., 1985). 23. Geoffrey Brewer, "An American in Shanghai," *Sales & Marketing Management,* November 1997, pp. 38–49. 24. Jim Hersma, personal correspondence. Used with permission. 25. Erika Rasmusson, "How to Manage Long-Term Leads," *Sales & Marketing Management,* January 1998, p. 77. 26. Betsy Cummings, "Do Customers Hate Salespeople? Only If They Commit One of These Deadly Sins of Selling," *Sales and Marketing Management,* June 2001, pp. 44–51; Kenneth A. Hunt and R. Edward Bashaw, "Using Buyer's Information Processing to Formulate Selling Strategies," *Industrial Marketing Management* 28, January 1999, pp. 99–107. 27. Robert B. Woodruff and Sarah Fisher Gardial, *Know Your Customer: New Approaches to Understanding Customer Value and Satisfaction* (Cambridge, MA: Blackwell Publishers, Ltd., 1996) p. 20. 28. Anne Millen Porter, "Rasing the Bar," *Purchasing,* January 14, 1999, pp. 45–50. 29. Jennifer M. George, "Salesperson Mood at Work: Implications for Helping Customers," *Journal of Personal Selling & Sales Management,* Summer 1998, pp. 23–30. 30. See Chad Kaydo, "In Search of a Decision Maker," *Sales & Marketing Management,* February 1999, p. 69. 31. Rackham, *Major Account Sales Strategy.* 32. Chad Kaydo, "In Search of a Decision Maker," *Sales & Marketing Management,* February 1999, p. 69. 33. Rackham, *Major Account Sales Strategy,* p. 30. 34. Jeffrey E. Lewin, "The Effects of Downsizing on Organizational Buying Behavior: An Empirical Investigation," *Journal of the Academy of Marketing Science* 29:2 (2001), pp. 151–164. 35. Nancy J. Adler,

International Dimensions of Organizational Behavior (Boston: Kent Publishing, 1986), p. 33. 36. Nanci McCann, "For Their Own Good, as Well as Yours: If You Can Offer Real Benefits, Someone Should Really Hear about Them," *Selling,* April 1995, pp. 23–24. 37. Dave Zielinski, "Going Global," *Presentations,* November 1998, pp. 57–63. 38. See Rob Zeiger, "Sex, Sales & Stereotypes," *Sales & Marketing Management,* July 1995, pp. 48, 51; Andy Cohen, "Topless Bars Dress Up Their Act," *Sales & Marketing Management,* July 1995, p. 54; Rob Zeiger, "Dancers: They're Not Here to Fall in Love," *Sales & Marketing Management,* July 1995, p. 56; David Dorsey, "Risky Business," *Sales & Marketing Management,* July 1995, p. 128; Mary MacKinnon, "How Topless Bars Shut Me Out," *Sales & Marketing Management,* July 1995, p. 53. 39. See Scott Heimes, "Video Conferencing: You Don't Have to Be Present to Present," *Presentations,* April 1997, pp. 32–45; Becky Waring, "Ready or Not," *Presentations,* October 1999, pp. 33–40. 40. See Desa Philadelphia, "Video Traveler," *Time: Time Bonus Section Inside Business,* February 2001, pp. Y2–Y4. 41. See Mary Gundermann and Cynthia Kadlec, "Meet Me in Cyberspace," *Successful Meetings,* August 1999, pp. 89–92. 42. Alison Overholt, "Virtually There," *Fast Company,* March 2002, pp. 112. 43. Robert Sullivan, "Out to Lunch," *Sales and Marketing Management,* April 2000, p. 110. 44. Betsy Cummings, "Do Customers Hate Salespeople? Only If They Commit One of These Deadly Sins of Selling," *Sales and Marketing Management,* June 2001, pp. 44–51. 45. Susan Roy, "Icebreakers," *Working Woman,* February 1996, p. 47. 46. Roy, "Icebreakers," p. 47. 47. Roy, "Icebreakers," p. 47. 48. See Anne M. Bachrach, "Master the Warm Call: How to Get Appointments with Difficult to Reach Prospects," *American Salesman,* December 1998, pp. 26–30. 49. See "Turning Objections into Sales Opportunities," *Sales & Marketing Management,* March 1999, p. 88. 50. Robyn Griggs, "Taking the Leads," *Sales & Marketing Management,* September 1995, p. 47. 51. Carol Davidson, "Sole of a Sale," *Selling Power,* July/August 1997, p. 22. 52. Dave Zielinski, "The Million Dollar Pitch," *Presentations,* July 2000, pp. 41–49. 53. Dave Zielinski, "Clock Work: How to Make the Most of Your Presentation Preparation Time," *Presentations,* February 2000, pp. 30–40. 54. Stephen Regenold, "Case Study: A Cracker of a Presentation," *Presentations,* February 2002, p. 18. 55. Don Beveridge, "The Seed of Success," *Industrial Distribution,* July 1999, p. 78.

CHAPTER 9

1. Based on personal correspondence with Karl Sooder (2/14/02). 2. Building partnerships and strong relationships is a process that starts when a lead is identified and continues throughout all postsale service and future calls. See Marvin A. Jolson, "Broadening the Scope of Relationship Selling," *Journal of Personal Selling & Sales Management,* Fall 1997, pp. 75–88. 3. Of course, many aspects of first impressions are outside the control of the salesperson. See, for example, Tony L. Henthorne, Michael S. LaTour, and Alvin J. Williams, "Initial Impressions in the Organizational Buyer–Seller Dyad: Sales Management Implications," *Journal of Personal Selling and Sales Management,* Summer 1992, pp. 57–65. The authors found that different first impressions were formed as a function of race and gender. 4. See Jim Hall, "Nail Your First Three Minutes to Avoid Going Down in Flames," *Presentations,* February 1999, p. 28; Eli Jones, Jesse N. Moore, Andrea J. S. Stanaland, and Rosalind A. J. Wyatt, "Salesperson Race and Gender and the Access and Legitimacy Paradigm: Does Difference Make a Difference?" *Journal of Personal Selling and Sales Management,* Fall 1998, pp. 71–88. 5. See, for example, Jeffrey Gitomer, "Your First Sales Statement Has No Words," *Business Journal—Milwaukee,* August 22, 1997, p. 12. 6. Oscar W. DeShields Jr., Ali Kara, and Erdener Kaynak, "Source Effects in Purchase Decisions: The Impact of Physical Attractiveness and Accent on Salespersons," *International Journal of Research in Marketing,* February 1996, pp. 89–101. 7. Sean Dwyer, Orlando Richard, and C. David Shepherd, "An Exploratory Study of Gender and Age Matching in the Salesperson–Prospective Customer Dyad: Testing Similarity–Performance Predictions," *Journal of Personal Selling and Sales Management,* Fall 1998, pp. 55–69. 8. Dave Zielinski, "The Gender Gap: Do Women Have to Be Better Presenters than Men?" *Presentations,* August 1998, pp. 36–45. 9. Julie Hill, "Changing Faces, Facing Change," *Presentations,* November 2000, pp. 42–50. 10. Dale Carnegie, a noted sales training consultant, would disagree with this advice. He suggests that not offering a handshake shows a lack of assertiveness. 11. Robin Eisner, "Get a Grip," ABCNews.com, http://abcnews.go.com/sections/living/DailyNews/handshake000 710.html, as viewed on 7/10/00. 12. See, for example, John Perry, "Palm Power in the Workplace," *The American Salesman* 46, October 2001, pp. 22–26. 13. See Julie Hill, "Getting Carded: Business-Size CD-ROMs Find a Niche," *Presentations,* June 2000, p. 15. 14. Erika Rasmusson, "The 10 Traits of Successful Salespeople," *Sales & Marketing Management,* August 1999, p. 34. 15. Ken Delmar, *Winning Moves* (New York: Warner, 1984), p. 4. 16. Peter Giuliano, "Did I Say That?" *Successful Meetings,* March 1999, p. 96. 17. Christopher McGinnis, "Sign Language," *Entrepreneur,* December 1995, p. 59. 18. Robert McGarvey, "Whoops!" *Entrepreneur,* August 1998, p. 114. 19. To learn what most buyers are looking for in a supplier, see Kevin R. Fitzgerald, "What Makes a Superior Supplier," *Velocity,* Spring 1999, pp. 22–49. 20. Neil Rackham, *SPIN Selling* (New York: McGraw-Hill, 1988). 21. Kevin J. Corcoran, Laura K. Peterson, Daniel B. Baitch, and Mark Barrett, *High Performance Sales Organizations: Best Sales Practices from Global Leaders* (Burr Ridge, IL: Irwin Professional Publishing, 1995), pp. 45–47. 22. Jim Meisenheimer, "The 12 Best Questions to Ask Potential Customers," *Cintermex,* March/April 1999, p. 25. 23. Brian Tracy, "Stop Talking . . . and Start Asking Questions," *Sales & Marketing Management,* February 1995, pp. 79–87. 24. Rackham, *SPIN Selling.* 25. Susan Greco, "Five Ways to Blow a Sale: Inc. 500 CEO's Share Their Biggest Sales Mistakes," *Inc.,* September 1996, p. 101. 26. Ray Hanson, personal correspondence. Used by permission. 27. See also Tim Becker, "Are You Listening?" *Selling Power,* June 1999, pp. 28–30; Rosemary P. Ramsey and Ravipreet S. Sohi, "Listening to Your Customers: The Impact of Perceived Salesperson Listening Behavior on Relationship Outcomes," *Journal of the Academy of Marketing Science,* 25:2 (1997), pp. 127–37. 28. Nancy J. Adler, *International Dimensions of Organizational Behavior* (Boston: Kent Publishing, 1986), p. 55. 29. See Libby Estell, "Unchained Profits," *Sales and Marketing Management,* February 1999, pp. 63–67; Bill Brooks, "Values and Sales Success," *The American Salesman* 46, November 2001, pp. 14–17; John R. Graham, "Sales Strategies for a Changed World," *The American Salesman* 46, January 2001, pp. 16–22; Robert McGarvey, "Ice Cubes to ESKIMOS," *Entrepreneur,*

August 2000, pp. 75–76; Betsy Cummings, "Do Customers Hate Salespeople?" *Sales and Marketing Management,* June 2001, pp. 44–51; Al Borowski, "To Connect with Audiences, Learn How to Build Rapport," *Presentations,* March 2000, p. 78. 30. Jim Hersma, personal correspondence. Used with permission. 31. Jerry Vass, "Ten Expensive Selling Errors," *Agency Sales Magazine,* July 1998, p. 38. 32. John E. Swan, I. Fredrick Trawick, and David W. Silva, "How Industrial Salespeople Gain Customer Trust," *Industrial Marketing Management,* 1985, pp. 203–11. 33. Todd Graf, personal correspondence. Used with permission. 34. Tracey Brill, personal correspondence. Used with permission. 35. Diane Sanchez, "Think Like Your Customer," *Sales & Marketing Management,* December 1998, p. 22. 36. Ibid. 37. Barbara L. Breaden, *Speaking to Persuade* (Fort Worth, TX: Harcourt Brace College Publishers, 1996). 38. Stanley F. Slater and John C. Narver, "Market Orientation and the Learning Organization," *Journal of Marketing,* July 1995, pp. 63–74. 39. See, for example, Melinda Ligos, "On with the Show," *Sales & Marketing Management,* November 1998, pp. 70–76; Jon Hanke, "Presenting as a Team," *Presentations,* January 1998, pp. 73–82; Donald W. Jackson, Jr., Scott M. Widmier, Ralph Giacobbe, and Janet E. Keith, "Examining the Use of Team Selling by Manufacturers' Representatives: A Situational Approach," *Industrial Marketing Management,* March 1999, p. 155.

CHAPTER 10

1. Tad Simons, "Study Shows Just How Much Visuals Increase Persuasiveness," *Presentations,* March 1998, p. 20. 2. See J. Brock Smith and Donald W. Barclay, "The Effects of Organizational Differences and Trust on the Effectiveness of Selling Partner Relationships," *Journal of Marketing,* January 1997, pp. 3–21; Patricia M. Doney and Joseph P. Cannon, "An Examination of the Nature of Trust in Buyer–Seller Relationships," *Journal of Marketing,* April 1997, pp. 35–51; David Strutton, Lou E. Pelton, and John F. Tanner, Jr., "Shall We Gather in the Garden: The Effects of Ingratiatory Behaviors on Buyer Trust in Salespeople," *Industrial Marketing Management* 25 (1996), pp. 151–62. 3. Mari Pat Varga, "Don't Lose That Thought—Keep a Presenter's Journal," *Presentations,* January 2001, p. 92. 4. See Arun Sharma and Rajnandini Pillai, "Customer's Decision-Making Styles and Their Preference for Sales Strategies: Conceptual Examination and an Empirical Study," *Journal of Personal Selling and Sales Management,* Winter 1996, pp. 21–33; Kevin Daley, "The Dog and Pony Show: Dead on Arrival," *Business-to-Business Marketer,* July/August 1998, p. 3. 5. For some specific advice about communicating during a presentation, see Caryn Meyers, "Mars & Venus in the Meeting Room," *Successful Meetings,* April 1999, pp. 46–50. 6. See Rebecca Ganzel, "Telling Stories," *Presentations,* May 1999, pp. 35–40. 7. John Ward, "Stories Clarify, Set the Tone, and Drive the Message Home," *Presentations,* November 1996, p. 24. 8. Michael Finley, "One Writer, One Projector and a Roomful of Lawyers," *Presentations,* October 1996, p. 90. 9. Julie Hill, "Laugh Lab," *Presentations,* March 2002, p. 18. 10. Dave Zielinski, "Going Global," *Presentations,* October 1998, p. 48. 11. Jon Hanke, "I Dug Your Laser Light Show, but . . ." *Presentations,* October 1998, p. 15. 12. Julie Hill, "The Tale of the Tablet Computer," *Presentations,* February 2002, p. 13. 13. Dave Zielinski, "Stop! Thief!" *Presentations,* July 2001, pp. 28–40. 14. See Mark Merritt, "The Great White Way: What's New In Electronic

Whiteboards," *Presentations,* September 2001, pp. 55–60; Wayne Kawamoto, "The White Stuff," *Presentations,* November 1999, pp. 73–78. 15. Demonstrations are especially important for some products, such as new technology. See Sarah Lorge, "Selling a Product That's Ahead of Its Time," *Sales & Marketing Management,* July 1999, p. 15. 16. This section was developed from Tad Simons, "Handouts That Won't Get Trashed," *Presentations,* February 1999, pp. 47–50. 17. For more information on the bidding process, see Richard Ilsley, "Winning Bidding," *Selling Power,* June 1999, pp. 22–25. 18. "Setting Sights with Statistics," *Sales & Marketing Management,* September 1995, pp. 32–33. 19. See Robert Carey, "High Anxiety: Calculating Return on Investment Is the Murkiest Concept in the Meetings Industry," *Successful Meetings,* October 1999, pp. 38–44. 20. Tad Simons, "Scared Speechless," *Presentations,* September 1998, p. 42. 21. See Mark Merritt, "Taming the Beast Within," *Presentations,* March 2002, pp. 29–36; Darlene Price and John Messerschmitt, "Try These 8 Power Points for Presenting More Confidently," *Presentations,* August 1999, p. 84; Ellen Cahill and Paul Cahill, "Presentation Paralysis Is an Easily Preventable Hazard," *Presentations,* September 1999, p. 80. 22. Randy Cunningham, "Good Presenters Are Never Content with Their Content," *Presentations,* April 2000, p. 102.

CHAPTER 11

1. See Jeffrey Gitomer, "Name of Sales Game Is Building Relationships," *Triangle Business Journal,* September 17, 1999, p. 16. 2. See Ray Dreyfack, "Speak No Evil: Keep a Civil Tongue While Taking Defensive Action," *Selling Power,* November/December 1999, p. 43. 3. Paul S. Goldner, "Overcoming Price Objection," *Agency Sales* 30, February 2000, pp. 61–63. 4. *Increase Your Selling Power* (Pittsburgh: Westinghouse Electric Corporation), sec. 3, pp. 4–5. 5. See H. E. Carroll, "Win the Sales Argument by Seeing It in Advance," *American Salesman,* September 1999, pp. 15–18. 6. Tad Simons, "Every Audience Is a Puzzle Waiting to Be Solved," *Presentations,* May 2001, p. 6. 7. Solomon, Proverbs 18:13. 8. See David Richardson, "Don't Take Q & A Sessions for Granted: Be Prepared," *Presentations,* May 1999, p. 74. 9. Personal correspondence; name of firm and industry withheld by request. 10. Melanie Berger, "Net Sales," *Sales & Marketing Management,* April 1998, pp. 90–91. 11. See Don Beveridge, "Overcoming Price Objections," *Industrial Distribution,* February 1999, p. 94. 12. Tracey Brill, personal correspondence. Used with permission. 13. See Erin Strout, "Ask S&MM," *Sales and Marketing Management,* May 2001, p. 74; Andy Cohen, "Don't Succumb to Price Pressures," *Sales and Marketing Management,* March 2001, p. 14. 14. Ronald E. Karr, "Do You Give Up Too Easily on Tough-to-Sell Prospects?" *American Salesman,* January 1999, pp. 11–17.

CHAPTER 12

1. "No More Commando Selling," *Sales & Marketing Management,* May 1986, pp. 29–30. 2. Jack Falvey, "For the Best Close, Keep an Open Mind," *Sales & Marketing Management,* April 1990, pp. 10, 12. 3. Tim Conner, "The New Psychology of Closing Sales," *American Salesman,* September 1987, p. 25. 4. Neil Rackham, *SPIN Selling* (New York: McGraw-Hill, 1988), pp. 19–51. 5. John Graham, "A Three-Step Sales System," *Personal Selling Power,*

November/December 1994, pp. 62–63. 6. Joan Leotta, "Effortless Closing," *Selling Power,* October 2001, pp. 28–31. 7. Tom Dellecave, Jr., "Missing Link," *Sales & Marketing Management,* August 1996, pp. 94–95. 8. Mary Lu Harding, "Total Cost of Ownership—Capital Equipment," *Purchasing Today,* September 2001, pp. 16–17. 9. Russ Berry, "You're Always Selling," presented as executive in residence, Baylor University's Center for Professional Selling, October 19, 1995. 10. Marvin A. Jolson, "Selling Assertively," *Business Horizons,* September/October 1984, pp. 71–77. 11. See Sergey Frank, "Global Negotiating: Vive les Differences!" *Sales & Marketing Management,* May 1992, p. 67. 12. See Paul B. Brown, "A Bird in the Hand," *Inc.,* August 1989, pp. 114–15. 13. Harvey B. Mackay, "Humanize Your Selling Strategy," *Harvard Business Review,* March/April 1988, p. 47. 14. Norton Paley, "Seeing the Small Picture," *Sales & Marketing Management,* January 1995, pp. 22–23. 15. Shirley Bednarz, "The Selling Blues: Myths That Sabotage Positive Sales Outcomes," *American Salesman,* September 1998, pp. 7–8. 16. Andy Cohen, "No Deal," *Sales & Marketing Management,* August 1996, pp. 51–54. 17. Richard Kern, "A Follow-up Program for Lost Sales," *Sales & Marketing Management,* November 1989, pp. 124–25. 18. Anne O'Kleefe, "Opportunity Calling," *Personal Selling Power,* November/December 1994, pp. 56–57. 19. Ted Pollock, "Service—More Important than Ever," *American Salesman,* September 1990, p. 26. 20. Jay Finegan, "Stand and Deliver," *Inc.,* November 1992, p. 140. 21. Chad Kaydo, "Five Steps to Wrapping Up a Sales Call," *Sales & Marketing Management,* January 1998, p. 21. 22. Mark Prude, "Making the Transition from College to Professional Life," presented at Baylor University, September 21, 1999.

CHAPTER 13

1. Weld Royal, "Keep Them Coming Back," *Sales & Marketing Management,* September 1995, pp. 50–52. 2. Christopher Power, Lisa Driscoll, and Earl Bohn, "Smart Selling," *Business Week,* August 3, 1992, pp. 46–48; Frederick F. Reichheld and Earl Sasser, "Zero Defections: Quality Comes to Services," *Harvard Business Review,* September/October 1990, pp. 105–11. 3. William O'Connell and William Keenan, Jr., "The Shape of Things to Come," *Sales & Marketing Management,* January 1990, pp. 36–41. 4. Deloitte & Touche Survey, reported in *Selling Power,* October 2001, p. 17. 5. Gary L. Frankwick, Stephen S. Porter, and Lawrence A. Crosby, "Dynamics of Relationship Selling: A Longitudinal Examination of Changes in Salesperson–Customer Relationship Status," *Journal of Personal Selling & Sales Management* 21, Spring 2001, pp. 135–146. 6. John Tashek, "How to Avoid a CRM Failure," *eWeek* 18:40, October 15, 2001, p. 31. 7. Tony Vavra, *Aftermarketing: How to Keep Customers for Life through Relationship Marketing* (Burr Ridge, IL: Business One/Irwin, 1992). 8. Tricia Campbell, "Service with a :-)," *Sales & Marketing Management,* March 1999, pp. 63–68. 9. "Salespeople's Selling Skills," *American Salesman,* April 1990, pp. 10–11. 10. Connie O'Kane, "Stop It! 15 Things You're Doing Wrong!" *ADVantages* May/June 1999, pp. 7–13. 11. Chad Kaydo, "As Good as It Gets," *Sales & Marketing Management,* March 2000, pp. 55–60. 12. The Forum Corporation, "Why Do Customers Stop Buying?" *Sales & Marketing Management,* January 1998, p. 14. 13. Millind Lele and Jagdish Sheth, *The Customer Is Key* (New York: John Wiley & Sons, 1987). 14. Malcolm Fleschner, "Bold Goals," *Selling Power,* June 1999, pp. 54–59. 15. "What Qualities Make Sales Representatives Valuable to Customers? Survey Shows That Being the Customer's Advocate Is Most Important," *Agency Sales Magazine,* June 1987, pp. 34–35. 16. James P. Morgan, "How the Top Ten Measure Up," *Purchasing,* June 4, 1992, pp. 62–63. 17. Ellen Garbarino and Mark S. Johnson, "The Different Roles of Satisfaction, Trust, and Commitment in Customer Relationships," *Journal of Marketing* 63, April 1999, pp. 70–87; Erika Rasmusson, "Winning Back Angry Customers," *Sales & Marketing Management,* October 1997, p. 131. 18. Stephanie Gruner, "How Can I Increase Sales?" *Inc.,* March 1997, p. 103. 19. Sarah Mahoney, "Think Before You Thank," *Selling,* July/August 1996, pp. 68–70. 20. Andy Cohen, "No Deal," *Sales & Marketing Management,* August 1996, pp. 51–54. 21. John Graham, "Turn Added Value into Added Sales," *Personal Selling Power,* January/February 1995, pp. 62–63. 22. James P. Morgan, "How the Top Ten Measure Up," *Purchasing,* June 4, 1992, pp. 62–63. 23. Justin Longenecker, Carlos Moore, William Petty, and Leo Donlevy, *Small Business Management: An Entrepreneurial Emphasis,* Canadian ed., (Scarborough, Ontario: Nelson, 1998). 24. Kathleen Schmidt, "Unisys Cuts Clear Path to International Recovery," *Marketing News,* September 27, 1999, pp. 4, 6. 25. William Keenan, Jr., "Direct Results," *Sales & Marketing Management,* January 1995, pp. 78–84. 26. Don Peppers and Martha Rogers, "Growing Revenues with Cross-Selling," *Sales & Marketing Management,* June 1999, p. 24. 27. "Quality Is Key for Purchasing," *Purchasing,* January 17, 1991, p. 137. 28. Sarah Lorge, "Can ISO Certification Boost Sales?" *Sales & Marketing Management,* April 1998, p. 19. 29. James P. Morgan and Shirley Cayer, "Working with World-Class Suppliers: True Believers," *Purchasing,* August 13, 1992, pp. 50–52. 30. James P. Morgan, "Supply Strategy: Buyer–Supplier Alliances," *Purchasing,* July 23, 1996, pp. 34B13–34B16. 31. Jean Graham, "A Simple Idea Saves $8 Million a Year," *Purchasing,* May 21, 1992, pp. 47–49. 32. Lisa M. Ellram, "The Supplier Selection Decision in Strategic Partnerships," *Journal of Purchasing and Materials Management,* October 1990, pp. 8–14. 33. Neil Rackham, "The Pitfalls of Partnering," *Sales & Marketing Management,* April 2001, pp. 32–33. 34. Keith Thompson, Helen Mitchell, and Simon Knox, "Organisational Buying Behaviour in Changing Times," *European Management Journal* 16:6, pp. 698–795. 35. Susan Fourneir, Susan Dobscha, and David Glen Mick, "Preventing the Premature Death of Relationship Marketing," *Harvard Business Review,* January/February 1998, pp. 42–51. 36. Gerard A. Athaid, Patricia W. Meyers, and David Wilemon, "Seller–Buyer Interactions during the Commercialization of Technological Process Innovation," *Journal of Product and Innovation Management* 13 (1996), pp. 406–21. 37. Laurie Freeman, "Beating a Strategic Retreat," *Business Marketing,* October 1996, pp. 1, 44. 38. Gilbert A. Churchill, Neil M. Ford, Orville C. Walker, Jr., Mark Johnston, and John F. Tanner, Jr., *Sales Force Management* (San Francisco: McGraw-Hill, 2000). 39. Paul Kelly, *Situational Selling* (New York: AMACOM, 1988). 40. This section is based on Kelly, *Situational Selling;* see also John F. Tanner, Jr., and Stephen B. Castleberry, "The Participation Model: Factors Related to Buying Decision Participation," *Journal of Business to Business Marketing* 1:3

(1993), pp. 35–61. 41. Achim Walter, "Relationship Promoters: Driving Forces for Successful Customer Relationships," *Industrial Marketing Management* 28, 1999, pp. 537–51. 42. Joe Sperry, "Recommended Reading," *NAMA Journal,* Fall 1998, p. 26. 43. John Schanck, "Dun & Bradstreet Shortens Sales Cycle for High-End Solutions," *Acclivus Update,* October 1999, pp. 1–5. 44. Paul Kelly, *Situational Selling,* (New York: AMACOM, 1988). 45. Ed Rigsbee, "Positioned as Partner," *Personal Selling Power,* October 1994, pp. 50–51. 46. Howard Scott, "Winning Back a Lost Account," *Nation's Business,* July 1996, p. 31R. 47. Robert Bly, *Keeping Clients Satisfied* (Englewood Cliffs, NJ: Prentice Hall, 1993). 48. Ron Willingham, *Integrity Selling,* (New York: Doubleday, 1987). 49. Tom Bassett, "Managing Conflict with Suppliers," *Purchasing Today,* December 2001, pp. 7–9. 50. Richard Porterfield, "The Basics of Avoiding Disputes," *Purchasing Today,* March 2001, p. 8. 51. John Yuva, "Trust and Business Go Hand-in-Hand," *Purchasing Today,* July 2001, pp. 49–53.

CHAPTER 14

1. See, for example, P. Anders Miller and P. Kelle, "Quantitative Support for Buyer–Seller Negotiation in Just-in-Time Purchasing," *International Journal of Purchasing and Materials Management,* Spring 1998, pp. 25–31. 2. See Sarah Lorge, "The Best Way to Negotiate," *Sales & Marketing Management,* March 1998, p. 92. 3. See Jenson J. Zhao, "The Chinese Approach to International Business Negotiation," *The Journal of Business Communication* 37, July 2002, pp. 209–37; Alma Mintu-Wimsatt and Jule B. Gassenheimer, "The Moderating Effect of Cultural Context in Buyer–Seller Negotiation," *Journal of Personal Selling and Sales Management* 20, Winter 2000, pp. 1–9; Y. Paik and R. L. Tung, "Negotiating with East Asians: How to Attain 'Win–Win' Outcomes," *Management International Review* 39:2 (1999), pp. 103–23; R. D. Gulbro and P. Herbig, "Cultural Differences Encountered by Firms When Negotiating Internationally," *Industrial Management & Data Systems* 99:2 (1999), pp. 47–54; H. S. Woo, "Cultural Characteristics Prevalent in the Chinese Negotiation Process," *European Business Review* 99:5 (1999), pp. 313–23; Hong Seng Woo, "Negotiating in China: Some Issues for Western Women," *Women in Management Review* 14:4 (1999), pp. 115–20; Jennifer George, Gareth Jones, and Jorge Gonzalez, "The Role of Affect in Cross-Cultural Negotiations," *Journal of International Business Studies* 29:4 (1999), pp. 749–72. 4. Beacon Expert Systems, Inc., 35 Gardner Rd., Brookline, MA (617) 738-9300. Information can be found at www.negotiatorpro.com/npro/negprosof.html. 5. Thomas A. Wood, "Team Negotiations in a Single Voice," *Purchasing Today,* July 2001, pp. 8–10. 6. The information in this section was developed from Kenneth Thomas, "Conflict and Conflict Management," in *The Handbook of Industrial and Organizational Psychology,* ed. Marvin Dunnette (Skokie, IL: Rand McNally, 1976). See also Lourdes Munduate, Juan Ganaza, Jose M. Peiro, and Martin Euwema, "Patterns of Styles in Conflict Management and Effectiveness," *International Journal of Conflict Management* 10, January 1999, pp. 5–24; Philip J. Moberg, "Linking Conflict Strategy to the Five-Factor Model: Theoretical and Empirical Foundations," *International Journal of Conflict Management* 12:1 (2001), pp. 47–68. 7. Joseph Conlin, "Negotiating Their Way to the Top," *Sales & Marketing Management,* April 1996, p. 62. 8. Ibid., pp. 58–65.

9. Anne Macquin and Dominique Rouzies, "Selling across the Culture Gap," *The Financial Times,* March 13, 1998, p. FTS10–11. 10. "Fractured English," *Have a Good Day,* January 1997, pp. 1–2. 11. William Donohue and Robert Kolt, *Managing Interpersonal Conflict* (Newbury Park, CA: Sage Publications, 1999), p. 56. 12. See Roger Fisher and William Ury, *Getting to Yes: Negotiating Agreement without Giving In,* 2nd ed. (Boston: Houghton Mifflin, 1991). 13. See Bob Oros, "Negotiating Skills: Coming to a Happy Selling Agreement," *ID: The Voice of Foodservice Distribution,* September 1998, p. 111; Dean Rieck, "The Rule of Reciprocity: 'I'll Do This for You. Then, You Do That for Me,'" *Direct Marketing,* January 1998, pp. 42–44. 14. Neil Rackham, "Winning the Price War," *Sales and Marketing Management,* November 2001, p. 26. 15. Michael Bohon, "Debriefing after the Negotiation," *Purchasing Today,* October 2001, p. 10–11.

CHAPTER 15

1. Pierre Desmet, "Estimation of Product Category Sales Responsiveness to Allocated Shelf Space," *International Journal of Research in Marketing* 15, December 1998, pp. 443–47. 2. Jaclyn Fierman, "The Death and Rebirth of the Salesman," *Fortune,* July 25, 1994, pp. 80–91. 3. Robert Sharoff, "Not Just Fun and Games," *Selling,* November 1994, pp. 32–36. 4. Lester E. Goodman and Paul A. Dion, "The Determinants of Commitment in the Distributor/Manufacturer Relationship," *Industrial Marketing Management* 30 (2001), pp. 287–300. 5. Martha C. Cooper, Douglas M. Lambert, and Janus D. Pagh, "Supply Chain Management: More than a New Name for Logistics," *The International Journal of Logistics Management* 8:1 (1997), pp. 1–14. 6. Mark Hurd, "What Is CRM?" Presentation at Baylor University, February 19, 2002. 7. Nancy McCann, "One Open Door Doesn't Lead to Another," *Selling,* November 1995, p. 23. 8. Janet Wagner, Richard Ettenson, and Jean Parrish, "Vendor Selection among Retail Buyers: An Analysis by Merchandise Division," *Journal of Retailing,* Spring 1989, pp. 58–79. 9. Scott Corriveau, "Mott's USA Empowers Brokers," *Sales and Marketing Strategies & News,* June/July 1996, p. 24. 10. Geoffrey Brewer, "Shout It Out," *Sales & Marketing Management,* February 1996, pp. 30–42. 11. "How Much Does It Cost to Close a Sale?" *Research Report SM17* (Bethesda, MD: Center for Exhibition Industry Research, 1996). 12. Wendy Hatoum, "Selling Your Soles," *Sporting Goods Dealer,* April 1993, pp. 40–42. 13. Ibid. 14. Robert Blattberg and Edward Cox, *Category Management* (Washington, DC: Food Marketing Institute, 1995). 15. This example is based on data presented in Christopher Hoyt and Hunter Hastings, "Re-Connect with the Consumer," *PROMO: The International Magazine for Promotion Marketing,* December 1993, pp. 14–15.

CHAPTER 16

1. Renee Zemanski, "A Matter of Time," *Selling Power,* October 2001, pp. 80–82. 2. Betsy Wiesendanger, "Bigger Sales, Same Budget," *Sales & Marketing Management,* July 1993, pp. 46–53. 3. Lawrence Tuttle, "Are You Ready to Improve?" *Personal Selling Power,* October 1994, pp. 38–44. 4. Michael Treacy and Fred Wiersema, "How Market Leaders Keep Their Edge," *Fortune,* February 6, 1996, pp. 88–98. 5. Erika Rasmusson, "Wanted: Profitable Customers," *Sales & Marketing Management,* May 1999, pp. 28–34. 6. Adel El-

Ansary and Waleed A. El-Ansary, *Winning Customers, Building Accounts: Some Do It Better than Others* (Jacksonville, FL: Paper and Plastics Education and Research Foundation, 1994). 7. Rob Smith, "For Best Results, Treat Business Decisionmakers as Individuals," *Business Marketing,* March 1999, p. 39. 8. William F. Kendy, "One More Sale per Week," *Selling Power,* October 2001, pp. 35–39. 9. Case study, "Northwestern National Speeds Quotes," *Sales and Marketing Strategies & News,* June/July 1996, p. 4. 10. Stephen Rush, "From Baseball to Business," *Nation's Business,* October 1996, pp. 48–52. 11. Sarah Lorge, "Improving Time Management," *Sales & Marketing Management,* February 1998, p. 112. 12. Steve Atlas, "Time to Organize," *Selling Power,* November/December 2001, pp. 35–38. 13. Michael Goldstein, "Getting Out from Under," *Successful Meetings,* October 1999, p. 28. 14. Joan Leotta, "Time Tyrants," *Selling Power,* April 2000, pp. 117–20. 15. Thomas Petzinger, Jr., "Bob Schmonsee Has a Tool for Better Sales and It Ignores Excuses," *Wall Street Journal,* March 26, 1999, p. B1. 16. T. J. Becker, "How to Make the Most of Downtime," *Selling,* October 1995, pp. 54–56. 17. Stuart Miller, "Beating the Clock—and Records," *Sales & Marketing Management,* February 1997, pp. 20–21. 18. Doug Loewe, "Long-Distance Manager," *Sales & Marketing Management,* October 1994, p. 25. 19. "Get Plugged In," *Sales & Marketing Management,* March 1999, pp. 58–61. 20. Tony Seideman, "Who Needs Managers?" *Sales & Marketing Management,* June 1994, pp. 15–17. 21. Melissa Campanelli, "The King of Email," *Sales & Marketing Management,* December 1994, pp. 13–16.

CHAPTER 17

1. Dennis Christiansen and Sudhir Tiwari, "Internal Selling: The #1 Issue That Keeps Strategic Account Managers Awake at Night," *NAMA Journal,* Summer 1998, pp. 11–12. 2. George Day, "The Capabilities of Market Driven Organizations," *Journal of Marketing,* October 1994, pp. 37–52. 3. Edmund Bradford and Francis Rome, "Applying Total Customer Management at DHL: How One Leading Organization Has Proved the Payoff," *Journal of Selling and Major Account Management* 2, Autumn 1999, pp. 117–23. 4. Andy Cohen, "Should Reps Collect the Bills?" *Sales & Marketing Management,* June 1996, pp. 53–54. 5. Richard C. Munn, "Marketers Must Align Themselves with Sales," *Marketing News,* November 9, 1998, p. 12. 6. Sarah Lorge, "Salespeople Are from Venus," *Sales & Marketing Management,* April 1999, pp. 27–33. 7. Kevin J. Clancy, "Perfecting the Marketing–Sales Balancing Act," *Business Marketing,* July 1998, p. 17. 8. Jo Yandle and Jim Blythe, "Intra-Departmental Conflict between Sales and Marketing: An Exploratory Study," *The Journal of Selling and Major Account Management* 2, Spring 2000, pp. 13–31. 9. Lawrence B. Chonko, John F. Tanner, Jr., and Ellen Reid Smith, "The Sales Force's Role in International Marketing Research and Marketing Research Information Systems," *Journal of Personal Selling and Sales Management,* Winter 1991, pp. 69–80. 10. Susan Greco, "The Customer Driven Bonus Plan," *Inc.,* September 1995, p. 89. 11. Michelle Marchetti, "Person to Person: How to Sell Your Boss," *Sales & Marketing Management,* May 1996, p. 43. 12. Shelby D. Hunt and Arturo Vasquez-Parraga, "Organizational Consequences, Marketing Ethics, and Salesforce Supervision," *Journal of Marketing Research,* February 1993, pp. 78–90. 13. Charles W. Schwepker, Jr., "Ethical Climate's Relationship to Job Satisfaction, Organizational Commitment and Turnover Intention in the Salesforce," *Journal of Business Research* 54 (2001), pp. 39–52. 14. Much of this section is based on the work of Richard P. Nielsen, "What Can Managers Do about Unethical Management?" *Journal of Business Ethics,* Vol. 6, 1987, pp. 309–20, and on "Negotiating as an Ethics Action (Praxis) Strategy," *Journal of Business Ethics,* Vol. 9, 1989, pp. 383–90. 15. Donna Wheeler, "Rockwell Automation Leverages Sales and Service to Team for Greater Success," *Acclivus Update,* Fourth Quarter 1999, pp. 3–5. 16. Andy Cohen, "Managing," *Sales & Marketing Management,* April 1996, pp. 77–80. 17. Henry Canady, "Team Selling Works!" *Personal Selling Power,* September 1994, pp. 52–58. 18. Tricia Campbell, "Getting Top Executives to Sell," *Sales & Marketing Management,* October 1998, p. 39. 19. Michele Marchetti, "Compensation Gamble," *Sales & Marketing Management,* July 1996, pp. 65–69. 20. William Moncrief, Shannon H. Shipp, Charles W. Lamb, Jr., and David W. Cravens, "Examining the Roles of Telemarketing in Sales Strategy," *Journal of Personal Selling and Sales Management,* Fall 1989, pp. 1–12. 21. Francy Blackwood, "Whose Customer Is It?" *Selling,* April 1996, pp. 76–77. 22. Steve Atlas and Elise Atlas, "Team Approach," *Selling Power,* May 2000, pp. 126–28. 23. Craig MacClaren, "Companies Find Benefits in the Team Approach," *Promo: The Magazine of Promotion Marketing,* April 1996, p. 80. 24. Nancy Arnott, "Selling a Relationship," *Sales & Marketing Management,* January 1995, p. 14. 25. Atlas and Atlas, "Team Approach." 26. Frank Jossi, "Pulling It All Together: Creating Presentations as a Team," *Presentations,* July 1996, pp. 18–26. 27. Nancy Chamberlain, "Out of Touch—Out of Luck," *Sales and Marketing Strategies & News,* September 2001, pp. 33–34.

CHAPTER 18

1. Laurie Freeman, "Fiorina Brings Marketing, Sales Savvy to HP's Top Post," *Business Marketing,* August 1999, pp. 3, 50. 2. Eileen Zimmerman, "So You Wanna Be a CEO," *Sales and Marketing Management,* January 2002, pp. 31–35 3. Darrel Wash, "A New Way to Classify Occupations by Education and Training," *Occupational Outlook Quarterly,* Winter 1995–96, pp. 29–40. 4. U.S. Department of Commerce, *Occupational Handbook Quarterly,* Spring 2000, pp. 28–39. 5. Cyndee Miller, "Job Picture for Marketing, Sales Brightest in Years," *Marketing News,* August 29, 1994, pp. 1–2. 6. Ana Maria Rendon, "Doing Business in Mexico," *Cintermex,* October 1999, pp. 22–24. 7. Lewis C. Rogers, "Sales Interview Preparation," Orion-careernetwork.com, May 16, 2001. 8. Jack Chapman, "Have You Considered Sales?" *Marketing News,* Fall 1996, pp. 17–18. 9. Eugene Johnson, "How Do Sales Managers View College Preparation for Sales?" *Journal of Personal Selling and Sales Management,* Summer 1990, pp. 69–72; Cliff Enico, "Essential Characteristics for Sales Success," *SAM,* May/June 2001, pp. 62–63. 10. Alan Farnham, "Are You Smart Enough?" *Fortune,* January 15, 1996, pp. 34–48. 11. Seymour Adler, "Personality Tests for Salesforce Selection: Worth a Fresh Look," *Review of Business,* Summer/Fall 1994, pp. 27–31. 12. John L. Munschauer, "The Resume: How to Speak to Employer's Needs," *CPC Annual,* 1992–93, pp. 27–41. 13. Gene Garofalo and Gary Drummond, *Sales Professional's Survival Guide* (Englewood Cliffs, NJ: Prentice Hall, 1987). 14. Margaret Littman, "Good Economy, Bad Candidates," *Marketing News,* April 10, 2000, pp. 12–13.

15. Dana James, "A Day in the Life of a Corporate Recruiter," *Marketing News,* April 10, 2000, pp. 1, 11. 16. Ramon Avila, Joseph Chapman, and Pamela Reigle, "A Business Perspective on the Student Portfolio," proceedings of the National Sales Conference, 1994, pp. 54–57. 17. Vadim Liberman, "Manager's Tool Kit," *Across the Board,* January/February 2002, pp. 78–79. 18. Joe Haley, "He Said, She Said," *ADvantages,* March/April 1999, p. 39. 19. Michael Adams, "Family Matters," *Sales & Marketing Management,* March 1998, pp. 61–66. 20. Ed Holton, "The Critical First Year on the Job," *CPC Annual,* 1992–93, pp. 72–75. 21. Jan Gelman, "If You Had $3,000 to Spend on Self-Improvement, What Would You Do?" *Selling,* September 1995, pp. 59–72; "3M Offers Sales Professionals a Career Development Tool," *3M Stemwinder,* June 1997, pp. 6–7. 22. Diane McGrath, "Continuous Learning," *Update,* Fourth Quarter 1998, p. 8. 23. Donna Cornachio, "How Not to Lose Your Job," *Sales & Marketing Management,* August 1996, pp. 58–63. 24. Ellen Pullins, Leslie Fine, and Wendy Warren, "Identifying Peer Mentors in the Sales Force: An Exploratory Investigation of Willingness and Ability," *Journal of the Academy of Marketing Science* 24:2 (1996), pp. 125–36. 25. Rick Ebel and Alan D. Fletcher, "Who Are Today's Buyers and What Do They Really Want?" *Promotional Products Business,* January 1999, pp. 71–84. 26. Sandra Fisher, "Stress, Part 1: Warning Signs and Identifying Characteristics," *Sales & Marketing Management,* November 1992, pp. 93–94. 27. Susan M. Keaveney and James E. Nelson, "Coping with Organizational Role Stress: Intrinsic Motivational Orientation, Perceived Role Benefits, and Psychological Withdrawal," *Journal of the Academy of Marketing Science* 21, Spring 1993, pp. 113–15. 28. Betsy Cummings, "Sales Ruined My Personal Life," *Sales and Marketing Management,* November 2001, pp. 45–50. 29. John F. Tanner, Jr., Mark G. Dunn, and Lawrence B. Chonko, "Vertical Exchange and Salesperson Stress," *Journal of Personal Selling and Sales Management,* Spring 1993, pp. 27–35. 30. Ibid. 31. Gilbert A. Churchill, Jr., Neil M. Ford, Orville C. Walker, Mark Johnston, and John F. Tanner, Jr., *Sales Force Management,* 6th ed. (New York: Irwin/McGraw-Hill, 2000). 32. Andy Cohen, "Facing Pressure," *Sales & Marketing Management,* April 1997, pp. 30–38. 33. John F. Tanner, Jr. and Stephen B. Castleberry, "Vertical Exchange Quality and Performance: Studying the Role of the Sales Manager," *Journal of Personal Selling and Sales Management,* pp. 17–27; Rosemary Lagace, "Leader–Member Exchange: Antecedents and Consequences of the Cadre and Hired Hand," *Journal of Personal Selling and Sales Management,* February 1990, pp. 11–19.

Glossary

ABC analysis Evaluating the importance of an account. The most important is an A account, the second most important is a B account, and the least important is a C account.

accommodating mode Resolving conflict by being unassertive and highly cooperative. When using this approach, people often neglect their own needs and desires to satisfy the concerns of the other party.

account opportunity Another term for the sales potential dimensions of the sales call allocation grid.

account share See *customer share*.

active listening Process in which the listener attempts to draw out as much information as possible by actively processing information received and stimulating the communication of additional information.

activity goals Behavioral objectives, such as the number of calls made in a day.

activity quota A type of quota that sets minimal behavioral expectations for a salesperson's activities. Used when the sales cycle is long and sales are few. Controls activities of salespeople.

adaptive planning The development of alternative paths to the same goal in a negotiation session.

adaptive selling Approach to personal selling in which selling behaviors and approaches are altered during a sales interaction or across customer interactions, based on information about the nature of the selling situation.

administrative law Laws established by local, state, or federal regulatory agencies, such as the Federal Trade Commission or the Food and Drug Administration.

adoption process Steps that a person or an organization goes through when making an initial purchase and then using a new product or service.

advantages Why a feature would be important to someone.

after-tax cash flows Used to evaluate a purchase; ensures that the company has enough cash to pay for the purchase.

agenda Listing of what will be discussed, and in what sequence, in a negotiation session.

agent Person who acts in place of his or her company. See also *manufacturers' agents*.

aggressive Sales style that controls the sales interaction but often does not gain commitment because it ignores the customer's needs and fails to probe for information.

ambush negotiating A win–lose tactic used by a buyer at the beginning of, or prior to, negotiations when the seller does not expect this approach.

amiable Category in the social style matrix; describes people who like cooperation and close relationships. Amiables are low on assertiveness and high on responsiveness.

analysis paralysis When a salesperson prefers to spend practically all of his or her time analyzing the situation and gathering information instead of making sales calls.

analytical Category in the social style matrix; describes people who emphasize facts and logic. Analyticals are low on assertiveness and responsiveness.

application form Preprinted form completed by a job applicant.

approach Method designed to get the prospect's attention and interest quickly.

articulation The production of recognizable speech.

assertive Sales manner that stresses responding to customer needs while being self-confident and positive.

assertiveness Dimension of the social style matrix that assesses the degree to which people have opinions on issues and publicly make their positions clear to others.

assessment center Central location for evaluating job candidates.

automatic replenishment (AR) A form of just-in-time inventory management where the vendor manages the customer's inventory, and automatically ships and stocks products at the customer's location based on mutually agreed-upon standards.

avoiding mode Resolving conflict in an unassertive and uncooperative manner. In this mode people make no attempt to resolve their own needs or the needs of others.

awareness phase The first phase in the development of a buyer–seller relationship, in which salespeople locate and qualify prospects and buyers consider various sources of supply.

backdoor selling Actions by one salesperson that go behind the back of a purchaser to directly contact other members of the buying center.

balanced presentation Occurs when the salesperson shows all sides of the situation—that is, is totally honest.

balance sheet method Attempts to obtain commitment by asking the buyer to think of the pros and cons of the various alternatives; often referred to as the *Ben Franklin method*.

banner advertising Ads placed at the top, sides, or bottom of a Web page, encouraging the viewer to visit a different website.

barriers Buyer's subordinates who plan and schedule interviews for their superiors; also called *screens*.

bartering The trading of goods for goods instead of for money.

benchmarking A process of comparing your activities and performance with those of the best organization or individual in order to improve.

benefit How a particular feature will help a particular buyer.

benefit approach Approach in which the salesperson focuses on the prospect's needs by stating a benefit of the product or service.

benefit summary method Obtaining commitment by simply reminding the prospect of the agreed-on benefits of the proposal.

bird dog Individual who, for a fee, will provide the names of leads for the salesperson; also called a *spotter*.

blitz Canvassing method in which a large group of salespeople attempt to make calls on all prospective businesses in a given geographic territory on a specified day.

body language Nonverbal signals communicated through facial expressions, arms, hands, and legs.

bonus Lump-sum incentive payment based on performance.

boomerang method Responding to objections by turning the objection into a reason for acting now.

bottom-up forecasting Forecast compiled by adding up each salesperson's forecast for total company sales.

bounce-back card Card returned from a lead that requests additional information.

brainstorming session Meeting in which people are allowed to creatively explore different methods of achieving goals.

breaking bulk Resellers selling in smaller quantities than they received from manufacturers and distributors in order to meet individual users' needs.

bribes Payments made to buyers to influence their purchase decisions.

browbeating Negotiation strategy in which buyers attempt to alter the selling team's enthusiasm and self-respect by making unflattering comments.

budget bogey Negotiation strategy in which one side claims that the budget does not allow for the solution proposed; also called *budget limitation tactic*.

budget limitation tactic See *budget bogey*.

business defamation Making unfair or untrue statements to customers about a competitor, its products, or its salespeople.

buyback A seller's guarantee to buy back unsold merchandise from the buyer.

buyer's remorse The insecurity a buyer feels about whether the choice was a wise one; also called *post-purchase dissonance*.

buying center Informal, cross-department group of people involved in a purchase decision.

buying community Small, informal group of people in similar positions who communicate regularly, often both socially and professionally.

buying signals Nonverbal cues given by the buyer that indicate the buyer may be ready to commit; also called *closing cues*.

canned presentation See *standard memorized presentation*.

cap A limit placed on a salesperson's earnings.

capital equipment Major purchases made by a business, such as computer systems, that are used by the business for several years in its operations or production process.

cash discount Price discount given for early payment in cash.

category captain The best supplier in a category that retailers often turn to for help in managing the category. This supplier partners with the reseller to gain insight into customer needs and to develop a program for increasing category profits.

category management In selling to retailers, a current trend in the area of full-line selling.

center-of-influence method Prospecting method wherein the salesperson cultivates well-known, influential people in the territory who are willing to supply lead information.

champion Person who works for the buying firm in the areas most affected by the proposed change and works with the salesperson for the success of the proposal; also called *advocate* or *internal salesperson*.

change agent Person who is a cause of change in an organization.

circular routing Method of scheduling sales calls that includes using circular patterns from the home base in order to cover the territory.

closed questions Questions that can be answered with a word or short phrase.

closing Common term for obtaining commitment, which usually refers only to asking for the buyer's business.

closing cues See *buying signals.*

cloverleaf routing Method of scheduling sales calls that involves using loops to cover different portions of the territory on different days or weeks; on a map it should resemble a cloverleaf.

cold call See *cold canvass method.*

cold canvass method Prospecting method in which a sales representative tries to generate leads for new business by calling on totally unfamiliar organizations; also called *cold calls.*

collaborating mode Resolving conflict by seeking to maximize the satisfaction of both parties and hence truly reach a win–win solution.

collusion Agreement among competitors, made after contacting customers, concerning their relationships with customers.

combination plan Compensation plan that provides salary and commission; offers the greatest flexibility for motivating and controlling the activities of salespeople.

Commerce Business Daily Publication that contains all the invitations for bids issued by the federal government.

commission Incentive payment for an individual sale; often a percentage of the sale price.

commission base Unit of analysis used to determine commissions: for example, unit sales, dollar sales, or gross margin.

commission rate Percentage of base paid or the amount per base unit paid in a commission compensation plan: for example, a percentage of dollar sales or an amount per unit sold.

commitment phase The fourth stage in the development of a buyer–seller relationship in which the buyer and seller have implicitly or explicitly pledged to continue the relationship for an extended period.

common law Legal precedents that arise out of court decisions.

compensation method Method used to respond helpfully to objections by agreeing that the objection is valid, but then proceeding to show any compensating advantages.

competence Whether the salesperson knows what he or she is talking about.

competing mode Resolving conflict in an assertive and noncooperative manner.

complacency Assuming the business is yours and will always be yours.

compliment approach Approach in which the salesperson begins the sales call by complimenting the buyer in some fashion.

compromising mode Resolving conflict by being somewhat cooperative and somewhat assertive. People using this approach attempt to find a quick, mutually acceptable solution that partially satisfies both parties.

computer-interactive whiteboard A sophisticated electronic whiteboard that allows users to access and control software applications on the computer, utilizing interactive meeting software tools.

computer-peripheral whiteboard An electronic whiteboard that is always connected to a computer and can do what an electronic copyboard can do; it can also save the session as a computer file.

concession Occurs when one party in a negotiation meeting agrees to change his or her position in some fashion.

consequence questions Questions that illustrate the consequences of a disadvantage in a competitor's product.

consignment Method of payment for goods in which the retailer makes no payment until the product is sold.

conspiracy Agreement among competitors, made prior to contacting customers, concerning their relationships with customers.

consultative selling philosophy Form of customized presentation in which salespeople identify the prospect's needs and then recommend the best solution, even when the best solution does not include the salesperson's own products or services.

contest Trade promotion a firm uses to increase sales by rewarding top salespeople with trips, extra money, or merchandise.

contract to sell Offer made by a salesperson that received an unqualified acceptance by a buyer.

conventional résumé Form of life history organized by type of work experience.

conversion goals Measures of salesperson efficiency.

conversion ratio Similar to a batting average; calculated by dividing performance results by activity results (for example, dividing the number of sales by the number of calls).

co-op advertising Advertising paid for by both retailer and manufacturer, often with some assistance in preparing the ad from the manufacturer.

corporate culture The values and beliefs held by a company and expressed by senior management.

coupon clippers People who like to send off for product information, even though they have no intention of ever buying the product or service.

creativity The trait of having imagination and inventiveness and using it to come up with new solutions and ideas.

credibility The characteristic of being perceived by the buyer as believable and reliable.

credible commitments Tangible investments in a relationship that indicate commitment to the relationship.

credulous person standard Canadian law stating that a company is liable to pay damages if advertising and sale presentation claims and statements about comparisons with competitive products could be misunderstood by a reasonable person.

creeping commitment Purchase decision process that arises when decisions made early in the process have significant influence on decisions made later in the process.

cross-selling Similar to full-line selling except that the additional products sold are not directly associated with the initial products.

cultural relativism A view that no culture's ethics are superior to those of another culture's.

cumulative discount Quantity discount for purchases over a period of time; the buyer is allowed to add up all the purchases to determine the total quantity and the total quantity discount.

curiosity approach Arousing interest by making an unexpected comment that piques the prospect's curiosity.

customer intentions survey Method of forecasting sales in which customers are asked how much they intend to buy over the forecasting period.

customer orientation Selling approach based on keeping the customer's interests paramount.

customer service rep Inbound salesperson who handles customer concerns.

customer share The percentage of business received from a company's accounts. Also called *account share* or *share of wallet.*

customer value The customer's perception of what he or she wants to have happen in a specific use situation, with the help of a product or service offering, in order to accomplish a desired purpose or goal.

customized presentation Presentation developed from a detailed and comprehensive analysis or survey of the prospect's needs that is not canned or memorized in any fashion.

databases Contain information on leads, prospects, and customers.

data mining The use of artificial intelligence and statistical tools to discover hidden insights in the volumes of data in a database.

deal Promotional discount offered by a manufacturer to a retailer, often (but not always) in exchange for featuring a product in a newspaper ad and/or a special display.

deception Unethical practice of withholding information or telling white lies.

deciders Buying center members who make the final selection of the product to purchase.

decoding Communication activity undertaken by a receiver interpreting the meaning of the received message.

deferred dating Scheduling payment of a bill at a later (deferred) date; gives a reseller time to sell the product in order to generate the cash needed to pay for it.

dependability Whether the salesperson will live up to promises made; is not something a salesperson can demonstrate immediately.

derived demand Situation in which the demand for a producer's goods is based on what its customers sell.

diagnostic feedback Information given to a salesperson indicating how he or she is performing.

digital asset management Software systems to archive, catalog, and retrieve digital media and text. Salespeople use these to easily create presentations.

digital sales assistant (DSA) Indicates any software tool that is designed to help salespeople get their message across. PowerPoint and Astound are two DSAs.

direct denial Method of answering objections in which the salesperson makes a relatively strong statement indicating the error the prospect has made.

direct request method Attaining commitment by simply asking for it in a straightforward statement.

disadvantage questions Questions that ask a customer to articulate a specific problem.

disguised interview Discussion between an applicant and an interviewer in which the applicant is unaware that the interviewer is evaluating the applicant for the position.

dissolution The process of terminating the relationship; can occur because of poor performance, clash in culture, change in needs, and other factors.

distribution channel Set of people and organizations responsible for the flow of products and services from the producer to the ultimate user.

document cameras Also called *visual presenters;* are similar to traditional overhead projectors in their ability to display transparencies. However, because they are essentially cameras, document cameras are also capable of displaying any three-dimensional object without the use of a transparency.

dormant accounts Accounts that have not purchased for a specified time.

draw Advance from the company to a salesperson made against future commissions.

driver Category in the social style matrix; describes task-oriented people who are high on assertiveness and low on responsiveness.

efficient customer response (ECR) system Distribution system that drives inventory to the lowest possible levels, increases the frequency of shipping, and automates ordering and inventory control processes without the problems of stockouts and higher costs.

ego-involved Refers to the perception of an audience member that presented subject matter is important to his or her own well-being. For a contrast, see *issue-involved*.

elaboration questions Questions that are positive requests for additional information rather than simply verbal encouragement.

electronic copyboard A projection device that can scan and print whatever is written on its surface. It is not connected to a computer.

electronic data interchange (EDI) Computer-to-computer linkages between suppliers and buyers for information sharing about sales, production, shipment, and receipt of products.

electronic whiteboard A digital version of an easel.

emotional intelligence The ability to effectively understand and use your own emotions and those of people with whom you interact. Includes four aspects: (1) knowing your own feelings and emotions as they are happening, (2) controlling your emotions so you do not act impulsively, (3) recognizing your customer's emotions (called *empathy*), and (4) using your emotions to interact effectively with customers.

emotional needs Organizational and/or personal needs that are associated with some type of personal reward and gratification for the person buying the product.

emotional outburst tactic Negotiation strategy in which one party attempts to gain concessions by resorting to a display of strong emotion.

encoding Communication activity undertaken by a sender translating his or her thought into a message.

encouragement probes Questions or nonverbal signals that encourage customers to reveal further information.

end users Businesses that purchase goods and services to support their own production and operations.

endless-chain method Prospecting method whereby a sales representative attempts to get at least one additional lead from each person he or she interviews.

e-selling Utilizing e-mail to generate leads.

ethical imperialism The view that the ethical standards that apply locally or in one's home country should be applied to everyone's behavior around the world.

ethics Principles governing the behavior of an individual or a group.

ethics review board May consist of experts inside and outside the company who are responsible for reviewing ethics policies, investigating allegations of unethical behavior, and acting as a sounding board for employees.

evaluative feedback Information to a salesperson indicating how he or she is performing.

exclusive sales territories Method that uses a prospect's geographic location to determine whether a salesperson can sell to that prospect.

excuses Concerns expressed by the buyer that are intended to mask the buyer's true objections.

executive summary In a written proposal, a summary of one page or less that briefly describes the total cost minus total savings, the problem to be solved, and the proposed solution.

expansion phase The third phase in the development of a relationship, in which it takes a significant effort to share information and further investigate the potential relationship benefits.

expense budget Budget detailing expenses; may be expressed in dollars or as a percentage of sales volume.

expert opinions Method of forecasting sales that involves averaging the estimates of several experts.

expert system Computer program that mimics a human expert.

exploration phase The second phase in the development of a relationship, in which both buyers and sellers explore the potential benefits and costs associated with the relationship.

expressed warranty Warranty specified through oral or written communications.

expressive Category in the social style matrix; describes people who are both competitive and approachable. They are high on assertiveness and responsiveness.

extranets Secure Internet-based networks connecting buyers and suppliers.

extrinsic orientation Orientation of salespeople characterized by viewing their job as a way to achieve rewards such as compensation given to them by others.

FAB When salespeople describe the features, advantages (why that feature is important), and benefits of their product or service.

face A person's desire for a positive identity or self-concept.

factual questions Questions that ask for factual information and usually start with who, what, where, how, or why.

fax Electronic document transfer device; short for *facsimile*.

feature (1) Quality or characteristic of the product or service. (2) Putting a product on sale with a special display and featuring the product in advertising.

FEB Stands for feature, evidence, benefit; technique useful in interviewing.

FEBA A method of describing a product or service where salespeople mention the feature, provide evidence that the feature actually does exist, explain the benefit (why that feature is important to the buyer), and then ask whether the buyer agrees with the value of the feature and benefit.

feedback See *diagnostic feedback* and *evaluative feedback*.

feel–felt–found method Method of helpfully responding to objections in which the salesperson shows how others held similar views before trying the product or service.

felt stress Persistent and enduring psychological distress brought about by job demands or constraints encountered in the work environment.

field sales manager First-level manager.

field salespeople Salespeople who spend considerable time in the customer's place of business, communicating with the customer face to face.

field support representative Telemarketer who works with field salespeople and does more than prospect for leads.

flip chart A large easel-type chart placed on the floor; used in making presentations to a group.

FOB (free on board) Designates the point at which responsibility shifts from seller to buyer.

FOB destination The seller has title until the goods are received at the destination.

FOB factory The buyer has title when the goods leave the seller's facility.

focus of dissatisfaction The person in the organization who is most likely to perceive problems and dissatisfactions; leads to the focus of power.

focus of power The person in the organization who can approve, prevent, or influence action.

focus of receptivity The person in the organization who will listen receptively and provide a seller with valuable information; leads to the focus of dissatisfaction.

follow-up Activities a salesperson performs after commitment is achieved.

Foreign Corrupt Practices Act Law that governs the behavior of U.S. business in foreign countries; restricts the bribing of foreign officials.

forestall To resolve objections before buyers have a chance to raise them.

forward buy Buying a larger-than-normal amount to take advantage of a lower price.

free on board See *FOB*.

freestanding insert (FSI) Advertisement that is printed separately and then inserted in a newspaper.

full-line selling Selling the entire line of associated products.

functional relationship Series of market exchanges between a buyer and a seller, linked together over time. These relationships are characterized as win–lose relationships.

functional résumé Life history that reverses the content and titles of a conventional résumé and is organized by what a candidate can do or has learned rather than by types of experience.

gatekeepers Buying center members who influence the buying process by controlling the flow of information and/or limiting the alternatives considered. Sometimes called *barriers* or *screens*.

geographic salesperson Salesperson assigned a specific geographic territory in which to sell all the company's products and services.

global account manager (GAM) Sales executive responsible for coordinating sales efforts for one account globally.

good guy–bad guy routine Negotiation strategy in which one team member acts as the "good guy" while another team member acts as the "bad guy." The goal of the strategy is to have the opposing team accept the good guy's proposal to avoid the consequences of the bad guy's proposal.

goodwill Value of the feelings or attitudes customers or prospects have toward a company and its products.

greeter Interviewer who greets the applicant and may conduct a disguised interview.

gross margin quota Minimum levels of acceptable profit or gross margin performance.

gross profit margin The net sales minus the cost of goods sold.

group interview Similar to *panel interview* but includes several candidates as well as several interviewers.

guaranteed price Price guaranteed to be the lowest. If the price falls, the buyer is refunded the difference between the original and new prices for any inventory still in stock.

halo effect How one does in one thing changes a person's perceptions about other things one does.

handouts Written documents provided to buyers before, during, or after a meeting to help them remember what was said.

high-context culture Culture in which the verbal part of communication carries less of the information in a message than the nonverbal parts. The sender's values, position, and background are conveyed by the way the message is expressed. Examples of high-context cultures include Japan, France, and Spain.

honesty Combination of truthfulness and sincerity; highly related to dependability.

house accounts Accounts assigned to a sales executive rather than to the specific salesperson responsible for the territory containing the account.

implication questions Questions that logically follow one or more problem questions (in SPIN®); designed to help the prospect recognize the true ramifications of the problem.

implied warranty Warranty that is not expressly stated through oral or written communication but is still an obligation defined by law.

impression management Activities in which salespeople engage to affect and manage the buyer's impression of them.

inbound Salespeople or customer service reps who respond to calls placed to the firm by customers rather than placing calls out to customers.

inbound telemarketing Use of the telephone, usually with a toll-free number, that allows leads and/or customers to call for additional information or to place an order.

incentive pay Compensation based on performance.

indirect denial Method used to respond to objections in which the salesperson denies the objection but attempts to soften the response by first agreeing with the prospect that the objection is an important one.

inflection Tone of voice.

influencers Buying center members inside or outside an organization who directly or indirectly influence the buying process.

influential adversaries Individuals in the buyer's organization who carry great influence and are opposed to the salesperson's product or service.

initiator The person who starts the buying process.

inside salespeople Salespeople who work at their employer's location and interact with customers by telephone or letter.

integrated marketing communications Coordinated communications programs that exploit the strengths of various communication vehicles to maximize the total impact on customers.

internal partnerships Partnering relationships between a salesperson and another member of the same company for the purpose of satisfying customer needs.

internal selling A communication process by which salespeople influence other employees in their firms to support the salespeople's sales efforts with customers.

interview Personal interactions between candidates and job recruiters for the purpose of evaluating job candidates.

intrinsic motivation Motivation stimulated by the rewards salespeople get from simply doing their job.

intrinsic orientation An orientation of salespeople characterized by seeking rewards from simply doing their jobs well.

introduction approach Approach method in which salespeople simply state their names and the names of their companies.

inventory turnover Measure of how efficiently a retailer manages inventory; calculated by dividing net sales by inventory.

invitation to negotiate The initiation of an interaction, usually a sales presentation, that results in an offer.

issue-involved Refers to the perception by an audience member that a subject is important although it may not affect him or her personally. For a contrast, see *ego-involved*.

job descriptions Formal, written descriptions of the duties and responsibilities of a job.

just-in-time (JIT) inventory control Planning systems for reducing inventory by having frequent deliveries planned just in time for the delivered products to be assembled into the final product.

keiretsu Group (more than two) or family of Japanese companies that form strategic partnerships to jointly develop plans to exploit market opportunities and to share the risks and rewards of their investments.

key accounts Large accounts, usually generating more than a specified amount in revenue per year, that receive special treatment.

kickbacks Payments made to buyers based on the amount of orders they place for a salesperson's products or services.

lead A potential prospect; a person or organization that may have the characteristics of a true prospect.

lead management system The part of the lead process in which salespeople carefully analyze the relative value of each lead.

lead qualification system A process for qualifying leads.

lead user Company that faces and resolves needs months or years ahead of the rest of the marketplace.

leapfrog routing Method of scheduling calls that requires the identification of clusters of customers; visiting these clusters and "leaping" over single, sparsely located accounts should minimize travel time from the sales office to customers.

learning organization Type of firm that acquires information about its environment and remembers this information so that it can guide organizational decision making even if employees in the organization change.

letters of credit Common method of international payment; similar to a personal check except that the company can collect cash from a customer's letter of credit only when the company can prove that the customer did not pay for the merchandise.

life-cycle costing Method for determining the cost of equipment or supplies over their useful life.

likability Behaving in a friendly manner and finding a common ground between the buyer and seller.

linear DSA A canned electronic slide presentation that forces the seller to follow a predetermined path through the slides and information.

list price Quoted or published price in a manufacturer's catalog or price list from which buyers may receive discounts.

lowballing Negotiation strategy in which one party voices agreement and then raises the cost of that agreement in some way.

low-context culture Culture in which the verbal part of communication carries more of the information in a message than the nonverbal parts. The sender's values, position, and background are conveyed by the content of the message. Examples of low-context cultures include the United States, Canada, Germany, and Switzerland.

lubrication Small sums of money or gifts, typically paid to officials in foreign countries, to get the officials to do their job more rapidly.

major sale Sale that involves a long selling cycle, a large customer commitment, an ongoing relationship, and large risks for the buyer if a bad decision is made.

manufacturers' agents Independent businesspeople who are paid a commission by a manufacturer for all products and services the agents sell.

markdown A discount offered to a customer. Industrial distributors often offer discounts if customers make large purchases (quantity discounts) or pay for merchandise quickly.

market (1) Mall where manufacturers show and sell products to retailers. (2) A short period of time when manufacturers gather to sell products to retailers.

market exchange Relationship that involves a short-term transaction between a buyer and a seller who do not expect to be involved in future transactions with each other.

marketing mix Elements used by firms to market their offerings: product, price, place (distribution), and promotion. Personal selling is part of the promotion element.

market share Percentage of total market sales that is accounted for by one product or total product category sales divided by brand sales.

markup The percentage of sales by which the price for the product is initially increased.

material requirements planning (MRP) Planning system for reducing inventory levels by forecasting sales, developing a production schedule, and ordering parts and raw materials with specific delivery dates.

merchandise markets Places where suppliers have sales offices and buyers from resellers visit to purchase merchandise.

mind share The degree to which a manufacturer's product receives attention from (occupies the mind of) the distributor.

minimum call objective Minimum that a salesperson hopes to accomplish in an upcoming sales call.

minimum position Negotiation objective that states the absolute minimum level the team is willing to accept.

missionary salespeople Salespeople who work for a manufacturer and promote the manufacturer's products to other firms. Those firms buy products from distributors or other manufacturers, not directly from the salesperson's firm.

modified rebuy Purchase decision process associated with a customer who has purchased the product or service in the past but is interested in obtaining additional information.

MRO supplies Minor purchases made by businesses for maintenance and repairs, such as towels and pencils.

multiattribute model Model describing how information about a product's performance on various dimensions is used to make an overall evaluation of the product.

multilevel selling Strategy that involves using multiple levels of company employees to call on similar levels in an account; for example, the VP of sales might call on the VP of purchasing.

multiple-sense appeals Appealing to as many of the senses (hearing, sight, touch, taste, and smell) as possible.

national account Prospect or customer that is covered by a single, national sales strategy; may be a house account.

national account manager (NAM) Sales executive responsible for managing and coordinating sales efforts on a single account nationwide.

need payoff questions Questions that ask about the usefulness of solving the problem.

needs satisfaction philosophy Form of customized presentation in which the prospect's unique needs are identified and then the salesperson shows how his or her product or service can meet those needs.

negotiation Decision-making process through which buyers and sellers resolve areas of conflict and arrive at agreements.

negotiation jujitsu Negotiation response in which the attacked person or team steps away from the opponent's attack and then directs the opponent back to the issues being discussed.

net present value (NPV) The investment minus the net value today of future cash inflows (discounted back to their present value today at the firm's cost of capital).

net price The price the buyer pays after all discounts and allowances are subtracted.

net profit margin The profit on the product, expressed as a percentage of sales.

net sales Total sales minus returns.

networking Establishing connections to other people and then using those networks to generate leads, gather information, generate sales, and so on.

new task Purchase decision process associated with the initial purchase of a product or service.

nibbling Negotiation strategy in which the buyer requests a small extra or add-on after the deal has been closed. Compared with lowballing, a nibble is a much smaller request.

noise Sounds unrelated to the message being exchanged between a salesperson and a customer.

nonlinear DSA An electronic slide presentation that allows the flexibility of choosing the order of presentation.

nonverbal communication Nonspoken forms of expression—body language, space, and appearance—that communicate thoughts and emotions.

North America industry classification system (NAICS) A uniform classification system for all businesses for all countries in North America.

objection Concern or question raised by the buyer.

offer Specific statement by a seller outlining what the seller will provide and what is expected from the buyer.

office scanning Activity in which the salesperson looks around the prospect's environment for relevant topics to talk about.

one-way communication Methods of communication, such as e-mail messages and letters, that have low levels of interactivity.

open-door policy General management technique that allows subordinates to bypass immediate managers and take concerns straight to upper management when the subordinates feel a lack of support from the immediate manager.

opening position The initial proposal of a negotiating session.

open questions Questions for which there are no simple yes–no answers.

opinion questions Questions that ask for a customer's feelings on a subject.

opportunity cost The return a buyer would have earned from a different use of the same investment capital.

optimistic call objective The most optimistic outcome the salesperson thinks could occur in a given sales call.

orders Written orders that become contracts when they are signed by an authorized representative in a salesperson's company.

original equipment manufacturer (OEM) Business that purchases goods (components, subassemblies, raw and processed materials) to incorporate into products it manufactures.

outbound Salespeople, customer service reps, prospectors, account managers, and field support telemarketers who place phone calls out to customers.

outbound telemarketing Using the telephone to generate and qualify leads to determine whether they are truly prospects or not; also used to secure orders and provide customer contact.

outlined presentation Systematically arranged presentation that outlines the most important sales points. Often includes the necessary steps for determining the prospect's needs and for building goodwill at the close of the sale.

outsourcing The purchase of goods and services from outside the firm that were previously produced inside the firm.

panel interview Job interview conducted by more than one person.

participative leadership Style of leadership that allows followers to make a contribution to decision making.

partnership Ongoing, mutually beneficial relationship between a buyer and a seller.

pass-up method Responding to an objection by letting the buyer talk, acknowledging that you heard the concern, and then moving on to another topic without trying to resolve the concern.

payback period Length of time it takes for the investment cash outflows to be returned in the form of cash inflows or savings.

performance feedback A type of feedback that salespeople often get from their supervisors that focuses on the seller's actual performance during a sales call.

performance goals Goals relating to outcomes, such as revenue.

personal selling Interpersonal communication process in which a seller uncovers and satisfies the needs of a buyer to the mutual, long-term benefit of both parties.

pioneer selling Selling a new and different product, service, or idea. In these situations the salesperson usually has difficulty establishing a need in the buyer's mind.

portfolio Collection of visual aids that can be used to enhance communication during a sales call.

postcard pack Cards that provide targeted information from a number of firms; this pack is mailed to prospective buyers.

postpone method Objection response technique in which the salesperson asks permission to answer the question at a later time.

postpurchase dissonance See *buyer's remorse*.

preferred supplier Supplier that is assured a large percentage of the buyer's business and will get the first opportunity to earn new business.

prequalification To help salespeople use their time wisely, firms determine whether leads are qualified before even turning them over to the field sales force.

price discrimination Situation in which a seller gives unjustified special prices, discounts, or special services to some customers and not to others.

primary call objective Actual goal the salesperson hopes to achieve in an upcoming sales call.

prime selling time Time of day at which a salesperson is most likely to be able to see a customer.

privacy laws Laws that limit the amount of information that a firm can obtain about a consumer or business and specify how that information can be used or shared with others.

probing method Method to obtain commitment in which the salesperson initially uses the direct request method and, if unsuccessful, uses a series of probing questions designed to discover the reason for the hesitation.

problem questions Questions about specific difficulties, problems, or dissatisfactions that the prospect has.

Procurement Automated Source System (PASS) A Small Business Administration database that contains information on federal purchasing agents working on federal contracts.

producer Firm that buys goods and services to manufacture and sell other goods and services to its customers.

product approach Approach in which the salesperson actually demonstrates the product features and benefits as soon as he or she walks up to the prospect.

production era A business era, prior to 1930, in which firms focused on making products with little concern for buyers' needs and developing products to satisfy those needs. The role of salespeople in this era was taking orders.

productivity goals Objective concerning how efficiently a salesperson works, such as sales per call. Efficiency measures indicate an output divided by an input.

profit quota Minimum levels of acceptable profit or gross margin performance.

prospect A lead that is a good candidate for buying what the salesperson is selling.

prospecting The process of locating potential customers for a product or service.

push money (PM) Money paid directly to the retailer's salespeople by the manufacturer for selling the manufacturer's product. See also *spiffs*.

qualifying a lead The process of determining whether a lead is in fact a prospect.

quantifying the solution Showing the prospect that the cost of the proposal is offset by added value.

question approach Beginning the conversation with a question or stating an interesting fact in the form of a question.

quick-response (Q) system Minimizing order quantities to the lowest level possible while increasing the speed of delivery to drive inventory turnover; accomplished by prepackaging certain combinations of products.

quota Quantitative level of performance for a specific time period.

rapport Close, harmonious relationship founded on mutual trust.

rate of change A critical element to consider about change; refers to how fast change is occurring.

rational needs Organizational and/or personal needs that are directly related to product performance.

reciprocity Special relationship in which two companies agree to buy products from each other.

references People who know an applicant for a position and can provide information about that applicant to the hiring company.

referral approach Approach in which the name of a satisfied customer or friend of the prospect is used at the beginning of a sales call.

referred lead Name of a lead provided by either a customer or a prospect of the salesperson.

reflective probes Neutral statements that reaffirm or repeat a customer's comment or emotion, allowing the salesperson to dig deeper and stimulate customers to continue their thoughts in a logical manner.

relational partnership Long-term business relationship in which the buyer and seller have a close, trusting relationship but have not made significant investments in the relationship. These relationships are characterized as win–win relationships.

relationship behaviors Actions taken by a manager to deal with a subordinate's feelings and welfare, develop support, or build the salesperson's self-confidence or commitment to the job or organization.

relationship manager The role of salespeople in the partnering era to manage the firm's resources to develop win–win relationships with customers.

relationship marketing The focus of marketing activities on establishing, developing, and maintaining cooperative, long-term relationships.

request for proposal (RFP) Issued by a potential buyer desiring bids from several potential vendors for a product. RFPs often include specifications for the product, desired payment terms, and other information helpful to the bidder. Also called *request for bids* or *request for quotes*.

requirements Conditions that must be satisfied before a purchase can take place.

resale price maintenance Contractual term in which a producer establishes a minimum price below which distributors or retailers cannot sell their products.

resellers Businesses, typically distributors or retailers, that purchase products for resale.

response time The time between sending a message and getting a response to it.

responsiveness The degree to which people react emotionally when they are in social situations. One of the two dimensions in the social style matrix.

retail salespeople Salespeople who sell to customers who come into a store.

return on investment (ROI) Net profits (or savings) expected from a given investment, expressed as a percentage of the investment.

revenue quota The minimum amount of sales revenue necessary for acceptable performance.

role accuracy The degree to which a salesperson's perceptions about the sales role are correct.

role ambiguity The degree to which a salesperson is not sure about the actions required in the sales role.

role clarity The degree to which a salesperson understands the job and what is required to perform it.

role conflict The extent to which the salesperson faces incompatible demands from two or more constituencies that he or she serves.

role stress The psychological distress that may be a consequence of a salesperson's lack of role accuracy.

routine call patterns Method of scheduling calls used when the same customers are seen regularly.

routing Method of scheduling sales calls to minimize travel time.

salary Compensation paid periodically to an employee independently of performance.

sale The transfer of title to goods and services by the seller to the buyer in exchange for money.

sales call allocation grid Grid used to determine account strategy; the dimensions are the strength of the company's position with the account and the account's sales potential.

sales era A business era, from 1930 to 1960, in which firms focused on increasing demand for the products they produced. The role of salespeople in this era was persuading customers to buy products by using high-pressure selling techniques.

sales puffery Exaggerated statements about the performance of products or services.

sales quota The minimum number of sales in units.

scope of change A critical element to consider about change; refers to the extent or degree to which the change affects an organization.

screens See *barriers*.

search engines The tools that individuals use to locate information on the Internet or on a specific website.

secondary call objectives Goals a salesperson hopes to achieve during a sales call that have somewhat less priority than the primary call objective.

seeding The seller sends the customer important and useful items or information prior to the meeting.

selective perception Occurs when we hear what we want to hear, not necessarily what the other person is saying.

selling See *personal selling*.

selling center A team that consists of all people in the selling organization who participate in a selling opportunity.

selling deeper Selling more to existing customers.

selling history How well a product or product line sold during the same season in the previous year.

services End-user purchases such as Internet and telephone connections, employment agencies, consultants, and transportation.

sexual harassment Unwelcome sexual advances, requests for sexual favors, and other, similar verbal (such as jokes) and nonverbal (such as graffiti) behaviors.

simple cost–benefit analysis Simple listing of the costs and savings that a buyer can expect from an investment.

situational stress Short-term anxiety caused by a situational factor.

situation questions General data-gathering questions about background and current facts that are very broad in nature.

small talk Talk about current news, hobbies, and the like that usually breaks the ice for the actual presentation.

sneak attack See *ambush negotiating*.

social style matrix Method for classifying customers based on their preferred communication style. The two dimensions used to classify customers are assertiveness and responsiveness.

soft savings The value of offset costs and productivity gains.

solo market exchange Both the buyer and the seller pursue their own self-interests because they do not plan on doing business together again.

spam A term used for unwanted and unsolicited junk e-mail.

speaking–listening differential The difference between the 120-to-160-words-per-minute rate of speaking versus the 800-words-per-minute rate of listening.

spiffs (push money) Payments made by a producer to a reseller's salespeople to motivate the salespeople to sell the producer's products or services.

SPIN® Logical sequence of questions in which a prospect's needs are identified. The sequence is situation questions, problem questions, implication questions, and need payoff questions.

spotter See *bird dog.*

standard industrial classification (SIC) A uniform classification system for an industry. The SIC system is being replaced by the new North America industry classification system (NAICS).

standard memorized presentation Carefully prepared sales story that includes all the key selling points arranged in the most effective order; often called a *canned sales presentation.*

statutory laws Laws based on legislation passed by either state legislatures or Congress.

stock keeping unit (SKU) A specific item that a reseller stocks; for example, a 5,000-watt Dayton professional-duty, portable, gasoline power generator is a SKU.

straight commission Pays a certain amount per sale; plan includes a base and a rate but not a salary.

straight-line routing Method of scheduling sales calls involving straight-line patterns from the home base in order to cover the sales territory.

straight rebuy Purchase decision process involving a customer with considerable knowledge gained from having purchased the product or service a number of times.

straight salary Compensation method that pays a fixed amount of money for working a specified amount of time.

strategic account manager (SAM) A company executive who coordinates all the salespeople who call on an account throughout the nation or the world. Also called *national account manager (NAM).*

strategic partnership Long-term business relationship in which the buyer and seller have made significant investments to improve the profitability of both parties in the relationship. These relationships are characterized as win–win relationships.

strategic profit model (SPM) Mathematical formula used to examine the impact of strategic decisions on profit and return on investment.

strength of position Dimension of the sales call allocation grid that considers the seller's strength in landing sales at an account.

stress interview Any interview that subjects an applicant to significant stress; the purpose is to determine how the applicant handles stress.

submissive Selling style of salespeople who are often excellent socializers and like to spend a lot of time talking about nonbusiness activities. These people are usually reluctant to attempt to obtain commitment.

subordination Payment of large sums of money to officials to get them to do something that is illegal.

suggested retail price Price the manufacturer suggests the store charge for the product.

superior benefit method Type of compensation method of responding to an objection during a sales presentation that uses a high score on one attribute to compensate for a low score on another attribute.

supply chain management Set of programs undertaken to increase the efficiency of the distribution system that moves products from the producer's facilities to the end user.

systems integrator Outside vendor who has been delegated the responsibility for purchasing; has the authority to buy products and services from others.

target position Negotiation objective that states what the team hopes to achieve by the time the session is completed.

task behaviors Actions taken by a manager to enable a subordinate to complete a task.

team selling Type of selling in which employees with varying areas of expertise within the firm work together to sell to the same account(s).

telemarketing Systematic and continuous program of communicating with customers and prospects via telephone and/or other person-to-person electronic media.

testimonial Statement, usually in the form of a letter, written by a satisfied customer about a product or service.

tests Personality or skills assessments used in assessing the match between a position's requirements and an applicant's personality or skills.

third-party-testimony method Method of responding to an objection during a sales presentation that uses a testimonial letter from a third party to corroborate a salesperson's assertions.

tickler file File or calendar used by salespeople to remind them when to call on specific accounts.

trade All members of the channel of distribution that resell the product between the manufacturer and the user.

trade discount Discount in which the price is quoted to a reseller in terms of a percentage off the suggested retail price.

trade fair The European term for *trade show.*

trade promotion Promotion aimed at securing retailer support for a product.

trade salespeople Salespeople who sell to firms that resell the products rather than using them within their own firms.

trade show Short exhibition of products by manufacturers and distributors.

trial close Questions the salesperson asks to take the pulse of the situation throughout a presentation.

trial order A small order placed by a buyer in order to test the product or the vendor. Not to be confused with *trial close*.

trust Firm belief or confidence in the honesty, integrity, and reliability of another person.

turnaround Amount of time taken to respond to a customer request or deliver a customer's order.

turnover (TO) Occurs when an account is given to another salesperson because the buyer refuses to deal with the current salesperson.

turnover How quickly a product sells; calculated by dividing net sales by average inventory.

24/7 service A phrase that highlights the fact that customers expect a selling firm to be available 24 hours a day, seven days a week.

two-way communication Interpersonal communication in which both parties act as senders and receivers. Salespeople send messages to customers and receive feedback from them; customers send messages to salespeople and receive responses.

tying agreement Agreement between a buyer and a seller in which the buyer is required to purchase one product to get another.

Uniform Commercial Code (UCC) Legal guide to commercial practice in the United States.

upgrading Convincing the customer to use a higher-quality product or a newer product.

users Members of a buying center that ultimately will use the product purchased.

value analysis Problem-solving approach for reducing the cost of a product while providing the same level of performance. See *quantifying the solution*.

value proposition A written statement (usually one or two sentences) that clearly states how purchasing your product or service can help add shareholder value.

variable call patterns Occur when the salesperson must call on accounts in a nonsystematic method.

variable routing Method of scheduling sales calls used when customers are not visited on a cyclical or regular basis.

vendor A supplier.

vendor analysis A formal method used by organizational buyers to summarize the benefits and needs satisfied by a supplier.

vendor loyalty Develops when a buyer becomes committed to a specific supplier because of the supplier's superior performance.

verbal communication Communication involving the transmission of words in face-to-face communication, over the telephone, or through a written message.

versatility A characteristic, associated with the social style matrix, of people who increase the productivity of social relationships by adjusting to the needs of the other party.

videoconferencing Meetings in which people are not physically present in one location but are connected via voice and video; seems to be growing in usage.

virtual sales call See *webcast*.

visual presenters Similar to traditional overhead projectors in their ability to display transparencies. However, because they are essentially cameras, visual presenters are also capable of displaying any three-dimensional object without the use of a transparency (also called *document cameras*).

voice characteristics The rate of speech, loudness, pitch, quality, and articulation of a person's voice.

warranty Assurance by the seller that the goods will perform as represented.

webcast A videoconference in which the meeting is broadcast over the Internet.

willingness Salesperson's desire and commitment to accomplish an objective or task.

win–lose negotiating Negotiating philosophy in which the negotiator attempts to win all the important concessions and thus triumph over his or her opponent.

win–lose relationship Type of relationship characterized by one or a series of market exchanges wherein each party is concerned only with his or her own profits and not with the welfare of the other party.

win–win negotiating Negotiating philosophy in which the negotiator attempts to secure an agreement that completely satisfies both parties.

win–win not yet negotiating A negotiation session in which the buying team achieves its goals while the selling team does not. However, the sellers expect to achieve their goals in the near future, thanks to the results of that negotiation session.

win–win relationship Type of relationship in which firms make significant investments that can improve profitability for both partners because their partnership has given them some strategic advantage over their competitors.

word picture Story or scenario designed to help the buyer visualize a point.

zoning Method of scheduling calls that divides a territory into zones. Calls are made in a zone for a specified length of time and then made in another zone for the same amount of time.

Company Index

ABC Gifts and Baskets, 359
Accrue Software, 199
Achieve Global, 561
ADT, 209
AeroMexico, 153
Aerovox, 438
Aetna, 285
Ailing & Cory, 11
Air France, 153
Albert Heijn, 48
Alcoa Aluminum, 46
Alco Chemical, 141
Allied Signal, 391
Allied Van Lines, 64
Allsteel, 408
Alpine Paper Company, 312
Amazon.com, 106
Ambassador Office Equipment, 281
AMC, 439
AMD, 193
American Airlines, 33, 36, 37, 153, 396, 540
American Distribution Systems (ADS), 393
American Express Financial Advisors, 193
American Flag Co., 447
American Optical, 263
American Supply Company, 386
Apple Computer, 451
Apprise Technologies, 200
Arrow Electronics, 12, 41, 42, 436, 439
Association Luxury Hotels International, 224
Astound, 285
Astra Pharmaceuticals, 388
AT&T, 43, 194, 521, 558
Automobile Protection Corporation (APCO), 386
Avid Sports, 97
Azimuth Partners, 386

Ballard Medical Products, 8
Barnes & Noble, 86
Baxter, 40, 49, 94, 376, 390, 525
BCI Consulting Group, 360
BehaviorScan, 450
Belden Wire & Cable, 199
Ben & Jerry's, 276
Benson Bakery, 394
Best Buy, 454
Bethlehem Steel, 389–390
Black & Decker, 435, 436, 452, 457
Boeing, 255
Bose Corporation, 377
Brazos Farm and Equipment, 436
Briggs & Stratton, 155–156
Brink Locking Systems, 281
Brio, 442
Bristol-Myers Squibb, 191, 226, 281
British Petroleum, 226
Business Resources Software, 169, 170

Cable & Wireless, 476
Cadenhead Shreffler Insurance, 199

Calvin Klein, 358
Campbell Soup Company, 11, 387, 388
Canadian Airlines, 282
Canon, 454
Cargill, 385
Carlton-Bates, 31
CarQuest, 394, 395
CBC Communications, 378
Cellular One, 209
Century Business Services, 397
Chicago Rawhide, 101
Choate Construction, 258
Chrysler Corporation, 102, 114
Ciba-Geigy, 393
Cifra, 391
Circle-6 Motel, 391
Circuit City, 451
Cisco Systems, 16, 331
Clairol, 561
Clarke, 226
Clark Equipment Company, 44–45
CNN, 189
Coca-Cola, 33, 92, 96, 397, 444, 509
Colgate-Palmolive, 412
Collier Electric, 380
Compaq, 12
CompuServe, 490
Computer Intelligence, 526
Computerland, 447
ConAgra, 439
Conectiv, 215
Conita Technologies, 526
Corporate Sport, Inc., 359
Cort Furniture, 344
Cott Beverages, 387
Crest, 523
Cub Foods, 409
Curtin Matheson Scientific, 11–12
Cutler and Buck, 437

D. A. Stuart Company, 215
Dale Carnegie, 561
Dallas Market Center, 455
Dartnell, 334
Datapro, 450
Dayton, 438
Deere and Company, 89
DEI Management Group, 184
Dell Computer, 17, 31, 86, 436
Dendrite International, 524
DeWalt, 435
DHL, 504
Dial, 481
Diamond Shamrock, 48
Disney, 6, 23
Dixie Bearing, 281
Dow Chemical, 12, 77
Driltech, 13
Drugstore.com, 553
Dun & Bradstreet, 43, 182, 215, 395–396, 526
Duplex Products, 42
Du Pont, 13–14, 15, 86, 180

Eagle Equipment, 193
eBay, 106

EDS, 503, 524
Edward Jones, 469
Eli Lilly, 520, 542
El Volcan, 397
Emerging Market Technologies, 198
emWare, Inc., 226
Enerpac, 23
Enron, 58
Excel, 285
Experian, 182

Federal Express, 23, 341, 477
Filter Queen, 388
FIND/SVP, 486
Firestone, 252
First National Bank of Shreveport, 196
Flexatard, 8
Florida Furniture Industries (FFI), 48, 385
Foley's, 449
Force Computers, 508
Ford Motor Company, 219, 505
Fram, 394, 395
Freedom Jet, 388
Freeman Exhibit Company, 474
Frito-Lay, 14, 93

Gateway, 31
Gaylord Container Corporation, 101
General Dynamics, 522
General Electric, 23, 376, 436, 438, 450, 538
General Motors Acceptance Corporation, 42
General Motors (GM), 84, 104–105
Giddings & Lewis Measurement Systems, 100
GlaxoSmithKline Pharmaceuticals, 209
GoldMine, 378
Gonher, 426
Goodyear, 311
Gould Inc., 49
Grafo Regia S.A., 507–508
Grocery Supply Company, 83

H. R. Challey, Inc., 544
Habitat for Humanity, 10
Hallmark, 440
Harley-Davidson, 511
Harris Corporation, 86
Health Choices, 439
Heineken, 48
Heinz, 87–88
Hershey Chocolate, 83
Herzog & Associates, 516
Hewlett-Packard (HP), 44, 48, 158–159, 189–190, 288, 290, 522, 523, 538
HHG Bekins Van Lines, 482
Hilton Hotels, 183
Hobart, 394
Holt Marketing, 556
Home Depot, 23, 435, 436, 438, 452
Home Made Brands, 345
Hoover, 215–216, 217

HQ Global, 226
Hughes Telecommunications, 372
Hunt-Wesson, 374
Huthwaite, Inc., 248, 252
Hyster, 91

IBM, 43, 46, 49, 64, 87, 95, 200, 313, 394, 459, 481, 490, 509, 525, 526, 544, 549
Ikon Office Solutions, 472, 482
iMarket, 193
InfoUSA, 183, 480
Insuror's of Texas, 522
Intel, 12, 31, 193, 436, 438, 439
International Computers Limited (ICL), 526
International Flavors and Fragrances, 88
International Wood Products (IWP), 379
Iomega Corporation, 378

J. I. Case, 104
J. R. Simplot, 89
J&L, 101
JCPenney, 16, 36, 37–38, 48, 438, 543
Jello, 259
Jewel, 409
John Deere, 359, 436, 444, 445
Johnson & Johnson, 228, 522
Johnson Controls Automotive Systems Group (ASG), 505
Johnson Electronics, 221, 222
Johnson Wax, 252, 255, 281, 345, 351, 477
JustSell.com, 216

Karr-Hunter Pontiac, 377–378
Keebler, 232
Keith Clark, 455
Kellogg, 385, 507–508
Kenneth Crosby Co., 101
Kestner's Department Store, 48
Kiwi, 458, 459
Kmart, 444
Knight Industries, 372
Kodak, 222
Kraft, 436, 439
Kraft/General Foods (KFG), 16–17, 45–46
Kroger, 409, 436, 439
Kubota, 257

Lands' End, 32
Lanyon Ltd., 60
Learning International, 250
Lego Systems, 442
Lever Brothers, 6
Levi Strauss, 37, 38, 48
Linz Jewelers, 442, 443
Lipton, 439
Lockheed Martin, 180, 182
Lone Star Foods, 350
Lotus, 49, 215, 286
Lowe's, 438

Lucent Technologies, 504, 538
Lufthansa, 286
Lutron Electronics, 121

M. D. Industries, 485
M. H. McIntosh, 190
McDonald's, 6, 89, 525
McGraw-Hill, 371
McKeeson Corporation, 86
Macromedia, 200
Macy's, 438, 449
Maddocks Systems, 524–525
Makita, 387
Marion/Merrell Dow, 477, 486, 487
Markel Corporation, 226
Marketing Logistics, 189
Marquis Communications, 387
Maximum Impact, 10
Mead, 390
Menasha Corporation, 384
Mercedes-Benz, 100
Merck, 14, 17, 285
Merrill Lynch, 492, 493, 545
Metamor Technologies, 514
Microsoft, 30, 31, 106, 290,
    456, 480
Midwest Communications, 179
Minolta Business Systems, 350, 481,
    540, 561
Monster.com, 548, 549
Moody's, 182, 217
Moore Business Forms, 351
Moore Industries, 388
Motorola, 12, 61, 194–195, 389, 522
Mott's USA, 449
MTS-Group Inc., 314
Murray, 444

Nabisco, 88–89
Nalco, 38
NASCAR, 6
National Adhesives, 353
National Cash Register (NCR), 32, 48
National Commercial Bank of
    Jamaica, 48
National Semiconductor, 107
NationsBank, 7
NCR, 521
Nekoosa, 225
Nestlé Foods, 221
Netscape, 30, 106
Nielsen, 12, 450
Nike, 86, 426

Norand Corporation, 344
Nortel, 35, 87
Northeast Utilities, 375
Northwestern Mutual Financial
    Network, 3, 57
Northwestern National Insurance,
    480–481
Novartis, 220, 542
Novell, 456
Noxell, 439–440
Nucor, 12

Oasis Technology Ltd., 48
Office Depot, 34
Olivetti, 376
Omnia Group, 350
Oracle Corporation, 191
Owens-Corning, 490

Panasonic, 221, 222, 440
Parker Hannifin, 157
ParkStock Computer
    Solutions, 239
PDP Inc., 264
Pennzoil, 6
PepsiCo, 183
Phillips, 219
Pillsbury, 390
Pioneer, 193
Pitney-Bowes, 484
Platinum Technology, 485
PowerPoint, 285, 286, 292
PPS Parking, 314
Precision Fabric Group (PFG), 447
Premier Industrial, 332
Private Business, Inc., 200
Procter & Gamble (P&G), 9, 40,
    155, 180, 287, 377, 436,
    439, 444, 521, 540, 542
ProspectMiner, 189
Prudential, 310
Publix, 9
Purcell Agricultural, 209

Quaker Oats, 409, 542
Quaker State, 426
Quaker Tropicana Gatorade, 275
Quantum Medical, 295

RadioMail, 490
Raleigh, 282
Ralph Lauren, 444
Ranir Corporation, 490

RCA, 520–521
Relizon, 40
Resonate, 189
Revlon, 14
Reynolds Metals Company, 11
Rice-a-Roni, 439
Ritchie Pharmacal, 361
Rockwell Automation, 521, 523
Rockwool, 377
Rooms To Go, 48
Roper Organization, 187
Ross/Flex, 372
Royal Bank of Canada, 477
RPG Digital Imaging, 523
Ryder Truck, 49
Ryerson Coil Processing, 101
Ryerson Steel, 310

Sabritas, 11
Safeway, 409
Sales and Marketing
    Executives, 561
Sam's Club, 391
San Antonio Spurs, 508
Scarborough Company, 480
Scott Paper Company, 100
Sears, 104
SecondWind, 459, 460
Servall Packaging Industries, 563
Seton Medical Center, 40
Shachihata, 230
Sherwin-Williams, 104
Siebel Systems, 480
Silverline Technologies, 481
Simmons, 387
Singer Sewing Machines, 32
SMART Technologies, Inc., 289
Snapper, 444
Sony, 219, 436
SOS Technology, 475, 476
Southland Corporation, 83
Spenco Medical Corporation, 90,
    448, 449, 450, 451, 458
Spiegel, 32
Spirit Graphics, 350
Standard & Poor's, 182, 217
Stanley Tools, 457
Starbucks, 36
State Farm Insurance, 14
Steak and Ale, 394
Street Fighter, Inc., 199
Sun Microsystems, 30
Synesis Corporation, 194

Target, 10, 446–447
Teradata, 503, 524
TESCO, 376
Texaco, 98
Texas Instruments (TI), 44
Text 100 Corp., 550
Thermafrost, 376
3M, 309, 557
Times Mirror Cable Television, 474
Tinker Toys, 442
Toledo Scale Company, 284
Tommy Hilfiger, 438, 444
Tom Thumb, 345
T/R Systems, 188
Turner Broadcasting System (TBS),
    189, 372

UARCO, 387
UMAX Technologies, 456
Unilever, 439
Unisource, 521
Unisys, 283, 387
United Airlines, 36, 37–38, 255
UPS, 224
US Foodservice, 407

Value Line, 182
Verizon, 386
Victory Tube Company, 397

W. W. Grainger, 85, 436, 438
Walker Interactive Systems, 88
Walker Muffler, 311
Wallace, 36, 37, 224, 362, 396,
    537–538, 559
Wal-Mart, 14, 64, 120, 377, 387,
    391, 436, 438, 442, 443,
    446–447, 461, 521–522
Wards, 217
Waterhouse Group, 169
Weldstar Company, 101
Westin la Cantera Resort, 224
Whirlpool, 36–37
Wilson Learning Corporation,
    250, 561
Wisdomware, 170
Wollin, 36–37
Worldwide Internet Solutions
    Network, 91
Wrangler, 37, 38

Xerox, 49, 187, 196, 231, 387–388,
    389, 514, 521, 524

Name and Subject Index

ABC analysis, 477–478
Access and image, 48
Accommodating mode, 417
Account classification, 476–481
Account opportunity, 478, 479
Account salespeople, 520–522
Account share, 480
ACT!, 385, 490
Active listening, 131–132
Activity analysis, 491–492
Activity goals, 474
Activity quotas, 512
Acuff, Frank, N–1
Adams, Michael, N–12
Adaptive learning, 8
Adaptive planning, 414
Adaptive selling, 19, 152–175
  alternative training systems for,
    168–170
  customer relationship management
    systems, 170
  diversity and, 154–157
  knowledge and, 157–161
    analyzing successes and failures,
      160–161
    approaches for developing,
      158–159
    categorizing, 158
    extrinsic orientation, 161
    feedback and, 159–160
    intrinsic orientation, 161
    manuals and trade
      publications, 159
    product and company, 18,
      157–158
    of sales experts, 159
    social style matrix and, 168
  presentations and, 154
  sales success and, 154–157
  social style matrix and; see Social
    style matrix
Adler, Nancy J., N–6, N–7
Adler, Seymour, N–11
Administration, 508
Administrative law, 69
Advantages, 258
Advertising, 6, 7, 19, 189–190
Advocates, 393
After the sale; see Long-term
  partnerships
Agenda, 419–420
Agent, 70
Age of Unreason, The (Handy), 279
Aggressiveness, 349–350, 351
Ainscough, Thomas, 174
Akin, Emily M., N–6
Alessandra, Anthony, 168, 174,
  342, N–5
Alexander, Joe F., 431
Allen, Chris, N–5
Alreck, Pamela, N–3
Alvarado, Ursula Y., 465
Alvarez, Mark, 23
Ambush negotiating, 418
Amiables, 164
  cues for recognizing, 165
  customer expectations for, 167

Amin, Sammy, 568
Analysis paralysis, 214
Analyticals, 164
  cues for recognizing, 165
  customer expectations for, 167
Anderson, Erin, N, N–1
Anderson, Eugene, 403
Anderson, Helen, 52
Anderson, James C., 270, N–5
Anderson, Kare, N–4
Anderson, R., 534
Anderson, Rolph E., 305
Anderson, Steve, 199
Anthony, William P., 118
Anticipating objections, 319–320
Appearance, 141–143
  casual dress codes, 141–142, 143
  hints for men, 142
  hints for women, 142–143
  matching the customer's
    dress, 141
Application form, 544
Appointments; see Making
  appointments
Approach, 244–246
Arckey, Ray, 9
Arend, Bill, 475, 476
Areni, Charles S., 271
Armstrong, Robert W., N–1
Arnott, Nancy, N–1, N–11
Articulation, 128–129
Assenheimer, Jule, N–2
Assertiveness, 162
  adjusting to, 168
  indicators of, 162
  obtaining commitment and,
    349–350, 351
  self-assessment of, 166
Assessment centers, 544–545
Assisted selling, 454
Assortments, providing, 438
Assumptive close, 356
Athaid, Gerald A., 500, N–9
Atlas, Elise, N–11
Atlas, Steve, 359n, N–11
Attitude
  positive, 318–319, 349
  wrong, 359
Automatic replenishment (AR),
  106, 446
Avila, Ramon, N–3, N–12
Avoiding mode, 417
Awareness stage, 46–47

Baatz, Elizabeth, N–4
Bachrach, Anne M., N–7
Backdoor selling, 66
Badovick, Gordon J., 368
Bagozzi, Richard P., 206, 568, N–6
Bahns, K. D., N–3
Baitch, Daniel B., N–7
Baker, Thomas L., 466
Balanced presentation, 262
Balance sheet method, 353
Baldauf, Artur, 28
Banks, Stan, 435
Banner advertising, 189

Barclay, Donald W., 28, 53, N, N–3,
  N–8
Barker, A. Tansu, 174, N–4
Barksdale, Hiram C., Jr., 28, 404, N
Barlow, Wayne, 551
Barnes, James H., 81
Barnett, Ted, 371
Barnett, Tim, 81, N–2
Barrett, Mark, N–7
Barriers, 227–228
Bartering, 32
Bashaw, R. Edward, 236, 339, N–6
Bass, Ken, 81, N–2
Bassett, Tom, 397, N–10
Bauer, Barbara, 350
Baugh, Frank, 492, 493
Beamon, Kelly, N–6
Bearden, William, 67n, 111n
Beck, Robert, 53
Becker, T. J., N–11
Becker, Tim, N–7
Bednarz, Shirley, N–9
Behavioral observation scale
  (BOS), 516
Bell, Michelle, N–1
Bellizzi, Joseph A., 534
Bello, Daniel C., 52
Belton, Beth, N–6
Benchmarking, 475
Benefit approach, 244–245
Benefit-in-reserve close, 356
Benefits, 256–258
  features compared to, 257, 259
Benefit statements, 347
Benefit summary method, 352–353
Ben Franklin method, 353
Berger, Melanie, N–8
Berkey, Steven, 397
Berman, Barry, 466
Berry, Leonard, N
Berry, Russ, 346, N–9
Berry, Wendell, N
Besser, Bill, 101
Bettman, James, N–4, N–5
Beveridge, Don, N–7, N–8
Beverland, Michael, 28
Bharadwaj, Sundar G., 404
Bhatnagar, Deepti, 432
Bialeszewski, Dennis, N–1
Bingham, Frank, N–3
Biong, Harold, N
Bird, Thomas, 49
Bird dogs, 194
Bishop, Bill, 206, N–5, N–6
Bitner, Mary Jo, 271
Blackwood, Francy, 127n, N–2, N–11
Blattberg, Robert C., 465, N–10
Blitz, 193–194
Blois, Keith J., 52
Bly, Robert, N–10
Blythe, Jim, N–11
Boardman, Bill, 350
Body language, 135–137
  culture and, 136, 137, 141, 146
  patterns, 137
  sending messages using, 138–140
Boedecker, Karl, N–2

Bohn, Earl, N–9
Bohon, Michael, N–10
Boles, James S., 28, 404, 534, N
Bolton, Dorothy, N–5
Bolton, Robert, N–5
Bonus, 512
  compensation plans including,
    512–515
Boomerang method, 327
Boone, Mary E., N–5
Boorom, Michael, 174, N–4
Borders, Aberdeen Leila, 466
Borowski, Al, N–8
Bosik, Darren, 206
Bostrom, Ulf, 404
Bottom-up forecasting, 511
Bounce-back card, 190
Bowe, John, N–1
Bowe, Marisa, N–1
Bowles, Erskine, N–2
Boyd, Larry, 295
Bradford, Edmund, N–11
Bradford, Kevin, 28, 53, N–4
Brainstorming session, 414
Breaden, Barbara L., N–8
Breaking bulk, 438
Brennan, Ross W., 174, 403, N–4
Brewer, Geoffrey, 568, N, N–6, N–10
Bribes, 63, 75, 76, 520
Brill, Tracey, 262, 264, N–8
Brooks, Bill, N–7
Browbeating, 424
Brown, Gene, 81, N–2
Brown, Paul B., N–9
Brown, Stephen, 403
Brown, Steven P., 236, 271, N–4
Brunelli, Mark, N–4
Bryant, Barbara, 403
Buchwald, Art, 500
Budget bogey, 423–424
Budget limitation tactic, 423–424
Budgets, expense, 511
Budman, Matthew, N–4
Building partnering relationships,
  30–53
  adaptability, 156
  characteristics of success at, 38–46
    commitment to mutual gain,
      44–45
    common goals, 44
    credible commitments, 45
    open communication, 43–44
    organizational support, 45–46
    trust; see Trust
  closeness to customers, 350
  concessions and, 426
  creativity and, 20, 224
  cross-cultural ethical problems, 77
  customer complaints, 380
  ethics and, 59
  evolution of personal selling, 32–33
  honesty, 263
  internal partnerships and, 505
  knowing your audience, 300
  long-term; see Long-term
    partnerships
  management and, 47–49

mentoring, 558
metaphors, 126
model of, 24
phases of, 46–47
with resellers, 460–461
responding to objections, 314
shelf space and, 439
summary, 50
"tag—you're it," 37
types of relationships, 33–38
using the Internet, 107
Buller, David B., 150, 270
Bunn, Michele, N–3
Burger, Philip, N–1, N–3
Burgoon, Judee K., 150, 270
Burnap, Herb, 351
Burns, Alvin, N–3
Busch, Karl R., 431
Bush, Victoria D., 174, 568
Business consultants, 5
Business defamation, 73
Business development managers, 5
Business Geographics, 218
Business-to-business channels, 12–14
Business-to-business selling,
    106–107, 436
Buyback, 453
Buyer's remorse, 356
Buying behavior and the buying
    process, 18, 82–119
organizational buying and selling,
    88–89
supplier evaluation and choice,
    98–102
    buying center needs, 100–102
    economic criteria, 99
    emotional needs, 98
    life-cycle costing, 99
    multiattribute model; see
        Multiattribute model of
        product evaluation and
        choice
    quality criteria, 99–100
    rational needs, 98
    service criteria, 100
    value analysis, 100
    vendor analysis, 102, 103
    vendor loyalty, 102
trends, 102–108
    business-to-business selling,
        106–107
    centralized purchasing, 104
    global sourcing, 104–105
    Internet, 106–107
    long-term customer-supplier
        relationships, 108
    outsourcing, 105
    purchasing agents, 104
    supply chain management,
        105–106
types of customers, 84–88
    consumers, 88
    government agencies, 86–87
    institutions, 87–88
    producers, 84–86
    resellers, 86
Buying center, 95
    individual needs of members,
        101–102
Buying community, 187
Buying signals, 346
Buzzotta, V. R., 168, N–5

Cahill, Ellen, N–8
Cahill, Paul, N–8
Campanelli, Melissa, N–11
Campbell, Alexandra J., N–1
Campbell, Tricia, N–9, N–11
Canady, Henry, N–5, N–11
Cann, Cynthia, N–1, N–3
Canned presentation, 154
Cannito, Michael P., 271, N–4
Cannon, Joseph P., N–8
Cap, 418

Capital equipment, 85
Caplan, Adam, 553
Capwell, Perri, N
Carbone, James, N–3, N–4
Career management, 536–575
    developing your skills, 560–561
    dual career path, 558–559
    goals, 556
    interviews; see Interviews
    learning your current and future
        jobs, 559–560
    making a good match, 539–543
        asking questions, 541
        corporate needs, 541–543
        corporate offerings, 542
        personal inventory, 540–541
        personal needs, 539–540
    mentoring, 558
    opportunities in selling, 538–539
    recruiting process; see Recruiting
        process
    self-directed development, 557–558
    stress management, 561–563
    transition from college, 556–557
Carey, Robert, N–8
Carlson, Les, 52
Carnegie, Dale, 243, N–7
Carnes, Tom, 212
Carroll, H. E., N–8
Case problems
    ACT!, 573–575
    AdTech, 52
    Arco, 149
    Audio Warehouse, 464–465
    Becky Grounds' interview, 565–567
    Boeing 717 jets, 303–304
    Calaway Park, 337–338
    Callaway Big Bertha C4 drivers,
        570–573
    Caterpillar wheel loaders, 234–235
    Closing styles at Emerald
        Cloud, 366
    Comcast, 173–174
    Discovery needs, 270
    Ericsson, 365–366
    FedEx, 430–431
    Fleet Management, 111–113
    Flow Master Controls, 529–530
    General Electric streamlines its
        purchasing practices, 111
    Headhunting, 80
    Help wanted, 567
    Identifying actual leads, 205
    JDE Electrical Corporation, 26–27
    McGraw-Hill, 499–500
    Nortel, 495–496
    Northern Farm Equipment,
        496–499
    Obtaining commitment, 367–368
    OfficeMax, 150
    Old account or lost account, 51
    Responding to objections, 338–339
    Right first job?, 567–568
    Role playing, 569–575
    Rosewood boat, 80–81
    Ryder Trust Rental-Leasing,
        400–402
    Salespeople, direct mail, or the
        Internet?, 27
    Social style matrix, 172
    Sony Handcam camcorders,
        268–269
    Strengthening the presentation,
        304–305
    Structural Steel Industries, 530–534
    3M's Digital Library Assistance,
        204–205
    Turning it Around, 402–403
    Twin Peaks of the Baking Business,
        463–464
    XanEdu online course-specific
        content, 235–236
Cash discounts, 345
    resellers and, 453

Castleberry, Stephen B., 133n, 150,
    151, 271, 568, N–4, N–5,
    N–6, N–9, N–12
Category captions, 460
Category management, 460–461
Cateora, Philip, 66n, N–4
Cayer, Shirley, N–3, N–9
Cecil, Jim, 206, N–6
Center-of-influence method, 186–187
Centralized purchasing, 104
Cha, Jaesung, 403
Challagalla, Goutam, 535, N
Chalmers, Sophie, 305
Chamberlain, Nancy, N–11
Champions, 393–394
Champy, James, N
Chang, Kuochung, 431
Change agent, 392–393
Chapman, Jack, N–11
Chapman, Joseph, N–12
Choate, Millard, 258
Choi, Gene, 16
Chonko, Lawrence B., 81, N–11,
    N–12
Chow, Simeon, N–4
Christiansen, Dennis, N–11
Chronister, Tom, 305
Churchill, Gilbert A., 37n, N–9,
    N–12
Ciemiewicz, Sean, 142
Cimperman, Wayne, 447–448, 449
Circular routing, 487
Clancy, Kevin J., N–11
Clark, Ralph, N–2
Clay, Jennifer W., 28
Clopton, Stephen W., 28
Closed questions, 129, 251–252
Closing, 342, 347–348; see also
    Obtaining commitment
Closing cues, 346
Cloverleaf routing, 487
Cobb, Brian, 209
Cocchiarella, Beth, 195–196
Code of ethics, 62
Cohen, Andy, 236, 339, 466, 505n,
    568, N–3, N–5, N–6, N–7,
    N–8, N–9, N–11, N–12
Cold calls, 193–194
Cold canvass method, 193–194
Cole, Tom, 490
Collaborating mode, 417
Colleagues, 454
    ethical relationship with, 68–69
Collins, Robert, N–5
Collusion, 74
Combination plans, 514–515
Comdex, 455, 456
Comer, James, 52
Comer, Lucette B., 28, 150, 174,
    368, N–4, N–5
Commission, 512–515
Commission base, 513–514
Commission rate, 513
Commitment
    buyer's objections and, 310
    during interviews, 554
    to mutual gain, 44–45
    obtaining; see Obtaining
        commitment
Commitment stage, 47, 389–395
    champions, 393–394
    change agents, 392–393
    communication, 390–391, 392
    complete commitment, 390
    corporate culture, 391–392
    determining the necessary
        resources, 394
    objections during, 310
    positioning the change, 394
    preferred suppliers and, 389
    securing, 390–392
    time-based strategy, 394–395
Common courtesy, 31
Common law, 69

Communication, 6–8, 120–151
    appearance; see Appearance
    breakdowns in, 122–123
    commitment to partnership and,
        390–391, 392
    cultural differences; see Cultural
        differences, communications
        and
    in a high-technology environment,
        143–145
    integrated marketing, 7–8
    methods, 6, 124–125
        strengths and weaknesses, 7
    noises and, 123
    open, 43–44
    price-related objections and,
        332–333
    successful salespeople and, 19
Company-related objections, 313–314
Company reputation, 332
Comparative cost-benefit analysis,
    296–297
Compensation
    ethics and, 518
    evaluation and, 512–515
Compensation method, 325–326
Competence, 41
Competing mode, 416
Competitors
    ethical relationships with, 69
    failing to monitor, 396
    interference with, 74
Complacency, 396–397
Compliment approach, 245–246
Compromising mode, 417
Compton, Jason, N–5
Computer-peripheral whiteboard, 288
Computers
    e-mail, 488–489
    paperwork and communication, 490
    time planning and, 484–485
    for visual presentations, 285–287
Concessions, 424–426
Confidential information, 66
Conflict, 44, 397–398
Conlin, Joseph, N–10
Conlon, Ginger, 392n, N–5
Conner, Tim, 342, N–8
Conners, Mary, N–5
Consignment, 453
Conspiracy, 74
Consumer channels, 13, 14
Consumers, 88
Contests, 459
Continuous yes close, 356
Contract to sell, 70
Control, 511–512
Conventional resumés, 545, 546
Conversion goals, 474–475
Conversion ratio, 493
Co-op advertising, 457
Cooper, Martha C., N–10
Cooper, Robert G., N–1
Cooper, Robert W., 77n, 81
Coordinating activities, 11
Copaceanu, Adriana, 359
Corbett, Charles, N–3
Corcoran, Kevin J., N–7
Cordon, Carlos, 377, N–1
Cornachio, Donna, N–12
Corporate culture, 391–392
Corriveau, Scott, N–10
Cost-benefit analysis, 296–297
Cost of goods sold, 442
Cousineau, Joe, 225
Cover letter, 549–550
Cox, Edward, N–10
Cravens, David W., 28, 534, N–11
Creativity, 19–20
Credibility, 261–264
Credible commitments, 45
Credit rating, 182
Credit terms, 345
Credulous person standard, 73

Creeping commitment, 92
Creyer, Elizabeth, N
Crissy, W. J. E., 487n
Cron, William L., 236
Crosby, Lawrence A., 271, 403, N–9
Cross, James, 28
Cross-selling, 388
Crowell, Donna, 44
Cruz, Clarissa, N–3
Cultural differences, 16, 19
  adaptive selling and, 154–157
  communication and, 44, 145–146
    body language, 136, 137, 141, 146
    rapport, 247
  ethics and, 58, 66, 75–77
  forms of greeting, 242
  gestures, 248
  negotiation and, 410, 414, 419,
    420–421
  relationships and, 36, 38
  sale call objectives and, 219
Cultural relativism, 76
Cummings, Betsy, 236, N–6, N–7,
  N–8, N–12
Cumulative discount, 344
Cunningham, H., 487n
Cunningham, Isabella, 487n
Cunningham, Randy, N–8
Customer complaints, 378–384
  achieving customer satisfaction, 384
  determining the facts, 381–382
  encourage buyers to tell the truth,
    380–381
  following through with action, 384
  offering a solution, 382–384
Customer orientation, 41–42
Customer relationship management
  (CRM) systems, 170
  resource allocation and, 480–481
Customer retention, 185
Customers
  consumers, 88
  ethics and, 63–67
    backdoor selling, 66
    bribes, gifts, and entertainment,
      63–65, 66
    confidential information, 66
    deception and, 63
    special treatment, 65
  getting the attention of, 243–246
    benefit approach, 244–245
    complement approach, 245–246
    halo effect and, 243
    introduction approach, 244
    product approach, 245
    prospect's name and, 243–244
    question approach, 246
    referral approach, 244
  government agencies, 86–87
  institutions, 87–88
  producers, 84–86
  resellers, 86
  servicing, 10–11
Customer service, 509
Customer service reps, 523
Customer share, 480
Customer value, 223, 372–374
Customized presentation, 154

Dahlstrom, Robert, N–2
Daily activity planning, 482–483
Dalaskey, Bob, 482
Daley, Kevin, N–8
Dant, Shrish P., 52
Darmon, Rene Y., 534
Dart, Jack, 175
Databases, 193
Data mining, 193
Davids, Meryl, N–2
Davidson, Carol, 230–231, N–7
Davies, Howard, N–5
Davis, Joe, 189, 490
Dawes, Philip, N–3
Dawley, David, 118

Dawson, William, 505n
Day, George, N–11
DayRunner, 484
Day Timer, 484
Deals, 452
DeCarlo, Thomas, 368, 568, N–5
Deception, 63
Deciders, 97–98
DeConinck, Jim, 534
Deeter-Schmelz, Dawn R., 28, 118,
  305, 534
Deferred dating, 453
DeKeno, Thomas, 174
Dellecave, Tom, Jr., N–9
Delmar, Ken, N–7
de los Santos, G., 431
DelVecchio, Susan, 28, N
Demonstrations, 289–292
Department of Labor, 476
Dependability, 18, 40–41
Derived demand, 89
de Rossiter, Cher, 481
de Ruyter, Ko, 52
DeShields, Oscar W., Jr., 431, N–7
Deshpande, Rohit, N–1
Desmet, Pierre, N–10
Diagnostic feedback, 159–160
DiCarlo, Frank, 358
Dickinson, Roger, 404
Digital asset management, 285
Digital sales assistant (DSA),
  285–286
DiMartino, Michael, 36
Dimitri, Ashraf, N
Ding, Cherng G., 431
Dion, Paul A., 466, N–10
Direct channel salespeople, 12
Direct denial, 324
Direct request method, 352
Discounting the cash flows, 298–299
Discounts, 344–345
  cash, 345, 453
  cumulative, 453
  financial, 453
  promotional, 452–453
  quantity, 452
  trade, 451–452
Disguised interviews, 554
Dissolution, causes of, 395–398
  complacency, 396–397
  conflict, 397–398
  failing to monitor competitors, 396
  failing to monitor industry, 396
  limited personal relationships,
    395–396
Dissolution stage, 47
Distribution channel, 12
  business-to-business, 12–14
  consumer, 13, 14
  resellers, 436–438
Distributor salespeople, 12
Diversity, 154–157
Dixon, Andrea L., 271
Dobscha, Susan, 53, N–9
Document cameras, 288
Domanski, Tomasz, N–3
Donaldson, Bill, 500
Donaldson, Thomas, N–2
Donath, Bob, N–4, N–5
Doney, Patricia M., N–8
Donlevy, Leo, N–9
Donnan, Michael P., 52
Donoho, Casey L., 271, 323
Donohue, William, N–10
Donovan, Ryan, 550
Dorfman, Larry, 386
Dorsch, Michael J., 52, N–2
Dorsey, David, N–7
Draw, 513–514
Dress for Success (Molloy), 142
Dreyfack, Ray, N–8
Driscoll, Lisa, N–9
Drivers, 162, 164

cues for recognizing, 165
  customer expectations for, 167
Drollinger, Tanya, 150, N–4
Drummond, Gary, N–11
Dsujan, Harish, N–5
Dual career path, 558–559
Dube, Cameron, 563
Duffy, Roberta, N–4
Duman, Jill, 305, N–5
Duncan, Tom, 28
Dunfee, Thomas, 81, N–2
Dunn, Gary, 381n
Dunn, Mark G., N–12
Dunnette, Marvin, N–10
Durrett, Joe, 45–46
Durvasula, Srinivas, 568
Dwyer, F. Robert, N–1
Dwyer, Sean, 174, 500, N–7

Ebel, Rick, N–12
Economic criteria, 99
Economies of scale, 48
Efficient consumer response (ECR)
  systems, 106
  resellers and, 446, 447
Ego-involved, 264–265
Ehrlich, Elizabeth, N–3
80/20 rule, 31, 476, 477
Eisner, Robin, N–7
El-Ansary, Adel, N–10–N–11
El-Ansary, Waleed A., N–11
Electronic copyboard, 288
Electronic data interchange (EDI),
  106, 447
  order processing and, 376
  resellers and, 447
  transactions and, 107
Electronic whiteboards, 288–289
Ellram, Lisa M., 53, N–1, N–3, N–9
E-mail, 488–489
Emotional close, 356
Emotional intelligence, 20–21
Emotional needs, 98
Emotional outburst tactic, 423
Encoding communication, 122
Endless-chain method, 185–186
End-user, 85–86
England, Robert, N
Enico, Cliff, N–11
e-Selling, 189
Estell, Libby, N–7
Estep, Paul, N–5
Ethical imperialism, 76
Ethics, 18, 56–81
  buyers' view of unethical
    behavior, 67
  checklist for decisionmaking, 63
  factors influencing behavior, 59–61
  good business and, 64
  international selling and, 75–76
  management of, 517–520
    field sales managers, 518–520
    open-door policies, 517–518
    sales executives, 517–518
    unethical requests, 518–520
  personal code of, 62
  personal selling and, 58–59
  policy for Motorola, 61
  relationships and, 62–69
    with colleagues, 68–69
    with competitors, 69
    with customers; see Customers,
      ethics and
    partnering, 59
    with the salesperson's company,
      67–68
  shelf space and, 439–440
Ethics review boards, 518, 519
Ettenson, Richard, N–10
Eure, Dr. Jack, 27
Euwema, Martin, N–10
Evaluation and compensation,
  512–515
Evans, Joel R., 466

Evans, Kenneth R., 175, 271, 404,
  535, N–6
Everett, Martin, N–3
Excel®, 414
Exclusive sales territories, 183
Excuses, 321–322
Executive summary, 294
Expansion stage, 47, 385–389
  cross-selling, 388
  expert guidance and, 386–387
  full-line selling, 387–388
  presence at buying time, 385
  repeat orders, 385–387
  servicing the product, 385–386
  special assistance, 387
  total quality management, 388–389
  upgrading, 387
Expense accounts, 67
Expense budgets, 511
Expert guidance, 386–387
Expert systems, 169
Exploration stage, 47, 374–384
  customer complaints; see
    Customer complaints
  follow-up, 377–378
  monitoring order processing,
    375–376
  personal visits, 378
  proper initial use of product or
    service, 376–377
  setting the right expectations, 375
  supply chain management, 377
Expressed warranty, 71
Expressives, 164
  cues for recognizing, 165
  customer expectations for, 167
Extranets, 106, 189
Extrinsic orientation, 161

FAB, 258
Face, 421
Faes, Wouter, N
Fahland, Mary, 101
Falvey, Jack, N–8
Fang, Tony, 174
Farber, Barry, N–5
Faris, Charles, N–3
Farmer, Jim, 264
Farnham, Alan, N–11
Farrell, Deb, 60
FAST (Field Automation Sales
  Team), 490
Father Troll, 346
Fay, Gene, 97
Features, 256–259
FEBA, 258
FEB (feature, evidence, benefit)
  technique, 553
Federal Aviation Administration, 86
Federal Trade Commission (FTC),
  69, 196
Feedback, 159–160
Feel-felt-found method, 326–327
Fein, Adam, N–1
Fellman, Michelle, 568
Felt stress, 563
Ferrell, Linda, N–2
Ferrell, O. C., 81, N–2
Festervand, Troy, N
Field sales managers, 515–517
Field salespeople, 15, 522–523
Field support rep, 523
  team selling and, 524, 525
Fierman, Jaclyn, N–1, N–10
Financial terms and conditions,
  344–346
Fine, Leslie, 81, 558n, N–2, N–5, N–12
Finley, Michael, N–8
Finn, David, N–2
Fiorina, Carly, 538
Fiorito, Susan, N–4
Fisher, Roger, 431, N–10
Fisher, Sandra, N–12
Fitzgerald, Kevin R., 118, 466, N–7

I-4   *Index*

Flaherty, Karen E., 534
Fleschner, Malcolm, N–9
Fleshman, Dan, 86
Fletcher, Alan D., N–12
Flexibility
    daily activity planning and, 485
    as reward in selling, 22
    successful salespeople and, 19
Flip chart, 284
FOB (free on board), 70, 345, 451
Focus of dissatisfaction, 225
Focus of power, 225
Focus of receptivity, 224
Follow-up, 358, 377–378
Food and Drug Administration, 69
Ford, David, 403
Ford, John, 118
Ford, Neil M., 37n, N–9, N–12
Forecasting, 511
Foreign Corrupt Practices Act, 76
Forenell, Claes, 403
Forestall, 321
Formal negotiation, 406–433
    nature of, 408–411
    negotiation meeting, 418–427
        agenda, 419–420
        ambush negotiating and, 418
        general guidelines, 420–421
        making concessions, 424–426
        preliminaries, 419–420
        recap of successful, 426–427
        win-lose negotiating; see Win-
            lose negotiating
    planning the session, 411–418
        company buyer and seller
            positions, 413–414
        conflict handling behavior
            modes, 416, 417
        individual behavior patterns,
            416–417
        information control, 418
        issues to be negotiated, 413
        location, 411
        objectives, 412–414
        team selection and management,
            414–416
        time allotment, 412
    win-lose; see Win-lose negotiating
    win-win, 408
    win-win not yet negotiating,
        426–427
Forward buy, 453
Foster, Richard, 534
Fournier, Susan, 53, N–9
Fox, Edward J., 465
Frambach, Ruud T., 119, N–3
Frank, Garry L., 77n, 81
Frank, Sergey, N–9
Franklin, Ben, 294, 295
Frankwick, Gary L., 403, N–9
Fredette, Michael, 403
Freeman, Laurie, N–9, N–11
Free on board (FOB), 345, 451
    destination, 70
Freestanding insert (FSI), 457
Friedman, Susan A., N–9
Fries, Daniel, 40, N–1
Frook, John Evan, 206
FSQS (friendly silent questioning
    stare), 323
Fulfer, Mac, 151
Full-line selling, 387–388
Functional relationships, 34–35
Functional resumés, 545–547
Furney, Marcy K., N–5

Galea, Christine, 198n, 224n
Ganaza, Juan, N–10
Ganzel, Rebecca, N–8
Garbarino, Ellen, N–1, N–9
Gardial, Sarah Fisher, 236, N–6
Gardner, Alston, 534
Gardner, Bill, 32
Garofalo, Gene, N–11

Garrison, Sue, N–6
Garvin, David, N
Gaski, John F., 466
Gassenheimer, Jule B., 432, N–10
Gatekeepers, 96–97
    appointments and, 227–228
Gates, Bill, 290
Gaulke, Sue, 305
Gelman, Jan, N–12
Generative learning, 8
Genger, Charles, N–5
Gentry, James W., 206
Geographic salespeople, 520
    SAMs and, 521, 522
George, Jennifer M., 271, N–6, N–10
Geraghty, Barbara, 248
Germain, Richard, N–4
Ghauri, Pervez N., 431
Ghinggold, Morry, 118
Giacobbe, Ralph, N–8
Giallourakis, Michael, N–1
Gibbs, Fiona, N–2
Gifts and entertainment, 63–66
Gilbert, Faye, N–4
Gilliland, David, N–3
Gilly, Mary C., N–5
Gilyard, Burl, 305
Girard, Joe, 180
Gitomer, Jeffrey, N–7, N–8
Giuliano, Peter, N–7
Glatzer, Ross, 556
Glazov, Shelia, 158
Glick, Daniel, N–3
Global sourcing, 104–105
Goals, 471–475
    activity, 474
    benchmarking, 475
    calculations of, 473
    career, 556
    common, 44
    conversion, 474
    nature of, 471–473
    need for, 471
    performance, 473–474
    relationship of, 471
    sales, 473–475
    setting, 471–475
Goel, Sanjay, N–3
Goldner, Paul S., 271, 339, N–8
Goldstein, Michael, N–11
Goleman, Daniel, N
Gomer, Roger, N
Gonzalez, Jorge, N–10
Good, David J., 175, 404, 534, N–6
Good guy-bad guy routine, 421–422
Good impressions; see Making the
    sales call, good impressions
Goodman, Lester E., 466, N–10
Good manners, 295
Goodwin, Cathy, 53
Gottlieb, Sid, 359
Government agencies, 86–87
Graf, Todd, 262, N–8
Graham, Jean, 389n, N–9
Graham, John L., N–5, N–8, N–9
Graham, John R., 236, N–6, N–7
Gramm-Leach-Bliley Act, 214
Greco, Susan, 206, 314n, N–5, N–7,
    N–11
Greeters, 554
Greising, D., N–3
Gremier, Dwayne D., 271
Grid analysis, 478–480
Griggs, Robyn, N–6, N–7
Gronstedt, Anders, N
Gross margin quotas, 512
Gross margin ROI, 443–444
Gross profit margin, 442
Group interviews, 555
Grove, L. J., N–2
Gruner, Stephanie, N–9
Guarantee, 71
Guaranteed prices, 451
Guinipero, Larry, 118

Gulbro, R. D., N–10
Gummesson, Evert, N
Gumünden, Hans Georg, 53
Gundermann, Mary, N–7
Gunthner, Rick, 505
Gupta, Susan Forquer, 500, N–3, N–6
Gurvis, Sandra, 568
Guzek, Elizabeth, N–3
Gwinner, Kevin P., 271

Haberle, Matt, 10
Hadaway, Farrand J., 368
Hair, Joseph F., Jr., 535
Haley, Debra, N–2
Haley, Joe, N–12
Hall, Jim, N–7
Halo effect, 243
Hamm, B. Curtis, 479n
Hanan, Mack, 271
Handfield, Robert, 118
Handouts, 292–293
Handshaking, 242, 243
Handy, Charles, 279
Hanke, Jon, N–8
Hanson, Ray, 258, N–7
Harding, Mary Lu, N–9
Hargie, Owen, N–4
Hart, Michael, 271
Hartley, Mark, 53
Hartley, Steven W., 28
Harvard Business Review, 140
Harvey, Paul, 449
Hastings, Hunter, N–10
Hasty, Ronald W., 534
Hatch, Denny, N–6
Hathaway, Patti, N–4
Hatoum, Wendy, N–10
Hausman, Michael, 224–225
Havila, Virpi, 52
Hawes, John, N–1
Hawes, Jon M., N–1
Hayajneh, Abdalla, 568
Heiman, Stephen E., N–6
Heimes, Scott, N–7
Hendrick, T., N–1
Henthorne, Tony L., 118, N–3, N–7
Herbig, P., N–10
Herndon, Neil, 466
Hersma, Jim, N–6, N–8
Herzog, Paul, N–5
Herzog, Steve, 516
Higgins, Jason, 331
High-and-wide relationship strategy,
    395–396
High-context cultures, 145
Hill, Julie, 20n, 305, N, N–7, N–8
Hobbs, Lawrence, 101
Hoffer, Eric, 558, 560
Holbrook, Morris, N–2
Holcombe, Marya W., 305
Holden, Reed, N–4
Holder, Dick, 11
Hollander, Stanley C., 404
Holton, Ed, N–12
Homburg, Christian, 403, 534
Honesty, 43
    responding to objections, 319
    during sales presentations, 263
Honeycutt, Earl D., Jr., 28
Hopkins, Tom, 561
Hotchkiss, Carolyn, 81, N–2
House accounts, 183, 521–522
Howell, Bob, 480
Howell, Roy, 404
Hoyt, Christopher, N–10
Hrsistodoulakis, Ilias, N
Hu, Jun-Chen, 432
Hult, G. Tomas M., 119, N–2, N–3
Humor, 279–280, 320
Hunt, Kenneth A., 236, 339, N–6
Hunt, Shelby D., 53, N, N–11
Hunt, V. D., N–3
Hunter, Joe, 377–378
Hunter, Shirley, 503

Hurd, Mark, N–10

Illegal business practices, 73–75
Ilsley, Richard, N–8
Image
    with consumers, 444
    selling, 453–455
    in the trade, 444–445
    turnaround and, 454–455
Immelt, Jeffrey, 538
Implication questions, 253–254
Implied warranty, 71
Impression management, 240
Inbound, 523
Inbound telemarketing, 194–195
Incentive pay, 512–515
Independence, 22
Indirect denial, 324–325
Industry, failure to monitor, 396
Inflection, 128
Influencers, 96
Influential adversaries, 213
Information acquisition, 8, 11–12
Information dissemination, 8–9, 11–12
Ingram, Thomas N., 67n, 81, 111n,
    174, 568, N–2
Initiators, 96
Inks, Lawrence W., 175, N–4
Inside salespeople, 15, 522–525
Institute for Supply Management, 92
Institutions as customers, 87–88
Integrated marketing
    communications, 7–8
Internal partnerships, 504–507
    global suppliers and, 505
    importance of, 504–505
    role of sales in learning
        organizations, 504–505
    selling internally, 505–507
Internal salespeople, 393–394, 505–507
International selling
    culture and; see Cultural differences
    ethical and legal issues, 75–77
Internet, 7, 30, 91–92, 106–107
    precall information via, 215–216
    prospecting via, 188–189
    recruitment via, 548, 549
Interviews, 544, 550–556
    during, 552–554
    after employment, 556
    cover letter, 549–550
    disguised, 554
    employment postings for, 548, 549
    follow-up, 555–556
    group, 555
    panel, 555
    personal contacts for, 547
    preparing for, 550–552
    questions asked during, 550, 551
    resumés, 545–546, 547
    stress, 554–555
Intrinsic orientation, 161
Introduction approach, 244
Inventory
    holding, 438
    just-in-time, 105–106, 446, 447
    return on; see Strategic profit
        model (SPM)
Inventory turnover, 443
Investing in accounts, 481–482
Invitation to negotiate, 70
ISO 9000, 389
Issue-involved, 265

Jackson, Donald W., Jr., N–8
Jacob, Rahul, N–1
James, Dana, N–12
Jamil, Maqbul, 271
Jap, Sandy, 404
Jeary, Tony, 305
Jeffrey, Brian, 339, N–6
Jennings, Darren, 557
Jennings, Richard G., 305
Jensen, Jens Wiik, 77

Jensen, Traci, 35–36
Johnson, Eugene, N–11
Johnson, Julie T., 28, 404, N
Johnson, Mark S., N–1, N–9, N–12
Johnson, Michael, 403
Johnson, Rob, 151
Johnston, Lauren, 537–538
Johnston, Mark, 37n, N–9
Johnston, Wesley J., 466, 534
Jolson, Marvin A., 349, 368, 500, N–7, N–9
Jones, Eli, N–7
Jones, Gareth, N–10
Joseph, Kissan, 339
Josephs, Sally, 81, N–2
Joshi, Ashwin W., 534
Jossi, Frank, N–11
Just-in-time (JIT) inventory control, 105–106, 446, 447

Kaczmarek, Stephen Kyo, 151, N–4
Kadlec, Cynthia, N–7
Kado, Chad, 250n
Kahn, Kenneth, 534
Kalakota, Ravi, N–1
Kalwani, Manohar U., N–1
Kaminski, Peter F., 368
Kang, Jikyeong, N–4
Kappauf, Alan, 215
Kara, Ali, N–7
Karr, Ronald E., N–8
Kassarjiam, H., N–2
Katrichis, Jerome, N–3
Katskikeas, Constantine S., 466
Kawamoto, Wayne, N–8
Kaydo, Chad, 107n, 206, 381n, N–4, N–6, N–9
Kaynak, Erdener, N–7
Keaveney, Susan M., N–12
Keele, P., N–10
Keenan, William, Jr., N–9
Keep, William, 404
Keillor, Bruce, 535
Keiningham, Timothy, N–3
Keiretsu, 38
Keith, Janet E., 272, N–8
Kellaris, James, N–2
Kellaris, Pratibha, N–2
Kelley, Bill, N–2
Kelley, Scott, N–2
Kelley, Steve, 521
Kellgren, Barbara S., 121
Kelly, Kevin, N–2
Kelly, Paul, 396, N–9, N–10
Kemp, Robert A., 77n, 81
Kendy, William F., N–11
Kennedy, Bill, 359
Kern, Richard, N–9
Key accounts, 521
Kickbacks, 63
Killen, Rhonda, 275
Kim, Jai-Beom, 377n
Klein, Noreen M., 272
Kleine, Robert E., III, 271
Knowledge base, 485
Knox, Simon, N–9
Koester, Jolene, 151
Kohli, Ajay K., 306, 535, N
Koloszyc, Ginger, 466
Kolt, Robert, N–10
Kondo, Mari, 432
Kotler, Philip, N
Kotzab, Herbert, 465
Krapel, Robert, 535, N–1
Kristof, Amy L., 568
Krohmer, Harley, 534
Kurland, Nancy B., 534
Kushner, Malcolm, 305
Kyzirdis, Panagiotis, 404

LaForge, Raymond W., 67n, 81, 111n, 479n, N–2
Lagace, Rosemary, N–2, N–12
Lamb, Charles W., Jr., N–11

Lambe, C. Jay, 500
Lambert, Douglas M., N–10
Lamons, Bob, 466
Landry, Timothy D., 271
Laneros, Robert, 53
Langlotz, Richard, 561, 562
Laris, Alexis, 174, N–5
Larrick, Richard, 432
Larsen, T., 534
Lasky, Jane, 156n
Lassk, Felicia G., 28
LaTour, Michael S., 118, N–3, N–7
Lattal, Alice, N–2
Lawler, Edmund, N–1
Lawrence, Barry, N–4
Leach, Mark P., 404
Lead management system, 199–201
Lead qualification system, 198–201
Leads, 180–184
  ability to pay, 182
  accessibility, 182
  authority to buy, 182
  eligibility, 182–183
  existence of wants or needs, 181
  managing, 199–201
  other criteria, 184
  qualifying, 180–181, 198–201
Lead user, 48
Leapfrog routing, 487
Learning organization, 8–9
  role of sales in, 504–505
LeClair, Debbie, N–2
Lee, Don Y., 466
Lee, Kendra, 189
Lefton, R. E., 168, N–5
Legal issues, 61, 69–76
  administrative law, 69
  common law, 69
  guidelines for, 75
  illegal practices, 73–75
  international, 73, 75–76
  misrepresentation or sales puffery, 72–73
  statutory law, 69
  UCC, 69, 70–72
Leigh, Thomas, 174
Lele, Millind, N–9
LeMay, Stephen, 53
Lemmik, Jos, 52
Lemon, Katherine N., 53
Leonard, Andrew, N–5
Leone, Peter J., 126n
Leotta, Joan, N–9, N–11
Letters of credit, 453
Leung, Kwok, 432
Leung, Thomas, K. P., N–5
Levy, Michael, 466, N–2
Lewicki, Roy J., 431
Lewin, Jeffrey E., 236, N–6
Li, Jianfeng, 432
Liberman, Vadim, N–12
Lichtenthal, J. David, 174
Liebeskind, Ken, 97n
Life-cycle costing, 99
Ligos, Melinda, 191n, 413n, N–4, N–8
Likability, 43
Lile, Marty, 361
Linear DSA, 286
Lineham, M., 558n
Liogs, Melinda, 143n
Listening to customers, 131–135
  active listening, 131–132
  clarifying information, 133–134
  concentrating on ideas being communicated, 134–135
  repeating information, 132
  restating or rephrasing information, 132–133
  speaking-listening differential, 131
  summarizing the conversation, 134
  testing skills at, 133
  tolerating silences, 143
List price, 451

Lists and directories, 191–193
Littman, Margaret, N–11
Litvan, Laura, N–1
Liu, Annie H., 404
Locker, Kitty O., 151, 294n, N–4
Locksin, Lawrence, N
Loewe, Doug, 490, N–11
Lohtia, Ritu, 52
Loie, Terry, N–2
Longenecker, Justin, N–9
Long-term partnerships, 370–404
  objections and, 311
  value of customers, 372–374
Lord, Danielle, 407
Lorge, Sarah, 119, 228n, 339, 431, N–3, N–5, N–6, N–8, N–9, N–10, N–11
Lotus 123®, 414
Loudness, 128
Low, Brian Koon Huat, N–6
Lowballing, 422–423
Low-context cultures, 145
Lowell, Dana, 505
Lubrication, 75
Lucas, George H., 271
Luk, Sherriff, T. K., N–5
Lummus, Rhonda, N–3
Lumpkin, James R., 368, N
Lundin, Rolf, 404
Luo, Jin-Lian, 432
Luo, Yadong, 431
Luostari, Scott, 126n
Lustig, Myron, 151
Lynch, Al, 543
Lysonski, Steven, 568

McCall, Kimberly L., 206
McCann, Nanci, N–7, N–10
McCasky, Michael, 140
MacClaren, Craig, N–11
McCorkle, Denny E., 431
McCrea, Bridget, 23n
McCreary, Don, N–1
McDonald, Margaret, N–5
McDowell, Raymond, 403
McElroy, James, 368, 568, N–5
McGarvey, Robert, N–6, N–7
McGee, Gail, N–2
McGinnis, Christopher, N–7
McGrath, Diane, N–12
McIlhenny, David, 305
Macintosh, Gerrard, 206, N
Mackay, Harvey B., 212, 217, 358, N–6, N–9
McKenzie, Samuel, 151
MacKenzie, Scott B., 534
MacKinnon, Mary, N–7
McLaughlin, Craig, 98
McMaster, Mark, N–6
McNeilly, Kevin, 534
Macquin, Anne, N–10
McQuiston, Daniel, 466
McRae, Brad, 432
McWilliams, Robert, N–3
Mahoney, Sarah, N–9
Maikish, Gus, 95–96
Main, Angie, 179
Maintenance, repair, and operating (MRO) supplies, 85–86
Major sale, 252
Making appointments, 223–231
  creativity and, 224
  focus of dissatisfaction and, 225
  focus of power and, 225
  focus of receptivity and, 224
  gatekeepers and, 227–228
  relationships with subordinates, 227–228
  responses to objections concerning, 231, 310
  right person, 224–226
  right place, 226–227
  right time, 226
  telephoning, 229–231

Making the sales call, 238–272
  building credibility during the call, 261–264
  ego-involved audience and, 264–265
  good impressions, 240–248
    developing rapport, 246–247
    four A's of, 240
    getting the customer's attention; see Customers, getting the attention of
    handshaking, 242, 243
    impression management, 240
    selecting a seat, 242–243
    very first impression, 241–242
    waiting for the prospect, 240–241
    when things go wrong, 247–248
  honesty, 263
  issue-involved audience and, 265
  offering the solution to the buyer's needs, 256–261
    assessing cues, 259–260, 261
    benefits, 256–259
    features, 256–259
    making adjustments, 261
    nonverbal cues, 259–260, 261
    selective perception and, 261
    trial close and, 261
    verbal probing, 260–261
  prospect's needs, 248–256
    additional considerations, 255
    closed questions, 251–252
    developing a strategy for the presentation, 256
    differentiating your product, 248, 250
    effective communication, 250
    need behind the need, 248–249
    open questions, 250–252
    reiterating pre-identified needs, 254–255
    SPIN® technique; see SPIN®
    twelve good questions to ask, 255
  selling to groups, 264–265
Management opportunities, 23–24
Managing within your company, 502–535
  administration, 508
  customer service, 509
  ethics; see Ethics, management of
  field sales managers, 515–517
  internal partnerships; see Internal partnerships
  manufacturing, 507–508
  marketing, 509–510
  sales management; see Sales management
  salespeople; see Salespeople as partners
  sales teams, 523–525
  shipping, 509
  technology and teamwork, 525–526
Mancuso, Joseph, 249
Mandel, Lawrence, 143
Mander, Bob, 143
Manning, Gerald, 168, N–5
Manufacturers' agents, 14
Manufacturing management, 507–508
Manzo, Ellen, 43–44
Marchetti, Michele, 206, N–2, N–6, N–11
Markdown, 442
Market exchanges, 33–35, 39
  solo, 33–34
Marketing, 509–510
Market share, 450–451
Marklein, Mary Beth, N–2
Marks, Steven, 466
Markup, 442
Marquette, Alexander, 239
Mast, Kenneth E., N–1
Mastrodonato, Frank, 101
Material requirements planning (MRP), 106
Matthyssens, Paul, 118

Maxham, James G., III, 535
Maxwell, Bill, 557
May, Eleanor, N–4
Maynard, Michael, 386
Mayo, Michael, 53
Meche, Melanie, 206
Medcof, John W., 404
Mehta, R., 534
Meisenheimer, Jim, 255n, 271, N–7
Melia, Marilyn Kennedy, N
Menon, Anil, 404
Mentoring, 558
Merchandise markets, 455
Merrill, David, 161–168, N–5
Merritt, Mark, 305, N–8
Messerschmitt, John, N–8
Metaphors, 126
Meyer, Bob, 8
Meyers, Caryn, N–8
Meyers, Patricia W., N–9
Michell, Paul, 377n
Mick, David Glen, 53, N–9
Millar, Bill, 236
Miller, Cyndee, N–11
Miller, Marlane, 168, N–5
Miller, P. Andres, N–10
Miller, Robert B., N–6
Miller, Stuart, N–11
Millman, Tony, 534
Minahan, Tim, N–3
Mind share, 440
Minifie, Jan, 388n
Minimum call objective, 220–221
Minimum position, 412
Minor-point close, 356
Minton, John W., 431
Mintu-Wimsatt, Alma, 432, N–10
Mirani, Robert, 466
Misrepresentation, 72–73
Missionary salespeople, 12–14
Mitchell, Helen, N–9
Mitchell, Scott, N–3
Mitchell, Tom, 466
Moberg, Philip J., N–10
Modified rebuy, 95
Moller, Kristian, 534
Molloy, John, 142
Moncrief, William, N–2, N–11
Mondoza, M. Teresa, 432
Money, R. Bruce, 432, N–5
Monoky, John F., N–6
Moon, Mark A., 500, N–3, N–6
Moore, Carlos, N–9
Moore, Deanne, 466
Moore, Ellen, N–3
Moore, Jesse N., N–7
Moorman, Christine, N–1
Moorman, Luci, 52
Morgan, Fred, N–2
Morgan, James P., N–1, N–9
Morgan, Robert, 53, N
Moriarty, Sandra, 28
Mornell, Pierre, 151
Morris, Michael, 432, N–3
Morrison, William F., 410n
Motivation, 18
    resellers and, 459
Mount, Ian, 568
Movondo, Felix T., N–1
Mowatt, Jef, 271
MRO supplies, 85–86
Multiattribute model of product
        evaluation and choice,
        114–118
    implications for salespeople,
        117–118
    important weights, 115
    overall evaluation, 116
    performance evaluation of
        characteristics, 114
    supplier selection, 116–117
    value offered, 116
Multilevel selling, 524
Multiple-sense appeals, 276

Multz, Jeff, 198
Mulvey, Al, 104
Munduate, Lourdes, N–10
Munn, John, 509
Munn, Richard C., N–11
Munschauer, John L., N–11
Murphy, Harry, 37
Murray, John, N–2
Mutual gain, 44–45
Myers, David, 228
Myers, Dawn, N–2
Myers, Jennifer, N–1
Myron, David, 481n

Napolitano, Lisa, 271, 392n, 500, N
Narayandas, Narakesari, N–1
Narus, James, N–5
Narver, John C., N, N–6, N–8
National account managers (NAMs),
        104, 521
National Association of Legal
        Secretaries, 455–456
National Association of State
        Purchasing Officials, 87
National Basketball Association
        (NBA), 97
Naumann, Earl, N–3
Need payoff questions, 254
Need-related objections, 311–312
Needs
    corporate, 542–543
    identification of, during interviews,
        552–553
    personal, 539–540
Negotiation, 408
    formal; see Formal negotiation
    internal selling and, 507
    non-negotiation versus, 408–409
    philosophies of, 408
Negotiation jujitsu, 424
Negotiator Pro, 414
Nelson, James E., N–12
Nelson, Michael, 226
Nemac, John, 206, N–5
Net present value (NPV), 298–299
Net price, 451
Net profit margin, 442–443
Net sales, 442
Networking, 187–188
Networld, 455
Neuborne, Ellen, 271
New task, 93
Newzell, Bob, 263n
Nibbling, 423
Nicholls, J. A. F., 28, 174, N–5
Nichols, Ernest, 118
Nielsen, Richard P., N–11
Noises, 123
Nolan, Johannah, N–1
Nonlinear DSA, 286
Nonverbal communication, 124,
        135–143
    appearance; see Appearance
    body language; see Body language
    commitment and, 348
    distance during interactions,
        140–141
    hidden emotions and feelings,
        137–138
    touching, 141
Norris, George A., N–5
North American Free Trade
        Agreement (NAFTA),
        120, 193
North American industry
        classification system
        (NAICS), 191
Nunn, Ed, 23–24
Nwakanma, Hudson, 568

Objections, 308–339
    effective response methods,
        322–330
        boomerang method, 327

        buying group and, 330
        compensation method, 325–326
        direct denial, 324
        feel-felt-found method, 326–327
        indirect denial, 324–325
        pass-up method, 327–328
        postpone method, 328–329
        probing method, 323
        steps in, 322–323
        using, 329–330
    major types of, 312
    need-related, 311–312
    other, 317–318
    preparing to respond to, 318–322
        anticipation, 319–320
        avoiding interruptions, 320
        evaluation, 321–322
        forestalling known concerns, 321
        positive attitude, 318–319
        truthfulness, 319
    price-related; see Price-
        related objections
    product-related, 312–313
    raising of, 310–311
    source-related, 313–315
    time-related, 316–317
    tough customers and, 334
Obtaining commitment, 340–368
    after, 355–358
        confirm the customer's choice,
            356–357
        cultivate for future calls, 358
        get the signature, 357
        no surprises, 356
        review actions, 358
        show appreciation, 357
    closing, 342
    closing the interview, 361–362
    examples of, 343
    failure at, 358–361
        dealing with, 360–361
        discovering the cause, 360
        good measures and, 361
        poor habits and skills, 360
        poor presentation, 360
        proper perspective and, 360–361
        recommend other sources, 361
        what "no" means, 359
        wrong attitudes, 359
    financial terms and conditions,
        344–346
    importance of, 343–344
    methods of, 351–355
        alternative choice, 355
        balance sheet, 353
        benefit summary, 352–353
        Ben Franklin, 353
        direct request, 352
        other traditional, 355, 356
        probing, 354–355
    process of, 342–343
    success at, 349–351
    timing of, 346–348
    today, 342
Occupational Outlook Quarterly, 538
O'Connell, Jim, 442
O'Connell, William, N–9
O'Connor, Jim, 126
O'Connor, Michael, 174, N–5
Offer, 70
Office scanning, 247
Oh, Sejo, N–1
O'Hanlon, Kevin, 426n
O'Hearn, John, 224
O'Kane, Connie, N–9
O'Kleefe, Anne, N–9
Oliva, Ralph A., N–4
Oliver, Richard W., N–3
One-way communication, 124
Onkvisit, Sak, N–2
Open-door policies, 517–518, 519
Opening position, 412
Open questions, 129, 250–252
Opportunity cost, 299, 315

Optimistic call objective, 221
Order processing, 375–376
Orders, 70
Organizational buying decisions,
        89–98
    buying center and, 95
    creeping commitment and, 92
    deciders and, 97–98
    gatekeepers and, 96–97
    influencers and, 96
    initiators and, 96
    steps in, 89–92, 98
    types of, 93–95
    users and, 96
Organizational learning, 8–9
    role of sales in, 504–505
Organizational support, 45–46
Original equipment manufacturers
        (OEMs), 84–85, 86
Oros, Bob, N–10
Ottinger, William F., 236
Outbound, 523
Outbound telemarketing, 194
Outlined presentation, 154
    example of, 155
Outsourcing, 105
Ouwerkerk, Cok, N–2
Overholt, Alison, 236, N–7
Owens, Jan P., N–6

Paduch, John, 386–387, 393
Pagh, Janus D., N–10
Paik, Y., N–10
Paley, Norton, N–3, N–9
Paliska, Stephen, 314
Panel interviews, 555
Paolozzi, Lisa, 485–486
Paperwork, 489–490
Pappas, James M., 534
Pardo, Catherine, 534
Parker, Sam, 143
Parrish, Jean, N–10
Partnerships, 35–38; see also Building
        partnering relationships
Parvatiyar, Atul, N
Pass-up method, 327–328
Patton, W. E., III, 271
Pavlovitch, Tim, 31
Payback period, 298
Pearce, Craig L., 535
Pearson, John N., N–3
Peelen, Ed, N–2
Peiro, Jose M., N–10
Pelton, Lou E., 272, 368, 466,
        535, N–8
Penney, James Cash, 36
Peppers, Don, 271, N–9
Performance evaluation, 490–493
    activity analysis, 491–492
    performance analysis, 492
    postcall analysis, 491, 492
    productivity analysis, 492–493
    sales evaluation measures, 493
Performance feedback, 159–160
Performance goals, 473–474
Perry, John, N–4, N–7
Perry, Monica, 535
Personal selling
    communication and, 6–8
    ethics and, 58–59
    evolution of, 32–33
    justification for, 19
    reasons for learning about, 4–5
Petach, Paul, N–5
Peters, Ray, 378
Peterson, Laura K., N–7
Peterson, Robert A., 271, N–4
Peterson, Robin, N–2
Pettijohn, Charles, 535
Pettijohn, Linda S., 535
Petty, William, N–9
Petzinger, Thomas, Jr., N–5, N–11
Philadelphia, Desa, 236, N–7
Pick, Polly, 404

Pifer, Norm, 141–142
Pillai, Rajnandini, 175, N–6, N–8
Pinkham, Will, 472–473
Pioneer selling, 312
Pipeline analysis, 480
Pitt, Leland F., 568
Plank, Richard E., 53, 151, 305
Planning the sales call, 208–236
  flow diagram of process, 210
  making appointments; see Making
    appointments
  objectives, 218–223
    buyer's, 223
    criteria for effective, 219–220
    examples of, 220
    minimum call, 220–221
    multiple call, 220–223
    optimistic call, 221
    primary call, 220, 221
    secondary call, 221
    for several calls, 221–223
    value proposition and, 223
  obtaining precall information,
    210–218
    information sources, 214–218
    Internet, 215–216
    noncompeting salespeople, 217
    other sources, 218
    privacy concerns, 214
    prospect/customer, 217
    prospect/customer as an
      individual, 212
    prospect's/customer's company,
      212–213
    reasons for, 210
    resources within your
      company, 215
    secondary sources, 217
    secretaries and receptionists, 217
    seeding, 232
  other activities, 231–232
Podsakoff, Phillip, 534
Pollard, Kimberly, 454n
Pollock, Ted, N–9
Porter, Anne Millen, N–6
Porter, Stephen S., 175, 403, N–4, N–9
Porterfield, Richard, N–10
Portfolios, 283–285, 553–554
Positive attitude
  obtaining commitment, 349
  responding to objections, 318–319
Postcall analysis, 491, 492
Postcard packs, 189–190
Postpone method, 328–329
Postpurchase dissonance, 356
Powell, Colin, 413
Power, Christopher, N–9
Pragman, Claudia, N–4
Preferred supplier, 389
Prequalification, 199
Presentations, 154
  balanced, 262
  interview, 553–554
  needs of the prospect and, 256
  objections during, 310
  poor, 360
  strengthening; see Strengthening
    the presentation
Presenting price, 346
Price, Darlene, N–8
Price, Glenn R., Jr., 3
Price discrimination, 74–75
Price-related objections, 315–316,
  330–333
  communication tools, 332–333
  establishing the value, 331–332
  up-to-date information, 331
Pricing terms, 451
Primary call objective, 220, 221
Prime selling time, 483
Pritchett, Lou, 40
Privacy laws, 214
Probing method, 323, 354–355
Problem questions, 253

Procurement Automated Source
  System (PASS), 87
Producers, 84–86
Product approach, 245
Product demonstrations, 289–292
Productivity analysis, 492–493
Product-related objections, 312–313
Product specialists, 522
Profit margin, 451–453
  gross, 442
  net, 442–443
Profit quotas, 512
Projectors, 287–289
Promotional allowances, 452–453
Promotions to build demand,
  457–458
Prospecting, 178–206
  characteristics of good prospects,
    180–184
  importance of, 180
  leads; see Leads
  overcoming reluctance toward,
    201–202
  sources and methods, 184–198
    ads, direct mail, etc., 189–190
    buying community, 187
    center-of-influence method,
      186–187
    cold calling, 193–194
    CRM systems, 193
    data mining, 193
    endless-chain method, 185–186
    Internet, 188–189
    lists and directories, 191–193
    networking, 187–188
    other, 198
    overview of, 185
    referrals, 184, 186
    sales letters, 196–197
    satisfied customers, 184–185
    secondary sources, 191–193
    selling deeper, 185
    seminars, 191
    spotters, 194
    telemarketing, 194–196
    trade shows, 190–191
Prospects, 180–184
Proving sales, 447–451
  market share, 450–451
  selling history, 449
Prude, Mark, 362, N–9
Publicity, 6, 7
Pullig, Chris, 535
Pullins, Ellen Bolman, 151, 558n,
  N–12
Pull strategy, 458
Purchasing agents, 104
Purchasing Magazine, 100, 101,
  384, 386, 387
Pusateri, Michael, 392n, 535
Push money (PM), 74
  resellers and, 459
Push strategy, 458

Qualifying the lead, 180–181
  system for, 198–201
Quality criteria, 99–100
Qualls, William, 404
Quantifying the solution, 296; see
  also Value analysis
Quantity discounts, 452
Question approach, 246
Questions, 129–131
Quick-response systems, 106
  resellers and, 446, 447
Quigley, Charles, N–3
Quinn, James Brian, N–3
Quota, 511
Quota setting, 511–512

Rackham, Neil, 218, 224, 225, 339,
  426, N–6, N–7, N–8, N–9,
  N–10
Raiffa, Howard, 413n

Rajala, Arto, 534
Rallapalli, Kumar C., 81
Rameseshan, B., 568
Ramsey, Rosemary P., 118, 305, 534,
  N–7
Randall, Cindy, 568
Randall, James, 568
Randall, Sheila, 534
Ranson, Robert, 52
Rapport, 246–247
Rasmusson, Erika, 305, 541n, N–1,
  N–6, N–7, N–9, N–10
Rate of change, 393
Rational needs, 98
Ray, Dana, 119, 175, N, N–4, N–5
Ray, Nina M., 466
Raymond, Mary Anne, 52
Reciprocity, 73
Recruiting process, 543–556
  application information sources,
    543–545
  cover letter, 549–550
  employment postings, 548, 549
  interviews; see Interviews
  resumés, 545–546, 547
  selecting salespeople, 543–545
  selling your capabilities, 545–556
Reece, Barry, 168, N–5
Reeter, Jeff, 57
References, 544
Referral approach, 244
Referrals, 184
Referred lead, 186
Rega, Michael, N
Regenold, Stephen, 305, N–7
Rehfeld, Barry, N–1, N–3
Reich, Robert, N–3
Reichheld, Frederick F., N–9
Reid, David A., 151
Reid, Roger, 161–168, N–5
Reigle, Pamela, N–12
Reilly, Tom, 271
Reinhardt, Andy, N–4
Reiss, Victor, 341
Rejection, dealing with, 360–361
Relational partnerships, 35–36
Relationship management, 47–49
Relationship marketing, 9, 33; see
  also Building partnering
  relationships
Rendon, Ana Maria, N–11
Repeat orders, generating, 385–387
Reporting work-time information
  and activities, 67
Reports, 490
Request for information (RFI), 88
Request for proposal (RFP), 293
Requirements, 347
Resale price maintenance, 74
Resellers, 86, 434–465
  buying considerations, 440–445
    image, 444–445
    other factors, 445
    return on inventory; see Strategic
      profit model (SPM)
    return on space, 444
  category management and, 460–461
  described, 436
  distributed channel, 436–438
  getting them to sell your products,
    438–440
  merchandise markets and, 455
  partnering with, 460–461
  role of, 437–438
  selling to, 445–455
    image, 453–455
    improving turnover, 446–447
    profit margin; see Profit margin
    proving sales, 447–451
    strategic profit model and,
      446–453
    turnaround, 454–455
  supporting the sales efforts of,
    456–460

  contests, 459
  motivation, 459
  promotions to build demand,
    457–458
  push money, 459
  training, 459–460
  trade shows and, 455–456, 457
Resource allocation, 475–482
  ABC analysis, 477–478
  account classification and,
    476–481
  customer relationship management
    software, 480–481
  grid analysis, 478–480
  investing in accounts, 481–482
  life and death and, 476
  resources to be allocated, 475
  where to allocate, 475–476
Response time, 124
Responsibility, 22
Responsiveness, 162
  adjusting to, 168
  indicators of, 163
  self-assessment of, 166
Resumés, 545–547
Return on investment (ROI), 297,
  440–445
  gross margin, 443–444
Return on space, 444
Revenue quota, 511
Rewards, 46
Rice, Gillian, 77n, 81
Rich, Gregory A., 534, 535, N–5
Richard, Orlando, 174, 500, N–7
Richardson, Bradley, 568
Richardson, David, N–8
Richardson, Lynne, 53
Richardson, Priscilla, 306
Ridnour, Rick M., 28, 133n, 150,
  151, 271, 568, N–4
Rieck, Dean, N–10
Rigdon, Edward E., 466
Rigsbee, Ed, N–10
Rink, David, N–1, N–2, N–3
Risk reductions, 101–102
Ritter, Thomas, 53
Rivers, L. Mark, 175
Roberts, Jenney, N–1
Roberts, Julie, N–3
Robertson, Kristen, 380
Robertson, T. S., N–2
Robertson, Thomas, N
Robinson, Patrick, N–3
Robinson-Patman Act, 74–75
Rodrigo, Elaine M., N–1
Rogers, Lewis C., N–11
Rogers, Martha, 271, N–9
Roitman, Marcy, 300
Role accuracy, 563
Role ambiguity, 563
Role conflict, 563
Role models, 518, 519
Role of salespeople in business, 5–9
  communication and, 6–8
  information and, 8–9
  relationship management and, 9
  sales jobs and, 14
Role-play cases, 569–575
  ACT!, 573–575
  Callaway Big Bertha C4 drivers,
    570–573
  making comments on, 570
  preparing for, 569–570
Role stress, 563
Rome, Francis, N–11
Roos, Johan, N–3
Rosa, Jose, 404
Rose, Gregory M., 174
Rose, Mike, 384
Rosenbloom, B., 534
Rosler, Randy, 224
Ross, Greg, 556
Ross, Sharon, 556
Ross, William, 81, N–2

Roth, Phillip, N
Roth, Sam, 217
Rotondo, Jennifer, 306
Rounds, Beth, 199
Routine call patterns, 486–487
Routing, 486–488
Rouzies, Dominique, N–10
Roy, Susan, N–7
Royal, Weld F., 568, N–9
Rubash, Arlyn, N–5
Rudelius, William, 28
Rudolph, Bettina, 403
Rush, Stephen, N–11
Russ, Frederick A., 534
Rust, Roland, N–3

Sabol, Barry, 53
Salary, 512–515
Sale, 70
Sales & Marketing Management, 541
Sales call allocation grid, 478–480
Sales calls
    essential elements of, 238
    making; *see* Making the sales call
    planning; *see* Planning the sales call
Sales Dashboard, 331
Sales force automation (SFA), 481
Sales goals, 473–475
Sales jobs
    continuum, 16
    creativity level of, 16
    describing, 14–15
    examples of, 16–17
    statistics on, 21
Sales letters, 196–197
Sales management, 510–515
    compensation and evaluation,
        512–515
    controls, 511–512
    ethics and, 517–518
    expense budgets, 511
    forecasting, 511
    quotas, 511–512
    sales executive, 510–515
    size and organization of sales
        force, 510
Salespeople, 2–28
    building partnerships model, 24
    case problems, 26–27
    characteristics of successful, 18–21
        communication skills, 19
        creativity, 19–20
        customer and product
            knowledge, 18
        dependability of, 18
        emotional intelligence, 20–21
        ethical sales behavior, 18
        flexibility, 19
        learning of, 21
        motivation, 18
        trustworthiness, 18
    communication and, 6–8
    field, 15
    functions of, 9–12
        coordinating activities, 11
        pie chart of, 10
        providing and preparing
            information, 11–12
        selling, 9–10
        servicing customers, 10–11
    inside, 15
    manufacturers' agents, 14
    missionary, 12–14
    price-related objections and, 333
    reasons for learning about, 4–5
    as relationship managers, 9
    rewards for, 21–24
        financial, 22–23
        independence and
            responsibility, 22
        management opportunities,
            23–24
    sales jobs; *see* Sales jobs
    trade, 12

    types of, 12–17
        business-to-business channels,
            12–14
        consumer channels, 14
Salespeople as partners, 520–525
    account, 520–522
    geographic, 520, 521, 522
    inside versus outside, 522–523
    product specialists, 522
    sales teams, 523–525
Sales portfolios, 283–285
Sales puffery, 72–73
Sales quotas, 511
Sales teams, 523–525
    technology and, 525–526
Salling, Scott, 12
Salmi, Asta, 52
Salmond, Deborah, N–1
Sanchez, Diane, N–8
Sanger, Ira, N–1
Sanger, Michael, 404, 500
Saren, Maki, 153
Sasser, Earl, N–9
Satterfield, Mark, 28
Saunders, David M., 431
Schaars, Teo, 355
Schanck, John, N–10
Scheraga, Dan, N–4
Schiffman, Stephan, N–5
Schippmann, Jeffrey, N
Schmidt, Kathleen, N–9
Schmitt, Melissa, 28
Schmonsees, Bob, N–5
Schorr, John E., 119
Schul, Patrick L., 271, 431
Schultz, Don E., 28
Schultz, Roberta J., 175, 404, 535,
    N–6
Schurr, Paul, N–1
Schwepker, Charles W., Jr., 81, 534,
    N–2, N–11
Scope of change, 393
Scott, Howard, N–10
Scott, Stan, N–3
Screens, 227–228
Search engines, 188–189
Secondary call objective, 221
Securities and Exchange
    Commission, 69
Seeding, 232
Seideman, Tony, N–11
Selective perception, 261
Self-management process, 470; *see
    also* Time and territory
    management
Sellers, Patricia, N–1
Selling center, 215
Selling deeper, 185
Selling history, 449
Selling internally, 393–394, 505–507
    seven principles of, 506
Selling opportunities, 538–539; *see
    also* Career management
Selling Scenarios
    activities of salespeople, 10
    assisted selling, 454
    casual dress, 143
    good ethics and good business, 64
    in hospital operating rooms, 228
    issues to be negotiated, 413
    price objections, 331
    rudeness, 292
    sales bloopers, 557
    selling the way people want to
        buy, 34
    seminars, 191
    supply chain management, 377
    team selling and, 526
Selnes, Fred, N
Selway, Mark, N–4
Seminars, 191
Sengupta, Sanjit, 535
September 11, 446–447
Service criteria, 100

Services, 85, 86
    price-related objections and, 332
    resellers and, 438
Servicing the product, 385–386
Settle, Robert, N–3
Sexual harassment, 68–69
Shakespeare, William, 539
Shanahan, Timothy, 101
Sharland, Alex, 432
Sharma, Arun, 175, 404, N–6, N–8
Sharoff, Robert, N–1, N–2, N–10
Shaw, John, N–2
Shay, Eileen, 32
Shein, Esther, N–6
Shelf space, 439–440
Shelton, Paula, 344
Shepherd, C. David, 28, 81, 133n,
    150, 151, 174, 271, 500,
    N–4, N–7
Shepherd, David, N–2
Sheridan, John, N–3
Shervani, Tasadduq, N
Sheth, Jagdish, N, N–9
Shih-Hsieh, Rick, 64
Shipp, Shannon H., N–11
Shipping, 509
Shipping costs, 345–346
Shroud, Howard, 83
Sieckman, Debra, 64–65
Siguaw, Judy A., 466
Silva, David W., N–8
Silverman, Brian, N–5
Simons, Tad, 126n, 151, N–8
Simonson, Alexander, N–2
Simple cost-benefit analysis, 296
Simpson, Penny, 466
Sims, Henry P., Jr., 535
Singh, Jagdip, 53
Singhapakdi, Anusorn, N–2
Sinkula, James, N
Sirdeshmukh, Deepak, 53
Sirgy, M. Joseph, 28
Siwolop, Sana, N–3
Skarmeas, Dionisis, 466
Skelly, Gerald, N
Slater, Stanley F., N, N–6, N–8
Slattery, John, 521
Slocum, John W., Jr., 236
Slutsky, Jeff, N–6
Slutsky, Marc, N–6
Small Business Administration, 87
Small talk, 246–247
Smeltzer, Larry, N–3
Smith, Chuck, 88
Smith, Daniel C., N–6
Smith, Ellen Reid, N–11
Smith, J. Brock, 28, 53, N, N–8
Smith, N. Craig, 81, N–2
Smith, Rob, N–11
Sneak attack, 418
Social style matrix, 161–168
    amiables, 164
    analyticals, 164
    assertiveness and, 162
    categories of, 162–164
    cues for recognizing, 165
    dimensions of, 161–162
    drivers, 162, 164
    expressives, 164
    identifying, 165
    illustrated, 163
    knowledge and, 168
    responsiveness and, 162
    sales presentation and, 165–167
    versatility and, 167–168
Sohi, Revipreet S., N–7
Sojka, Jane Z., 28
Sollner, Albrecht, 368
Sonnenberg, Frank, N–1
Sooder, Karl, 240, N–7
Source-related objections, 313–315

Spam, 189
Sparks, John R., 271
Speaking-listening differential, 131
Special assistance, 387
Specialty Advertising Association
    International (SAAI), 455
Speech rate, 127–128
Spekman, Robert, 500, N–1
Sperry, Joe, N–10
Spiffs, 74
    resellers and, 459
SPIN®, 129, 252–254
    conclusions about, 254
    described, 252
    implication questions, 253–254
    major sales and, 252
    need payoff questions, 254
    problem questions, 253
    situation questions, 253
    using the technique, 253
Spinks, Nelda, 206
Spiro, Rosann, 271, N–4
Spotters, 194
Sprague, David, N–3
Srivistava, Rajesh, 535
Stafford, Thomas, 175
Stanaland, Andrea J. S., N–7
Standard industrial classification
    (SIC), 191
Standard memorized
    presentation, 154
Standing-room-only close, 356
Starr, Karen, N–5
Statutory law, 69
Stein, Judith, 305
Stephens, Ronald, 534
Stevens, Cynthia Kay, 568
Stevens, Ruth P., 206, N–5, N–6
Stinchfield, Chad, 200
Stock keeping unit (SKU), 438
Stoddard, James E., 28
Stoltman, Jeffrey, N–2
Straight commission, 513
Straight-line routing, 487
Straight rebuys, 93–95
Straight salary, 513
Strategic account managers (SAMs),
    521, 522
Strategic partnerships, 36–38
Strategic profit model (SPM),
    440–444
    cost of goods sold, 442
    formula for, 440–441
    gross margin ROI, 443–444
    gross profit margin, 442
    illustrated, 441
    inventory turnover, 443
    net profit margin, 442–443
    net sales, 442
    selling to resellers, 446–453
        improving turnover, 446–447
        profit margin, 451–453
        proving sales, 447–451
Strategic Selling (Miller and
    Heiman), 218
Straughn, Katherine, N–4
Streeter, Sabin, N–1
Stremersch, Stefan, 119, N–3
Strengthening the presentation,
    274–306
    characteristics of strong
        presentations, 276–277
    dealing with the jitters, 299–300
    handouts, 292–293
    product demonstrations, 289–292
    value analysis; *see* Value analysis
    verbal tools, 278–280
    visual tools; *see* Visual tools for
        presentations
    written proposals, 293–295
Strength of position, 478–479
Stress interviews, 554–555
Stress management, 561–563
Strout, Erin, 292n, 306, N–1, N–8

Strutton, David, 272, 368, 466, 535, N–8
Stuart, Elenora, N–3
Stump, Rodney L., 500
Subach, Frank, 101
Submissiveness, 349–350, 351
Subordination, 75
Suggested retail price, 451
Sujan, Harish, 175, N–4
Sujan, Mita, 175, N–4, N–5
Sullivan, Pauline, N–4
Sullivan, Rawlie, N–5
Sullivan, Robert, 236, N–6, N–7
Summay, Al, 440
Superior benefit method, 325–326
Supply chain management, 105–106
Sviokla, John, 175
Swan, John E., 53, N–1, N–2, N–3, N–8
Swenson, Michael J., 271
Switching jobs, 68
Switzer, Fred, N
Syracuse, Lisa, N
Systems integrators, 182
Szymanski, David M., 272, N–4, N–5

Tanner, John F., Jr., 28, 37n, 81, 119, 272, 368, N–2, N–5, N–8, N–9, N–11, N–12
Target position, 412
Tashek, John, N–9
Taylor, Albert, 535
Team selling, 523–526
Teas, R. Kenneth, 368, N–5
Technology
    access to, 48
    increased efficiency and, 49
    team selling and, 525–526
Telemarketing, 194–196
Telemarketing Sales Rule, 195
Telephone Consumer Protection Act, 195
Telephone contact, 488–489
Tellefsen, Thomas, 174
Tepper, Bette, 466
Test, Alan, 272
Testimonials, 282–283
Tests, 544
Thatcher, Margaret, 413
Third-party-testimony method, 327
35mm slides, 285
Thomas, Kenneth, 417n, N–10
Thomke, Stefan, 404
Thompson, Keith, N–9
Tickler file, 485
Time and territory management, 468–500
    goals; see Goals
    implementing, 482–485
        computerized planning, 484–485
        daily activity planning, 482–483
        flexibility, 485
        planning process, 483–485
        prime selling time and, 483
    making more calls, 485–490
        e-mail, 488–489
        paperwork and reports, 489–490
        routing, 486–488
        telephone, 488–489
        zoning, 488
    performance evaluation; see Performance evaluation
    resource allocation; see Resource allocation
    self-management process, 470
    value of time, 470
Time-related objections, 316–317
Tiwari, Sudhir, N–11
Total quality management (TQM), 388–389
Tracy, Brian, 239, N–7

Trade discounts, 451–452
Trade fairs, 456
Trade promotions, 451–452
Trade salespeople, 12
Trade shows, 190–191
    resellers and, 455–456, 457
Training, 46
    resellers, 495–460
Traits of top salespeople, 541
Trawick, I. Fredrick, N–1, N–2, N–3, N–8
Treacy, Michael, N–10
Trial closes, 347–348
    verbal probing as, 260
Trial order, 351
Trumfino, Ginger, N
Trust, 40–43
    commitment and, 342
    competence and, 41
    consumer orientation and, 41–42
    dependability and, 40–41
    honesty and, 43
    likability and, 43
Trustworthiness, 18
Truthfulness; see Honesty
Tully, S., N–3
Tung, R. L., N–10
Turnaround, 454–455
Turnbull, Peter W., 174, 403, N–4
Turner, Gregory B., 53
Turnover (TO), 315
    improving, 446–447
    inventory, 443
Tuten, Tracy L., 53, 466, N–1
Tuttle, Lawrence, N–10
Twain, Mark, 231, 248
24/7, 2
Two-way communication, 122–125
Tying agreements, 74
Tzokas, Nikolas, 404, 500

Ulwick, Anthony, 404
Uniform Commercial Code (UCC), 69, 70–72
U.S. Army, 553
University of Michigan, 426
Upgrading, 387
Upselling, 387
Urban, David J., 53, 466, N–1
Urbaniak, Anthony J., 206
Ury, William, 431, N–10
Uschok, Jeffrey, 42n
Users, 97
Usunier, Jean-Claude, 431

Valero, Greg, 466
Value analysis, 100, 296–299
    comparative cost-benefit analysis, 296–297
    net present value, 298–299
    opportunity cost, 299
    other methods, 299
    payback period, 298
    return on investment, 297
    simple cost-benefit analysis, 296
Value proposition, 223
Valvo, Povert, N–3
van Bruggen, Gerrit H., N–5
Van Der Pool, Lisa, 101n
Vansyckle, Joseph, 553
Varga, Mari Pat, N–8
Varma, Anoop, N–4
Variable call patterns, 487
Vasquez-Parraga, Arturo, N–11
Vass, Jerry, 262, N–8
Vassey, Michael J., 28
Vavra, Tony, N–9
VCRs, 285
Veie, Ellen, N–3
Vendenbempt, Koen, 118
Vendor analysis, 102, 103

Vendor image, 444–445
Vendor loyalty, 102
Venkatesh, R., 306, 535
Verbal communication, 124–135
    listening to; see Listening to customers
    questions, 129–131
    strengthening presentations with, 278–280
    voice characteristics, 127–129
    words, 125–127
Verbeke, Willem, 206, 568, N–2, N–6
Vermillion, Leslie J, 28, 174
Versatility, 167–168
Videoconferencing, 226–227
Vincher, Andrew, N
Virtual sales calls, 226–227
Visual presenters, 288
Visual tools for presentations, 280–289
    catalogs and brochures, 281–282
    charts, 280–281
    comparison of, 284
    computer hardware and software, 285–287
    media used for, 283–289
    models, samples, and gifts, 281
    pictures, ads, maps and illustrations, 282
    sales portfolios, 283–285
    testimonials, 282–283
    test results, 283
    35mm slides, 285
    VCRs, 285
    visual projectors, 287–289
Vitell, Scott J., 81, N–2
Vogel, Robert, N–4
Voice characteristics, 127–129
Volery, Thierry, N–1
Volkema, Roger J., 432
Vollman, Thomas E., 377, N–1
Von Hipple, Eric, 404
Voss, Bristol, N–2

Wagner, Janet, N–10
Wagner, Judy A., 272
Wagner, Robert, 459
Waldrop, Dawn E., 272
Walker, Bob, 558
Walker, Gail, 387
Walker, Orville C., Jr., 37n, N–9, N–12
Walle, Don Vande, 236
Walsh, J. S., 558n
Walter, Achim, 53, N–10
Ward, John, N–8
Ward, Scott, N–2
Wareham, John, 292n
Waring, Becky, 432, N–7
Warner, Fara, 272
Warner, Justin, 469
Warnke, Phil, 561
Warranties, 71–72
Warren, Wendy, 558n, N–12
Wash, Darrel, N–11
Washington, Katie, 557
Waterhouse, Steve, 169
Weaver, Trent, 350
Webcasting, 226
Weber, John A., 466
Webster, Frederick E., Jr., N–2
Weeks, William, 81, 272
Weilbaker, Dan C., 272
Weiss, W. H., N
Weiss, Wendy, 306
Weitz, Barton, 28, 53, 175, 466, N–1, N–2, N–4
Welles, Edward O., N–6
Wells, Barron, 206
Welsch, Lawrence, N–3
Wentz, , Alyson Hendrickson, N–1
West, Vicki, 388n

Weydahl, Allan, 38, 48
Wheeler, Donna, N–11
White, Richard, N–3
White, Tiffany Barnett, 53
Whiteboards, 288–289
Whiteford, Vicki, 361
Whittler, Tommy E., 306
Wichern, Virginia, 309
Widmier, Scott M., N–8
Wierenga, Berend, N–5
Wiersema, Fred, N–10
Wiesendanger, Betsy, N–10
Wilemon, David, N–9
Willars, Antonio, 426
Williams, Alvin J., N–3, N–7
Williams, Katherine, 432
Willingham, Ron, N–10
Willis, Tom, 34
Wilson, David, 404
Wilson, Elizabeth, N–3
Wilson, Timothy, 404
Wind, Yoram, N–3
Winer, Russell S., 53
Win-lose negotiating, 408, 421–424
    browbeating, 424
    budget limitation tactic, 423–424
    emotional outbursts, 423
    good guy-bad guy routine, 421–422
    lowballing, 422–423
    strategy for dealing with, 422
Win-lose relationship, 35
Win-win negotiating, 408
Win-win not yet negotiating, 426–427
Win-win relationships, 35–38
Wisdom Ware, 485
Withey, John, N–4
Wolven, Tom, 11
Wong, Yiu-hing, N–5
Woo, Hong Seng, N–10
Wood, Charles M., 53
Wood, Thomas A., N–10
Woodall, W. Gill, 150, 270
Woodruff, Robert B., 236, N–6
Woodward, Nancy, 151, N–4
Woolford, Scott, 485
Word-of-mouth communication, 6, 7
Word picture, 126–127
    strengthening presentations and, 278–279
Workman, John P., Jr., 534
Wotruba, Thomas, N–1, N–2
Wright, Jeff, 537
Written proposals, 293–295
Wuyts, Stefan, 119, N–3
Wyatt, Rosalind A. J., N–7

Yandle, Jo, N–11
Yarbrough, John F., 300n
Yarmoff, Louise, 481n
Yee, Siew Min, N–1
Yellin, Sue, 229
Yoder, Eric, 206
Young, Clifford E., 479n
Young, Robert, 151, N–4
Yovonvich, B. G., N–1
Yovonvich, G. B., N–1
Yuva, John, N–10

Zaguroli, Jim, 372
Zahorik, Anthony, N–3
Zaltman, Gerald, 306, N–1
Zeiger, Rob, N–7
Zemanski, Renee, N–10
Zhao, Jensen J., 432, N–10
Zielinski, Dave, 151, 236, 306, N–4, N–7, N–8
Zimmerman, Eileen, N–11
Zimmerman, Susan, N–1
Zitka, Linda, 42
Zoning, 488